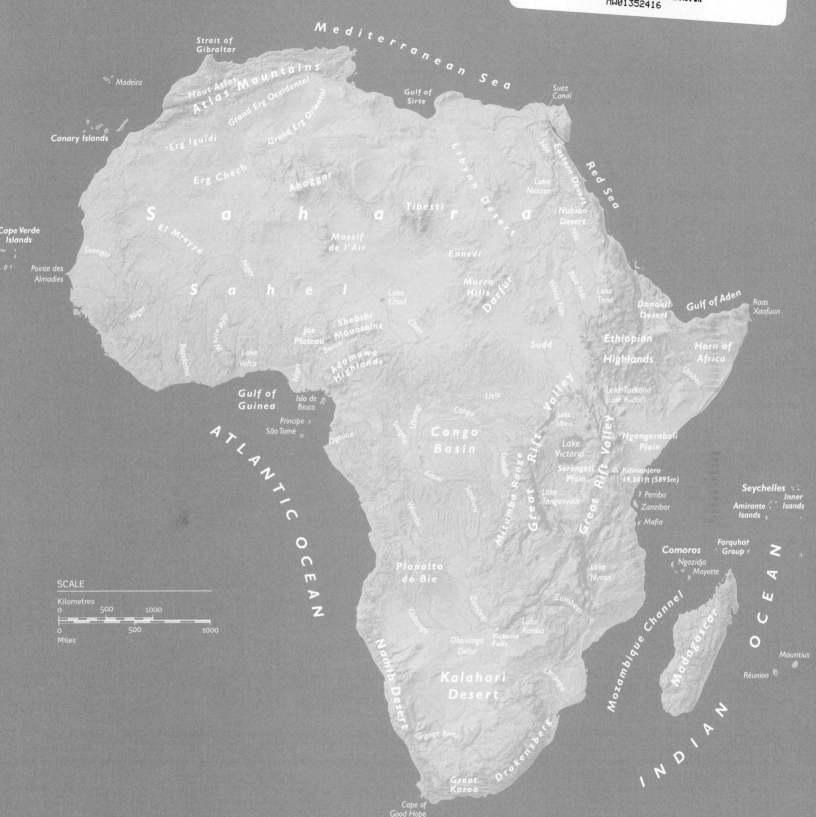

AFRICA

AFRICA

THE DEFINITIVE VISUAL HISTORY OF A CONTINENT

DK London

Senior Editors	Simon Beecroft, Laura Sandford
Senior Art Editors	Jane Ewart, Lisa Lanzarini
Senior US Editor	Megan Douglass
Editors	Ankita Awasthi Tröger, Bridget Giles, Ian Fitzgerald, Scarlett O'Hara, James Smart, Anna Streiffert Limerick, Marcus Weeks
CGI Author and Researcher	Justine Willis
CGI Coordinator	Phil Gamble
CGI Artworks	Peter Bull Art Studio
Senior Cartographic Editor	Simon Mumford
Managing Editor	Carine Tracanelli
Managing Art Editor	Anna Hall
Senior Production Editor	Andy Hilliard
Production Controller	Jack Matts
Picture Researcher	Sarah Hopper
Jacket Design Development Manager	Sophia M.T.T.
Publishing Director	Jonathan Metcalf
Associate Publishing Director	Liz Wheeler
Art Director	Karen Self

DK Delhi

Art Editor	Debjyoti Mukherjee
Deputy Managing Art Editor	Vaibhav Rastogi
Senior Jacket Designer	Suhita Dharamjit
Senior Jackets Coordinator	Priyanka Sharma Saddi
Senior DTP Designer	Harish Aggarwal
DTP Designers	Bimlesh Tiwary, Anita Yadav
Hi-res Coordinator	Jagtar Singh
Pre-production Manager	Balwant Singh
Production Manager	Pankaj Sharma
Design Head	Malavika Talukder

First American Edition, 2024
Published in the United States by DK Publishing
1745 Broadway, 20th Floor, New York, NY 10019

Copyright © 2024 Dorling Kindersley Limited
DK, a Division of Penguin Random House LLC
24 25 26 27 28 10 9 8 7 6 5 4 3 2 1
001–324350–Apr/2024

All rights reserved.
Without limiting the rights under the copyright reserved above, no part of this publication may be reproduced, stored in or introduced into a retrieval system, or transmitted, in any form, or by any means (electronic, mechanical, photocopying, recording, or otherwise), without the prior written permission of the copyright owner.
Published in Great Britain by Dorling Kindersley Limited

A catalog record for this book
is available from the Library of Congress.
ISBN: 978-0-7440-6010-2

Printed in the UAE

www.dk.com

This book was made with Forest Stewardship Council™ certified paper – one small step in DK's commitment to a sustainable future.
Learn more at
www.dk.com/uk/information/sustainability

Use of historical language
Names of organizations and words used on historical images included in this book retain the language and terminology of their time. Some of this language is now outdated, and is deemed insensitive, inappropriate, and offensive. It is a reflection of its time, and does not reflect the opinions of the publisher or of our contributors.

contents

1 African prehistory
5 MYA – 3500 BCE

African prehistory	14
Africa's environment	16
Namib Desert	18
The shifting Sahara	20
Cradle of humanity	22
The rise of sapiens	24
Stone tools	26
Out of Africa	28
Origins of human culture	30
Rock art	32
The development of agriculture	34
The Bantu migrations	36

2 Early civilizations
3000 BCE – 600 CE

Early civilizations	40
The Age of the Pharaohs	42
Ramses II	44
The Ramesseum	46
Egyptian artifacts	48
Kerma and Kush	50
Nubian temple	52
Napata and Meroë	54
Taharqa	56
Writing systems	58
Nok terra-cotta figure	60
The Kingdom of Aksum	62
Carthage	64
Kingdoms of the northwest	66
Hannibal	68
Roman North Africa	70
The arrival of Islam	72
Christian states of the northeast	74

3 African empires
600 – 1900 CE

African empires	78
Languages	80
The development of East African trade	82
The rise and fall of Wagadou	84
Dogon settlement	86
Riches of the trade routes	88
The Empire of Mali	90
Mansa Musa	92
Djinguereber Mosque	94
Timbuktu manuscript	96
The Aghlabids and Fatimids	98
The Almoravid and Almohad dynasties	100
Koutoubia Mosque	102
The Songhai Empire	104
Askia Muhammad I	106
Kanem-Bornu	108
Rise of the Yoruba	110
The Oyo Empire	112
The Igbo states	114
Nri bronzes	116
Medieval Ethiopia	118
The splendor of Gondar	120
Bete Giyorgis, Lalibela	122
The Ayyubids, Mamluks, and Ottomans	124
Nomads: Bedouin, Tuareg, and Maasai	126
The Kingdom of Benin	128
Oba Ewuare	130
Benin Bronze with oba and attendants	132
Royal power	134
Great Zimbabwe	136
The Great Enclosure	138
The Mossi States	140
Kingdoms of the Luba, Lunda, and Lozi	142
Luba "memory board"	144
The East African Sultanates	146
The Eastern slave trade	148
Textiles	150
Pastoralists and hunter-gatherers	152
Mundari cattle camp, South Sudan	154
Mythology and folklore	156

4 European encounters
1440–1914

European encounters	160
The Atlantic slave trade	162
West African griots	164
Europe in Africa	166
Cape Town	168
Madagascar	170
Ranavalona I	172
Kingdoms of the Great Lakes	174
Rwanda and Burundi	176
The Kingdom of Dahomey	178
Njinga Mbande	180
The Kingdom of Kongo	182
Mangaaka power figure	184
The Sultanate of Zanzibar	186
Stone Town	188
The Asante Empire	190
Osei Tutu	192
The Sokoto Caliphate	194
The Tukulor Empire	196
West African art and craft	198
European explorers	200
Map of Bamum	202
Christian missionaries	204
Shaka and the Zulu Kingdom	206
Cetshwayo	208
The scramble for Africa	210
Congo Free State	212
The African diaspora	214
Colonial wars	216
Resistance and uprisings	218
Jaja of Opobo	220
Exploitation and administration	222

5 The age of independence
1914–1994

The age of independence	226
Early independence movements	228
Africa and World War II	230
Pan-Africanism	232
Independence from France	234
Independence of Libya and Egypt	236
Gamal Abdel Nasser	238
Independence from Britain	240
Kwame Nkrumah	242
Capturing the new mood	244
Africa and the Cold War	246
Independence from Portugal	248
Samora Machel	250
The fight for Zimbabwe	252
South Africa and apartheid	254
Anti-apartheid poster	256
The legacy of colonization	258
A new political generation	260
The rise of the military	262
Civil wars	264
Africa's Great War	266
The end of apartheid	268
Nelson Mandela	270

6 Contemporary Africa
1994–

Contemporary Africa	274
Reclaiming cultures	276
Beadwork	278
Religions	280
Protecting environments	282
Lagos	284
Sports	286
Feminisms	288
Ellen Johnson Sirleaf	290
Cinema	292
Musical instruments	294
Popular music	296
Bottle-top sculptures	298
Art and activism	300
Writers	302
The future of Africa	304

National histories	306
Glossary	386
Index	388
Acknowledgments	398

contributors

FOREWORD AND CONSULTANTS

David Olusoga (foreword)
David Olusoga is a British-Nigerian historian, broadcaster, presenter, and BAFTA-winning filmmaker. His books include the award-winning *Black and British: A Forgotten History*. In 2022, he received the British Academy President's Medal.

Dr. Nemata Blyden
Dr. Nemata Blyden is Professor of 19th Century African American History at the Carter G. Woodson Institute, University of Virginia. She teaches and publishes widely on African, African American, and African diaspora history.

Dr. Marie Rodet
Dr. Marie Rodet is a Reader in the History of Africa at SOAS (School of Oriental and African Studies), University of London. Her expertise is on the modern history of French-speaking West Africa.

Steven Snape
Steven Snape is Honorary Professor of Egyptian Archaeology at the University of Liverpool. His research interests focus on the sacred landscape of dynastic Egypt. He is the author of *Ancient Egypt: The Definitive Visual Guide* (DK, 2021).

AUTHORS

Dr. Morenikeji Asaaju
Dr. Morenikeji Asaaju is Cadbury Postdoctoral Fellow in African Studies at the Department of African Studies and Anthropology, University of Birmingham, UK. Her thematic interests are in gender, marriage, family, and the slave trade.

Dr. Abidemi Babalola
Dr. Abidemi Babatunde Babalola received his PhD from Rice University, Texas. He is an Andrew Mellon Fellow at the British Museum and a Marie Curie Postdoctoral Fellow at the Cyprus Institute, and has published widely.

Prof. Jane Bryce
Prof. Jane Bryce is a scholar of African literature and cinema. She is widely published in a range of academic journals and essay collections, and is the author of *Zamani: A Haunted Memoir of Tanzania* (Cinnamon Press, 2023).

Obert Mlambo
Obert Bernard Mlambo is Associate Professor of Classical Studies and History at the University of Zimbabwe. He is the author of *Land Expropriation in Ancient Rome and Contemporary Zimbabwe* (Bloomsbury, 2022).

Patience Motsatsi
Patience Motsatsi is a lecturer at the University of South Africa, specializing in Education and Academic Excellence, Organizational Studies, Colonization and Decolonization, Media Studies, and Culture and Identity.

Dr. Butholezwe Mtombeni
Dr. Butholezwe Mtombeni holds a PhD in History from the University of South Africa, where he is a lecturer in African History. His research interests include the Zulu people, gender, religion, slavery, and social and agrarian history.

Dr. Girma Negash
Dr. Girma Negash is Associate Professor of History and current Head of the Department of History at Addis Ababa University, Ethiopia. His book, *The Education of Children Entangled in Khat Trade in Ethiopia*, was published in 2017.

Prof. Raphael Chijioke Njoku
Prof. Raphael Chijioke Njoku teaches History and Global Studies at Idaho State University. He has published 12 books and 50 academic articles, including *West African Masking Traditions and Diaspora Masquerade Carnivals* (2020).

Philip Parker
Philip Parker studied International Relations at Johns Hopkins School of Advanced International Studies. He is a specialist in medieval and military history and the author of DK's *Eyewitness Companions: World History* (2010).

Luke Pepera
Luke Pepera is a writer, broadcaster, and historian of African history and cultures. He is the author of *Motherland: 500,000 Years of African History, Cultures, and Identity* (Weidenfeld & Nicolson, 2025).

Dr. Marilee Wood
Dr. Marilee Wood, an Honorary Research Associate in the School of Geology, Archaeology, and Environmental Studies at the University of the Witwatersrand, specializes in glass beads traded into Africa in the Islamic period.

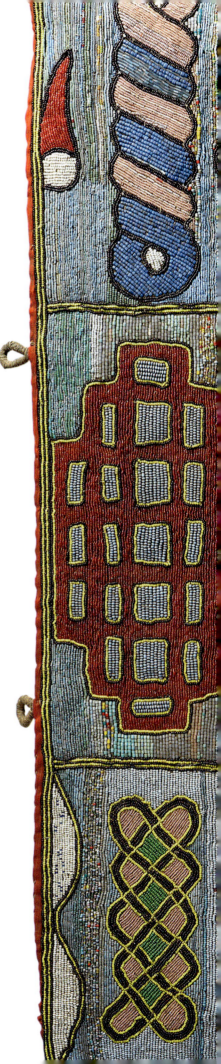

▷ **Beaded tunic**
This highly decorative, beaded tunic would have been worn by a Yoruba king, or *oba*, on important occasions.

▷ **Following page**
Ewe *kente* cloth from Eastern Ghana or Togo

Foreword

Africa is the continent upon which humans first emerged and, therefore, where the history of us all began. Yet Africa's astonishing past—even today—remains poorly understood. This book is a huge, sweeping introduction to the history of the African continent and its many diverse peoples.

That diversity is astounding; greater in Africa than in any other continent. There are around 3,000 ethnic groups living on the continent today who, between them, speak around 2,000 languages. Behind that incredible diversity lies a long history of movement, migration, and adaptation; a history within which numerous African states and empires have risen and fallen over the centuries.

The scope of this book is thus inevitably vast. It begins in Africa's prehistory and introduces the reader to those very first humans who walked the immense spaces of Africa when it was the "cradle of humankind." It goes on to show how those early African peoples became the creators of the world's very first civilizations and cultures. The book then explores the age of Africa's great empires, before introducing the reader to colonial European empires in Africa, and the independence struggles of the late 20th century that toppled them. Finally, it takes us to modern Africa, with its massive and youthful populations, vibrant music, cinema, and art, and its growing megacities, like Lagos—the city of my birth.

This book also confronts the most painful chapters in Africa's history. It explores how Africa became a source of enslaved people—first to the Arab world from the 7th century onward. From the 16th century, Africa was ravaged by the Atlantic slave trade, which sparked wars and disastrously disrupted African societies as at least 12 million Africans were trafficked to European colonies in the Americas. Later, this book examines how toward the

end of the 19th century almost the whole of the continent was colonized and exploited by European imperial powers—despite constant resistance from African peoples.

Another theme addressed by this book is how Africa has been imagined and misrepresented by non-African peoples—in maps, through legends, and within the racial and cultural theories that were used to "justify" slavery and imperialism.

The real Africa, which was concealed behind those myths, is a continent of cultural sophistication whose people have their own sense of history. It is also a continent whose landscapes are almost as diverse as its people. Through stunning photography, this book offers a glimpse of Africa's ancient deserts, sweeping grasslands, and verdant rainforests. The history of Africa has always mattered to me. My work as a historian has repeatedly led me back to African history, as I have sought to understand how Africans were seen by the outside world and how they interacted with the various peoples, from different continents, with whom they have had contact for centuries. For far too long, Africa's place in global history has been underappreciated. This book is an effort to bring to the reader the remarkable story of the continent upon which human history first began.

David Olusoga
British–Nigerian historian and broadcaster

Introduction

Africa is a land of great diversity. Hot deserts sit alongside high mountain ranges formed over billions of years by immense geological forces. Lush rainforests border extensive grasslands. The continent's topography exists on an epic scale, with awe-inspiringly spectacular coastlines and some of the world's longest rivers; largest lakes; most stupendous waterfalls; and widest, deepest valleys.

The pages that follow explore how those landscapes were formed, then focus on the historical events that make Africa truly unique. Some 2 million years ago, the first humans emerged on the continent, either in East Africa or possibly farther south. As they evolved, our early ancestors learned to hunt, to master their environment, to form communities, to manufacture tools, and to create culture. They moved around their continent and, eventually, beyond it. As they did so, the first civilizations were born. One of these, of course, was Egypt. But the Nile Valley in which it developed was also home to other early African civilizations such as Kush, Kerma, Napata, Meroë, and Aksum, all of which feature here, alongside lesser-known but important cultures like that of the Nok of West Africa.

In classical antiquity, North Africa was home to the mighty Carthaginian Empire and was one of the key sites involved in Rome's rise to power. By this time, a distinction had emerged between the "Mediterranean" North Africa and the regions of Africa south of the Sahara, which remains to this day. This idea was reinforced by the arrival in Africa of Christianity, which would go on to spread across the west and south, and the later advance of Islam in the north. After this era, great African empires formed: Wagadou in present-day Ghana, for example, and the Mali and Songhai empires. Their stories, and those of many other kingdoms and peoples, are told here through their art, artifacts, archaeology, and architecture, and through the biographies of their leaders and the customs and practices of Indigenous groups such as the Asante, Bedouin, Maasai, Tuareg, Yoruba, and Zulu.

The medieval period saw Africa develop deeper contacts with Europe, the Middle East, and Asia. Trade became an important aspect of these contacts, with states importing cloth, glass, ceramics, and spices, and exporting gold, ivory, leather goods, timber, and many other items. The period saw an escalation in the enforced trafficking of people from

△ **Emblem of office**
This c. 18th-century ceremonial ivory sword, or *udamalore* ("sword of the well-born"), symbolized power and was worn by chieftains in Oyo, a Yoruba state in modern Nigeria.

Africa, which had begun in the 7th century with the slave trade between Africa's northern and eastern states and the Arab world. The arrival of European explorers in West Africa in the 15th century led to many more millions of Africans being transported to the Americas in the Atlantic slave trade.

Imperialism and beyond

An examination of the complex relationship between Africa and Europe forms an important part of this book. The Portuguese arrived first, exploring the West African coast, followed by the British, Dutch, French, and others. By the end of the 15th century, Europeans had established military and commercial outposts on African soil. From these beachheads, as many as 15 million enslaved people would be forced to work on plantations in the Americas.

The "Africa" the Europeans encountered was not the "primitive" or "dark" continent that they later portrayed it to be, but a place of sophisticated cultures. Many of the continent's great empires continued to thrive—some in part due to their entanglement in the slave trade. Old kingdoms such as that of Kongo in Central Africa endured alongside newer powers like the West African kingdom of Dahomey. Islamic Sultanates, notably that of Zanzibar, along the East African coast enjoyed a golden age.

From the early 19th century onward, Europe increasingly involved itself in Africa's affairs. Explorers and Christian missionaries paved the way for the era of formal colonization that followed. African people resisted fiercely and sometimes successfully, but from around 1880 to the 1960s the majority of the continent was under European control—a short but highly significant period in Africa's long history. It was the aftermath of World War II, Cold War politics, and liberation movements within Africa that finally ended imperialism.

Independence was not a magic cure for all the issues that affected Africa in the wake of colonization—such as poverty, political instability, corruption, over-powerful militaries, and a lack of economic development. But through self-rule, African nations are regaining control of their own destiny. Today, people across the continent are increasingly contextualizing the past, celebrating it, and using history to understand the present—and building a future based on confidence in who Africans are and what Africa can be.

◁ **Winged arrowhead**
Cut in flint, this sharp-edged Neolithic arrowhead was made in North Africa. It measures 1½ in (3.6 cm) in length and would have been used for hunting.

1

African prehistory

5 MYA–3500 BCE

African prehistory

Africa is a continent of diverse climates and landscapes. It is also the home of humankind, the origin point from which the first anthropoids (primates that resembled humans) emerged from apelike creatures, evolved over millions of years into *Homo sapiens*—modern humans—and spread across the rest of the world.

Early origins

Africa spans around 5,000 miles (8,000 km) from the north to its southern tip, and 4,600 miles (7,400 km) east to west. Geologically, the continent was formed about 180 million years ago by the breakup of the "super-continent" Pangaea, which split into Africa, South America, Arabia, Madagascar, India, Australia, and Antarctica. Most of Africa sits on a single tectonic plate (the African Plate) that extends into the middle of the Atlantic Ocean. The eastern edge of the plate is bordered by the Arabian Plate, situated in the northeast, and the Somalian Plate, which extends from the Horn of Africa to the Southern Cape. The fault lines where these plates join are responsible for geological formations such as the Ethiopian Highlands and the Great Rift Valley.

The landscape of Africa has changed over millions of years, shaped by tectonic movement and the effects of successive ice ages and interglacial warmer periods. The continent today is characterized by a hot, dry north that encompasses the Sahara; a central band of tropical forests and savannas, or grasslands, either side of the Equator; and the more temperate south, with its plateaus and mountains, such as the Drakensberg range.

The first humanlike creatures emerged around 5 million years ago, descended from the order of primates that includes apes and monkeys. Why this happened in Africa and nowhere else is a mystery, as is where in Africa it originally happened. Two million years ago, *Homo erectus* ("upright man") appeared in Africa, and the human story took a great step forward. This species evolved into *Homo sapiens* ("wise man") 1.7 million years later. Numbers of both species moved out of Africa, spawning subspecies and other species (such as the Neanderthals) that all, with the exception of *Homo sapiens*, eventually died out.

The birth of culture

As well as being the birthplace of humanity, Africa is also where culture and society were born. The first humans did not exist as solitary creatures that only came together to mate. From the beginning, our ancestors lived and worked together. Initially, and for many hundreds of thousands of years, humans were hunter-gatherers, traversing the landscape with the changing seasons in search of food, water, and shelter. By necessity, those early hunters began to fashion tools and weapons from stones and figured out how to make and control fire. Cooking with fire allowed humans to improve their diet, which helped make their bodies more efficient and their brains bigger. Humans began to express themselves through art and body adornment, such as jewelry. In time, in Africa and beyond, humans learned how to gain some control over their environment. Settled agriculture arose, towns and cities were built, civilizations emerged, and the next phase of human development began.

◁ **The Makapansgat pebble, found in South Africa**

c. 180 million BCE Breakup of the Pangaea supercontinent; Africa and other separate landmasses form

c. 5–4 million BCE Evolution of *Australopithecus afarensis*, the earliest human ancestor

c. 3–2 million BCE Evolution of *Homo habilis* ("handy man"), the first of the *Homo* species and the first toolmaker

c. 3 million BCE Makapansgat pebble is thought to be the oldest known object that hominids recognized as having a symbolic face

c. 2 million BCE Emergence of *Homo erectus*, the first species with humanlike proportions

AFRICAN PREHISTORY | 15

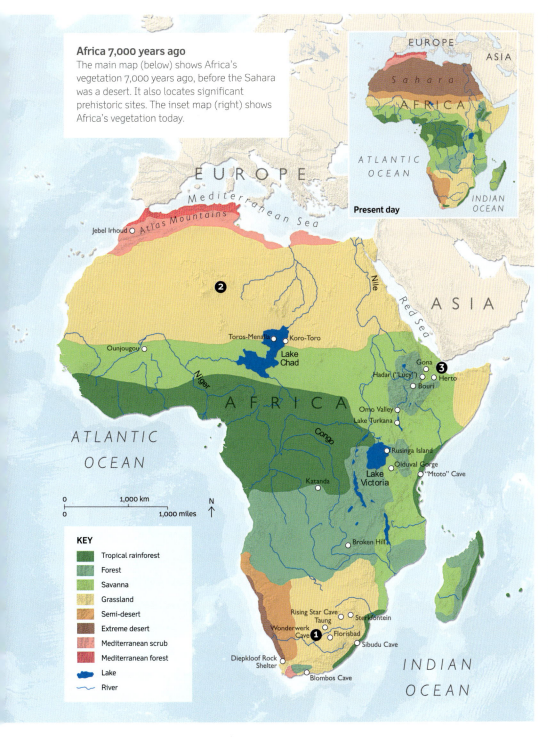

Africa 7,000 years ago
The main map (below) shows Africa's vegetation 7,000 years ago, before the Sahara was a desert. It also locates significant prehistoric sites. The inset map (right) shows Africa's vegetation today.

KEY
- Tropical rainforest
- Forest
- Savanna
- Grassland
- Semi-desert
- Extreme desert
- Mediterranean scrub
- Mediterranean forest
- Lake
- River

❶ South Africa's Wonderwerk Cave

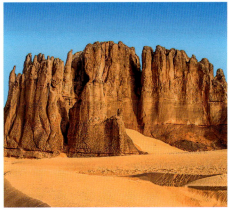

❷ Tassili n'Ajjer, Algeria, a site of ancient cave art

❸ Laas Geel Caves, Somalia

---

c. 1.75 million BCE The first "out of Africa" migrations by small groups of *Homo erectus*

c. 430,000 BCE First appearance of Neanderthal species in Europe and Asia

c. 300,000 BCE First appearance of *Homo sapiens*

c. 150,000 BCE The first languages begin to develop

c. 73,000 BCE The first rock art appears, in South Africa

c. 40,000 BCE *Homo sapiens* becomes the sole surviving human species

c. 9000 BCE Domestication of livestock begins

c. 3500 BCE Earliest migrations of Bantu-speakers across Africa

△ **Coastal desert**
Considered to be the world's oldest desert, the Namib stretches for almost 1,200 miles (2,000 km) along the Atlantic coast of Southern Africa.

Africa's environment

The continent's rich and varied topography

Africa's varied climatic zones—deserts, mountains, islands, rainforests, and temperate coastal plains—and its plant and animal life have shaped the history of this vast continent for millennia.

Africa covers more than 12 million sq miles (30 million sq km), contains the world's longest river and largest hot desert, and is second only to Asia in size. Its tallest peaks are Kilimanjaro in Tanzania at 19,341 ft (5,895 m) and Mount Kenya at 17,057 ft (5,199 m). East Africa is also home to the Great Rift Valley, a vast sequence of trenches and valleys that includes Lake Assal in Djibouti, 509 ft (155 m) below sea level. Africa's great mountain ranges include the Atlas Mountains of North Africa, East Africa's Ethiopian Highlands, and the Drakensberg Mountains in South Africa.

These high areas are the source of some of Africa's mighty rivers, including the Congo, Niger, Zambezi, and Orange. The Nile is the world's longest river, running 4,132 miles (6,650 km) from Lake Victoria— the world's largest tropical lake—to Egypt's Nile Delta. Africa's river systems have enabled civilizations to flourish, with the Niger supporting the empires of Ghana, Mali, Songhai, and Kanem-Bornu, while Egypt's population hugs the Nile.

Climate and civilization

The equator cuts Africa in two, bringing heavy rainfall and warm temperatures to a central belt of rainforests. This region is rich with plant life, including majestic mahogany trees and spectacular orchids, and animal life, including chimpanzees and elephants.

North and south of this lush rainforest stretch different climatic zones, with conditions generally becoming drier farther from the equator. To the

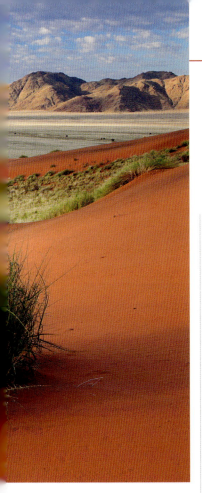

"I am an African. I owe my being to the hills and the valleys ... the ever-changing seasons."

THABO MBEKI, FORMER PRESIDENT OF SOUTH AFRICA, 1996

northeast, toward the Horn of Africa (Eritrea, Ethiopia, and Somalia) lies a temperate rainforest that the ancient Greeks saw as an earthly paradise, with plentiful rainfall and rich soil. As the land rises into the Ethiopian Highlands, the climate becomes drier and hotter, and human settlement relatively sparse.

To the west of here, woodlands and vast grasslands fringe the central rainforests and provide a home for megafauna such as giraffes, hippos, and lions. Farther north, the Sahel runs across north-central Africa from Mali to Sudan. Its minimal rainfall and coarse soil mean vegetation is mostly thin and shrubby, although in medieval times the region was more verdant and supported a considerable population.

Deserts, forests, and bush

The world's largest hot desert, the Sahara, along with the Egyptian, Libyan, and Nubian deserts, lies to the north of the central savannas. These desert landscapes contain rock-strewn plains, dunes, sand seas, and oases where camels and human travelers have quenched their thirst for thousands of years. The Atlas Mountains separate the Sahara from the fertile and more populous plains that border the Mediterranean.

South of the equator, from central Gabon to Tanzania and down to Botswana in Southern Africa, the central belt of rainforest transitions to grassland and forests, and parts of Botswana's Okavango Delta, Zambia, Zimbabwe, and Tanzania are sparsely populated but abundant with wildlife. In the Indian Ocean, Madagascar is one of the world's largest islands, with unique flora and fauna.

Southern Africa is generally dry, with grass or bush, and the Kalahari and Namib deserts stretching to the southwest. There are small mountain ranges such as the Karas, as well as large national parks, while the tip of South Africa has a Mediterranean-like climate. In Southern Africa, human settlement is most dense close to major rivers and seas, with drier regions supporting thinner or nomadic populations.

△ **Forest habitat**
The largest living primates, mountain gorillas, make their home in the rainforests of the Congo Basin. These forests, the largest in Africa, cover 1 million sq miles (1.6 million sq km).

▽ **Lake Nakuru**
Flamingos gather at Kenya's Lake Nakuru, one of the Rift Valley lakes, 5,755 ft (1,754 m) above sea level.

Namib Desert

A gemsbok stands in the Namib, a desert that stretches for almost 1,200 miles (2,000 km) along the coasts of Angola, Namibia, and South Africa. The Namib is believed to be the world's oldest desert, existing in an arid state for at least 55 million years. Beyond a few coastal cities, the region is virtually uninhabited by humans. But there is life. Vegetation includes grasses, lichens, and even some trees. Beetles, geckos, and snakes are found across the region; birds throng the coast; and antelope, elephants, and lions can be found in the north. Gemsbok, a variety of oryx, are particularly well suited to hot conditions thanks to adaptations including a vein-packed nose that cools their blood.

The shifting Sahara
Changing climate of the world's largest hot desert

The Sahara occupies around 3.5 million sq miles (9 million sq km), or one-third of Africa's total landmass. Today, the Sahara is a place of endless sands, rocks, and mountains. But more than 5,000 years ago, the region was a lush, verdant land.

Evidence of the past
Early travelers have left eyewitness accounts of the Sahara, including Muslim scholar Ibn Battuta's famous book *The Rihla* (*The Travels*) in the 14th century. But to reconstruct the ancient ecology of the Sahara, scientists use archaeological remains and paleoclimate (historical climate) evidence, such as pollen found in sediment. Earlier than about 5,000 years ago, these sources indicate, the Sahara had regular rainy monsoon seasons that created networks of rivers, rivulets, and lakes. At this time, the region supported diverse flora, including grasslands and forests, and fauna, including river animals such as fish and crocodiles. These wetter conditions also encouraged the establishment of vibrant settlements and transhumance (the movement of livestock around different regions). Rock carvings and paintings in Tassili, southern Algeria, dating from more than 6,000 years ago, show people and animals, including elephants, giraffes, hippos, and rhinos, that flourished in the vast, lush savanna before desiccation set in.

Examination of ocean sediments along West African coasts, including dust, pollen, and other materials deposited by the wind, suggests that about 8,000 years

△ **Lake Chad**
A freshwater lake with a surface area that varies by season as well as year by year, Lake Chad is the remaining portion of a larger ancient sea sometimes called Mega Chad. It covers territories in four countries: Nigeria, Cameroon, Niger, and Chad.

△ **Shrinking waters**
Satellite images taken over several decades provide startling visible evidence of the shrinking of the once "Great" Lake Chad. It now spans less than a tenth of the area it covered in the 1960s. Many initiatives, such as planting trees to avoid soil erosion, are being taken by local communities to protect their lake environment.

△ **The Sahel**
The Sahel is a region of grasslands, forests, savannas, and shrublands between the Sahara to the north and the Sudanian savanna to the south. Deforestation and drought have caused much of it to turn to desert—a trend that is likely to continue.

"We found much water ... in pools left by the rains."

IBN BATTUTA, *THE RIHLA (THE TRAVELS)*, 1354

ago the middle of the Sahara experienced a period of dryness. This period lasted about 1,000 years, forcing a wave of migration to the north and south and marking a cultural shift among the ancient inhabitants. Those who returned after the dry period survived on a more diverse diet, moving from hunting and gathering to cattle herding and dairy production.

Desert on the move

The current more intense period of dryness set in some 5,000 years ago, forcing further migrations from the Sahara as groups of people moved to the better-watered grasslands and forests of West Africa and northeastward into Egypt's fertile Nile Delta. These movements helped foster a cultural interaction on which ancient Egypt's 3,000-year-old civilization was built. For around 2,000 years, the Sahara's climate has been relatively stable. However, scientists at the University of California Los Angeles (UCLA) have shown that the desert is now expanding steadily southward by 0.9 miles (1.5 km) a year. Lake Chad in West-Central Africa, which provides food and water to more than 50 million people, has shrunk by 95 percent since 1960, threatening the lives of many in the region. Trends indicate that this drift will continue until at least 2050. However, some models of future climate change suggest that the West African monsoon could strengthen again naturally, which would trigger an increase in green vegetation: a new chapter in the story of the Sahara.

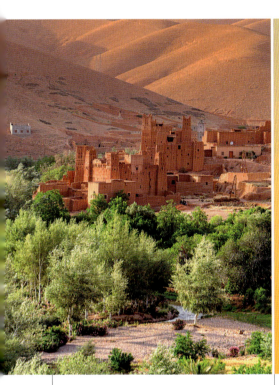

△ **Desert settlement, Morocco**
Communities in desert settlements in the High Atlas Mountains in Morocco are highly vulnerable to the effects of climate change. Many barely scrape a living as laborers and agriculturalists, and face the constant threat of drought.

△ **Ships of the desert**
Dromedary camels were first introduced to the Sahara around 200 CE as part of trade caravans from the Arabian Peninsula. Their tremendous endurance, strength, and ability to withstand the effects of intense heat and food and water deprivation make them ideally suited to the harsh desert environment.

△ **The hammada**
The majority of the Sahara is a type of desert known as hammada, meaning "rock" in Arabic. These landscapes consist of high, hard, rocky plateaus, generally lacking in vegetation, where most of the sand has been removed through wind erosion.

Cradle of humanity

From *Ardipithecus* to *Australopithecus*

A wealth of fossil finds across the continent of Africa provides evidence for the earliest humans, who evolved from the family of hominids, or "great apes" (chimpanzees, orangutans, and gorillas), about 5–4 million years ago (MYA).

△ **Facial reconstruction**
Researchers re-created the face of a 4–3.3-million-year-old hominid, known as "Lucy," using sophisticated forensic techniques.

The confirmation of humanity's African origins began in the 1920s. Ever since, experts have been reconstructing humankind's family tree, tracing its branches back over millions of years to show how evolution progressed not in a straight line, one species after another, but contingently.

In 1924, the Australian anthropologist Raymond Dart discovered a child's skull at Taung, in South Africa. "Taungboy," as Dart described the 2.8-million-year-old fossil, was the first specimen found of the upright-walking bipedal early human, or hominin, *Australopithecus afarensis* ("the southern ape from afar").

At this time, the scientific community believed that humans originated in Europe or Asia, not Africa, and many dismissed Dart's assertion that *Australopithecus afarensis* represented a "missing link" between apes and humans. In time, however, scientists recognized his claim, helped in part when the paleontologist (a scientist who studies fossils) Robert Broom discovered adult *australopithecine* remains in South Africa in 1936.

Following Dart's and Broom's discoveries, similar, older finds in Tanzania, Ethiopia, and Kenya left little doubt as to humankind's place of origin. In 1978, the British paleoanthropologist Mary Leakey found sets of

> "The **driving force of evolution** is **environment**."
>
> YOHANNES HAILE-SELASSIE, 2019

CRADLE OF HUMANITY | 23

◁ **Place of origin**
Olduvai Gorge in Tanzania is one of the world's most important sources of hominin fossil remains and early stone tool artifacts.

3.5-million-year-old footprints made by upright-walking hominins at Laetoli, south of Tanzania's Olduvai Gorge. This complemented her earlier discovery at Olduvai Gorge in 1959 of what is now known as *Australopithecus boisei*, which lived 3–2 MYA and had a larger cranium than *Australopithecus afarensis*. This species was later linked with *Paranthropus robustus*, a hominin found in Southern Africa.

Unlike *Australopithecus boisei*, *Paranthropus robustus*, which lived 2–1.2 MYA, was able to make tools. *Homo habilis*, an advanced species of *Paranthropus robustus*, is credited with creating sharpened stone tools that allowed it to hunt game effectively and harvest wild roots and crops for food.

The past reveals the present
A landmark find came in 1974, when French geoscientist Maurice Taieb's team in Hadar, Ethiopia, excavated "Lucy," an apelike creature 3 ft 8 in (1.1 m) tall and weighing 65 lb (29 kg). "Lucy" was a small-brained bipedal hominid, classed as *Australopithecus afarensis*, who lived 4–3.3 million years ago. Her ability to stand upright and walk placed her species in a prominent position in the human evolution tree.

In 1998–1999, a team led by paleoanthropologists Louise and Meave Leakey made another important discovery in Lake Turkana, Kenya. *Kenyanthropus platyops* lived 3.5 MYA and its flat facial features and small teeth have led some to believe that this species is a direct ancestor of modern humans. Then, in Ethiopia in 2009, came the earliest find yet—the 4.4-million-year-old *Ardipithecus ramidus*. An older fossil, the 7-million-year-old *Sahelanthropus tchadensis* from Chad, is not yet fully accepted as a true human ancestor due to doubt as to whether the species could walk on two legs.

How humankind developed in Africa, and why some species thrived while others died out, depended on a number of factors. The tool-making capabilities of some species played a role, as did Africa's ecology, with its climate, landscape, flora, and fauna determining which species prospered. With each new fossil discovery, our understanding of human evolution expands.

△ **"Lucy" skull**
Scientists have reconstructed the skull of "Lucy" from fragments of bone. Her third molars ("wisdom teeth") are erupted and slightly worn, indicating that "Lucy" was fully adult.

◁ **Find from Ethiopia**
Yohannes Haile-Selassie, a paleoanthropologist from Ethiopia, helped discover the skull of an *Australopithecus anamensis*, an ancestor of *Australopithecus afarensis*. The two species coexisted for around 100,000 years.

Figures were painted using ground-up minerals mixed with water, saliva, blood, fat, or urine

Elaborate decorations on limbs and torso

△ **Rock paintings of Tassili n'Ajjer**
This rock art, from Tassili n'Ajjer, Algeria, dates to c. 6000 BCE. Of all ancient human species, only *Homo sapiens* seems to have created figurative art, a skill demonstrating its ability to understand and represent the world.

The rise of sapiens

Tracing the birth of humankind

From the Latin for "wise man," *Homo sapiens* is the species to which all modern humans belong. It first appeared in Africa and developed a complex culture and technology that allowed it to adapt to a wide range of different environments.

Homo sapiens, the first recognizable humans, evolved in Africa. Scientists view Southern Africa or Ethiopia as the likeliest sites, although the earliest remains discovered so far were found in Jebel Irhoud in Morocco, and date from around 300,000 years ago.

Like all of humankind's ancestors, *Homo sapiens* derived from primates, the zoological order whose groups also include monkeys and apes. Indeed, humans (*Homo*) are actually part of the ape "superfamily" Hominoidea. The *Homo* genus of the Hominoidea family tree branched off around 3 million years ago (see pp.22–23) and evolved through a number of species, including *Homo habilis*, *Homo erectus*, and *Homo heidelbergensis*. *Homo sapiens* is the most recent *Homo* species and has outlived all the others, which have gone extinct.

The defining characteristic of *sapiens* against all earlier species is that it had a bigger brain, housed in a high-vaulted, thinly walled skull. Why this bigger brain developed is the subject of scientific debate, but some environmental and cultural factors are generally agreed. *Sapiens* came about at a time when Earth's climate was relatively dry and cold. Food and water were scarce, meaning that our ancestors had to invent strategies for finding and keeping sustenance when they could. In this respect, *sapiens* profited from earlier *Homo* species' development of the first stone tools and their harnessing of fire as a means of keeping warm and cooking food.

Origins of the species

With their bigger brains and the evolutionary experience of hundreds of thousands of years of toolmaking by earlier species, *sapiens* made and used cutting and hunting implements that were better and more effective than ever before. Being able to gather, store, and cook food—particularly meat—more efficiently allowed *sapiens* to evolve into a strong, healthy, long-lived, practical, organized, and intelligent species. All of these characteristics in combination ensured that *sapiens* would flourish where other species, which possessed only some of these characteristics, would die out.

In addition, the earliest *sapiens* discovered that those groups able to accumulate knowledge, share it, and pass it on to others were more likely to thrive. Devising ways of working together (or against each other) allowed groups of *sapiens* better chances of survival, especially in harsh, unforgiving environments as they moved around, and ultimately out of, Africa. Cooperation by necessity means communication, and this led to the emergence of language and, in time, art, religion, culture, social organization, and the first civilizations—and *sapiens* becoming who we are today.

SEARCHING FOR **AFRICA'S EARTH MOTHER**

In recent decades, scientific studies have sought to discover the origin site of humankind by looking at mitochondrial DNA, which is found within cells and inherited only by females. Comparing mitochondrial DNA in the oldest *Homo sapiens* fossils with that of Indigenous populations in parts of Africa, the aim is to discover people with the strongest or longest unbroken genetic links. A study among the Khoisan people (below) of northern Botswana placed the Makgadikgadi basin region as a strong candidate, but the quest to find the definitive "Mitochondrial Eve" continues.

▷ **Brain development**
A comparison of the "Turkana Boy" skull (above right) with a *sapiens* skull (right), found in Ethiopia and dating to 200,000 years ago, shows the remarkable increase in cranium size.

△ **Turkana Boy**
This model is based on a *Homo ergaster* skeleton from c. 1.6 million years BCE, discovered in 1984 in Kenya and known as "Turkana Boy." From a species predating *Homo sapiens*, he appears remarkably "modern."

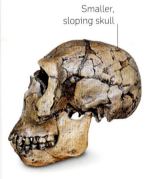

Smaller, sloping skull

HOMO ERGASTER SKULL

Large cranium holds bigger brain

HOMO SAPIENS SKULL

Stone tools

Inventing the earliest implements

Africa's Stone Age began 3.3 million years ago and ended around 2000 BCE. In modern times, archaeologists have uncovered a wide variety of tools and artifacts used by humankind's ancient ancestors, including sharp flakes, arrowheads, hammerstones, hand axes, and other utensils.

▷ **Stone Age selection**
These tools are from a find of 300,000-year-old artifacts at Jebel Irhoud, Morocco. "Limace," "Unifacial," and "Levallois" describe different "flaking" styles.

LIMACE — Flaked on both sides
UNIFACIAL — Flaked on one side only
LEVALLOIS — Edges flaked off by hammer

Expertly rendered serrated edge

Patch of iron-rich pink in otherwise blue-gray jasper

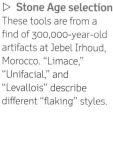
Green jasper

Skillfully created symmetrical shape

Slender carved shaft

Inward-curving wings

△ **Regional rarity**
Discovered in Mali, this scraper was made 280,000–500,000 years ago. It is 2.75 in (7 cm) in length and is of a style and material unique to West Africa.

△ **On the hunt**
Sharp items like this 195,000-year-old projectile point from Omo Kibish in Ethiopia were attached to sticks to use as spears for hunting animals.

△ **Neolithic arrowhead**
Found in the western Sahara, this slender arrowhead measures 1.77 in (4.5 cm) long and dates from about 10,000 BCE–2000 BCE.

△ **Saw-toothed tool**
Designed with double faces, this elongated cutting implement dates from the Neolithic era. Discovered in Mali, it measures 6.45 in (16.4 cm) in length.

STONE TOOLS | 27

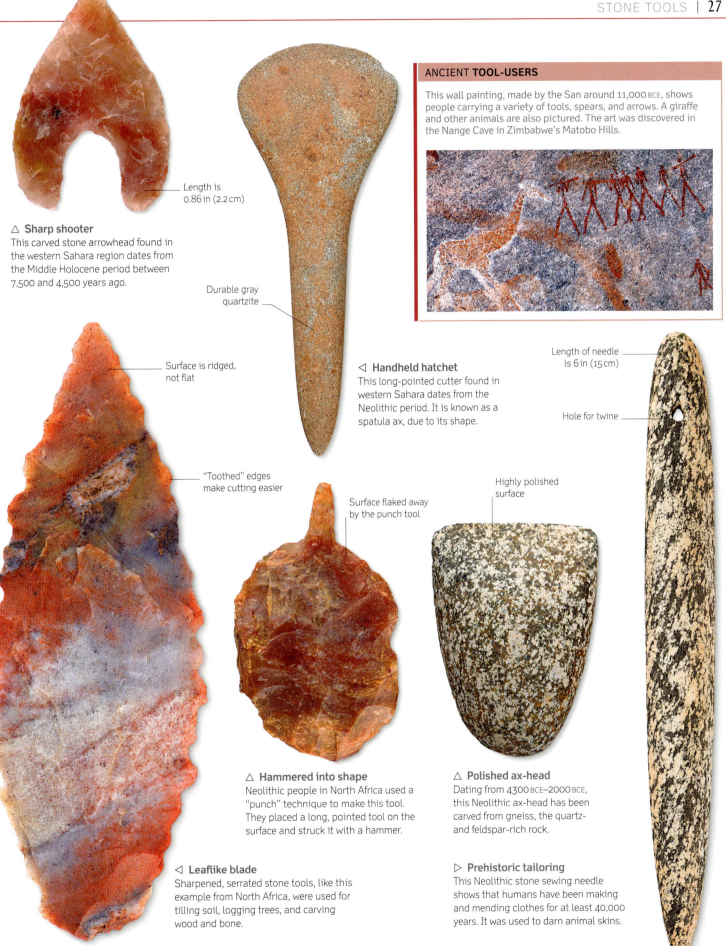

Length is 0.86 in (2.2 cm)

△ **Sharp shooter**
This carved stone arrowhead found in the western Sahara region dates from the Middle Holocene period between 7,500 and 4,500 years ago.

Durable gray quartzite

ANCIENT **TOOL-USERS**
This wall painting, made by the San around 11,000 BCE, shows people carrying a variety of tools, spears, and arrows. A giraffe and other animals are also pictured. The art was discovered in the Nange Cave in Zimbabwe's Matobo Hills.

Surface is ridged, not flat

◁ **Handheld hatchet**
This long-pointed cutter found in western Sahara dates from the Neolithic period. It is known as a spatula ax, due to its shape.

Length of needle is 6 in (15 cm)

Hole for twine

"Toothed" edges make cutting easier

Surface flaked away by the punch tool

Highly polished surface

△ **Hammered into shape**
Neolithic people in North Africa used a "punch" technique to make this tool. They placed a long, pointed tool on the surface and struck it with a hammer.

△ **Polished ax-head**
Dating from 4300 BCE–2000 BCE, this Neolithic ax-head has been carved from gneiss, the quartz- and feldspar-rich rock.

◁ **Leaflike blade**
Sharpened, serrated stone tools, like this example from North Africa, were used for tilling soil, logging trees, and carving wood and bone.

▷ **Prehistoric tailoring**
This Neolithic stone sewing needle shows that humans have been making and mending clothes for at least 40,000 years. It was used to darn animal skins.

Out of Africa
The first human migrations

Groups of early humans moved from their homelands and out of Africa in phases, with the first, *Homo erectus*, dispersing about 2 million years ago, followed by *Homo sapiens* around 60,000 years ago.

Homo sapiens (modern humans) was not the first species to leave Africa. Fossil records show that small numbers of an earlier human ancestor, *Homo erectus* ("upright man"), made their way through the Middle East and on to Europe and parts of southeast Asia and China around 2 million years ago, surviving for hundreds of thousands of years.

The Ubeidiya archaeological complex in northern Israel, for example, contains the remains of *Homo erectus* dating from 1.5 million to 700,000 years ago, alongside a variety of "Acheulean" tools—oval and pear-shaped hand axes that were first developed in Africa around 1.76 million years ago. It is believed that Acheulean toolmaking (of which the oldest examples have been found in Ethiopia) emerged from Oldowan technology, a very early form of tool manufacture from around 2.9 million years ago associated with the Olduvai Gorge in Tanzania. These finds offer additional confirmation of a lineage of early human—and technological—evolution spreading outward from the African continent.

◁ **Pointing the way**
These finger bones date from c. 85,000 BCE and were found in the Arabian Peninsula—one of the routes by which *Homo sapiens* left Africa.

Beyond Israel, it is thought that *Homo erectus* arrived in China 700,000 years ago. The remains known as "Peking man" found in northern China in 1921 are recognized as *Homo erectus pekinensis*, a subspecies of *Homo erectus*. Further subspecies made it to Indonesia between one million and 500,000 years ago (*Homo erectus erectus*, or "Java man") and to Europe around 500,000 years ago (*Homo heidelbergensis*, or "Heidelberg man").

Evolutionary steps

Although *Homo erectus* was dispersed widely across the world, it failed to thrive in great numbers. Around 300,000 years ago, it was joined outside Africa by the first migratory *Homo sapiens*. As with *Homo erectus*, Israel appears to have been an early stopping-off point for the new species. Archaeological digs at the Mislaya Caves on the slopes of Mount Carmel, in northern Israel, have uncovered a 200,000-year-old *Homo sapiens* jawbone and teeth, together with advanced flint tools and sophisticated hand axes.

This may have been part of an advance wave of *Homo sapiens* migrations that were ultimately failures. It was not until around 60,000 years ago that the species began to leave Africa in larger numbers and successfully flourish in new locations. Reconstructions of the era's climate indicate that conditions in Africa (particularly the east of the continent) were dry, with sea levels much lower than today, and this made it easier for populations to move north and east, toward the Middle East, Europe, and Asia across land bridges between continents that have since disappeared beneath the rising waters of the oceans. The arid, drought-like conditions in their African homelands may also have made *Homo sapiens*' exodus

▽ **On the move**
Waves of humanlike *Homo* species moved around and out of Africa from 2 million years ago. The Americas were the last landmasses early humans reached.

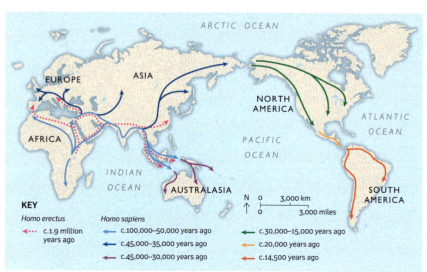

◁ **Leaving a mark**
Dating to c. 20,000–6000 BCE, these fossilized *Homo sapiens* footprints lie at the base of Ol Doinyo Lengai, an active volcano in Tanzania. The depth and angle of the prints indicate they were made by people jogging.

Layer of volcanic ash and mud in which prints are preserved

Indentation of footprint, one of 400 left by up to 20 individuals

necessary, forcing them out in search of water, nutrient-rich plants, and a varied diet. In 2020, footprints from hundreds of elephants, cattle, and horses were discovered in a dried lake in Saudi Arabia, along with the footprints of three humans—the oldest evidence of *Homo sapiens* in Arabia—demonstrating the close ties between the movements of early humans and the animals they hunted. Finally, there is simply the possibility that *Homo sapiens* migrated spontaneously, as populations in Africa became more dense.

As *Homo sapiens* settled in new areas, they coexisted and to some extent interbred with other species, such as *Homo erectus* and *Homo neanderthalensis* (Neanderthals). Eventually, *Homo sapiens* began to supplant all other species, and, by between 40,000 and 15,000 years ago, all *Homo* species except *sapiens* had died out.

SOUTH-TO-EAST EXODUS

Scientists and anthropologists continue to speculate on the movements of our ancestors within and out of Africa. One scenario suggests an early migration from Southern Africa into East Africa in around 70,000–60,000 BCE when a naturally climate-induced wet corridor opened up. *Homo sapiens* from the south of Africa showed the earliest and clearest examples of complex toolmaking and self-expression, including rock art depicting humans and animals. Transferring these new skills and abilities to existing populations in the east could have provided the means for further migratory exploration beyond the continent.

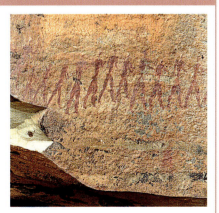

SAN ROCK ART, SOUTH AFRICA

Origins of human culture

The conscious creation of things

As human evolution progressed, from *Homo erectus* to *Homo sapiens*, the first stirrings of culture developed. Toolmaking, the use of fire, social organization, and communication through art and language emerged.

As the era of *Homo erectus* came to an end and that of *Homo sapiens* began, the development of culture accelerated, diversified, and became more sophisticated. This is not "culture" in its modern sense—though it certainly paved the way for it and contains elements of it—but more a shift in the way that humans acted, how they thought, and how they expressed those thoughts. The period runs roughly from 300,000 BCE, when *Homo sapiens* (modern humans) first emerged, to around 40,000 BCE, when it was on the way to becoming the sole surviving human species.

Causes, effects, and cultural shifts

A significant factor that allowed culture to develop was early humans' mastery of fire. This happened around 2 million years ago, in the era of *Homo erectus*. At sites such as Wonderwerk Cave in South Africa and Koobi Fora in northern Kenya, scientists have found evidence of controlled fire use, including remnants of burned bone and plants, and what appear to be hearths. Using fire to cook meat and fish had an evolutionary outcome. Cooked food took less of the body's energy to digest than raw food—and the energy saved was channeled toward evolving a smaller, more efficient digestive tract and a larger, more powerful brain. Evolution progresses slowly, so it would be hundreds of thousands of years before these changes came to fruition, in the shape of *Homo sapiens* and its contemporaries such as Neanderthals, found in Europe and Western Asia.

A bigger brain allowed early humans to see the world differently, and begin to attribute meaning and significance to the things they experienced. It also gave them the ability to remake the world in ways that better suited their needs and wants. Tools are a good example of this process at work. The earliest tools, found in places such as Kenya and Ethiopia, were made around 3.3 million years ago and were simple rock hammerstones and sharp flakes and shards of stone. By the time of *Homo sapiens*, tools had evolved into far more complex and practical items, designed for specific purposes and relatively easy to use (see pp.26–27). Discovered at many sites, particularly in North and East Africa, and dating to around 300,000 years ago, these tools included blades, awls (piercing tools), points, scrapers, and burins (chisels). By at least 90,000 years ago, barbed points made of

△ On point
This 90,000-year-old harpoon head was found at an archaeological site on the Semliki River in the Democratic Republic of the Congo. The harpoon is carved from bone.

◁ Art supplies
This sea snail shell, used for mixing paint, was found in South Africa's Blombos Cave. At c. 100,000 years old, it is among the oldest art objects ever discovered.

Motif of lines

△ Early engravings
At 60,000 years old, the engravings on these ostrich shell water containers are early examples of graphic art. These fragments were discovered at the Diepkloof Rock Shelter, South Africa.

bone—like those discovered at sites on the Semliki River in the Democratic Republic of the Congo—were used to spear fish. Other composite tools, including axes, arrows, and bows, were made of materials such as stone, animal hide, and wood. Many of these designs are still in use today.

What these sophisticated tools showed was that humans were now able to think in abstract and symbolic terms. Not coincidentally, at around the same time humans were producing new and better tools, they also began to make art. One of the first ways humans left their mark was through rock art and cave paintings, the oldest of which—patterns made with an ocher crayon on a piece of rock—dates from around 73,000 years ago and was found in South Africa. Mark-making began to be used to represent the world and express or invoke beliefs and expectations, complementing the other form of communication humans acquired at around this time: language.

Birth of the decorative arts

Initially, humans would probably have decorated practical objects in some way—carving ax handles or inscribing patterns onto bowls, for example. Eventually, this morphed into the making of decorative items purely for their own sake, or for possibly ceremonial or symbolic purposes.

From around 130,000 BCE, humans began to bury their dead, as evidenced by sites in Europe and Asia. The earliest intentional burial site found in Africa is at Panga ya Saidi, a cave site on the Kenyan coast that dates back 78,000 years—where a three-year-old child whose head appears to have been laid on a support, like a pillow, is buried.

Artifacts and ornaments have been found at burial and other sites. In 2014–2018, a team of archaeologists in Morocco found 33 shell beads dating from around 150,000–130,000 BCE that were designed to have been strung on some form of cord and worn as decorative items. Body piercing and tattooing seem also to have been practiced: bones of a 12,000-year-old man found in Tanzania show teeth damage thought to have been caused by a piercing on the lower lip.

With most of the elements associated with the creation of culture in place by 40,000 years ago at latest, the scene was set for the next phase of human development. This was the era of settled agriculture, the building of towns and cities, and the formation of the first civilizations.

△ **Patterned plaque**
This ocher plaque, dating to c. 70,000 BCE, is engraved with possibly the first geometric pattern made by a human hand. It was found in Blombos Cave, South Africa.

▽ **Cave of wonders**
The 100,000-year-old sediments in South Africa's Blombos Cave contained some the earliest and richest cultural artifacts made by early humans yet discovered.

Rock art

Visual representation in the Neolithic era

Art forms such as drawings and paintings (known as pictographs), carvings and inscriptions (petroglyphs), rocks arranged in patterns (petroforms), and carved motifs (engravings) are modes of expression as old as humankind. Africa offers rich and varied examples of rock art created in all of these techniques.

Creating a visual record

Archaeologists have discovered millennia-old artwork over the entire continent, from Namibia and South Africa to Mali and Niger in West Africa, across the Sahara to the plains of Egypt and south to Uganda, Tanzania, and Kenya. The study and interpretation of these paintings, carvings, and rock formations offers a wealth of insights into a long-vanished past.

This artwork reveals that our earliest ancestors shared a common interest in documenting their existence. The similarity of works found across the whole expanse of Africa suggests that the impulse or need for expression was common to peoples as they began to form into groups and acquire the first trappings of domesticity and civilization.

Africa's Neolithic cave paintings, drawings, carvings, and sculptured forms are the earliest images of how peoples were organized, where they found shelter, how they moved and migrated across the land, how they gathered food, what and how they hunted, and much more. In the absence of written records or, in many cases, lacking extensive archaeological remains, ancient art has also supplied the modern

△ **Designs in the desert**
The engravings at southeast Algeria's Tin Taghirt site were made around 8000 BCE by nomadic pastoralists and include representations of cattle, buffalo, and crocodiles. This antelope appears to be sleeping with its head resting on a forelimb.

△ **Stencils and paintings**
Egypt's Wadi Sura ("Valley of Pictures") is famed for its Neolithic rock art, which is more than 7,000 years old. The "Cave of Beasts," as it is known to archaeologists, features thousands of painted animals, including elephants, ostriches, and giraffes, and, as here, depictions of human figures and stencils of small hands.

△ **Preserved by nature**
The "Great God of Sefar", in Tassili N'Ajjer, Algeria, was painted around 12,000 years ago and is more than 10 ft (3 m) high. The Sahara's hot, dry climate has helped preserve much rock art, including the image of this mysterious, horned, faceless figure.

> "Africa's **rock art** ... is the **common heritage** of humanity."
>
> KOFI ANNAN, FORMER UN SECRETARY-GENERAL, 2005

world with invaluable information on how humanity's ancestors thought about issues such as gender and sexuality, ethnicity, religious beliefs, and fertility, as well as how they entertained themselves with music and dance, wore decorative clothing and headdresses, made technological advances, and developed a material culture and lived their daily lives.

Methods and impulses

The earliest rock art discovered in Africa so far is in Namibia (see right). Early humans experimented with production techniques and invented methods for communicating their artistic impulses. They ground colored rocks into fine powders—for example, ocher for yellow, orange, and brown, limestone for white, and hematite for red—and used charcoal for black and shells for more white. They mixed these with binding agents such as plant sap, animal fat, or saliva, and applied them to walls using their hands or with brushes made from feathers, animal hair, or the ends of chewed sticks. Sometimes, they drew with solid lumps of pigment or blew powdered pigment onto surfaces through a pipe.

Why Neolithic people created rock art is open to question. It is thought that the main reasons were to express religious beliefs, to appease or ask for help from spirits or providence, to celebrate a good hunt, or to simply make something beautiful or interesting.

△ **Animal magic**
Seven quartzite slabs found from 1969–1972 in a cave in Namibia depict human and animal figures and have been dated to around 28,000 BCE. Archaeologists called the cave "Apollo 11" after the then-recent NASA moon mission.

△ **Expressive figures**
The hunter-gatherer San people created many images on rock surfaces in South Africa's Cederberg Mountain region, many as recently as 2,000 years ago. These dancing women are thought to be involved in a ritual or ceremony.

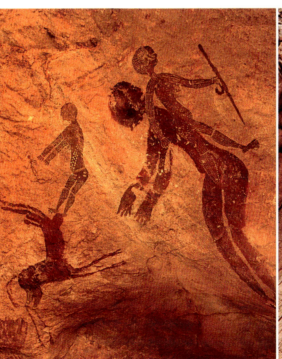

△ **Everyday life**
Among the 15,000 examples of rock art that have been identified so far in Algeria's Tassili N'Ajjer National Park are many scenes of daily and social life that display remarkable naturalistic realism. Such depictions include people hunting and herding animals, and, as here, what appears to be children taking part.

△ **Set in stone**
Dabous, in Niger's Ténéré Desert, hosts prehistory's most extensive collection of animal petroglyphs. The celebrated "Dabous Giraffes" are at least 6,000 years old and were probably carved and etched into the soft sandstone using flint tools.

△ **Cattle drive**
Livestock is rounded up for inspection in this Egyptian tomb painting from c. 1350 BCE. Cattle herding in Egypt began around 6000 BCE.

The development of agriculture

Cultivation and settlement in Africa

From the late Neolithic period, farming became established across the African continent in different ways and at different rates. This had a profound effect on how African societies were organized.

Although humans originated in Africa (see pp.22–23), agriculture did not. The first farmers emerged around 12,000 years ago in the area known as the "Fertile Crescent." This was the well-watered land between the Euphrates and Tigris rivers that included modern-day Lebanon, Syria, southern Turkey, Iraq, and western Iran. From here, the understanding of how to domesticate animals and cultivate plants and crops spread east to India and China, and southwest to the Nile Valley.

Agriculture and settlement

Egypt was the first place in Africa to acquire knowledge of agriculture—the management of crops, livestock, fish, and forestry for food and other purposes. It is no coincidence that the continent's first settled civilization also developed there. Hunter-gatherers tend to operate in small groups, always on

Animal-hide binding

Wooden handle

◁ **Ancient multi-tool**
This model of an adze (a type of ax) used in Egypt c. 1981 BCE has a copper blade. Adzes were used for cutting, chopping, and planing wood.

the move, their time largely spent finding sources of food, preparing it, and seeking suitable places to shelter. Settled communities, by contrast, are larger and more diverse. Once they master the principles of agriculture, people in these communities have more time for other pursuits. Religions develop, social hierarchies are established, leaders emerge, and complex forms of social organization can then arise.

One outcome of settlement is that there is now time for the manufacture of tools to begin. The first farmers were able to plant crops and improve yields through the use of a variety of tools. At first, these were fairly crude stone items (see pp.26–27), ridged, shaped, and sharpened to clear overgrown land, make furrows in soil, and cut down harvests.

This activity began to take place in small pockets of Egypt in the Lower Nile Valley around 6000 BCE, and by 3000 BCE—around the time of the First Dynasty in c. 3100–2890 BCE—agriculture was well established. By this time, agriculture in Africa had spread west and southwest into the modern-day countries of Libya; Morocco; and the southern, non-desert parts of Mauritania. Barley and wheat were cultivated, and cattle, sheep, and goats domesticated. Saharan rock paintings from the 5th millennium BCE begin to show cattle herding and milking as well as hunting scenes, and the cattle are often depicted in huge herds.

The crops grown

Plant and animal domestication took place later in regions south of the Sahara, some time in the 3rd millennium BCE. This probably occurred spontaneously in the area around modern-day Nigeria and Cameroon rather than being imported from Egypt. Millet was the first cereal crop cultivated south of the Sahara, followed by sorghum—a nutrient-rich cereal grain that remains one of the continent's most important crops. These grains were probably initially grown as food for animals; it is likely that Africa's first farmers domesticated livestock long before they began to grow crops for their own consumption.

In addition to millet and sorghum, in West Africa people began to grow rice between 2,000 and 3,000 years ago along the floodplains in a bend in the Niger River. A type of rice called *Oryza glaberrima* is native to the regions of Africa south of the Sahara and is one of the world's two cultivated rice species (the other being *Oryza sativa*, which is found in Asia). Africa is still a major producer of rice today, and the crop ranks fifth among the continent's cash exports after cassava (a potato-like root vegetable), sugar cane, and corn—which were all introduced by Portuguese colonizers after 1500—as well as yams, an indigenous tuber similar to the sweet potato.

"The **best** of mankind is a **farmer**; the best food is **fruit**."

ETHIOPIAN PROVERB

Farming spreads south

While agriculture was developing in West Africa, it was also spreading farther south from Egypt into what is today Sudan, and across into the Great Lakes region and to East Africa. In Ethiopia, however, farming probably developed independently of any outside influence, as it did in West Africa, as early as 5000 BCE. The crops grown in Ethiopia were indigenous rather than introduced from other regions. They included the cereal grains *tef* and *dagusa*, also known as finger millet; *enset*, a banana-like plant used to make flatbreads, pancakes, and porridge; and *nug*, a flowering herb grown for its oil and edible seeds.

The development of African agriculture proceeded more slowly south of the equator. Bantu-speaking people migrating out of West and Central Africa brought their knowledge of farming with them as they gradually traveled farther south from c. 2500 BCE. Settled agriculture was not practiced in any significant way in Southern Africa until around 250 CE—more than 6,000 years after the continent's earliest farmers had planted their first crops in Egypt around 4,350 miles (7,000 km) away.

▽ **Farmer at work**
This 4th-century CE carved relief once decorated the walls of the Ghirza Mausoleum in western Libya. It shows a farmer using a tool to harvest a wheat crop.

The Bantu migrations
The spread of farming and iron-making culture

Around 3,500 years ago, Bantu-language speakers began leaving their home near the border of modern-day Nigeria and Cameroon. They dispersed techniques of farming and iron-smelting to hunter-gathering groups across the continent.

△ **Migration routes**
This map gives an approximate indication of the migration paths that different Bantu-speaking groups are thought to have taken across Africa.

Evidence for the Bantu migrations is mainly linguistic, drawing on the strong language resemblances in vastly different areas. Scholars believe this movement may have been caused by climatically induced overpopulation: following a period of cold, dry, erratic weather about 10,000 years ago (known as the Younger Dryas), the Earth gradually became warmer, wetter, more stable, and richer in carbon dioxide (today's epoch, known as the Holocene).

Plant life became increasingly abundant and, instead of frequent foraging, the Bantu-speaking groups stayed longer in specific areas, where they collected and stored as much of the local foods as possible. This increase in the availability of food meant that their societies could sustain a greater number of people. To feed the higher numbers, they began cultivating local produce, working the land harder for longer, and developing a wider range of tools to increase efficiency and productivity.

◁ **Lydenburg pottery fragment**
This pottery fragment, c. 500 CE, was retrieved from Lydenburg, South Africa, one of the areas populated by the Bantu-speakers.

Eventually, their populations grew so large they were unsustainable, and some Bantu-speaking groups migrated in search of other fertile lands. Other Bantu-speaking groups migrated to the edges of the Central African forest, which, from 2000 BCE, was traversable, inhabitable savanna—although the core of the forest remained dense and inhospitable.

Learning and spreading new skills

In 500 BCE, a new climatic shift took place: the climate, and the sea surface, became warmer, prompting more rainfall, which washed away the soil in the Central African forest. Trees were unable to grow and savanna replaced the dense vegetation at the heart of the forest. Some of the Bantu-speakers moved into it, occupying areas such as modern-day north Gabon; others migrated into what is now eastern Congo, before using nearby waterways to migrate east and south. By around 300 BCE, some of them had ventured as far as the Great Lakes of East Africa.

▷ **Ironworkers**
A watercolor, made around 1650 CE by Italian missionary Giovanni Antonio Cavazzi da Montecuccolo, shows ironworkers in the Bantu-speaking Kingdom of Kongo forging weapons and tools.

> "Iron … **so pure** that I doubt in Europe they would achieve **such perfection.**"
>
> CAVAZZI DA MONTECUCCOLO, FROM HIS HISTORY OF CONGO, MATAMBA, AND ANGOLA, 1687

There, they met farmers and skilled iron-tool users who spoke the languages of Central Sudan, and from them they acquired greater knowledge about farming.

Many diverse hunter-gathering groups populated the areas into which the Bantu-speakers had moved since 2000 BCE. The Bantu-speaking communities conquered or displaced these people, or adapted to their environments, exchanging knowledge and cultural practices. Hunter-gatherers adopted ironworking technology from the Bantu-speakers, who in turn borrowed words and customs from hunter-gatherers.

Multiple migrations

Between 300 and 200 BCE, some of the Bantu-speakers who had been influenced by the Central-Sudan-language-speakers migrated back west, along the south edge of the Central African forest, into north Angola. There, they encountered Bantu-speakers who, rather than settling in north Gabon or moving east following the climatic shift of 500 BCE, had migrated down Africa's west coast to south Congo. By 1 CE, many had settled in north Angola and adopted the ironworking, farming culture of the Central-Sudan Bantu-speakers.

Some of the north Angolan Bantu-speakers migrated south, moving deeper into Angola, gradually spreading themselves over much of southwest Africa; others went east, into the Democratic Republic of the Congo and Zambia, settling there by 500 CE. Meanwhile, between 100 and 200 CE, instead of migrating westward, some of the Central-Sudan-speaking Bantu who had settled near the Great Lakes traveled south and east, finally settling in Kenya, Tanzania, and possibly Somalia. Between 300 and 400 CE, some of them had continued farther south, moving first into Zambia and Malawi, before entering Zimbabwe and South Africa.

In this way, the Bantu-speaking people from West Africa gradually spread a sophisticated ironworking, farming culture across most of the continent of Africa.

△ **San archer**
This detail from a cave painting, c. 6000 BCE, in the Cederberg Mountain range in South Africa, shows a San artist's representation of an archer. Bantu-speakers helped spread methods of farming and ironworking to peoples across Africa, including hunter-gatherer San-speaking groups.

◁ **Precious collar**
Wealthy ancient Egyptians wore beaded necklaces known as *wesekh*, or broad collars. The faïence beads in this collar, made in 1353–1336 BCE, symbolize fruits and flowers.

2

Early civilizations

3000 BCE–600 CE

Introduction

During ancient times, a variety of peoples and civilizations thrived in Africa, particularly in the north. Some were known to non-African cultures, such as those of Assyria, Greece, and Rome; others rose and fell, unknown beyond their own—often considerable—spheres of influence in Africa.

Kingdoms of the Nile

The most notable ancient African civilization was Egypt, whose long and complex history embraces not just the Old, Middle, and New Kingdoms, but the state's incorporation into the Roman Empire and the later arrival of Coptic Christianity and Islam.

South of Egypt, in what is now Sudan, Kerma flourished from around 2500 BCE, followed by the Kingdom of Kush and the ancient Nubian city-state of Meroë. Farther south, present-day Eritrea and Ethiopia were home to the little-known D'mt along with the extensive Aksum Kingdom.

Early colonizers and hidden histories

North Africa's coast was home to several cultures that helped shape the history of the ancient world. Carthage, in modern Tunisia, was founded by traders from the East Mediterranean seaboard and, in the Punic Wars, battled with Rome to dominate the Mediterranean. To the west of Carthage lay Mauretania, while farther east was Cyrenaica. Surrounding and at times subsuming them all was the vast, shifting territory of Numidia.

Beyond the Nile and the Mediterranean, however, were African civilizations unknown to the contemporary "Western" chroniclers on whom we have tended to rely today for much of our knowledge of the ancient world. Now, modern research methods and archaeology are helping to expand our knowledge of once little-known cultures such as the Nok, which existed up to 3,500 years ago in present-day Nigeria, and the Sao civilization, which flourished from as early as the sixth century BCE in what is now Chad.

A shared heritage

By looking at Africa's earliest civilizations, we recognize the diverse influences that shaped the continent's different cultures, and the importance of recognizing those diverse influences within a shared "African" context. It is clear that while parts of Africa in ancient times developed with little or no contact with outside civilizations, large areas of the continent were impacted and indeed changed by their contacts with Rome, Greece, and Phoenicia, for example, and by the effects of Christianity or Islam on their cultures.

It may be argued, indeed, that the Carthaginians and some later rulers in Egypt (of Phoenician and Macedonian descent respectively) were of different ethnicities to Black Africans who lived south of the Sahara. But this does not necessarily mean that they are less African than those with a longer lineage on the continent or whose cultures had less contact with the wider world. What an examination of Africa's earliest civilizations reveals is the diversity of development experienced by its peoples who, at the same time, share a heritage on the continent that makes all of them Africans.

◁ **Anthropomorphic figure from Sao civilization**

c. 5000 BCE People begin to settle in Egypt

c. 3000 BCE Egypt is unified as a single state under King Narmer

c. 2500 BCE Kerma culture begins to flourish

c. 1500 BCE Earliest evidence of Nok culture in West Africa

EARLY CIVILIZATIONS | 41

❶ The ancient ruins of Kerma

❷ Nubian pyramids at Meroë

❸ The Ezana Stone, Aksum

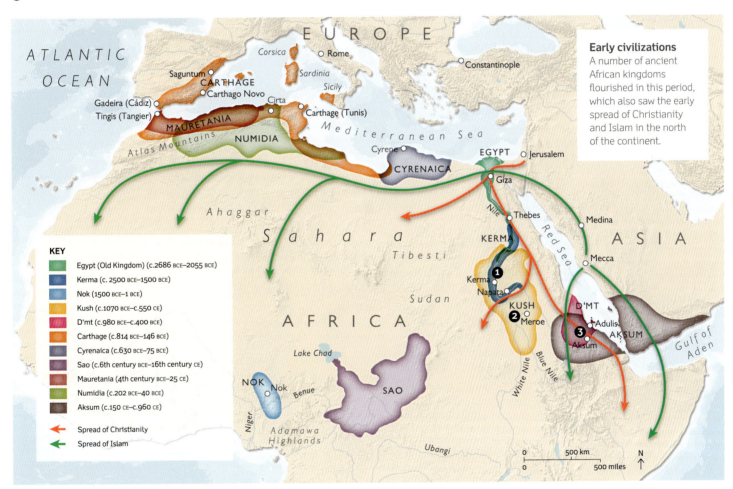

Early civilizations
A number of ancient African kingdoms flourished in this period, which also saw the early spread of Christianity and Islam in the north of the continent.

KEY
- Egypt (Old Kingdom) (c.2686 BCE–2055 BCE)
- Kerma (c. 2500 BCE–1500 BCE)
- Nok (1500 BCE–1 BCE)
- Kush (c.1070 BCE–c.550 CE)
- D'mt (c.980 BCE–c.400 BCE)
- Carthage (c.814 BCE–146 BCE)
- Cyrenaica (c.630 BCE–75 BCE)
- Sao (c.6th century BCE–16th century CE)
- Mauretania (4th century BCE–25 CE)
- Numidia (c.202 BCE–40 BCE)
- Aksum (c.150 CE–c.960 CE)
- → Spread of Christianity
- → Spread of Islam

c.1070 BCE Kingdom of Kush forms to the south of Egypt

980 BCE Origin of D'mt Kingdom in modern-day Eritrea and northern Ethiopia

c.630 BCE Kingdom of Cyrenaica established by colonists from Greece

202 BCE Establishment of Amazigh (Berber) Kingdom of Numidia in northwest Africa

25 BCE Ancient Amazigh kingdoms of Mauretania annexed to Rome

c.814 BCE Founding of Carthage by Phoenician settlers from Tyre (a city in modern-day Lebanon)

c.500 BCE The Sao civilization develops to the south of Lake Chad

30 BCE Egypt becomes a part of the Roman Empire

c.150 CE The Kingdom of Aksum is established

The Age of the Pharaohs
Ancient Egypt under absolute rule

The Old, Middle, and New Kingdoms of ancient Egypt flourished in the third and second millennia BCE, an era that saw the state's greatest political, artistic, and architectural accomplishments.

Egypt's first settled cultures developed around 10,000 BCE. By 6000 BCE, climate change and overgrazing led to the creation of the Sahara, forcing people to concentrate into villages, towns, and cities along the Nile. This was predynastic Egypt, where, under cultures such as the Badari and Naqada, deities such as Osiris, Isis, and Set and some of the forms of local government and tax collection associated with the later Egyptian civilization were introduced. These developments culminated in the rule of Narmer, a chieftain-king from southern Egypt who, around 3200 BCE, headed north and conquered the Nile Delta, unifying the region into a single kingdom.

Societal organization

In time, Egypt's kings became known as pharaohs, a word meaning "great house," indicating the palace in which the king lived. Not just the head of state, the pharaoh was also Egypt's religious leader, the divine intermediary between the people and the gods. The pharaoh's authority included the power to make laws, collect taxes, and wage war. The pharaoh also owned all of the country's land and its people. Below the pharaoh, the state was administered by an upper class of priests, officials, and military officers. Then came a middle class of merchants and artisans, followed by a lower class of laborers and land-workers.

△ **Palette of King Narmer**
Found at Hierakonpolis, the first African city, this palette (c. 3200 BCE) is thought to depict the unification of Upper and Lower Egypt.

A golden age

The Age of the Pharaohs is divided into three eras: the Old, Middle, and New Kingdoms. The Old Kingdom lasted from c. 2686 to 2055 BCE, and followed the so-called "Early Dynastic Period" inaugurated by Narmer's son, Hor-Aha, which saw Memphis emerge as the capital of newly united Egypt. The most remarkable visual symbols of the Old Kingdom are the Great Pyramids of Giza and the Sphinx—a sculpture thought to represent the godlike power of the king. On a practical level, the organization of Egypt into a regulated state took place during the Old Kingdom.

There was a period of political instability at the end of the Old Kingdom. Order was restored—and the Middle Kingdom initiated—with the reign of Montuhotep II (c. 2055–2004 BCE). He reunited Egypt, initiated ambitious building programs, and began to expand Egypt's borders to the south and west, after which the state enjoyed a golden age of peace and prosperity. However, by c. 1700 BCE regional unrest undermined the power of successive pharaohs; within 150 years the Middle Kingdom was over.

The New Kingdom

The first ruler of the New Kingdom was Ahmose I and his sister-wife Ahmose-Nefertari (1550–1525 BCE). Later New Kingdom pharaohs included Hatshepsut, Thutmose III, Amenhotep III, Tutankhamen, and

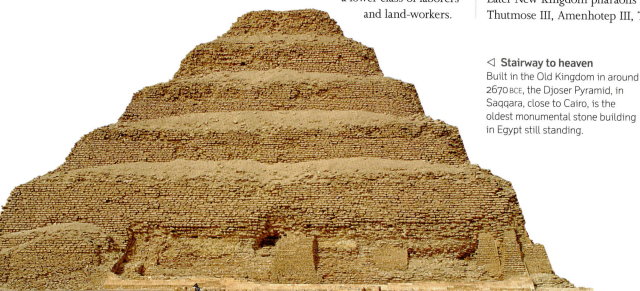

◁ **Stairway to heaven**
Built in the Old Kingdom in around 2670 BCE, the Djoser Pyramid, in Saqqara, close to Cairo, is the oldest monumental stone building in Egypt still standing.

A HOLY CITY

Abydos in southern Egypt is one of the country's oldest and most sacred cities. It is home to many temples and pharaonic burial sites including those of kings in the Early Dynastic Period. One of the city's most extraordinary ancient buildings is the temple of the New Kingdom pharaoh, Seti I (reigned c. 1294–1279 BCE), whose wall carvings include the Abydos King List (right). It is inscribed with the names, in hieroglyphics, of 76 Egyptian pharaohs from the legendary king Menes to Seti I himself.

KING SETI I AND HIS SON RAMSES II, SHOWN ON THE ABYDOS KING LIST

Ramses II and III. The great temple complexes at Luxor and Karnak and the Valley of the Kings were all either built or reached their greatest extent in the New Kingdom. The Book of the Dead, Ancient Egypt's most famous text, was composed in this era.

Decline and fall

The New Kingdom's last pharaoh was Ramses XI (1099–1069 BCE). His long reign—the longest since Ramses III—was followed by political volatility, economic decline, and a smallpox epidemic that left the state vulnerable to a succession of foreign rulers that included Libyans, Nubians, Assyrians, and Persians. The Macedonian Greeks arrived in 332 BCE and installed the Ptolemaic dynasty, which was still in power 300 years later when the Romans defeated the last pharaoh, Cleopatra VII, and her lover Mark Antony at the Battle of Actium in 31 BCE. The three-millennia-long Age of the Pharaohs ended the following year, when Cleopatra died by suicide.

△ **Face from the past**
Weighing 24 lb (11 kg), the solid gold funerary mask of New Kingdom pharaoh Tutankhamen was among the treasures discovered in his tomb in the Valley of the Kings in 1922.

◁ **Representing power**
As queen, regent, then pharaoh, Hatshepsut was one of Egypt's few female rulers. At her own request, she was depicted in sculpture as a man, as here.

> "**Respect the nobles**, support **your people**, fortify your **borders**."
>
> ADVICE FROM *THE TEACHING FOR KING MERYKARA*, WRITTEN DURING THE MIDDLE KINGDOM

The *Uraeus* is a symbol of kingship in the form of a cobra snake

"**A savage lion** … advancing **bravely** and returning only when he has **triumphed**."

POEM ON RAMSES II'S "VICTORY" AT KADESH, INSCRIBED ON KARNAK TEMPLE

Khepresh, or war crown

Heqa scepter, denoting power and dominion

Pleated robe with hieroglyphic inscriptions

Ramses II
This magnificent, life-size statue, which dates from the first half of his reign, depicts the king as a young man, wearing the robes and emblems of office.

Ramses II

Egypt's greatest and most powerful king

Ramses II (r. 1279–1213 BCE) was one of Egypt's most influential leaders, famous for his military campaigns in the Middle East and his impressive building programs, including the spectacular rock-cut temples at Abu Simbel.

Few of Egypt's kings were as revered as Ramses II, also known as Ramses the Great. He was the third ruler of the 19th Dynasty (1293–1185 BCE), one of the three New Kingdom dynasties in Egypt between 1550 and 1069 BCE. In boyhood, Ramses joined his father, Seti I, on military exploits, and he became king in 1279 BCE, at the age of 24. Ramses ruled for 66 years, making him one of the few pharaohs to take part in two of the Heb Sed festivals that were held every 30 years to rejuvenate the pharaoh.

The rise of the warrior-king

Under Ramses II, the New Kingdom rose to its greatest heights in military strength and stability. To establish a base for his military campaigns in Syria, Ramses founded a new capital in the Nile River Delta in his name, Pr-Ramesses (House of Ramses). His early successes included campaigns in Nubia to the south and an assertion of Egypt's foothold in Libya and Syria. In western Syria, the king attempted to dislodge the Hittite Empire at the famous battle of Kadesh in 1274 BCE. The outcome was inconclusive, but Egyptian propaganda depicted Ramses as the courageous victor (see opposite). The two sides eventually signed a peace treaty in 1259 BCE.

Ramses was an adept self-publicist, and his building programs served as potent symbols of his wealth and power. His construction projects include the temple of Karnak at Thebes and, near the border with modern Sudan, the magnificent rock-cut temples at Abu Simbel, as well as cities, monuments, and colossal statues. Among his greatest architectural achievements was his mortuary temple in Thebes, the Ramesseum (see pp. 46–47). He also memorialized his principal wife, Nefertari, with a tomb in Thebes and a temple—next to his own—at Abu Simbel.

Ramses' reign was one of the longest and most glorious in Egyptian imperial history. He strengthened the country's borders, increased its wealth, and widened its scope of trade. After Ramses died c. 1213 BCE, aged about 90 years, nine more pharaohs took his name in honor of their illustrious forebear.

△ **Queen Nefertari**
This detail from Nefertari's tomb in Thebes shows her bearing two ritual vessels.

▽ **King's temple**
The entrance to Abu Simbel is flanked by four rock-hewn statues of Ramses II that are 66 ft (20 m) tall.

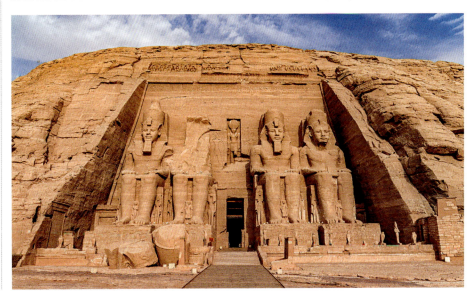

- **c. 1303 BCE** Ramses II is born to King Seti I and Queen Tuya
- **c. 1289 BCE** Appointed Prince Regent by Seti I at the age of 14
- **1279 BCE** Ramses II is crowned king
- **1274 BCE** Battle of Kadesh
- **c. 1277 BCE** Construction of Ramses' mortuary temple, the Ramesseum, begins
- **1255 BCE** Abu Simbel is completed
- **1259 BCE** Peace treaty with the Hittites is signed
- **1213 BCE** Ramses dies and is succeeded by his son Merneptah

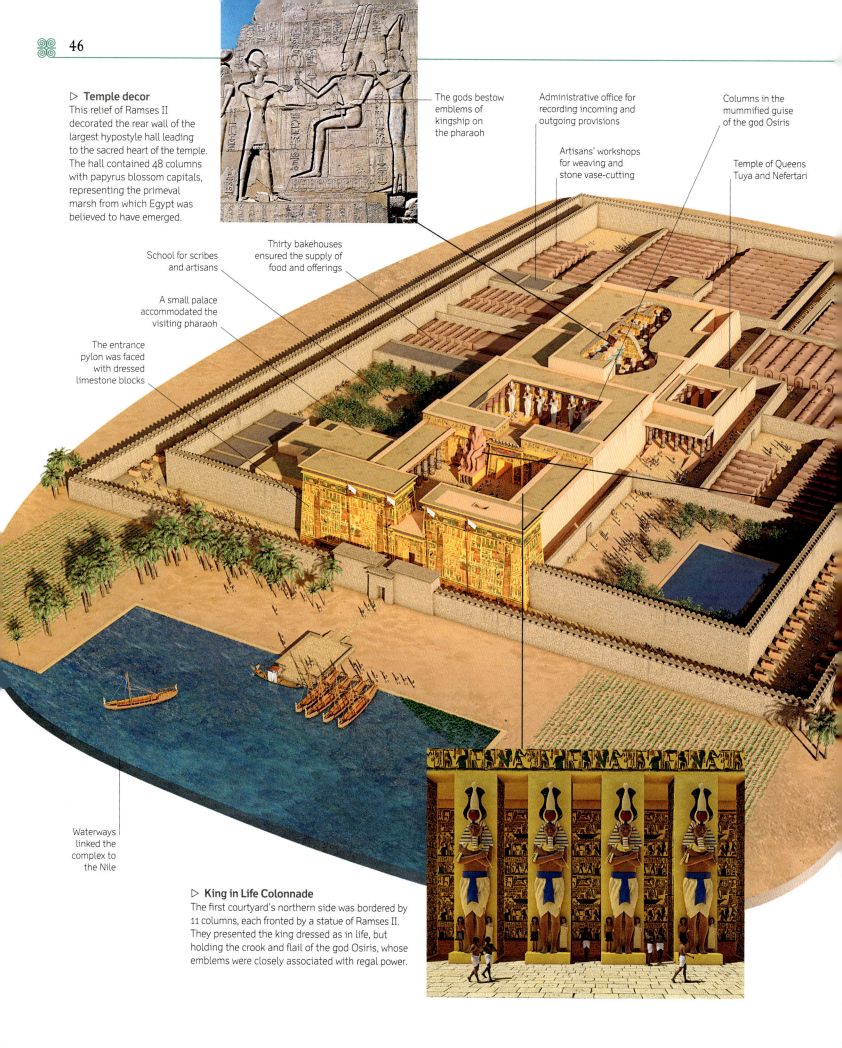

▷ **Temple decor**
This relief of Ramses II decorated the rear wall of the largest hypostyle hall leading to the sacred heart of the temple. The hall contained 48 columns with papyrus blossom capitals, representing the primeval marsh from which Egypt was believed to have emerged.

The gods bestow emblems of kingship on the pharaoh

Administrative office for recording incoming and outgoing provisions

Columns in the mummified guise of the god Osiris

Artisans' workshops for weaving and stone vase-cutting

Temple of Queens Tuya and Nefertari

Thirty bakehouses ensured the supply of food and offerings

School for scribes and artisans

A small palace accommodated the visiting pharaoh

The entrance pylon was faced with dressed limestone blocks

Waterways linked the complex to the Nile

▷ **King in Life Colonnade**
The first courtyard's northern side was bordered by 11 columns, each fronted by a statue of Ramses II. They presented the king dressed as in life, but holding the crook and flail of the god Osiris, whose emblems were closely associated with regal power.

The Ramesseum

Thebes (present-day Luxor), Egypt

The Ramesseum was built for Ramses II as his mortuary temple, dedicated both to the worship of his cult after his death, and to the god Amun. Designed to demonstrate Egypt's power and wealth, the complex introduced a new level of monumental architecture and was an inspiration for succeeding pharaohs, particularly Ramses III. The walls tell a story of Ramses II's greatness on earth and in heaven, with brightly painted reliefs depicting his military victories and kinship with the gods. Beyond the sacred temples at its core, the Ramesseum was a hub of economic activity, even during the pharaoh's lifetime. A vast arrangement of outbuildings included kitchens, artisans' workshops, a scribes' school, and dozens of storerooms.

▽ **Mansion of Millions of Years**
In Ramses II's day, the Ramesseum was referred to as his "Mansion of Millions of Years." Construction began in the second year of his reign (c. 1278 BCE) and lasted some 20 years. This reconstruction depicts the complex as it may have looked upon completion.

◁ **Royal stores**
This model of a Middle Kingdom granary shows scribes recording deliveries of grain. The Ramesseum had dozens of such storerooms, demonstrating the king's ability to provide for the gods and his people.

◁ **Processional avenues**
Surrounding the complex on three sides, the processional avenues are unique to the Ramesseum. This reconstruction shows how the northern avenue, lined by jackals, may have looked. Excavations indicate that sphinxes with the head of Ramses II lined the other avenues.

A columned treasury housed the most precious items

The shoulder bears the statue's name: "Sun of Princes"

The granite was polished to a sheen

The statue had a chapel dedicated to its own cult

◁ **The Sun of Princes**
A monumental colossus of Ramses II dominated the first courtyard. Hewn from a single block of pink granite and shipped in one piece along the Nile from the quarries of Aswan, farther south, it was nearly 59 ft (18 m) tall and weighed more than 1,100 tons (1,000 metric tons).

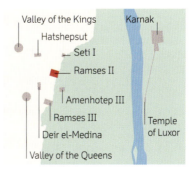

◁ **Thebes**
C. 1150 BCE
Ramses II built his temple on the west bank of the Nile at Thebes, in close proximity to the great temples of Karnak and Luxor on the east bank. The Ramesseum was linked to the river by channels.

Egyptian artifacts
Treasures from across the ages

Ancient Egypt has bequeathed to the world a vast collection of beautiful decorative and practical items, jewelry, and artworks that show the full range of the culture's creativity and crafting excellence, while simultaneously offering fascinating glimpses of everyday life in this civilization.

△ **Animal statuette**
This hippopotamus figure, from c. 1900 BCE, is molded from faience, a ceramic composed of ground quartz. The brilliant blue glaze represents the life-giving waters of the Nile.

Lotus inscriptions symbolize rebirth and regeneration

△ **Heavenly delights**
This fresco from palace official Nebamun's tomb dates from c. 1350 BCE. The scene shows the entertainments he will enjoy in the afterlife.

Arghul (double flute)
Dancers providing entertainment

△ **Scarab amulet**
This thumbnail-size, glazed steatite (soapstone) scarab beetle amulet from c. 1460 BCE was recovered from Queen Hatshepsut's funerary temple.

Hatshepsut's name in hieroglyphs
Engraved cartouche (pharaoh's name in hieroglyphs)

△ **Royal representations**
Once brightly painted, this life-size sandstone statue from c. 2490 BCE is an idealized embodiment of Pharaoh Menkaura and one of his wives.

Tripartite wig is a symbol of elite status
Kilt typically worn by pharaohs

△ **Happy couple**
This statue of Demedji, an official, and his wife Hennutsen dates from c. 2450 BCE. Non-royal statuary has a "rougher," less refined finish.

Finely carved hairstyle

△ **Arm defenders**
This gold and lapis lazuli bracelet was owned by Pharaoh Shoshenq II (d. 885 BCE). The design incorporates the protective Eye of Horus.

▷ **Journey to the afterlife**
This *Book of the Dead* papyrus from c. 1275 BCE shows a heart weighed against a feather from the goddess Maat to assess if its owner can enter *Duat*, the underworld.

Ani, the scribe who commissioned the papyrus
Anubis, the jackal-headed god of funerary rites
Ammit, the beast-goddess that devours hearts that "fail" the feather test

△ **Decorative detail**
Inlays were flat stone carvings fixed to shrine walls and niches. This one shows a solar god, Shepsi, and dates from the 4th century BCE.

△ **Fit for a king**
This alabaster jar is inscribed with the name of Pharaoh Ramses II (r. 1279–1213 BCE).

△ **Floral displays**
These amphorae, dating from the 19th–20th Dynasties (left) and the 18th Dynasty (right), display similar decorative styles, painted with garlands of flowers and vegetation.

▷ **Unusual instrument**
Although nominally a necklace, this item, called a *menat*, was usually carried, and the beaded strands shaken, during religious ceremonies.

▽ **Neck protector**
Broad collar necklaces were popular throughout ancient Egyptian history. Dating from c. 1750 BCE, this example features rows of colored faience beads.

△ **Death duties**
This glazed steatite figurine shows the shabti ("servant") of the 16th-century BCE official Seniu. The hieroglyphs list the servant's obligations toward his master in the afterlife.

▷ **In memoriam**
Wooden coffins included a likeness of the deceased, along with spells and images of other family members. This one houses a man known as Khonsu.

Kerma and Kush

Early civilizations of the Sudan

The Nubian civilization of Kerma, in modern-day northern Sudan, prospered from 2500–1500 BCE and for a time rivaled Egypt as a regional power. Kerma was followed by the more Egyptophile Kingdom of Kush.

Named after its capital city, the Kerma civilization grew out of a Neolithic culture known as the A-group, which emerged around 3500–3000 BCE, at the same time as predynastic Egypt (see pp.42–43). The A-group traded—and, it appears, competed—with its northern neighbor. By 2800 BCE, however, Egypt's First Dynasty had established its regional ascendancy, forcing the A-group Nubians southward. Here, they evolved into a culture known as the C-group, which became the precursor to the Kerma state.

◁ **Place of worship**
The monumental temple known as the Western Deffufa dominates Kerma. The word *deffufa* derives from the Nubian term for a mudbrick building.

Rise and fall

By 2000 BCE, Kerma was well established in Upper Nubia, an area corresponding to central and southern Sudan—"Upper" refers to regions upstream on the Nile, therefore farther south. Over the next three centuries, Kerma also conquered Lower Nubia (downstream on the Nile, or farther north), bringing its territory up to the border with Egypt. Perhaps inevitably, the two civilizations clashed. Egypt, by now in its expansionist Middle Kingdom period, dominated at first. However, when Egypt's power declined after 1650 BCE, Kerma seized the opportunity to consolidate its control of Upper and Lower Nubia. The city of Kerma encompassed around 10,000 people and its rulers built palaces, tomb complexes, and *deffufas*—large temples. Between 1575 and 1550 BCE, Kerma allied with Hyksos—Canaanites who occupied the Nile Delta—and threatened the survival of the remaining Egyptian state based at Thebes. Egypt's Middle Kingdom had collapsed and a spell of military and political turmoil, known as the Second Intermediate Period, ensued.

This turmoil encouraged Kerma and Hyksos to strike at Egypt. However, the establishment of the New Kingdom after 1550 BCE restored order in Egypt. Within 50 years, a resurgent Egypt had conquered and colonized Kerma. Sporadic rebellion continued for a couple of hundred years, but over time Kerma became increasingly Egyptianized and tied to Egyptian imperial government, and was never to regain its position as an autonomous power.

The people of Kerma left no written records, and it is not known which language they spoke. The names of only a few of their kings survive. As well as the royal family, Kerma had elite classes of priests and merchants and sizable urban populations at its capital city and at the town of Sai Island in the Nile River. The economy was based on agriculture and trade, though there is also evidence of gold mining. Kerma was also endowed with cattle, dairy products, ebony, ivory, and incense—and produced fine bronzework and pottery, including blue glazing known as faïence.

A change of the guard

As Kerma's civilization began to wane, a new Nubian culture was on the rise: the Kingdom of Kush. Egyptian texts refer to "Kush" as a general name for Upper Nubia, but scholars also use the term to refer to

Crown, with double *uraei* (cobras) representing Nubia and Egypt

◁ **Badges of office**
This statue of a Kushite king was made c. 713–664 BCE. The king's name was engraved on his belt, but is now indecipherable.

△ **Nubian delegation**
Nubian tribute-bearers appear in the top three rows of this painting, the original of which dates to 1353–1327 BCE and appeared in the tomb of Amenhotep, the viceroy of Kush.

the kingdom that emerged in Nubia after the Egyptian New Kingdom. Unlike Kerma, the Kushite rulers borrowed from Egyptian culture, especially in royal art and state religion. The chief state deity was Amun, a god associated with kingship, whose cult was celebrated at temples in Kush's capital city, Napata, and at many other places. Kush also had the good fortune to emerge just as the great age of the pharaohs was drawing to a close, leaving it well placed to fill the power vacuum left by Egypt's decline.

Historians believe the Kushite rulers were in charge of the state religion and maintained the houses of the gods. But many specifics of the early Kushite civilization's social and economic organization remain unclear. More visible would be the later Kushite civilization that emerged in the 8th century BCE, based first in Napata and then Meroë (see pp.54–55).

▽ **Royal ornament**
This gold ram's head amulet was once strung on a Kushite ruler's necklace. A ram's head was the symbol of the god Amen.

"We realized that **the tombs, palaces, and temples** stood out from Egyptian remains … **We were in another world.**"

ARCHAEOLOGIST CHARLES BONNET, ON UNCOVERING ANCIENT KERMA'S RUINS

Nubian temple
Dating from the 1st century BCE, the Lion Temple at Naga in modern-day Sudan is carved with figures in relief on all four of its sides. The southern side, shown here, depicts the gods Horus (with a falcon's head) and Apedemak (with a lion's head), and the Nubian (or Kushite) king Natakamani and his wife Queen Amanitore paying homage to the gods. Apedemak was the Nubian god of war, while Horus was an Egyptian deity, marking a fusion of cultures at this time.

Napata and Meroë

The later kingdoms of Kush

Beyond Egypt's southern border lay Nubia, a territory from which arose cultures whose civilizations would compete with, absorb, submit to, and—in the case of Meroë—ultimately outlast the pharaohs.

For two millennia after 3000 BCE, Egypt dominated Africa's Nile region (see pp.42–43). But other African civilizations rivaled Egypt's power, in particular the kingdoms of Kerma and Kush (see pp.50–51). By 1450 BCE, however, Kerma had disappeared and Egypt was experiencing a period of political instability and economic decline. Kush, the newest of these civilizations, filled the power vacuum, and for the next 1,000 years held sway over the region south of Egypt known as Nubia.

◁ **Royal artifact**
This gold "shield ring" was found within the pyramid of Queen Amanishakheto, who was ruler of Kush from approximately 10 BCE–1 CE.

Ram-headed god, Amun

The capital of Kush was Napata, and around 750 BCE it was the base from which the Kushite king Kashta launched his conquest of Upper Egypt. His son and successor, Piye, annexed the rest of Egypt, and so-called "Nubian Pharaohs" ruled Egypt and Kush until an Assyrian invasion forced them out in the 660s BCE (see pp.56–57). The Kushites regrouped in their stronghold of Napata, but within two generations a resurgent Egypt went on the attack. Egyptian attempts to reconquer the northern part of Kushite territory may have been a factor that encouraged King Aspelta to move his capital from Napata 150 miles (240 km) upriver to Meroë.

Meroë's history is traditionally divided into four Meroitic periods. The first, from 542–315 BCE, saw the city grow steadily and witnessed the construction of

NAPATA AND MEROË | 55

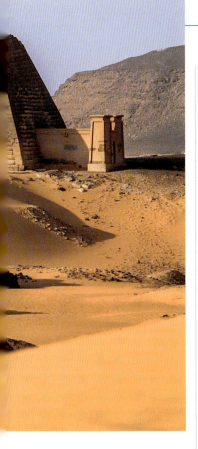

△ **Pyramids of power**
Almost 200 royal tomb pyramids were built at three sites in and around Meroë, ranging in height from 20–98 ft (6–30 m).

the earliest of the royal pyramid tombs that would be erected over the next several hundred years and are today the civilization's most distinctive archaeological remains. The second and third Meroitic periods took the kingdom into the 1st century CE. More pyramids were built, along with grand palaces, temples, residences, and industrial buildings and warehouses, attesting to Meroë's importance as a major center of iron production and as a trading crossroads between North Africa, Central Africa, and Asia.

In the fourth Meroitic period, from the 1st to the 4th centuries CE, the kingdom came to the attention of Rome. After taking Egypt, the emperor Augustus invaded Nubia in 23 BCE, but withdrew the following year having plundered Napata. Meroë remained more or less unmolested by Rome after this, surviving for another three centuries until its final destruction by the new Aksumite Empire (in present-day Ethiopia) in 350 CE.

Meroitic culture

As a long-lasting Nubian power, Meroë is today cited as an early example of a successful "Africanized" civilization, especially in contrast to the more Mediterranean- and Middle Eastern–facing Egypt. In truth, both states were highly culturally and ethnically diverse—although contemporary references by writers to the "Ethiopians" (a synonym for Black Africans) of Nubia perhaps indicates a greater preponderance of peoples from south of the Sahara there than in Egypt.

One unusual aspect of Meroitic society was the position of the *kandakes*—the queens, queen mothers, and female relatives of the king. They held great power in Meroë, especially when serving as regents to child monarchs. Shanakhdakheto, the first known *kandake*, is said to have ruled without a king, holding sole power from 170–150 BCE, while it was the warrior-queen Amanirenas who fought the Romans in Nubia following their attack on Napata in 23 BCE. Almost a century later, *Kandake* Amanikhatashan sent cavalry and archers to fight for Rome during the First Jewish-Roman War of 66–73 CE.

▷ **Stele of Nubian Queen**
A stone stele from the late 1st century BCE shows warrior *Kandake* Amanishakheto (right) being embraced by the protector goddess Amesemi.

> "[Meroë has] the **biggest concentration** of **pyramids in the world.**"
>
> MAHMOUD SULIMAN BASHIR, NATIONAL CORPORATION FOR ANTIQUITIES AND MUSEUMS, SUDAN

Victorious king
In this c. 7th-century BCE relief added to the 15th-century BCE temple complex at Karnak, in Upper Egypt, King Taharqa grasps the hair of multiple defeated enemies.

Taharqa

A Nubian king of Egypt

Hailing from Egypt's southern neighbor, Taharqa initiated the last great age of pyramid-building. As a warrior-pharaoh, his long-running fight with the mighty Assyrian Empire defined his reign.

Taharqa was born to Piye, Nubian ruler of the Kushite kingdom of Napata in modern-day Sudan. He was a cousin of the Kushite pharaoh of Egypt, Shebitku, and joined the imperial court at Thebes when he was just out of his teens. In 701 BCE, in his early twenties, Taharqa led an Egyptian-Kushite force against an Assyrian army that was laying siege to Jerusalem, the capital of Egypt's neighbor, Judah. According to the Bible's Book of Kings, "Tirhakah" (who scholars identify as Taharqa) and the Judeans won the ensuing Battle of Eltekeh; the Assyrian king, Sennacherib, by contrast claimed a victory for his side.

In 690 BCE, Taharqa became Egypt's ruler, probably after usurping his predecessor, Shabaka. As both monarch of the Kingdom of Kush and pharaoh of Egypt, Taharqa was the main regional bulwark against the expansionist Assyrian emperor, Esarhaddon. In 674 BCE, Taharqa repulsed an Assyrian invasion force. Three years later, however, the Assyrians captured Egypt's capital, Memphis, forcing Taharqa into exile in the south. He retook Memphis in 669 BCE, but Esarhaddon's successor, Ashurbanipal, soon reasserted Assyrian hegemony. An Assyrian vassal, Necho I, replaced Taharqa, who never regained full control of Egypt. He died in Thebes in 664 BCE.

Building a legacy in Egypt and Nubia

Throughout his reign, Taharqa had maintained an ambitious building program. In the 680s BCE, he ordered the construction of a temple to the sun and fertility god, Amun-Re, at Kawa in his native Nubia. He also rebuilt and restored several other temples to Amun-Re across his empire. Most strikingly, he restarted the practice of pyramid-building after 1,000 years, creating the first and largest of 20 or so pyramids at Nuri, in modern Sudan, erected between c. 670 BCE and c. 310 BCE.

◁ **Royal statue**
Shown here as a bronze statue, Taharqa was pharaoh and *qore* (king) of the Kingdom of Kush. He was fourth of the five "Kushite Pharaohs" who made up Egypt's 25th Dynasty.

△ **Kiosk of Taharqa**
This is the only remaining example of the ten 69-ft (21-m) columns that lined Karnak's Kiosk of Taharqa, a vast chamber built as part of the processional route of the god Amen out of the temple.

> "I was **brought from Nubia** among the **royal brothers** that **his Majesty** had brought."
>
> TAHARQA'S TEMPLE INSCRIPTION AT KAWA

- **725 BCE** Birth of Taharqa
- **705 BCE** Taharqa is taken to Thebes
- **690 BCE** Taharqa becomes pharaoh
- **680 BCE** Building of Amun-Re temple, Kawa
- **670 BCE** Work begins on Pyramid of Taharqa at Nuri
- **674–669 BCE** Wars against Esarhaddon of Assyria
- **668 BCE** Ashurbanipal becomes Assyrian king
- **664 BCE** Death of Taharqa

Writing systems
From ancient symbols to modern scripts

Some of the earliest marks or symbols made by early humans have been found in Africa. Examples include symbolic patterns engraved on 60,000-year-old ostrich eggshells, found at Diepkloof, South Africa (see p.30), and symbols and patterns painted on cave walls at Wonderwerk, in northern South Africa. Rocks by the Kharga oasis in present-day Egypt bear traces of writing-like inscriptions, called "Proto Saharan" by some scientists, that date from at least 4000 BCE.

Ancient scripts
In around 3000 BCE, hieroglyphic writing developed in Egypt. Egyptian hieroglyphs were initially used as simple labels, but soon developed into a complex writing system using a mixture of both phonetic and pictorial signs. Ancient Egyptians also used an abbreviated, cursive form of the hieroglyphic script, known as Hieratic, which could be written at a greater speed. In the 1st century BCE, an even simpler script, called Demotic (from a Greek word meaning "popular script"), came into everyday, general use, such as for writing documents.

In around 800 BCE, an alphabetic script known as Meroitic arose in Nubia (modern-day Sudan). Meroitic takes two forms: a cursive script, derived from Demotic, and hieroglyphs, developed from Egyptian hieroglyphs. The cursive form could be written with a stylus and was used for general records on parchment or papyrus. The hieroglyphic form appears mainly as royal or religious inscriptions in stone.

△ **Egyptian hieroglyphs**
Hieroglyphs can be read from right to left, left to right, or top to bottom. The direction in which humans and animals face indicates the starting point of the text. In this right-facing wall-carved inscription, the text is intended to be read from right to left.

△ **Meroitic**
Shown here on a stone inscription from the 1st century BCE, Meroitic was used to write the language of the kingdom of Meroë in modern-day Sudan. The script is not fully deciphered, but scholars know how the letters sounded: there are vowels, and consonants are assumed to be followed by "a," unless another vowel is provided.

△ **Punic**
This Punic inscription on a funerary stele in Carthage, Tunisia, dates from 300–200 BCE. Punic was spoken in Carthage until about the 4th century CE and was derived from the earlier Phoenician alphabet, with influences from coastal Amazigh (Berber) languages.

From the 1st century CE in Ethiopia, the Ge'ez script, based on Arabic and consisting of 231 characters, was used; it is one of the oldest writing systems in continuous use in the world.

Since at least the 10th century CE, people throughout Africa have used an Arabic-derived script called Ajami to write phonetic renderings of about a dozen languages, including Swahili, Wolof, and Hausa. The rediscovery of Ajami texts, from love letters to business records, provides historians with valuable insights into everyday life in Africa.

Many parts of Africa developed ideographic scripts, which use symbols to represent ideas. In parts of Central and Southern Africa, Sona pictograms are mnemonic devices for remembering fables, riddles, and proverbs. The system was documented in drawings by European visitors in the 17th century, but may date back to antiquity. *Adinkra* symbols, developed by the Akan people in Ghana, represent concepts and aphorisms, and are printed on fabric for events such as weddings and funerals.

In recent times, scripts have been developed for specific languages. Created in the 1980s, Adlam transcribes the Fula language, spoken by 25 million people in West Africa, and can be typed on phones and computers. The Luo script, developed in 2009–2012, transcribes the Dholuo language spoken in East Africa. In North Africa, Tifinagh, used for writing Amazigh (Berber) languages, has been modernized as Neo-Tifinagh for use on computers and phones.

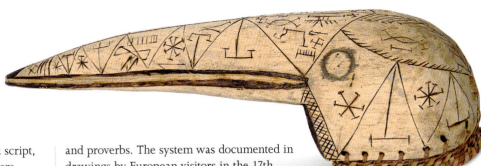

△ **Nsibidi headdress**
This wooden, bird-beaked headdress is engraved with Nsibidi script using a heated tool or fine flame. Developed by secret societies in what is now Nigeria in around 2000 BCE, Nsibidi comprises nearly 1,000 symbols.

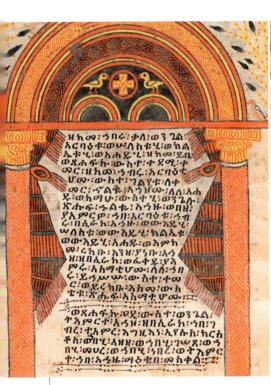

△ **Ge'ez**
This illuminated manuscript of the Christian Bible was created at a monastic center in Ethiopia around the beginning of the 15th century CE. The text is in Ge'ez, a Semitic language still used in religious ceremonies in the region.

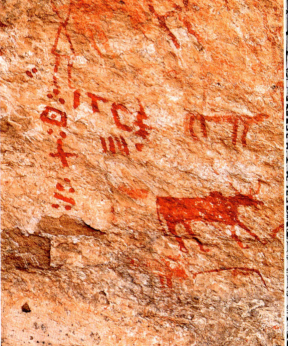

△ **Libyco-Berber**
A cave painting at Tadrart Acacus, Libya, dated to between 12000 BCE and 100 CE, shows Libyco-Berber script alongside pictograms of animals. The Libyco-Berber alphabet developed into Tifinagh, a script used to write the Amazigh languages spoken across North Africa today.

△ **Adinkra**
This early example of Ghanaian *adinkra* mourning cloth, dating from 1817, features 15 symbols, including *nsroma* (stars) and *dono ntoasuo* (double *dono*, or talking, drums). The patterns were printed using carved calabash (gourd) stamps and a vegetable-based dye.

> "These works **define our history**. They **define who we are**."
>
> — ALHAJI LAI MOHAMMED, MINISTER OF INFORMATION AND CULTURE, NIGERIA, 2020

Nok terra-cotta figure

Celebrating the artistry of West Africa's oldest civilization

In 1943, a British archaeologist in Nigeria named Bernard Fagg noticed a terra-cotta head that had been used on a scarecrow in a local yam field. Recognizing the object was of great antiquity and of a style not seen before, Fagg began to search for and collect similar sculptures. By Fagg's estimate, the sculptures had been made around 500 BCE—much earlier than any civilization known to have existed in that region. Fagg named this largely forgotten West African culture the Nok, after the village where several of the finds had been located.

Sophisticated culture

Radiocarbon dating has since shown that the Nok flourished even earlier than Fagg thought, from 1500 BCE, disappearing around 1 CE. As yet, little is known about Nok life and culture. What has been established, however, is that the Nok were imaginative and technically advanced. Excavations at artifact sites have revealed iron-smelting furnaces—13 at one dig close to the village of Taruga. Scientists have dated the furnaces to 280 BCE, which would make the Nok people the first to master iron smelting south of the Sahara. As many of the terra-cotta heads were found in and around smelting sites, some historians believe the sculptures were intended as objects of worship, used to bring good luck in the manufacture of iron tools, weapons, and decorative objects.

To date, close to 200 terra-cotta sculptures have been retrieved across the 30,000 sq miles (80,000 sq km) of Nok territory, centered on the town of Jos—suggesting that the Nok civilization was large and widespread. Surviving Nok terra-cotta pieces range in size from 4 in (10 cm) to 4 ft (1.22 m) tall (based on sculptural fragments). Craftworkers made the sculptures not by a casting process, but by carving individual pieces of clay—such as an arm, head, leg, or beads—and then joining them together to form a single composite work that was fired in a furnace. Some scholars have argued that the Nok's creativity may have influenced the sculptors of the 14th-century Yoruba Ilé-Ifè culture (see pp.110–111), whose naturalistic, copper-alloy, life-size heads are among humanity's greatest artistic achievements.

Distinctive styling

The object shown here is a particularly complex example of Nok terra-cotta work. Its date of manufacture is not known, but it contains details typical of Nok sculpture including the oversize, cylindrical heads with elongated features such as the distinctive oval-shaped eyes. This sculpture was one of three items purchased against Nigerian law by the French government in 1998 and, with post-factum consent from the Nigerian government, is currently displayed in the Musée du Quai Branly in Paris.

△ **Female figure**
Subjects are often shown seated, sometimes with their hands on their knees or in stylized poses. The purpose, if any, of Nok sculpture is still unknown.

- Finely worked headwear
- Perforations allowed heat to be equalized during the firing process
- Figures carved separately and added to main structure
- Triangular or oval-shaped eyes are an identifying characteristic of Nok sculptures
- Sculpture is 21 in (54 cm) in height and appears to be the base of a larger piece

◁ **Nok sculpture**
This is a rare example of a Nok sculpture with multiple heads. After controversially acquiring the piece, France signed an agreement with Nigeria to lease it for 25 years.

The Kingdom of Aksum

East Africa's first Christian state

The Kingdom of Aksum ruled a large tract of East Africa for four centuries. A great trading hub, it was an entry and exit point into the continent for peoples, products, ideas, and faiths.

Centered around what is today the Tigray Region of northern Ethiopia, the Kingdom of Aksum was founded around 150 CE. At its height, it controlled parts of modern Eritrea, Djibouti, and Somalia, as well as territory across the Red Sea in Yemen. Little is known of Aksum's origins. Its earliest myths claim it was the home of the Queen of Sheba (ruler of the Kingdom of Saba or Sheba in southwestern Arabia) and the resting place of the Ark of the Covenant (a gold chest said to have held the tablets of the law in Judaism and Christianity). Though both assertions are implausible, they illustrate how this part of the continent was considered a cultural crossroads.

The capital, also called Aksum, was located on a high, fertile plateau 6,560 ft (2,000 m) above sea level. It sat at the intersection of the major trading routes south and west into Africa, north toward the Middle East and the Mediterranean, and east across the Indian Ocean to Asia from the Red Sea port of Adulis. Ivory and gold were the main products bought and sold here, along with frankincense, myrrh, obsidian, rhinoceros horn, emeralds, salt, livestock, textiles, iron, steel, weapons, olive oil, glassware, and much more. Enslaved people were also traded here.

One of the kingdom's most significant imports was Christianity. It arrived south of the Sahara in the 4th century CE, introduced as the state religion by Aksum's king, Ezana I (r. 320s–c. 360). This was possibly a diplomatic move by Ezana to align his kingdom's faith with that of its most important trading partner, the eastern Roman Empire in Constantinople. Around 270 CE, Aksum became the first African nation to mint its own coinage. It was manufactured according to standardized Roman imperial weights and matched the compositions of Roman coins. Aksumite coins have been found as far away as Israel and India.

Expansion and challenge

Aksum reached its peak between the 3rd and 7th centuries. The city of Aksum's population numbered up to 20,000, and art and architecture—including distinctive stone stelae—flourished there. Erected as grave markers, the stelae were carved to resemble multi-storied royal palaces or houses of the nobility. Ruins of one stele indicate it was 97 ft (30 m) tall.

As well as trade, Aksum acquired power and prosperity through conquest. The early Aksumite king Gedara expanded into southern Arabia at the beginning

△ **Carved stelae**
Aksum's commemorative stelae are tall structures with representative doors and windows carved into their facades. This, in the Northern Stelae Park in Aksum city, stands 79 ft (24 m) high.

Gold coin shows ears of wheat or barley

100 percent pure silver

Bronze coins were the most common

▷ **Use of coins**
Aksum introduced Roman-style coinage in the 3rd century CE. This was at a time when other states south of the Sahara were using shells, beads, or bartered goods as currency.

△ **Popular story**
Known as "Sheba's Palace," these extensive remains at Dungur, close to Aksum city, actually date from the 7th century CE—1,700 years after the biblical queen's era.

of the 3rd century CE, and Ezana I conquered the Sudanese city-state of Meroë (see pp.54–55) a century later. Around 520, Aksum's King Kaleb (also known as Saint Elesbaan) sent a large naval force to subdue the Himyarite kingdom in what is today southern Yemen. This was done partly at the request of the Byzantine emperor, Justin I, who wanted to punish the Himyarites for their persecution of Christians. This conquest saw Aksum's empire reach its greatest extent.

Within a decade, however, rebels in the Himyarite kingdom were challenging Aksum's authority. Aksum struggled to retain its Arabian holdings for the next 50 years, until, around 575, it was driven out of the peninsula by an army invading from the Sassanian Empire (modern-day Iran).

Aksum under threat

On the African mainland, nomadic herding peoples such as the Afar, the Saho, and the Beja migrated into Aksum territory. Their livestock overgrazed the land, and this degraded the soil, leading to crop failures and famine that destabilized the state. More significantly, the rapid spread of Islam across North and East Africa after its founding in 610 presented Christian Aksum with an existential threat. By 648, the Rashidun Caliphate based in Medina had taken control of the Red Sea, cutting off Aksum's access to the Indian Ocean. The caliphate also assumed control of the overland trade routes that Aksum had benefited from for so long. Now isolated and surrounded, Aksum's inhabitants abandoned their capital, moving farther inland to the Ethiopian highlands and founding a new capital whose name and location are lost to history.

The kingdom continued for several hundred years, but was much diminished. The exact date of its demise is not known, but at some point between 900 and 1200 its lands were taken by the Zagwe dynasty, who were based at Lalibela in northern Ethiopia (see pp.122–123). The remains of the city of Aksum were designated a UNESCO World Heritage Site in 1980.

▷ **Man of God**
This 10th-century Byzantine painting shows King Kaleb (r. 514–542). Also known as Saint Elesbaan, he abdicated in old age and retired to a monastery.

"And so went **in peace** to his land this **Christ-loving Kaleb** and all his army with him."

THE BOOK OF THE HIMYARITES

Carthage
The empire that rivaled Rome

Carthage in North Africa was a Phoenician settlement that went on to rule much of the Mediterranean. This wealthy trading empire became a target for Roman plans for dominance in a great rivalry that brought about its eventual downfall.

The Phoenicians, one of the great peoples of antiquity, emerged in modern-day Lebanon and Syria. They came to prominence as important sea traders in the mid-12th century BCE, and in around 814 BCE settlers from the Phoenician city of Tyre founded Carthage in what is now Tunisia, North Africa. The city-state became the richest in the ancient world with a multiethnic African culture, encompassing many Indigenous Amazigh (Berber) people.

Carthage has roots in myth. According to the Roman poet Virgil, the Phoenician founder of Carthage, Elissa, renamed Queen Dido by Virgil, met Aeneas, a hero of the Trojan war. They fell in love, but Aeneas left Dido and the queen cursed him, foreshadowing the enmity that was to arise between Carthage and the Romans, who claimed descent from Aeneas.

Trading empire
Carthage's site was a fine one: the port occupied a key position on maritime trade routes and had access to fertile land for agriculture. By the middle of the 6th century BCE, the city had grown powerful. In addition to Northern African territory, Carthage eventually encompassed much of Sicily, as well as Corsica, Sardinia, and parts of modern-day Spain.

Carthage traded heavily with the Iberian Peninsula, although its traders also crossed the Sahara, ferrying between Africa and Europe everything from wine and ivory to ostrich eggs, as well as trading silver and tin with other Phoenician cities in the Mediterranean. Tin, possibly sourced from the Canary Islands and Britain, was an important ancient article of trade, since it was used to make bronze.

As Carthage rose to power, the Phoenician heartland was fading. The city-states in modern-day Lebanon and Syria fell under the sway of the Assyrians, the Babylonians, the Persians, and finally Alexander the Great. Yet Phoenician culture continued to shape Carthage. The Carthaginians spoke a Semitic language, Punic, and their religion was of Phoenician origin, involving worship of the gods Baal Hammon, Eshmun, Bes, and Melqart, and the goddess Tanit.

△ **Miniature mask**
This 3rd-century BCE mask, made from glass paste, is believed to have been a funerary pendant.

◁ **Carthaginian god**
This limestone carving of Baal Hammon, the weather deity and chief god of Carthage, dates from the 2nd century CE. At this time, Carthage was under Roman control but worship of Phoenician deities continued.

> "Carthage ... rich in **wealth** and most **harsh** in the **arts of war**."
>
> VIRGIL, *THE AENEID*

By the 3rd century BCE, the city of Carthage had as many as 500,000 inhabitants, mostly of African heritage, and the empire had fought wars against Greeks and Libyans. Initially, relations with Rome were friendly, but as Rome grew in strength the two empires clashed over Sicily.

Wars with Rome

The First Punic War (264–241 BCE) ended with Sicily becoming a province of the victorious Romans. In the Second Punic War (218–201 BCE), Rome and Carthage fought over the Iberian Peninsula, and the great Carthaginian general Hannibal (see pp.68–69) surprised the Romans by crossing the Alps and attacking Italy from the north. He won several battles before his final defeat in 202 BCE at Zama, Tunisia.

Carthage was now a weakened state, confined to North Africa. But the Romans still desired the kingdom's rich farmland, and the Roman statesman Marcus Porcius Cato demanded the destruction of Carthage, convinced that Rome could never be safe while it remained. He ended many senatorial addresses, irrespective of the subject of debate, with the famous words "Delenda est Carthago" ("Carthage must be destroyed"). In the Third Punic War (149–146 BCE), despite fierce resistance, Rome destroyed Carthage and killed many of its people.

It was the end of an empire, but not the end of the city. Carthage was rebuilt and became one of the wealthiest Roman cities. Punic (Carthaginian) and Amazigh culture persisted through such writers as Numidian-born Apuleius (c. 124–170).

▽ **Antonine Baths**
Built in the 2nd century CE, the now-ruined Antonine Baths of Roman Carthage were the largest Roman baths in Africa.

Kingdoms of the northwest

Carthage's ancient neighbors

Carthage and Egypt may be North Africa's most famous ancient states, but in the northwest, the Amazigh (Berber) kingdoms of Numidia and Mauretania flourished for hundreds of years.

North Africa supported several ancient civilizations. To the west of Carthage (see pp.64–65) stood Mauretania and Numidia. These were the kingdoms of the Amazigh, who had lived in the Maghreb for thousands of years. Mauretania included parts of what is now Algeria and Morocco. Its first known ruler, Baga, reigned in the 3rd century BCE, but evidence of trade with Carthage goes back still further. The kingdom had close relations with Numidia to the east in modern Algeria. According to the Roman historian Sallust, the Numidians had nomadic ancestors, although they later adopted a more settled existence, built great monuments and tombs, and traded with what would become Spain.

Rival states

Numidia was divided into two states: the Massylii in the east and the Masaesyli in the west. Both were famous for their nimble, javelin-wielding horse riders. At the start of the Second Punic War, in 218 BCE, the Massylii were allied with Carthage and the Masaesyli with Rome. But in 206 BCE, the new king in the east, Masinissa, allied with Rome instead, since he believed it would prevail in the war. The western king, in opposition to him, joined Carthage. When the war ended in 201 BCE, the Romans gave all of Numidia to Masinissa.

Masinissa and his descendants ruled a large kingdom, which now extended beyond the Atlas Mountains in the south, but in 118 BCE civil war broke out between his grandson Adherbal and Jugurtha, the illegitimate son of Mastanabal, Masinissa's youngest son.

△ **Jugurtha**
This coin, minted in c. 50 BCE, decades after the Jugurthine War, depicts Jugurtha on the right kneeling in chains before the Roman dictator, Sulla.

△ **Juba I**
Juba I, depicted on a coin from around 50 BCE, sided with Pompey in the Roman civil war of 49–45 BCE.

△ **Juba II**
This Mauretanian coin shows Juba II, who was educated in Rome and ruled both Numidia and Mauretania as a client king.

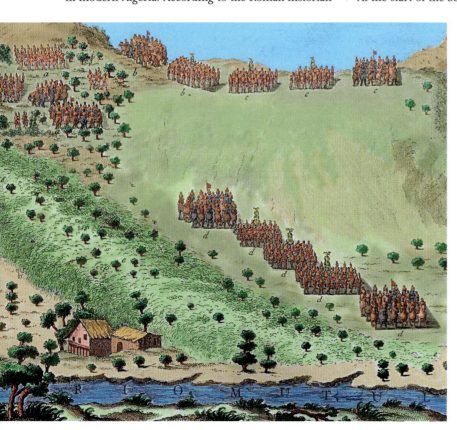

◁ **Jugurthine War**
Numidian forces under Jugurtha (in the woodland at the top left) face the Roman legions of Quintus Caecilius Metellus during the Jugurthine War.

KINGDOMS OF THE NORTHWEST | 67

Jugurtha besieged the Numidian capital, Cirta (modern Constantine, in Algeria), and when Adherbal surrendered, killed him and all armed adult males that he found. Romans were among the dead, and Rome declared war. During the Jugurthine War (112–106 BCE), Jugurtha was captured and executed.

Numidia remained independent, but when civil war broke out between Julius Caesar and Roman general Pompey in 49 BCE, King Juba I took Pompey's side. In 46 BCE, the two armies met at Thapsus on the Tunisian coast, and Juba, foreseeing defeat, died by suicide. After the war, western Numidia came under Mauretanian rule and the eastern part became a Roman province, Africa Nova. In 40 BCE, western Numidia was annexed to Africa Nova.

Juba's son, Juba II, is said to have been one of the most educated Roman citizens of the time. He ruled Africa Nova (30–25 BCE) and then Mauretania (25 BCE–23 CE) as a client king—a monarch who ruled only with Rome's consent—and married Selene II, daughter of Queen Cleopatra VII of Egypt and Roman politician and general Mark Antony.

Rome finally annexed Mauretania in 44 CE, putting the whole northwest under direct control. The region supplied grain to the empire, and many cities grew significantly and gained Roman infrastructure—the Mauretanian city of Volubilis acquired a basilica and a temple. In 428 the Vandals, a Germanic peoples, invaded the region, and the Mauro-Roman Kingdom, an independent Amazigh state in what is now Algeria, challenged both the Vandals and the Byzantine conquerors. The Byzantines eventually occupied the kingdom from 578, until the forces of the Rashidun and Umayyad Caliphates ousted them in the 7th century. But the kingdoms of the northwest left their mark: Amazigh, or Tamazight, is now an official language of Morocco and Algeria.

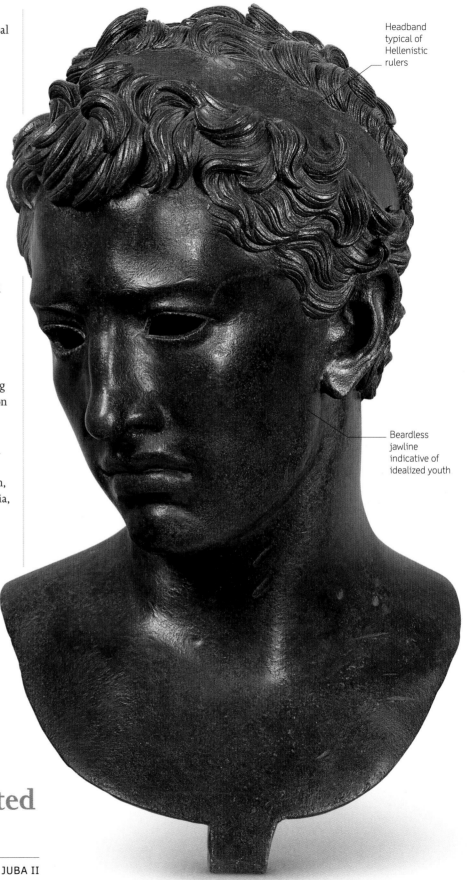

Headband typical of Hellenistic rulers

Beardless jawline indicative of idealized youth

▷ **Bust of Juba II**
This bronze head of Juba II, dating to around 25 BCE, was found in Volubilis, then part of Mauretania, near the modern-day Moroccan city of Meknes.

"One of **the most gifted rulers** of his time."

GREEK HISTORIAN PLUTARCH ON JUBA II

◁ **Bust of Hannibal**
This Roman marble bust, dating from the 2nd century BCE and thought to be of Hannibal, was found at the ancient city of Capua in southern Italy.

Decorated helmet

"**What else** do you believe the Alps are, but **high mountains**?"

HANNIBAL TO HIS ARMY,
AS REPORTED BY ROMAN HISTORIAN LIVY

Paludamentum (military cape)

Hannibal

Africa's most famous general

Hannibal commanded the armies of Carthage against the Romans during the Second Punic War (218–201 BCE). He crossed the Alps and won a succession of crushing victories, bringing Rome to its knees, before being overcome at Zama.

In the third century BCE, the powerful North African empire of Carthage clashed with Rome in the Punic Wars (see pp.64–65). Hannibal, born in 247 BCE, swore hostility to Rome from childhood and spent much of his life fighting Carthage's great rival.

In 221 BCE, Hannibal became commander of the Carthaginian army and began expanding Carthage's territory in the Iberian Peninsula. After his forces sacked the city of Saguntum in Spain in 219 BCE, the Romans declared war. Hannibal's response was to strike at Rome's heart, and in 218 BCE he chose to attack from the north by marching across the Alps.

During the crossing, Hannibal lost many men and several of the war elephants he rode on, but in Italy his skillful tactics and strong leadership helped him outwit his opponents time after time. The Romans adopted delaying tactics but faced him again at Cannae, southeast Italy, in 216 BCE, where Hannibal's troops surrounded and almost destroyed a larger Roman and Italian army. Hannibal subsequently established winter quarters at Capua in southern Italy, an area noted for its wealth and power. The Romans laid siege to Capua in 212 BCE. Hannibal attempted to draw the Romans away from the city by mounting his own siege of Rome itself—unsuccessfully, as Capua fell to the Romans shortly afterward.

In 203 BCE, after 15 years in Italy, Hannibal was recalled to North Africa to face a Roman invasion of Carthage. The following year, at the Battle of Zama, the Roman general Scipio defeated the Carthaginians and stripped Carthage of its European territories.

Final act

Hannibal was not finished. As a statesman in Carthage, he attempted to eliminate corruption and restore the economy. He then used his battlefield experience to command troops for the Seleucid Empire of the Eastern Mediterranean and the Kingdom of Bithynia, in what is now Turkey. He is said to have died by suicide c. 183 BCE, when, finally cornered by the Romans, he took poison concealed in a ring.

△ **Silver shekels**
These silver Carthaginian shekels, showing a man wearing a laurel wreath and an elephant and its rider, were produced in Spain in the 3rd century BCE.

◁ **Crossing the Alps**
The Italian Renaissance artist Jacopo Ripanda painted *Hannibal in Italy* c. 1510. Hannibal's armies included war elephants and an Amazigh (Berber) cavalry.

247 BCE Born in what is now Tunisia

221–219 BCE Defeats the Olcades and Carpetani in Spain and captures Saguntum

218 BCE Second Punic War begins and Hannibal crosses the Pyrenees, then the Alps, with his army

216 BCE Hannibal's forces are victorious at the Battle of Cannae in Italy

207 BCE A Carthaginian army under Hannibal's brother Hasdrubal is defeated in northern Italy

202 BCE Having returned to North Africa, Hannibal's army is defeated at Zama in what is now Tunisia

201 BCE Rome and Carthage agree a peace treaty, ending the Second Punic War

c. 183 BCE Dies in exile in modern-day Turkey

Roman North Africa

Annexation and assimilation with the Mediterranean world

△ **Roman culture**
Along with its troops and administrators, Rome imported its culture to North Africa. The theater at Sabratha, in modern Libya, is one of 230 still standing in the region.

In 146 BCE, Rome defeated the great Mediterranean power Carthage in the third and final Punic War. So began the empire's advances into North Africa—an occupation that would continue for the next 600 years.

By the 1st century BCE, both Cyrenaica (modern Libya) and Egypt had been brought under Roman control, followed by the territories encompassing the North African coast and all cultivable lands north of the Sahara. The last kingdom taken by Rome was Mauretania, to the far west, annexed in 40 CE. This extended Rome's imperial frontier along a border more than 4,000 miles (6,500 km) long.

Collectively, the Romans called these territories (excluding Cyrenaica and Egypt) *Africa*, possibly derived from the name of an Amazigh (Berber) people, the *Aourigha* (pronounced "Afarika"). In time, Rome divided the region into four provinces: *Africa Proconsularis* (Tunisia and coastal Libya); *Numidia* (eastern Algeria); *Mauretania Caesariensis* (the remainder of Algeria); and *Mauretania Tingitana* (northern Morocco).

Lines of defensive forts, called Limes, along the provinces' borders were manned by troops including the Third Augustan Legion. Their role was to stave off external attacks, control internal dissent, and safeguard the region's rich resources of wheat, wine, corn, and olive oil. These goods were mostly exported overseas, to Italy, along with large quantities of ivory and cedarwood, used for ship construction and house building.

Rome expropriated the best agricultural land from Imazighen (Berbers) and Indigenous groups and consolidated it into estates. Land in the mountains, borderline desert areas, and other zones that were hard to farm were left to the Imazighen. Whatever crops they managed to produce were subject to Roman taxes and tithes.

△ **Artistic legacy**
This lion mosaic from the House of Liber Pater in Sabratha dates from the mid-4th century CE.

With Roman control came Romanization. The authorities encouraged the inward migration of settlers, including merchants, magistrates, other civic officials, and former Roman soldiers—enticed with rewards of free land for their years of military service. The Romans rebuilt existing settlements and cities such as Carthage (in modern Tunisia) and Leptis Magna (in modern Libya) according to Roman town-planning models, and established new, wholly Roman cities, such as Timgad (in modern Algeria) around 100 CE.

Divisions and decline

The Romans also achieved the Romanization of North Africa through assimilation. They progressively extended Roman citizenship throughout the 1st and 2nd centuries, allowing locally born men of ability to attain positions of power. The high point of this process came in 193, when Leptis Magna–born Septimius Severus became the first Roman emperor of African origin. In 212, Septimius's son and successor Caracalla extended Roman citizenship to free peoples across the empire, which increased opportunities for social advancement among the inhabitants of North Africa and other provinces. Despite these attempts at integration, Roman North Africa remained divided along class and ethnic lines. Roman and Romanized citizens controlled its towns and coastal cities, while peoples whose culture, language, and way of life remained distinctly Amazigh populated more rural and marginalized areas.

Rome was in decline by the 5th century, its control in Africa, as elsewhere in the empire, falling away. But all of the civilizations of North Africa—including Egypt and Cyrenaica—continued to be connected with those of the Mediterranean, with cities such as Alexandria and Carthage important centers of Christian scholarship and worship. The region's destiny would change again in the decades and centuries to come, but its contact with Rome left an imprint that is still visible today.

NORTH AFRICA'S GREATEST THEOLOGIAN

St. Augustine (*right*) was one of the most significant examples of the cultural exchange resulting from Rome's control of North Africa. A man of Amazigh heritage, Augustine (354–430 CE) rose to become not just the bishop of Hippo Regius in Numidia (modern Algeria), but one of the foremost theologians and philosophers of the early Roman Catholic church. His writings helped lay the foundation for much of medieval and modern Catholic thought, including the concept of original sin.

Pharos Lighthouse was one of the Seven Wonders of the World

Walls once stood 30 ft (9 m) high

Romans introduced camels to North Africa c. 200 CE

◁ **Major city**
Alexandria was, after Rome itself, one of the largest and most populous cities of the empire. This engraving shows it in the 16th century.

The arrival of Islam
The Muslim empire expands into Africa

Following the establishment of Islam in the 7th century CE, an Islamic empire spread rapidly from Arabia into Africa, as Muslim conquests displaced the Christian rule of the Byzantine Empire.

Muhammad, the founder of Islam, was born in Mecca, Arabia, in around 570 CE. By the time of his death in 632, Islam had grown from having a handful of followers to being the predominant religion of the Arabian Peninsula, unifying the previously disparate Arabic peoples in a single, powerful Islamic nation.

Initially, the new religion's doctrine of a single deity met with hostility from adherents of polytheistic religions. Muhammad and his followers faced persecution and were forced to flee from Mecca. Many went with Muhammad to the city of Medina, but some sought refuge in Abyssinia (present-day Ethiopia and Eritrea) in 614, a migration known as the First Hijra. Despite requests to surrender them to the Meccans, King Najasi (r. 614–630) of the Christian Kingdom of Aksum gave them safe haven, and himself went on to convert to Islam.

Most of the Muslims sheltering in Abyssinia later returned to Medina, but some remained, and established the first mosques in Africa, notably at Zeila in present-day Somalia and Massawa in Eritrea. Under Islamic rule, Arabia prospered, and after Muhammad's death his successors, the Rashidun caliphs, expanded its influence into neighboring regions to form an Islamic empire.

During the reign of the second caliph, Umar, Islamic forces conquered Egypt in 641, took much of Persia and the Levant, and, the following year, went on to occupy what is today Libya. This involved some cunning strategy: when Muslim soldiers attacked Tripoli, seven of them managed to enter secretly and, by inciting riot, gave the false impression that the Muslim forces had already entered the city en masse.

Eastward expansion

By the time the Rashidun Caliphate was succeeded by the Umayyad dynasty, the Islamic Empire extended as far as present-day Tunisia. Forces led by General Uqba Ibn Nafi then made further inroads into the Maghreb, the western part of North Africa, and in 670 established the city of Kairouan as a military base. This became the capital of the Islamic province of Ifriqiyya (a name sharing the same root

◁ **African protector**
This 14th-century manuscript illustration shows the King of Aksum refusing to surrender Muslim refugees to the Meccans.

> "**All those who listen to me** shall pass on **my words to others.**"
>
> MUHAMMAD, FINAL SERMON (c. 630 CE)

THE BLUE QUR'AN

Produced in Kairouan, Tunisia (or, possibly, Córdoba, Spain) and believed to date from the late 9th or early 10th centuries, the Blue Qur'an is one of the most celebrated early Qur'anic manuscripts. It takes its name from the unusual indigo-colored parchment on which the text is written. Most striking is the gold calligraphy in Kufic script (the oldest calligraphic form of the various Arabic scripts).

as "Africa"), and the site of a magnificent mosque. The push westward along the Mediterranean coast continued through the 670s, and by 681 Islamic forces had reached present-day Morocco. General Uqba failed to occupy Tangier, however, and it would be another century until Morocco became a Muslim state.

Campaigns and conquest

A key moment in the conquest of North Africa came in 695, when Muslim forces invaded Carthage, an important Byzantine stronghold. The Muslims were initially victorious, but the Byzantine army eventually repulsed them. Later, in 698, the Muslims retook Carthage, sacking the city to prevent it falling under Christian rule again.

Soon after, General Musa Ibn Nusair began a campaign against the Imazighen (Berbers) in the quest to extend the Umayyad Empire across the Maghreb. The Imazighen put up a fierce resistance, but their queen, Al-Kahina, was slain in the Battle of Tabarka, and the Muslims continued their conquests, reaching the Atlantic coast in 708. Almost all of North Africa was now under Muslim control, and, in place of the Christian social order, an Islamic society was set up, which persists to the present time.

◁ **The Great Mosque of Kairouan, Tunisia**
Distinctive horseshoe arches line the colonnade alongside the courtyard of the Mosque of Kairouan, which was established in 670 CE, but extensively rebuilt in the 9th century.

Christian states of the northeast

The establishment of Christianity in northern Africa

The Christian Church in northern and northeastern Africa can trace its roots back as far as 1st-century Ethiopia and Egypt, developing into a distinctively African Orthodox tradition.

△ **Aksumite gold coin**
King Ezana of Aksum's conversion to Christianity was marked by a change in design of the coinage from a pagan disk and crescent motif to the Christian cross.

▽ **Ethiopian convert**
This illustration from the Menologion of Basil II (c. 1000 CE) depicts the conversion and baptism of the Ethiopian eunuch by Philip the Evangelist.

According to the Acts of the Apostles, the first African convert to Christianity was described as an Ethiopian eunuch, who was returning home from Jerusalem when he met Philip the Evangelist, who baptized him. In Ethiopian tradition, this event marked the foundation of the Ethiopian Church, but it was almost 300 years until Christianity was formally adopted here in the 4th century CE.

In Egypt, the apostle St. Mark established the Coptic Orthodox Church in Alexandria around 42 CE. This was initially linked to the Greek-speaking Orthodox Church, but by the 2nd century had developed distinctive characteristics, including worship in the local languages and the use of the *Agpeya*, a breviary or prayer book in the Coptic language. Also in the 2nd century, Christianity began to rise in the western half of North Africa, specifically in the Roman province of *Africa Proconsularis*, situated in present-day Tunisia and parts of Algeria and Libya. This community was linked to the Church of Rome.

Christian communities were also growing in northeastern Africa. The kingdom of Aksum, situated in modern-day Ethiopia, Eritrea, northern Djibouti, and eastern Sudan, was first to formally adopt the religion, after the conversion of King Ezana of Aksum around 330. This marked the establishment of the Ethiopian Orthodox Church, linked to the Coptic Orthodox Church of Alexandria.

▷ **Ethiopian cross**
This processional cross with typically elaborate, stylized design was created by the Tigrinya people of Tigray province in about 1500.

Spread and schisms

From Aksum, Christianity began to spread into neighboring Nubia to the north. In about 350, Aksum invaded the Meroitic kingdom, in modern-day Sudan, causing its decline and eventual collapse. It was replaced by three smaller kingdoms: Nobatia, Makuria, and Alodia. The Nobatian king and aristocracy officially converted to Orthodox Christianity in 543, and Alodia followed suit soon

"Philip and [the Ethiopian] went down into the water and Philip baptized him."

ACTS OF THE APOSTLES 8:37

Text in classical Ge'ez script

Page made of vellum (prepared animal skin)

▷ **Illuminated manuscript**
This tempera and ink painting is one of 20 from an illuminated manuscript of the Four Gospels that monks in the Amhara region of northern Ethiopia created in the 14th or 15th centuries. This scene depicts the appearance of the resurrected Christ.

after. Christian influence had also made its way into Makuria in the 6th century, and after it annexed the kingdom of Nobatia at the beginning of the 8th century, it, too, officially adopted the religion.

Although the Coptic Orthodox Churches were initially a part of the Greek Orthodox Church of Alexandria, differences of belief developed between them. This culminated in a schism in 451, separating the Oriental (Coptic) Orthodox Churches of Africa from the Eastern (Greek) Orthodox Church. The dispute centered around the nature of Christ: while the Eastern Orthodox Church took the mainstream Christian view (shared with the Roman Catholic Church) that Jesus has two distinct natures, divine and human, the Oriental Orthodox Churches held that Jesus' two natures are united as one. Indeed, the Ethiopian Orthodox Tewahedo Church contains in its name the Ge'ez (Classical Ethiopic) word for "united as one"—*tewahedo*.

Another schism came in the Maghreb, this time between the Roman Church of Carthage and a breakaway sect, Donatism, which flourished in the 4th and 5th centuries. Donatists presented a challenge to the Christian clergy by arguing that ministers must be faultless for their ministry to be effective. The Donatist church survived until the arrival of Islam in North Africa in the 7th century (see pp.72–73).

◁ **Royal leopard**
Brass leopards, symbolizing royal power, decorated the palace of the *oba* of Benin, a mighty kingdom in what is now Nigeria. Skilled artisans used the lost wax method to create detailed sculptures and plaques, known as bronzes.

3

African empires

600–1900 CE

African empires

Several African empires such as Napata, Meroë, and Aksum had emerged during antiquity, but numerous kingdoms across the continent entered their golden age during the medieval period and beyond. These empires were made rich by networks of international trade and they developed wealthy elites. Potent belief systems, including Islam and Christianity, became closely linked with state power. The kingdoms also developed and utilized writing systems, as part of a sophisticated bureaucracy, and nurtured distinctive, world-class artistic traditions.

Empires in the North and West

The first medieval empires to rise to prominence were North African. After the fall of Rome at the end of the 7th century, a succession of caliphates ruled great swathes of the region, spreading Islam as they went. The Fatimid Caliphate stretched as far east as the Arabian Peninsula, while the Almoravids conquered much of North Africa and Spain and reached south to Gao, in what is now Mali.

The Almoravids clashed with the Wagadou Empire (ancient Ghana), one of the great powers in the West African Sahel between the 9th and 16th centuries. The mighty Mali Empire that followed was founded in the early 13th century by the Mandingo (Malinke) warrior-prince Sundiata Keita and peaked during the reign of Mansa Musa a century later. In the 15th century, the Songhai dominated the region and its rich trade routes, which crossed the Sahara and reached into Central and East Africa.

To the west of these kingdoms, in what are now Senegal and the Gambia, the Jolof Empire prospered between the 14th and 16th centuries. To the south, in modern-day Ghana, Osei Tutu and his childhood companion Okomfo Anokye founded the Asante Empire in the early 18th century. In what is now Nigeria, the Oyo formed a Yoruba kingdom with a cavalry that was the scourge of surrounding states from the 17th to the 19th centuries. Among their conquests was the 18th-century Kingdom of Dahomey, in modern-day Benin, which was eventually overrun despite its use of European firearms.

East, Central, and Southern Africa

In the northeast of the continent, around modern-day Ethiopia, the Zagwe dynasty ruled from the 11th to the 13th century. Its most famous king, Lalibela, commissioned magnificent rock-hewn churches at a site that now bears his name. The Zagwe were overtaken by the Solomonids who formed the Ethiopian Empire, which was only briefly colonized by Europeans and survived until the 20th century.

Much of Central and Southern Africa was less densely populated, but the Christian Kingdom of Kongo, founded in the 14th century in what is now Angola, grew rich on commerce and endured for six centuries. East of there, between the 12th and 16th centuries, the super-state of Great Zimbabwe profited from Indian Ocean trade and built a capital whose massive stone walls still stand. In today's South Africa, in the 19th century, the warrior-king Shaka used groundbreaking tactics to strengthen the Zulu Kingdom, which redrew the map of Southern Africa before falling to European colonizers expanding their own empires.

◁ **Gold pendant crafted by the Asante people**

9th century CE The Wagadou (Ghana) Empire enters its peak, powered by trade in gold, ivory, and horses

969 Tunisia's Fatimid Caliphate conquers Egypt, and soon makes Cairo its capital

c. 1120 The Amazigh (Berber) Almoravid Caliphate stretches from Mauritania to Spain

c. 1200 The Yoruba empire of Ife, well known for its sculptures, emerges in what is now Benin

12th–13th centuries Great Zimbabwe becomes the heartland of a Shona kingdom

AFRICAN EMPIRES

Major empires
This map shows African empires that existed from the medieval era onward. Most sit by the coast, near major rivers, or on trading routes, which brought many benefits.

KEY
- Wagadou Empire (600–1000)
- Kanem-Bornu Empire (c.800–1893)
- Aghlabid Emirate (800–909)
- Zagwe Kingdom (c.900–c.1200)
- Fatimid Caliphate (909–1171)
- Sultanate of Kilwa (957–1513)
- Almoravid Caliphate (1050s–1147)
- Almohad Caliphate (1121–1269)
- Kingdom of Benin (1180–1897)
- Ife Empire (1200–1420)
- Kingdom of Zimbabwe (1220–1450)
- Mali Empire (1230–1660)
- Ethiopian Empire (1270–1974)
- Oyo Empire (c.1300–1896)
- Kongo Kingdom (c.1390–1862)
- Songhai Empire (1464–1591)
- Mossi States (1500–1895)
- Luba Kingdom (1585–1889)
- Lunda Kingdom (c. 1665–c. 1887)
- Lozi Kingdom (c.1700s–1890)
- Asante Empire (1701–1901)
- Zulu Kingdom (1816–1887)
- Sultanate of Zanzibar (1856–1964)

❶ Great Zimbabwe's Hill Complex

❷ The rock-cut Church of Saint George, Lalibela

❸ The Larabanga Mosque in what is now Ghana

c. 1270 The Solomonic dynasty defeats the Zagwe dynasty and founds the Ethiopian Empire

c. 1350 The Jolof Empire, once a vassal of the Mali Empire, gains its independence

1580s The Luba Empire emerges in what is now the Democratic Republic of the Congo

1700s The Oyo Empire wages war on the Kingdom of Dahomey, eventually defeating its rivals

1901 After two centuries of rule, and four wars with the British, the Asante Empire finally falls

c. 1312 Mansa Musa becomes ruler of the Mali Empire, gathering immense wealth

1460s Under Sunni Ali, the Songhai Empire adopts Islam and dominates much of West Africa

1623 The Kingdom of Kongo defeats a Portuguese army in what is now Angola

1816 Shaka becomes ruler of the Zulu nation and begins building a powerful army

Languages
From Arabic to Zulu

Around 2,000 different languages are used in Africa, some spoken by millions of people, others on the verge of extinction. In addition, nonverbal means of communication include beadwork and "talking" drums. Spoken languages are grouped into several major families, their geographical spread reflecting thousands of years of communication and settlement.

The largest family, Niger-Congo, includes Bantu languages such as Swahili, Zulu, and Shona, as well as the Mande and Dogon languages of West Africa. Thanks in part to the movements of Bantu-speaking peoples, it is the most widespread language group. Most Niger-Congo languages use tone to change word meaning and feature noun classification (in which nouns are grouped by theme).

Afro-Asiatic languages are spoken in North Africa and the Horn of Africa. They include Semitic (such as Arabic, spoken across much of North Africa), Chadic (including Hausa, spoken primarily in northern Nigeria and southern Niger), Cushitic (such as Oromo, spoken in Ethiopia and parts of Kenya), and Amazigh (Berber) languages, as well as Ancient Egyptian. Most Afro-Asiatic languages require syllables to start with consonants, and share a common set of pronouns.

Between these two large language groups, some peoples in the Sahel and Sahara speak the Saharan, Nilotic, and Sudanic languages. More than 100 languages fall into these families, which can be grouped together as Nilo-Saharan languages, and are characterized by their use of different tones to change

△ **Bantu-speakers**
Bantu-speaking peoples live across Central and Southern Africa—the musicians shown in this 19th-century Italian print are from modern-day Angola. Bantu-speakers use around 500 distinct but related languages in the Niger-Congo language family.

△ **San storyteller**
The San peoples are hunter-gatherers from Southern Africa with a rich storytelling tradition that is both a regular pastime and a way to preserve a threatened culture. The San, like the pastoralist Khoikhoi, speak a variety of languages that feature clicking sounds, which function as consonants.

△ **Tuareg**
The Tuareg (shown here in a 19th-century European depiction) are an Amazigh people who live in Niger, Mali, Algeria, Libya, and Burkina Faso. Tuareg languages are part of the Afro-Asiatic language family; the most widely spoken dialect is Tawellemet.

> "If you know … the **language of your culture** … that is **empowerment**."
>
> NGŨGĨ WA THIONG'O, KENYAN WRITER, 2017

meaning and by rules of vowel harmony (in which two sets of contrasting vowels never coexist in the same word). Many speakers live in Sudan or South Sudan, although Songhai languages (deriving from the empire of the same name) are spoken in West Africa.

In contrast to these thriving language groups, many of Africa's most ancient languages are endangered. Once widespread, the hunter-gatherer San and the pastoralist Khoikhoi have been forced to the margins of their homelands, which mainly lie in Southern Africa. One of the most notable features of the speech of the Khoikhoi and San is their use of clicking sounds, produced when air is released in a burst past the tongue, teeth, and palate. These clicks have been borrowed by Bantu languages such as Xhosa and Zulu, but are not found on any other continent. Some languages, such as Khoikhoi (spoken in Namibia, Botswana, and South Africa) and Sandawe (Tanzania), are used by many thousands of people, but others have been driven to extinction.

Languages from outside Africa also have a significant presence, with English an official tongue in over 20 nations, especially in Southern and East Africa, and French widely used in West Africa. Creole languages such as Krio (Sierra Leone) and Kreyol (Liberia) are also spoken, while Madagascar's Malagasy is the westernmost Austronesian language in the world, having been introduced by traders from the Malay archipelago more than 1,500 years ago.

△ **Message beads**
Aroko is a form of nonverbal communication used by the Yoruba of West Africa. Meaning is determined by different combinations or colors of leaves, cowrie shells, weapons, and beads.

△ **Nilotic speakers**
The Nilotic-speaking Samburu (pictured) are cattle and sheep herders, who mostly live in northern Kenya. Nilotic languages are part of the Nilo-Saharan linguistic family and are spoken by more than 50 million people across East Africa.

△ **Talking drum**
Griots (poets and musicians) in West Africa have used talking drums as a storytelling tool for centuries. The instrument can be played to mimic the rhythm and tone of human speech, but was also used to spread messages between villages, conveying news over long distances more rapidly than a horse and rider.

△ **N|uu language**
South African government minister Nathi Mthethwa hands a N|uu dictionary to Ouma Katrina Esau, one of the remaining fluent speakers of this San dialect. Esau created a school to pass on the language, which has 45 clicks, 30 non-click consonants, and 39 vowels.

The development of East African trade

Trade and transformation in East Africa

East Africans have been trading with people in the Persian Gulf, along the Arabian Sea, and on the coast of the Indian Ocean for 2,000 years, taking advantage of the prevailing winds to journey to and from Asia.

From at least the 1st century BCE, Cushitic (ancient Somali) livestock herders were bartering goods with traveling Arab merchants. These contacts continued for the next 200 years, with the Cushites setting up trading ports on the coast along the Horn of Africa, including one known today as Hafun West, where archaeological finds include pottery fragments from the region occupied by modern-day Iraq.

The Bantu-speakers and sea trading

By the 1st and 2nd centuries CE, Bantu-speaking people (see pp.36–37) from the Great Lakes region around modern-day Burundi, Rwanda, and the Democratic Republic of the Congo (DRC) had migrated eastward, displacing or assimilating Indigenous groups as they progressed. On reaching East Africa's coast, they founded new settlements and took over those already constructed by the migratory Cushite pastoralists. Rhapta in modern Kenya, for example, had been established in the 1st century BCE by the Cushites and was known to the Romans, but only became a major sea-trading center under Bantu-speakers 200–300 years later.

Generally speaking, the prevailing winds in the region blew from west to east in the summer, making this the season for traders to sail to Asia or up and down East Africa's coastline. They would buy and sell goods such as the elephant ivory and animal skins that were popular in Arabia, India, and China. Merchants traveled in a vessel called a *mtepe*, a long, square-sailed cargo boat. The wooden planks of its hull were sewn together using coir, the hairlike husk of a coconut shell, which made the boats notoriously leaky. By winter, with the winds blowing east to west, Asian merchants arrived in East Africa with grain, glass beads, and pottery to trade for local produce.

All of this activity made East Africa's ports diverse and ever-changing places. Their inhabitants were not simply sailors and traders, but also acted as middlemen, facilitating deals between Arab, Indian, and Iranian merchants, and with local suppliers and vendors along the coast as well as much farther inland.

Birth of a new culture

From the 8th to the 12th centuries, East Africa's trading links with the nations across the Arabian Sea and the Indian Ocean intensified. Iran and the

△ **Chinese connection**
This tomb pillar from the East African settlement of Kunduchi (in modern-day Tanzania) is embedded with plaques from medieval China, evidence of links between the two regions.

◁ **Port of call**
Ancient ruins at Gedi (in modern-day Kenya) include a palace with arched gateways, as well as houses, tombs, and a mosque. Gedi was a coastal trading center during the medieval period.

- Mountains with rivers running down to the sea appear inland from the East African coast
- Mecca is at the center of the map
- The "Mountains of the Moon," the fabled source of the Nile River
- The representations of India, China, and South Asia owe more to guesswork than informed knowledge on the map-maker's part
- Straits of Gibraltar
- The Iberian Peninsula of Spain and Portugal

▷ **World turned upside-down**
This 1154 world map by Arab cartographer Mohammed al-Idrisi is displayed as his contemporaries would have seen it: with Africa at the top and Europe below.

southern Arabian territory of present-day Yemen became particularly important destinations for African merchants. A range of goods, including gold, ivory, and rock crystal, were traded for textiles, glass beads, and ceramics as part of a rich cultural exchange. In addition, enslaved people were trafficked across the region (see pp.148–149). With ports and city-states such as Shanga and Pemba (islands off Kenya and Tanzania, respectively) and Kilwa (in Tanzania) growing in size, population, and reputation, East Africa's wealthier citizens now lived in homes built from a stonelike coral called *porites* rather than the usual mud, wood, and leaves, and they imported large quantities of Arabian pottery and Chinese porcelain to display as a visible sign of their status.

Arrival of Islam

Islam also made an impact, with many East Africans adopting the faith, observing whichever branch of the religion—Sunni or Shia—was practiced by the Muslims they transacted with. The growing cosmopolitanism of East Africa's trading centers led to major social change. With large numbers of Indian, Chinese, Iranian, and particularly Arab people settling in East Africa, the population's composition began to alter. As incomers began to mix with and intermarry among the Islamized Bantu-speaking people, a new culture and language known as Swahili emerged. Today, Swahili is still the name given to both the language and the people of much of the East African coastal region.

△ **The usual view**
When Mohammed al-Idrisi's map is shown in a more recognizable orientation, Africa, Europe, and Asia are easier to visualize.

The rise and fall of Wagadou

An empire built on gold and trade

On the southern edge of the Sahel, the Wagadou (Ghana) Empire emerged in the 6th century CE as the first great trading state of West Africa, thriving for seven centuries until its eventual collapse in the 14th century.

△ **Prime location**
At its height in the 1050s, the Wagadou Empire dominated trade passing between the goldfields to its south and the Muslim states of North Africa.

Wagadou (Ghana), meaning "the land of gold," arose among the Soninke peoples of modern-day southeastern Mauritania and western Mali around 600 CE. The existence of a stone-built town at Dhar Tichitt in the southwestern Sahara, dating from about 1600 BCE, suggests that the empire developed from several existing local cultures.

The rulers—known as the *ghana*—of the new state enjoyed considerable wealth. This was partly due to the availability of copper and salt, which could be traded and on which tolls could be levied. The region's position on trans-Saharan trade routes carrying gold from sources at Ghiyaru, Bure, and Bambuk on the Senegal and Upper Niger also brought wealth, and the *ghana* possessed a monopoly on the gold itself, of which most citizens were allowed to possess only the dust.

Much of what we know about Wagadou comes from early Arab travelers who passed through it (see box), beginning with the astronomer Ibrahim al-Fazari (d. 777). The first king was said to have been Dyabe Sissé, whose successors expanded to the east and west, seeking to dominate all routes through the Sahara. They built relations with the Sanhaja Amazigh (Berber) rulers of Aoudaghost north of Wagadou, and with the buffer states at Sili and Takrur in the west.

The capital city

Described as possessing an army of 200,000 men, including 40,000 archers, the Wagadou kings ruled from a capital at Koumbi Saleh, which was divided into two sections. The royal city—which Arab writers called *al-Ghaba* ("the grove")—housed the palace, which was surrounded by a stone wall and circular wooden huts for the majority of the population. It was also the site of the wooden-domed royal tombs and sacred copses where Wagadou priests carried out their rituals.

Islam had reached Wagadou by the 11th century, and the other district was the Muslim town, which had twelve mosques, special food shops, and resident Islamic legal scholars. Modern excavations suggest

Corded patterning

Netlike decoration

◁ **Wagadou crafts**
Pottery vessels provided storage and a way to transport everyday items such as grain, and have been found at many Wagadou sites.

▷ **Trading post**
Ouadane, once an important stage on the gold-trading route north of Aoudaghost in the southwest Sahara until its decline in the 13th century, now lies in ruins.

that the site may have held a population of 15,000. It occupied around 110 acres (45 hectares), and had two large cemeteries outside its walls.

The decline of Wagadou

Trade routes gradually moved farther east due to desertification, which had extended the borders of the Sahara southward. Border regions such as Takrur broke away and eventually the Wagadou Empire became far less significant. The last great king was probably the *ghana* Tunka Menin, who ascended the throne in 1063. Menin succeeded his maternal uncle to become king—Wagadou royal succession was matrilineal. In 1054, the Almoravids—a movement of Islamic renewal with its roots in the desert fringes of Mauretania—(see pp.100–101), swept south and captured the important Amazigh trading town of Aoudaghost. In 1076, they sacked Koumbi Saleh—a devastating blow to Wagadou.

Although Wagadou recovered a little after the Almoravid Empire collapsed in the 1140s, it was unable to bring together the rival Soninke chieftaincies or compensate for the loss of revenue from the gold trade. The capital, Koumbi Saleh, could no longer support the large population it once held. Instead, Wagadou was obliged to pay tribute to the growing Mali Empire (see pp.90–91), and by the mid-13th century Koumbi Saleh had disappeared.

> **ARAB TRAVELERS**
>
> Most of our information about Wagadou comes from Muslim Arab writers who had heard accounts from other travelers. The geographer al-Yaqubi mentioned the kingdom briefly in the 9th century, followed by a more detailed description by another geographer, al-Masudi (d. 956 CE). Historian and geographer al-Bakri, from Córdoba, describes the trans-Saharan trade routes, including those in the Wagadou Empire, in his *Book of Routes and Realms*, written in the 1060s.

"From every donkey **loaded with salt** … the king takes a duty of **one gold dinar**."

ABU UBAYD AL-AZIZ AL-BAKRI, 1068

Dogon settlement
On the Bandiagara Escarpment in Mali's central plateau, these adobe buildings are houses and granaries for the Dogon people. The Dogon arrived here around the 15th century when the area was occupied by the Tellem people, who had been here since the 11th century. Some Tellem were pushed out; others intermarried and became part of the Dogon community. There is evidence that the Dogon drew on Tellem customs in their own faith. The approximately 600,000 Dogon live as farmers, mainly near the top or bottom of the cliffs—where there is a water supply—and the area is also a popular place for tourists.

Riches of the trade routes

The exchange of goods, people, and ideas

The trade routes that crossed the Sahara, known as the trans-Saharan trade routes, carried gold, salt, and enslaved people, bringing huge wealth and influences that helped shape Africa's economic, cultural, and political development.

African merchants have traded across the continent and beyond since ancient times. From at least Egypt's Old Kingdom in the 3rd millennium BCE, the vast sand sea of the Sahara (see pp.20–21), far from being a barrier, proved a highly effective conduit for trade. Here, merchants went in search of products available in Africa south of the Sahara, such as ivory and hides, in exchange for grain and manufactured goods. The immense hardships of desert travel during this period channeled the trade from oasis to oasis along certain routes, where towns began to spring up, eventually deriving great wealth from the provisions sold to travelers and the tolls imposed on them.

Caravans of gold

Farther west, a network of routes developed, carrying gold, spices, kola nuts, and other forest products, as well as enslaved people, in exchange for jewelery, textiles, and salt, which was scarce in West Africa. From the northern terminus of the trade—towns such as Sijilmasa (in modern-day Morocco), Tripoli (in Libya), and Kairouan (in Tunisia)—caravans of merchants traveled south. From around the 3rd century CE, the merchants used camels to carry both goods and people. The ability of these animals to travel long distances without food and water made the journey less risky and arduous.

The trade greatly enriched African rulers south of the Sahara, giving rise from the 6th century to the formation of larger empires such as Ghana, whose kings controlled access to the Bambuk goldfields beyond the Senegal River. Farther east, the Kanem-Bornu Empire (see pp.108–109) flourished on the fringes of Lake Chad. In addition, trade brought with it the exchange of ideas and beliefs, including the transmission of Islam (see pp.72–73). The religion began to penetrate North Africa from the 8th century, although it did not become established among rulers and the bulk of the populace for several centuries yet.

The newfound wealth helped the growth of trading hubs like Gao, Djenné, and Timbuktu, which became centers of learning and of industries—such as textile production—as well as the focus of competition between rival powers. Later, they developed into substantial towns, with royal palaces and mosques, including the Djinguereber mosque at Timbuktu, built

△ **Gold dinar**
The Islamic Almoravid dynasty based in Morocco minted this mid-12th-century coin from gold traded across the Sahara.

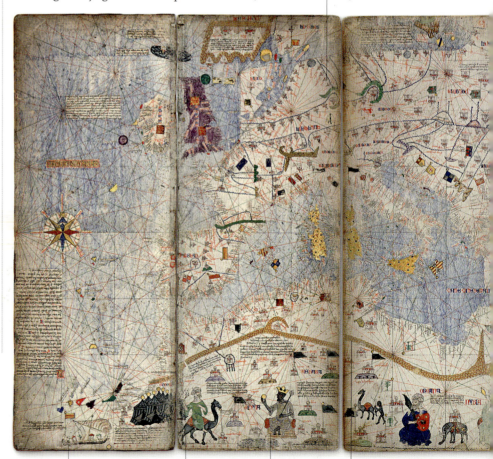

▷ **The Catalan Atlas**
Created in 1375 by a cartographer in Majorca, this map situates North Africa and the Sahara region at the bottom left. The Atlas demonstrates the significant European interest in the lucrative trade routes that had developed across Africa.

European sailors en route to Africa | Camel-riding desert trader | Mansa Musa of Mali | Gold band representing Atlas Mountains | Europe in 1327. The discovery of new goldfields at Bure (modern-day Guinea) led trade routes to shift slightly to the east, bypassing Ghana, which had lost the key trading town of Aoudaghost by 1050. A new empire, Mali, founded by Sundiata Keita in the 1230s, would eclipse Ghana as the preeminent power in the region.

Mali profited so much from trans-Saharan trade that its ruler Mansa Musa (see pp.92–93) went on a pilgrimage to Mecca in 1324–1325, during which he spent and gave away such vast quantities of gold that it caused the overall value of gold to decrease for at least a decade afterward. Mali was, in turn, eclipsed by the Songhai Empire (c. 1464–1591), which again relied for its wealth on the profits from trading gold and enslaved people northward.

By this time, however, the ancient trading routes were already endangered. From the 1440s, the arrival of the Portuguese in Africa opened up alternative sea routes for trade, and the beginnings of the transatlantic slave trade destabilized new regions of coastal West Africa.

The decline of trade

In 1591, the Moroccan sultan Ahmad al-Mansur sacked Timbuktu, bringing the Songhai Empire to an end. Although trade across the desert continued, and even became easier with the advent of modern roads and railroads in the 19th century, the demand for gold among Mediterranean states had also slackened. By 1600, the heyday of the trans-Saharan trade routes was over.

△ **Ivory salt cellar**
Created by West African craftspeople for a European market, the snakes on this exquisitely carved ivory salt cellar represent wealth.

> "We came next to [the oasis of] **Tisarahla** … where the caravans halt."
>
> IBN BATTUTA, *THE TRAVELS*, 1354

Caravan with camels, on the Silk Road, China

Sultan of Babylon (Cairo, Egypt) | Legendary Queen of Sheba | Trading ships on the Red Sea | Islands along the coast of China | Kingdom of Taprobane (Ceylon, now Sri Lanka)

△ **Impressive landmark**
The Great Mosque of Djenné, in modern-day central Mali, was built around the 13th century, though the current structure dates to 1907.

The Empire of Mali

The creation of Africa's most famous empire

Born from the defeat of a king said to have been a sorcerer, the Mali Empire stretched across West Africa in the 13th and 14th centuries. Its wealth in gold made it famous from Europe to Mecca.

Between the 9th and 11th centuries, the Ghana Empire dominated the region around the Niger River (see pp.84–85). Its empire encompassed Mande, the homeland of the Mandingo (also known as the Mandinka or Malinke), in what is now southern Mali and northeastern Guinea. But after a disastrous war in the 11th century with the Almoravids, an Islamic dynasty centered on modern Morocco, its grip weakened and several provinces began to break away.

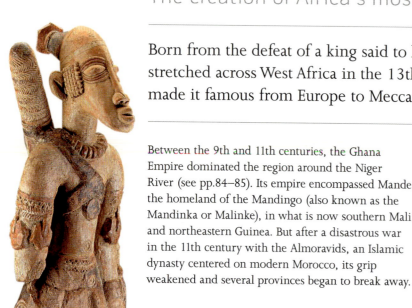

◁ **Archer figure**
This terra-cotta archer, dating from the 13th–15th centuries, is depicted in ceremonial military attire and may represent warriors who were allies of the Malian emperor Sundiata Keita.

By the 12th century, Mande had conquered the nearby Kingdom of Do, as well as other towns around the Niger, to create the Kingdom of Mali.

Sumanguru and the Lion King

Mali was not the only nation to rise in Ghana's wake. Under its ruler Kemoko Kanté, the Kingdom of Sosso conquered much of the declining empire. When he died, his son Sumanguru continued to expand Sosso territory. An impressive but reportedly cruel leader, Sumanguru was believed to have mystical powers, and is remembered as the inventor of the *balafon*, a xylophone made from gourds. Sumanguru sacked Mande nine times, but each time the Mandingo regrouped and counterattacked. However, when the

Malian king Maghan died in around 1218, he left the crown to his less military-minded son, Dankaran Tuman, who sued for peace. Unable to maintain the support of his people, Dankaran fled Mande. His younger brother, Sundiata—or Mari-Diata (Lion King)—returned from travels across the Ghana Empire and led the Mandingo to war. He raised an army of troops and cavalry, and at the Battle of Kirina in around 1235, he defeated Sumanguru's army.

The victorious Sundiata conquered the lands of the Sosso and created an oral constitution, named *Kurukan Fuga* after the plain on which it was agreed, that made him ruler of the Mali Empire. His generals conquered the gold fields of Bondu and Bambuk to the south and desert trading towns to the north, and by Sundiata's death his empire stretched west and east to the Senegal and Niger rivers respectively.

Prosperity and decline

The empire's central West African location and its control of goldmines, fertile land, and trade routes put it in a commanding position. Taxes on the trade in gold, salt, copper, ivory, and enslaved people made its kings wealthy. Yet Sundiata's descendants struggled to make a mark, and several decades of instability caused by succession rivalries followed his death in around 1255. The empire still prospered, thanks in part to powerful court officials, and Islam became increasingly influential.

In around 1307, Mansa Musa ascended to the throne, and the empire reached its peak. Musa (see pp.92–93) almost doubled its possessions, conquering the cities of Gao and Timbuktu and enslaving thousands of captured people. But while he spent most of his reign in conflict with his non-Muslim neighbors, he encouraged closer links with the sultanates of North Africa.

By now, the multiethnic and multilingual Mali Empire supported a large army that included mail-clad cavalrymen and archers. Muslim scholars gathered in libraries and universities in cities such as Timbuktu. For several decades after Musa's death in around 1337, Mali's golden age continued. But the empire's size made it hard to defend. Arguments over the succession weakened Mali, and rebellions gradually shrank its borders in the 14th and 15th centuries. Portuguese ships challenged for trade, the nomadic Tuareg raided settlements, and by the early 16th century, the Songhai (see pp.104–105) had taken over much of the empire. Mali remained a regional power, but its legendary riches were long gone.

> ### FOUNDER OF **THE MALI EMPIRE**
> Much of our knowledge of Mali's founder, Sundiata Keita, comes from the *Epic of Sundiata*, a poem that mixes history and myth and was originally recited by *griots* (storytellers). According to the poem, Sundiata was born to King Maghan and a formerly enslaved woman named Sogolon. The young prince was disabled from birth, but miraculously learned to walk. He left Mande and grew into a skilled warrior and statesman. Finally, his people, the Mandingo, called him back to lead them and he commanded a large army made up of calvary and infantry—as had been foretold by prophecy.
>
> **HORSEMAN FIGURINE, MALI, 13TH–14TH CENTURIES**

▷ **Seated figure**
This 13th-century sculpture from Djenné in present-day Mali may represent mourning, though its exact meaning is unknown.

Toes and other expressive, intimate details bring the sculpture to life

Bumps are thought to depict ornaments or sores from illness

Wealthy emperor
Mansa Musa is represented on the 1375 Catalan Atlas of the Jewish-Spanish cartographer Abraham Cresques. Musa's crown and orb are rendered in vivid gold, the source of his great wealth.

Mansa Musa

The greatest ruler of the Mali Empire

Mansa Musa oversaw the growth of the Mali Empire in the 14th century. His pilgrimage to Mecca was one of the most notable events of the medieval age.

Born into the Mali Empire's royal family, Musa became *mansa*, or emperor, around 1307. His predecessor headed a fleet of ships on an expedition that sought to discover whether any lands lay beyond the Atlantic Ocean—and was never seen again.

The Mali Empire reached its greatest extent during Musa's reign, encompassing large areas of present-day Guinea, Senegal, Mauretania, and the Gambia, as well as Mali itself. Mali's imperial might was backed by impressive resources, too. As well as gold and salt deposits, Musa's empire also benefited from the lucrative trade in ivory. Such were Mali's riches that Mansa Musa has often been described as the richest man that has ever lived.

Raising Mali's public profile

In 1324, Musa embarked on the *Hajj*, or pilgrimage, to Mecca that every devout Muslim is expected to attempt. His reasons for making the long and hazardous journey from West Africa to Arabia were complex. Piety played a role, as did guilt—a year earlier Musa had caused his mother's death by accident, and his court counselors advised him to visit the tomb of the Prophet Muhammad in Medina, close to Mecca, as penance.

Going on the *Hajj* also gave Musa an opportunity to display his wealth and prestige to the outside world. He reportedly traveled to Mecca and Medina with 60,000 porters bearing gifts made of gold, 500 silk-clad servants, and 15,000 camels laden with sacks of gold, perfume, salt, and provisions. His retinue gifted and spent so much gold while staying in Cairo that they debased the precious metal's value there for more than 10 years afterward.

Once in Mecca, Musa recruited a number of scholars to help modernize his empire. Chief among these was the Andalusian lawyer, poet, and architect Abu Ishaq al-Sahili, whose finest creation was the Djinguereber Mosque in Timbuktu. This, and other mosques, *madrasas* (centers of learning), and schools, turned Timbuktu from a busy trading hub into the home of one of the world's first universities.

△ **Timbuktu texts**
Under Mansa Musa, Timbuktu's libraries grew to hold countless texts on science, medicine, and, as shown here, mathematics and astronomy.

▽ **Seat of learning**
Built during Musa's reign, Sankoré Madrasa in Timbuktu was a great medieval seat of learning.

1235 Mali's empire founded by Sundiata Keita, Musa's great-uncle

c. 1307 Musa becomes *mansa* (emperor) of Mali

1324/5 Mansa Musa's pilgrimage to Mecca and Medina

1325 Mali conquers Gao, capital of the rival Songhai people

1325/6 University of Timbuktu established

1327 Djinguereber Mosque commissioned

1330 Timbuktu invaded by neighboring Mossi kingdom, but later recaptured

c. 1337 Death of Mansa Musa

Djinguereber Mosque

Timbuktu, present-day Mali

The city of Timbuktu benefited from a strategic location on a trans-Saharan trade route between goldfields to the south and salt mines to the north. It began to prosper in the 14th century under Mansa Musa, who promoted Islam and established the first of the city's three great mosques: Djinguereber. In the 15th to 16th centuries, through its mosques and trade network, Timbuktu developed into a renowned center of religious and intellectual learning, with a prestigious university attracting scholars from North Africa and beyond. In 1591, Morocco invaded, bringing the city's golden age to an abrupt end.

▷ **A Timbuktu library**
As a city of scholarship, Timbuktu became renowned for the production and trade of quality manuscripts on a wide variety of subjects. Tutors of the university built up prized collections in their personal libraries, and often drew on these to lead the study and copying of texts in their own homes.

The roof was constructed using *golettes* (small sticks) overlaid with mudbricks.

Tuareg tents made from wood and straw matting

Extensions to the original prayer hall arcades feature arches

Wells provided the community with easy access to water

The main courtyard provided additional prayer and teaching space

Long drainpipes reduce erosion by rain

DJINGUEREBER MOSQUE | 95

◁ **Focus of prayer**
The prayer hall is cool and dim, with simple mudbrick arcades. A molded frieze confers special significance on the *qibla* wall and *mihrab* (prayer niche) and may date to the 16th century.

△ **Secondary courtyard**
The courtyards of Timbuktu's mosques provided space for prayer, theological discussion, and study: much of the university teaching took place there, in individual tutor groups. The secondary courtyard at Djinguereber, reconstructed here, also allowed access to the main minaret.

Palm wood *torons* provide support, built-in scaffolding, and decoration

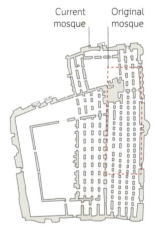

▷ **Evolution of Djinguereber Mosque**
Excavations suggest the original mosque, built around 1325 for Mansa Musa, had a simple rectangular plan (marked in red on this floor plan of the current building). It has since been remodeled and enlarged several times, most notably in 1570–1583.

The conical minaret is situated above the *mihrab* in the prayer hall

The *qibla* wall indicates the direction of prayer

Camel trains from the Sahara desert brought in salt slabs weighing 55–66 lb (25–30 kg) apiece

Manuscripts were among the most valuable trade goods

ANNUAL RESTORATION

The distinctive earthen architecture of Timbuktu's mosques is durable, but requires regular maintenance to survive weathering by wind, sand, and rain. Restoring the mosques is an important tradition, carried out annually at the request of the relevant imam and directed by one of two families of master masons, who claim descent from the original builders of the 14th century. Using the decorative wooden posts (*torons*) in the minaret as scaffolding, local residents replaster the surface with fresh mudbrick. Every member of the community contributes in some way, be it labor, money, or materials.

REPLASTERING THE DJINGUEREBER MOSQUE

△ **Djinguereber district**
Djinguereber district lay on a north–south trade route at the southwest limit of old Timbuktu. This reconstruction depicts the area in the 1580s, at the peak of Timbuktu's prosperity and renown. Trade was thriving, and the Great Mosque had just been reconstructed on a grand scale.

> "The **word of God** and the treasures of **wisdom** are only to be found **in Timbuktu**."
>
> — 15TH-CENTURY MALIAN PROVERB

Timbuktu manuscript
Written records of West Africa

Red Morocco leather used to encase pages

Timbuktu's position between the southern Sahara and the Niger River in West Africa made it a crucial medieval trading post. However, for all the gold that passed through this legendary city, its greatest legacy has arguably been cultural. Part of the Mali Empire in the 13th century, Timbuktu became known for its mosques, *madrasas*, and libraries.

In Timbuktu, students and scholars wrote, translated, and collected hundreds of thousands of texts. The city's written works, collectively known as the Timbuktu Manuscripts, represent a unique treasure, and span 900 years, with the oldest texts dating from around the 12th century. Many of the manuscripts are written in the Arabic and Spanish languages, but also in Ajami, an Arabic-derived script used to write other local languages, including Songhai, Fula, and Bambara, reflecting the variety of cultures that interacted with Timbuktu's heritage.

Classification and preservation
The collection includes some of the earliest known Islamic texts of philosophy and mathematics, while astronomy, medicine, botany, architecture, music, law, and history are also represented. Multiple copies of the Qur'an are present, as well as religious treatises and guides to morality, while literary works include the *Epic of Sundiata* (see pp.90–91), an account of the founding of the Mali Empire.

The Timbuktu Manuscripts are significant to many African countries and their diasporic communities. They are evidence of the vibrant civilization of West Africa, a testament to the resilience and strength of its people, and a reminder of the region's rich written, as well as oral, cultures.

Yet these texts, many of which date from the Mali and Songhai Empires in the 14th to 16th centuries, have often been under threat. After a Moroccan invasion in the late 16th century, Timbuktu declined, although new works continued to be written. Under French colonial control (1892–1960), Arabic education was neglected, and more manuscripts were damaged, lost, or entered private ownership.

In 2012, Tuareg militants occupied Timbuktu, destroying thousands of manuscripts that did not meet their interpretation of Islam. Librarians battled to save the texts, with a team led by Malian librarian Dr. Abdel Kader Haïdara saving thousands of manuscripts and smuggling them via all-terrain vehicles, carts, and boats to Mali's modern-day capital, Bamako. While many documents have been lost, others have been stored or digitized by Malians, as well as by global giants such as Google, which has uploaded 40,000 for public use under the banner "Mali Magic." Mali's ancient gold may be gone, but its scholarship lives on.

▽ **Decorated Qur'an**
This 12th-century Qur'an, one of the finest of the Timbuktu Manuscripts, comes from the collection of Dr. Abdel Kader Haïdara.

Decorative panel enhances the text

The Arabic script used is typical for 12th-century Morocco

Note records that this Qur'an was owned by several Moroccan kings

The rise and fall of the Aghlabids and Fatimids

Two great powers in North Africa

Eastern North Africa, conquered by Muslim armies around 700 CE, gave rise to two immensely powerful dynasties—the Aghlabids, who ruled for a century, and the Fatimids, who ruled for more than 200 years.

Until the late 8th century, the Arab Islamic Abbasid dynasty controlled Egypt and North Africa. However, in parts of the empire, a series of local rulers began to govern more or less independently. In 800, Ibrahim ibn al-Aghlab, the commander of a small Abbasid garrison, quelled a rebellion by Arab soldiers and seized the important city of Kairouan. He was rewarded with the province of Tunisia and ruled the region for 12 years, founding the Aghlabid dynasty, paying lip service to the Abbasids but in reality operating independently.

Aghlabid rule

Al-Aghlab moved the capital to al-Abbasiya, just outside Kairouan, and built a series of *ribats*, or fortified garrison posts. His successor Ziyadat Allah I (r. 817–838 CE) faced a serious challenge when the *jund*, the troops of Arab descent, rebelled in 824, an uprising that took three years to suppress. In part as an outlet for these disaffected *jund* troops, the Aghlabids invaded Sicily in 827, leading to a Muslim occupation of the island for 200 years.

Aghlabid rule was opulent, financed by a fixed tax that paid for a lavish lifestyle and a series of grand building projects. These included the Great Mosque at Sousse, and reconstruction of the Zitouna Mosque in Tunis and the Great Mosque at Kairouan, all completed in the reign of Abu Ibrahim Ahmed (r. 856–863). However, the Aghlabid emirate descended into tyrannical bloodshed, as Ibrahim II (875–902) massacred *jund* garrisons and put down an Amazigh (Berber) revolt. In 903, Ibrahim's grandson Ziyadat Allah III (r. 903–909) killed his own father, Abdullah II. Ziyadat Allah also went on to murder his brother.

The Fatimids take over

Order was restored by a new dynasty, the Fatimids, whose origins lay with a Shia missionary, Abu Abdullah al-Shii. He had converted the Kutama Amazigh of eastern Algeria, raised them in revolt against the Aghlabids, and by 909 had taken Kairouan. Abu Abdullah was executed by his superior, Ubaydullah al-Mahdi, who declared himself caliph and imposed Shia Islam on Tunisia. In 914, he launched an invasion into Egypt. The Egyptian forces repulsed the attack and Ubaydullah al-Mahdi instead concentrated on securing his power base, building a capital at Mahdia in 916, and invading Idrisid Morocco, an Arab Muslim dynasty (788–974) whose capital Fès he took in 921.

△ **Fatimid goldwork**
This 11th-century pendant shows filigree and cloisonné enamel of birds. It is a rare surviving example of the fine work of Egyptian goldsmiths from the Fatimid era.

△ **Fatimid miniature**
This painting shows two traders weighing merchandise on a set of scales. Fatimid merchants profited from Egypt's strategic position between Africa and West Asia.

THE RISE AND FALL OF THE AGHLABIDS AND FATIMIDS | 99

The Fatimids continued the Arab conquest of Sicily, but struggled to hold together their extensive empire. They lost control of northern Morocco to the Umayyad Caliphate of Córdoba between 931 and 973, and faced a serious revolt from 944 by Abu Yazid (known as "the old man on the donkey"), an Amazigh rebel of humble origins who became a spiritual leader and gained support for his opposition to the Fatimids.

Peak of Fatimid power

It took twelve years to put down Abu Yazid's uprising, after which the Fatimids regrouped, partially retaking Algeria in 958 and, under al-Mansur (r. 946–953), building a new capital at al-Mansuriyya south of Kairouan. In 969, Caliph al-Muizz (r. 953–975) ordered the invasion of Egypt. A weakened Ikshidid dynasty of Muslim Turks, which controlled Egypt and Syria at this time, offered little resistance. Al-Muizz's general Jawhar al-Katib had established a new capital at al-Qahira (Cairo) and in 973 the Fatimid court moved to Egypt, never to return.

Control of Tunisia was now handed to Zirid governors (Sanhaja Amazigh from modern-day Algeria), who rapidly installed an independent dynasty. The Fatimids also overran Syria and Palestine and secured peace in Egypt. As part of their campaign to promote Shia Islam, the Fatimids built *madrasas* and mosques in Cairo, including the splendid al-Azhar.

End of the Fatimids

Fatimid rule was briefly threatened in the mid-11th century by the migration of nomadic Arab peoples, the Banu Hilal and Banu Sulaym. After the Fatimids successfully diverted these groups westward toward Tunisia, they instead wrought devastation on the Zirids.

Infighting, aggravated by famines, led to provinces in the east and far west breaking away, and in 1099, the capture of Jerusalem by the Christian crusaders dealt a devastating blow to Fatimid prestige. In 1073, the caliph al-Mustansir sent an army officer, Badr al-Jamali, to restore order. Al-Jamali executed dissident commanders and his success established a military regime and reduced the power of the caliphs. In 1171, the Kurdish general Saladin took over the office of vizier and deposed the last Fatimid caliph, putting an end to the dynasty.

> "We will **defend you and protect you** against [enemies]. We will **not let you be harmed** …"
>
> FATIMID COMMANDER JAWHAR'S PROMISE TO THE EGYPTIANS, CITED IN SCHOLAR IDRIS AL-DIN'S *UYUN AL-AKHBAR*, 1467

▽ **Clay plate**
This 12th-century plate from Egypt shows Fatimid art and uses a lusterware technique. Metallic oxide glaze applied before firing leaves a shimmering, yellow-gold surface.

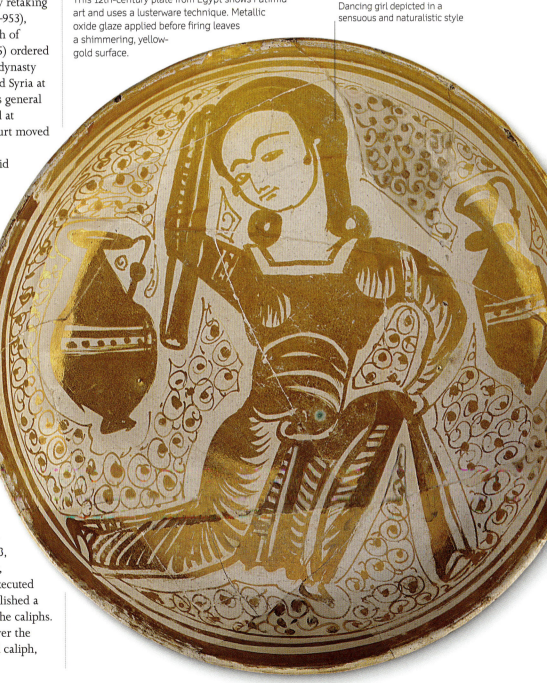

Dancing girl depicted in a sensuous and naturalistic style

The Almoravid and Almohad dynasties

Conquerors of the Western Mediterranean

From the 10th century, several Muslim dynasties emerged across North Africa. While the Fatimid Caliphate, a dynasty of Arab origin, controlled the east and central region, in the west two short-lived but influential powers emerged.

△ **Empire builder**
Possible portrait of Almoravid commander Abu Bakr ibn Umar, from a 15th-century Spanish map. As well as founding Marrakech, ibn Umar spread Islam to the southern edges of the western Sahara.

The Almoravid dynasty—the name deriving from the Arabic *al-Murabitun*, meaning "men of the *ribat*," a fortified place of religious practices—was founded in the 11th century. From the 1040s, a Muslim theologian, Abdallah ibn Yasin, began preaching among the Sanhaja. These nomadic Amazigh (Berber) peoples had until then practiced their own religion. Abdallah ibn Yasin's interpretation of Islam emphasized the importance of conquest as a means of spreading the word of the Prophet Muhammad. Among his many supporters was Yahya ibn Umar, leader of the most powerful Sanhaja group, the Lamtuna. Together, Ibn Yasin and Ibn Umar established the Almoravid dynasty.

The Almoravid dynasty
Yahya ibn Umar died in 1056 and Abdallah ibn Yasin in 1059. By this time, the Almoravids controlled the most important trans-Saharan trading cities in the region, Sijilmasa and Aoudaghost, and had conquered most of western North Africa. Yahya ibn Umar's brother, Abu Bakr ibn Umar, founded the city of Marrakech around 1070, making it the imperial capital, and from here the Almoravid Empire began to grow. In 1086–1087, the Almoravids took control of the *al-Andalus* region of southern Spain and Portugal, and by the early 1100s their empire had penetrated as far south as modern Senegal, covering an area 1,900 miles (3,000 km) long from north to south.

◁ **Lighting the way**
This early 12th-century engraved Almoravid lamp shows the fine craftsmanship of which the warlike dynasty was capable. The handle may depict a lion or a wolf.

The Almoravids' successes were spectacular but short-lived. Barely a century after the dynasty was formed it collapsed when, in 1147, a new rival in the region—the Almohads—killed the last Almoravid king, Ishaq ibn Ali, and took the capital, Marrakech.

Almohad ascendancy and defeat
The Almohad Caliphate, as it came to be known, had grown out of an earlier rebellion against Almoravid rule by Masmuda Amazigh peoples in the Atlas Mountains. The rebels' leader was Muhammad ibn Tumart, who died around 1130, and whose adherence to Sufism, a mystical branch of Islam, contrasted with the more austere beliefs of the Almoravids.

Having toppled the Almoravids, the Almohads inherited their Western Mediterranean empire in North Africa and Iberia. They administered it by

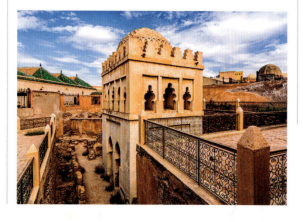

◁ **Almoravid pavilion**
The exquisitely decorated Qubba al-Ba'adiyyin in Marrakech dates from the early 12th century and is one of the few surviving examples of Almoravid architecture in the city.

Design of lions and harpies (human-headed birds)

> "When you strive after **much-desired glory**, cease not to aspire until you **reach the stars**."
>
> IBN TUMART, QUOTING 10TH-CENTURY POET AL-MUTANABBI

operating a huge fleet based at Rabat on the Atlantic coast. Such was the fleet's reputation that the great Muslim warrior Salah al-Din Yusuf ibn Ayyub (commonly known as Saladin) called for its help during the Third Crusade in 1183, and it held its own against major powers such as Pisa, Genoa, and Venice. However, the caliphate's fortunes begin to decline after a land defeat against southern Spain's Christian kingdoms at the Battle of Las Navas de Tolosa in 1212. After a series of revolts in the Almohads' North African heartland, the dynasty's end came when the Banu Marin, an Amazigh people from northern Morocco, captured the capital Marrakech in 1269.

Almoravid shroud
This fragment of an early 12th-century shroud was made during the Almoravid conquest of southern Spain. Its intricate design is woven with red, green, and light brown silk and gold thread.

102 | AFRICAN EMPIRES

△ **Inside the prayer hall**
Row upon row of rhythmic horseshoe arches divide the vast prayer hall into 17 naves, capable of accommodating 25,000 worshippers. The central nave leads to a decorative *mihrab*, the focal point for prayer, at the midpoint of the *qibla* wall.

- All worshippers face the *qibla* wall
- The pattern of arcades creates a sense of order
- Mats provide a clean, individual space to pray

▷ **Inside the courtyard**
The courtyard—centered on an ablutions fountain—provided a calm space for the faithful then, as now, to cleanse and prepare themselves for prayer in keeping with Muslim practice. It was laid out over a garden belonging to the destroyed Almoravid palace.

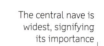

- The central nave is widest, signifying its importance
- The *mihrab* is at the midpoint of the *qibla* wall
- The imam and rulers accessed the prayer hall through private chambers
- The *qibla* wall indicates the direction of prayer
- The hall contains 112 columns

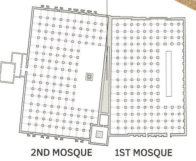

- A triangular area shows the difference in alignment

2ND MOSQUE | 1ST MOSQUE

◁ **The two mosques**
As seen in this plan, both mosques shared one minaret and an almost identical layout, but their orientation differed. The second mosque may have been built to better align with the desired direction of prayer.

Koutoubia Mosque

Marrakech, present-day Morocco

In 1147, the Almohad dynasty, an Amazigh (Berber) Muslim people from the Atlas Mountains, captured Marrakech from the Almoravid dynasty. In a show of supremacy, the Almohad ruler, Abd al Mu'min (r. 1130–1163), destroyed the Almoravid palace and constructed a great mosque in its place. Within a decade, for reasons that remain unclear, Abd al Mu'min began building a second mosque next to the first. This second mosque, still in use today, became the most important in the Almohad dynasty. Its landmark minaret is quintessentially Almohad, and closely resembles two other great towers: the Giralda in Seville (Spain) and the (unfinished) Hassan Tower in Morocco's modern capital, Rabat. Historically, this district was the booksellers' quarter, hence the name "Koutoubia," from the Arabic for booksellers: kutubiyyin.

- Three golden spheres top the minaret
- The minaret is 250 ft (77 m) tall
- A ramp allowed the *muezzin* to ride up the tower on horseback to give the call to prayer
- The mosque is built from local pink brick and sandstone
- Booksellers traded outside the mosque

△ **Koutoubia mosques**
This reconstruction depicts the two mosques around 1200. They are believed to have coexisted for several decades before the first mosque was demolished, though it is not clear what function the first mosque served during that time.

△ **Intricate stonework**
The ornamental elements on the minaret reappear frequently in Almohad architecture. Each face bears different patterns of horseshoe and polylobed arches—some blind, some open—intricately carved in symmetrical arrangements.

MASTERFUL MINBAR

In 1137, the Almoravid ruler 'Ali ibn Yūsuf commissioned Andalusian artisans to create a minbar (pulpit) for his mosque in Marrakech. They delivered a masterpiece: an eight-stepped wooden structure exquisitely paneled with intricately carved and inlaid patterns and inscriptions using colored woods and bone. Recognizing its quality, Abd al Mu'min saved it for the Koutoubia Mosque, where, according to historical accounts, it rolled magically into position when needed. Evidence suggests it may have used a counterbalance mechanism, perhaps triggered by the imam's footfall.

MEDIEVAL MINBAR

The Songhai Empire
The rise and fall of one of Africa's great states

After a slow rise to power, the Songhai Empire grew to control the Niger River in West Africa. It became rich on trans-Saharan trade and spread Islam across the region before internal strife weakened it fatally.

The Songhai people emerged in the northwest African kingdom of Gao (also known as al-Kawkaw) around the 9th century. This stretch of the western Sahel, known as the Sudan region, was home to fertile savanna and the Niger River, which offered abundant opportunities for fishing and trade.

Farming, fishing, and war

Songhai society had three divisions of trades: fishermen (*sorko*); hunters (*gabibi* or *gow*); and agriculturists (*do*), who specialized in arable farming and cattle rearing. Although the Songhai gained territory and grew more prosperous in the 10th century, their rise to greatness was gradual. Their heartland, in what is now Mali, was a long way from the gold-producing areas of Bambuk and Bure to the southwest, and they had many rivals.

From the 11th century, the Songhai had to protect their territory from the neighboring Mandingo (Malinke), Sosso, and Soninke, and in the 14th century, Gao fell under the yoke of the Mali Empire (see pp.90–91). As the Mali Empire started collapsing in the late 14th century, the Songhai won their independence, but it was only with the defeat of the nearby Mossi, Dogon, and Fulani during the late 15th century and early 16th century that the kingdom became an empire. Trans-Saharan trade had been significant for centuries, but its extension into territories such as the Hausa Kingdoms, in what is now northern Nigeria, made Songhai a major hub of desert-caravan and river routes connecting North and West Africa.

Sunni the Great

Sunni Ali, who came to the throne in 1464, became the first emperor of the Songhai. Under his reign, the Songhai expanded their land through conquest until they controlled all the major trading ports along the Niger—extending their authority further than the Empire of Mali ever had. Now trade flowed between the salt mines of Taghaza in northern Mali and great commercial cities such as Djenné and Timbuktu.

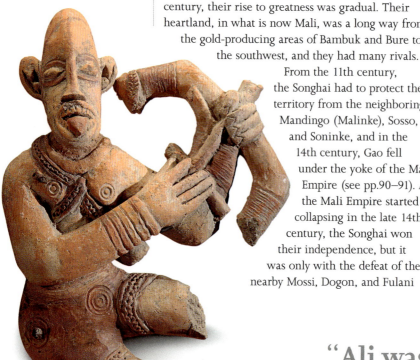

▽ **Archer figure**
This figure of an archer was made on the Niger Delta between the 11th and 17th centuries. The Songhai Empire had a professional army of infantry and cavalry.

> **HISTORIES OF THE SONGHAI**
>
> The 17th-century chronicles, *Tarikh al-Sudan* ("History of the Sudan") and the *Tarikh al-fattash* ("The Researcher's Chronicle"), are important primary sources for the history of the Songhai Empire. The books were written by Muslim scholars in Timbuktu.
>
>
>
> PAGE FROM THE *TARIKH AL-SUDAN*

> "**Ali was always victorious** … his armies were **never defeated**."
>
> THE *TARIKH AL-SUDAN* ON SUNNI ALI

△ **City of scholars**
The fabled city of Timbuktu, shown in a 19th-century European drawing, became an important place of learning during the Mali Empire and remained so under the Songhai.

Fine North African horses were traded for gold, ivory, and the enslaved people who had been captured during the empire's wars of expansion.

In the oral tradition of the griots (narrators of those traditions), Sunni Ali is remembered as Sunni Ali Ber, meaning "Sunni the Great," a strong and wise ruler who commanded the powers of magic. But in the histories that Muslim scholars wrote in the 17th century (see box, left), he is depicted as a bloodthirsty tyrant, who was capable of great generosity but also committed numerous acts of cruelty and treated the scholars in Timbuktu with contempt.

The rise of Islam

As the Songhai Empire expanded, its belief system was shifting. Islam had spread from the Maghreb along the trade routes, and was stronger in the west and in great river cities such as Djenné and Timbuktu, which were key centers of education. But it had not yet become the faith of the state, with pre-Islamic Songhai beliefs a strong force, especially among pastoralists and in the historic Songhai nucleus around Gao.

Sunni Ali followed both Islamic and Songhai beliefs, and sought to balance the two groups, but his son Sunni Dao, who succeeded to the throne in 1492, favored the pre-Islamic Songhai belief that everything contains a spirit or soul. Only a year later he was deposed by one of his generals, Askia Muhammad I (see pp.106–107). Askia made Islam the state religion, established Islamic schools and a university at Timbuktu, and encouraged conversion throughout the empire. In the years that followed, Islam became the basis not just of the state religion, but also of royal authority, spreading its culture and practices to distant lands. Askia conquered the desert trading post of Agadez (in modern-day Niger), fought campaigns against the Hausa Kingdoms, and extended the empire west toward the coast.

Power and decline

By now, the empire was at its peak, ruling a vast strip of inland West Africa that took in much of modern Mali, Niger, Mauritania, Nigeria, Senegal, Guinea, Gambia, Burkina Faso, and Côte d'Ivoire, as well as parts of southern Algeria. Timbuktu now rivaled the old Songhai heartland around Gao and the early-16th-century Andalusian traveler Leo Africanus wrote admiringly of its "corn, cattle, milk, and butter … in great abundance" and its "magnificent and well-furnished court."

In the decades that followed, Askia's children and grandchildren tussled for power, as the lack of an internal succession system saw instability weaken the Empire. The Songhai's crucial role in West Africa's gold and salt trade continued through the 16th century, but also made it attractive to other powers. Moroccan raids culminated in an invasion, and in 1591 the country's Saadi Sultanate, equipped with muskets and cannons, crushed the Songhai forces. The remaining Songhai elite fled to the Songhai and Dendi provinces, in southwestern Niger, but would never regain their great empire.

Lance confers high status on the bearer

Hunter's hat

Seated position denotes authority

▷ **Seated hunter**
A Bamana maker crafted this figure of an idealized male leader as early as the 16th century, when the Bamana people were part of the Songhai Empire. The Bamana later founded an empire of their own.

Askia Muhammad I
The Songhai's mightiest emperor

Under Askia Muhammad I's rule, Songhai became the largest empire West Africa had ever seen. Askia established a unique and efficient bureaucracy and made Islam the state religion, transforming West Africa.

△ **Malian manuscript**
This medieval manuscript, written in Arabic and Songhai, comes from Timbuktu. Askia Muhammad was a keen promoter of scientific and Muslim scholarship in the city.

Askia Muhammad was a prominent minister in the late 15th-century court of Sunni Ali, the first king of the Songhai. Ali had expanded his empire from the Songhai heartland in what is now Mali to control much of the area around the Niger River. On Ali's death in 1492, his son, Sunni Dao, succeeded him. But Askia Muhammad desired the throne and challenged the succession. In 1493, his forces defeated the king's armies and he founded the Askia dynasty.

A devout Muslim, Askia took the *Hajj* to Mecca in 1497, building a hostel for Songhai pilgrims and reportedly bringing 300,000 gold pieces with him—a third of which he gave away as alms. He continued to allow non-Muslims to practice their own religions, as they had done under the Sunnis, but he was keen to spread his Islamic faith. At home, he recruited Islamic scholars from Egypt and Morocco, set up centers of learning in cities including Gao, Djenné, and Walata, and enforced the veil for Muslim women.

War and justice

Askia built a large standing army of cavalry and archers, and used it to expand his borders west into what is now Senegal, northeast to the Saharan city of Agadez, in modern Niger, and southeast into the Hausa Kingdoms of Nigeria. The resulting empire was one of the largest Africa had ever seen.

Askia was also an astute administrator. He established an efficient bureaucracy, which was responsible for taxation and justice. He divided the kingdom into provinces with governors to oversee them and set up a council of ministers that included a commander of the fleet, a minister of forests and fisheries, and a master of the court.

This administration, unparalleled in West Africa at the time, allowed Askia to expand Songhai trade across the Sahara, with commerce reaching as far as Europe and Asia. But by the 1520s, Askia was aging and had become blind. He spent his last years as a powerless witness to dynastic rivalries that weakened his empire. In 1528, one of his sons, Askia Musa, deposed him in a bloodless coup.

△ **The tomb of Askia**
This wood and mud structure, built during Askia's reign, is believed to contain his tomb. The 55-ft- (17-m-) high building includes a mosque that is still used for worship.

c. 1443 Born in the Songhai city of Gao

1492 Songhai king Sunni Ali dies, and is succeeded by his son, Sunni Dao

1493 Askia wins the Battle of Anfao and seizes the throne

1497 Askia takes the *Hajj* to Mecca, staying until 1498

c. 1500 Songhai armies capture territory in modern Niger and Burkina Faso

c. 1510 The Songhai fight campaigns against the Fulani in Senegal

1537 Askia dies and is buried in a tomb that still stands today

1591 The Songhai Empire, weakened by civil war, falls to Moroccan troops

Terra-cotta horseman

This sculpture from Mali dates to between the 12th and 16th centuries. Successive West African empires developed cavalry, including Wagadou (Ghana) and Mali. Under Askia, the Songhai cavalry reached its peak as a formidable force.

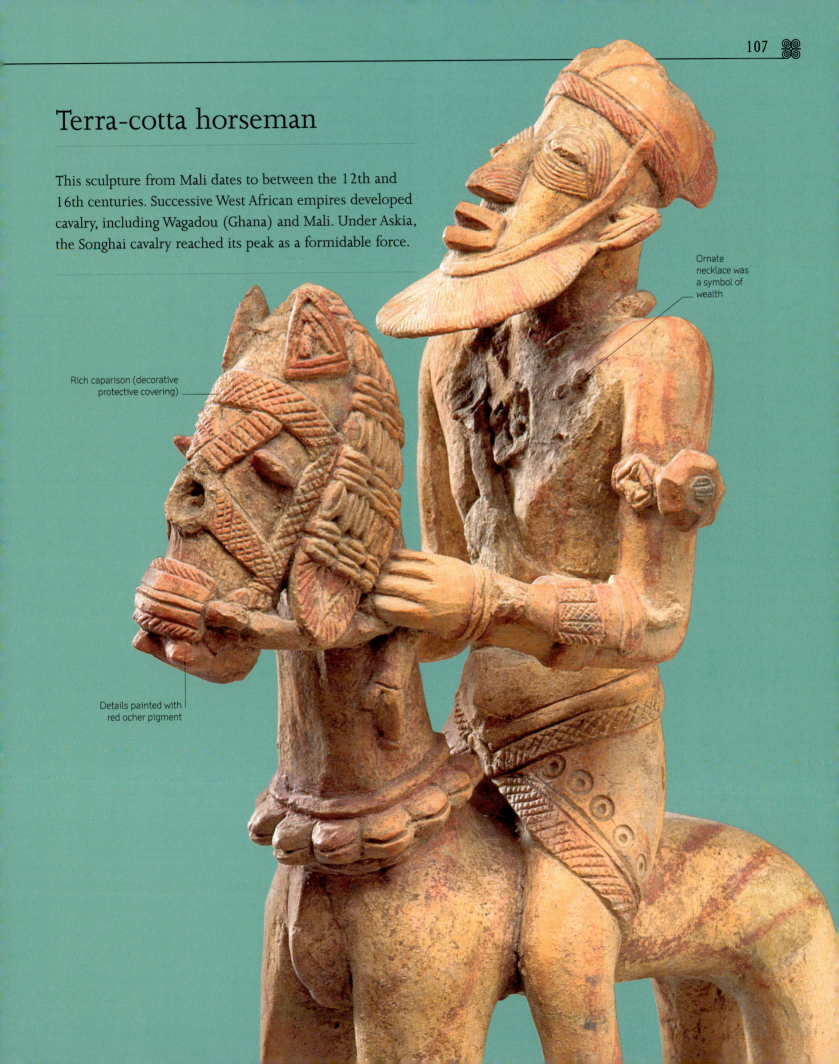

Rich caparison (decorative protective covering)

Details painted with red ocher pigment

Ornate necklace was a symbol of wealth

△ **Mounted warriors**
Heavily armored cavalry formed the heart of the Bornu army, enabling it to dominate vast areas.

Kanem-Bornu

A major empire in northern Central Africa

Centered around the shores of Lake Chad, the Empire of Kanem-Bornu was one of Africa's longest-lasting states. It dominated the region from the 10th to the 19th centuries.

△ **Horse protection**
This brass horse harness is ornately worked, an indication of the importance of the cavalry to the Bornu.

The origins of the Kanem state are probably linked to the nomadic Zaghawa people who migrated south from Amazigh (Berber) communities in North Africa around the 7th century. They settled on the edges of the Sahara north of Lake Chad. Their ironworking skills and use of horses enabled them to dominate local communities and control the trading routes that led to the Mediterranean.

Arab travelers, such as al-Ya'qubi in the 9th century and Ibn al-Nadim in the 10th, wrote that the Zaghawa created a state based on a sacred kingship, with a royal capital at Njimi northeast of Lake Chad. Toward the end of the 11th century, a Muslim noble named Humai ibn Salamna drove out the ruling Zaghawa dynasty and founded the Sayfawa dynasty that would rule Kanem-Bornu for 770 years, making it one of the world's longest reigning royal houses.

A Muslim state

Although Islam had already reached Kanem, Humai was the first Muslim *mai* (king), and his successor Dunama (r. 1098–1151) performed the *Hajj* to

> "Before the **age of our Sultan**, [non-Muslims] used to wander about in the **land of Bornu** … Idris [Alawma] **stopped all this**."
>
> BOOK OF THE BORNU WARS, IBN FARTUWA, 1576

△ **Royal audience**
Visitors to the Bornu court in the 19th century have an audience with the *mai*, who is, as tradition demanded, seated inside a cage made from bamboo.

Mecca three times. Under *Mai* Dunama Dabbalemi (r. 1221–1259), Kanem reached its peak, with its borders extended to the Fezzan, an arid region that lay to the north. However, his destruction of the *mune*, a sacred object said to protect the power of the king but which Dabbalemi associated with non-Islamic local religion, angered many of the people and weakened the monarchy. The 13th and 14th centuries were marked by struggles to maintain the Kanem Empire: four *mais* died in war with the Sao, a powerful people to the west, and an equal number fighting Bulala pastoralists from 1377 to 1387. There were also civil wars between the descendants of *Mai* Idris and *Mai* Dawud. By 1387, the court had abandoned Njimi and fled west across Lake Chad, establishing a new capital at Ngazargamu (in modern-day northern Nigeria).

A new empire
The Sayfawa rulers established the Bornu Empire, although it remained unstable until the accession of *Mai* Ali Gaji (r. 1470–1503), who fortified Ngazargamu. His son Idris Katakarmabe (r. 1507–1529) managed to drive the Bulala out of the old Kanem capital, Njimi. Skirmishes with the Bulala over Kanem continued for a century, leading the Bornu *mais* to seek allies elsewhere, including with the Ottoman commander and *Pasha* of Tripoli, Turgut Reis, in the mid-16th century. Meanwhile, the empire's expansion to the south and west continued with the occupation in 1532 of the Amazigh Sultanate of Agadez in the Aïr mountains.

The Bornu Empire reached its peak in the reign of Idris Alawma (r. 1570–1619), who conquered the Hausa peoples of northern Nigeria, aided by a camel cavalry and Turkish musketeer recruits. Idris also reformed the administration and integrated local groups who had previously been semi-independent. Less able successors faced challenges from Agadez and the state of Kwararafa in Hausaland, as well as from Tuareg warriors. The last great *mai*, Hajj Ali, defeated attacks on Ngazargamu by both Agadez and Kwararafa in 1668. He was followed by *mais* who struggled with famines and a declining grip on vital trade routes. A devastating defeat against Mandara rebels from northern Cameroon in 1781 shattered the Bornu army. Then, in 1808, Fulani Muslims, led by Usman dan Fodio (see pp.194–195), attacked Bornu and proclaimed a jihad (holy war) against nonobservant Muslims. *Mai* Dunama Lefiami called for the help of an Islamic scholar, Muhammad al-Kanemi, who saved Bornu by rallying resistance and repelling the Fulani, becoming effective ruler until his death in 1837.

The Sayfawa *mais* remained monarchs in name only until 1846, when al-Kanemi's son Umar deposed the last one and declared himself *shehu* (sheikh). The Bornu Empire struggled on for a few more decades until a Sudanese military leader named Rabih az-Zubayr conquered it in 1893. In 1900, French colonial forces killed Rabih and reestablished the *shehu*. Today, descendants of al-Kanemi still rule the Bornu state, which is located in northeastern Nigeria.

▽ **Fine craftwork**
This highly decorated women's cotton robe was created in Bornu state, Nigeria, and dates from the 19th century.

Brightly colored silk embroidery

Rise of the Yoruba

An iconic African culture

The Yoruba claim descent from Oduduwa—their founder king. From their beginnings as a highly spiritual, artistic people, this West African ethnic group would create a powerful city-state and worldwide diaspora.

There are around 45–50 million Yoruba-speaking people in West Africa, the vast majority living in Nigeria. The first Yoruba settlement was Ilé-Ifè in the southwest of the country, whose earliest archaeological artifacts date from the 4th century BCE. In Yoruba mythology, the city was built by their founder and first king, Oduduwa. Among those who follow Indigenous beliefs, Ilé-Ifè is the Yoruba's most important religious site and the seat of their spiritual leader, the *Ooni*.

Ilé-Ifè was also a center of art. During the city-state's "golden age" from 1000–1500, artisans produced some of Africa's finest stone, terra-cotta, and bronze sculpted heads depicting royal and political figures. In addition, Ilé-Ifè was the only African state south of the Sahara able to manufacture the colored glass beads that were widely exchanged as currency and were used as decorative items on royal and religious regalia. The city-state's position as sole supplier of these valuable items made Ilé-Ifè wealthy.

Despite its affluence and technological expertise, Ilé-Ifè declined due to political divisions and emigration. By the 17th century, the wealth and power had moved away to other city-states such as Ilesha, and, especially, Oyo (see pp.112–113). Founded around 1300, Oyo was the largest and the most powerful Yoruba city-state by the mid-18th century, its empire covering southern Nigeria, the Kingdom of Dahomey, and parts of Benin.

Power and trade

Yoruba culture centered around large towns and cities rather than dispersed villages. The centralized power structure, based around divine kingship, that had developed in Ilé-Ifè was used in many other city-states. Each Yoruba state was organized slightly differently, but most were ruled by a powerful—but not absolute—monarch, or *oba*, who was assisted by a prime minister, an administrative body, and an advisory council of elders and religious officials. Trade brought goods and revenue, with salt, leather, horses,

△ **Mythical monument**
This 18-ft- (5.5-m-) tall granite stele in Ilé-Ifè is known as "Oranmiyan's Staff." Oranmiyan was the son of Oduduwa and the founder of the Oyo dynasty.

▷ **Capturing a king's likeness**
This copper alloy mask is said to represent the Ilé-Ifè ruler Obalufon II, who reigned in the 14th century. It was probably used in religious rites.

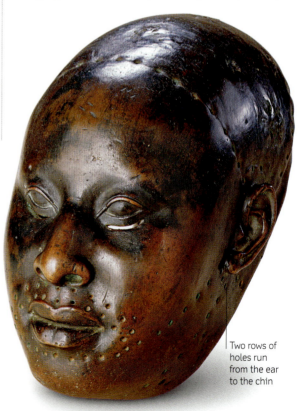

Two rows of holes run from the ear to the chin

> "All the [peoples] of the **Yoruba Nation** trace their **origin from Oduduwa** and the City of Ilé-Ifè."
>
> S. O. JOHNSON, *THE HISTORY OF THE YORUBAS*, 1959

RISE OF THE YORUBA | 111

- A bird connects the *Ooni* to Oduduwa
- Cap is divided into three sections representing youth, adolescence, and old age
- Beaded veil hides the *Ooni*'s face

◁ **Ceremonial crown**
The *Aare*—sacred beaded crowns—symbolize power and authority for the Yoruba. The *Ooni* of Ilé-Ifè still wears a headdress like this during festivals.

kola nuts, ivory, and textiles bought and sold among the Yoruba and their neighbors. Humans were also trafficked extensively, as captives in warfare and as part of the Atlantic slave trade (see pp.162–163) that saw at least one million Yoruba transported to the Americas.

An enduring culture

The city-states began to decline in the late 18th century. Most could not resist the incursions into their territory by the Muslim Fulani people, whose Sokoto Caliphate became West Africa's dominant empire in the late 18th century (see pp.194–195). In 1900, most of the Yoruba were absorbed into the British Empire's Southern Nigeria Protectorate.

Today, the Yoruba are Nigeria's second-largest ethnic group, with around 20 percent of the population. Yoruba culture remains important in the diaspora, particularly Brazil, where the popular Candomblé religion blending Catholic, Yoruba, and other African ritualistic practices has several million followers.

▷ **Yoruba deity**
This 12th–15th century copper alloy head represents Olokun, the Yoruba deity of the sea, wealth, and glass bead-making—Ilé-Ifè's profitable and prestigious industry.

- Decorative headdress with rosette
- Striped facial markings, or "scarifications"

The Oyo Empire
Yoruba's most powerful state

The Yoruba state of Oyo was one of many powerful competing kingdoms in West Africa. From the 17th century until the beginning of the 19th, Oyo held sway, thanks to its innovative political structure and military strength.

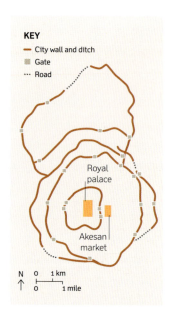

City defenses
The multiple concentric walls at Oyo-Ile comprised ditches and embankments, and were constructed during the heyday of the Oyo Empire for protection against attacks.

According to Yoruba history, Oranmiyan (sometimes called Oranyan), the son of Oduduwa, founder of the Yoruba people (see pp.110–111), established the city of Oyo-Ile around 1300 CE and his descendants expanded it into the Oyo Empire. Historical evidence shows that Yoruba farmers in southwest Nigeria set up an organized political entity around the 9th century and cemented Oyo-Ile's status as a metropolis between the 13th and the 15th centuries. By the late 15th century, as a result of its stable political system and a strong army, Oyo's influence was growing.

Dynamic statecraft

Like other Yoruba states and kingdoms, Oyo was ruled by an *oba*, or king. In Oyo, the king was known as the *alaafin* ("the owner of the palace"). As the head of state, the *alaafin* was owed both the loyalty of the people and the tribute of goods and army recruits from local chieftains and leaders of conquered territories. The *alaafin*'s power was not absolute, however. A privy council, the *Oyo Mesi*, consisted of seven of the state's most powerful noblemen and was headed by a prime minister, or *bashorun*. No *alaafin* could assume the throne without the *Oyo Mesi*'s approval, and any *alaafin* who ignored their advice—and whose behavior threatened the empire—could be banished, forced to abdicate, or compelled to die by suicide. There were *alaafins* in Oyo into the 21st century. The power-sharing government exercised authority through its army.

Some time around 1535, a devastating invasion by the Nupe people to the east forced Oyo's rulers to abandon Oyo-Ile and resettle at Igboho for about 80 years. They reorganized their state along militaristic lines. Its large, semi-standing army was supplied with arms and armor that included elephant- and ox-hide shields and formidable 9-ft (2.7-m) swords. Oyo was one of a few states to adopt the use of cavalry, which gave it a competitive advantage against infantry-only enemies. By the early 17th century, Oyo had retaken all of the territory lost to the Nupe, including the capital Oyo-Ile, to which a triple ring of walls and earthen barriers was added. The walls stood up to 24 ft 6 in (7.5 m) high, with an outer wall 13 miles (21 km) long.

Expansion and destabilization

From the early 17th century, Oyo State began to build an empire. Oyo had subdued the Nupe and taken control of the territory occupied by the other Yoruba towns and city-states. It was also receiving tribute from the Kingdom of Benin (see pp.128–129) in the southeast in return for not attacking it, and had conquered the Kingdom of Dahomey (see pp.178–179) to the west. In 1764, Oyo led a coalition of armies that repelled an invasion by the powerful Asante Empire (see pp.190–191). Oyo's territorial expansion gave it control of the southern end of the trade route from North Africa to what is now the Nigerian coast, allowing it to collect vast sums in taxes from merchants. These taxes were

Oyo palace
The thatched-roof palace of the *alaafin* of Oyo was a multi-room and multi-chamber building. The complex housed the royal family and palace administrators.

THE OYO EMPIRE | 113

△ **Royal portrait**
Wearing a veiled beaded crown and holding an *irukere* (fly whisk), Adeniran Adeyemi II, *alaafin* of Oyo State, poses with his son in 1950. His political sympathies led to exile in 1954.

"**Oyo** had reached the **zenith** of its territorial **expansion** by the middle of the **18th century**."

PROFESSORS ARIBIDESI USMAN AND TOYIN FALOLA, 2019

Edun ara (sacred stone) embedded in battle-ax

▷ **Thunder god**
This *ose Sango* (Shango's staff) represents the Shango deity – the god of thunder and fire, who was worshipped during the 18th century. His might is symbolized by a double-edged battle-ax.

Ayan (drummer)

Worshipper of Sango

paid in money—usually cowrie shells—or as tributes, with customs officials taking a portion of the traded goods, which included gold, ivory, leather, cloth, and salt. Enslaved people were also traded.

It was during the Oyo's expansionist period that the annual Bere festival was initiated. Taking place in January or February, it both celebrated the yearly harvest of valuable *bere* grass in Yorubaland and served as a means by which vassal states paid tribute to the *alaafin*. They did this by bringing bundles of *bere* grass to the capital to re-thatch the roof of the royal palace. Another important source of produce for Oyo was its colony of Ede-Ile (south of Oyo-Ile), whose reserves of clay were used for pottery and iron ore for smelting.

Oyo's power began to wane in the early 19th century, when its regions and vassal states began to chafe against central control. The destabilization this caused was followed in the 1830s by attacks from Muslim jihadists known as the Fulani—who would go on to establish the Sokoto Caliphate (see pp.194–195). As Oyo's empire dissolved, a number of Oyo refugees established a new city-state to the south, at Ibadan. This became Oyo's new power base, from which it was able to reassert a small degree of its former influence. However, by the late 19th century, the European-controlled slave trade further weakened the Yoruba states. In 1900, Britain forced Yorubaland—including the Oyo territories—into its Southern Nigeria Protectorate. Oyo still exists today as a thriving city, with a majority Yoruba population, within Oyo State.

The Igbo states
A unique civilization of the Niger Delta

Igbo people lived in egalitarian village-based communities in the forests of southeastern Nigeria. This distinctive culture traded widely, developed exceptional craft making abilities, and was known for freeing enslaved people.

Around a fifth of Nigeria's population today is made up of Igbo people, with sizable groups in nearby Cameroon, Gabon, and Equatorial Guinea. But while the Igbo have a shared language, they have never formed a single nation.

Archaeological discoveries—particularly jewelery, ceramics, and finely worked bronze items—from the town of Igbo-Ukwu in the south of Nigeria suggest that a sophisticated Igbo society existed from at least the 9th century CE. Communities to the east and west of the Niger River formed groups made up of several villages, with many Igbo people living as subsistence farmers, cultivating crops of nutritious root vegetables such as cassava, yams, and taro. These communities spoke different dialects, and today the Igboid language has several dialects including Delta Igbo, Enuani Igbo, Ika Igbo, Ikwerre, and Ukwuani.

Igbo political organization was broadly democratic, and accounts from Portuguese traders—who first arrived in the region in the 15th century—describe groups governed by consultative assemblies of the common people, led by councils of elders. Discussions took place in the market square and the aim was to reach a consensus on local disputes. In these communities there was no "ruler," though elders were male and the position was generally passed on to other male relatives.

Igbo culture

Glass beads from the Middle East, palm-leaf textiles, and bronze artifacts—including cups, pendants, and swords—found in Igbo-Ukwu suggest technological sophistication and wide trade links. Symbols called *nsibidi*, drawn on gourds, drinking vessels, and houses, conveyed information about sexual relationships, land and property, or local crimes and journeys. The Igbo developed a calendar with four days in a week, seven weeks in a month, and thirteen months in a calendar year, with the thirteenth month having an extra day.

Unlike many West African peoples, the Igbo did not practice slavery for much of their history. They did operate a system of indentured servitude, but the differences in status between the free people

△ **Igbo terra-cotta statue**
This 19th- or 20th-century figurine shows a woman holding a child. Igbo culture featured expressive statues known as *ntekpe* (meaning "children of the shrine"), which are linked with healing and worship.

"Among **the Igbo** ... **proverbs** are the **palm oil** with which **words are eaten**."

CHINUA ACHEBE, *THINGS FALL APART*, 1958

◁ **Igbo ceremonial dress**
Igbo people are seen here in a photograph from the early 20th century wearing ceremonial dress, including headdresses, feathered pieces, and tall metal leg bands.

and servants appear to have been limited. Olaudah Equiano, an Igbo man who was forced into enslavement in the Americas in the 18th century, reports in his memoir of the experience (see box, right) that the servants did not do more work than the rest of the community, and had the same clothing and food, though they were not permitted to eat with people who were free-born.

Kingdoms and conquest

In the late medieval period, increasingly centralized states developed. The neighboring empire of Benin, which reached its peak in the 16th century, ruled over some of the western Igbo people. However, the Igbo formed several kingdoms, especially in the eastern regions. According to oral tradition, the kingdom of Nri was established around the 9th century, and had political and religious dominion over about a third of Igbo territory by the 17th century. The state, ruled by priest-kings called *eze nri*, who managed trade, was known for setting enslaved people free. Its artists produced many exceptional bronzes that have survived to this day (see pp.116–117).

By this time, other Igbo-dominated communities, including Onitsha and Arochukwu, had kings or priest-kings. The European demand for enslaved people to work in the Americas from the 16th century had led to conflict and territorial shifts, and the Aro people of Arochukwu fought a series of campaigns against the neighboring Ibibio people in the southeastern region of modern-day Nigeria in the 17th and 18th centuries. Nri populations declined, while the Aro and other nearby Igbo and non-Igbo communities traded in increasing numbers of enslaved people.

Igbo people were also captured and enslaved by the Efik people, who had settled in the Cross River Delta, near the border with Cameroon. The area, which was known as Old Calabar, became a major port for enslaved people, and was governed by the Ekpe (Leopard) society, made up of wealthy Efik men.

British influence

In 1807, Britain, which had shipped large numbers of enslaved people to its colonies, prohibited slavery and put pressure on other nations to do the same. As the trade declined, British influence grew, and European merchants established trading posts in Igboland, where the plentiful palm trees were a ready supply of oil.

Many people converted to Christianity, but Igbo identity remained strong. After Nigeria gained its independence from Britain in 1960, the Igbo-dominated state of Biafra, in southeastern Nigeria, went on to declare its independence from Nigeria in 1967. Nigeria crushed and reabsorbed the state in 1970, and many Igbo have since felt marginalized by Nigeria's Hausa and Yoruba majorities. Igbo nationalists continue their struggle for recognition through celebrations of Igbo culture and calls for increased autonomy.

OLAUDAH EQUIANO

In 1789, an Igbo man published a memoir that helped end slavery. *The Interesting Narrative of the Life of Olaudah Equiano* describes Equiano's youth in Igboland in the 1740s and '50s, his capture, and his life as an enslaved person in Britain, North America, and the Caribbean. As the first popular "slave narrative," it made a significant contribution to the abolitionist cause. Equiano went on to buy his freedom, and returned to London where he married. He died in 1797, but his memoir has been repeatedly reprinted and adapted.

△ **Igbo woman**
This photograph of an Igbo woman wearing brass anklets was taken in 1922 by British anthropologist Northcote Thomas. Women played a key role in trading in the Igbo marketplace.

Surface is decorated with carved symbols

▷ **Brass anklet**
Dating from around 1930, this is an Igbo brass anklet or *ogba*. Anklets were a status symbol for young Igbo women. They were worn in pairs, with smaller anklets on the lower leg and larger ones toward the knee.

Nri bronzes

Fine decorative craftwork

The Nri culture, which developed among the Igbo of eastern Nigeria around the 9th century CE, created a series of exquisite bronzes. Excavated mainly from three sites at the town of Igbo Ukwu, these artifacts employed a sophisticated version of the lost wax technique (see pp.132–133) using latex.

◁ **Bowl on stand**
Produced during the 9th or 10th century, this is a leaded bronze bowl resting on top of a bronze stand. It is decorated with small raised coils.

Fine exterior decoration

Inward sloping rim with spiral pattern

△ **Roped pot**
Cast in two pieces and standing 12½ in (32 cm) high, this water pot is slightly oval-shaped. It is decorated with raised lines and an elaborate ropelike design of two intertwining strands.

Lip on which to rest the altar

△ **Altar stand**
Carved with snakes, frogs, female figures, and male figures with wavy hair and wearing two necklaces, this open cylinder measuring 10½ in (27 cm) in height was an altar stand.

Four rows of loops indicate hair or headdress

△ **Pendant**
This ornament in the shape of a human head is 3 in (8 cm) high, with a loop for attaching to a pendant. The oblique lines on the face indicate scarification.

▷ **Fly whisk handle**
A small bronze figure riding an animal (probably a horse) sits atop a base, which was fitted to a fly whisk. The oversize human figure has scarification marks to indicate high status.

Scarification marks

Decorative beading

▷ **Ceremonial bowl**
All cast in one piece, with a single handle on one side, this bowl is 10 in (26 cm) in diameter. It is decorated with patterns of triangles and quatrefoils.

Underside of the bowl decorated with three bands of quatrefoil patterns

NRI BRONZES | 117

Crescent-shaped clawlike object

Loops of wire with beads

Five whorls spiral in a clockwise direction

Spiral dot pattern around the rim

◁ **Ritual vessel**
Shell-shaped, this hollow vessel is decorated with raised circles in lozenges and spirals, and surmounted by a leopard, its spots all carefully detailed.

◁ **Bird pendant**
Showing a bird roosting on a pair of eggs, this exceptionally fine pendant ornament has chains of beaded wire attached to it.

△ **Shell**
A water sprinkler made for use in ceremonies, this piece is in the form of a triton shell and is 11 in (28.5 cm) long. The ornamental pointed end is perforated.

Single handle at one end

Bird with its head between two eggs

Grooved metal for ear

Curved ram's horn

Cricket or fly

◁ **Decorated bowl**
The underside of this leaded bronze bowl has rings of decoration. It can be hung by the handle so the decoration can be seen.

△ **Pendant fitting**
This ram's head pendant attachment forms part of a series of animal-shaped pendant fittings. The series included leopards and elephants.

Chain links for attaching to pendant

Medieval Ethiopia: the Zagwe and Solomonids

East Africa's Christian empires

The East African kingdom of Aksum was replaced by the Zagwe dynasty, which in turn succumbed to the Solomonids. This Orthodox Christian empire fended off several Islamic incursions and the dynasty reigned until 1974.

Much of modern-day Ethiopia and Eritrea is made up of the ancient kingdom of Aksum (see pp.62–63), which arose in the 2nd century CE. Aksum's dominance ended between the 8th and 12th centuries, when the Zagwe people assumed control of the kingdom's territory.

The Zagwe heartland was northern Ethiopia's Lasta Mountains. On seizing power, the Zagwe moved the kingdom's capital from Aksum to Roha (sometimes called Adefa). How the Zagwe deposed the Aksumites is not clear, and the names of the dynasty's earliest rulers are lost to history. The most notable Zagwe king was Gebre Meskel Lalibela (r. 1181–1221). The Zagwe had carved 11 extraordinary Christian churches into the rocks at Roha (see pp.122–123). Legend says that the churches were built in one night during Lalibela's reign, though historians agree that they were actually built over the course of the Zagwe dynasty. The capital city was renamed Lalibela in honor of the king and it became an important pilgrimage site.

The Zagwe Kingdom's economy was based on farming, but this was supplemented by trade in ivory, gold, and enslaved people with states around the Arabian Gulf. Much of this trading took place in the Red Sea port of Dahlak Island and later at Zeila in the Gulf of Aden.

According to most accounts of Zagwe's history, the dynasty's end came about as a result of regional unrest and palace intrigues, which weakened the last (or, in some sources, penultimate) Zagwe ruler, Yitbarek. He was defeated and killed at the Battle of Gaynt Qirqos in 1270 by a prince of the Amhara people of northwest Ethiopia named Yekuno Amlak. Yekuno established the Solomonic dynasty, which would reign for 700 years.

△ **King of kings**
In this colorful 15th-century Ethiopian icon, King Gebre Meskel Lalibela is shown on horseback and carrying a spear.

King Solomon's heirs
Yekuno Amlak claimed descent from Ethiopia's first emperor, Menelik I, the supposed son of King Solomon and the Queen of Sheba—this

> "The excellent and **hallowed** ... glorified and blessed, **wearer of purity** ..."
>
> DESCRIPTION OF KING LALIBELA, *GADLA LALIBELA* (ACTS OF LALIBELA)

Symmetrical latticework design

◁ **Sign of faith**
This early 15th-century copper alloy cross was designed to be used in religious processions, and to ward off evil spirits.

△ **Christian place of worship**
The Debre Damo Monastery on a mountain in northern Ethiopia is only accessible by rope. It dates from the 6th century, indicating how long the Christian faith has existed in the area.

is where the name "Solomonic" came from. The Solomonids' territory expanded and contracted over the centuries, but their stronghold always remained the highlands in northern Ethiopia. For this reason, and because of the Solomonids' strict adherence to the Ethiopian Orthodox Church, the state Yekuno Amlak established was also known as the Christian Highland Kingdom. To ensure the new state's stability, after each Solomonic king named his chosen heir, all other possible claimants to the throne were imprisoned for life in a mountain fortress called Amba Geshen in northern Ethiopia.

Initially, the dynasty had no capital city. Instead, it set up what the 14th-century Arab historian Al-Umari called "tent capitals," moving the royal court from place to place. This was in part an effort to incorporate newly conquered territories in the north toward Beja and south toward Berara into the Solomonids' expansionist empire. The most successful Solomonic ruler was Amda Seyon I (r. 1314–1344), who annexed regions to the north and south of the highland heartlands, as well as land along the Red Sea coast.

These last conquests were part of the Christian Solomonids' long-running conflicts with the emerging Islamic sultanates of East Africa (see pp.146–147) such as Adal (incorporating areas of modern Somalia and Sudan) and Ifat (parts of modern-day Ethiopia, Djibouti, and Somaliland). Religious rivalries and trade disputes led to two centuries of intermittent warfare, which ended in 1543 when the Solomonids were able to fend off an attempted conquest by Ahmad ibn Ibrahim al-Ghazi of the Adal Sultanate. They were only able to do this, however, with help from the Portuguese. This was a sign that their empire was in decline and that Europeans were playing an ever more active role in African affairs.

By the mid-16th century, the Solomonids' best days had already passed, although later rulers such as Fasilides would temporarily revive the empire's fortunes, building a permanent capital city at Gondar (see pp.120–121) in 1636, for example. The dynasty continued to reign until 1974.

△ **Yekuno Amlak**
This wall portrait may show the Solomonic king, Yekuno Amlak. He is shown holding symbols of his kingship and his Orthodox Christian faith.

- Cherubic angel is one of 123 that decorate the ceiling
- Wooden beam supports
- Murals show the evangelists Matthew, Mark, Luke, and John
- St. George slaying the dragon
- The Trinity: God the Father, Jesus the Son, and the Holy Spirit

△ **Illustrated shrine**
Gondar's Debre Birhan Selassie Church was built by Fasilides' grandson, Emperor Eyasu II. It was damaged by lightning and rebuilt in the 1880s. Almost every surface in its interior is covered in murals depicting stories from the Bible.

The splendor of Gondar

A city fit for royalty

Founded by Emperor Fasilides in the 17th century, Gondar was the capital of the Ethiopian Empire for two centuries. This wealthy and cosmopolitan city became known for its stone architecture, including a royal castle and many churches.

For centuries, Ethiopia's emperors moved their court around the country in great processions, exploiting the best agricultural land and forests for firewood. By 1636, Fasilides (r. 1632–1667) decided a permanent capital would better allow him to conduct the affairs of government and manage his growing empire.

The chosen place was Gondar, which sat on a high, fertile plain, close to the caravan routes running to and from modern-day Sudan and the Red Sea. At its height in the 17th and 18th centuries, Gondar had a population of 10,000 people, many of them traders, artisans, and court officials. Its greatest architectural treasure is the Fasil Ghebbi ("the Royal Enclosure"), a complex of palaces, fortresses, churches, a swimming pool, and other buildings. Much of the compound was built under Fasilides, but significant portions were constructed by the Empress Mentewab in the mid-18th century. These include the castle that bears her name and a grand banqueting hall.

Gondar was the capital of a Christian empire, with nobles and wealthier residents occupying the Qagn Bet district. Those who practiced other faiths tended to live in their own areas: Muslims occupied the Addis Alem quarter, while many of Ethiopia's large population of Jews occupied the Kayla Mayda neighborhood.

Into the present

Gondar was replaced as Ethiopia's capital by the eastern city of Mekele in the 1880s, but remains an important religious center and popular tourist destination. Today, Fasil Ghebbi is a UNESCO World Heritage Site, in recognition of the Royal Enclosure's variety of finely detailed Nubian, Indian, Arab, and Baroque buildings and artistic styles.

△ **Empire-builder**
No contemporary images of Fasilides exist. This stamp, designed by 20th-century Ethiopian artist Afewerk Tekle, depicts him beside the capital city he created.

◁ **Palatial surroundings**
Fasilides' Castle is the most intact building in the Fasil Ghebbi ("Royal Enclosure"). It stands 105 ft (32 m) tall, with a crenelated parapet and four towers topped by egg-shaped domes.

Bete Giyorgis, Lalibela

The church of Bete Giyorgis (House of St. George) in northern Ethiopia was hewn out of volcanic rock 800 years ago. The area in the Amhara region, 370 miles (600 km) north of Addis Ababa, is named after King Lalibela (r. c. 1181–1221). Eleven rock-hewn churches were built there during the Zagwe dynasty—and according to legend, all built during Lalibela's reign. Their names recall those of the biblical Jerusalem: House of Golgotha and House of St. Michael and Bethlehem, for example. Bete Giyorgis is cruciform in shape and, like all the churches, was carved from the top down using chisels, axes, and other types of blades.

The Ayyubids, Mamluks, and Ottomans

Three major empires in Egypt

A succession of great empires ruled medieval Egypt. The Ayyubids made Cairo the capital of the Arab world, before the Mamluks rose in the 13th century, and the Ottomans expanded Egypt's borders and strengthened its economy.

△ **Muhammad Ali**
This oil painting of Ottoman *pasha* Ali from 1841 is by French artist Auguste Couder. Regarded as "the great modernizer" of Egypt, Ali took power from the Mamluks and brought in economic as well as military reforms.

The Fatimid Caliphate, which followed Shia Islam, had conquered Egypt in 969 CE. However, by the 12th century it was riven by internal disputes and weakened by campaigns against Christian Crusaders, paving the way for its fall to the Ayyubid dynasty.

The Ayyubids

Syrian general Salah al-Din Yusuf ibn Ayyub, known in English as Saladin, joined a military expedition to Egypt led by his uncle Shirkuh. Saladin assassinated the Fatimid caliph, prevented the Frankish rulers taking Egypt, and on the death of Shirkuh was appointed vizier in 1169. He abolished the Fatimid Caliphate in 1171, established the Ayyubid dynasty, and announced that the region would return from Shia to Sunni Islam. Saladin enjoyed great military success, defeating the Crusaders in 1187 and reclaiming Jerusalem for Islam. He united Muslim-controlled territories in Egypt and the Middle East into an Ayyubid empire, declaring himself sultan, a secular title, rather than caliph. Under Ayyubid rule, canals were dug to irrigate farmland, the profitable Red Sea trade grew, and banking developed. In Cairo, *madrasas* (Islamic schools) and hospitals were built, science flourished, and the city became the intellectual center of the Islamic world.

Saladin was succeeded by his brother al-Adil, who largely continued his policies, in 1198. The Ayyubid Empire was not a centralized state: instead, it was a

▷ **A Mamluk welcome**
This Italian painting shows an unnamed Mamluk governor (seated) receiving a Venetian consul—Niccolò Malipiero (wearing red)—and his retinue in Damascus in 1511.

Cupola of the great Umayyad Mosque

coalition of principalities, ruled by family members. Under Sultan al-Kamil (r. 1218–1238), the Ayyubids ceded Jerusalem to the Crusaders and made a peace in 1229, which lasted for 10 years. However, remaining an independent state required a strong military, and the sultanate relied on Mamluks, enslaved people from the Eurasian steppe who had converted to Islam and trained as professional soldiers. As their numbers grew, Mamluks became an increasingly powerful caste.

The Mamluks

Ayyubid sultan al-Salih Ayyub was killed in another crusade and by 1250, a rebel group of Mamluks had set their own sultan, a general named Aybeg, on the throne. Over the next decade, armies of the Mongol Empire (which reached across Asia into northern Europe) swept through the Arabian Peninsula, sacking Baghdad in 1258, but in 1260, an Egyptian Mamluk army defeated them, bolstering Mamluk legitimacy. The Mamluks would rule Egypt for almost 300 years. Artisans and scholars who had fled Mongol attacks came to Egypt, and mosques and *madrasas* were built, cementing Cairo's status as an Islamic cultural center.

Egypt prospered as the leading power in the Arab world. Islam continued to spread, and Egypt's substantial Coptic Christian minority were persecuted, although many Copts continued to hold key roles in government bureaucracy. However, the transition of power from one Mamluk sultan to the next was often violent, and by the 15th century, plagues and poor governance took their toll on the kingdom.

The Ottomans

Relations between Turkey's Ottoman Empire and the Mamluks had long been adversarial, with both states vying for control of the spice trade and the holy cities of Islam (Mecca, Medina, and Jerusalem). In 1517, the ascendant Ottomans conquered Egypt, as well as Mamluk territory in the Middle East (Syria). Mamluk culture and social organization persisted at a regional level, but the ruler of Egypt was a viceroy or *pasha* appointed by the Ottoman sultan in Istanbul and answerable to him. Turkish rule seems to have improved administration and the economy, and Egypt became a major source of revenue for the Ottomans, although its cultural achievements faded. In the 1550s, its southern boundary was pushed into Nubia (in modern-day Sudan), and the port of Massawa (now in Eritrea) was taken from the Portuguese, helping to ensure Ottoman dominance of Red Sea trade.

While most early *pashas* were Turks, the Mamluks continued to be elite within Egyptian society and grew to wield increasing power. By the early 18th century, Ottoman authority was limited to recognizing the autonomy of the ruling Mamluk faction in exchange for a guarantee of annual payments to Istanbul.

In 1798, the French seized Egypt, but were ejected by British and Ottoman troops, and in 1805 Ottoman commander Muhammad Ali seized power. He reformed the civil service and expanded Egyptian territory. The state was only nominally Ottoman but Ali believed he was powerful enough to challenge the sultan, and he conquered Ottoman Syria in 1831. Ali's successors became increasingly subject to European interventions, and in 1882 Egypt became a British protectorate.

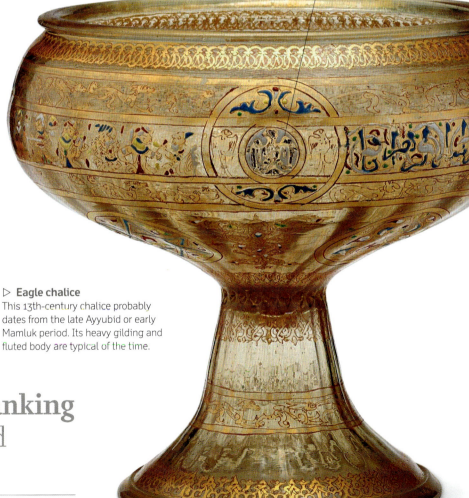

The central emblem shows an eagle

▷ **Eagle chalice**
This 13th-century chalice probably dates from the late Ayyubid or early Mamluk period. Its heavy gilding and fluted body are typical of the time.

> "So many of the **high-ranking** about me have discarded **mercy** as a **weakness**."
>
> SALADIN

Nomads: the Bedouin, Tuareg, and Maasai

Nomadic peoples of the Sahara and East Africa

The Bedouin and the Tuareg made the Sahara their own, while the Maasai dominated the dry savanna of the Great Lakes. Together, these roaming pastoralists have helped shape African history and cultures.

The Sahara has not always been an arid desert (see pp.20–21). Around 10,000 years ago, lush, green conditions supported Stone Age cultures, with a large population of nomadic pastoralists and sedentary agriculturalists. Around 5,000 years ago, as the climate grew drier, the desert expanded and the population decreased. However, in the thousands of years since, several peoples—including the Tuareg and Bedouin—have adapted to life here. These nomads were primarily pastoralists, relying on their herds of livestock to provide them with food and income. They also practiced some forms of agriculture, such as growing dates and other fruits, and vegetables including okra and eggplant.

Mobile populations

The Tuareg are descended from Amazigh (Berber) peoples who have inhabited North Africa for thousands of years. In the first few centuries CE, the Tuareg are believed to have spread south from what is now Morocco into the Sahara. As Arab peoples arrived from the Middle East from the 8th century onward, the Tuareg converted to Islam and moved deeper into the desert and the Sahel that borders it to the south. Many lived in tents or small villages as semi-nomadic pastoralists, with groups controlling trade routes across the desert and raising cattle such as zebu.

From around the 11th century, the Bedouin migrated from the Middle East into North Africa; today, they inhabit a wide region stretching from northern Mauritania to Egypt. Their herd animals—goats, sheep, cattle, and camels—shaped their movements, with many moving from farmland into the desert in the winter. The Bedouin fought the existing Amazigh population, occupying crucial desert oases and spreading Arabic and Islam.

To the east, the Maasai are believed to have originated in the Nile Valley of what is now South Sudan, on the Sahara's edge. They spread throughout the semi-arid plains of the Rift Valley region of Tanzania and Kenya, using spears and *orinka* (throwing clubs) to dominate the area of fertile grasslands. They shared a language, *maa*, with some local groups living as semi-nomadic pastoralists and hunters, and others following their cattle in a fully nomadic life, traveling long distances in search of pasture and water.

Trading cultures

The Bedouin, Maasai, and Tuareg have played a major role in the histories of North and East Africa, thanks in part to their ability to survive in arid environments. The Bedouin and Tuareg were integral to the trans-Saharan trade in gold, spices, salt, ivory, kola nuts, and cowrie shells, as well as enslaved people (see pp.88–89). Camels were introduced from the Middle East in antiquity and became increasingly common after the 5th century CE. These animals can carry

△ **Tuareg cross**
These crosses, also known as Agadez crosses after the Nigerien city of the same name, are made by the Tuareg people. This example bears Arabic inscriptions from the Qur'an.

◁ **Desert nomad**
The cartographer of the 1375 "Catalan Atlas" depicts a turbaned nomad, possibly a Tuareg, on a camel. Next to him is a tented encampment.

Bedouin tents
This 19th-century image shows a Bedouin family and their tents in the Sahara. Tents, constructed from fabric made of camel hair and vegetable fibers, were designed to be easily erected, dismantled, and transported.

heavier loads than horses, and their adaptations to arid conditions allowed the nomads to travel farther, as well as exploit camel milk and wool. As empires rose, particularly in West Africa, the nomads of the desert opened up new routes across the Sahara.

The cultures of these nomadic peoples have also enriched Africa. The Bedouin are known for their oral poetry, *nabaṭi*, which dates to at least the 14th century and addresses a wide range of subjects including history, eulogies, social commentary, and riddles. Maasai culture maintains a focus on cattle and martial pride, with its acrobatic *adumu*, or jumping dance, performed at weddings, religious rites, and other significant occasions. The Tuareg are famous as makers of weapons and jewelery, such as Tuareg cross pendants, as well as music, which has found modern expression through the "desert blues" of acts such as Mali's Tinariwen.

Nomads in the modern age

The desert peoples have faced many challenges. European maritime dominance reduced the importance of trans-Saharan trade, and successive governments have sought to increase their control of once-remote regions. Some Tuareg groups have long argued—and fought—for independence from Mali, while, in Tanzania, Maasai are resisting their peoples' eviction from lands now used as private game reserves.

The nomads of the desert remain a significant presence—several million Bedouin live in Africa and the Middle East, the Maasai number almost a million, and over two million Tuareg live in nations including Niger, Mali, and Burkina Faso. But they often find themselves marginalized, as governments struggle to integrate seasonal herders into economies that depend on urban areas and settled agriculture.

Maasai jumping
Maasai men in the Maasai Mara, Kenya, demonstrate the *adumu*, a jumping dance that may have its origins in training drills for hunting and combat.

The Kingdom of Benin

Rule of the *obas*

One of the most prominent West African empires from the medieval period, the Kingdom of Benin was a resource-rich trading giant and military powerhouse in a region of fiercely competitive rivals.

The Edo people who populated the Kingdom of Benin originally called it "Ubini," which the Portuguese corrupted into "Benin." According to Yoruba history, Oranmiyan, a prince from Ilé-Ifè (see pp.110–111), founded the kingdom in the 12th or 13th century. He and his descendants established themselves in what became Benin City (in modern Nigeria), a metropolis encompassing some 500 small settlements within high walls.

△ **Absolute monarch**
This Italian lithograph from c. 1820 is a European view of an *oba* riding among his people. The *oba* was a revered figure who personally owned everything of value in the state.

An entrepreneurial empire

The kingdom was ruled by a powerful king, or *oba*, although chieftains and local rulers were permitted to exercise self-rule so long as they paid tribute (in the form of goods or enslaved people) to their monarch. In 1440, the royal prince Ewuare (see pp.130–131) seized power, becoming the first warrior-ruler who established Benin as a major force in West Africa. He and his successors extended the kingdom's territory further east toward the borders of modern Cameroon and west as far as Ghana.

One of the main motivating factors for the kingdom's expansion was economic. The state's kings realized that dominion over large sections of West Africa's coastline enabled them to control Africa's Atlantic trade routes, through the imposition of taxes, tolls, and other levies on the ports that did business with other African nations and with Europe. In particular, Ewuare's son and successor, Ozolua, expanded Benin's trade with Portuguese merchants in the 1480s, trading glass beads, cotton, ivory, rubber, palm oil, and, most importantly, gold and pepper.

The Kingdom of Benin also participated in the slave trade, though not as extensively as Portugal would have liked. From 1516, for example, the king prohibited the sale of enslaved males to Europeans, as he needed them for his own army. At its height, Benin was able to put 100,000 armed men in the field and, around 1590, it expanded to the coastal city of Lagos, built a military base, and took over the control of a major port.

Masters of metalwork

The kingdom's wealth and military might gave it the economic power and access to valuable minerals to develop a rich material culture. Pottery-making and textile manufacture were two areas of expertise, but by far the Kingdom of Benin's most abiding—and contested—artistic legacy came in the form of its metallurgical accomplishments, particularly the "Benin Bronzes" (see pp.132–133). Created from the 13th to the 18th centuries, they comprise thousands of expertly worked bronze and brass pieces, mostly in the form of reliefs, plaques, and sculptures made to decorate the royal palace in Benin City and in many cases showing the military prowess of ancient Benin and its trading activities with the

▷ **Queen Mother**
This bronze head depicts Idia, the powerful mother of King Esigie (r. 1504–1550). Idia raised an army to ensure her son became king.

> "**Great Benin**, where the king resides, is **larger than Lisbon.**"
>
> PORTUGUESE SHIP CAPTAIN
> LOURENÇO PINTO, 1691

△ **King of Benin**
This photograph shows King Eweka II c. 1920. The British did not abolish the Kingdom of Benin's monarchy and today *obas* sit on the throne in Nigeria.

Portuguese. The kingdom's expertise in crafting beautiful items in metal also included jewelery and other ornamental objects.

A change in the balance of power

The golden age of the Kingdom of Benin lasted around 150 years, from the accession of Ewuare until the death of the last of the "warrior-kings," Ehengbuda, in 1601. From here, the state was weakened by a series of civil wars and succession disputes and went into a decline that was initially gradual but accelerated rapidly at the end of the 19th century, when British forces invaded the kingdom.

For centuries, the kingdom had accrued its wealth by acting as an intermediary between European traders and African vendors. But by the 19th century, Britain had replaced Portugal as the main European nation involved in West Africa, and the power dynamic began to change. Whereas Portugal's interests in the region were primarily commercial, Britain's were overtly imperial—at least, that is what the *oba* Ovonramwen believed when he cut off all trading links with the British in the mid-1890s and, as the dominant power broker for all trade in the region, blocked Britain from doing business with Benin's neighbors. Britain sent an allegedly peaceful but nevertheless provocative diplomatic mission to assert the country's "right" to trade. When Benin soldiers attacked and killed several members of the mission at the kingdom's borders on January 4, 1897, London used the attack as a pretext to invade.

The following month, more than 1,000 British troops entered the capital and in just under three weeks they deposed the king, razed Benin City's royal palace to the ground, and killed hundreds of citizens. Britain then forcibly incorporated the state into its empire, first as part of the British Niger Coast Protectorate and later as part of colonial Nigeria. In retaliation for "provoking" Britain's incursion, the British expeditionary force ruthlessly looted the kingdom's treasures, particularly the Benin Bronzes. Today, many of them are still held in Britain, the US, and Germany, though in recent years progress has been made in repatriating some of the items from a number of museums.

By the turn of the 20th century, British colonial administrators had eliminated the last pockets of resistance and rebellion against British rule, and the former Kingdom of Benin would remain under imperial control until Nigeria's independence movement restored the country's freedom in 1960.

Oba Ewuare

Benin's greatest warrior-king

A transformative ruler, Ewuare boosted the monarch's power in the Kingdom of Benin, expanded the state's territory at the expense of its neighbors, and achieved godlike status among his people.

The third son of the *oba* ("king") Ohen, Prince Ogun seized power after his father's death, defeating his own brother Uwaifiokun in a violent coup and taking the regnal name Ewuare, meaning "the trouble has ceased." He became the first—and greatest—of his country's so-called "warrior-kings."

Before his rule, monarchs in the Kingdom of Benin (see pp.128–129) shared power with local chiefs; under Ewuare, the king became the sole authority—although Ewuare was also careful to appoint a council of advisors made up of both royal officials and local leaders (including some representing areas with a history of rebellion and resistance). To emphasize his power, Ewuare made the monarchy hereditary, removing the local leaders' right to select the new king on the death of the old one. Ewuare also changed the name of the kingdom from Ubini to Edo (although the old name persisted in some quarters, especially among European traders who corrupted "Ubini" into "Benin" and inadvertently gave the kingdom the name by which it is known today).

From king to god

Having remade the kingdom's politics, Ewuare revamped its army. He increased its size and organization, and used it to win territory from Igbo-controlled lands to the east and Yoruba-dominated regions to the west. Internationally, Ewuare began to agree trade deals with Portuguese merchants. At home, he became a patron of the arts, especially ivory- and wood-carving, and the creation of bronze statuary (see pp.132–133). The earthworks and defensive walls and ditches he constructed around Benin City's royal palace are among the finest building projects of the age. For his achievements, the king became "Ewuare the Great," and was said to possess magical, semi-divine powers—so, too, was each subsequent *oba*.

It is not known how Ewuare died, but by the time of his passing the kingdom of Benin had become perhaps the main regional force in West Africa. After a few years of tumult—one of Ewuare's sons was assassinated, the second deposed—Ewuare's third son, Ozolua, became *oba* in 1480 and carried on his father's expansionist policies.

▽ **Ceremonial cleansing**
The kingdom of Benin's rulers used this bronze water container in the form of a sacred leopard to wash their hands in purification rituals at court.

△ **Emblem of authority**
Kings and local leaders wore artfully carved ivory or brass bracelets like this one from c. 1550–1680 to symbolize their power and status.

---

c. 900s Area around Benin City first settled

c. 1180 Eweka I becomes the first *oba*

c. 1434 Ewuare's brother Uwaifiokun becomes *oba*

1440 Ewuare seizes power

c. 1470 Ewuare renames his kingdom Edo

1472 First contact between the Portuguese and the *oba*

1473 Death of Ewuare

1601 Death of Ehengbuda, the last of the warrior-kings

Head of state

A brass likeness of an *oba*. This sculpture dates from the 16th century, but is typical of the way in which Benin's kings were represented.

Woven cap accessorized by coral beads

Eyes and other facial features are stylized and symmetrical

Decorative coral strands hang from each ear

Attendant shelters the *oba*'s head

Armed guard flanks the *oba*

Horse wears decorative bridle

> "These artifacts speak to **who we are** and speak to **our history**, our religion, our **values and ethics**."
>
> LAL MOHAMMED, NIGERIA'S CULTURE MINISTER, 2022

Benin Bronze with oba and attendants

A West African portrait of power

The Kingdom of Benin (in modern-day Nigeria) was a powerful West African state between the 12th and 19th centuries (see pp.128–129). Among the kingdom's most important cultural legacies are the thousands of artifacts known as the "Benin Bronzes." Produced between the 13th and 16th centuries, they include jewelery, ornaments, ritual artifacts, and decorative items. However, they are best known for the plaques and sculptures that mainly depict the kingdom's *obas* (kings), royal family, and important state figures.

Production of the artwork

It was probably during the rule of *Oba* Oguola (r. 1274–1287) that production of the pieces began. The most distinctive works were created in the era of *Oba* Ewuare (see pp.130–131), who came to power in 1440. He commissioned pieces to be hung exclusively in the royal palace in the capital city of Edo (also called Benin City). These would reflect the ruler's power and authority, as well as display his state's culture, traditions, and religious practices. They were made of bronze, brass, or a copper alloy. The earliest artifacts were produced by heating, hammering, and manipulating the metal, but over time this evolved into the more technically complex "lost wax" process. In this method, a model of the sculpture or plaque is made in wax—which is easier to work and allows for more elaborate designs—that is then coated in clay. When the clay is fired in a kiln, the wax melts, leaving behind an impression of the object on the clay's hollow interior. Molten bronze or brass poured into the hollow cools and solidifies into the metalworks.

Many of these pieces were looted by colonial powers in the 19th and 20th centuries; some have eventually been repatriated to Nigeria from museums and collections outside Africa. The issue of their acquisition and return remains controversial (see pp.128–129).

Representation of majesty

The c. 16th-century copper alloy plaque shown here is of an unnamed *oba*, identifiable by the beaded coral regalia worn by Benin's rulers from this period. His high status is also indicated by him being the only figure on horseback. He is surrounded by attendants and officials, their differing sizes representing their relative importance. This item shows Portuguese influences—horses were transported to the kingdom by Portuguese traders, as were the coral beads around the *oba*'s neck. The cross-shaped rosettes in the background may indicate the influence of Christianity, also imported to the country by the Portuguese.

◁ **Royal procession**
The *oba* is deliberately shown larger than his subjects and attendants, as a sign of his royal power. He holds the hands of his subjects in a fatherly, inclusive gesture.

△ **Palace performer**
This 14th- or 15th-century bronze figure of a court musician is shown playing a horn and wearing a leopard print—an animal associated with an *oba*.

Royal power
Rulers with divine powers or military might

More than 5,000 years have passed since the reign of the earliest African monarchs—the first pharaohs of a united Egypt c. 3100 BCE. Royal power in African societies has been expressed in diverse ways, usually by male rulers, though Queen Njinga of Ndongo ruled in her own right, while Nefertiti, the wife of the pharaoh Akhenaten, and the *iyoba* or queen mother in Benin, both had a major influence over their state's affairs.

A sacred leader

Common to many rulers is the idea of sacred kingship, where the head of state acts as a mediator with the gods, or is himself divine. In ancient Egypt, pharaohs were deemed earthly manifestations of the god Horus (shown as a falcon and representing power). Among the Bunyoro people of what is now Uganda, the ruler depended on his control of sacred shrines, and his ancestors had to pass a test set by a deity. Divine kingship, however, encompassed great differences in the practical power of rulers. The Luba people of Central Africa believed that the king's power should not be absolute, so a council—the *bambudye*—acted as an intermediary between the king and the people. The vast Oyo state had layers of government. Its ruler, the *alaafin*, could not act without the consent of the *Oyo Mesi*, a council of seven leaders (see p.112). In the Nri Kingdom of the Igbo, the idea of a divine king remained: the *eze nri* was a priest-king who held religious but not political power in a system that lasted until British conquest in 1911.

△ **Nefertiti**
The wife of pharaoh Akhenaten, and queen from 1353 to 1336 BCE, Nefertiti was one of the most powerful women in Egyptian history, ruling at a time of huge artistic and religious changes and elevated by her husband to be virtual coruler.

△ **Saladin**
Beginning as a lowly army officer, Saladin became vizier of Egypt and, after deposing the last Fatimid caliph in 1171, sultan. He united Muslim forces and conquered an empire, his power dependent not on birth or divine powers, but on the might of his armies and his political skills.

△ **Lalibela**
According to Ethiopian tradition, Emperor Gebre Meskel (r. 1181–1221) ordered the building of 11 rock-cut churches in northern Ethiopia to show the power of the Christian Church, which underpinned his rule. They are known by the emperor's birth name, Lalibela.

> "I warn you against shedding blood ... blood never sleeps."
>
> SALADIN, SULTAN OF EGYPT

Power and wealth

Medieval rulers, such as Saladin, the founder of the Ayyubid dynasty (see pp.124–125), were warriors who commanded great armies. The kings of Wagadou (ancient Ghana) and *mansas* of Mali, such as Musa, enjoyed resources greater than those of European royalty. The Asante Empire, which covered a large area, created a system from the reign of Osei Kwadwo (1764-1777) onward with ministers, provincial governors, and a treasury into which taxes flowed.

The coming of Europeans undermined many African rulers, but for others it cemented their status, as they derived new wealth from trade. The Zulu State built power from its military successes and conquests. Religions also acted as potent sources of authority: the kings of Ethiopia from the 13th century claimed descent from the Biblical king Solomon, and dynasties in North Africa, including the Fatimids of Tunisia in the 10th century, and the Almoravids in northwest Africa from the 12th century, based their authority on their rulers' adherence to Islam.

As colonialism progressed, local rulers were often the only recognized source of the continuation of a tradition and acted as mediators with colonial powers. Monarchs such as the *kabakas* of Buganda (in Uganda) and the *shehus* of Borno survived centuries of foreign control to reemerge as figures of authority and, in Morocco and Eswatini, as ruling heads of state. King Mswati III in Eswatini still reigns as an absolute monarch today, and is part of an almost 300-year-old dynasty.

△ **Iyoba**
This 18th-century bronze statue of an *iyoba* or queen mother is from the West African state of Benin. The *iyoba* acted as the chief advisor to the *oba* (her son), and commanded her own regiment in wartime, the only woman permitted to do so.

△ **Prempeh II**
Asantehene (king) from 1931–1970, Prempeh was four years old when the British conquered Asante in 1896. After 40 years in exile he returned, and as the power of local rulers grew, he became the first president of Ghana's National House of Chiefs in 1969.

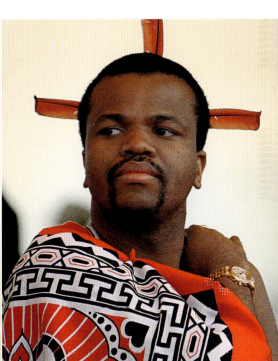

△ **Mswati III**
King since 1986, Mswati III is a member of the Dlamini dynasty that has provided all Eswatini's kings since Ngwane III founded the state in 1745. He is Africa's only remaining absolute monarch and representative of a pattern of rule once widespread throughout the continent.

Great Zimbabwe

The mighty walled cities of a lost Shona empire

Great Zimbabwe was the architectural and artistic high point of a powerful Shona civilization that endured for six centuries. Its people traded gold and ivory across the Indian Ocean and built vast fortified complexes whose ruins still stand today.

The Zimbabwe culture was centered on large settlements, including the city we now know as Great Zimbabwe, which was founded around the 9th century in modern-day southeastern Zimbabwe. In the 13th and 14th centuries, the city supported more than 10,000 people, and became the grand capital of a kingdom of the Zimbabwe culture that reached as far as present-day Mozambique. In Shona, the name Zimbabwe means "big stone house" and Great Zimbabwe was a city of immense scale—the largest in Southern Africa at the time.

The earliest origins of the Zimbabwe culture date to 2,500 years ago, when Bantu-speaking peoples from Central Africa migrated to Southern Africa (see pp.36–37) and met the Indigenous San hunter-gatherers. Bantu-speakers known as the Shona settled in the plains and forests of the Shashe-Limpopo Basin around 500 CE. They grew crops and herded cattle, gradually displacing the San. The area, where modern-day Zimbabwe, Botswana, and South Africa meet, was not immediately prosperous, and the population declined after 700 CE, but around 900 CE settlement resumed, and the region became a hub.

Cattle were the principal form of wealth in this Iron Age society, representing power and status. The region's grassland made good grazing, and the Shona began to exchange goods along the Limpopo River with the Swahili, fellow Bantu-speakers who lived on the coast of what is now Kenya, Tanzania, and Mozambique. The Swahili kingdoms were part of a commercial network that crossed the Indian Ocean, connecting East and North Africa with the Arabian Peninsula, India, Indonesia, and even China. As trade links grew stronger, iron, salt, ivory, cattle, fish, snail and mussel shells, chert (a rock used for tools and to create sparks for fires), and beads made from ostrich eggs traveled up and down the great river.

Great Zimbabwe's rise

The Shona population grew through the 11th and 12th centuries, and the cattle economy evolved into what became known as the Zimbabwe culture. A class-based society, centered on Great Zimbabwe, emerged in which the ruling elite profited from the labor of traders, food producers, and artisans, and acquired new luxury trade goods such as Chinese porcelain and glass beads.

Great Zimbabwe was not yet dominant, though. Its predecessor as the capital was Mapungubwe, some 170 miles (270 km) to the south in what is now South

◁ **Prestigious complex**
The Great Enclosure may have been used as a royal palace or a grain store, while the plains that surround it supported large numbers of cattle.

Africa. In the 12th century, the population of Mapungubwe may have reached 5,000 people. By the 13th century, the Mapungubwe people were mining gold, which they traded and used to make objects such as scepters, bowls, headdresses, and animal figures.

Great Zimbabwe was also growing increasingly sophisticated, with tall walls and elaborate buildings. When the Little Ice Age changed the climate in the 12th century, the interior of Southern Africa became colder and dryer, leading to Mapungubwe's decline and eventual abandonment in the early 13th century. This increasingly arid climate also presented challenges to the inhabitants of Great Zimbabwe, who took care to preserve water. Huge pits on the site are believed to have been used to harvest surface water and store groundwater, which was used during dry seasons. These measures may have contributed to the city's rise to replace Mapungubwe, since Great Zimbabwe was able to sustain a significant population, as well as livestock and agriculture.

Towering walls and soapstone birds

Today, archaeologists divide Great Zimbabwe into three key areas. The Hill Complex, which began to be constructed in the 10th century, was probably either the home of the king or a ceremonial site—it may have been used for rain-making rituals. Both it and the 14th-century Great Enclosure were surrounded by huge mortarless walls, with the Hill Complex's up to 20 ft (6 m) thick and more than 33 ft (10 m) tall. The nearby Valley Complex, which dates from between the 14th and 16th centuries, included many stone buildings. Avian soapstone sculptures, known as "Zimbabwe birds," stood on columns in the city, and may represent totem animals. The presence of 15th-century potsherds, beads, woven goods, and golden artifacts show that the empire continued to thrive, and Portuguese traders were aware of its existence. However, by the mid-15th century Great Zimbabwe was declining, possibly due to shortages of food, water, or gold. It was eventually abandoned, with a new city at Khami, near Bulawayo in what is now southwestern Zimbabwe, rising to prominence in the 16th and 17th centuries. Other migrants from the city are believed to have founded the Kingdom of Mutapa, which became the main power in Eastern Zimbabwe and Mozambique between the 15th and 17th centuries.

After Great Zimbabwe's collapse, different Shona groups used the ruins for religious purposes. By the late 19th century, white colonists had begun to arrive in Zimbabwe, and the ruins' history was disputed, with some Europeans suggesting they could not be the work of Black Africans and might instead have been built by the Phoenicians or the Biblical King Solomon.

In 1931, the British archaeologist Gertrude Caton-Thompson described Great Zimbabwe as of "Bantu origin and of a medieval date," but the white minority government of Rhodesia (see pp.252–253) continued to downplay the ruins' Bantu connection. Modern archaeology has confirmed that the Shona constructed the city, which is now a UNESCO World Heritage Site. It gave its name to Zimbabwe, which became independent in 1980, and Great Zimbabwe sits at the center of the nation's coat of arms, while a Zimbabwe bird adorns its flag.

Rim is decorated with symbols

△ **Divination bowl**
This plaster cast of a wooden platter, decorated with a crocodile, was found near Great Zimbabwe in the late 19th century. It is thought to be a divination bowl.

Thin sheets of gold covered wooden carving (now decayed)

Holes where tiny gold nails once held covering in place

△ **Luxury item**
Found in a grave in the ruins of Mapungubwe, the 800-year-old Golden Rhinoceros of Mapungubwe shows the Zimbabwe culture's wealth and sophistication.

" … there is **a fortress** built of stones of **marvelous size**, and … no mortar joining them."

PORTUGUESE CAPTAIN VICENTE PEGADO, 1531

The Great Enclosure

Great Zimbabwe, Masvingo, Zimbabwe

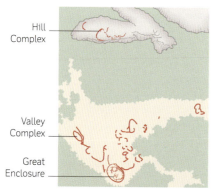

The site
Great Zimbabwe comprises three main groups of ruins: the Hill Complex, which shows the earliest evidence of settlement; the Great Enclosure, where the masonry reaches its zenith; and the Valley Complex, a collection of smaller-scale stone enclosures where artifacts from Central Africa and Asia have been found.

Zimbabwe birds
Among the most famous finds from Great Zimbabwe are eight distinctive bird figures carved from soapstone. While each is unique, several blend avian features with human features such as toes and lips. It is thought they may represent significant ancestors of Great Zimbabwe's people.

Chevrons appear on all eight bird monoliths

Masters of masonry
The smooth, curving walls were constructed from local granite. No binding mortar was used: instead, the masons carefully positioned rectangular blocks in even layers, tapering gently upward for maximum stability. A stonework chevron frieze, the significance of which is unknown, spans a 171-ft (52-m) length of the outer wall.

The core is packed with irregular blocks

The daga platform may have had ritual significance

The solid 33-ft (10-m) conical tower is thought to be symbolic

At its thickest, the outer wall is 18 ft (5.5 m) at the base and 12 ft (3.6 m) at the top

The outer wall is 820 ft (250 m) long and around 33 ft (10 m) high

The monumental dry stone ruins at Great Zimbabwe are the largest south of the Sahara. Built by ancestors of modern-day Zimbabwe's Shona people, the site is one of many stone settlements in the region, but its relative scale suggests it served as the capital of a kingdom. Among the ruins, the most imposing is the Great Enclosure, an enormous elliptical structure 820 ft (250 m) in circumference, within which lower walls interconnect to form a series of courtyards around individual homesteads. Archaeologists are still working to understand exactly how this enclosure was used. One theory is that it was a royal residence; another is that it served as a site for ritual ceremonies.

THE GREAT ENCLOSURE | 139

▷ **Great entrances**
The Great Enclosure's monumental entrances originally had lintels, at least two of which were wooden. No evidence suggests the immense walls were built to be defensive; they may have been intended to protect the privacy of an elite group.

△ **Typical dwelling**
Homesteads had separate huts for cooking and sleeping made of *daga* (a mix of clay and gravel). *Daga* was also molded to create hearths and raised surfaces for sitting, sleeping, and storage.

Open communal area

Individual homesteads are separated by stone walls

The entrance buttresses are not structural but restrict the view into the enclosure

Buttresses may have provided privacy, or controlled movement

The height and thickness of the walls is uneven

A narrow passageway leads to the conical tower

Huts had conical thatched roofs

Huts and *daga* walls may have been painted

△ **Use of the Great Enclosure**
This reconstruction depicts the Great Enclosure as it may have looked in the 14th century, when Great Zimbabwe flourished. Archaeological finds indicate that metalworking, weaving, pot-making, and soapstone-carving were important activities.

The Mossi States

Powerful nations united

A shared ancestry, ethnicity, religion, political system, and social hierarchy allowed the Mossi States—a West African confederation of nations—to survive and thrive for at least 500 years, until the end of the 19th century.

The Mossi States were a collection of kingdoms in West Africa whose territory encompassed parts of modern-day Burkina Faso, Côte d'Ivoire, and Ghana. Many details of the states' origins and histories are lost, but most sources agree there were up to 20 states, of which five were particularly influential: Ouagadougou, Tenkodogo, Fada N'gourma, Zondoma (replaced eventually by Yatenga), and Boussouma. Although each kingdom was independent, they acted collectively in areas such as foreign affairs, trade, and war. This made the Mossi Empire, as it is sometimes known, one of Africa's strongest forces.

Beginning and growth

According to historical records, anthropological study, archaeology, and Mossi legends and stories, the Mossi originated some time between the 11th and 14th centuries. The culture's foundation myth tells how the Mossi people emerged from the union of a fugitive princess named Yennenga and an elephant hunter called Rialé (see box, opposite). Their son Ouédraogo is said to have founded Tenkodogo, which was then ruled after his death by his son, Zoungrana. His two other sons, Diaba Lompo and Rawa, founded Fada N'gourma and Zondoma respectively. Ouédraogo's grandson Oubri founded the Ouagadougou dynasty, supposedly around 1050. It was the actual or imagined existence of these ancestral and ethnic links that allowed the Mossi States to collaborate effectively.

Over the next several hundred years, the Mossi States concentrated on strengthening their economic and military power. By the 15th century, this empire was one of the most effective in West Africa. It successfully resisted the neighboring Songhai Empire (see pp.104–105) to the north, and from the early 18th century onward formed trading links with powers including the Mali and Massina empires, as well as the Sokoto Caliphate (see pp.194–195) and the nearby states and kingdoms of the region's Fula

Scarification patterns mark passage to adulthood

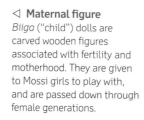

◁ **Maternal figure**
Biiga ("child") dolls are carved wooden figures associated with fertility and motherhood. They are given to Mossi girls to play with, and are passed down through female generations.

▽ **House of worship**
In a largely Muslim region, the Mossi kingdoms resisted becoming Islamic states, although many Muslims lived here and mosques, such as this one in Ouagadougou, were built.

△ **Animal mask**
Masks were worn at important Mossi events, such as funerals. Each local group had its own representative spirit animal. This one is *wan-nyaka* ("the little antelope").

people. Disputes over matters such as religions, borders, or resources sometimes broke out into violence, but in general most of West Africa's states were evenly matched enough to avoid upsetting the area's balance of power. The Mossi States, for example, were not actively expansionist and preferred to defend the territories they already controlled.

The Niger and Volta rivers ran through Mossi lands, and this allowed the states to grow wealthy by controlling the flow of goods along these important trading waterways. Mossi farmers exported cattle and crops such as millet, sorghum, and cotton. The main imports were salt and highly prized, caffeine-containing kola nuts. The Mossi were also renowned as skilled ironworkers and produced both weapons and decorative items for domestic use and export. Unlike most of their neighbors, the Mossi States were not involved in the slave trade.

Power and belief

Despite each of the Mossi states being autonomous, Ouagadougou (in modern-day Burkina Faso) was preeminent among its peers. Ouagadougou's capital city, also called Ouagadougou, was the seat of the *morho naba* ("great king") of the Mossi people. More a spiritual figure than a ruling monarch, the *morho naba* was believed to channel a supernatural force—known as *naam* and derived from the Mossi's creator-god Wende—that gave him the power to lead other people. The *morho naba* oversaw the Mossi people in their rites and ceremonies that included the sacrifice of animals to appease Wende and the spirits they believed inhabited the natural world. The Mossi also practiced ancestor veneration. Other belief systems such as Islam and Christianity had only limited success in converting the Mossi.

Mossi society was strictly stratified. The *nakombse* were the elite few who could trace their lineage back to the states' founders and who therefore possessed *naam* and enjoyed a divine right to rule; the *tengbiise* were the people whose forebears had been the first inhabitants of the lands the *nakombse* first conquered and had become assimilated into the Mossi States.

During their height, the Mossi States ensured mostly peace and prosperity, as a result of their strong economy, stable social structure, ability to cooperate with each other, and the relatively settled balance of power in West Africa. This ended in 1896, when French forces invaded the Mossi States and incorporated them into France's Upper Volta colony. The last king of Ouagadougou, Wobgo, died in exile in the Gold Coast (modern-day Ghana) in 1904, and the regions of West Africa that France had colonized would not gain their independence until 1960.

LEGENDARY PRINCESS

Princess Yennenga—the legendary "mother of the Mossi"—embodied two important aspects of this West African culture: the martial and the maternal. She was trained in combat by her father Nedega, ruler of the Dagbon Kingdom in possibly the 11th or 12th century. She fought her first battle at 14, and was so skilled a fighter that her father barred her from marrying, fearing that family life would deprive his kingdom of a great warrior. This caused Yennenga to flee the kingdom in disguise on horseback. In Mandingo (Malinke) territory to the north, she married a local hunter, Rialé, and they had a child, Ouédraogo, whose descendants and kinship groups would go on to found the Mossi nations.

BRONZE FIGURINE OF PRINCESS YENNENGA

Kingdoms of the Luba, Lunda, and Lozi

Central Africa's most renowned trio of states

From the late 16th century, much of Central Africa was under the sway of the neighboring Luba, Lunda, and Lozi kingdoms. All three coexisted more or less peacefully for around three centuries.

The Luba people emerged from what is today the southeast of the Democratic Republic of the Congo (DRC), in a marshy region of lakes and rivers known as the Upemba Depression. The first Luba leader of note was the semi-mythical Kongolo Mwamba, who is said to have established a kingdom in 1585. His nephew and successor, Kalala Ilunga, conquered vast lands to the west and inaugurated many of the Kingdom of Luba's traditions. From his time on, the kingdom had a political culture of a king (or *mulopwe*), revered as a living god, who ruled alongside an advisory council. A fair and balanced governance was ensured by a committee-based decision-making process, a respect for authority (embodied in the person of the king), and adherence to the Luba religion's values of ethical conduct.

The Kingdom of Luba flourished for 300 years, and was known for its arts, especially wood carving and—often accompanied by music—poetry. Weakened by a succession dispute in the 1880s and the depredations of slave traders from East Africa raiding its lands, the kingdom finally succumbed to the imperial ambitions of Belgium. In the mid-1880s, Belgian colonization fragmented and split the Kingdom of Luba, forcing it into the Congo Free State, a colony established as the personal property of the Belgian king, Leopold II (see pp.212–213).

◁ **Ornamental instrument**
Cowrie shells were used as currency throughout West and Central Africa, and as decorations symbolizing wealth and status—as on this late 19th-century Lunda whistle.

Lunda Kingdom

The histories of the Lunda and the Luba kingdoms are inextricably linked. The Lunda people originated in an area along the Kalanyi River in the south of the DRC, close to the homelands of the Luba. The kingdom was founded some time in the mid-17th century after an exiled Luba prince named Ilunga Tshibinda took up residence in a region to the south called Ba Lunda. His son, Yao Nawedji, became the first Lunda ruler. The kingdom adopted a governmental model of monarchy supported by an advisory council similar to that of the Luba. This gave the state political stability. Economically, Lunda benefited from the highly profitable trade in enslaved

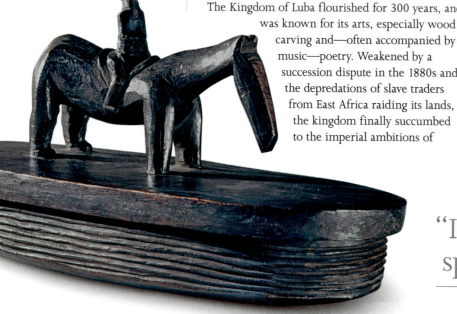

▽ **Domestic art**
This food dish is typical of the zoomorphic, or animal-themed, pottery, ironmongery, and wood-worked items produced by the Lozi.

> "I am the **great rock** that spreads all over **the lands**."
>
> *MULOPWE* KALALA ILUNGA, 16TH-CENTURY LUBA KING

people, salt, ivory, copper, and forestry products such as timber. The wealth this generated allowed Lunda's rulers to commission a variety of artwork, particularly carved wooden sculptures.

The Kingdom of Lunda collapsed in the late 19th century, when it was invaded by the neighboring Chokwe people. A much-diminished rump kingdom survived for a few more years, but this came to an end in 1887, when the Congo Free State took over the remaining Lunda lands.

Power-sharing in the south

The southern part of the Luba-Lunda states were occupied by the Lozi (sometimes called the Silozi) people in an area known as Barotseland. The name Lozi means "plain" and refers to the floodplain of the Zambezi River, along which most of the people lived. Each Lozi village had its own leader and ruling council, but the state was nominally a kingdom with a powerful and revered monarch, or *litunga*, whose court was based in the dry season at Lealui, close to the Zambezi, and in the wet season at Limulunga on higher ground. The annual decampment of the king and his court from Lealui to Limulunga was marked by a festival known as the *Kuomboko* (literally, "to get out of the water").

The British maintained an interest in Lozi lands from the late 19th century, but, as the region proved to be a poor source of valuable minerals such as gold and copper, imperial interference was minimal. In 1964, the Lozi heartland of Barotseland was incorporated into the newly independent Zambia.

◁ **Seat of power**
This stool was intended for a Luba chieftain. It was carved for ceremonial use and was highly symbolic: the female figure represents divine motherhood as the origin of royal authority.

△ **Cultural crossover**
Lunda rulers commissioned skillful artists from client peoples such as the Chokwe to create artwork, such as this figure of the mythical Lunda hero, Chibinda Ilunga.

> "**Wakupile luzi bipa** [A person holding flies with clenched fists]."
>
> LUBA PROVERB DESCRIBING THE *BANA BALUTE* AS KEEPERS OF SECRET KNOWLEDGE

Luba "memory board"

History in your hands

The Luba people of what is today the Democratic Republic of the Congo (DRC) had a unique means of recording their history, laws, and customs. Known as *lukasa* ("the long hand," or "claw"), these handheld wooden boards were crafted in an hourglass shape that represented, all at once, the Luba landscape, the royal court, the human body, and a turtle (the Luba monarchy's symbolic spirit animal). Each *lukasa* was studded with colored beads, shells, and metal, and scored with lines and symbols. This arrangement of shapes and objects was a sophisticated narrative device—a memory board—encoding vital information.

The people charged with interpreting *lukasa* were members of the Mbudye (or Bambudye) Society, an elite organization of mostly male diviners, storytellers, and spiritual teachers known as *bana balute* ("memory men"). The *bana balute* had to master successive levels of specialized knowledge before they were permitted to decipher and interpret the *lukasa*'s intricate designs and motifs. To do so, they ran their right hand over the board's beads, shapes, and ridges while declaiming aloud its stories and instructions. The arrangement of items on a *lukasa* was more a guide than a set narrative. No two memory men read the same *lukasa* in the same way; indeed, an individual *bana balute* would read the same memory board differently on different occasions, depending on where and to whom he was giving his recital.

The information on a *lukasa* was displayed in one of three styles. *Lukasa lwa nkunda* ("the long hand of the pigeon") record, among other things, the history of the Luba kings and the society's myths and legendary heroes; *lukasa lwa kabemba* ("the long hand of the hawk") feature information on the structure of the Mbudye Society alongside political, cultural, and social instructions for the Luba people; and *lukasa lwa kitenta* ("the long hand of the sacred pool") were made for individual Luba rulers and, it is said, contained secret spiritual information shared only with the king. None of this last style of *lukasa* remain in existence.

Partial interpretation

As with most surviving *lukasa*, the style of the one shown here and its precise meaning are not entirely known. What is clear is the significance of some of its symbols and their patterns of arrangement. Human faces, for example, represent Luba chiefs, kings, and Mbudye members; colored beads organized into rectangles, lines, ovals, and circles describe the layout of a chief or king's household, or the configuration of the Mbudye Society's meeting places, with lines also representing significant roads or migration routes. The carved and incised edges of the *lukasa* supposedly echo the shell markings of a turtle.

LUBA "MEMORY BOARD" | 145

Memory man
A Luba *bana balute* recites from a *lukasa* in this 1989 photograph taken in the DRC, showing that the practice of oral storytelling and instruction by this elite group continues.

Story board
This late 19th- or early 20th-century *lukasa* is 10 in (25 cm) long and about 5½ in (14 cm) wide. A row of carved mounds called *lukala* divide the board into female (left) and male (right) sides.

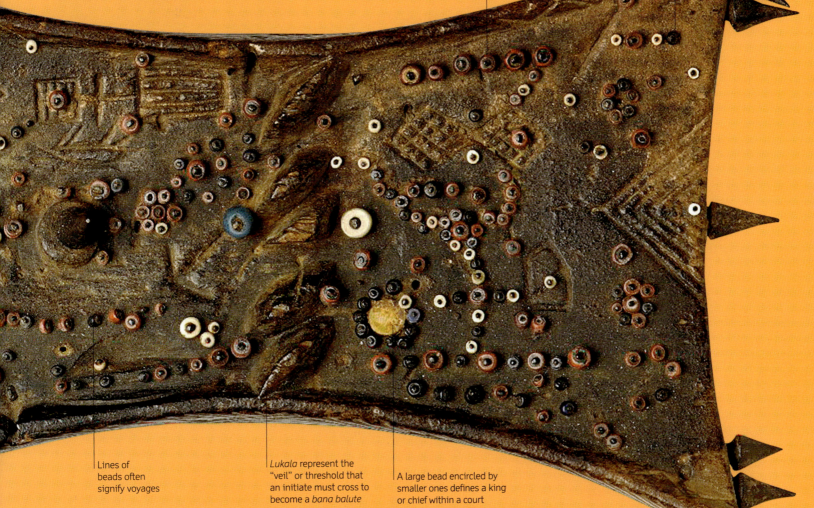

Beads and shells are attached to the board by slivers of wood or handmade iron wedges

Colors denote specific historical figures or events

Tapered ends represent stylized crocodile heads

Lines of beads often signify voyages

Lukala represent the "veil" or threshold that an initiate must cross to become a *bana balute*

A large bead encircled by smaller ones defines a king or chief within a court

△ **City of Kilwa**
The island of Kilwa was developed by Persian traders and later taken over by the Portuguese, who built this fort at Gereza. Despite its wealth, the Islamic city was not well defended.

The East African Sultanates

Trade with Persia, India, and Asia

Between the 8th and 15th centuries, much of East Africa became a trading hub for Islamic settlers who were based in powerful city-states known as the East African Sultanates.

Communities along the coast of East Africa where the modern-day countries of Somalia, Kenya, Tanzania, and Mozambique lie became significant trading posts for Islamic merchants who arrived by sea from Arabia and Asia. The Indigenous Bantu-speakers living in the region practiced pastoralism and their attention had been pointed more toward the African interior. When merchants from the Islamic world, as well as from India and farther afield, began arriving and settling along the coast, the focus of life in the region shifted outward and transformed this part of the continent into one of the most diverse in Africa for its time.

Influences from the east

Transoceanic trade became part of East African life, its activity dictated by the prevailing winds that blew across the Gulf of Aden and the Indian Ocean. From November to March, west-to-east monsoon winds brought Asian merchants to East Africa, their wooden

▽ **Attractive items**
Merchants from Asia traded their jewelery, such as this beaded necklace found at Kilwa Kisiwani, textiles, spices, and porcelain for African gold and ivory.

dhows laden with cotton, silk, porcelain, glassware, and spices. When the winds changed direction from April to October, traders set sail for the east, their hulls filled with gold, ivory, tortoiseshell, ambergris (a substance excreted by sperm whales, which is used in perfume manufacture), incense, spices, iron, animal hides, and enslaved people. These journeys took several months, and sailors and travelers often put down roots in the port cities they visited, getting married, forming friendships, and bringing new ideas, cuisines, languages, and ways of life along with them.

Islam reaches East Africa

One major import the visitors brought was Islam, possibly arriving with Shia Muslim refugees from Oman, which was Sunni-Muslim dominated, in the 8th century. Between 1050 and 1200, people from the city of Shiraz (Shirazi) settled in the region around modern-day Mogadishu, in Somalia. Some scholars dispute that the settlers came from Persia—however, they were certainly Muslim and helped spread the faith along the East African coast.

By the 12th century, the Shirazi had reached Kilwa, an island off Tanzania. It became the center of an empire that a century later extended along the East African coast from Somalia in the north to Tanzania in the south. The Kilwa Sultanate, as it was called, dominated East Africa's lucrative trade in gold for 200 years. Its capital, Kilwa Kisiwani, boasted stone-built houses and the empire minted its own copper coins—one of the first places in Africa south of the Sahara to do so.

Islamic sultanates

With the success of Kilwa acting as encouragement, other, mainly Arabic, incomers set up commercial outposts along the East African coast, and these city-states came to be known as the East African Sultanates. Shanga, on the Kenyan island of Pate, was an early Islamic center (its first mosque was built in the 8th century), followed by Kizimkazi on the Tanzanian island of Unguja (also called Zanzibar), and Mogadishu in Somalia, along with other city-states. Apart from the unquestionably powerful Kilwa, none of these places were "sultanates" in the traditional sense. The term really only indicates that they were all predominantly Arabic-Islamic in origin.

▷ **Establishment of Islam**
An 1882 illustration of the Fakhr al-Din Mosque in Mogadishu, Somalia, indicates the presence of Islam in the African city. The mosque was built in the 13th century.

◁ **Wealthy city-state**
This illustration from 1572 shows the thriving city-state of Kilwa. By the 15th century, it was the most powerful city on the East African coast.

Trade continued along the coast and across the Persian Gulf and Indian Ocean, but now the commercial relationships between merchants and city-states were subject to taxes and tariffs that paid for the mosques, royal palaces, and other impressive Arab-style buildings that still decorate East Africa's coast.

Although the Sultanates were wealthy, they were not militarily strong. The first Portuguese explorers arrived offshore in the late 15th century and within a century had plundered the Sultanates' cities and destroyed their trade. Despite their collapse, however, the Sultanates had changed East Africa irrevocably. The merging of Islamic and other non-African people with local Bantu-speaking populations had created a new language and culture known as Swahili. In essence, Swahili is a Bantu tongue but written in Arabic script (and including some Arabic vocabulary). "Swahili" derives from the Arabic *sahil* ("coast"), so it can be translated as "people of the coast." Today Swahili, or, more accurately, Kiswahili, is the most commonly spoken language in East Africa, and Islam is widely practiced among the people of the coast.

وكُنتُ أحسبُ أنّه سيُنبطُ بزرِّ سرزاليِ ويُعلى السمةِ على فاحلوِ الحبيِّ جلفَت ما أغلقتْ
بل قال إنَّ العبدَ إذا أُبرزَ ثمنُه وخفّتْ مؤنتُه بُرِّكَ بمولاهُ والنجفُ عليه مولاهُ فانٍ

لا وترجينَّك هذا الغلامَ النبيهَ بأن أخفَّ ثمنُه عليكم مائتي درهمٍ شيئٍ
واشكُرني ما جئتَ فقلتُ المبلغَ في الحالِ كما نقدني في الرخصِ الغالِ ولم

Slave market

This page from the *Maqamat* of Al-Hariri, a 13th-century illustrated manuscript, shows traders and enslaved people at a market in what is now Yemen. Enslaved Africans in the Middle East were forced to work in homes and as laborers, concubines, or soldiers, though some rose to positions of power.

Visitors to the market

Enslaved people put on sale in the marketplace

The Eastern slave trade

A trade that prospered in the face of abolition

Enslaved people were transported across the Sahara and the Indian Ocean for centuries. Like its transatlantic equivalent—which it outlasted—this slave trade changed societies and tore many Africans from their roots.

Slavery in Africa dates back at least 3,000 years, to ancient Egypt. Later empires such as the Romans, the Byzantines, and the Sasanians of Iran also enslaved Africans.

As the caliphates of the Middle East and North Africa grew in the 8th and 9th centuries CE, Muslim merchants began to buy enslaved people along a commercial frontier that stretched across the Sahara and into the Horn of Africa. Empires such as Wagadou (see pp.84–85) and Kanem-Bornu (see pp.108–109) enslaved people in raids, while Amazigh (Berber) and Arab enslavers led captives on grueling marches across the Sahara. On the east coast, Arab and Swahili enslavers used the Indian Ocean and Red Sea to ship people, as well as commodities such as gold, to North Africa, Europe, the Middle East, and Asia, in exchange for spices, textiles, precious stones, and other goods.

The trade in enslaved people shattered communities and was used to build powerful empires, especially in West Africa. The Atlantic slave trade (see pp.162–163) intensified these pressures but also rerouted the trade so that while Atlantic ports were busier than ever, trade across the Sahara declined.

Indian Ocean trade

By the late 18th century, the transatlantic trade was under pressure from abolitionists, and it was banned by the British Empire in 1807. But in East Africa the slave trade thrived as never before. French sugar and coffee plantations across the Indian Ocean relied on the labor of enslaved people, while Brazilian enslavers wary of British patrols off the coast of West Africa

▷ **Camp in the Congo Basin**
This 19th-century engraving shows a camp at Boyoma Falls, in the modern-day Democratic Republic of the Congo. Raids into the interior targeted enslaved people and ivory.

◁ **Tippu Tip**
Trader Tippu Tip worked for several Zanzibar sultans. Born around 1832, he became one of the most notorious enslavers in Africa before his death in 1905.

switched to East Africa, transporting enslaved people, mainly of Bantu-speaking origin, from modern-day Mozambique. Zanzibar became the richest sea port in tropical Africa, and enslaved people labored in its clove plantations and were shipped to date plantations in the Persian Gulf. However, the days of large-scale slave trading were drawing to a close. In 1873, the British shut down the slave market in Stone Town, Zanzibar's capital (see pp.188–189), and banned slave shipments by sea.

The impact of the trade across the Sahara and the Indian Ocean was immense. Huge numbers of people were taken from their communities and forced into servitude. While individual traders and rulers became wealthy, the suffering of some populations was horrific. Meanwhile, the persistence of slavery, and the dislocation of people caused by it, provided European colonialists with an opportunity and an excuse to intervene across Africa.

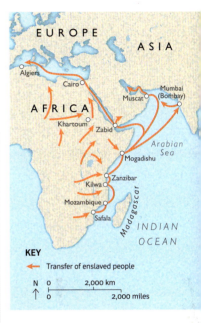

△ **Routes to slavery**
Slave-trading networks connected Africa south of the Sahara with the powerful states of the Middle East and the spice trade ports of Asia.

Textiles

The threads of a continent

Textiles in Africa have a rich history. Fabrics have been used for clothing, decoration, and trade, while different motifs, textures, and dyes often signify the individual wearer's ethnicity or status. There are many African textile traditions, but some common threads can be seen across the continent.

Most textiles have historically been handmade, by curing animal hide or using looms and shuttles to weave materials such as cotton, silk, hemp, wool, palms, tree bark, and bamboo. Decorative touches include introducing intricate sewn or drawn designs, adding beads, or dyeing and printing with colors derived from plants such as chile peppers, indigo, and cashew bark. Roles differ by region: men are the main weavers among the Asante of Ghana, while among the Kuba people in the Democratic Republic of the Congo (DRC), men weave the cloth and women transform it into garments, baskets, and other items.

Fabrics and decoration

Historically, the availability of local materials shaped production. In North Africa, flax was a key crop for the ancient Egyptians, and was used for clothing (alongside linen and wool), sails, and the strips used to wrap mummies. Amazigh (Berber) herders used their flocks' wool to produce clothing and rugs, and Amazigh rugs and carpets remain a major export.

In West and Central Africa, the leaves of palm trees have been used to produce raffia cloth. In forested regions of East, West, and Central Africa, meanwhile,

△ **Yoruba shawl, Nigeria**
Aso-oke is a Yoruba fabric that dates back to at least the 15th century. There are several main types, based on their colors. This shawl is a magenta cotton and silk weave called *alaari*. *Aso-oke* is worn on special occasions, such as festivals and weddings.

△ **Kuba raffia, Democratic Republic of the Congo**
The Kuba people of the DRC make a unique, velvetlike cloth using fibers of the raffia palm. Women artists embroider the surface of the cloth with geometric patterns (shown here). They also use the appliqué process, by which patterns are cut from one piece of cloth and sewed onto cloth of a different color.

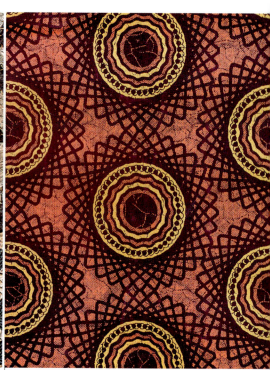

△ **Shweshwe prints, South Africa**
Shweshwe is a cotton fabric characterized by bright colors and geometric patterns. It is mainly used for Sotho (South Africa and Lesotho) clothing, and takes its name from Moshoeshoe I, the first ruler of Lesotho, who popularized its use in the 19th century.

> "Every piece [of kente cloth] has a **name and a meaning**. The cloth **speaks**."
>
> KWASI ASARE, GHANAIAN MASTER WEAVER, 2020

bark was stripped from a range of trees and boiled to make it malleable, then beaten with wooden hammers and dried in the sun. The Baganda people of Uganda are particularly well known for mutuba-tree bark cloth, which continues to be worn on formal occasions.

Patterns of trade also shaped fabrics and decoration. Around 2,000 years ago, Arab merchants introduced cotton to Ethiopia: the long, cotton *shamma* robe is a popular item of clothing in the country today. In Madagascar, silk and cotton, introduced by the sea trade with Asia, joined materials such as raffia, wool, and bark. For much of their history, the Maasai of Tanzania and Kenya mainly wore leather from sheep and cattle, but they are now known for striped and checkered *shuka* cloth, which became popular after trade with Europe brought cotton in the 19th century. In West and Central Africa, Dutch merchants during the 19th century introduced a colorful fabric with *batik*-inspired printing, which is known as *ankara*.

Many of the continent's best-known textiles are from West Africa. Nigeria's Yoruba use resist-dyeing (in which parts of the fabric are marked with substances such as wax so they resist the dye) to produce *adire*, a patterned indigo cloth. The Akan of Ghana began interlacing strips of silk and cotton around the 17th century to make *kente* cloth, which was used for royal robes. These fabrics are often used to communicate: *adinkra* cloth of the Asante, for example, carries symbols that represent proverbs, historical events, and cultural values.

△ **Dorze cloth, Ethiopia**
Weaving is an important trade for the Dorze people of southern Ethiopia. Huts and fences are made from interlaced local bamboo, while the borders of bright cotton clothing and blankets often feature intricate patterns.

△ **Mbuti bark cloth, DRC**
The Mbuti people make bark cloth, used for clothing and bedding, by beating and soaking bark until it becomes soft enough to work with. The Mbuti are hunter-gatherers from the Democratic Republic of the Congo's northeastern rainforests and the fabric's patterns sometimes show forest maps or song structures.

△ **Kente cloth, Ghana**
Traditionally made from handwoven strips of silk and cotton, *kente* cloth has long been worn by the Akan royalty of West Africa. The fabric is often used for special occasions and celebrations and, as machine-made *kente* print, is popular around the globe.

Pastoralists and hunter-gatherers

The San, Khoikhoi, Nuer, and Oromo

Across Southern and East Africa, peoples hunted, foraged, herded livestock, and developed unique cultures. These groups have lived off the land for generations, but clashed with African and European empires.

Several semi-nomadic peoples have lived for centuries in the grasslands and deserts of Southern and East Africa. Their resourcefulness and perseverance is reflected in their long histories. One group, the San, are believed to be the oldest surviving culture in Africa, and their rock art stretches back over 20,000 years.

The San and Khoikhoi

The San people are Indigenous hunter-gatherer groups, whose origins can be traced back to the region that is now modern-day Botswana, as well as parts of Namibia, Angola, Zambia, Zimbabwe, and South Africa; their populations are still spread across these regions today. The various San communities speak different languages and practice different religions, but have much in common. The San way of life is based on hunting animals such as antelope with bow and arrow and gathering edible plants and insects. These peoples are customarily mobile, with small, egalitarian groups staying in lightweight shelters as they forage or gathering in longer-term habitations, especially near waterholes during the dry season.

The Khoikhoi are another Indigenous group from Southern Africa, with a distinct cultural and linguistic heritage from the San. They are believed to have originally inhabited the southwestern region of Africa, which includes modern-day South Africa, Namibia, and northern Botswana. Today, Khoikhoi communities live mainly in Namibia and South Africa. This people's way of life is based on herding and trading cattle, sheep, and goats.

In the last few thousand years, waves of Bantu-speaking peoples (see pp.36–37) spread into San and Khoikhoi lands in Southern Africa. However, both peoples remained widespread until European colonization intensified in the 18th and 19th centuries, when many were killed or displaced from the most productive lands. Some San and Khoikhoi remain dedicated to pastoral ways of life, while others work on farms or in cities.

◁ **Leather bag**
San bags are used to carry hunting equipment, food, charms, and tobacco. Animals are usually hunted and skinned by men, before the hide is sewn and decorated by women and men.

◁ **San village**
San gather outside a hut in Nyae Nyae Conservancy. This community-managed area in Namibia is a San ancestral heartland, home to several San villages.

The Nuer and Oromo

Like the Khoikhoi, the Nuer, who are believed to have originated in what is now central Sudan, built their society around cattle. Cattle products were used in everything from clothing to shields, with dung used as toothpaste and burned to keep away pests. As Arab peoples expanded into their homeland, the Nuer moved into the grassland and marshes of South Sudan and western Ethiopia, defeating and absorbing communities of a local people, the Dinka, as they went. In the early 20th century, the Nuer faced the imposition of British colonial control in northeast Africa. Since Sudan gained its independence in 1956, Nuer forces have been involved in the conflicts for South Sudan's independence (gained in 2011).

The Oromo are fellow East African pastoralists. In the 16th and 17th centuries, they migrated from southeastern Ethiopia, conquering territory until they occupied much of southern and central Ethiopia. While most Oromo in the south remained cattle herders, more settled agriculture was increasingly widespread in other parts of the country. Today, the Oromo are the largest ethnic group in Ethiopia, mostly practicing Islam or Christianity.

△ **Hunting bow**
This San bow would be used in conjunction with arrows sometimes tipped in diamphotoxin, a poison derived from beetle larvae.

▽ **Village scene**
An 18th-century Dutch depiction of a Khoikhoi village shows a group of dancers and musicians.

Mundari cattle camp, South Sudan
The Mundari people from South Sudan are descendants of the original settlers of the Nile Valley, who first domesticated animals and practiced agriculture at least 5,000 years ago. A species of long-horned cow called Ankole-Watusi forms the central focus of the Mundari people's lives, their culture, and their religion. Regarded as sacred, these animals bring social status and the possibility of getting married and starting a family, since dowries are fixed in units of cattle. While older people and maternal relatives often live in towns, younger members of the community usually reside in camps with the cattle, where they care for and graze the flock.

Mythology and folklore

Beliefs and legends in African cultures

In African societies—as in most cultures—mythology, stories, and ancient beliefs reveal much about how people viewed the origins of their world, and their place and role within it.

Myths can encode a civilization's values and contain profound symbolism, which is of deep importance to the society where they originated. This makes them much more than colorful stories documenting old beliefs and superstitions. Africa's history contains many mythologies formulated across different eras by widely diverse cultures.

Origin stories and supreme beings

Many cultures have their own narrative that explains how life began. It may involve a pantheon of gods or one supreme being. Ancient Egypt's origin stories describe the world as created from the tears, saliva, and other bodily fluids of the gods. These tales clearly symbolize fertility, birth, and growth. In the Egyptian pantheon of deities, gods and goddesses embody qualities, physical objects, or important moments in life such as war, death, love, fertility, the harvest, and wine.

The creation mythology of the Yoruba of West Africa involves a supreme being, Olodumare, who empowered a lesser deity named Obatala to create humans. In some versions of the myth, only Olodumare could animate Obatala's humans with the breath of life. Yoruba religion also recognized other deities (known as *orisha*). These include: Orunmila, counselor of the gods and god of wisdom, knowledge, and divination; Eshu, a trickster figure; Ogun, a god of war and iron; and Shango, a god of thunderstorms.

In Southern Africa, the mythology of the San people of the Cape region included belief in shape-shifting figures such as IKaggen, a kind of divine artisan responsible for creating and maintaining the universe. IKaggen could assume many forms, including an eland bull, a snake, and a caterpillar, but was usually a praying mantis. In one telling of his story, he created the moon by throwing one of his shoes into the sky.

Bantu-speakers inhabit much of Africa south of the Sahara. While Islam and Christianity are the dominant religions among them today, their faith was once based around ancestor veneration and the worship of tutelary deities (protector gods of specific places or professions). These Bantu-speakers believed in a supreme being, whose name varied from place to place, but they also consulted diviners for advice and help in spiritual matters.

Like the Bantu-speakers, the Asante of what is now Ghana also worshipped a supreme deity. His name was Nyame, though he was also sometimes called Onyankopon. He created all things and then separated himself from the human world, ascending heavenward in the tradition of sky-gods found in many other religions worldwide.

Animal legends

A variety of animals also play important roles in beliefs across African cultures. A common tale across the continent involves two creatures, often a lizard and a chameleon but sometimes a dog and a goat,

- Anansi sits at the center of the web
- Shaft is intricately carved
- Wood covered in gold leaf

◁ **Symbol of office**
On this palace official's staff from West Africa, the spider's web represents the trickster god Anansi. The spider is considered wise and cunning.

◁ **Spirit of the water**
This painted wooden figure shows Mami Wata, a water spirit who is feared and venerated in West, Central, and Southern Africa. The spirit represents wealth and success.

MYTHOLOGY AND FOLKLORE | 157

◁ **Brass fan**
Priestesses of Osun, the Yoruba goddess of beauty and fertility, carried brass fans in their rituals celebrating her power and authority.

Different birds are depicted

Snakes decorate the rim

Stylized palm leaves

Decorative carved handle

THE DOGON CREATION STORY

The creation myth of the Dogon people of Mali says that the supreme deity, Amma, created the first living creature, Nommo. Not content with being the sole living person, Nommo divided himself into four pairs of twins, from which the human race descended. In Dogon tradition, when a person dies their spirit returns to Amma after a ritual known as a *dama* is performed by masked dancers on stilts.

> "**Anansi**, the child of Nsia, the mother of Nyame, the **Sky-god**."
>
> AKAN/ASANTE DESCRIPTION OF ANANSI

and explains why humans are not immortal like the gods. The chameleon was sent to tell people that they would be allowed to live forever. But he was too slow and was overtaken by a lizard, who informed humans that the gods had decided to make them mortal after all. This was why the Zulu of Southern Africa regarded seeing a chameleon as a bad omen. Other animal-based fables involve trickster rabbits, gullible hippos, and helpful elephants delivering homilies on how to live good lives. In West Africa, the trickster spider god Anansi was the protagonist of a great many myths and legends.

Human spirits

Occasionally, real humans achieved legendary status. Chaminuka was a holy leader among the Zezuru, a branch of the Shona people of modern-day Zimbabwe. When he died in 1883, Chaminuka's spirit reportedly "spoke" through the mediums Mutota and Pasipamire. One of his prophecies that they channeled was the building of a large settlement "at Harare"—the city that is today Zimbabwe's capital.

Africa's myths and folklore bear witness to world views where the sacred and the secular are intertwined. Even today, old beliefs and mythologies continue to exert much power and influence.

◁ **Asante gold**
This pectoral badge, called an *akrafokonmu* ("soul washer's disk"), was worn for protection by members of the Asante court in modern-day Ghana. The Asante Empire became wealthy through the trading of gold mined from its territory.

4

European encounters

1440–1914

European encounters

Aside from the northern Mediterranean coast, large areas of Africa remained unknown to the rest of the world until the arrival of Portuguese explorers in the 15th century. Henry the Navigator and Bartolomeu Dias were among the first Europeans to sail along Africa's west coast, ushering in an era of European exploration that saw Portuguese mariners mapping the coastlines and hinterlands of Senegal, the Gambia, and Guinea between 1444 and 1447. In 1497–1498, their compatriot Vasco da Gama rounded the Cape of Good Hope and sailed along the eastern coast of Africa to India—looting Arab merchant ships and attacking the island of Mozambique along the way.

An unfair exchange of resources

The Portuguese, and the other Europeans who followed, were not interested in exploration for its own sake. What drew them to Africa—and convinced them to stay and establish settlements and set up trading agreements—was the continent's wealth of resources. Gold and rubber were especially sought after, but it was one "commodity" above all that defined the complex relationship between Europe and Africa: people. With Portugal, Spain, and Britain establishing empires in the Americas from the early 16th century, people were needed to work the farms and plantations. West Africa in particular (but also East Africa and the Sahara) had a plentiful supply of enslaved people who had been captured in intra-African conflicts and could readily be bought in exchange for weapons, gunpowder, iron, textiles, and other items. States such as the Dahomey and Asante empires in West Africa and the Sakalava Empire in Madagascar grew wealthy from the 16th to the 18th centuries based in part on slavery.

Farther south, in 1652 Dutch navigator Jan van Riebeeck set up a fresh food supply station in what would become Cape Town. When Britain seized the Cape Colony from the Dutch in 1806, replacing one foreign power with another, the tone was set for future European actions. Europeans became less interested in trading with Africans or building relationships with local leaders: the emphasis now was on appropriating resources and assuming political and military control of territory. Commerce gave way to colonialization.

At the Berlin Conference of 1884–1885, the main colonial nations met without the involvement of any African nations and agreed their spheres of influence on the continent. The resulting "Scramble for Africa" allowed imperialists such as King Leopold II of Belgium and Britain's Cecil Rhodes free rein to expand and exploit their nations' colonial holdings. Religion, too, became a tool of empire building, with missionaries criss-crossing the continent in order to spread a faith that sought to replace local beliefs with a "Europeanized" version of Christianity. The colonizers attempted to justify their actions—and their success in colonizing most of Africa—by claiming that they were bringing "civilization" to people they saw as "inferior." Consequently, between 1884 and 1914, the African continent was partitioned into protectorates, colonies, and free-trade areas, with the Europeans' control imposed by their superior weaponry and industrialized military might.

◁ **Portuguese traders depicted on a bronze plaque from Benin, 16th/17th century**

1444 Portuguese explorers round Cap-Vert, Africa's westernmost point

1456 Portugal's Luis Cadamosto reaches the Cabo Verde Islands, off Senegal

1488 Bartolomeu Dias becomes the first European to round the Cape of Good Hope

1497–1498 Vasco da Gama sails around Southern Africa to India

1560 Jesuit missionaries sail up the Zambezi River

EUROPEAN ENCOUNTERS | 161

Africa colonized

The inset map (right) shows the routes of the Portuguese explorers in the 15th century and areas of colonial presence in 1878 (see key, below). The map below shows the extent of colonialization in 1914, less than 40 years later.

KEY
- Colonized by Britain
- Colonized by France
- Colonized by Portugal
- Colonized by Spain
- Colonized by Belgium
- Colonized by Italy
- Colonized by Germany
- Independent state

Voyages sponsored by:
- Henry the Navigator (1418–60)
- Dias (1487–88)
- da Gama (1497–98)

▲ Portuguese explorer Vasco da Gama

▲ Map of West Africa, 16th century

▲ Southwest African queen Njinga (c. 1583–1663)

1652 Dutch mariner Jan van Riebeeck establishes a settlement on the site of Cape Town

1806 Britain seizes the Cape Colony from the Netherlands

1884–1885 Berlin Conference partitions Africa between the European nations

1908 Belgium annexes the Congo Free State from its own king, Leopold II, due to his misrule

1790 Scottish explorer Mungo Park travels up the Niger River

1871 Missing Scottish missionary and explorer David Livingstone is found alive at Lake Tanganyika

1879 The Zulu of Southern Africa defeat British forces at the Battle of Isandlwana

1914–1918 World War I and its aftermath lead to weakening of some colonial powers in Africa

The Atlantic slave trade

The largest-ever forced transoceanic migration

Between the 16th and 19th centuries, European traders and merchants transported 12–15 million enslaved Africans to a life of hardship and forced them to labor on sugar and tobacco plantations in the Americas.

In the mid-15th century, European mariners began to explore the world. The west coast of Africa was an early port of call; merchants and adventurers were drawn there by tales of vast gold reserves and the potential riches of unknown lands. By 1488, Portugal's Bartolomeu Dias had rounded Africa's southernmost tip, the Cape of Good Hope, opening for the first time a sea route from Europe to Asia; four years later, Christopher Columbus crossed the Atlantic to the Americas. The world was connected as never before, with unmapped territories opened up for commerce, settlement, development—and exploitation.

Origins of the slave trade

In this age of interconnectedness, West Africa emerged as a vital maritime hub between Europe, Asia, and the Americas. West Africa had ports, gold mines, supply stations—and what traders of the time saw as another valuable resource: people. As early as the 1480s, Portugal and the Kingdom of Kongo (see pp.182–183) had been exchanging guns for enslaved prisoners of war, who were then transported to the sugar plantations that Portugal had established on the island of São Tomé (off Gabon). Along with the Cabo Verde Islands (off Senegal), São Tomé became both a testing ground for the viability of a slave-labor-based agricultural system and a way-station for the transport of enslaved Africans.

When the huge territory of Brazil became a Portuguese colony in the 1530s, the demand for enslaved Africans increased. In addition to Kongo, West African states including Luanda, Benguela (both modern Angola), and Dahomey (modern Benin) began to trade enslaved Africans—mostly captives from local wars—for European luxuries, clothing, and weapons.

The trade in enslaved people intensified from the 1650s. Export crops, such as sugar and tobacco, were in high demand and the owners of plantations in the Americas and the Caribbean had a limitless need for enslaved African labor, especially after it was discovered that the Indigenous peoples the colonizers intended to enslave had no natural immunity to "Western" infections such as flu and scarlet fever. Some sources estimate that 95 percent of the Indigenous population died in the decades after the Europeans arrived.

Horror and abolition

West African coastal states contributed to the Atlantic slave trade, playing an important role in its structure. African leaders decided how many people they wanted to sell and their sex and age, compelling European traders to take often high quotas of women and children, despite their preference for men, viewed as the most profitable workers. Some 70 percent of women and 90 percent of children who entered the Americas between 1500 and 1800 were shipped from Africa. The journey from Africa to the Americas, known as the Middle Passage, was notoriously

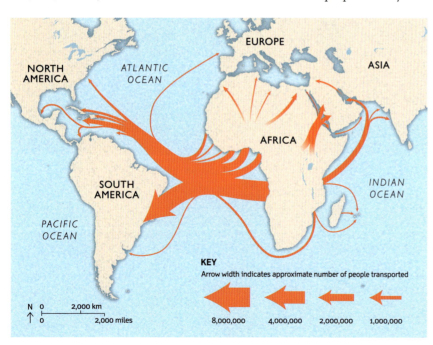

▽ **Uprooted peoples**
The largest numbers of Africans were trafficked to the Americas, with smaller, but significant, numbers to the Middle East, Asia, and Europe.

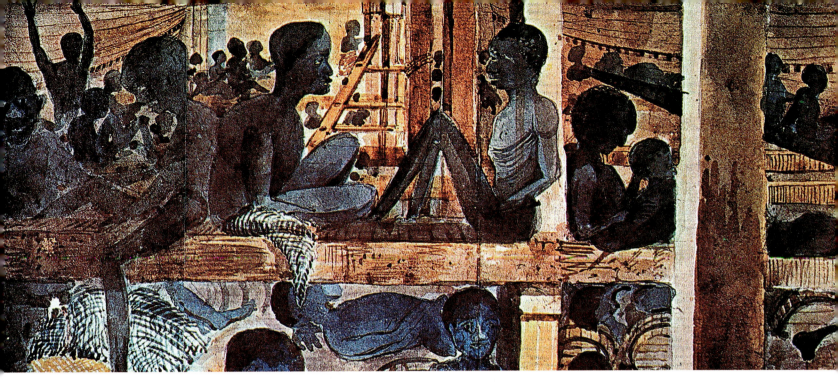

△ **Life below deck**
A watercolor of a Spanish ship captured by a British anti-slavery patrol in 1846 provides an eyewitness view of the cramped conditions on board.

dangerous. Enslaved Africans were shackled and packed in confined and squalid conditions. The voyage took between six and eight weeks and mortality rates were high, with frequent outbreaks of dysentery, smallpox, measles, flu, and scurvy.

By the early 18th century, religious groups, including Quakers, Methodists, and Baptists in the US and Britain, had begun to call for the slave trade to end. Enslaved people also put pressure on the colonial system by staging revolts both on ships and in the Americas. In 1803, Denmark abolished the trade, followed by Britain in 1807, the US in 1808, and most other countries by the 1830s. Although British, French, and US ships would patrol coasts to enforce the ban, compliance was not strict since slavery itself was not abolished until the 1860s.

While the end of the slave trade was a welcome development, it would ultimately lead to a new set of geopolitical dynamics. In 1884, the European powers met in Berlin to arrange the partitioning of Africa among each other (see pp.210–211). By 1914, these imperial powers had fully colonized the continent.

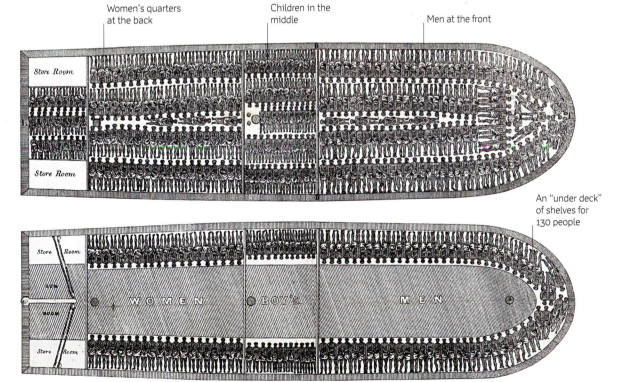

▷ **Ship plan**
This diagram of the *Brookes*, a British ship, was published by abolitionists in 1787. It shows how 454 enslaved Africans were crammed into the hold and transported to the Americas.

West African griots

In West Africa, *griots* are chroniclers of history, who for centuries have preserved the oral history, genealogies, and stories of people such as the Mandingo (Malinke), Fulani, Hausa, Songhai, and Tukulor. In African languages, they are known by many names, including *jeli* or *jali* in Mande (the Mandingo language) and *arokin* in Yoruba. Many *griots* sing their narratives, often providing their own instrumental accompaniment. Historically, they formed a specialized group, with marriage taking place only with other *griots*, and families of *griots* acting as advisors to kings and emperors. *Griots* would be called upon to settle disputes, and each village had its own *griots* to relate local histories.

Europe in Africa

Early intervention on the continent

European interference in Africa did not begin with 19th-century colonization. Initially based on trade, Europe's earlier presence in the continent developed into something more sinister and exploitative.

The first Europeans to reach Africa south of the Sahara were Portuguese mariners in the 1440s. Over the next four centuries, virtually every corner of the continent was mapped and studied by European explorers, merchants, and missionaries. In the process, they opened up Africa—not always willingly—to the trade in goods and humans, foreign settlement, the exploitation of its resources, the spread of Christianity, and, ultimately, imperialism.

The huge plantations in the Americas established by Europeans in the 16th century, growing crops such as sugar and cotton, required vast amounts of labor. By the late 19th century, 15 million Africans had been enslaved and shipped across the Atlantic (see pp.162–163) to work on these plantations. In the 19th century, the end of feudalism and the agricultural and industrial revolutions that followed saw the economies and the populations of Europe's nations grow, along with their need for new markets, products, raw materials, and resources. All were in plentiful supply in Africa.

European routes into Africa

The wealthy and hugely influential *Vereenigde Oost-Indische Compagnie* (VOC, or Dutch East India Company) was set up in 1602 to carry out trade activities in Asia. To make the journey from Europe to Asia easier, in 1652 the Dutch navigator Jan van Riebeeck established a supply and maintenance station for the VOC's ships at what would become Cape Town (see pp.168–169). This marked the beginning of Dutch involvement in South Africa that would spread from a small fortified settlement to subjugation, wars, land expropriation, and colonization across the country.

Although Britain's entry point into African affairs was via its active participation in the Atlantic slave trade, by the early 19th century it was using its opposition to the slave trade—which it had abolished in its own empire in 1807—as an excuse to increase its interference in Africa. To give the Royal Navy the bases it needed to stop British commercial vessels collecting enslaved people from West Africa, Britain took over parts of Sierra Leone, the Gambia, and the Gold Coast in 1808, 1816, and 1821 respectively. In addition to this, Britain had seized the Cape Colony, around the Cape of Good Hope in South Africa, from its trading rivals the Dutch in 1795. Within a century, Cecil Rhodes, a British mining magnate, had formed the British South Africa Company (BSAC) and pushed north from the Cape into what would become Rhodesia (modern-day Zimbabwe). In doing so, he took control of the region's rich reserves of gold, diamonds, and other minerals, and ultimately paved the way for the British government to exploit these resources.

Other European nations followed similar routes to greater involvement in Africa. France's trading relationships with North Africa began in the early 16th century, bringing the region within its sphere of influence by the start of the age of imperialism in the

△ **Triangular trade**
From the early 16th century, enslaved Africans were taken to the Americas to produce materials that were in turn transported to Europe and manufactured into goods. These goods were then transported to Africa and exchanged for more enslaved people.

▽ **Cultural exchange**
This 16th-century ivory salt cellar was carved in Benin, West Africa. It is possibly a depiction of the Portuguese merchant for whom it was made as a gift.

19th century. French merchants in West Africa set up similar arrangements. In Senegal, the trading post of Saint-Louis, established in 1659, gave France a foothold in Africa south of the Sahara. From here it extended its interference into Mauritania, Côte d'Ivoire, Niger, and elsewhere two centuries later.

Germany's presence in Africa began in 1682, when the then-independent state of Brandenburg-Prussia (Germany was not unified until 1871) founded two small settlements in modern-day Ghana, and established the Brandenburg African Company to explore business opportunities in the region.

Impact on African life and society

The Europeans' arrival in Africa had far-reaching consequences. European-introduced diseases such as cholera, yellow fever, meningitis, TB, measles, and smallpox decimated African populations. States unwilling or unable to trade produce for Western weaponry declined faster than those that did. South Africa's Zulu, for example, actively rejected the use of guns and rifles in favor of their habitual, but ultimately ineffective, spears and shields (see pp.206–207). Christian missionaries converted Africans from their Indigenous belief systems (see pp.204–205) by the millions, irrevocably changing the continent's religious landscape.

Europe's relationship with Africa before colonization saw many of the unequal power relationships, social changes, economic exploitations, and military interventions put in place that made imperialism, when it came, easier to impose and longer-lasting.

ENGLAND'S SLAVE-TRADING COMPANY

Set up in 1660, England's Royal African Company (RAC), whose emblem is shown here, was an early example of a state-endorsed commercial enterprise. It transported 187,697 people to the Americas, branding on the chest of each one the organization's initials.

△ **Commemorative box**
William IV, *Stadtholder* (leader) of the Dutch Republic, was given this presentation box by the Dutch West India Company (WIC) in 1749. It contained his letter of appointment as the WIC's Governor. Each finely carved detail depicts an aspect of the WIC's activities in Africa.

TOP VIEW — Enslaved people at a market | Figure representing the ivory trade | Real gold nugget embedded in lid | Figure representing panning for gold | Coat of arms of William IV | Ornamental *rocaille* carving in gold | Mercury, the god of trade, shown holding the company logo | Map of West African coast between Senegal and Angola | VIEW OF BASE | Side plaque depicts Dutch forts in West Africa | FULL VIEW

△ **New arrivals**
This 1680 work shows the Dutch fleet sailing into Table Bay—a far cry from the two ships Jan van Riebeeck arrived with in 1652.

Cape Town

One of South Africa's most historically important cities

South Africa's oldest and second-largest (after Johannesburg) city was founded in the mid-17th century. It grew from a humble Dutch naval supply station into a vibrant metropolis—albeit one with a troubled and contested history.

The Indigenous inhabitants of southern Africa were the Khoisan, an umbrella term covering the Khoikhoi and San people. As nomadic herders and hunter-gatherers, they moved with the seasons, their migrations based on a deep understanding of the land, its climate, water sources, vegetation, and animals. Their way of life was founded on a strong sense of community, with extended families often living together and an emphasis on the well-being of the group over the individual—important elements in furnishing feelings of belonging among people who were always in motion, rarely settling in towns or villages. Their vast territory covered modern South Africa, Namibia, Botswana, Zimbabwe, and Angola.

The Khoisan way of life would change forever on April 6, 1652, when the Dutch navigator Jan van Riebeeck arrived. The Dutch East India Company (see pp.166–167) had commissioned Van Riebeeck to establish a resupply station halfway along the route for ships making the long voyage between Europe and the East Indies. The Suez Canal would not be built until 1869, so European ships heading for Asia had to sail around Africa, navigating in the process the treacherous Cape of Good Hope, some 37 miles (60 km) along the coast from Cape Town.

◁ **Maritime map**
This nautical chart from 1752 shows the Cape of Good Hope region. The fort that would eventually evolve into Cape Town is indicated just north of Table Mountain.

▷ **Dressed to impress**
A young Khoikhoi woman wears a fur cape, beaded skirt, anklets, necklaces, bracelets, and earrings, in a colored woodcut by Belgian artist Auguste Wahlen.

"!ke e: /xarra //ke [diverse people unite]"

MOTTO ON THE COAT OF ARMS OF SOUTH AFRICA, WRITTEN IN THE EXTINCT KHOISAN LANGUAGE, |XAM

Van Riebeeck set up a small market garden with the intention of supplying fresh fruit and vegetables to passing ships. In doing so, he founded the first permanent European settlement in South Africa. Before long, the Khoisan were trading their livestock in return for European products, including tobacco, alcohol, and worked iron. Local figures such as the Khoi chieftain Autshumao acted as translators and intermediaries—and, in the case of his niece, Krotoa, served as ambassadors and even peace negotiators in times of conflict.

By 1654, several Dutch farmers had built farms, van Riebeeck's small market garden expanding into something much larger and more commercially focused. Instead of only looking outward, seeing their small harbor colony as a stopover en route to Asia, the Dutch turned inward, looking for the ways and means to exploit the territory inland from the Cape.

A disputed land

The encroachment of Dutch farmers and settlers into Khoisan pastures and hunting grounds restricted these nomadic people's lifestyle and made conflict inevitable. This came in 1659, when the Khoisan stopped trading cattle with the Dutch and tripled the price of other livestock. In retaliation, the Dutch confiscated Khoisan cattle—initiating the First Khoi-Dutch War, which ended the following year with defeat for the Khoisan. In 1670, the Khoisan chieftain Gonnema, whose people were known as the Cochoqua, attacked Dutch settlers who had looted the Cochoqua's cattle. This became the prelude to the Second Khoi-Dutch War (1673–1677), resulting in another Khoisan defeat. Both conflicts had disastrous consequences for the Khoisan. The Dutch disempowered influential clan chiefs and forced the Khoisan people into the less productive lands of the interior.

This "internal exile" of the Khoisan paved the way for further Dutch settlement and intensive agriculture, which was sustained by slavery. Britain temporarily annexed the Cape colony in 1795, and again more permanently in 1806. The British ended the slave trade the following year and this, along with the large influx of British settlers into the region, antagonized the Dutch. In 1836, the Cape's Dutch inhabitants embarked on the Great Trek, a mass migration north to escape British rule. In doing so, they intruded on both Khoisan and Zulu lands, displacing Indigenous peoples and fomenting unrest. Cape Town, meanwhile, thrived. Between 1891 and 1901 its population grew from 67,000 to 171,000, and on May 31, 1910, Cape Town became the capital of the new Union of South Africa.

As a result of its location and the circumstances of its foundation, Cape Town became a highly cosmopolitan city. Intermarriages between European settlers; enslaved people; the Khoisan; and other, smaller groups such as the Xhosa people of the Eastern Cape region, produced what, for its time, was a multiracial and uniquely heterogeneous population.

▷ **Settled community**
Not all Khoisan were migratory. Some lived in *kraal* (small villages), as captured in this c. 1835 lithograph. Note the tethered giraffe in the foreground.

Madagascar

An island at the crossroads

Lying off the coast of modern-day Mozambique, the island of Madagascar was well situated in the Indian Ocean to facilitate trade between East Africa and Asia from medieval times onward.

First settled in the early Middle Ages, Madagascar had a population of ethnically mixed Austronesian (Asian) and Bantu-speaking (African) peoples divided into distinct groups. Among these were the Sakalava ("people of the long valley") from western Madagascar. Seminomadic pastoralists, they kept large zebu (humped cattle) livestock before developing into skilled seafarers and, by the early 16th century, they emerged as the island's dominant group under their king, Andriamisara.

◁ **By royal appointment**
Also known as "the Great," Radama I, depicted in a painting from 1905, was the first king of Madagascar recognized by a European state.

Sakalava dynasties

The source of Sakalava power was the cattle and enslaved people they exchanged for guns with Omani and European traders. These weapons, which no other Madagascan peoples possessed, allowed Andriamisara, and later his son Andriandahifotsy, to assert Sakalava dominance across the island. But the Sakalava did not favor a centralized power structure. Instead, they divided areas into separate kingdoms. Some, like Menabe and Boina, ruled by Andriandahifotsy's sons Andriamanetiarivo and Andriamandisoarivo respectively, were relatively strong. Others, however, proved too small and weak to withstand the attentions of peoples that emerged as rivals around the mid-1750s. These peoples included the Betsimisaraka and the Merina—who had begun to transact with overseas traders, giving them access to firearms.

Under their leader Ramaromanompo (r. 1712–1754), the Betsimisaraka ("the many inseparables") from eastern Madagascar gained strength through alliances with local leaders and conquest of rivals. But they—and the Sakalava—would be subdued by the Merina ("the elevated ones"), who emerged out of the central highland plateau. Their regional power base grew in the 16th century, led by their queen, Rafohy. This growth continued until King Andrianampoinimerina (r. 1787–1810) established the Merina as a preeminent force.

European intrusion

Merina power reached its greatest extent under Andrianampoinimerina's son, Radama I. Just 18 years old when he came to the throne in 1810, Radama introduced Westernizing policies and welcomed in Christian missionaries. His skeptical attitude toward his people's religious practices, especially their devotion to rituals involving *sampy* (sacred amulets), angered the Merina's conservative elites.

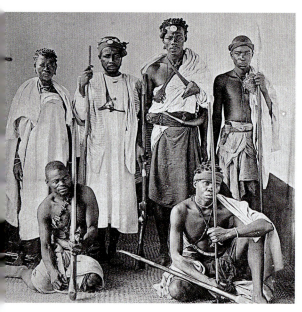

▽ **Men at arms**
The Sakalava, photographed here c. 1900, dominated Madagascar for around 150 years. They were superseded first by the Merina and then the French.

> "**Ny ranomasina no valapariako** [The border of my rice fields **is the sea**]."
>
> KING ANDRIANAMPOINIMERINA ON HIS AMBITION TO UNITE MADAGASCAR

- Elongated wooden poles, called *tandotrano*, indicate aristocratic houses
- Steep hillside on which Antsahatsiroa, a wealthy suburb of the capital, Antananarivo, is built

Keen to extend his kingdom, Radama embarked on several wars of conquest, on some of which he was accompanied by James Hastie, a British government civil agent in Madagascar. Radama's willingness to involve Britain in his country's affairs was not universally popular among his people. Nevertheless, Radama's pro-Western, Anglophone stance led to Britain recognizing him as king of Madagascar in 1817, when the two nations signed an alliance. Britain then supplied Radama with the arms and military training that allowed him to conquer two-thirds of the island. He abolished the slave trade, established schools and churches, and codified the Malagasy language in writing for the first time.

Radama died in 1828, aged 36, revered as a military genius and great nation builder. He was succeeded by his wife, Ranavalona I (see pp.172–173), whose opposition to Radama's Westernization was met with aggressive European interference, especially from France. In 1896, the French suppressed the last remnants of Indigenous power and Madagascar became a French colony until 1960.

△ **Iconic construction**
Madagascar's architecture of tall, sloping roofs, shown here in a photograph from 1856, during the reign of Queen Ranavalona I, is unique in Africa. It resembles styles in Borneo, from where Madagascar's earliest settlers arrived.

Royal carriage
A 19th-century illustration shows Ranavalona I being transported through the crowds on a *filanzana*, a seat supported by two long poles.

Ranavalona I

Powerful absolute ruler of Madagascar

Ranavalona I (r. 1828–1861) was a ruthless and autocratic leader who suppressed her own subjects and made use of forced labor. But she presented a fierce and effective resistance to colonial interests in Madagascar.

Little is known for certain about the early life of Ranavalona I, but most sources agree she was born Rabodoandrianampoinimerina in 1778 in Merina (see pp.170–171). Her father saved the life of King Andrianampoinimerina (r. 1787–1810), whose uncle plotted to kill him. In gratitude, the king adopted Ranavalona into the royal family and she later married his son, the future king Radama I. Their marriage was childless—although Ranavalona later had a child with Madagascar's prime minister—so when Radama became king, he had no children to succeed him.

After Radama's early death in 1828, Ranavalona seized power from the rightful heir, the son of Radama's eldest sister, and became the absolute ruler of most of Madagascar and the first female ruler of the kingdom of Merina since its founding in 1540.

Sovereignty and independence

Ranavalona's reign was marked by efforts to protect Madagascar from European encroachment. In 1829, she repelled a French naval attack in the north of the island, albeit assisted by an outbreak of malaria among foreign forces. Thereafter, she stepped up her policies of self-sufficiency and isolationism. She also restricted missionary activities, banned her subjects from practicing Christianity, and engaged in wars to expand her realm over the island. According to some scholars, she made significant use of the practice of *fanompoana* (forced labor). In 1857, she foiled a plot by her son, Rakoto, among others, to topple her from power.

Following Ranavalona's peaceful death in 1861, aged around 83, Madagascar was governed by a series of weak rulers and entered a period of decline. It was declared a French colony on August 6, 1896.

△ **Trial of the conspirators**
This French engraving from 1861 depicts the trial of those who plotted Ranavalona's overthrow. The Queen executed many of the locals who were involved and banished the Europeans.

△ **Coronation gown**
Despite her hostility to European influences, Ranavalona's striking coronation gown is believed to have been designed by a French tailor.

> "I will **not cede** the **thickness of one hair of my realm!**"
>
> — RANAVALONA I

1778 Ranavalona is born in the kingdom of Merina

1828 Ranavalona ascends to the throne following the death of Radama I

1829 French forces launch an unprovoked attack on Madagascar

1831 A ban on Christian baptism and marriages is introduced

1835 Ranavalona bans her subjects from practicing Christianity

1840 Persecution of the Christians begins

1857 Ranavalona thwarts a plot by her son Rakoto to dethrone her, but pardons him

1861 Ranavalona dies and is succeeded by Rakoto (Radama II)

Kingdoms of the Great Lakes: Bunyoro and Buganda

Power and privilege in East Africa

Among the many kingdoms in the region of the Great Lakes, Bunyoro and Buganda were the two most significant. These two powerful states dominated the region through trade and their absolute rulers.

The Great Lakes are scattered across the East African Rift, a huge geological scar that first appeared 25 million years ago. The region contains some of the world's largest and deepest lakes, including Lake Victoria, Lake Tanganyika, and Lake Malawi, and its abundance of water, fertile volcanic soil, and good climate made it an excellent incubator for emerging civilizations. These include the Kitara Empire of c. 1200 BCE–900 CE from which successor states including Bunyoro and Buganda emerged. Today, the area comprises Uganda, Burundi, Rwanda, the Democratic Republic of the Congo, Ethiopia, Kenya, Tanzania, Malawi, Zambia, and Mozambique.

The kingdom of Bunyoro

One of the most successful Great Lakes civilizations was the kingdom of Bunyoro, northwest of Lake Victoria in present-day Uganda. Founded around the 12th century, Bunyoro was at its height from the 16th to the 19th centuries, dominating the region's lucrative salt trade through its control of the extensive Kibiro saltworks on the shores of Lake Mwitanzige

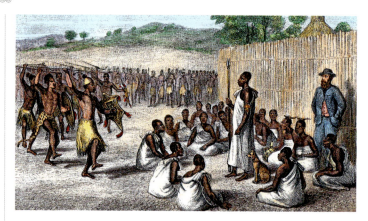

△ **On parade**
This European woodcut from 1864 depicts *Kabaka* Mutesa I. Under Mutesa, Christian missionaries, Muslim preachers, and Western commercial interests made inroads into Buganda.

(formerly Lake Albert). Bunyoro's metallurgy was also highly sought after and it traded heavily in ivory, cattle, and crops. Politically, Bunyoro's kings held absolute power and they personally appointed the chiefs that governed each of the state's provinces.

The state went into decline from the late 18th century, when the neighboring kingdom of Buganda occupied two of its provinces, while another province, Toro, seceded and took the money-making saltworks with it. Bunyoro also lost its dominance of the ivory trade in the mid-19th century. A few decades later, when Bunyoro's *omukama*, or king, Chwa II Kabalega tried to resist imperial incursions by the British and

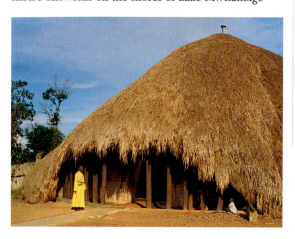

◁ **Royal resting place**
The Kasubi Tombs, in Kampala, Uganda, contain the remains of four Bugandan 19th- and 20th-century kings. The site is an important religious center for the Buganda people today.

King of Bunyoro
In this photo from 1922, Bunyoro's king Duhaga II is flanked by two chiefs. The chinstraps of their ceremonial beaded caps are fringed with "beards" of colobus monkey fur.

the Ottoman Empire, he was overthrown and, in 1899, exiled to the Seychelles. Bunyoro was forcibly incorporated into the British Empire, subjected to what has been called a "scorched earth" policy. The guerrilla war against the British, which had begun in 1894, led to widespread famine and the deaths of an estimated three-quarters of Bunyoro's population.

Power struggles in Buganda

Bunyoro's neighbor Buganda was located along the northern shore of Lake Victoria. A powerful local chief named Kato Kintu founded it in the 14th century and became the first *kabaka*, or king. Rulers relied on a first minister, or *katikkiro*, to administer the state. On the death of each *kabaka*, Buganda's clans would often battle for the throne. It was not unknown for a *kabaka* to murder his brothers and other potential rivals in order to secure his position.

Despite Buganda becoming the Great Lakes region's largest state and strongest military power, its constitutional instability would ultimately contribute to its decline. When in 1884 the *kabaka* Mutesa I died, Britain took advantage of the resulting political infighting to impose its authority. It forced through the Buganda Agreement of 1900, which formalized British control and made the kingdom a British protectorate. Buganda's economy expanded during the colonial period when it became a producer of coffee and cotton—although most of the resulting wealth was exported to the UK.

After Uganda won its independence in 1962, four monarchies in the country—Bunyoro, Buganda, Toro, and Busoga—were abolished in 1967, but were reinstated in 1993 following civil unrest. The kingdoms still exist, albeit in reduced states and with their monarchs occupying largely ceremonial roles.

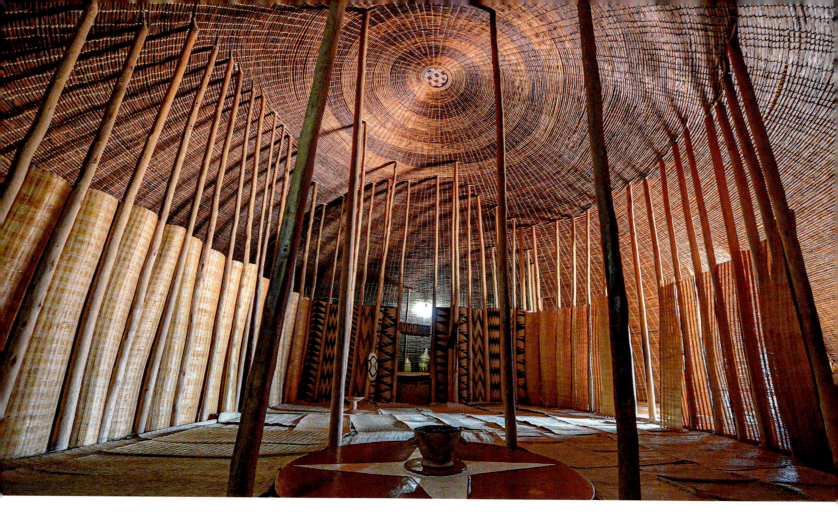

△ **The King's Palace**
This thatched, beehive-shaped building is a modern reconstruction of the palace of the king of Rwanda. It is the centerpiece of the King's Palace Museum in Nyanza, southern Rwanda.

Rwanda and Burundi

Countries with a shared history

The Hutu and Tutsi have coexisted in Africa's Great Lakes for centuries. Both groups were part of the kingdoms of Rwanda and Burundi from about the 15th to the 17th centuries, but colonialism stirred tensions that lasted into independence.

The first known inhabitants of the landlocked nations of Rwanda and Burundi, the hunter-gatherer Twa people, settled in the forests of the Great Lakes region before 3000 BCE. From around the 5th century CE, the hills and high plains of Rwanda and Burundi received waves of southbound Hutu migrants, most of whom were small-scale farmers. The Twa were pushed to the margins when minor Hutu kingdoms began to emerge in the 12th century, before the Tutsi arrived from the north around the 15th century. The martial Tutsi, whose herds of distinctive, long-horned ankole cattle grazed large areas of land, then began to dominate.

The Kingdom of Rwanda

A centralized state, the kingdom of Rwanda, emerged in the 15th or 16th century. Some believe its roots go back to the ancient godlike Tutsi leader Gihanga I. Over the years, a succession of kings, or *mwami*, expanded Rwanda from its beginnings near the modern-day capital, Kigali. The kingdom followed a broadly feudal system (the *ubuhake*) in which Tutsi landowners offered protection and land to Hutu farmers in exchange for food and labor. The Twa were mistreated and

◁ **Inyambo cattle**
Prized in Rwanda and Burundi, long-horned ankole cows are referred to as *inyambo*, "the cattle of kings," because of their close ties and importance to royalty, wealth, and status.

considered low status. This structure, with a Tutsi aristocracy and Hutu vassals, lasted for centuries, although there was social mobility, including marriages between Tutsi, Hutu, and Twa people. Over time, the state became more unified, with a justice system and a grain supply network controlled by the king. Under Kigeli IV (r. 1853–1895), the kingdom reached its greatest extent—which still forms Rwanda's borders today.

Social relationships in Burundi

The kingdom of Burundi (or Urundi) was established by Ntare I in the late 17th century. His family became known as the *ganwa*, an ancestral group considered distinct from the Tutsi and the Hutu. Between 1796 and 1850, Ntare IV doubled Burundi's territory by conquering neighboring states, and strengthened his power by punishing disobedient local chiefs. The Hutus and Tutsis shared a common language but the Tutsi also wielded power here, although the social contract (or *ubugabire*) that governed relationships seems to have been more equitable than Rwanda's *ubuhake*.

German and Belgian rule

The hilly terrain and relatively stable governance of Rwanda and Burundi meant incursions by Europeans were limited. However, the Berlin Conference of 1884–1885 (see pp.210–211) designated the region part of German East Africa. When King Kigeli IV died in 1895, there was a scramble for the throne, which the German colonialists took advantage of, increasing their influence over Rwanda. In Burundi, Germany forced King Mwezi Gisabo to sign a treaty submitting to its authority in 1903. During World War I, Germany was forced to cede both colonies to Belgium, which introduced a divide-and-rule policy, sponsoring the dominant Tutsi minority as allies who could

rule at the expense of the Hutu. In Burundi, Hutu farmers staged a series of uprisings, which Belgium suppressed. Relations between the Hutus and Tutsis had been largely peaceful in the precolonial era but, under increasing repression, the Hutu sought change.

△ **Royal ceremony**
King Yuhi V of Rwanda (center) is pictured in Kigali around 1930. In 1931, he was deposed by Belgian administrators and replaced by his son, Mutara III.

Independence and conflict

Nationalist feelings grew and in a referendum in 1960, the Hutus elected Hutu representatives and rejected the Tutsi monarchy, leading to Rwanda and Burundi gaining independence in 1962. However, tensions mounted and Tutsi groups led attacks in 1964 and 1990 in Rwanda. In 1994, soldiers and militia murdered around 800,000 Tutsi, moderate Hutu, and Twa in the Rwandan genocide. Efforts at reconciliation have made progress, but the scars remain. In Burundi, Mwambutsa IV became the head of state in 1962 but after a coup in 1966, instability has continued. Burundi became a republic that was effectively a military dictatorship, and conflicts in 1972 and 1993 led to the genocide of thousands of Hutu and Tutsi. The tensions stoked by colonizing powers remain, and Burundi regularly ranks as the poorest nation in Africa.

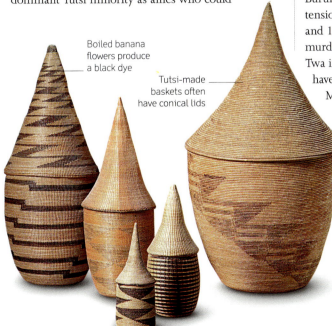

Boiled banana flowers produce a black dye

Tutsi-made baskets often have conical lids

◁ **Woven baskets**
These miniature grass baskets from Rwanda and Burundi were made in the first half of the 20th century. They were usually crafted by Tutsi women.

The Kingdom of Dahomey

Nation of the Fon people of Benin

Founded in about 1600 on the Abomey plain in present-day Benin, the Kingdom of Dahomey grew to become a major West African power, and an important center in the Atlantic slave trade.

△ **King of Dahomey**
King Ghezo, who ruled from 1818–1859, expanded Dahomey's military forces and won its independence from the Oyo Empire.

At the turn of the 17th century, a coalition of Fon peoples founded a nation on the inland Abomey plain of present-day Benin. However, the area lacked resources and was not on any trade routes. International trade along the coastal regions, by contrast, particularly in enslaved people, increased during the 16th century. West Africa provided European traders with a ready supply of labor for their colonies in the Americas. The Allada and Whydah groups on the coast prospered from providing enslaved people, captured from other groups. The Fon built a military force that could protect their people from exploitation and push south to profit from the lucrative Euro-American trade.

Expansion and interference

The Kingdom of Dahomey, as it became, developed a sophisticated, militaristic society, and over the next century expanded its empire: by the 1720s it had conquered the coastal kingdoms of Allada and Whydah, important ports for the Atlantic slave trade. As a major supplier of enslaved people, captured in its conquests and in raids on neighboring countries, Dahomey had to defend itself from attack by the powerful Oyo Empire to the west. Unable to completely resist the Oyo forces, Dahomey remained an autonomous nation, but was made a tributary state of the Oyo Empire in 1730.

Nevertheless, the kingdom flourished, and its king, Agaja, instituted reforms to the administrative system, and introduced the Annual Customs, a festival with military parades and Vodun ceremonies, including human sacrifice. Dahomey expanded while the slave trade increased through the 18th century, but it was not until 1827 that King Ghezo freed his country from the Oyo Empire.

Soon, however, he faced British forces, who blockaded Dahomey's Atlantic ports to end the slave trade. Ghezo eventually gave in to some of Britain's demands, ceasing the supply of enslaved people and ending human sacrifice, but he resisted pressure to adopt Christianity and give up the Indigenous Vodun religion.

European interest in the region continued and in 1892 France invaded Dahomey and won control of the kingdom in 1894, incorporating it into the colony of French Dahomey in 1904. It finally regained independence as the Republic of Dahomey in 1960, later becoming the Republic of Benin.

▷ **Royal procession**
In this 20th-century copper and wood model, a Fon king is carried in his hammock in a procession of musicians and attendants.

Flintlock musket

Child soldier

△ **Female fighting force**
The female soldiers of Dahomey, known as the *Mino*, are pictured with male warriors in a French newspaper in the 1890s. Originating as the King's bodyguard in the 18th century, the *Mino* were recognized as a permanent fighting force during the reign of King Ghezo.

Njinga Ana de Sousa Mbande
Queen Njinga used her recently adopted Christian names to impress the Portuguese, but she also asserted her equality with them by proudly wearing the finest Ndongo clothing, jewels, and feathers—as this European portrait shows.

Njinga Mbande

A warrior queen

Regarded today as the "Mother of Angola," Queen Njinga led the Mbundu people of Ndongo and Matamba in resistance against Portuguese colonization from the 1620s until her death in 1663.

Born into the royal family of Ndongo, in present-day Angola, Njinga Mbande grew up at a time when European powers, notably the Portuguese, were seeking to expand their lucrative slave trade. Her father became *ngola* (the root of the name Angola and "ruler" in the local Kimbundu language) and ensured she was schooled in government, diplomacy, the military, and the Portuguese language.

In 1617, Njinga's brother Mbandi succeeded their father. Mbandi was a tyrannical ruler, killing anyone he suspected of being a rival, even members of his family. Njinga fled to neighboring Matamba, but Mbandi, who was inept and lacked Njinga's diplomatic skills, recalled her to Ndongo in 1621, to act as ambassador to the Portuguese Governor in Luanda. With her Portuguese, and having been baptized as a Christian to gain respect from the Europeans, she asserted Ndongan independence, and negotiated an end to hostilities.

Ngola Njinga

After Mbandi's death in 1624, Njinga became *ngola*, despite opposition to the idea of a female ruler. The Portuguese took advantage of this unrest, renewing the fight for control of Ndongo. Njinga had hoped to regain the territory lost by her brother to neighboring states and the Portuguese, but instead was forced out of Ndongo, and replaced by a Portuguese puppet ruler. Undeterred, she returned to Matamba, where she became ruler, and consolidated her forces.

Meanwhile, Portugal was at war with the Dutch, who took Luanda in 1641. Njinga saw an opportunity, and entered an alliance with the Dutch, which enabled her to regain much of Ndongo. However, the Portuguese retook Luanda and the Dutch withdrew. In 1656, Njinga negotiated a peace treaty with the Portuguese that recognized Njinga as *ngola* of Matamba and Ndongo in return for concessions to the Portuguese for their slave trade. Njinga set up trade routes into Central Africa, welcomed formerly enslaved people, and set a precedent for Angolan resistance to colonization.

△ **Leading an army**
Queen Njinga is shown at the head of a Matamban military unit, armed with a bow and arrow. This was during her campaign to regain Ndongo from the Portuguese.

▷ **A powerful diplomat**
Njinga is negotiating with the Portuguese Governor in this engraving. She is shown using one of her servants as a seat to avoid the humiliation of standing throughout the meeting.

1621 Njinga appointed ambassador to the Portuguese by her brother, *Ngola* Mbandi

1624 After the death of her brother, Njinga becomes *ngola* of Ndongo

1626 The Portuguese declare war on Njinga

1628 Njinga forced to retreat from Ndongo

1631 Mbundu invade neighboring Matamba

1641 Njinga makes an alliance with the Dutch after they oust the Portuguese from Luanda

1656 Njinga signs treaty with the Portuguese, who recognize her as the ruler of Ndongo and Matamba

1663 After Njinga's death, her sister Mukambu assumes the throne

The Kingdom of Kongo

Rise and fall of an African superpower

One of premodern Africa's largest and wealthiest states, Kongo dominated much of western Central Africa for centuries, before succumbing to internal tensions in the face of Portuguese imperial interest.

△ **A Catholic king**
King Afonso I (r. 1509–1542), depicted in an 18th-century Portuguese illustration, opened Kongo to Portuguese and Christian influence.

The Kingdom of Kongo was a collection of states that came together around 1390 under the chieftain Lukeni lua Nimi. The territory he and his successors ruled over covered much of present-day Angola, the Republic of Congo, and the Democratic Republic of the Congo. Although he was advised by a council of aristocratic elders known as the *mwisikongo*, the king, or *mwene*, exercised absolute power. Authority was administered across his vast domain by local governors, part of whose role it was to collect tributes to the king in the form of ivory, grain, palm wine, and animal skins.

This system of government helped guarantee Kongo's stability, as did its trade in ivory, cow skins, salt, raffia cloth, gold, copper, and enslaved people. The common currency in Kongo and other African nations was cowrie shells, known as *nzimbu*. Neighboring states, such as Ndongo and Matamba (in modern Angola), were not part of Kongo but very much within its sphere of influence.

Christianity, culture, and conquest

A new era began when the Portuguese explorer Diogo Cão arrived in 1483. Within 10 years, Kongo's king Nzinga a Nkuwu had converted to Christianity, taking the name João I. This "Europeanization" continued when the Kongolese titles for regional leaders were abolished in favor of labels such as "Duke," "Marquis," and "Count." João I's son and successor Afonso I established Christianity as the state religion. He claimed that a heavenly vision of the cross, St. James, and the Virgin Mary had inspired him to victory at the Battle of Mbanza Kongo in 1509, in which he defeated his brother and rival claimant to the throne, Mpanzu a Kitima. Kongo's version of Christianity fused Catholic beliefs with Kongolese cosmology, such as using the Kongolese term for the supreme being, Nzambi a Mpungu, instead of "God"; in devotional art, too, Jesus was often represented as an African. At the same time, local beliefs remained, and some Kongolese rejected Christianity, seeing it as the means by which the Portuguese exercised social control.

Afonso I's death in 1542 initiated a period of disputed successions and instability. This ended with the accession of Alvaro I in 1568, supported by the Portuguese who, in return, were granted concessions and land in the province of Luanda (modern Angola). This gave the Portuguese a base from which to pursue their imperial ambitions, most notably the seizure of Kongo's copper mines and greater access to the region's slave trade. European interference escalated over the next decades, leading to several Kongo-Portuguese wars—the first of which ended in defeat for Portugal at the Battle of Mbanda Kasi in January 1623.

◁ **Cultural cross-currents**
The central section of this triple crucifix dates from the 16th–17th centuries. The Jesus figure displays the "Africanized" features characteristic of Kongolese Christianity.

> "**Each day**, traders are kidnapping **our people**."
>
> AFONSO I IN A LETTER TO THE KING OF PORTUGAL, 1526

THE KINGDOM OF KONGO | 183

Four figures at the top—two holding daggers, two clasping their hands in prayer

The fortunes of the Kongolese and the Portuguese fluctuated over the next half century, complicated by the arrival and interference of Dutch colonial adventurers from the mid-1620s. The three sides variously fought alongside and against each other in a series of shifting alliances—while Kongo's leaders were at the same time battling factional infighting between two branches of the royal family known as the Kimpanzu and Kinlaza. In 1670, Kongo's troubles came to a head when the Portuguese invaded Soyo, a powerful Kongolese province intent on declaring its independence. When the Soyo army defeated the Portuguese at the Battle of Kitombo in October that year, the consequences were far-reaching. Although the battle led to the Portuguese withdrawing from Kongo's affairs for 200 years, it only weakened the kingdom: Kongo was at that moment mired in civil war and did not welcome the emergence of a confident, militarily successful Soyo.

A disunited kingdom

By the early 20th century, Kongo was still nominally ruled by monarchs, but the kingdom had disintegrated into its constituent states, with local leaders and foreign trading corporations in control. In 1862, civil unrest in Kongo led its king, Pedro V, to ask the Portuguese for help. In return, he was forced to submit Kongo to Portugal as a vassal state. Following a rebellion in 1914, Portugal formally converted the state into a colony, its kings little more than figureheads. Portugal had already detached parts of southwestern Kongo as part of its Angola holdings in 1885, and that same year Belgium incorporated part of eastern Kongo into the Congo Free State (renamed the Belgian Congo in 1908). These developments saw the region subjected to a new phase of imperial entanglement (see pp.212–213 and pp.248–249).

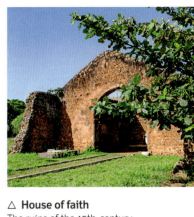

△ **House of faith**
The ruins of the 15th-century Cathedral of the Holy Savior of Congo stand in Kongo's capital, São Salvador. To encourage the adoption of Christianity, King Afonso built churches on existing holy sites.

Carved pattern echoes Kongolese textile designs

Four figures at the base form the "legs" of the knife holder

▷ **Ivory souvenir**
From the 16th century, Portuguese sailors commissioned Kongolese craftsmen to create objects to send home, like this skillfully carved ivory knife case, with lid, featuring a variety of figures.

Base identifies this as a display item

> "He who **spoke falsely** or bore **false witness** [before the *mangaaka*] **should die**."
>
> R. E. DENNETT, BRITISH TRADER

Mangaaka power figure
Divine protection—or retribution

In western Central Africa, *nkisi makondo* are wooden human-shaped sculptures imbued with spiritual power. When Europeans encroached into the Kingdom of Kongo in the late 19th century (see pp.182–183), they posed a threat to the authority of Kongo's leaders, which led the Kongolese to respond in the form of *mangaaka*, or "power figures," an addition to the many types of *nkisi makondo*. Often more than 3 ft (1 m) high, *mangaaka* represented a being with divine authority, able to impose social order and justice. Priests used them in rituals to resolve disputes and dispense punishments: to go against the judgment of the *mangaaka* was to invite terrible retribution.

Creation and preparation
To create *mangaaka*, carvers would work with a *nganga*, or spiritual specialist, who provided advice about the careful preparation that was needed before the figure could be activated, or imbued with its full power to protect or destroy. Made from weather-resistant hardwood, the figures were often placed outdoors.

The head was the most carefully carved part, its eyes usually inlaid with ceramic tiles with iron nails for pupils. The carvers used tools of hand-forged iron, with stone flakes, clamshells, and abrasive leaves to create the finishing touches. Hands on hips and leaning forward, the *mangaaka* was depicted with the attributes of a chief, such as a raffia *mpu* or headdress, a long beard, and raffia armbands. The lower part was less well defined but a cavity was sculpted in the abdomen, coated with a layer of resin, into which sacred objects would be placed. Ritual objects were also hidden behind the eyes, and the figure coated in black pigment, with details picked out in red or white.

Symbol of resistance
Once the *mangaaka* was complete, the *nganga* activated it and pronounced its judgments. Each time a judgment was made, the *nganga* hammered an iron object, such as a nail, into the wood, most often near the abdominal cavity, the center of the figure's spiritual power. These sharp objects included blades, and even fragments of bullets or musket parts.

The Yombe people from Kongo who created the *mangaaka* hoped the figures would protect them from intruders. The *mangaaka* became powerful symbols of resistance to the Europeans, who were therefore anxious to remove them, sending out expeditions for this purpose. A naval party from the British anti-slavery vessel HMS *Archer* was responsible for the first recorded seizure of a *mangaaka*, in 1865. Those *mangaaka* that survived ended up in foreign museums and private collections, but, before they were taken, the *nganga* seem to have ritually deconsecrated them, as none survive with the original sacred objects intact.

▷ **Striking artistry**
This 19th-century *mangaaka* is 4 ft (118 cm) tall. Its clothing and posture were intended to suggest divine power and strike fear into those who transgressed against the moral codes of Yombe society.

Nails are some of the 380 iron objects hammered into the figure

MANGAAKA POWER FIGURE | 185

Mpu chief's hat

Ceramic eyes are inlaid with a pupil made of iron

Remains of fixing for long beard

Abdominal cavity for sacred objects

Hands on hips and forward-leaning posture projects fearless authority

Wooden base carved with power symbols

Armband carved in imitation of raffia adornments worn by chiefs

The Sultanate of Zanzibar

An Arabian outpost in East Africa

From the 18th century, Zanzibar, now part of Tanzania, was controlled by the Sultanate of Oman. The island developed into such an important commercial center that it eventually became the sultanate's capital.

△ **Visionary leader**
The Omani leader Sayyid Said recognized Zanzibar's potential as a commercial and trading center. "I am nothing but a merchant," he once said—with approval rather than sorrow.

Situated on the southeast corner of the Arabian Peninsula, Oman was one of the key states plying the sea-trading routes between the Spice Islands of Indonesia and the coast of East Africa—off which lay the island of Zanzibar. Oman's control of Zanzibar fluctuated throughout the 18th century and into the early 19th century until, in 1806, Sayyid Said initiated a long and stable reign. Although he had only just turned 15, Said had already executed his cousin Badr bin Saif, who had briefly usurped the throne, and sidelined his brother, Salim bin Sultan, who their father had intended would reign alongside Said. The new sultan, it seemed, was a man of ambition.

Oman shifts its center of gravity

In 1823, Said signed a treaty with Britain banning the trade in enslaved people between his Muslim subjects and any western Christian powers. Significantly, the treaty did not exclude slave trading along the East African coast, leaving Said free to invest in people-trafficking in Oman's sometime colony of Zanzibar. Once there, Said also helped make the island a hub for the lucrative trade in African elephant ivory and expanded Zanzibar's already large clove plantations so the island became the world's largest source of the sought-after spice.

In 1840, Said transferred the Sultanate of Oman's capital from Muscat to Stone Town, in Zanzibar. Three years earlier, Said had conquered Mombasa, in

> **A BOLD PRINCESS**
>
> One of Sultan Said's 36 children lived a notably colorful life. Born in 1844, Sayyida Salme (below, in regal attire) learned to ride and shoot, and taught herself to read, which was unusual for women in her culture at the time. In Zanzibar, she met a young German merchant and moved to Germany with him, where they married. Later in life, Sayyida wrote her autobiography—the first East African woman to do so. She died in 1924 and was buried with a treasured bag of Zanzibar sand.

Distinctive circular motifs

▽ **Double comb**
This beautifully carved wooden comb, dating from the 19th century, shows the skill and artistry of artisan makers in Zanzibar and surrounding coastal regions.

"[O]ur own **prosperity** dates from the time of **my father's conquest** ... **of Zanzibar**."

SAYYIDA SALME ON HER FATHER, SULTAN SAYYID SAID

modern Kenya, on the African mainland, securing his supply lines of enslaved people and African goods such as ivory for export via Zanzibar; Oman had become peripheral to Said's needs.

As the state's ruler went, its religious culture followed. Omanis were followers of a branch of Islam known as Ibadism, and many Ibadi scholars migrated to Zanzibar with Said, turning the new capital into a center of religious learning. Muslim academics from across East Africa followed suit.

From sultanate to independence

Said's death in 1856 was the beginning of the end of Zanzibar's golden age. Two of his sons quarreled over the succession, resulting in the division of his territories. One son, Thuwaini, took control of Oman while another, Majid, became the first Sultan of Zanzibar. Britain's Viceroy and Governor-General of India, George Canning, mediated the dispute between the brothers, which led to Britain playing an increasing role in Zanzibar's affairs.

By 1890, Zanzibar had become a British protectorate; its sultans held office but no power. This was demonstrated in uncompromising fashion when a pretender to the throne, Khālid ibn Barghash, seized power from Britain's preferred candidate, Ḥamud ibn Moḥammed. After Khālid ignored an ultimatum to stand down, Britain declared war at 9 a.m. on August 27, 1896, sending in five Royal Navy ships to bombard Zanzibar's Royal Palace and Harem. Khālid surrendered within as little as 38 minutes, giving the Anglo-Zanzibar War the distinction of being considered the shortest conflict in history.

Ḥamud was installed as Zanzibar's sultan, but the Omanis' time was running out. Britain terminated its protectorship in 1963. A year later, the last sultan, Jamshid bin Abdullah Al Said, was deposed in the Zanzibar Revolution. Led by Ugandan John Gideon Okello, this socialist revolution saw the deaths of 20,000 people—mostly Arabs and Indians. In April 1964, Zanzibar merged with the recently independent mainland nation of Tanganyika to form what was later that year named Tanzania.

▷ **Grandee's chair**
This *kiti cha enzi* ("Chair of Power") dates from the 19th century, during Omani rule in Zanzibar. Unique to the region, such chairs were used by high-ranking officials on formal occasions and were offered to visiting foreign dignitaries as a sign of respect.

Decoratively woven string

Delicate inlay of bone and ivory

Frame design was inspired by prototypes from Europe or possibly Egypt

Stone Town

Capital of the Zanzibar Sultanate (present-day Tanzania)

From its humble beginnings as a fishing village, Stone Town developed into one of the most famous trading ports along the East African coast. Its location on the island of Zanzibar attracted competing foreign powers, which were eager to control a lucrative trade in enslaved people and commodities such as ivory between the African mainland, the Arabian Peninsula, Asia, and beyond. During the 19th century, the Omani sultan Sayyid Said moved his capital from Arabia to Zanzibar, recognizing its potential to extend the wealth and power of the sultanate. He encouraged local clove production and expanded international trade, transforming Stone Town into a thriving commercial hub with a multicultural population.

Distinctive architecture

Stone Town's buildings fused Swahili materials with the cultural traditions and tastes of its international residents. Behind the waterfront lay a dense maze of alleyways, characterized by townhouses of local coralline ragstone. Plain Arab-style frontages with decorative doorways neighbored narrow Indian shopfronts overhung by wooden balconies designed to catch sea breezes.

Sultan Said's Omani-style palace, the Beit al-Sahel, dominated the seafront, showing the sultanate's primacy. Successive sultans added extra palaces and embellishments, incorporating Indian-style elements. Under Sultan Barghash bin Said (r. 1870–1888), a prolific builder and enthusiast for new technology, Stone Town acquired its iconic landmark: the Beit al-Ajaib or House of Wonders.

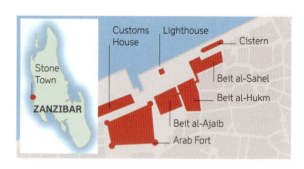

△ **Stone Town origins**
Stone Town developed on a peninsula offering safe anchorage on Zanzibar's west coast. Sultan Said encouraged the building of stone houses in his new capital, resulting in its name.

▽ **Waterfront palace complex**
This reconstruction depicts the sultan's palace complex as it appeared under Sultan Barghash in the mid-1880s, shortly after the House of Wonders was built. The architecture reflects the mix of Swahili, Arab, and Indian influences characteristic of Stone Town.

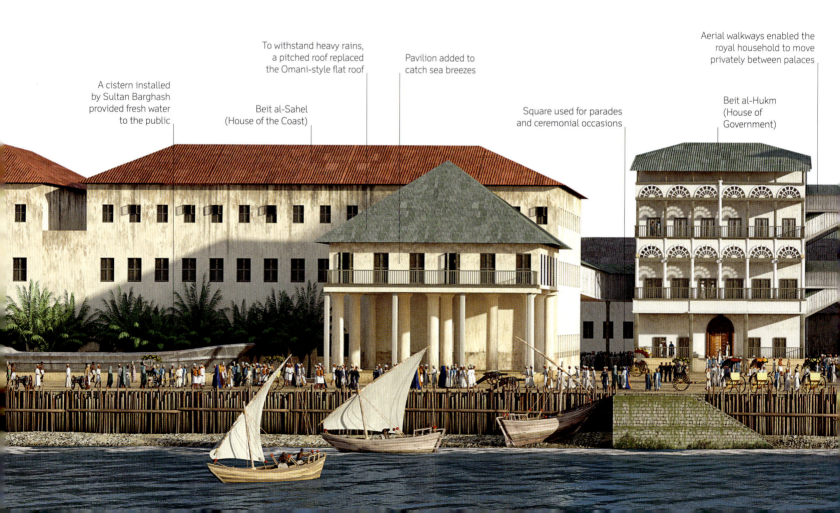

STONE TOWN | 189

1896: SULTANS UNDER FIRE

In 1890, Zanzibar became a British protectorate and the sultanate's independence and authority waned. In 1896, when the then sultan died suddenly, his cousin Khālid ibn Barghash (son of Sultan Barghash) tried to assume the sultanship. The British, however, had a different successor in mind: one more amenable to British interests. When Khālid refused to stand aside, the British Navy bombarded the palace complex, destroying Beit al-Hukm, the lighthouse, and much of Beit al-Sahel. In the following years, the area was relandscaped: Beit al-Sahel was rebuilt on a smaller scale, gardens were laid over the site of Beit al-Hukm, and the House of Wonders was remodeled to incorporate a clock tower with the original lighthouse clock. The waterfront was forever changed.

DAMAGED PALACE COMPLEX, 1896

▷ **Inside the House of Wonders**
The House of Wonders was an expression of Sultan Barghash's faith, modernizing instincts, wealth, and foreign influences, on a scale never before seen in Zanzibar. The sultan held court in paneled rooms arranged around a covered courtyard furnished with electric lights, European marble and silverware, and gilded doors inscribed with Qur'anic verses.

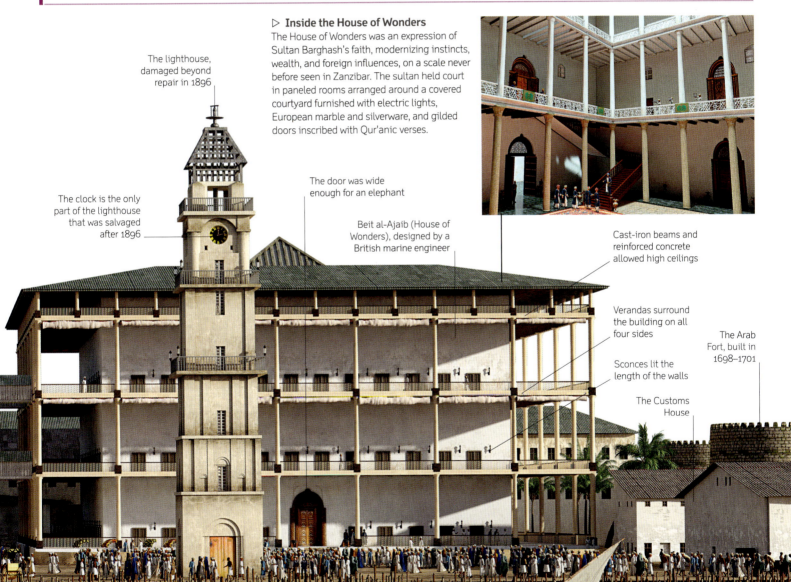

- The lighthouse, damaged beyond repair in 1896
- The clock is the only part of the lighthouse that was salvaged after 1896
- The door was wide enough for an elephant
- Beit al-Ajaib (House of Wonders), designed by a British marine engineer
- Cast-iron beams and reinforced concrete allowed high ceilings
- Verandas surround the building on all four sides
- Sconces lit the length of the walls
- The Arab Fort, built in 1698–1701
- The Customs House

The Asante Empire

West Africa's great imperial powerhouse

Growing from a small kingdom into West Africa's most significant state, the Asante Empire dominated Ghana's "gold coast," using its wealth and power to fend off British interference for almost a century.

The Akan people of what is now Ghana had long been divided into a number of autonomous groups when, in the late 17th century, war forced them together.

Denkyira was the wealthiest, strongest, and most actively expansionist Akan state. In 1694, its new leader, Ntim Gyakari, turned his attention to Denkyira's smaller but growing rival, the Asante Kingdom, which had been founded by the Okoyo of south-central Ghana. Shortly before Gyakari came to power, the Asante king, Osei Tutu, had seized territory from Denkyira and refused to give it back or pay the reparations Ntim Gyakari demanded of him. Unable to accept such a slight, Gyakari declared war.

In the conflict that followed, Osei Tutu put together an alliance of Akan peoples and states opposed to Denkyira's often tyrannical rule and, in 1701, the so-called "Kwaman Alliance" (named after the Asante capital) defeated Denkyira at the Battle of Feyiase. Ntim Gyakari died in combat and Denkyira became a member state of the new Asante Empire.

Establishing an empire

To establish the new order, the empire's capital was moved to Kumasi, in modern-day central Ghana, and Osei Tutu was ceremonially presented with the Golden Stool. This was a clever piece of political theater organized by Tutu's trusted advisor, *Okomfo* (priest) Anokye, who, according to legend, summoned from heaven a golden seat, or stool, that landed in Tutu's lap—proof of his divine right to rule.

As *Asantehene*, or king, of the Asante Empire, Tutu was not an absolute monarch but was "first among equals." The empire he ruled operated along federal lines, with chiefs and regional leaders, or *Amanhene*, exercising a degree of local power and forming the membership of a law-making and advisory council known as the *Asantemanhyiamu* (which translates as the

△ **Asante royal family**
Asantehene Prempeh I with the *Asantehemaa* (Queen Mother). In 1900, the British exiled him to the Seychelles for 24 years.

△ **The Asante court**
Thomas Edward Bowditch's watercolor *Cape Coast Castle to Ashantee* (1819) captures the color and pageantry of the Asante court at its imperial height.

▽ **Gold weights**
These brass figures were used to weigh gold. Rather than create simple round or square weights, the Asante cast decorative figures.

"When **a king** has **good counselors**, his reign is **peaceful**."

ASANTE PROVERB

"Great Council") that met each year. Okomfo Anokye drafted "The Seventy-Seven Laws," which served as the codified constitution of the Asante Empire.

When Tutu died in 1717, the *Asantemanhyiamu* approved the accession of his successor—and this became the method by which all Asante kings were anointed (the nominee for kingship having been chosen from a list of candidates by the widowed queen). Once in place, the new king was acknowledged as the imperial leader and served as the empire's highest legal authority, chief executive, and military commander-in-chief.

It was in this latter capacity especially that the second Asante emperor, Opoku Ware I, excelled. By the end of his reign in 1750, he had expanded the empire's borders to their widest extent, defeating neighboring peoples such as the Bono, Akyem, Akwamu, and Ga-Adangbe of present-day Ghana, Côte d'Ivoire, and other West African states. But empires that expand by conquest are often unsettled. The fifth Asante king, Osei Kwame Panyin, died by suicide in 1803 as a bitter civil war threatened the country. By this time, Britain was expanding its colonial control in West Africa, ultimately leading to the series of Anglo-Asante Wars that finally brought down the empire in 1901.

A golden age

Across its history, the Asante Empire was sustained economically by its large gold reserves (which were panned from rivers rather than mined), its trade in agricultural produce, and the manufacture of high-quality crafted goods. The empire was also involved in human trafficking, supplying enslaved people to British and Dutch traders in return for arms. As West Africa's leading precolonial power, the Asante Empire was blessed with a wealth of natural resources and a sophisticated, decentralized political culture that allowed it to thrive for two centuries.

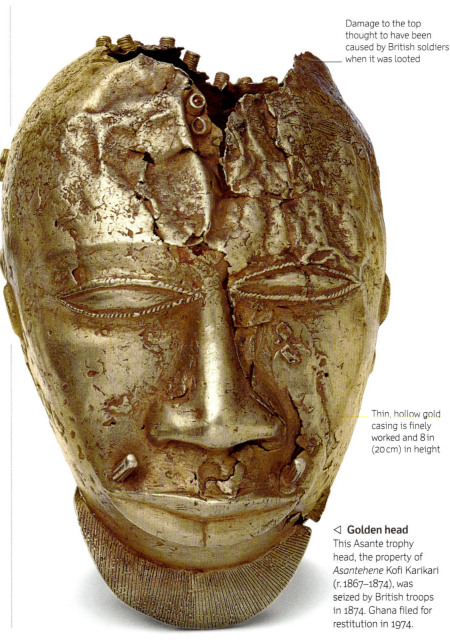

Damage to the top thought to have been caused by British soldiers when it was looted

Thin, hollow gold casing is finely worked and 8 in (20 cm) in height

◁ **Golden head**
This Asante trophy head, the property of *Asantehene* Kofi Karikari (r. 1867–1874), was seized by British troops in 1874. Ghana filed for restitution in 1974.

Osei Tutu

The founder of the Asante Empire

In 1701, Osei Tutu led a coalition of states against the reigning kingdom of Denkyira. Tutu's inventive tactics helped him defeat the Denkyira and found the Asante Empire, which would dominate West Africa for centuries.

△ **Asante architecture**
This 19th-century engraving depicts houses in the Asante Empire's capital, Kumasi, which Osei Tutu founded.

In the late 17th century, the Akan states occupied the forested coastal regions of modern-day Ghana, Togo, and Côte d'Ivoire. They were dominated by Denkyira, which had become the largest and wealthiest kingdom after conquering several of its neighbors with the help of muskets bought from European traders. But the rulers of Denkyira became tyrannical, demanding ever-higher tributes (payments) from states they had conquered and executing rulers who couldn't pay.

Princely upbringing

Osei Tutu was a prince of Kwaman, an Akan state inhabited by the Asante. Born around 1660, he spent some of his youth in the nearby state of Akwamu and also served, probably as a page boy, in the court of Boamponsem, the ruler of Denkyira. In Akwamu, Tutu learned about political and military tactics, and in Denkyira, he met a young man named Anokye—the son of an Akan noble—who became his chief advisor.

By the 1680s, Tutu succeeded to the throne of Kwaman, which had expanded its territory to become the heart of an Akan kingdom. When he defied the tribute demands of Boamponsem's successor, Ntim Gyakari, and conquered Denkyira lands, the rulers of the other Akan states agreed to back him. Open war broke out in 1699, with Tutu using nimble formations, pincer tactics, and firearms to gain an advantage. At the Battle of Feyiase in 1701, Tutu and his "Kwaman coalition" defeated the Denkyira, killing Gyakari and sacking the kingdom's capital, Abankeseso.

Tutu created a single state, the Asante Empire. Anokye, who had taken the title Okomfo ("priest"), used a stool—a traditional part of a king's regalia—to cement the union. In around 1717, Osei Tutu was at war with the rival Akyem state when a sniper's bullet hit him. It is said that he had believed the Akyem to be a lesser force so had not worn armor, and was killed instantly. Under his successor, Opoku Ware I, Osei Tutu's empire continued to flourish and expand.

Fine detailing, and all other parts, are carved from a single block of wood

◁ **Symbol of power**
For centuries, Akan rulers have used stools (*dwa*) as a symbol of royal authority.

> "Ankah me nim a [If only I knew]."
>
> OSEI TUTU'S LAST WORDS, APPARENTLY AT UNDERESTIMATING THE AKYEM IN BATTLE

- **c. 1660** Born in the town of Kokofu Anyinam, modern-day Ghana
- **c. 1678** Taken to Denkyira palace and meets Okomfo Anokye
- **c. 1680** Succeeds to the throne of the Akan Kingdom of Kwaman
- **1689** The Kwaman coalition is officially formed, and prepares for war with Denkyira
- **1695** Establishes Kumasi as capital city of Asante Empire
- **1701** Battle of Feyiase, where Tutu's Kwaman coalition defeats the Denkyira
- **c. 1701–1702** Tutu and Anokye use the symbol of the Golden Stool to form a single state, the Asante Empire
- **c. 1717** Killed in battle against the neighboring Akyem people

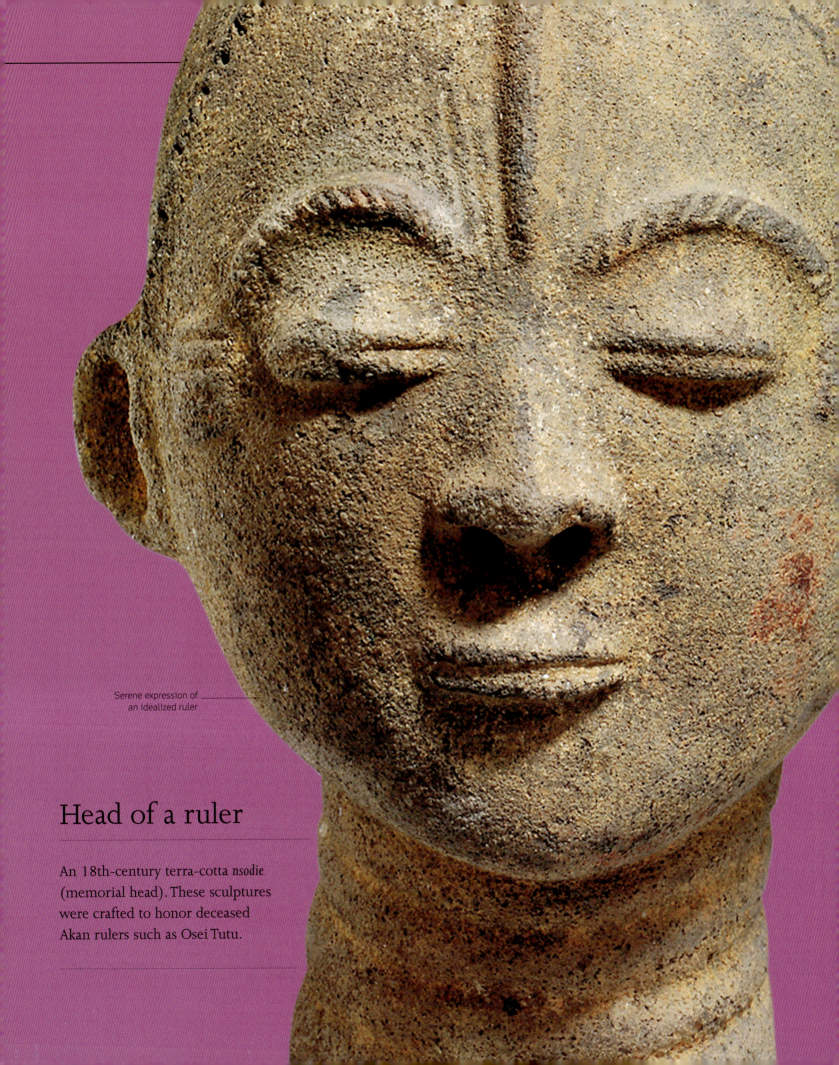

Serene expression of an idealized ruler

Head of a ruler

An 18th-century terra-cotta nsodie (memorial head). These sculptures were crafted to honor deceased Akan rulers such as Osei Tutu.

The Sokoto Caliphate

Forging an Islamic state

One of Africa's largest 19th-century empires, the Sokoto Caliphate was founded by the devout Muslim scholar Usman dan Fodio and expanded to include much of West Africa.

A Sunni Muslim state established in the early 19th century in modern-day Nigeria, the Sokoto Caliphate was previously a collection of seven independent city-states forming the Hausa Kingdoms, which had been in existence for 700 years.

The city-state of Gobir was part of the Hausa Kingdoms and although it was culturally Islamic, its rulers did not demand strict religious adherence. Muslim cleric Usman dan Fodio, by contrast, had an uncompromising faith. His preaching on the greed, corruption, and abuses of Sharia law by Gobir's elites brought him supporters, but also the enmity of his state's leaders. In 1802, a failed assassination attempt on Usman authorized by Gobir's king, Yunfa, drove him into exile. Usman took his supporters with him and two years later, when Yunfa declared war on Usman, he responded by declaring jihad—holy war—against Yunfa.

△ **Ceremonial head**
Sokoto's last independent caliph was Sultan Muhammadu Attahiru I. He was deposed after five months in power in 1903, and killed by the British at Mbormi five months later.

◁ **Hausa palace**
The royal palace in Bauchi, northeast Nigeria, is decorated with Hausa symbols. The Bauchi Emirate was established c. 1810 by Yakubu, one of Usman dan Fodio's army commanders.

Beginnings of the caliphate

In the early 19th century, it was common practice in Islamic states for disaffected religious groups to declare jihad against rulers or countries whose beliefs they questioned. In Sudan, West Africa, for example, more than a dozen jihadi leaders displaced old rulers and established new states.

In the Hausa states, Islamic fundamentalism was strongest among the Fulani people, whose number included Usman dan Fodio. His jihad against Yunfa set off a chain reaction, with Muslim groups in the other Hausa Kingdoms also rising up against their political leaders. The groups acted independently, but all recognized the authority of Usman, the man his followers had anointed as *Amir al-Mu'ninin* ("Commander of the Faithful"). Usman and his supporters took control of the kingdom of Gobir in 1808, and by 1812 the other Hausa Kingdoms had also fallen. In their place the insurgents established the Sokoto Caliphate, named after its capital city in what is today northwest Nigeria.

The Sokoto Caliphate was not a unified nation but an association of 30 Muslim emirates. By 1812, Usman had retired from politics to return to teaching and a life of religious study and was succeeded by his son, Muhammad Bello. As caliph (supreme religious leader), Muhammad Bello and each of his successors would receive the annual visit of tribute from the ruler, or emir, of each of the emirates. Such was the authority of the caliph that—despite the large number of emirates that made up the Sokoto Caliphate and the diversity of peoples and ethnic groups comprising it—no caliph was ever deposed by his subjects.

A military and economic powerhouse

By the end of Muhammad Bello's rule in 1837, the Sokoto Caliphate was the most populous empire in West Africa, numbering up to 20 million people. Muhammed Bello and his brother Abdullahi were gifted military leaders and conquered new territories. At its height, the Sokoto Caliphate extended 1,000 miles (1,600 km) from northern Cameroon in the east to Burkina Faso in the west. The caliphate became known as a center of art and culture, as well as for Muslim scholarship. The city of Sokoto was endowed with two large mosques, the Masallacin Shehu and the Masallacin Bello, and a royal palace. All of this was paid for by the spoils of conquest and the profits from the trade in cotton cloth, sorghum, brassware, spices, kola nuts, salt, potash, and leather goods. The empire's agricultural economy was powered largely by enslaved labor.

△ **Trading power**
This colored engraving of Sokoto's market was produced in 1853. It shows a bustling market with livestock and produce near the Sokoto River.

Collapse of the caliphate

By the end of the 19th century, the Sokoto Caliphate had begun to fracture. Abdurrahman dan Abi Bakar became caliph in 1891 but he was thin-skinned and a poor decision-maker. He alienated his emirs, weakening the state when France, Germany, and Britain were seeking to extend their influence in West Africa.

By the time Abdurrahman died in 1902, the British had decided to act. On the pretext of helping to resolve trade disputes, and to protect its own interests in the region, Britain sent troops into the caliphate in January 1903. They defeated the emirates and, in March 1903, Abdurrahman's successor was deposed and replaced by a purely ceremonial caliph, Muhammadu Attahiru II. The Sokoto Caliphate's time as an independent empire was over—although Sokoto's sultans, each of them a direct descendant of Usman dan Fodio, continue to wield a degree of influence over their people to this day.

> "If the king is Muslim, **his land is Muslim**; if he is an unbeliever, his land is **a land of unbelievers**."
>
> USMAN DAN FODIO

The Tukulor Empire
Conversion and conquest

The Tukulor Empire burned brightly but briefly in West Africa. Its founder, Al-Hajj Umar Tal, was a scholar and pilgrim who began a holy war, creating a 19th-century kingdom that survived for half a century.

△ **Resisting the French**
Umar Tal's son Ahmadu ruled much of the Tukulor Empire in the late 19th century. He coordinated resistance against the French colonizing forces.

By the early 19th century, the Islamic caliphates of the Fulani and Sokoto were expanding across West Africa. Meanwhile, European powers, once happy to trade with the kingdoms of the interior, were beginning to seek outright rule. Instability brought opportunity and, propelled by firearms and radical Islam, the Tukulor Empire took full advantage. This West African state began as the dream of one determined scholar and ended up stretching from Senegal to Timbuktu.

A pilgrim's empire
The Tukulor Empire was founded by Umar Tal, who was born in 1797 in Futa Toro, an arid region on the banks of the Senegal River. He studied at a *madrasa* (religious school) and took the pilgrimage to Mecca in his twenties, gaining the title "Al-Hajj."

Umar traveled for two decades, visiting Medina, Cairo, and Syria. In Mecca, an increasingly respected Umar was appointed the West African leader of the Tijaniyya, an Islamic order that foregrounded discipline and followed the mystic doctrine of Sufism. While a guest of Muhammad Bello, the sultan of the Sokoto court in modern-day Nigeria, he married the sultan's daughter and was groomed for leadership. In 1838, after Bello's death, Umar and a growing band of followers returned to Futa Toro determined to unite the Western Sahel under one ruler and one faith.

Wars, decline, and legacy
Umar initially failed to gain sufficient support in Futa Toro, and in the 1840s he established a *ribat* (sanctuary) in Fouta Djallon to the south, in what is now Guinea. He gathered soldiers, religious teachers, and European firearms for a holy war. His followers included members of the Tukulor people of Futa Toro and the Fulani people of Fouta Djallon. He even sought an alliance with the French, but they refused, wary of encouraging a potential rival.

During the late 1840s and 1850s, Tukulor troops struck at neighboring kingdoms and skirmished with the French, who were augmenting their military with local troops, and had begun to construct roads and

> "**Do you not know** that **Al-Hajj** ... has the capacity to **destroy you** ... and **all your trade**?"
>
> — AL-HAJJ UMAR TAL IN A LETTER TO THE FRENCH, 1854

French-made blade

Sheath made of leather and brass

THE TUKOLOR EMPIRE | 197

△ **The Great Mosque**
In the 1840s, Al-Hajj Umar built the Great Mosque of Dinguiraye in what is now Guinea, photographed here in around 1900. The exterior of its impressive domed roof was thatched.

forts in the region. The Tukulor won victories against the Bambara—an empire weakened by clashes with the Fulani of nearby Masina—before defeating Masina in 1862. Umar's empire now covered much of modern-day Senegal, Guinea, Mauritania, and Mali.

The Tukulor occupied Timbuktu in 1863, but an allied force of Fulani, Tuaregs, and Moroccans eventually halted their wars of expansion. On Umar's death in 1864, his son Ahmadu and nephew Tidiani each governed parts of the empire, but struggled to hold the sprawling kingdom together. The French encroached on Tukulor territory, building alliances with disgruntled local rulers, and eventually conquering cities. In 1893, Ahmadu fled to Sokoto, and the empire crumbled, with French West Africa taking control of Tukulor lands in 1897.

In West Africa, the Tukulor Empire is remembered for its heroic resistance to the French, but also for further dividing the region's peoples, making the French advance easier. Perhaps the empire's most significant legacy was to help spread Islam across the Sahel, where it remains the dominant religion.

Handle in the shape of a bird's beak

△ **Prized weapon**
Often described as "the sword of Umar Tal," this blade actually belonged to his son, Ahmadu. The French took it in 1893, only returning it to Senegal in 2019.

West African art and craft

A wide range of artistic artifacts

West Africa has a rich and diverse artistic heritage. Its artwork is often intricately connected to the social and religious ceremonies of its many different peoples, and imbued with ceremonial or ritual significance. Its artifacts encompass sculptures in wood, ivory, metal, and stone, and include masks, headdresses, and figures.

△ **Sande helmet mask**
The women's initiation society of Liberia, Sierra Leone, Guinea, and Côte d'Ivoire—called the Sande—is probably unique in creating masks to be worn exclusively by women.

◁ **Kongo nkisi figure**
Materials and amulets are attached to the Kongo nkisi figure by a nganga priest, to add spiritual power to the work.

▷ **Bwa plant mask**
Representing invisible forest spirits, the plank masks of the Bwa people of Burkina Faso, known as nwantantay, are highly stylized and abstract.

△ **Asante fertility figure**
The Asante akuaba figure with its distinctive disk-shaped head is for women hoping to conceive. The stylized features emphasize ideals of beauty and fertility.

◁ **Dahomey sculpture**
A bocio, or power sculpture, from Dahomey depicts a member of the royal family. These wooden figures were adorned with cloth and various organic materials.

▷ **Fon silver buffalo**
This lavishly silver-plated wooden buffalo was commissioned by the 19th-century king Ghezo of Dahomey as a symbol of wealth.

Shells and beads form a design of a stylized spider, associated with wisdom

Beaded collar

△ **Head of an oba**
This cast bronze head depicts a recently deceased *oba*, or ruler, of Benin, and was commissioned by his successor.

△ **Guéré mask**
The masks of the Guéré people of Côte d'Ivoire typically include cloth, hair, and metal objects attached to a painted wooden base.

Carved mudfish

Stylized hairstyle

Elaborate necklace

Portraits of Portuguese traders

△ **Pendant mask**
This 16th-century representation of Idia, the first *Iyoba* or Queen Mother of Benin, was sculpted from ivory for her son, King Esigie.

△ **Ejagham headdress**
Made of antelope skin over a wooden form, this headdress was created by the Ejagham people of Nigeria and Cameroon.

Decorative painted band

Decorative zigzag border

Glass beads

△ **Helmet mask**
Richly decorated with shells and beads, this mask from the Bamum kingdom of Cameroon indicates the privileged status of its owner.

△ **Moon mask**
This Baule mask from Côte d'Ivoire depicting the moon is an example of masks representing natural phenomena worn during *gbagba* dance performances.

△ **Wan-balinga mask**
A central feature of the funeral ceremonies of the Mossi people of Burkina Faso, Wan-balinga masks are worn exclusively by dancers of the farming community.

European explorers
Into the African interior

Europe's trading interactions with Africa were at first confined to the coasts. By the 19th century, European explorers had spread deep inland and trade developed into a vastly more complex network of contested relationships.

The Greeks and then the Romans, respectively, gave the names "Libya" and "Africa" to the territory now known as North Africa (see pp.70–71). However, their knowledge of—and interest in—Africa south of the Sahara was more limited. For Greek historians such as Herodotus, the interior was the "mysterious" source of the Nile, or, according to Homer, the origin of "the remotest of men," the Ethiopians. Later Roman writers such as Sallust portrayed Africa south of the Sahara as a "wild," "exotic," and "unknown" place.

Exploring a continent

Europeans' knowledge of Africa remained limited until the 15th and 16th centuries, when, primarily, Portuguese explorers began to chart its west coast.

Between 1444 and 1447, the Portuguese visited the seashores of Senegal, Guinea, and the Gambia, and mapped the Cape Verde Islands in 1456 and the Bissau islands in 1462. This led, in 1488, to Bartolomeu Dias becoming the first European to sail around the Cape of Good Hope on Africa's southernmost tip, a journey that itself paved the way for Vasco da Gama's voyage to India via the Cape 10 years later. And with each point of contact came trade: European wheat, cloth, and weapons in exchange for African gold and enslaved people. In the 16th century, the Portuguese repeated a similar pattern of exploration followed by the trade in goods and humans along Africa's eastern coast.

Although mariners had charted Africa's full outline by the late 16th century, its interior remained largely unexplored by Europeans for another 200 years. (Muslim enslavers, meanwhile, established several trade routes traversing the desert kingdoms of the Sahara.) By the early 19th century, Europeans desired knowledge of Africa beyond its coast. British, French, Italian, German, and Belgian explorers ventured ever-deeper inland. This facilitated further trade and the spread of Christian missions, followed by more formal colonial control when Europeans began to use

△ **Travels to the interior**
Scotland's Mungo Park (1771–1806), included in this German anthology of travelers' accounts, was one of the first Europeans to travel through Central Africa.

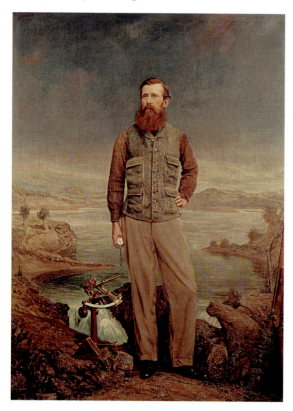

◁ **The river man**
In 1858, John Hanning Speke (1827–1864) traveled to a body of water he named Lake Victoria—correctly surmising it was the source of the Nile River.

"Here at last I stood on the **brink of the Nile**; most **beautiful was the scene** …"

JOHN HANNING SPEKE, 1863

military force to protect the African lands they held. They believed that these tactics were necessary, seeing themselves as "opening" Africa to the emerging global trading economy.

During the 1830s and 1840s, Europeans made comprehensive explorations of regions south of the Sahara. They charted areas that had previously been shown as blank on their maps, including the Congo Basin, Burundi's Great Lakes region, and the territory of the modern Democratic Republic of the Congo, Kenya, Malawi, Mozambique, Rwanda, and Zambia. Explorers collected and preserved much important ethnographic data concerning languages, cultures, and customs—although racist bias and prejudice often undermined the accuracy of their interpretation.

Cultures and conquest

By 1875, men such as John Hanning Speke, Sir Richard Burton, David Livingstone, and Henry Morton Stanley (see box, right) had completed the European exploration of Africa, after which geologists surveyed the continent, chiefly to locate new mineral sites for exploitation. The revelation of the continent's mineral wealth led to conflicts between the Africans who possessed it and the Europeans who desired it.

During this period, European colonizers partitioned Africa into spheres of influence and colonies, often imposing ethnic and political divisions where there had been none before. This in turn resulted in Africans' loss of political independence and the marginalization of Indigenous cultures. In short, cultural and political imperialism followed military imperialism, seeking to impose European customs onto African societies.

As well as military and police forces, imperial administrators, and commercial enterprises, Christian missionaries played an important role in the Europeanization of colonized African states. With the regions south of the Sahara less technologically advanced than Europe at this time, colonizing nations could easily portray Africa's people as "savages" in need of both God's salvation and the "civilizing" largesse of the West.

△ **Keeping a record**
Germany's Heinrich Barth (1821–1865) was as much an ethnographer as explorer. He collected oral histories and made many sketches, such as this view of Kano, in Nigeria.

FROM GLORY TO CONDEMNATION

The shift in public perception of Henry Morton Stanley (1841–1904) symbolizes the changing reputations of all European explorers over time. Originally lionized as the man who found David Livingstone (see pp.204–205) and as a successful explorer and colonial administrator, more recently Stanley (right, with his adopted African son, Kalulu) has been criticized as the archetypal "white savior" figure, and as a cruel taskmaster and rapacious imperialist, not least in the ruthless land expropriations he carried out for King Leopold of Belgium in Congo Free State (see pp.212–213).

> "[Njoya] preserved ... his kingdom's **physical boundaries** when **European colonialists** were erasing them ..."
>
> LANISA KITCHINER, CHIEF, AFRICAN AND MIDDLE EASTERN DIVISION, LIBRARY OF CONGRESS, 2022

Map of Bamum

Indigenous African cartography

During the German occupation of what is now Cameroon, Ibrahim Njoya, fon (ruler) of the Kingdom of Bamum from 1886 to his death in 1933, steadfastly defended his people's independence while working strategically with the colonizers to his advantage wherever possible. As well as devising an alphabet for writing the Bamum language and producing a written history of the people, he made a detailed map of the kingdom. He astutely realized that, in carving up the continent, the European colonizers laid claim to territory by making maps, and he set out to do the same to assert Bamum's existence as an independent nation—and to allow him to allocate land rights and resolve land disputes within his kingdom. In 1912, he established a group of surveyors to begin the task of mapping Bamum.

New mapping techniques

The first surveying expedition, consisting of around 60 individuals led by Njoya himself, made its way around the perimeter of the kingdom on foot, covering roughly two-thirds of the territory before the rainy season forced them to stop. In the absence of modern surveying equipment, they devised their own methods, timing their walks to estimate distances and gathering information from local guides. Interrupted by the death of the king's mother, followed by the turmoil of World War I, the survey was completed in 1920.

Njoya's surveyors created their own cartographic system. The map is oriented east–west rather than north–south, as indicated by the disks at the top and bottom, symbolizing the rising and setting sun. Although the true shape of Njoya's kingdom was triangular, the mapmakers stretched the kingdom's western boundary to produce a rectangular shape, with a symmetrical river system, creating a sense of unity that projects the king's power, even over the landscape. The size and centrality of the capital, Foumban, is exaggerated to emphasize its importance. Towns, villages, and landmarks are marked with labels using Njoya's alphabet.

▽ **Royal city**
Njoya's palace, indicated by the grid of red squares, lies within the walled capital city, Foumban.

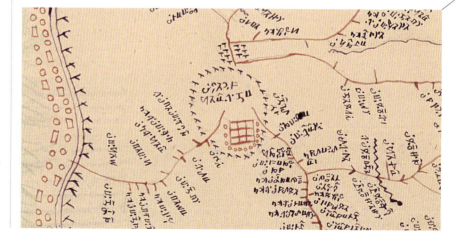

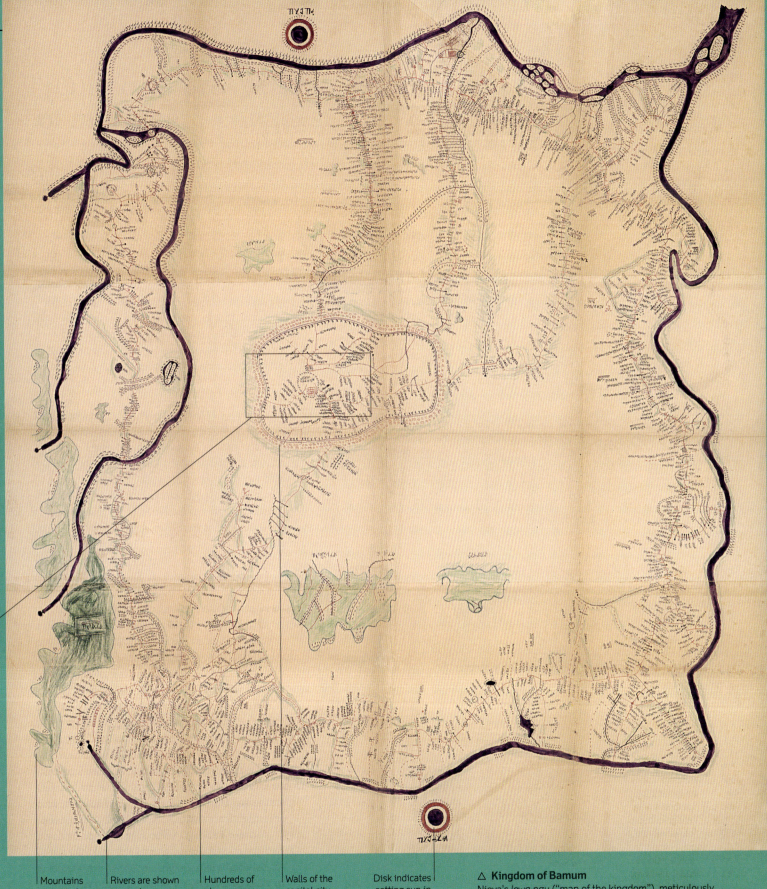

Mountains indicated in green

Rivers are shown in purple

Hundreds of place names border the edges of the kingdom

Walls of the capital city, Foumban

Disk indicates setting sun in the west

△ **Kingdom of Bamum**
Njoya's *lewa ngu* ("map of the kingdom"), meticulously charting the extent of his people's occupation of the land, is created on paper with ink and colored pencils and measures 39 in (100 cm) by 35 in (90 cm).

Text is mainly Visigothic, but contains notes in Latin and Arabic

Sacred bulls, shown here in the biblical story of the Adoration of the Golden Calf, appear in many cultures, including in ancient Egypt

△ **Mozarabic Bible**
Christianity had been established in North Africa and beyond before the rise of Islam in the 8th century. Mozarabs, who created this León Bible of 960, are Spanish Christians who lived under Muslim Amazigh (Berber) rule and adopted Arabic language and culture.

The illuminations are by a scribe and artist named Sanctus and his master Florentius

Christian missionaries

Conversion across the continent

Until the late 18th century, Christianity's influence in Africa had been limited to regions in the north. Christian missionaries in the 19th century transformed the continent's religious landscape—and had a profound impact on its history.

Some Africans embraced Christianity in its earliest days. The religion had spread to areas including Alexandria in Egypt, Cyrenaica in what is now Libya, and ancient Nubia by the 2nd century CE, and Aksum in Ethiopia by the 4th century CE. Yet the faith barely reached beyond these strongholds for centuries.

Christianity began to spread again as European influence increased. In the 15th century, Catholic Portuguese traders brought the faith to Kongo, in Central Africa. But it was the largely Protestant missionary enterprises of the late 18th and 19th centuries that had the greatest impact. Groups such as Britain's Church Missionary Society, which sent expeditions to the colony of Sierra Leone in the 1840s, emerged from growing evangelist movements in Europe and North America. Africans played a crucial role in missions founded by Europeans and also established missions on their own. For example, Samuel Ajayi Crowther, a formerly enslaved Yoruba man, opened a mission in the Niger Delta and became the first Black African Anglican bishop. From the 1880s, Africans began to found Africanized churches that incorporated local religious ideas, practices, and songs.

Religion and colonialism

Some missionaries, both European and African, struggled to convert local people. Others transformed communities via their faith and their encouragement of "legitimate commerce" in goods such as palm oil and sugar at the expense of the slave trade. Missionaries founded schools and orphanages, encouraging the rise of an educated elite. Today, around half of Africa's population practices Christianity. However, European missionaries discouraged Indigenous customs and divided communities. Education emphasized the achievements of Europe and North America. Indeed, religion and colonialism often went hand in hand.

David Livingstone, of the London Missionary Society (LMS), mapped wide areas of Central and Southern Africa for the British in the 1840s and '50s, and saw the Zambezi River as "God's Highway"—a route along which both Christianity and "civilization" could travel. Crowther urged that the British "pacify" the Niger Delta. In 1888, missionaries François Coillard and Charles Helm are said to have willfully mistranslated treaties for the Lozi and Ndebele of Southern Africa, resulting in territorial losses to British colonial enterprises. Christian missionaries did not just change hearts: they reshaped nations.

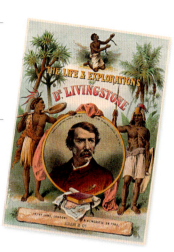

△ **Christian explorer**
Livingstone wrote about his extensive African travels in *The Life and Explorations of David Livingstone*, first published in 1870.

> "Spending so much of **my life in Africa ... is a privilege**."
>
> DAVID LIVINGSTONE, 1858

▷ **Mission school**
A nun teaches reading and writing to a group of Zulu children in an outdoor class at Mariathal Mission School in 1910, in what is now KwaZulu-Natal, South Africa.

Shaka and the Zulu Kingdom

A powerful southern force

In the early years of the 19th century, the Zulu Kingdom was one of several competing nations in Southern Africa; by the 1820s, under King Shaka, it had become a regional superpower.

The Zulus' ancestors arrived in the lands today known as South Africa around the 2nd millennium BCE, during the Bantu migrations (see pp.36–37). They emerged from the Nguni branch of Bantu-speaking inhabitants of East Africa's Great Lakes region. The Zulu developed in the 17th century as semi-nomadic, pastoral groups, inhabiting the region now called KwaZulu-Natal on South Africa's east coast. These groups grew, consolidating into larger ones and establishing settled communities with powerful chieftains. They became wealthy on the cattle, grain, and goods gained by conquering nearby chiefdoms.

Creation of a kingdom

In the first decade of the 19th century, the Zulu competed with other local groups, such as the Mthethwa, Ndwandwe, and Swazi, for land and resources, which were in short supply after drought

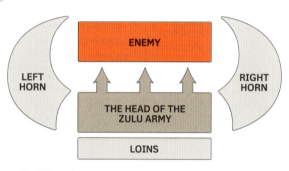

△ **Buffalo soldiers**
Shaka invented the immensely successful "Buffalo Horns" battle tactic. "Head" troops engaged the enemy's front and the "horns" attacked the flanks. The "loins" were reserves.

and famine affected the region from 1800–1808. Under the leadership of Dingiswayo, who became king in 1806, the Mthethwa ruled a confederacy of local groups, which included the Zulu. One of his most able military commanders was a young Zulu man called Shaka. The illegitimate son of the Zulu king Senzangakhona kaJama, Shaka had lived among the Mthethwa from childhood with his mother, Nandi.

When Senzangakhona kaJama died in 1816, Dingiswayo helped Shaka to seize the Zulu throne, provided that he remained a vassal of the Mthethwa. Following Dingiswayo's death in 1817, however, Shaka embarked on a series of conquests that saw him assume control of the entire territory of South Africa. Under Shaka, all conquered peoples became Zulu, and Zulu customs, including the rule of law upheld by chiefs, were imposed throughout the kingdom, forging a national identity among what had been a diverse group of peoples.

From Shaka onward, all power in the Zulu State was centralized under the king. Before this, the monarch had ruled in consultation with chiefs and advisors.

AN UNCOMPROMISING KING

Born c. 1787, Shaka kaSenzangakhona, known as Shaka Zulu, ran his state on martial lines. Boys as young as six were enrolled in his army, at first to carry supplies. When a warrior was unsuccessful in battle or showed cowardice, his family was executed. But it was not fear of failure alone that motivated Shaka's army. Soldiers were highly trained, and lived together in military stockades. Shaka introduced a variant of the long *assegai* throwing spear—the short *iklwa* stabbing spear used in hand-to-hand combat. A ruthless leader, Shaka became increasingly erratic in later life, and is said to have executed many people for not sufficiently mourning the death of his mother. He was assassinated in 1828 by two of his half-brothers.

STATUE OF SHAKA IN THE ZULU CAPITAL, ULUNDI

SHAKA AND THE ZULU KINGDOM | 207

▷ **Communal life**
Most Zulu families and clans lived in *kraals*, defensible enclosures with room for livestock and several beehive-shaped huts called *iQukwane*, usually built by women.

Under Shaka, local leaders and the chiefs of conquered peoples were still allowed to administer their own areas and keep some powers—settling land disputes or overseeing local legal affairs—but had to pay tributes to Shaka and the kings that followed in the form of local produce. Dissent was not tolerated, and Zulu lands were dotted with military garrisons to ensure law and order was kept.

The end of an era

The Zulu Kingdom rose to power during a period known as the *Mfecane* ("the crushing"). Its wars of conquest, along with famine and regional conflicts among local peoples such as the Matabele, the Tsonga and the Ndwandwe, saw two million people lose their lives. This made Southern Africa highly unstable, a situation Shaka's successors were unable to rectify, especially as Boer settlers from Britain's Cape Colony and British imperialist forces began to encroach on Zulu lands from the 1840s. In 1879, Zulu king Cetshwayo (see pp.208–209) attempted to drive the British from his territory. The British deposed him, and they and the Boers took over his kingdom.

During the apartheid era, South Africa's Zulus were confined to the KwaZulu homeland and denied civil rights—as were Black South Africans in the rest of the country's homelands (see pp.254–255). Today, many of South Africa's 10–12 million Zulus still live in the region, now called KwaZulu-Natal, one of the country's nine provinces. Although part of the parliamentary democracy of South Africa, KwaZulu-Natal boasts its own Zulu king. While the monarch has no legislative power, he controls through a state-operated trust around 30 percent of KwaZulu-Natal's land and exerts a considerable degree of political and social influence among his people.

▽ **Defensive weapons**
These Zulu warriors photographed c.1875 carry ox-hide *umbumbolozo* shields. At 36in (91cm), they were shorter than the Shaka-era 60in (152cm) *isihlangu* shields.

King in exile
Cetshwayo is photographed in London, where he adopted Western dress but wore his *isicoco*—a head-ring for Zulu men. He negotiated his return to the Zulu Kingdom with Prime Minister Gladstone and Queen Victoria.

Cetshwayo

The last great king of the Zulu Kingdom

Cetshwayo was a skillful negotiator and an uncompromising leader whose success and popularity brought him into direct conflict with Southern Africa's colonial occupiers at the end of the 19th century.

▵ **Capture of Cetshwayo**
The British spent nearly two months searching for Cetshwayo after the Battle of Ulundi, finally capturing him in a remote *kraal* (village).

Physically imposing at more than 6 ft 6 in (2 m) tall, Cetshwayo literally fought his way to the throne of the Zulu nation: in 1856, the power struggle between Cetshwayo and his brother Mbuyazi for the right to succeed their father, King Mpande, was settled at the Battle of Ndondakusuka. Mbuyazi was killed, along with at least another five of his brothers. At this point, Cetshwayo became the Zulu Kingdom's de facto ruler for 16 years, until formally taking power in 1873, a year after Mpande's death (which was initially concealed).

Mpande had been a reluctant ruler, ceding some of his land to the British and Afrikaners rather than risk conflict with them. Cetshwayo took a different approach to kingship, adopting an anti-Western stance and encouraging other African rulers to do the same. At the same time, he negotiated skillfully with colonial powers over border disputes. Eager to avoid giving the British a reason to destroy his kingdom, Cetshwayo would strategically move his army away from the borders of British colonies.

Engaging with the enemy

Sir Henry Bartle Frere, the British High Commissioner for Southern Africa, decided to force the issue. In December 1878, after Zulu troops made minor border incursions into British-controlled Natal, Frere ordered Cetshwayo to disband his army and relinquish his sovereignty. Cetshwayo's refusal led to the first battle of the Anglo-Zulu War, at Isandlwana in 1879, which the Zulu won. After a Zulu defeat at the Battle of Ulundi later that year, the British exiled Cetshwayo to the Cape Colony and then, in 1882, to England, where he petitioned British politicians for his return. Britain annexed Cetshwayo's former realm and, in 1883, permitted him to return to "rule" a portion of it. He died the following year of a heart attack, though rumors persist that he was poisoned.

◁ **Zulu shield**
In battle, the 20,000-strong Zulu army carried wooden and oxhide shields, like the one shown here, and *assegai* (spears), while the British used Gatling guns and rifles.

▽ **City of fire**
The British burned the Zulu capital Ulundi following Cetshwayo's defeat there in the final, decisive battle of the Anglo-Zulu War.

- **c. 1826** Birth of Cetshwayo in Eshowe, modern-day South Africa
- **1873** Cetshwayo becomes king of the Zulu nation
- **1878** Negotiations with Sir Henry Bartle Frere
- **1879** Anglo-Zulu War fought between the British Empire and the Zulu Kingdom
- **1881** Cetshwayo begins his campaign to reinstate the Zulu monarchy
- **1882** Cetshwayo meets with Queen Victoria in England
- **1883** Cetshwayo returns to Zulu Kingdom
- **1884** Death of Cetshwayo on February 8

The scramble for Africa
Carving up a continent

As the 19th century ended, Africa became subject to Europe's increasing desire for imperial control. Without the involvement of any African leaders, rival European nations agreed the division of the continent between themselves.

By the mid-19th century, several European nations had established trading posts across Africa. Some, notably Britain and France, had already acquired colonies in South Africa, Algeria, and elsewhere. Christian missionaries and adventurers returned from Africa's interior with tales of its peoples; spectacular landscapes; and untapped riches of gold, timber, minerals, and resources. Explorers investigated and mapped the continent. In Europe's eyes, Africa had been "discovered" and now was ripe for exploitation.

Colonization and cooperation

The Industrial Revolution made the nations of the West wealthy and powerful. It also left them hungry for raw materials and new markets, both of which they saw in Africa. With the international slave trade abolished by the mid-19th century, Europe turned its focus to securing trading and territorial rights within Africa itself, often employing deceptive contracts that dispossessed African rulers of their lands. Other tools of colonization were quinine—introduced from the 1850s—which lowered mortality rates from malaria, enabling Europeans to live in areas where the disease was prevalent, and new weapons, such as the breech-loading repeater rifle and the Maxim machine gun.

European nations' biggest fear was competition from each other—and they tackled the issue through collusion. Convened by the German chancellor Otto von Bismarck, the Berlin Conference of November 15, 1884–February 26, 1885, saw 13 European powers and the US meeting to agree between them spheres of influence in Africa. No African nations or peoples were represented at the conference—the Sultan of Zanzibar had requested to attend, but Britain refused.

As well as giving each country the right to claim a territory if it had treaties, flags, or people on the ground (a policy known as "effective occupation"), the European powers demarcated lands where future colonies could be established and set up free trade areas that mutually benefited European interests.

Remaking Africa in Europe's image

The agreements made at Berlin had far-reaching consequences. The Belgian king Leopold II was handed sole ownership of a vast territory, the Congo Free State (see pp.212–213). Today, as the Democratic

△ **European greed**
This French caricature from 1885 satirizes the Berlin Conference, showing Germany's chancellor Bismarck offering slices of Africa to his guests.

▷ **Camel Corps**
Britain's Egyptian Camel Corps stand guard, c.1900. Many camel drivers were Egyptians, either hired or press-ganged into supporting and supplying British and imperial troops.

Republic of the Congo, it still bears the scars of his, and later the Belgian government's, misrule. Similarly, Britain's claim to the territories forming modern-day Nigeria joined together historically divided lands and ethnic groups such as the Hausa-Fulani, the Yoruba, and the Igbo. After Nigeria achieved independence in 1960, longstanding tensions between the three groups erupted into civil war in 1967. The arbitrary drawing of borders that separated peoples and forced together ethnicities was repeated across Africa, for example by the British in Somalia, Kenya, and Zimbabwe.

The Berlin Conference recognized French power in West Africa and Britain's primacy in East Africa, from Egypt to South Africa in an almost unbroken line. Germany's interest in what are today Tanzania, Togo, and Namibia was accepted, as was Portugal's right to Mozambique, Angola, and Guinea, among others. New players—notably Italy, with colonies in modern-day Eritrea, Somalia, and Libya—would seize other regions. Before the Berlin Conference, 10 percent of the continent was under foreign control; by 1918 the figure was closer to 90 percent. Only Liberia and Ethiopia maintained their sovereignty.

The Berlin Conference did not initiate the scramble for Africa, but it accelerated the process of imperial expansion already underway, giving it a formally approved structure in a published set of terms and conditions known as the General Act. By adopting Britain's tactic of using anti-slave-trade agreements to "justify" imposing their control on African affairs, and by claiming they were bringing the benefits of modern civilization to Africa, Europe's imperialists added a moral gloss to an immoral system that would endure for another 75 years.

◁ **Unfair burden**
Europe's colonists routinely exploited their power. This pith-helmeted official in the French Congo makes four young men carry him.

Congo Free State
Colonial corruption in Central Africa

Leopold II of Belgium privately owned a huge, resource-rich region at the heart of the continent, which he named the Congo Free State. Having seized the region in 1885, Leopold ruthlessly exploited both its natural treasures and its people.

It was the writings of Welsh-American journalist Henry Morton Stanley (see pp.200–201) that captured the imagination of the Belgian monarch Leopold II in the 1870s. Stanley had in 1871 famously "found" the Scottish missionary and explorer David Livingstone, who had gone missing while searching for the source of the Nile. Leopold hired Stanley to act as his agent in Central Africa, where he was interested in securing territory, resources, and trading agreements.

From 1879–1884, Stanley traveled the region, setting up treaties with local leaders, who were not properly informed of their content or aware that agreeing meant handing over control of their land to Leopold. Stanley also oversaw the building of a highway connecting the Congo River to local trade routes, helping to make the area's economic potential easier to exploit. Leopold, meanwhile, had established organizations such as the *Association Internationale Africaine* and the *Association Internationale du Congo* to carry out nominally philanthropic, missionary, and anti-slavery work, but which mainly provided a respectable front for his activities.

This had the desired effect. At the Berlin Conference of November 1884 (see pp.210–211), Leopold's claim to Central Africa was formally recognized; in 1885, he announced the creation of the Congo Free State.

Exploited land

Leopold treated the Congo Free State, 76 times larger than Belgium, as if it were his personal kingdom. It encompassed 905,000 sq miles (2.34 million sq km) of land and 15 million people—a large proportion of whom objected to Leopold's rule and the vast majority of whom suffered oppression and expropriation during the state's two decades of existence. Leopold appointed only a small number of administrators, wanting to retain personal control. Instead, he formed the *Force Publique*, a private force of mercenaries notorious for their acts of torture, beating, murder, and sexual assault that caused millions of deaths.

Congo Free State was blessed with natural resources, including ivory and, most abundantly, rubber. Leopold soon saw opportunities for European corporations to exploit these resources within the country. When

△ **Threatened culture**
This *ndop* figure represents an 18th-century Kuba king. The Kuba people's culture was one of many to be suppressed under Leopold.

> "Leopold's Congo state is **guilty of crimes against humanity**."
>
> BLACK AMERICAN BAPTIST MINISTER AND POLITICIAN GEORGE WASHINGTON WILLIAMS, 1890

◁ **Hard harvest**
Rubber tapping was labor-intensive and dangerous. Workers sliced into rubber vines, allowing latex sap to coat their bodies, which was later scraped off—taking skin and hair with it.

from 1887 Dunlop, and then Michelin, began mass-producing bicycle inner tubes and pneumatic tires, the global demand for rubber skyrocketed, and Leopold granted companies such as the Anglo-Belgian India Rubber Company (Abir) concessions to run large swathes of Congo Free State in exchange for their investment in infrastructure, particularly road and rail. These concessionary companies' activities were unregulated. Extreme violence was meted out to those who refused to work or who did not collect enough rubber. With all resources devoted to rubber harvesting, agricultural production was neglected, resulting in crop failures and starvation.

By the turn of the century, the violence, coercion, and displacement suffered by the Indigenous people of the region became impossible for the international community to ignore: journalist E. D. Morel described Congo Free State as a "monstrous outrage." A 1904 report by British consul Roger Casement revealed the extent of Leopold's misrule and led to the arrest and punishment of several corporate figures and Congo Free State officials.

End of European rule

In 1908, Leopold was compelled to transfer control of the Congo Free State to the Belgian government, which renamed it the Belgian Congo. The economy gradually shifted away from rubber toward increasing investment in mining, but again there was forced cultivation of specific export crops such as cotton. Opposition to foreign rule continued, and many Congolese objected to—and resisted—paying taxes to Belgium. The colonial authorities met these acts of defiance with violence; a large number of inhabitants left the country to work in European-run mines and farms in neighboring states.

Belgium continued to administer the new state until it achieved independence in 1960, eventually becoming the Democratic Republic of the Congo.

△ **Ill-gotten gains**
This satirical image from c. 1905 makes the point that Leopold II of Belgium built his fortune on the bones of the people in the Congo Free State.

ARMY OF **OPPRESSION**

The *Force Publique* was the paramilitary arm of the Congo Free State. It protected the exploitative activities of the concessionary companies and stamped down on protest. Established in 1886, it consisted of Belgian soldiers and European mercenaries commanding troops recruited or conscripted from the local region and farther afield, including the West and East coasts. At its height, the *Force Publique* numbered 19,000 men. It was involved in many atrocities and its name was a byword for brutality.

Coffee plantation
Enslaved Africans pick coffee on a plantation in Brazil, where slavery was only abolished in 1888. Around 5.5 million Africans were transported to Brazil to work on plantations.

The African diaspora

People of African descent around the world

Africans have migrated from the continent since ancient times, but the 200-million strong diaspora of people of African descent was largely created by the enslavement and transportation of millions of Africans between the 15th and 19th centuries.

The African Union considers the African diaspora as "people of African origin living outside the continent, irrespective of their citizenship and nationality." In one sense, because human life began on the continent (see pp.22–23), the whole world is filled with an African diaspora. However, the movements that forced millions of people of African descent away from the continent are mostly political and financial.

Africans first reached Europe in Roman times, when North Africa was part of the Roman Empire. Indeed, Septimius Severus, who was born in Libya, became Roman emperor in 193 CE. Other Africans settled in the medieval Islamic world, often trafficked as enslaved people (see pp.148–149). There was also a small African population in Tudor London and Renaissance Portugal. These people were musicians, skilled tradespeople, diplomats, or part of wealthy households or the royal court.

The slave trade and the diaspora

The largest diaspora movement by far, however, was an entirely involuntary one: the transportation by Europeans of an estimated 11 million Africans across the Atlantic in the slave trade that devastated the African continent over four centuries. This was what led to a diaspora that today comprises more than 200 million people of African or mixed descent, around 43 million of these living in the US and roughly 10 million in Europe. Many countries in the Caribbean now have a majority of their population of diaspora

Sojourner Truth
Born into enslavement in New York State (at that time a state where slavery still existed), Truth escaped in 1826 and became an outspoken opponent of slavery and an advocate of Black American and women's civil rights.

> "Africa is our **center of gravity**, our cultural and spiritual mother and father … no matter **where we live** …"
>
> JOHN HENRIK CLARKE, AFRICAN AMERICAN HISTORIAN (1915–98)

descent. Smaller diaspora groups include the Siddi people of India and Pakistan taken there by the Arab slave trade, as well as the 100,000-strong Afro-Turk community in Turkey who were brought there in Ottoman times.

Impact of the diaspora

The forced migration of so many African people had a profound impact on many areas of society. The diaspora gave rise to political movements, especially in campaigns to abolish slavery, where works by formerly enslaved people such as Olaudah Equiano's *The Interesting Narrative* (1789) helped galvanize anti-slavery movements, and activists such as Sojourner Truth (1797–1883) and Frederick Douglass (1818–1895) played a key part in its abolition in the US at the end of the Civil War.

Diaspora Africans, with their international connections, were key to the development of the ideology of Pan-Africanism (see pp.232–233), with campaigners such as the Jamaican Marcus Garvey (1887–1940) and the American sociologist and historian W. E. B. Du Bois (1868–1963) laying the foundations for a movement that linked the diaspora with African politicians.

The end of colonial empires brought a further diaspora, as Africans moved from now independent colonies to the former colonial power. Some settled, others stayed for a while to study or work before returning to Africa. Often they were invited by the governments there to fill labor shortages. France, for example, received African migrants mainly from its former colonies in North and West Africa. While some diaspora Africans came voluntarily, others arrived as refugees from civil war, famine, or religious or political persecution.

New cultures emerge

Where Africans from many different cultures had been enslaved and forced to live together, this led to a loss of cultures and at the same time the emergence of new hybrid cultures. Religious systems such as Haitian Vodou, Cuban Santeria, or Brazilian Candomblé owed much to African origins, particularly from among the Yoruba people, but developed a vitality all of their own. In plantations where enslaved people had no shared language, creoles—adaptations of the colonial language tinged with African influences—arose, such as Haitian Creole, which is today the national language of Haiti. Over time, diaspora Africans also had a strong influence on the arts and music in particular, with jazz developing from work songs of enslaved African Americans, and calypso and reggae emerging in the diaspora populations of the Caribbean.

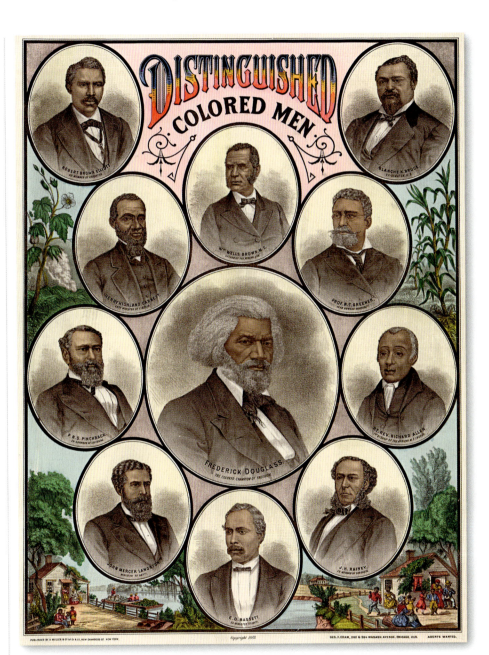

△ **Frederick Douglass**
Shown here on a poster from c.1884, Douglass is in the center, surrounded by other activists. The poster uses the language of the time, which today would be considered offensive.

Colonial wars

A continent in crisis

The 19th century saw unprecedented levels of European expansion into Africa, usually through war and conflict, followed by colonizing powers attempting to impose control over Indigenous populations.

△ **Stolen goods**
Following the British Army's attack in 1897, the colonial military looted the sculptures and other treasures from the razed Benin royal palace.

In the late 19th century, imperialist nations sought to exploit Africa's natural resources and establish strategically important military bases from which they could protect other territories they had colonized around the world. This "Scramble for Africa" was formalized by the Berlin Conference of 1884–1885, where the European powers agreed to partition Africa between them (see pp.210–211). The colonial frontiers might have been established on a map, but the colonial powers still had to occupy and take possession of lands by force. Across the continent, conflicts and wars broke out as European armies continued to meet African peoples who resisted European colonization.

The Anglo-Asante Wars had begun in 1824 when the Asante Empire (see pp.190–191) in modern-day Ghana resisted British encroachment. In the first conflict, the Asante defeated the British forces and forced a retreat. The second conflict, from 1863 to 1864, ended in a stalemate, but the third, between 1873 and 1874, resulted in defeat for the Asante, when the British occupied and burned Kumasi, the capital. Seeking greater control of the region, the British attacked the Asante again in 1894 and overthrew King Prempeh I in 1896. A final conflict in 1900 resulted in the complete annexation of the Asante Empire, until Ghana achieved independence in 1957.

Resistance and defeat

In North Africa, France invaded the city of Algiers in 1830, initiating more than a century of French rule in the region that would see hundreds of thousands of

▷ **Epic victory**
Zulu soldiers triumph at the Battle of Isandlwana, one of the British Army's worst colonial defeats—and a landmark moment in African opposition to imperialism.

GHANA'S GREAT REBEL QUEEN

Yaa Asantewaa (right, depicted in a statue in Ghana) was queen of Ejisu, a territory of the Asante Empire and an implacable opponent of colonialism. In the Fifth Anglo-Asante War in 1900, she led troops into battle against British forces in the Asante city of Kumasi, only to be captured and exiled to the Seychelles. She is revered as a Ghanaian heroine.

French settlers arrive and the attempted suppression of the Indigenous Muslim population. Armed uprisings against the French marked the period. Algerian religious and military leader Emir Abdelkader led a coalition of local peoples, and by 1839 controlled two-thirds of Algeria. By 1847, however, the French had brutally crushed his resistance.

In Southern Africa, the Anglo-Zulu War was fought in 1879 when the British invaded the Zulu Kingdom. At the Battle of Isandlwana in January, a large army of Zulu troops inflicted a heavy defeat on the smaller but much better armed British forces. By July, British reinforcements had deposed the Zulu king Cetshwayo (see pp.208–209), ending the independence of the Zulu nation. Now Britain turned to the white Afrikaners, or Boers, of the Transvaal and Orange Free State republics, seeking overall dominance in a region rich in diamond and gold fields. The Anglo-Boer War of 1899–1901 resulted in Britain taking control of much of Southern Africa.

Like Cetshwayo, Samory Touré was the leader of a nation which resisted the colonizing armies. Touré's Wassoulou Empire (also called the Mandinka Empire), which encompassed parts of present-day Mali, Sierra Leone, Guinea, Côte d'Ivoire, and Liberia, fought France when it invaded in 1882. For several years, Touré held back the French in what would be known as the Mandinka Resistance Wars. By 1898, however, France's soldiers made a concentrated assault against Touré, capturing his lands and exiling him to Gabon.

A year earlier, Britain had used an army of 5,000 soldiers, armed with Maxim guns—weapons that could fire hundreds of bullets a minute—to destroy the 600-year-old Kingdom of Benin (see pp.128–129). In this and countless other wars, Europeans used their superior firepower to impose military control, followed by civilian colonial government, on Africa. However, occupation would lead only to decades of uprisings and resistance from colonized peoples who demanded their freedom and independence.

△ **Resistant ruler**
Samory Touré's Sunni Muslim empire resisted French encroachment for almost 20 years. Samory was the great-grandfather of independent Guinea's first president, Ahmed Sékou Touré.

" ... the most dangerous antagonist the **Europeans have had to deal with**."

THE NEW YORK TIMES ON SAMORY TOURÉ, 1898

Resistance and uprisings
The fight for freedom intensifies

From the mid-19th century to 1914, Europe colonized the whole of Africa, except for Liberia and Ethiopia. Across the continent, Africans resisted imperial rule—through strikes, tax revolts, uprisings, and full-scale armed rebellion.

African reactions to the arrival of Europeans were mixed. Some groups, particularly the victims of internal warfare and intra-African slave raiding, welcomed the newcomers in the hope they would bring peace and protection. Others questioned the Europeans' motives for interfering in African affairs.

Confronting oppression

By the middle of the 19th century, it was clear the Europeans intended more harm than good—and that Africans would have to find effective ways to oppose them. The fates of the Asante Empire and the Zulu Kingdom (see pp.216–217) after taking on British imperial forces in open warfare indicated that a directly confrontational approach would not always work. But sometimes it did. At the Battle of Adwa in 1896, for example, the Ethiopian army of Emperor Menelik II killed 4,000 Italian soldiers, thwarting the invaders' attempts to expand the territory they already controlled in Eritrea farther into the Horn of Africa.

That same year, Mbuya Nehanda, a priestess of the Shona people of Rhodesia (modern Zimbabwe), led a revolt against the British South Africa Company's colonization of her lands. Another spiritual leader, Sekuru Kaguvi, supported her, and both were inspired by the large-scale but unsuccessful uprisings by the region's Ndebele people a year earlier. The British captured and executed Nehanda and Sekuru, and Nehanda in particular became a folk heroine, memorialized through songs, novels, and poems.

In 1904, Namibia's Herero people revolted against their economic exploitation by Germany, and were suppressed in especially brutal fashion. The Germans summarily executed many Herero fighters, and tens of thousands of men, women, and children died from starvation and disease when they were herded into

△ **Spiritual leaders**
Mbuya Nehanda (left) and Sekuru Kaguvi (right) were *svikiro*, mediums said to speak with the gods. The British hanged both rebel leaders in 1898.

◁ **Hero in exile**
The Herero chief Samuel Maharero led the 1904 rebellion against Germany's control of Namibia. This 1907 image shows him in exile in Bechuanaland (modern Botswana).

> "**Let us die fighting** rather than … as a result of **maltreatment** [or] **imprisonment**."
>
> SAMUEL MAHARERO IN A LETTER TO FELLOW CHIEF HENDRIK WITBOOI, 1904

△ **Ethiopian victory**
This painting depicts the Battle of Adwa that took place on March 2, 1896. Emperor Menelik II (top left, with umbrella) and the Empress Taitu (bottom left, on horseback) watch as their troops prepare to engage—and defeat—Italy's colonial soldiers.

concentration camps or fled the country to seek refuge. The following year, Germany crushed the Maji-Maji uprising in Tanganyika (modern Tanzania) organized by Kinjikitile Ngwale. A charismatic religious prophet, Ngwale supplied his followers with holy water instead of weapons to protect them from the Germans' bullets, with tragic results.

Pragmatic approaches

By the end of World War I, violent opposition to colonialism gave way to more measured and strategic responses: educated Africans demanded they be included in civic life; farmers resisted the colonial powers' attempts to control which crops they produced; and mine and port workers in Southern, West, and East Africa organized trade unions to fight for better pay and working conditions. In the Belgian Congo (today the Democratic Republic of the Congo) the Christian cleric Simon Kimbangu promised imperial liberation for the many followers of his new religious movement of Kimbanguism. The Belgians arrested him in 1921 and, charged with undermining security, he spent the remaining 30 years of his life in prison. In southeastern Nigeria, the Aba Women's War of 1929 saw thousands of women engage in sit-ins and other demonstrations at their exclusion from economic and public life by British colonial administrators. When one of their rallies turned violent, soldiers opened fire and killed at least 50 people. Ultimately, their activism worked, and the British reformed the region's governance to include more Indigenous participation.

Resistance to colonial rule was clearly not just about violent confrontation. Africans practiced countless acts of rebellion, large and small, on a daily basis. Sometimes this meant armed insurrection; on other occasions it meant something more mundane, such as deliberately giving visiting imperial officials wrong directions so they would get lost. In all instances the intention was the same: to let the European colonizers know that their presence in other people's lands was not welcome.

Powerful figure
King Jaja became a millionaire through his business acumen in Opobo, Nigeria. Yet the British decided his power and influence was an affront to their imperial ambitions and set out to remove him.

Jaja of Opobo

The palm-oil king of the Niger Delta

Enslaved as a child, Jaja of Opobo founded a 19th-century city-state that dominated West Africa's palm oil trade. As well as wealth and power, it brought him into conflict with Britain's colonial ambitions in the region.

Jubo Jubogha was born into the Igbo community of what is now Nigeria around 1821, and was enslaved as a child. His enslaver controlled several trade routes in the Niger Delta, a network of swamps and creeks through which goods—chiefly palm oil, used as a lubricant for industrial machinery and in soap, as well as for cooking—passed on their way to the coast.

When his enslaver died, the young man, who would become better known as "Jaja," took control of the business. He soon led a merchant group called Anna Pepple House on Bonny Island, a kingdom on the Delta. After a clash with other traders, Jaja and his allies headed 25 miles (40 km) east to found an independent settlement named Opobo.

Palm oil and power

Jaja was a strong leader with an eye for opportunity, and grew to dominate the regional trade in palm oil. Jaja became Opobo's king, and was determined to maintain the independence of his rapidly modernizing operation. By the early 1870s, he was sending part of his stock directly to Liverpool and other British ports. He confined European traders to Opobo, away from markets farther inland, and did not allow European missionaries in his kingdom.

Jaja embraced aspects of European culture. He sent his children to study in Glasgow, Scotland, and built a secular school in Opobo, staffed by white Europeans.

◁ **Palm fruits**
The yellowy-red pulp of oil-palm fruits is pressed to produce palm oil. Oil palms are native to West Africa.

During the Anglo-Asante Wars in what is now Ghana, he sent troops to aid the British. Yet the British would show no loyalty to Jaja. The Berlin Conference of 1884 (see pp.210–211) imposed direct European control on many African nations, and Opobo was designated British territory. Jaja resisted, and refused to remove taxes on British traders. The British arrested him in 1887 and exiled him to the Caribbean. By 1891, Jaja had negotiated his return, but died on his way home.

▽ **Palm oil market**
Igbo traders show calabash gourds filled with palm oil to a European buyer in a market in Southern Nigeria around 1900.

---

c. 1821 Jubo Jubogha, later known as Jaja of Opobo, is born

1869 After a clash with the established trading post of Bonny, Jaja founds the Opobo city-state

1873 Jaja's troops support the British army during the Anglo-Asante Wars

1884 Opobo is given to the British by the Berlin Conference

1885 Jaja's men use boom chains to limit access to the Opobo River

1887 Jaja is deposed and exiled to Saint Vincent and Barbados, in the Caribbean

1891 Jaja is finally granted leave to return to Opobo, but dies during the voyage

1903 A bronze monument honoring Jaja is erected in Opobo

Exploitation and administration

Governing the colonies

△ **Internment**
Suspected insurgents are held captive in a British concentration camp during the anti-colonial Mau Mau rebellion (1952–1960). Many suffered torture and abuse at the hands of British soldiers.

As colonial rule became firmly established in Africa, the European occupiers introduced various methods of administration in their colonies to best exploit the wealth of resources of the continent.

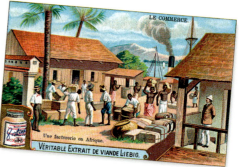

△ **Trading post**
Europeans established trading posts, called factories, on coasts or rivers, in order to influence and control trade, and generate profits for the metropole (imperial homeland).

With improvements in communications in the late 19th century, the European powers began to explore the heart of Africa in search of tradable resources to fill the gap left by the ending of the lucrative slave trade, acquiring lands through means such as treaties with local leaders (see box, right). As they did so, they developed various forms of colonial governance. At the onset of colonialism, European nations permitted the establishment of private companies, such as the British South Africa Company formed in 1887, which were granted the administration of large expanses of land. The rationale behind this form of company rule was the need to administer the colonies while minimizing expense for the colonizing nation. However, many companies proved unsuccessful because they generated only minimal profits for their stakeholders. By the mid-1920s, various forms of European governance had replaced company rule.

The major colonial players were Britain (which took control of the lion's share of Africa), France, Germany, Belgium, Italy, Portugal, and Spain. For the most part, these powers imposed their rule in order to extract resources with the minimum cost, but occupied only what was necessary for exploitation of the territory.

Systems of colonial rule

The French, Germans, Portuguese, and Belgians generally subjected their colonies in West and Central Africa to some form of direct rule, with a central colonial government that removed autonomy from Indigenous peoples. Britain, on the other hand, chose a form of indirect rule to govern its colonies in East Africa and Nigeria. Indirect rule granted African rulers some autonomy to choose their own leaders and local forms of government, but the colonizers had free rein to profit from exploring and exploiting the land, and from establishing trading posts.

In Southern Africa, a more common form of colonialism was by settler rule. This differed from other forms of colonial government in that migrants from Europe, who intended to make the colonies their permanent home, handled the administration. They established their status by direct rule, rather than by treaties with Indigenous peoples. Settlers from Britain, Germany, the Netherlands, and Portugal colonized regions in South Africa, Southern and Northern Rhodesia (present-day Zimbabwe and Zambia), Mozambique, Namibia, and Angola. Settler rule was also the model in the British colony of Kenya, and in the French colony of Algeria.

Under systems of colonial administration, communications from the interior to the coast were improved, with the building of roads and railroads. But this was all to the colonizers' benefit, and achieved by oppression of the local people. In Togo, for example, German colonizers coerced local people to build railroads and forced farmers to turn their land over to cotton rather than food crops. German administrators were authorized to punish by fines, whipping, and imprisonment, with little oversight.

Africans put up fierce resistance to all forms of colonial rule. This was especially violent in Kenya, where the British military forced the Kikuyu people from their territory in the central region. In the early 1950s, a secret society, the Kenya Land and Freedom Army, which the British called the "Mau Mau," stepped up attacks on European settlers and Kikuyus loyal to the government. Thus began the Mau Mau rebellion, lasting from 1952–1960, the most prolonged and violent response to colonial rule, and a harbinger of the eventual withdrawal of the European powers.

SIGNING TREATIES

In the late 19th century, European colonizers acquired territory through the signing of treaties with local African leaders—the French are pictured here signing an agreement with the Kingdom of Tamisso, in modern-day Guinea. Treaties offered "protection" from aggression or invasion in return for the right to carry out exploration and conduct trade, which ultimately gave the European power free rein to exploit the African state's resources.

> "**The colonial regime** owes its legitimacy **to force.**"
>
> FRANTZ FANON, *THE WRETCHED OF THE EARTH*, 1961

◁ **Pretoria station**
Crowds greet the arrival in 1893 of the first train at Pretoria train station, built to boost economic activities associated with the gold-mining industry.

◁ **Unique art form**
The craft of Zulu basketry, which had declined in the 1930s during colonization, has been revived as a symbol of national pride by South African artists such as Beauty Ngxongo, who wove this basket with *ilala* palm fiber.

5

The age of independence

1914–1994

The age of independence

The decolonization of Africa was a process that broadly took place from the early 1950s onward. The first postwar independence movements took hold in North Africa, starting with Libya in 1951, and then spread to West Africa with the independence of Ghana in 1957, and from there eastward and south. One year alone, 1960, called the Year of Africa, saw 17 nations gain their independence, including Mali, Senegal, and Madagascar from France, Somalia and Nigeria from Britain, and the Democratic Republic of the Congo from Belgium. While independence was more easily won in some places than in others, decolonization was rarely anything less than a radical and multilayered operation.

The seeds of independence

It is contested how much African decolonization was a top-down or bottom-up movement. It varied from place to place, but in all cases the role of educated African political elites was consequential. From around the 1880s, young African nationalists were able to travel and study abroad, exposing themselves to a cross-pollination of revolutionary ideas. Political impetus was provided by the freedom movements of earlier times, including the American Revolution of 1775–1791, the French Revolution of 1789, and the Haitian Revolution of 1791–1804. African intellectuals also absorbed the newly emerging Pan-Africanism of figures such as the Jamaican activist Marcus Garvey (see pp.232–233). The early years of the 20th century witnessed an upsurge of resistance to colonial rule, with educated African elites agitating the masses, initiating action against the colonists, and establishing nationalist political parties (see pp.228–229).

World wars and decolonization

Millions of Africans' participation and sacrifice in World War I led to increased African calls for self-determination. The period saw revolts against colonial rule, such as John Chilembwe's armed uprising against the British in 1915. In World War II, many more millions of Africans fought for the freedom of the West and increasingly believed that they should share this freedom, too. The Atlantic Charter, agreed in 1941 between Britain and the US (see pp.230–231), asserted that all people had a right to self-government. This and the signing of the United Nations' Universal Declaration of Human Rights in 1948 further motivated Africans to demand independence. In the 1940s and '50s, grassroots nationalist movements sprang up across Africa, spearheaded by many inspirational figures, including Funmilayo Ransome-Kuti in Nigeria and Bibi Titi Mohammed in Tanzania.

The main era of decolonization coincided with the Cold War (see pp.246–247), whose protagonists vied for influence among the emerging independent African nations. Meanwhile, the presence of entrenched white settlers in some states and longstanding rivalries between ethnic groups and peoples ensured that the process of decolonization was in several cases marred by violence, political turmoil, widespread unrest, and organized insurrections—though some nations also achieved independence through peaceful negotiations around the conference table.

◁ **Commemorative stamp from Ghana**

1900 Henry Sylvester Williams organizes the first Pan-African Conference, in London

1910 South African independence from Britain; power assumed by all-white government

1914 Marcus Garvey founds the Universal Negro Improvement Association

1915 Unsuccessful Chilembwe uprising in Nyasaland (Malawi) against British rule

THE AGE OF INDEPENDENCE

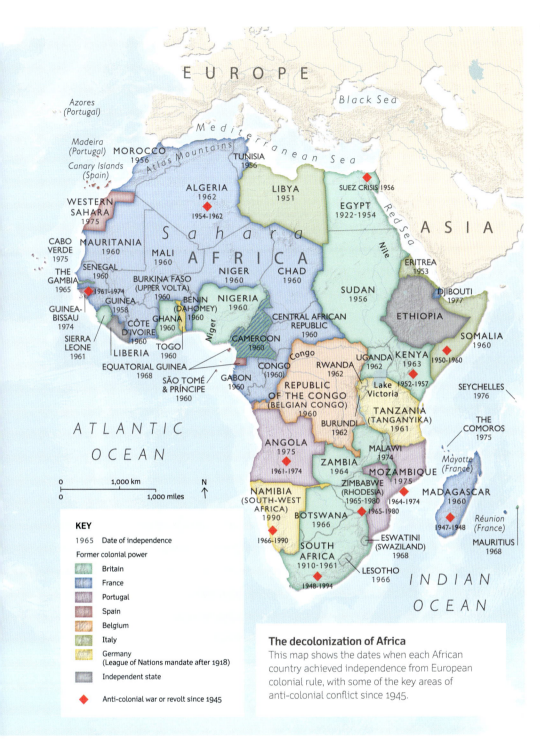

The decolonization of Africa
This map shows the dates when each African country achieved independence from European colonial rule, with some of the key areas of anti-colonial conflict since 1945.

▲ Marcus Garvey (1887–1940)

▲ Funmilayo Ransome-Kuti, Nigerian activist

▲ Bibi Titi Mohammed, "Mother" of Tanzania

1922 Egyptian independence from Britain, following revolution in 1919

1951 Libya becomes first nation to win independence after World War II

1963 Kwame Nkrumah helps establish the Organization of African Unity

1967–1970 Biafra War in Nigeria (independence 1960)

1919 W. E. B. Du Bois organizes the first Pan-African Congress, in Paris

1948 The Universal Declaration of Human Rights enshrines the rights and freedoms of all human beings

1954 Algeria's bloody war of independence from France begins (ends 1962)

1965 Rhodesia declares independence from Britain

1980 Rhodesia's independence formally recognized when the country becomes Zimbabwe

Early independence movements

Organized resistance grows

African peoples resisted the expansion of European colonial control from the 1870s and, after World War I, early nationalist movements emerged, seeking greater freedoms and ultimately independence.

Africans repeatedly challenged the increasing expansion into African lands by European powers from the mid-19th century, despite the Europeans' superior military might. There was organized military resistance against the French led by cleric Abd-al-Kadir in the Maghreb in 1847, and headed by Samory Touré (c. 1830–1900) of the Wassoulou Empire up to 1898. Similarly, the Asante Kingdom fought against the British up to 1901. However, all suffered heavy losses, though rebellions against the brutality of colonial governments continued. The *Chimurenga* Resistance in Zimbabwe in 1896–1897 saw the Shona and Ndebele peoples rise up, provoked by the British South Africa Company's confiscation of the best land (see pp.166–167). The Maji-Maji revolt against German colonial rule in Tanganyika in 1905 was sparked by the use of forced labor, and the Zulu leader Bambatha kaMancinza's rebellion against a poll tax in South Africa in 1906 was another manifestation of a continued will to oppose colonizers.

Impact of World War I

Following World War I, many European administrators left Africa, having been conscripted or co-opted into war work, and the colonial powers now decided to involve Africans who had a secondary education in the running of the colonies. Hundreds of thousands of Africans were requisitioned as military laborers and soldiers, fighting in campaigns in East and West Africa, but also in the Middle East, and—particularly in the French forces—on the Western Front. Many Africans resented the sacrifices being asked for little tangible reward, and groups such as the Borgawa people in French Dahomey and the Egba in 1918 in British southern Nigeria rose up in revolt. Having pleaded in vain for a moderation of the cruel treatment of African laborers on plantations in Nyasaland (modern-day Malawi), in January 1915 the Baptist pastor John Chilembwe led an insurrection against the British. Although Chilembwe's revolt was brutally put down within weeks, it represented a new form of resistance, melding Christianity with the desire of Africans to have a nation-state of their own.

In the post-war period, Africans established a number of independent churches, such as the Kimbanguist Christian Church founded by Simon Kimbangu in the

△ **Algerian resistance**
Islamic scholar Abd-al-Kadir, shown here on an Algerian stamp, led the resistance to the French invasion of the Maghreb from 1830 until his surrender in 1847.

▷ **First party**
This photograph shows the founders of the South African Native National Congress. This was Africa's first Black political party, which in 1923 became the African National Congress.

◁ **African soldiers**
Members of the King's African Rifles stand to attention in this photograph from World War I. The regiment was raised in East Africa and saw service during the war in Somaliland.

modern-day Democratic Republic of the Congo in the 1920s, which acted as a focus for opposition to colonial governments. Up to and including the 1920s, when the continent's economies suffered a slump, workers became increasingly organized, with strikes in ports and mining towns and the formation of the first Black trade unions, such as the Industrial Workers of Africa in South Africa in 1917.

Colonial response and nationalist parties
In an attempt to find ways to hold on to the lands that they had colonized, European governments turned to an elite group of educated urban Africans for help. The French imperialist notion of the *mission civilatrice*, through which they expected African colonies to eventually be integrated culturally and politically into France, led the government to grant limited political representation to these groups. In 1914, the Senegalese Blaise Diagne became the first African elected to a post in the French government. The British adopted a different approach, establishing legislative councils, such as that set up in 1922 in Nigeria, which included a limited number of African members in an attempt to diffuse opposition from African nationalist groups.

The desire for independence, however, led to the founding of nationalist parties, such as the South African Native National Congress in South Africa in 1912 and the Nigerian National Democratic Party in 1923. A series of political organizations in North Africa, most notably the Destour in Tunisia in 1920, and the Wafd Party in Egypt in 1919, also became prominent. While these parties made incremental improvements in conditions for Africans and gained a small say in colonial administration, their greatest impact was as forerunners of the mass-participation African political parties of the 1950s and '60s.

Pan-Africanism
In the UK, several activists were involved in setting up the West African Student's Union (WASU), which became a hub for anti-colonial thinkers, including Ghanaian Kwame Nkrumah (see pp.242–243), Nigerian law student Ladipo Solanke, and Sierra Leonean doctor Herbert Bankole-Bright. Organizations like this that asserted Pan-Africanism (see pp.232–233) helped build solidarity among colonized nations. The notion of *Négritude*, a cultural identity shared by every African, promoted by the Martiniquan Aimé Césaire (1913–2008), also fueled the desire for independence. These ideas encouraged the next generation of nationalist parties, which built on the foundations laid by the early nationalist movements to create an irresistible momentum for self-rule.

▷ **Hat protest**
John Chilembwe, leader of the 1915 Nyasaland uprising, wears a hat in this sculpture. A colonial edict had forbidden Africans from wearing a hat in the presence of Europeans.

The figure of Chilembwe stands five times larger than that of Chorley

Chilembwe's friend John Chorley was a white missionary

Africa and World War II
The war that led to Africa's independence

World War II changed Africa. The participation in the war of up to one million Africans encouraged movements that pushed for colonial reforms and independence once the conflict was over.

World War II made a major impact on Africa in June 1940, when Italian forces in Ethiopia and Eritrea seized British Somaliland and moved into British Sudan and Kenya. Although Britain launched a successful counteroffensive, it was only achieved with the help of reinforcements from South Africa, East Africa, West Africa, and India.

As the war developed, human and material resources were mobilized across Britain and France's African colonies. Encouraged by Allied anti-Nazi recruitment campaigns, tens of thousands of Africans joined the war. They believed that they were fighting what the British called in their Swahili propaganda messages *vita vya Uhuru* ("a war for independence").

At the beginning of the war, in British West Africa, the Royal West African Frontier Force (RWAFF) grew from 8,000 to 146,000. Altogether, nine regiments came from the British West African colonies alone. These servicemen fought battles against the Axis Powers in East Africa, storming the

▽ **United nations**
In this poster from c.1942, Allied troops—including those from the British Empire—march together in a "V for Victory" formation.

AFRICA AND WORLD WAR II | 231

▷ **Commando emblem**
This is a badge of the African Commandos. Created in 1943, this division of the French army included riflemen from Algeria and Morocco.

Arab *lateen* sail and the crescent emblem of Northwest Africa

Italian divisions on the Juba River, in modern-day southern Somalia, and driving the fascists to complete defeat in Somalia and Ethiopia. They later went farther afield, facing the Japanese in Burma and Ceylon (now Myanmar and Sri Lanka respectively).

Under duress, Africans donated cash, groundnuts, cotton, rubber, palm oil, palm kernel, food, and resources to support Allied forces. The war economy brought young people seeking opportunities to the cities to work and earn a living. The economic boom stimulated the rapid growth of communications facilities, and with it the spread of ideas and ideologies such as democracy, capitalism, communism, human rights, and self-determination.

Fighting for freedom

By presenting themselves as champions of equality and freedom against the racism and tyranny of the Axis powers, the Allies gave the colonies hope that they were fighting for their own freedom, too. This was encapsulated in the Atlantic Charter (see box, below) agreed by British prime minister Winston Churchill and US president Franklin D. Roosevelt.

By the end of the war, Britain and France had already backtracked from the principles of the Atlantic Charter, claiming that its terms only applied to Europeans, though the US affirmed that it believed all people had the right to self-determination. This led to the unusual situation in the 1950s and 1960s of British and French attempts to oppose or slow down independence movements being resisted by the US—supported by its Cold War enemy (see pp.246–247), the equally anti-imperialist Soviet Union (USSR).

While many Africans believed they had earned the right to rule themselves, the war gave them the opportunity to fight for that right. The imperial powers recognized this; it is one of the reasons why they tried to restrict the freedom of movement of returning veterans to colonial cities such as Lagos, Nairobi, and Freetown in an effort to prevent them from influencing their fellow Africans. Nevertheless, Africans now had knowledge of military tactics, of strategy, and of working together. They saw the vulnerabilities of the white occupiers and realized that Africans had powerful allies in countries such as the US and the USSR (both of which wanted to gain influence in Africa).

Furthermore, after the war Britain and France—the two main colonial powers—were bankrupt and could no longer afford to maintain their empires. They held out for several more years, but by the mid-1950s Sudan and then Ghana had won their independence. By 1960, 17 African nations had followed suit.

△ **Fighting for France**
African male and female soldiers of the Free French Army load a mortar in the Western Desert of North Africa in 1942.

THE ATLANTIC CHARTER

As a result of the Atlantic Conference of 1941, the US and Britain set out the principles they expected the post-war world to live by. Known as the Atlantic Charter, it declared that all subject peoples should have the right to self-determination—to choose the type of government they desired to live under. This led to the fall of the British Empire.

> "**We have been told** what we fought for … nothing but **freedom**."
>
> — NIGERIAN VETERAN WRITING TO AFRICAN NATIONALIST HERBERT MACAULAY

Pan-Africanism

African bonds of solidarity

Pan-Africanism, a cultural and ideological movement to strengthen solidarity between Africans, including those in the diaspora, has deep historical roots. Its origins lie in resistance against enslavement and liberation struggles against European colonization.

African organizations had been campaigning against oppression for centuries. Abolitionist groups such as the Sons of Africa, led by Olaudah Equiano and Ottobah Cugoano in the 1780s, protested against the trafficking of enslaved people. The Haitian Revolution from 1791 led the French colony of Saint-Domingue to become Haiti—the first former colony in the western hemisphere to become slavery-free and independent—and inspired hopes for an independent political destiny. Activists such as Martin Robison Delany (1812–85), the first African American officer in the Union army, and Edward Wilmot Blyden (1832–1912), an influential Liberian politician and writer, argued that Africans must return to Africa (in particular, Liberia) to attain real freedom.

Arguing for Pan-Africanism

The first formal Pan-African Congress met in Paris in 1919, bringing together delegates from Africa and the Caribbean to call for a global effort to end injustices against Black people. Among its key movers was the American academic W. E. B. Du Bois, who argued for the study of African history and cultures and the cultivation of a specifically African consciousness that colonialism had suppressed. In the 1920s, Jamaican

△ **Ottobah Cugoano (c. 1757–c. 1792)**
Born in present-day Ghana, enslaved, and transported to Grenada, Cugoano gained his freedom after being brought to England in 1772. He became a prominent abolitionist, giving speeches and writing one of the earliest firsthand accounts of slavery.

△ **W. E. B. Du Bois (1868–1963)**
Sociology professor and founder of the National Association for the Advancement of Colored People (NAACP) in 1911, Du Bois was the prime mover behind the early Pan-African congresses and believed that improving the economic and educational status of Black people would help bring about their liberation.

△ **Amy Jacques Garvey (1896–1973) and Marcus Garvey (1887–1940)**
Amy Garvey played a leadership role in her husband Marcus's Universal Negro Improvement Association (UNIA), which championed Black separatism and migration back to Africa.

> "If **Europe** is for the **white man** … then surely **Africa** is for the **Black man**."
>
> MARCUS GARVEY

journalist Marcus Garvey opposed the idea of equality through integration, arguing for self-reliance and economic development for Black people.

In the 1940s, the focus of Pan-Africanism shifted from the diaspora to the continent itself. Building on the arguments of Du Bois and Garvey, Senegalese poet Léopold Senghor developed the idea of *Négritude*—that Africans share a particular cultural identity and should reject assimilation and European cultural domination—which became very influential in Francophone colonies.

The Fifth Pan-African Congress in Manchester, UK, in 1945, attended by nationalist leaders including Kwame Nkrumah, Julius Nyerere, and Ahmed Sékou Touré, emphasized the importance of unity among Africans once they had won their independence. The 1959 Sanniquellie Declaration called for a "Community of Independent African States," leading in 1963, with Nkrumah's guidance, to the Organization of African Unity.

New movements

Disillusionment with failed projects for unity created other forms of Pan-Africanism. The Black Power movement that emerged in the US in the 1960s was led by Malcolm X (1925–1965), who argued for mass action and assertive reclaiming of Black heritage and rights, and the Black Consciousness movement in South Africa, championed by radical Steve Biko (1946–1977), focused on liberating the minds of Black people as a key weapon in their fight for freedom.

△ **African arts**
This poster advertises the First World Festival of Black Arts in Dakar, Senegal, in 1966—an event that drew around 2,500 delegates from 40 countries.

△ **Léopold Senghor (1906–2001)**
President of the West African Students' Association in Paris in the 1930s, Senghor was a writer and theorist of the *Négritude* movement. He became a member of the French Assembly and the first president of independent Senegal in 1960.

△ **Aimé Césaire (1913–2008)**
A poet and playwright from Martinique, Césaire made the cultural identity of Africans a prominent theme of his poetry and coined the term *Négritude*. He was a member of the French Assembly for 48 years, always arguing passionately against colonialism and racism.

△ **Angela Davis (1944–)**
Philosopher, feminist, anti-war campaigner, and Black rights activist, Davis maintained that feminism needed to fight not only gender-based oppression but also race- and class-based oppression. She was *Time* magazine's Woman of the Year in 1971.

Independence from France

Breaking free from French control

The African countries colonized by the French pressed for independence, with France offering only limited reforms. Eventually, most were successful and the process was largely peaceful, though marred by the brutal Algerian War.

△ **Ahmed Sekou Touré**
Guinea's first president, Sekou Touré, shown on a stamp, headed a campaign to reject the French Community Proposals in 1958. Guinea was the only country to do so.

World War II had a profound effect on independence movements in France's African colonies. Around one million Africans fought in the conflict and the ordeal fostered a sense of their national identities and a commitment to free themselves of foreign rule.

Independence movements in North Africa

As early as 1943, Algerian politician Ferhat Abbas drew up his *Manifesto of the Algerian People*, calling for "the condemnation and abolition of colonization." When France failed to honor its promise of self-rule for Algeria after World War II, the FLN (*Front de Libération Nationale*, or National Liberation Front) vowed to win it by force. The Algerian War of Independence began in 1954 and would last for eight years.

To Algeria's west, Morocco's *Istiqlal* independence party took a different approach. The party persuaded Morocco's longstanding precolonial ally, the US, to support its case for independence in the United Nations, putting international pressure on France to quit the country. Meanwhile, Tunisia's *Neo Destour* independence movement, with Habib Bourguiba among its leaders, organized strikes and demonstrations, and threatened armed struggle—adding to the fierce pressure also coming from Algeria on the colonial power. Morocco and Tunisia both gained their independence in 1956.

Reforms and decolonization

In 1946, France amended its constitution to create the French Union. This new political arrangement abolished France's colonies and incorporated them into the French state. It also allowed the former colonies to elect deputies to sit in France's parliament, the National Assembly. In response, the Côte d'Ivoire politician Félix Houphouët-Boigny formed the *Rassemblement Démocratique Africain* (RDA or African Democratic Rally), a coalition of West African nationalist parties that acted together to push forward their decolonization agenda. Houphouët-Boigny even held several ministerial posts in France's government, from 1957–1959, as leader of the largest party in France's African colonies. He was the first Black nationalist politician to hold high office in France.

While the RDA was united in its opposition to colonization, its members were divided over aiming for total independence or retaining some links with France. In 1958, the new government in France reinvented the French Union as the French Community, offering its

◁ **Triumphant return**
Tunisian nationalist leader Habib Bourguiba is greeted by huge crowds in Tunis on his return in June 1955 following three years of exile imposed by the French government.

△ **Victory parade**
FLN troops parade through Algiers on July 3, 1962, the day independence was declared, ending a bitter conflict that had lasted eight years and caused up to 1.5 million Algerian deaths.

African territories investment funds and a degree of self-rule if they chose to remain in the Community. Only Guinea chose to leave, becoming independent on October 2 that year. This was just a small breach in France's colonial edifice, but it was significant. It came at a time when the war in Algeria was escalating and Cameroon's left-wing nationalist UPC (*Union des Populations du Cameroun*, or Union of the Peoples of Cameroon) was conducting a guerrilla campaign against colonial forces that left thousands dead.

It was becoming clear that France was losing control of its former colonies and the French Community's limited political reforms and promises of financial support were not enough. Although only Guinea had officially made the break from France, other RDA members began questioning their choice to remain. France's days as an imperial power in Africa were numbered. It had neither the will nor the resources to resist the mass defection of its former colonies. In 1960, Cameroon, Senegal, Togo, Mali, Madagascar, Benin, Niger, Upper Volta (Burkina Faso), Côte d'Ivoire, Chad, the Central African Republic, Congo, Gabon, and Mauritania gained their independence. Algeria followed in 1962, and Comoros and Djibouti in 1975 and 1977 respectively. The African states' independence was achieved largely peacefully, with most of the former colonies choosing to maintain some business, military, and political links with France.

Independence of Libya and Egypt

The long road to self-rule

Centuries of competing Ottoman, Italian, and British control led to distrust and growing resistance in Libya and Egypt. The leaders of their freedom movements had to act cleverly and determinedly to achieve their aims.

Since the 9th century BCE, the North African regions of Tripolitania, Fezzan, and Cyrenaica had endured Phoenician, Roman, Islamist, and Ottoman rule. The Italians arrived in 1912 and as imperialist occupiers, they renamed these territories "Libya" in 1934. The majority of Italy's time there was marked by fierce resistance, particularly in Cyrenaica, led by Omar al-Mukhtar, a teacher and prominent figure in the region's powerful Sufi Muslim clan, the Senussi.

A disunited state

The area was put under Allied control after World War II. Britain administered Tripolitania and Cyrenaica; France took Fezzan. Libyan nationalists, the US, and the United Nations put pressure on the British and French, forcing them to leave. When they did so, they invited the religious leader and former resistance fighter Muhammad Idris to become the first monarch of a united Kingdom of Libya in 1951. Knowing that his new state was extremely poor as well as disunited—"Libya" had never existed before as a single political entity—Idris reluctantly agreed. Few people in Tripolitania, Fezzan, and Cyrenaica had ever campaigned for a united Libya, and local leaders and chiefs in all three regions had no intention of giving up their power.

What little revenue the country received came from international aid provided by the UK and the US in particular, which were allowed to establish military airfields and naval bases in Libya in return.

Impact of oil production

The regime of King Idris limped along in this way until, in 1959, the country's first successful oil well went on stream. Commercial oil production would transform Libya from one of the world's most impoverished nations to among its wealthiest. Hundreds of thousands of Libyans migrated to the cities and ports in search of work and opportunities in the oil-rich state. When these failed to materialize, and the thousands of millions of petrodollars flowed instead into the coffers of Idris, unrest grew.

On September 1, 1969, a group of twelve junior army officers, led by a young captain named Muammar Qaddafi, seized power in a bloodless coup that easily toppled Libya's corrupt and inefficient government. A new phase in the country's history was about to begin.

△ **National hero**
This Libyan 10-dinar note shows the Cyrenaican freedom fighter Omar al-Mukhtar, the "Lion of the Desert." He drew on his experience of desert warfare to resist Italian colonizers.

> "We were under **trusteeship**; we were **colonized**; and now we are **independent**."
>
> MUAMMAR QADDAFI, 2009

Egypt under foreign control

Part of the Ottoman Empire since 1517, Egypt fell under British dominion with the opening of the Suez Canal in 1869. Egypt built the waterway with France, but economic mismanagement, corruption and looming bankruptcy forced the country's ruler, Ismail Pasha, to sell all of his government's shares in the Suez Canal to Britain in 1875. By 1878, British and some French commercial and political representatives were sitting in on Egyptian government cabinet meetings.

The foreign control of a large area of Egyptian territory provoked widespread nationalist anger. Its first manifestation was the 'Urabi Revolt of 1879, an army mutiny that turned into an anti-British uprising. Britain suppressed the uprising and used the incident for its own ends, informally taking over the country in what has been called a "veiled protectorate."

Resistance builds

Egyptians across the country resisted. The middle classes flocked to support nationalist movements such as El-Nahda ("Renewal"), after being excluded by the British occupiers from high-level political and administrative roles. The general population also protested against Britain's heavy-handed approach to law and order, encapsulated by the Denshawai Incident of 1906, where four Egyptians were summarily tried and executed after allegedly attacking a British army officer.

Britain formally took over Egypt as a protectorate at the outbreak of World War I. At the war's end, Egyptian nationalists formed the Wafd ("Delegation") Party with the intention of attending the Paris Peace Conference and winning international support for self-rule. When Britain blocked this by exiling the Wafd leaders to Malta, Egypt rose up in the Egyptian Revolution of 1919. Its wave of riots, strikes, and demonstrations left at least 800 dead. Nationalist sentiment was too strong to be ignored by the British any longer. On February 28, 1922, the government of Britain unilaterally declared Egyptian independence.

Independence and the Suez Canal

The terms of the independence declaration that Britain had imposed—without consulting the Egyptians—meant that Britain retained control of the Suez Canal, as well as influence over the country's foreign affairs and defense. It was not until 1952 that the British were finally completely ejected from Egypt, when the military coup led by army officer Gamal Abdel Nasser (see pp.238–239) seized power. He went on to remove British influence from the Suez Canal by nationalizing it in 1956.

△ **First king**
Formerly sultan of Egypt, from 1917, Fuad I became independent Egypt's first king (r. 1922–1936) when Britain declared the country's independence in 1922.

▽ **Journey to freedom**
Students take over a trolley car in Cairo during the 1919 Revolution. This was Egypt's first nationwide rebellion against British control, and one in which women also played a vital role.

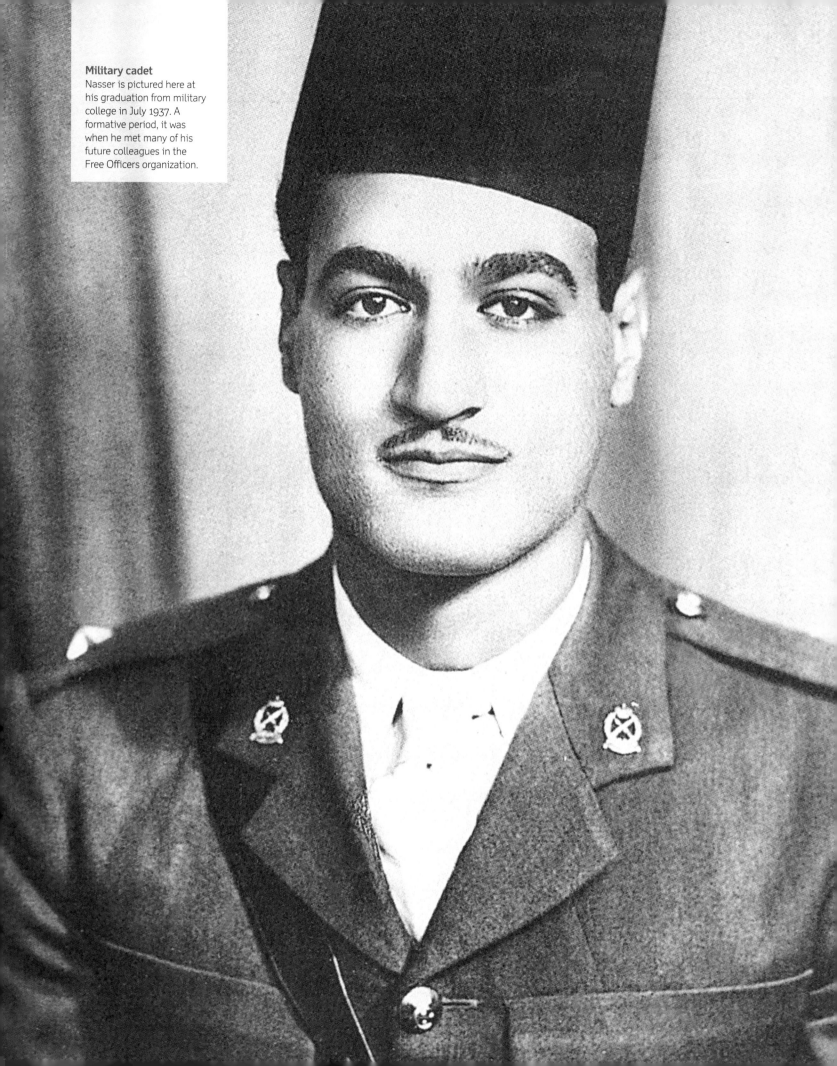

Military cadet
Nasser is pictured here at his graduation from military college in July 1937. A formative period, it was when he met many of his future colleagues in the Free Officers organization.

Gamal Abdel Nasser

Leader of an independent Egypt

A towering figure of Arab nationalism and one of the most important modern African politicians, Gamal Abdel Nasser steered an independent course for Egypt that often set it at odds with the West.

Gamal Abdel Nasser was born in Alexandria, Egypt, and became involved in politics early. When he was 18 years old, he joined a demonstration against Egypt's 1936 treaty with the British, which allowed British military bases to stay in the country. Graduating in law, Nasser joined the Military Academy in 1937, and saw service in Sudan, making useful contacts such as future Egyptian president Anwar el-Sadat. He also fought in the Palestine War against Israel in 1948, and was wounded.

Rise to power

Nasser became an instructor at the Military Academy but, dissatisfied with the peace Egypt had made with Israel and what he saw as a corrupt Egyptian monarchy that had lost touch with the people and alienated the military, he formed a secret group of dissident officers. On July 23, 1952, these Free Officers launched a coup against the nationalist party Wafd. They toppled King Farouk and installed a Revolutionary Command Council headed by Mohamed Naguib. Nasser was the coup's real instigator and he removed Naguib and installed himself as prime minister in 1954. He established a one-party state based on socialist ideals.

On July 26, 1956, now president, Nasser nationalized the British-controlled Suez Canal, sparking a military intervention by Britain, France, and Israel. This was a defining moment for Pan-Arabism, as the US forced the British and French into a humiliating withdrawal and made Nasser a hero.

Nasser promoted a Pan-Arab agenda, though he ruthlessly suppressed opposition at home. In 1957, he helped form the United Arab Republic with Syria, though it dissolved following an uprising by dissatisfied Syrian army officers in 1961. Egypt became embroiled in Yemen's Civil War in 1962, and the devastating losses in the Six-Day War with Israel in 1967 led Nasser to attempt to resign, but public pressure persuaded him to stay.

Eventually, he began to loosen state security and enhance support for the Palestinian Liberation Organization. In 1970, he started negotiations with the US to reach a peace deal with Israel, but then suffered a heart attack and died. He was given a hero's funeral and was succeeded as president by his former colleague Anwar el-Sadat.

◁ **Support for Arafat**
Nasser in 1969 with Yasser Arafat, leader of the al-Fatah faction of the Palestinian Liberation Organization (PLO). Nasser helped promote Arafat to be the dominant Palestinian leader.

▽ **Funeral tribute**
A soldier stands guard in front of a photographic tribute and wreaths of flowers for Nasser at his funeral in 1970.

- **1918** Born in Alexandria to a postal worker father
- **1938** Graduates as a second lieutenant from the Military Academy
- **1952** With Mohamed Naguib and other Free Officers launches revolution that topples the monarchy
- **1954** An alleged assassination attempt galvanizes support for Nasser
- **1956** Elected president after inauguration of New Constitution; nationalizes the Suez Canal
- **1957** Forms the United Arab Republic with Syria
- **1967** Defeat in Six-Day War and attempted resignation
- **1970** Dies of a heart attack and is succeeded by Anwar el-Sadat

△ **Independence dance**
A crowd in Accra, Ghana, watches dancers rehearse for Ghana's Independence Day on March 6, 1957. Events were attended by foreign dignitaries, including Martin Luther King, Jr.

Independence from Britain

Unstoppable momentum for change

After years of struggle by nationalist parties and liberation movements, the 1960s saw an acceleration in the pace of independence that left almost all of Britain's former African colonies free by the end of the decade.

By the middle of the 20th century, developments in Africa were key to the growing calls for freedom. Economic changes brought increasing prosperity for some Africans and demands from others for a share of it. For example, on the Gold Coast (later Ghana), cocoa exports rose from 1,000 to 240,000 tons annually between 1900 and 1951. Across the colonies occupied by Britain, railroads and roads the British instigated and local workers built increased economic activity and helped bind together disparate Indigenous peoples.

The emergence of a generation of young nationalist leaders, who had received an advanced education and were determined to put it at the service of the cause

◁ **Future president**
Nnamdi Azikiwe, the Governor-General of Nigeria, features on the cover of *Drum* magazine in March 1961. Azikiwe later became president of the newly independent Nigeria.

for independence, also played an important part. When World War II was over, the British government focused on improving Britain's domestic economy, with little left over to invest in its colonial empire. There were also growing international calls for the rights of colonized peoples for self-determination, while the meeting of African leaders at the Fifth Pan-African Congress in Manchester in 1945 (see pp.232–233) added moral weight to calls for freedom.

The pace accelerates

Impatience with the slow progress of some existing organizations, such as modern-day Ghana's United Gold Coast Convention, prompted young, assertive leaders such as Kwame Nkrumah (see pp.242–243) to form their own parties. Nkrumah's Convention People's Party, with its memorable slogan "self-government now," was founded in 1949. By 1951, he had led the CPP to victory in assembly elections. After he became prime minister in 1952, full independence was inevitable.

British concessions to African self-determination were initially timid, but once Britain had begun the process, its African colonies took control of it. In Tanganyika (later Tanzania), a legislative council was only established in 1945 and had just four African appointees out of 15 members, but the foundation in 1954 of the Tanganyika African National Union under Julius Nyerere created a political body with whom the British were forced to engage. Nyerere had huge support and he urged nonviolence, so Britain's only hope for a peaceful transition to independence was via him. In Nigeria, divisions between Igbo and Yoruba hampered moves for self-determination, but the National Council of Nigeria and the Cameroon, founded in 1944 with Nnamdi Azikiwe as secretary, argued against parties based on Nigeria's ethnic groups and so created a common front against British rule. By 1957, Nigeria had a prime minister empowered to choose his own cabinet.

Once African leaders saw that the British would grant only limited additional rights, they demanded greater freedom and set the increasing pace of change. Nkrumah had won Ghanaian independence in March 1957, while Nigeria gained its independence in 1960 (with Azikiwe initially as governor-general). Tanganyika became independent in 1961, with Julius Nyerere as prime minister. Problems in Uganda with rival political groups based around the Baganda Kingdom and Bunyoro state delayed progress, but by October 1962 it, too, was independent. The vocal European settler lobby impeded Kenyan independence, and the British fought a bloody anti-insurgency campaign against a group they called the "Mau Mau rebels," who led an anti-colonial uprising from 1952 to 1960. Nationalist leaders united behind Jomo Kenyatta, and in 1963, the British flag was lowered and Kenyatta became prime minister, remarking, "We shall build a country where every citizen may develop his talents to the fullest."

During the 1960s, almost all Britain's African colonies became independent states. The Seychelles followed in 1976 and Zimbabwe (formerly Southern Rhodesia, see pp.252–253) in 1980. By that point, Ghana was into its third decade of independence and Britain's substantial colonial empire in Africa had finally unraveled.

△ **First leader**
A Kenyan 10-cent coin bears the head of Jomo Kenyatta, who led the country to independence in December 1963.

▷ **Tanzanian independence**
Julius Nyerere celebrates the granting of internal self-government to Tanganyika in 1960, with him as prime minister However, he makes it clear his objective is total independence.

Young leader
In this photo portrait of Kwame Nkrumah as a young man, he wears Ghanaian *kente* cloth. His considered choice of clothing sends a message to the world about his ambition for his country to be free from British rule.

Kwame Nkrumah

Ghanaian nationalist leader

A nationalist politician in the colony of the Gold Coast, Kwame Nkrumah led his country to independence from Britain and became the first prime minister and president of the newly formed Republic of Ghana.

The founder of the independent nation of Ghana, Kwame Nkrumah was born and brought up in the Gold Coast, then under British colonial control. He trained as a teacher, and took up various teaching posts, before moving to the US and then to London to study economics, sociology, and philosophy. At this time, Nkrumah also became increasingly involved in Black nationalist politics and Pan-Africanism (see pp.232–233). His political ideas, like those of other African nationalist leaders such as Robert Mugabe and Samora Machel, were shaped by Marxism and Leninism, which he encountered during his studies.

Liberation movement
Upon his return to the Gold Coast in 1947, Nkrumah ran the United Gold Coast Convention (UGCC), the colony's first true political party, established that same year with the aim of effecting gradual constitutional change leading to self-government. In 1949, he founded his own party, the Convention People's Party (CPP). Making deliberate moves to reach people all across the country, especially in rural areas, he quickly gained support for his growing movement.

In 1950, the British authorities sentenced Nkrumah to three years in prison for his role in organizing mass strike action in Accra against the colonial government, demanding self-rule. He was released in 1951, after the CPP won a landslide victory in the election—the first in Africa to be held under universal suffrage. In 1952, Nkrumah became prime minister, in an arrangement overseen by the British. Retaining his resolve to achieve total independence, he led the CPP to success in two more elections, in 1954 and 1956, putting additional pressure on Britain. In 1957, the Gold Coast attained independence from Britain, adopting the name Ghana. Three years later, Nkrumah became its first president.

Overthrow and exile
In 1966, amid wage freezes and tax increases, and with many workers on strike, Ghana's military and police forces overthrew Nkrumah's government in a violent *coup d'état*. Nkrumah was on a state visit abroad at the time of the coup, and never returned to his home country. Instead, he moved to Guinea where he lived until ill health prompted him to seek treatment in Romania, where he died in 1972.

◁ **Memorial statue**
Nkrumah's statue stands in the Kwame Nkrumah Memorial Park in Accra and marks the spot where he declared Ghana's independence. A mausoleum houses the bodies of him and his wife Fathia.

△ **Bust of Nkrumah**
A 25-pesewa coin bearing the head of Nkrumah, with the inscription *Civitatis Ghanensis Conditor* ("Founder of the Ghanaian State").

1909 Born in Nkroful, Gold Coast

1949 Founds the Convention People's Party (CPP)

1951 CPP wins landslide victory in first free election

1952 Appointed prime minister of Gold Coast

1957 Ghana wins its independence

1960 Elected first president of Ghana

1966 Exiled to Guinea following his overthrow in a *coup d'état*

1972 Dies in Romania

Capturing the new mood
Photographs taken by Benin-born, Senegal-based Roger DaSilva epitomize the confident mood of African nations on the brink of self-rule in the 1950s and '60s. Primarily a portrait photographer, DaSilva also captured street scenes, nightclubs, and much else—in this image, an elegantly dressed man poses next to his car in front of DaSilva's studio in Senegal's capital, Dakar. With access to cheaper film and user-friendly cameras after World War II, photographers such as DaSilva, Seydou Keïta in Mali, and Lazhar Mansouri in Algeria began to document the optimism, modernity, and fashion consciousness of the era.

Africa and the Cold War

Caught between East and West

The post-war rivalry between the US and the USSR had a profound effect on Africa. Some African states profited from the Cold War, but many more experienced conflict and chaos.

The end of World War II saw one global conflict replaced by another. From 1945 to 1991, the US and the Soviet Union (USSR) faced each other in a state of political and military tension as they competed for power and influence around the world. In Africa, both the US and the USSR involved themselves in national politics, propping up supportive regimes and toppling uncooperative ones. However, the process was not entirely one-way. In the postcolonial period, some newly independent nations played on US–USSR rivalries to further their own interests.

Non-aligned stance

Having staged a military coup in 1952, Egypt's Gamal Abdel Nasser (see pp.238–239) needed to secure his regime by seizing the British- and French-controlled Suez Canal. He managed this in 1956 by gaining the backing of the USSR and the US. Egypt had strong links with the USSR, and the US pointedly failed to support its ally Britain in order to win favor with pro-USSR Egypt. Over the next two decades, Egypt aligned itself with both the USSR and the US as its own needs—not theirs—dictated.

Like Egypt, other newly independent African states were intent on not becoming pawns of either the US or the USSR, mainly by practicing a policy of non-alignment. The Non-Aligned Movement (NAM) was established in 1961 by anti-imperialist nations committed to maintaining a neutral position in the Cold War. The non-alignment of many of Africa's states made them an awkward prospect for the US and the USSR, both of which attempted to buy their favor through aid, trade, weapons, and development cash. Much of this funding was diverted into the bank accounts of corrupt leaders and kleptocratic bureaucracies, though neither Cold War superpower appeared to be very concerned about this. As most of Africa's liberation movements had been left-leaning, the US had to work harder than the USSR to win—or pay for—the support of African nations.

◁ **On parade**
Soldiers of Angola's UNITA movement parade with a flag bearing the image of their leader Jonas Savimbi. He fought for 28 years against the Marxist MPLA movement until his death in 2002.

Left-wing African leaders such as Ghana's Kwame Nkrumah, Tanzania's Julius Nyerere, and Guinea's Sékou Touré became adept at manipulating this situation, playing off the two Cold War powers against each other by tempering their friendliness toward Moscow or Washington when they believed their backing for one state or the other was being taken for granted. This ensured that they received a constant flow of funds and support from both Cold War capitals—sometimes simultaneously.

Proxy wars

However, not all African states were able to use east–west rivalries to their advantage, and a number of them fell victim to US and USSR interference. There were a number of so-called "proxy wars" across Africa during the Cold War, when the US and the USSR acted out their

▷ **Cold War art**
Figures on the Tiglachin Memorial in Addis Ababa, Ethiopia, celebrate the 10th anniversary of the revolution in 1974, which brought the Marxist Derg regime to power.

△ **Luxor tour**
Egypt's President Nasser (center) shows a group including Soviet leader Nikita Khrushchev (in the hat) around Luxor in 1964, at the height of the Egyptian-Soviet rapprochement.

own aggression by backing rival sides in conflicts. This frequently led to bloody civil wars that left hundreds of thousands dead and states bankrupt and destroyed. Such wars included the Congo Crisis of 1960–1965, the Namibian War of Independence of 1966–1990, and the Angolan Civil War of 1975–2002 where the USSR sent in Cuban troops to back the Marxist MPLA. The Ogaden War of 1977–1978 involved Ethiopia's pro-USSR, Marxist–Leninist Derg regime and the breakaway Somali Democratic Republic, which was backed by the US.

Lingering legacy

By the late 1980s, liberation movements that had drawn on Soviet help had secured power in Angola, Mozambique, Ethiopia, and Zimbabwe. However, with the collapse of the USSR in 1991, the Cold War came to an end.

Nonetheless, the effects of the period continue to be felt in Africa, particularly in the political and economic instability it engendered. Today, the US continues to pursue its interests in Africa, alongside Russia and an increasingly ambitious China.

Independence from Portugal

A violent struggle for freedom

Nationalist movements in Angola, Mozambique, and Guinea-Bissau demanded freedom from their Portuguese occupiers. They each fought guerrilla wars against Portuguese forces, which led finally to independence.

△ **Skillful leader**
Amílcar Cabral adeptly ran PAIGC's campaign for independence for Guinea-Bissau. He was assassinated eight months before the country achieved its independence.

The Africans of Angola, Mozambique, and the smaller territory of Guinea-Bissau on the coast of West Africa had had to deal with the Portuguese occupying power since the 15th century. The slave trade had ended in the 1860s and the Portuguese had more or less left the interior of the region and withdrawn to the coast. The meeting of colonial powers at the Berlin Conference of 1884–1885 called upon Portugal to exercise "effective occupation" of its African colonies (see pp.210–211), encouraging migration there and the exploitation of their land for cheap raw materials.

In the early 20th century, private companies backed by the Portuguese government took the most fertile lands and coerced Africans into forced labor. Africans paid high taxes and received low wages from the private enterprises using their land, and this injustice built support for African leaders who wanted change.

The liberation movements that arose in the 1950s found ready recruits. In Angola, politician Agostino Neto formed the *Movimento Popular de Libertação de Angola* (MPLA) in 1956, and in 1961 activist Holden Roberto established the *União das Populações de Angola* or UPA (later *Frente Nacional de Libertação de Angola* or FNLA).

The fight gains momentum

Also in 1961, cotton plantation workers in Baixa de Cassanje began to protest against their poor treatment and nationalists attempted to free political prisoners in Luanda. The Portuguese army responded violently, killing as many as 20,000 Africans. At least 150,000 Angolan refugees were forced to flee to Congo, though the struggle against Portugal continued. Portugal called in 20,000 troops to control Angola's vast area. Angola's liberation armies continued to make progress, which was only hampered by the divisions between them. In 1965, rebel leader Jonas Savimbi split from the FNLA (the majority of whose membership were from the northern Bakongo people) and set up *União Nacional para a Independência Total de Angola* (UNITA) to represent the Ovimbundu people of central Angola. Despite the divisions, by 1970, the liberation forces had pushed back the Portuguese armies into the main towns.

In Mozambique, in 1960, Portuguese troops massacred pro-independence demonstrators in the town of Mueda. Armed resistance groups rose up and merged to form *Frente de Libertação de Moçambique* (FRELIMO) in 1962. Led by former anthropology

◁ **Mozambique's resistance**
FRELIMO fighters ride a truck in Mozambique's northern Cabo Delgado province in 1973 during the later stages of the war for independence.

professor Eduardo Mondlane, the group aimed to create a socialist society as well as gain independence. After FRELIMO launched a full-scale uprising in 1964, the Portuguese army detained and tortured civilians and forcibly relocated villagers. By 1967, FRELIMO controlled around a fifth of the country and Portugal had 50,000 troops involved in the war. The assassination of Mondlane in 1969 halted FRELIMO's advance. However, military commander Samora Machel replaced Mondlane and by 1971, FRELIMO's progress toward the capital Lourenço Marques (modern-day Maputo) had resumed.

In Cabo Verde and Guinea-Bissau in West Africa, the nationalist Amílcar Cabral formed *Partido Africano para a Independência da Guiné e Cabo Verde* (PAIGC) in 1952, to work for independence. These territories had been so neglected by the Portuguese that there was only one doctor for every 100,000 Africans. In 1961, Cabral announced an armed struggle, launching raids from bases in Guinea. PAIGC set up its own alternative state, which included more than 125 elementary schools.

In 1968, Marcelo Caetano replaced the Portuguese dictator António Salazar, though he also sought to hold on to the African colonies. In 1970, FRELIMO, the MPLA, and PAIGC issued a joint statement calling for policy change. In September 1973, PAIGC declared the independence of Guinea-Bissau, though fighting continued in Mozambique and Angola. In 1974, General António de Spínola became president of Portugal and promised to transfer power to the African territories, bringing about a ceasefire.

Independence at last

Portugal's colonial empire now rapidly wound up. In January 1975, Portugal signed the Alvor Agreement with the MPLA, FNLA, and UNITA, giving Angola independence, though fighting broke out between the groups as they jockeyed for power. In Mozambique, a deal was signed with FRELIMO and June 25, 1975, was set as independence day. Similar agreements granted independence to Cabo Verde and São Tomé & Príncipe, where there had been no fighting. The departure of the Portuguese was chaotic, with hundreds of thousands of settlers fleeing the former colonies. In Angola, there was no recognized government to hand over to and a decades-long civil war broke out. However, West Africa had now freed itself of Portuguese control.

▽ **MPLA victory**
A poster commemorates the MPLA's 1976 victory in the Angolan War of Independence. The MPLA's flag is on the left and that of Angola on the right.

Military discipline
Samora Machel is dressed in full military uniform in April 1984 in Mozambique. By this time, the often authoritarian president headed a one-party state that put dissidents in brutal "reeducation" camps.

Samora Machel

East African opponent of colonialism

An army commander and anti-imperialist, Samora Machel became Mozambique's first president after securing the country's independence from Portugal. He nationalized key institutions and supported Africa's freedom movements.

Growing up in Mozambique's agricultural Gaza Province in the 1940s and '50s, Machel saw how the country's Portuguese rulers exploited Black farmers like his father, telling them which crops to grow and threatening their rights to their land. Machel also watched as many poor Mozambicans left the country for low-paid work in neighboring South Africa's mines—some, like his own brother, dying in accidents there. While working in a hospital, Machel led protests against Black nurses being paid less than their white equivalents.

Committing himself to driving out the Portuguese, Machel journeyed to Tanzania and joined the independence organization FRELIMO (*Frente de Libertação de Moçambique*, or the Liberation Front of Mozambique), which the Portuguese had outlawed. He rose through the ranks, becoming head of the movement's guerrilla forces, then army commander, and finally, in 1970, the leader of FRELIMO itself.

Putting theory into practice

FRELIMO won Mozambique's independence in June 1975 and Machel became the country's first president. A self-declared Marxist-Leninist, he introduced wide-ranging socialist policies, nationalizing the land, health, rented housing, and the assets of the Catholic Church. He also supported the independence movement in Rhodesia and the anti-apartheid campaign in South Africa. In response, the leaderships of the two states established in 1977 a new political and paramilitary organization, RENAMO (*Resistência Nacional Moçambicana*, or the Mozambique National Resistance), which was diametrically opposed to FRELIMO. Violence between FRELIMO and RENAMO continues to this day.

Samora Machel died in a plane crash over South African airspace in 1986. A South African-established investigation declared the accident was due to pilot error, but many in Mozambique still suspected the apartheid regime of foul play.

△ **Tragic memorial**
The Samora Machel Monument marks the site in South Africa where Machel's plane crashed and contains several pieces of the wrecked aircraft. Steel tubes represent the 35 lives lost in the crash.

◁ **Brothers in arms**
Machel (left) with Eduardo Mondlane, his predecessor as FRELIMO leader. Mondlane was killed in 1969 by a package bomb. His assassin has never been named.

1933 Born in the village of Madragoa

1954 Studies nursing in the capital city, Lourenço Marques (now Maputo)

1962 Joins FRELIMO, founded that year in modern-day Tanzania

1964 FRELIMO begins its armed pro-independence campaign

1966 Machel assumes command of FRELIMO's armed forces

1970 After a disputed leadership campaign, Machel becomes FRELIMO's president

1975 Mozambique secures its independence from Portugal

1977 RENAMO is founded and launches a violent insurgency against Machel's regime

1980 Machel makes a state visit to the newly independent Zimbabwe (formerly Rhodesia)

1986 Dies in a plane crash in Mbuzini, South Africa

The fight for Zimbabwe

The armed conflict that created a new country

△ **Independence day**
On April 18, 1980, Zimbabwe became independent from Britain and crowds across the country celebrated.

A struggle that began with a 19th-century colonial war finally ended after a 20th-century war of liberation, as Zimbabwe's Black majority fought to free itself from the white-minority state of Rhodesia.

In the 19th century, the area now known as Zimbabwe was home to several ethnic groups, including the Shona and Ndebele. The Shona occupied Mashonaland, in the north, while the Ndebele had moved to Matabeleland, in the southwest, after splitting from the Zulu Kingdom. From the 1880s, European colonists, led by Cecil Rhodes's British South Africa Company, began to invade the region. They took land and cattle—crucial commodities on which both the Shona and Ndebele were dependent—and imposed taxes, leading to the First *Chimurenga* (meaning "uprising" in the Shona language) in 1896–1897, when the Ndebele and Shona revolted against the British administration. The British crushed the uprising and appropriated the region as a colony in 1898. The war marked the beginning of organized armed resistance in Zimbabwe.

Migrants from Britain settled in the colonies of Southern Africa. Southern Rhodesia, as Zimbabwe was then known, became self-governing in 1923, though rules surrounding property ownership meant that the vote was effectively restricted to white settlers. The settlers offered prime farmland to new arrivals, and restricted Black people to unproductive areas or

△ **First prime minister**
Robert Mugabe speaks to a crowd in Harare in the 1980s. Mugabe ruled Zimbabwe as prime minister (1980–1987) and then president (1987–2017).

> "Africa **must revert** to what it was before the imperialists divided it. These are **artificial divisions** which we ... will seek to **remove**."
>
> ROBERT MUGABE, AT A SPEECH IN SALISBURY (NOW HARARE), 1962

forced them to work on white farms. Black people were economically marginalized, and some workers suffered from forced labor and settler brutality. Unrest bubbled in Black townships, and activists called for equal employment rights and the right to vote.

Second Chimurenga

After World War II, African nationalism grew (see pp.230–231) and neighboring Malawi and Zambia gained their independence in 1964. A year earlier, two rival revolutionary groups had formed in Southern Rhodesia. The Zimbabwe African People's Union (ZAPU), led by Joshua Nkomo, had primarily Ndebele members, while the Zimbabwe African National Union (ZANU), led by Robert Mugabe, was dominated by the Shona. The Second *Chimurenga* began in 1964, with ZAPU and ZANU forces fighting the Rhodesian army and clashing with each other.

Southern Rhodesia's white minority, which never made up more than around eight percent of the population, offered little in the way of compromise. As the conflict intensified, fears that Britain would open the franchise to the Black majority led Prime Minister Ian Smith to declare Southern Rhodesia's unilateral independence from Britain in 1965. A new constitution that offered "non-Europeans" several seats in parliament failed to quell Black Africans' resistance to white-minority rule. Guerrillas disrupted transportation and communications in the cities, and neighboring Zambia and Mozambique provided bases for anti-government forces.

Toward independence

Facing increasing international isolation and escalating internal resistance, the Smith regime announced a political settlement in 1978, on the condition that the police and army remained under white control. The elections in 1979 were still skewed toward the white minority, but resulted in a victory for the United African National Council (UANC) of Bishop Abel Muzorewa, which supported Black majority rule but had not advocated armed struggle. The new government failed to win international recognition, and continued resistance led the warring parties to the negotiating table a few months later. The Lancaster House talks, between the British government, the Patriotic Front (a coalition formed by ZAPU and ZANU), the UANC, and Smith's Rhodesia Front began in London in October 1979. The parties agreed on new elections, a new constitution, and a cease-fire, ending the Second *Chimurenga*. But the burning issue in the negotiations was land, with the white minority holding the vast majority of fertile farmland. Robert Mugabe fought hard for radical change, but accepted the principle that white landowners would be compensated for any land sales.

In the 1980 election, ZANU-PF (ZANU Popular Front) won a majority, with Robert Mugabe as prime minister and clergyman Canaan Banana as president. The country, now known as Zimbabwe, finally had its independence. ZANU-PF increased its majority in the 1985 election, allowing for reforms such as the removal of the last "whites-only" seats in parliament. In 1987, the opposition ZAPU joined with ZANU-PF.

However, the issue of land reform has never gone away. White farmers, who continued to own a high proportion of arable land, increasingly began to be forced off their land in the early 21st century. This fed into wider economic and social instability, and an increasingly unpredictable Mugabe was finally forced out in 2017, with ordinary Zimbabweans hoping the new government could turn troubles such as ferocious inflation and corruption around.

THE ROLE OF WOMEN IN THE STRUGGLE

Women played critical roles in the war of liberation. One of their first roles was carrying arms, often at night, to the front lines. By 1977, they had been integrated into combat roles, and held training and leadership positions. Women also galvanized support for the struggle among rural villages. By the end of the war, women made up an estimated third of the ZANU fighting force.

South Africa and apartheid

Racism on a national scale

South Africa's white leadership held out against sharing power or integrating with the country's majority Black population. Instead, it institutionalized ethnic discrimination and adopted white supremacy as official state policy.

△ **Permit to travel**
A Black woman in Cape Town displays her "interior passport," showing that she is only allowed within the city limits during working hours.

The Union of South Africa was proclaimed in 1910 and from the beginning power rested with the country's minority white population, which was mainly Boer—settlers of Dutch, German, or Huguenot (French Protestant) descent. For the next eight decades, South Africa's leaders marginalized the country's majority Black population by introducing discriminatory laws. The Natives Land Act of 1913 and the Natives (Urban Areas) Act of 1923 between them prescribed where Black people could live, for example, while the tellingly-named Master and Servant Act allowed (white) employers to whip (Black) workers. The so-called Hertzog Bills of 1936 disenfranchised the few wealthy Black South Africans who had been qualified to vote.

By the late 1940s, white South Africa was enjoying a post-war economic boom, but millions of Black people remained poor. Hundreds of thousands lived on the fringes of major cities in illegal squatter camps, in dismal conditions and working for low pay. When Black people began to campaign for their rights, South Africa's white electors reacted in 1948 by voting into power the uncompromisingly white supremacist National Party (NP). Once in office, the NP set about introducing its program of state-sanctioned racial discrimination that it called apartheid ("apartness").

First acts of oppression

Apartheid legislation began with 1949's Prohibition of Mixed Marriages Act, followed by a law forbidding interracial sexual relations. To clarify what "race" meant, the Population Registration Act of 1950 established three categories: "Whites," "Coloreds" (multiracial heritage), and "Blacks." A fourth category, "Asian," was added later. A series of Land Acts put 80 percent of South Africa's farmland under white control. Beaches, parking lots, public restrooms, restaurants, and even graveyards were segregated, and people of color were forced to carry pass books—essentially internal passports—allowing them to enter certain areas. Only white South Africans could join a trade union or be elected to the country's parliament.

South Africa's people of color reacted to apartheid in a number of ways. In 1949, the main anti-apartheid organization, the African National Congress (ANC), introduced a Program of Action calling for resistance to white domination through active opposition. Inspired by a new generation of leaders such as Nelson Mandela, Oliver Tambo, and Walter Sisulu rising through its Youth Wing, the ANC grew increasingly

◁ **Enduring defiance**
Soweto protesters vent their anger in 1980—showing how state repressions like the one that suppressed the earlier Soweto Uprising in 1976 failed to end public defiance.

confrontational as South Africa's governments became more oppressive. The "defiance campaign" it organized in 1952, for example, encouraged the burning of pass books. In 1955, a group called the Congress of the People drew up a Freedom Charter that declared "South Africa belongs to all who live in it, Black or white." At a public meeting to adopt the charter, 150 attendees were arrested and charged with high treason. Other groups such as the South African Indian Congress, the Colored People's Organization, Trade Unions, and the Pan Africanist Congress also actively opposed apartheid.

Segregation and resistance

In 1959, the government of prime minister Hendrik Verwoerd passed the Promotion of Bantu Self-Government Act. It established 10 "Bantustans," or Black homelands, including QwaQwa, Transkei, and KwaZulu. These Black-only regions were allowed some self-government but were ultimately state-subsidized ghettos, with high rates of crime, poverty, ill health, unemployment, and disease. Each Bantustan was established as home to a particular ethnic or linguistic group (KwaZulu was the Zulu people's homeland, for example), deliberately emphasizing the differences between Black populations and making it difficult for them to work together. Between 1961 and 1994, some 3.5 million Black people were relocated to Bantustans. In 1970, Black people were stripped of their South African citizenship by being defined as legal citizens of the homeland in which they lived.

In March 1960, 7,000 people protested against pass book laws in the township of Sharpeville. Police fired on them, and at least 67 were killed and 180 wounded, leading to national and international condemnation. The ANC was one of several resistance groups to set up military units in the aftermath of the "Sharpeville Massacre." Between 1960 and 1963, the ANC's *Umkhonto we Sizwe* ("Spear of the Nation") armed wing carried out almost 200 attacks, mostly bombings, against state buildings and institutions. No deaths were recorded in this period, at the end of which the *Umkhonto we Sizwe* leader Nelson Mandela was captured and imprisoned in Cape Town's Robben Island prison, becoming in the process an international figurehead of the anti-apartheid movement (see pp.270–271).

By the end of the 1960s, many African states had fought for and won their independence, while South Africa's people of color remained unfree. But the opposition to apartheid would only grow—at home and abroad. This ensured that the struggles of the 1950s and '60s were not in vain and ultimately contributed to the end of apartheid (see pp.268–269).

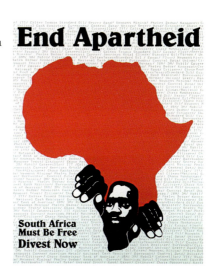

△ **International support**
This anti-apartheid poster was made by the American artist and activist Lincoln Cushing in 1985, displaying solidarity with the Black South African cause.

◁ **Homeland housing**
These homes are in eastern South Africa's QwaQwa homeland, established for the country's Besotho people. The single-story houses were "self-built" by residents under supervision.

> "The act of **creating art** should complement ... **liberating the country for my people**."
>
> THAMI MNYELE, MEDU COFOUNDER

▷ **Imagining the future**
Made in 1981, this Medu Art Ensemble poster depicts and predicts both the end of apartheid and the election of Nelson Mandela as democratic South Africa's first president, an event that would happen in 1994.

Anti-apartheid poster

Art as a weapon of struggle in South Africa

In 1978, Black South African exiles in Gaborone, Botswana, founded Medu Art Ensemble. The aim of the group was to organize resistance to apartheid through literary, musical, and artistic works, as well as with conferences, workshops, and other events. Members of Medu—which means "roots" in the Sepedi-Sotho language spoken in northeast South Africa—called themselves "cultural workers," to emphasize that their activities were a necessary social, ethnic, and political task rather than merely art for art's sake, which they viewed as elitist.

At its height, Medu comprised 60 "cultural workers," campaigners whose works drew attention across the continent and beyond to South Africa's inequalities. In 1982, Medu held its most influential event, the week-long Culture and Resistance Festival and Symposium in Gaborone that attracted human rights activists, political agitators, and members of the public from Africa, Europe, and the Americas. The event included politically themed concerts, exhibitions, talks, and activities. Attendees explored aspects of life under apartheid, including censorship and land and labor policies, and promoted Pan-Africanism, civic education, and the role artists could play in bringing about social change in South Africa.

This symposium and Medu's other activities brought the group's message to a wider audience than ever before—convincing South Africa's government that it needed to take action against it. On June 14, 1985, up to 50 members of the South Africa Defense Force (SADF) crossed the border into Botswana and launched Operation Plecksy, a targeted search-and-destroy raid on anti-apartheid activists based in Gaborone, including members of the Medu Art Ensemble. SADF operatives murdered at least 12 people, four of whom were members of the collective, including one of its founders, the artist Thami Mnyele. A decimated Medu was disbanded in the aftermath of the attack.

Art and propaganda

An important aspect of Medu's output was its political posters, which usually displayed striking imagery and direct and inspiring messages and slogans such as "The People Shall Govern" and "Unity, Democracy, and Courage." As all Medu work was banned in South Africa, it took a dedicated and courageous network of sympathizers to smuggle posters across the borders and hang them in public spaces, much to the chagrin of the country's leaders.

US-born artist Judy A. Seidman made the poster shown here. Seidman lived and worked in Zambia and Swaziland (now Eswatini) before moving to Gaborone and joining Medu in 1980. This piece, like Medu's other output, shows how opposition groups inside and outside South Africa used art as a means of promoting and effecting change to help undermine the country's undemocratic apartheid regime.

The legacy of colonization

Far-reaching impacts of European misrule

European powers brought new infrastructure and trade to Africa—but they also exploited its resources. Communities were divided and African cultures and learning were sidelined, leaving independent states with a legacy of instability.

By the 1970s, most African nations had won their independence, but their colonial past shaped their development. These states were not organic nations, but lines on a map drawn by 19th-century European colonizers. The empires of Europe ignored the size, natural resources, ethnic mix, religions, and trading relationships that might make viable, long-term states. These arbitrary borders led to instability, civil wars, and the marginalization of some groups.

Many African nations have struggled to reconcile their territory and peoples. In Nigeria, which became independent from Britain in 1960, colonial borders had brought together over 250 ethnic groups. Clashes between the largest ones, the Hausa-Fulani, Yoruba, and Igbo, led to a conflict that ended the First Republic in 1966. In Sudan, also previously occupied by Britain, tensions between Muslim Arabs in the north and Dinka and other groups who practiced Christianity and local religions in the south led to bloodshed and the 2011 secession of South Sudan.

Colonizing powers did not just divide Africa into different states. Missionaries converted numerous people to Christianity, while industries, from mining and agriculture to colonial administration, trained their staff. The positive impacts of this included increased literacy and numeracy, but colonial education and missionary work often spread European learning and faith at the expense of local cultures, religions, and crafts. Some taught entirely in languages

△ **Graduation ceremony**
Founded in 1960, the *École nationale d'administration* in Madagascar trained senior civil servants for the newly independent nation.

▷ **Uganda Railway**
This 1908 poster shows the railroad that connected Mombasa and Lake Victoria. Constructed by mainly Indian workers, it consolidated British power over East Africa's Great Lakes.

"[T]he struggle against colonialism does not end with **the attainment** of **national independence**."

GHANAIAN PRESIDENT KWAME NKRUMAH, 1963

such as English or French, and European writers and thinkers were held up as exemplars. Meanwhile, although European laws provided a framework for newly independent states, laws such as the British penal code that outlawed same-sex sexual acts in countries like Uganda institutionalized prejudice.

While colonial education introduced new ideas and prepared some Africans for nationalist agitation, most training was focused on the needs of the colonial administration, with Africans taking on less skilled or low-ranking jobs. On the eve of independence in 1959, Belgian Congo had no Congolese people in the senior grade of the civil service due to the paucity of colonial education policies.

Cash crops and transportation

European nations' use of colonies to supply raw materials resulted in a focus on cash crops such as groundnuts, palm oil, rubber, timber, coffee, cocoa, tea, tobacco, cotton, and spices; and minerals like copper, gold, and diamonds. Large farms and mines were established and infrastructure, such as railroads, modern roads, telegraphs, electric power, bureaucracy, hospitals, and pipe-borne water and sewage systems, was set up around these resources. Many Africans were encouraged or forced to leave their lands to serve resource production, contributing further to uneven development and social instability.

Land transportation connected these production hubs with ports that could export goods to Europe and beyond. In East Africa, great railroads were built under British and German rule, but they were designed to help colonial nations exploit the Great Lakes region's immense resources and cement their power there, not to assist local communities.

Struggle for self-reliance

When states gained their independence, colonial infrastructure aided international trade, but had not been designed for self-reliance. Foreign influence, termed neocolonialism (see pp.260–261), often continued to disadvantage African economies. European powers had little interest in encouraging the development of a manufacturing base or balanced agriculture. Longstanding crops such as sorghum, fonio, and millet were pushed off the land, leaving many African nations dependent on the large-scale import of wheat and corn. Meanwhile, skewed trade arrangements limited the profits and benefits received by African economies. Many nations emerged from colonization dependent on a limited number of exports (such as coffee in Kenya, oil in Libya, and copper in the Democratic Republic of the Congo) whose value can shift dramatically, creating instability.

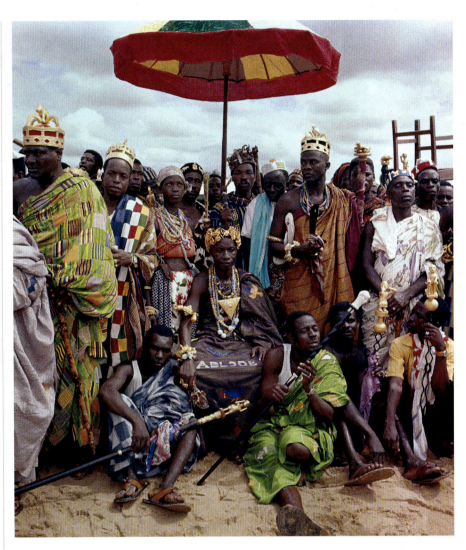

Local elites, such as the Tutsi of Rwanda and Burundi, who worked closely with Europeans, often inherited power after independence, and fought to maintain it as marginalized groups struggled for equality. In parts of Southern Africa, white settlers who had grown used to superior farmland and political influence used a mix of legal tools and state violence to maintain their privileged position, as seen most notoriously in apartheid South Africa (see pp.254–255).

△ **Ewe chiefs**
Colonial borders created an identity crisis among the Ewe of West Africa, whose homelands were divided between Ghana, Benin, and Togo. Since independence, some Ewe have campaigned for a consolidated state.

THE TEXTILE TRADE

Cotton is widespread in Africa, and is grown primarily as an export crop—this 1964 stamp celebrates Zambia's industry. During the scramble for Africa in the late 19th century, the availability of cheap cotton, which was required by an expanding European population, was a major reason for colonial investment in the continent. Today, price fluctuations and the subsidies enjoyed by European and North American competitors mean profits from the crop are often marginal.

△ **Liberation artwork**
Ethiopian artist Afewerk Tekle's stained-glass work *The Total Liberation of Africa* is situated in the headquarters of the United Nations Economic Commission for Africa in Addis Ababa.

A new political generation

Taking up the reins of power

The political leaders who came to prominence from the 1930s onward—many of whom had been exposed to new political ideas via Western educations—went on to face the immense task of leading newly independent African nations.

European colonizers used education to produce workforces that could administer African colonies for colonial gain. But schools and colleges also helped shape a new elite that campaigned for self-rule and would govern new nations. These leaders were mostly men from privileged backgrounds, and their Western education differentiated them from the majority of the population, who had less access to schooling.

An influential early figure was Nnamdi Azikiwe (1904–1996), who gained an education at religious schools before continuing his studies in the US. In 1937, he returned to his native Nigeria, where he published nationalist newspapers and grew increasingly prominent, becoming president in 1960. Azikiwe was Igbo, but also spoke Yoruba and Hausa, helping him appeal to a multiethnic electorate.

Azikiwe's eloquence and mix of international and church-school learning was shared by other members of the new generation. While working as a newspaper editor in the Gold Coast colony (now Ghana), Azikiwe briefly mentored another leader-in-waiting, Kwame Nkrumah (see pp.242–243). Nkrumah studied socialist literature in the US, before returning to the Gold Coast to become an impassioned campaigner for independence. Hastings Banda studied in the US and Britain before returning to his home country, Malawi (then British-ruled Nyasaland), in 1958 to advocate for independence, becoming prime minister in 1963 and, from 1966, an increasingly autocratic president.

Many of the new generation had strong cultural as well as political interests. Léopold Senghor (1906–2001), who became Senegal's first president in 1960, was a poet and one of the founders of the *Négritude* literary and artistic movement, which sought to foreground African and Black identities and experiences. The long-standing Tanzanian president Julius Nyerere (1922–1999) translated several plays by William Shakespeare into Swahili and wrote widely on nationalism and liberation, while Kenya's Jomo Kenyatta (c. 1894–1978) authored a study of the culture and society of the Kikuyu people of Kenya.

Kenyatta's long career saw him campaign against colonial land seizures and endure jail as a suspected terrorist before becoming prime minister (1963–1964) and president (1964–1978) of Kenya. Not all leaders enjoyed such lengthy careers. The transition from colonies to independent nations proved challenging, thanks in large part to colonization's divisive legacy (see pp.258–259). Nkrumah was forced from power by a coup, while Azikiwe was ousted by the Nigerian military. Other leaders, including Nyerere and Senghor, became increasingly autocratic.

New challenges

While this generation might not have all fulfilled their early promise, they played a pivotal role in the fight for independence and the development of ideas. They fused beliefs such as socialism and nationalism into African forms—stressing political and economic self-reliance—and used their colonial education to articulate the aspirations of the newly enfranchised electorates and drive their new nations forward.

△ **New leaders**
African heads of state gather in Kinshasa, Democratic Republic of the Congo (then Zaire), for the 1967 summit of the Organization of African Unity. Julius Nyerere (sixth from left) and Jomo Kenyatta (ninth from left) are among those pictured.

However, while generations of leaders have upheld Africa's independence, regions such as Europe and North America still wield influence, while China's power increases. Neocolonialism has made the questions the postcolonial generation pondered as vital as ever. How can African nations stand on their own, tap into their wealth of science and culture, and indigenize democracy for political and social peace? And are African leaders—often wealthy and with elite educations—mere gatekeepers for neocolonialism?

These questions have a practical impact. In West and Central Africa, 14 nations that were formerly under French control still use the CFA franc and are required to deposit a percentage of their GDP in the Bank of France as a trust. Such issues are the responsibility of another generation of leaders, such as Macky Sall of Senegal, Alassane Ouattara of Côte d'Ivoire, Paul Biya of Cameroon, Paul Kagame of Rwanda, and Sahle-Work Zewde of Ethiopia. They face a struggle to live up to the intellectual weight of their predecessors, and a mighty challenge to build a better world.

ORGANIZATION OF AFRICAN UNITY

The Organization of African Unity (OAU) was founded in 1963 to increase collaboration between its 33 member states, and to resist colonialism and neocolonialism. Its inaugural conference (pictured here) was held in 1963 in Addis Ababa, Ethiopia. Pan-African integration has been a major theme for the continent's leaders, and has also been encouraged through a series of meetings of the Pan-African Congress (see pp.232–233), which first convened in 1919, and set itself against imperialism and discrimination. The OAU contributed to African unity on the world stage, but was criticized for doing little for ordinary Africans. In 2001, it was succeeded by the African Union, which has 55 members, covering almost the entire continent.

The rise of the military
Taking power by force of arms

In the decades after independence, military coups were a regular occurrence in Africa. The reasons behind these destabilizing events are complex and varied—not least the impact and legacy of colonization itself.

The end of European colonial rule had a profound effect in many African states. While the process of decolonization was mostly carried out peacefully, nations such as Britain and France did not always give up their imperial holdings willingly. In many cases, minimal preparation was done to ensure a smooth transition of power. Incoming political leaders, often with no experience of holding office, inherited countries riven with social, political, and economic problems. In many countries, the imperial power had provided a single focus for opposition groups; with the foreign powers gone, opposing factions turned on each other. Popular unrest followed, and military coups became a means of effecting regime change.

Numbers and causes
More than 200 coups have taken place in Africa since the 1950s. Around half have been successful. The most intense period of coup activity was during the 1960s and 1970s, with a coup or attempted coup every 55 days; 90 percent of African states had some form of coup experience in this era. Geographically, West Africa had the highest proportion of coups, accounting for 44.4 percent of them from 1958–2008.

It is, of course, not the case that Africa is simply predisposed toward military coups. The causes are multiple and complex, in large part arising as a result of how the colonial empires left the continent. Poverty, lack of economic development, political corruption, ethnic rivalries, and religious divisions are common factors. Additionally, what South African politician and strategist Joel Netshitenzhe has described as an ongoing "thirst for Africa's resources" (for example, for minerals and oil) from external powers has led to corruption and oppression. Added to this, from the Cold War onward (see pp.246–247), the US, the Soviet Union (USSR), the former colonial powers, and—from the early 2000s—China and Russia have sought to increase their influence in the continent. This has boosted the power of the military in many states, sometimes acting as proxies for non-African nations or as the beneficiaries of the political disruption they cause.

Coups across the continent
Africa's first post-war military coup took place in Egypt. In July 1952, a group of young army officers led by Mohamed Naguib and Gamal Abdel Nasser toppled the corrupt and incompetent regime of the country's hereditary ruler, King Farouk I. Naguib and Nasser's coup was backed by the anti-colonial US and USSR—which trumped the opposition the insurgents faced from imperialist Britain and France.

As well as inspiring other independence movements throughout Africa, the Egyptian Revolution of 1952 showed that military coups worked as a means of seizing power, especially with help from abroad. The military coup that overthrew Ghana's president Kwame Nkrumah (see pp.242–243) in 1966, for

▽ **Council of war**
Gamal Abdel Nasser (seated, third right) sits with his fellow coup plotters. Having ousted Egypt's king in 1952, Nasser would rule the country from 1956 until his death in 1970.

THE RISE OF THE MILITARY | 263

"Everywhere that the **struggle** for **national freedom** has triumphed … there were **military coups** that overthrew their leaders."

AHMED BEN BELLA, PRESIDENT OF ALGERIA (1963–1965)

△ **Political ringmaster**
Zaire's dictator Mobutu Sese Seko makes political capital from a fight between boxers Muhammad Ali and George Foreman, with the line, "Ali and Foreman have confidence in Mobutu."

example, was backed by Britain and the US because of the African leader's communist leanings. Similarly, in the newly independent Republic of the Congo (now the Democratic Republic of the Congo), prime minister Patrice Lumumba was executed in 1961 in an army-led rebellion in part orchestrated by his country's former colonial occupier, Belgium. This happened after Lumumba tried to nationalize his country's lucrative (and Belgian-controlled) uranium, rubber, and copper industries. His replacement, General Mobutu Sese Seko, was a corrupt and murderous dictator. He became president in 1965 and held power until 1997, running his state—which he renamed Zaire in 1971—as a kleptocracy and amassing a fortune as his country sank into poverty.

In Mali, when the first post-independence president Modibo Keïta began to advocate socialist-style policies, France secretly assisted the 1968 military coup led by Lieutenant Moussa Traoré that brought him down.

Some argue that martial regimes stabilize (however temporarily) the states they take over because such regimes impose strict obedience, as well as fear and repression. However, the violent careers of Uganda's Idi Amin and Nigeria's Sani Abacha, to name but two, show how military dictatorships bring economic decay and corruption on their nations. More often than not, military rule only leads to autocratic rule and more governmental fragility. Sudan—plagued by corruption, civil unrest, and dire poverty—has experienced more than a dozen military coups since 1950, the most recent in 2023.

Coups in perspective

In fact, military coups are only a regular occurrence in around a dozen of the 54 countries that make up Africa. The development of strong civil institutions can make the overthrow of governments unlikely and unnecessary, as has been the case in South Africa since the end of apartheid. Some states, including Botswana and Senegal, have never experienced a coup at all. Countries such as Morocco, Kenya, and Cameroon have only ever experienced unsuccessful military coups; other states saw coups solely in the instability of the post-independence era. Ghana's series of coups, for example, took place between 1966 and 1984, the last successfully put down by Jerry John Rawlings's government. Rawlings was himself a military officer who had staged coups in 1979 and 1981. He led a military junta until 1992, after which he resigned from the military and founded the National Democratic Congress (NDC). He served his allotted two terms as president and oversaw the peaceful transfer of power to an elected member of the opposition. Ghana has since seen decades of stable democracy.

▽ **Military leader**
Mali's Moussa Traoré, pictured here in 1982, took power in a 1968 coup and was himself overthrown in a military takeover in 1991.

Civil wars

Power struggles across the continent

At least 20 African nations have experienced civil wars. Their causes include colonialism, religious or ethnic divisions, corruption, leadership failures, poverty, and foreign interference in domestic affairs. While no single factor explains the scale of Africa's armed struggles, the impacts of imperialism laid the groundwork for many of them. As foreign powers left, they were replaced by national leaders who had been afforded little to no experience in government, and who had inherited weak economies and undeveloped political institutions. In addition, large areas of Africa were rich in resources. The former colonial powers, as well as the US, the Soviet Union (USSR), and, later, Russia and China, used all means at their disposal, both fair and foul, to gain access to them.

The First Sudanese Civil War, which began in 1955, saw mainly Christian southern Sudan attempt to separate itself from the majority Muslim north. Britain, the USSR, and Egypt supported the north, while Ethiopia, Uganda, and Israel endorsed the south. After 500,000 deaths, the war ended in 1972 with the establishment of the Southern Sudan Autonomous Region. A second civil war from 1983 left two million dead before a peace deal was brokered in 2005. South Sudan gained its independence six years later, but remains a troubled region, while in Sudan armed conflict flared up again in 2023.

In the Nigerian Civil War (1967–1970), the Igbo people of the country's southeast attempted to declare an independent Republic of Biafra. Once again, the

△ **Nigerian Civil War (1967–1970)**
This soldier from the putative Biafran Republic carries an injured comrade in 1968. Igbo attempts to form a country of their own in the southeast of Nigeria led to civil war. The Nigerian government eventually mounted a food blockade to force Biafra's surrender.

△ **Ethiopian Civil War (1974–1991)**
Eritrean women played a vital role in the Ethiopian Civil War, in which Eritrea won independence from Ethiopia. As soldiers, they made up over a third of the Eritrean People's Liberation Front (EPLF), a left-leaning nationalist organization that also supported women's rights and worked to improve literacy.

△ **Ugandan Civil Wars (1980–present)**
This "night commuter" is one of an estimated 30,000 young people in Uganda who, fearful of kidnap or worse by marauding rebel groups, leave their homes each evening to seek safety in NGO-run public shelters.

> "Virtually all of **Africa's civil wars** were started by politically **marginalized** or **excluded** groups."
>
> GEORGE AYITTEY, GHANAIAN ECONOMIST AND POLITICAL COMMENTATOR, 2010

triumvirate of Britain, the USSR, and Egypt supported the established government against the secessionists. One million citizens died in a conflict that lasted for three years and resulted in defeat for the breakaway republic and marginalization of the Igbo in the Yoruba- and Hausa-Fulani-dominated state.

Difficult path to peace

The misrule and state-sanctioned violence that have afflicted Uganda since independence in 1962 put the country into a 25-year-long tailspin of poverty, dictatorship, and societal breakdown. The result, in 1987, was the ongoing insurgency against the corrupt regime of Yoweri Museveni by the Lord's Resistance Army (LRA). Led by the self-styled Christian warrior Joseph Kony, the LRA has no coherent aims, apart from a desire to destroy its opponents. LRA violence has dislocated 2 million Ugandans and Kony's militias have abducted 60,000 civilians—most of them turned into child soldiers and enforced sex workers.

The Somali Civil War began after a coup ousted the country's dictator, General Siad Barre, in 1991. The conflict has claimed a million Somali lives in violence, famine, and disease. The aims of its many competing forces (Islamic, socialist, nationalist, separatist) are so diverse that the prospect of peace appears distant.

The best antidote to war, as shown by countries like Botswana, Namibia, and Ghana, is to establish stable, democratic governments that effectively manage the sociocultural diversity in African societies.

△ **First Liberian Civil War (1989–1996)**
This masked militiaman is a member of the National Patriotic Front of Liberia (NPFL), the rebel group that won Liberia's first civil war in 1996. The NPFL leader Charles Taylor was himself ousted in a second civil war ending in 2003.

△ **Rwandan Civil War (1990–1994)**
The civil war in Rwanda saw a brutal genocide take place among the Tutsi and Hutu people. At the war's end, two million defeated Hutus fled to neighboring Zaire (now the Democratic Republic of the Congo)—many abandoning their machetes, as shown here. Tens of thousands of Hutus died in further civil conflicts in Zaire.

△ **South Sudanese Civil War (2013–2020)**
Soldiers celebrate the 34th anniversary of the founding of the Sudan People's Liberation Army (SPLA) in 2017. South Sudan gained independence from Sudan in 2011, but a power struggle between its leaders erupted into ethnic violence and civil war.

Africa's Great War

The world's deadliest conflict since World War II

A year after the First Congo War (1996–1997), the Second Congo War (1998–2003), sometimes called Africa's Great War, broke out. It involved multiple African countries and claimed around 5.4 million lives.

The African region known as the Congo has been troubled since at least 1885, when Belgium's king, Leopold II, assumed personal ownership of what was then called the Congo Free State (see pp.212–213). Ever since, the country's changing name—the Belgian Congo, the Republic of the Congo, the Democratic Republic of the Congo, Zaire, and, from 1997, the Democratic Republic of the Congo (DRC) once more—has reflected its unstable and often violent fortunes.

The Second Congo War marked a particularly volatile period in the state's history. The roots of the conflict were in the First Congo War (1996–1997), the civil struggle that ended the dictatorship of Mobutu Sese Seko, president of what was at that time called Zaire. The man who usurped and replaced Mobutu was Laurent-Désiré Kabila, a dissident, a revolutionary, and the leader of the Alliance of Democratic Forces for the Liberation of Congo (AFDL). The state Kabila inherited was riddled with corruption, failures of leadership, poverty, and institutionalized violence. Vested interests at home and abroad (mostly Belgium and the US) vied for control of the country's abundant mineral wealth.

Foreign influences

Kabila was swept to power in 1997 by an alliance of Mobutu's opponents that included the governments of neighboring Uganda and Rwanda. Just as the US and Belgium had gained access to the DRC's natural resources in return for supporting Mobutu in power, so Uganda and Rwanda expected a similar quid pro quo from Kabila. They also wanted unrestricted freedom to take action against the Hutu militias that had fled to the DRC (then called Zaire) after perpetrating the 1994 genocide against the Tutsi people of Rwanda. When, a year after the end of the First Congo War, Kabila made it clear that none of these concessions would be forthcoming, Uganda and Rwanda switched sides and began to support the new president's opponents. This development marked the beginning of the Second Congo War.

◁ **All-powerful leader**
Mobutu Sese Seko seized power in 1965. With Western support, he was the DRC's president-dictator for 32 years and was one of Africa's most corrupt leaders.

The main party against Kabila in the DRC was the Rally for Congolese Democracy (RCD). It was backed by Uganda and Rwanda, and headed a coalition of rebel factions, disaffected regional parties, and other groups that felt excluded by Kabila's rule. The war itself was not a single conflict but rather a series of contests, with multiple fronts and a shifting alliance of states and militias. At various times, Kabila's supporters included Angola, Chad, Namibia, and Zimbabwe, as well as the Allied Democratic Forces (ADF), an Islamic group, and the Lord's Resistance Army (LRA), a notoriously brutal Christian force. Most of these pro-Kabila countries and groups were motivated more by their mistrust of Uganda and Rwanda's territorial ambitions than their belief in the DRC's government. To complicate matters, Uganda and Rwanda's opposition to the DRC did not mean they fully supported each other: the two countries' forces came to blows over rival territorial ambitions more than once during the Second Congo War.

Ongoing challenges

Laurent-Désiré Kabila was assassinated by one of his bodyguards in 2001. He was succeeded by his 29-year-old son, Joseph, who agreed to take part in the South Africa–brokered peace talks of 2002–2003 that ended the war. A transitional government was established in

◁ **Displaced people**
Up to 600,000 Hutu refugees fled the DRC (then Zaire) in 1996 at the start of the First Congo War, returning to their ethnically divided home nation of Rwanda.

the DRC and the UN deployed a peacekeeping force to monitor the fragile cease-fire between the conflict's many armed groups. In 2006, Joseph Kabila was named president in the DRC's first democratic elections since independence. He was reelected in 2011 and stood down in January 2019 after losing the 2018 election to opposition candidate Félix Tshisekedi.

Despite these moves toward democracy, the DRC is far from stable and peaceful today. The issues that fueled the war—foreign interference, corruption, economic inequality, ethnic differences, resource conflicts, ideological and religious schisms, and poverty—have not gone away. Armed factions and rebel groups, some backed by the DRC's neighbors, continue to fight. In pursuit of territory gains and control of resources, rebel forces have committed acts of alleged genocide, for example against the DRC's Twa (or Batwa) and Bambuti people, situated in the northwest and northeast of the country respectively. In 2005, the UN's International Court of Justice ruled that Uganda had violated the DRC's sovereignty and looted resources worth billions of dollars. The DRC demanded $10 billion in reparations from Uganda. This was arbitrated down to $325 million. In 2022, Uganda paid its first installment of $65 million.

SHIFTING ALLIANCES

Citizens celebrated when soldiers from Laurent-Désiré Kabila's Alliance of Democratic Forces for the Liberation of Congo (AFDL) marched unopposed into the DRC's capital Kinshasa in May 1997 (below). Formed less than a year earlier, in October 1996, the army was a loose coalition of mainly Rwandan, Ugandan, Burundian, and Congolese dissidents who opposed Mobutu Sese Seko. After a short-lived peace, many of these same soldiers turned against Kabila, initiating the Second Congo War.

The end of apartheid

Equality comes to South Africa

The steady growth of opposition to apartheid in South Africa from the 1970s onward showed that "people power"—combined with international support—could bring down even the most oppressive of regimes.

△ **Men of the moment**
Nelson Mandela and F. W. de Klerk join hands in unity in 1994. A year earlier, both men were awarded the Nobel Peace Prize for their efforts to remake South Africa.

The first two decades of apartheid (see pp.254–255) had been marked by largely peaceful protest and acts of defiance. The next 20 years, however, were marked by increasing levels of direct confrontation, violence, and an ever-more confident and organized anti-apartheid movement.

The people fight back
By the beginning of the 1970s, it was clear that the nature of South African resistance to apartheid was changing. Government crackdowns in the mid-1960s had seen many leaders of the outlawed African National Congress (ANC), the main anti-apartheid organization, arrested or exiled. These events opened the way for a new generation of activists, such as the charismatic Steve Biko (see box, below) and other figures in the Black Consciousness Movement (BCM). As a grassroots operation, the BCM preached the gospel of resistance in Bantustans and townships, convincing Black South Africans that they could be liberated through their own efforts. It was a way of thinking that influenced one of the anti-apartheid movement's defining incidents.

In June 1976, a series of protests by Black students in the Johannesburg township of Soweto escalated from a demonstration about their curriculum into a challenge against apartheid itself. Government troops opened fire on the "Soweto Uprising" demonstrators, killing at least 176 of them. In response, the ANC reactivated its armed wing, *Umkhonto we Sizwe* ("Spear of the Nation"), which had been unused since the imprisonment of its leader Nelson Mandela in 1963.

Support from around the world
With anti-apartheid groups within South Africa becoming more assertive, populist protest movements outside Africa joined the fight for freedom. In October 1970, around 10,000 people gathered in London's Trafalgar Square to protest against British arms sales to South Africa. Throughout the 1980s, activists in the UK, the Netherlands, and the US ran a concerted campaign to protest against the energy company Shell's activities in South Africa. In the UK alone, the "Boycott Shell" movement contributed to the company losing almost 7 percent of its share of the gasoline market—a deficit that was in part passed on to the South African government in the form of lost taxes and revenues.

Anti-apartheid agitation was not confined to protest groups and activist organizations. In 1973, the United Nations' General Assembly officially denounced apartheid, and in 1977 the UN Security Council introduced an embargo on arms sales to South Africa.

As the 1970s ended, South Africa's government was increasingly embattled. The anti-apartheid movement was not deterred by the white authorities' violent attempts to repress protest, and international pressure for change was mounting. From 1983, prime minister P. W. Botha began to introduce piecemeal reforms, including offering limited voting rights to Asian and "Colored" (the apartheid-era term for people of mixed race) South Africans. But when the US and the British Commonwealth introduced damaging trade

THE "FATHER OF BLACK CONSCIOUSNESS"

Born in South Africa's Eastern Cape in 1946, Stephen Bantu Biko, or Steve Biko, rose to prominence in the late 1960s as an anti-apartheid student activist. He was a leading light of the Black Consciousness Movement, which rejected the support of white liberals (believing it paternalistic and condescending) and held that Black people alone should solve their own problems. Biko's uncompromising stance, combined with his grassroots activism in student, community, and health programs, made him a target. After his arrest in September 1977, he was beaten to death while in custody. Biko's funeral (pictured here) became one of the defining moments of the anti-apartheid movement at home and around the world.

> "We are starting a **new era** of **hope**, **reconciliation**, and **nation building**. We are **one nation**."
>
> — NELSON MANDELA, 1994

△ **Democracy in action**
Citizens line up to vote at a Soweto primary school in April 1994. This was South Africa's first democratic election and the first one where all Black people were allowed to vote.

and business sanctions against South Africa in 1985, it was clear that apartheid's time was running out. Faced with economic, political, and even cultural isolation across the globe, South Africa's government began to acknowledge that only a constitutional revolution would work.

The birth of democracy

In 1990, President F. W. de Klerk lifted the 30-year ban on the ANC and other anti-apartheid groups and released political prisoners, notably Nelson Mandela after 27 years in jail. A dialogue was opened between the government and opposition parties, mainly the ANC, and De Klerk and Mandela drew up a new constitution as apartheid laws were repealed and Black people were given the vote. In 1993, Mandela and de Klerk were awarded the Nobel Peace Prize "for their work for the peaceful termination of the apartheid regime, and for laying the foundations for a new democratic South Africa."

The country held its first democratic elections in April 1994. The ANC took 62 percent of the vote and headed a new coalition government of national unity that also included the National Party and the mainly Zulu Inkatha Freedom Party. On May 10, 1994, Nelson Mandela was inaugurated as South Africa's first Black president.

▷ **Champion of change**
A committed Black rights activist, Winnie Mandela was Nelson Mandela's second wife (from 1958–1996) and was known to her supporters as "the mother of the nation."

Peace advocate
Wearing his trademark colorful silk shirt and HIV/AIDS-awareness pin, Nelson Mandela appears in 2000 at peace talks for Burundi, which was then engaged in a bitter civil war. Even in his 80s, Mandela played an active role in world politics.

Nelson Mandela

South Africa's first Black president

Nelson Mandela was a lawyer, an activist, a prisoner, a president, and a celebrity. This transformative politician is still revered globally as a symbol of freedom and as a founder of modern South Africa.

Born into a powerful Xhosa family in 1918, Nelson Mandela attended Christian missionary schools, and trained as a lawyer in Johannesburg. As a young man, he became interested in the politics of African nationalism and joined the youth wing of the African National Congress (ANC) in 1944 (see pp.254–255).

Mandela's rise up the ANC's ranks came as South Africa—then a self-governing dominion of the British Empire—moved toward apartheid. Mandela spoke at rallies and pushed for radical action. As repression intensified, he became an anti-apartheid figurehead, and was repeatedly arrested and imprisoned.

Hardship and triumph

Mandela grew increasingly determined to fight for freedom. In 1960, police killed 69 protesters in Sharpeville, near Johannesburg, and the following year Mandela cofounded *Umkhonto we Sizwe* ("Spear of the Nation"), the ANC's paramilitary wing. The group launched acts of sabotage, and in 1962 Mandela received military training in Morocco and Ethiopia. Later that year, he was arrested in South Africa. Mandela turned his trial into political theater, declaring in a three-hour speech that equality was "an ideal for which I am prepared to die." He avoided the death penalty, but was imprisoned in 1962 and sentenced to life imprisonment in 1964.

By the 1980s, internal resistance was growing and South Africa was an international pariah. Mandela had remained popular throughout his imprisonment, and was finally released in 1990. He became president of the ANC in 1991 and negotiated the end of apartheid with President F. W. De Klerk (see pp.268–269).

Elected the country's first Black president in 1994, Mandela prioritized the dismantling of apartheid through racial reconciliation. He appointed politicians from De Klerk's National Party to government roles and created a Truth and Reconciliation Commission to investigate crimes committed by government forces and the ANC.

Nelson Mandela served only one term in office, stepping down in 1999 to campaign and raise money for rural development and HIV/AIDS treatment. But the impact of this freedom fighter turned man of peace is unparalleled.

△ **Young activist**
A young Mandela wears a beaded necklace and a kaross (blanket) during his time in hiding from the police in South Africa in 1961.

▽ **A free man**
Mandela and his then wife Winnie greet crowds in Cape Town on his 1990 release from prison. Mandela spent over 27 years behind bars.

1918 Rolihlahla Mandela is born—he is given the name Nelson by a school teacher

1944 Joins the youth wing of the African National Congress (ANC)

1961 Co-founds *Umkhonto we Sizwe*, the ANC's military wing

1964 Imprisoned for life for sabotage and conspiracy to overthrow the government

1990 Release from prison, after massive global controversy at his imprisonment

1991 Becomes president of the ANC and leads negotiations with the government

1994 Elected president in South Africa's first election with universal suffrage

2013 Dies after a respiratory infection at home in Johannesburg

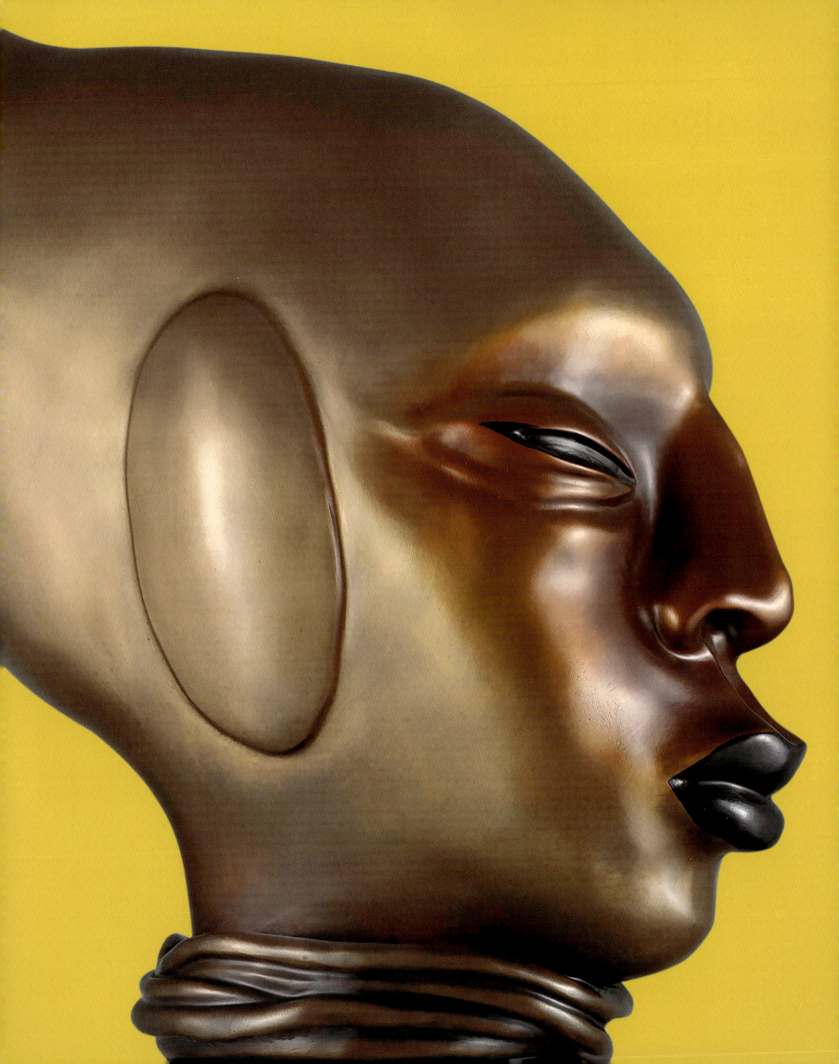

◁ **Afrofuturistic art**
The presence and importance of women in Africa's past and present is visualized in this large bronze sculpture, *The Seated III* (2019), by Kenyan artist Wangechi Mutu.

Contemporary Africa

1994–

Contemporary Africa

Huge strides toward African freedom and self-determination were made in the 20th century. In its closing decades, two events became beacons of hope: Zimbabwe's hard-won independence in 1980 and the 1994 victory of the African National Congress in South Africa's first free elections.

Many nations have thrived in the modern age. Countries including Botswana and Mauritius have been democratic for the entirety of their postcolonial history, and cities such as Lagos, Cairo, and Kinshasa (see pp.284–285) have become global powerhouses. Organizations like the African Union have sought to increase collaboration between African nations, while major global events such as the 2010 World Cup, hosted in South Africa, have put the continent in the spotlight.

Growth and challenges

Progress has been remarkable. Child mortality across the continent has fallen consistently for 50 years, and healthy life expectancy has increased. The spread of internet access and peer-to-peer payment networks has helped drive growth. Dams, railroad and bridge building, land reclamation, and new data centers and undersea internet cables have transformed physical and digital spaces. Some projects have been supported by foreign investment, particularly from China, indicating both the continued impact of neocolonialism and the recalibration of world power.

However, Africa's difficulties have not vanished. Rwanda suffered a genocidal conflict in 1994 and other nations have endured civil wars or long-standing insurgencies. Much of Central Africa remains under authoritarian rule. The Arab Spring of the early 2010s led to elections in Tunisia and Egypt, but popular movements have often met with mixed success, resulting in civil wars in countries like Mali and Libya. Diseases including malaria have wreaked havoc, although COVID-19 deaths in Africa have so far been among the world's lowest. Despite these ongoing challenges, and growing threats such as climate change—which brought severe floods to West Africa in 2022 and Libya in 2023—Africa's power and potential continues to rise. By 2100, it is estimated that a third of the world's population will be African, as the continent takes center stage.

New voices

Since the 1990s, African voices have been growing in prominence, with talented artists, filmmakers, athletes, and leaders pushing boundaries and setting new standards. Musical genres such as Nigeria's Afrobeats, Senegal's *mbalax*, and Egypt's *mahraganat* (or electro-*shaabi*) are increasingly influential, while African artists are reinvigorating existing traditions, often combining African heritage with new technology, as in Nigerian Dennis Osadebe's pop art-inspired "Afrofuturist" paintings. In cinema, Nigeria's Nollywood is Africa's best known, but across the continent filmmakers, performers, actors, and comedians are exploding into the global mainstream. Authors are exploring African identities and choosing to write in their own languages rather than English, while athletes have dominated sports including soccer and distance running—as the continent continues to nurture and celebrate African talent.

◁ **Magodi-Noxolo (2020) by South African ceramicist Zizipho Poswa**

1994 Nelson Mandela becomes South Africa's first Black president

1997 Zaire's longstanding President Mobutu is ousted and the nation becomes the Democratic Republic of the Congo

1999 Rwanda's National Unity and Reconciliation Commission is formed

2001 The African Union forms. It now has 55 member states across the continent

2002 The First Ivorian Civil War begins after a military rebellion

CONTEMPORARY AFRICA | 275

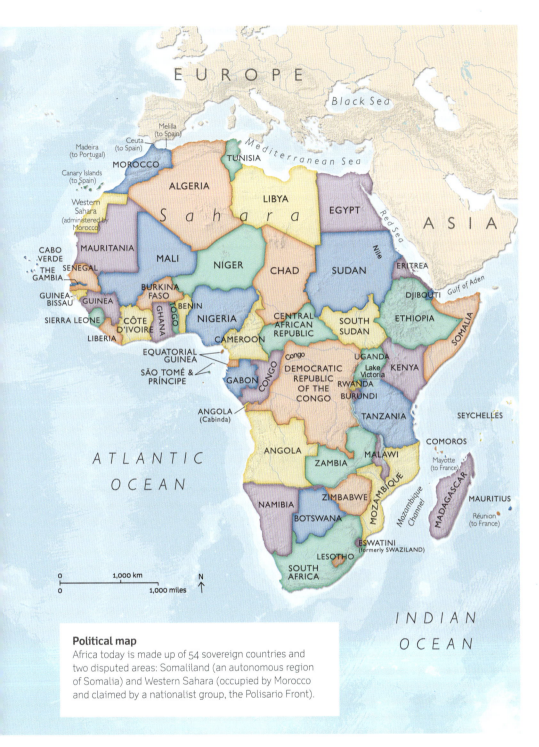

Political map
Africa today is made up of 54 sovereign countries and two disputed areas: Somaliland (an autonomous region of Somalia) and Western Sahara (occupied by Morocco and claimed by a nationalist group, the Polisario Front).

▲ The Hillbrow Tower, Johannesburg, South Africa

▲ Fans at the 2022 Africa Cup of Nations

▲ Runway show at Lagos Fashion Week, 2022

2008 Africa's population reaches a billion; by 2023, it is nearly 1.5 billion

2009 Islamist militant group Boko Haram begins an insurgency in Nigeria

2011 After decades of conflict, South Sudan gains its independence from Sudan

2013 The Ebola virus claims victims in West Africa, particularly in Sierra Leone, Liberia, and Guinea

2019 The largest-yet Africa Cup of Nations, held in Egypt, is won by Algeria

2022 COP27 is held in Egypt, the first time the UN climate change conference has been held in Africa

2023 African Union made a permanent member of the G20 (or Group of 20) forum for international economic cooperation

Reclaiming cultures

Preservation, renewal, and reinvention

During the colonial era, many European powers attempted to suppress the practices of African cultures. Today, people across the continent are reclaiming and reinventing cultures and values via politics, language, and art.

Oppressive colonial policies discouraged the use of African languages, technologies, and artistic expressions, and even after independence, Western cultures and customs continued to spread. However, African cultures have deep roots, and many people have increasingly sought to embrace and redefine these longstanding practices.

Some peoples have consciously chosen to use their own languages, with the Khoi and San languages added to the South African curriculum, and Kenyan author Ngũgĩ wa Thiong'o eschewing English for Gikuyu. In Kenya, the Maasai are creating a digital archive of their entire community's shared intellectual property and language. Other campaigns include the digitizing of the vast libraries of centuries-old documents that form the Timbuktu Manuscripts of Mali (see pp.96–97).

The European occupation of African countries led to the theft of many ancient and valuable objects that hold cultural and historical significance for local communities, many of whom are demanding these objects back. Some museums in Europe have begun to return the bronze sculptures looted from Benin (see pp.128–129) in modern-day Nigeria. Egyptian mummies have been sent back to Egypt from Ireland and the US, and efforts to return other great cultural works, including a Ugandan throne held by the UK, continue.

Elsewhere, art forms are being revitalized. In Bamako in Mali, the *bogolan* custom of producing and dyeing patterned fabric has been re-created and celebrated. In the north of Tanzania, Jita elders are working to restore their cultural heritage, in particular their dance styles. In Port Harcourt and Calabar in Nigeria, projects involving young people have reclaimed the art of mask-making and masquerades, blending historical practices with commentary on contemporary life and politics.

△ **Benin cockerel**
Okukor is one of the Benin Bronzes produced by artisans in the Kingdom of Benin. The British stole the work in 1897, and it was returned to Nigeria in 2021.

◁ **Zulu coronation**
Misuzulu ka Zwelithini is recognized as the king of the Zulu nation at a 2022 ceremony in Durban, the first such Zulu coronation since South Africa became a democracy in 1994.

New forms are also being born from older, existing traditions. Contemporary artists have been inspired by the geometric murals of the Ndebele people of South Africa and the sinuous abstraction of Nigerian uli art, while others have Africanized Western genres such as pop art. The music of nations across Africa has been revived in everything from Cameroonian *makossa* and Ghanaian highlife to Tanzanian *bongo flava*.

Political renewal

Pan-African collaboration is an important part of the reclaiming of the continent's cultures. The African Union (see pp.304–305) gathers heads of state, but grassroots efforts to foster unity are just as vital. Zimbabwe's Pan African Women's Organization brings together women from across Africa, while events such as the Panafrican Film and Television Festival of Ouagadougou (FESPACO) gather creative voices. Youth movements, meanwhile, show a new generation eager to challenge the status quo, with the Ghana Youth Party (GYP) campaigning on unemployment and access to education, and Y'en a Marre ("Fed Up"), a group of rappers and journalists, mobilizing the young Senegalese to vote on issues such as land reform.

Campaigns for land rights and sovereignty strive to reclaim nations that vanished from the map when Europeans redrew African borders at the end of the 19th century. Numerous African peoples are advocating for the autonomy of their native land, with South Sudan's 2011 independence from Sudan a significant result. Groups such as the Oromo and Tigray (Ethiopia), Kabyle (Algeria), Igbo (Nigeria), and Tuareg (Mali) are pushing for independence via a mix of strikes, advocacy, and military means. The Canary Islands, one of a handful of territories still under European control, has an active nationalist movement. These efforts, and many other drives to preserve and renew African cultures, are ongoing.

△ **Uli-inspired tapestry**
The Beauty Within, a 2019 tapestry by Nigerian artist Jennifer Ogochukwu Okpoko, recalls *uli* art, in which Igbo women paint curves and other shapes on people and buildings.

▽ **Ndebele art**
Artist Esther Mahlangu is pictured in front of her home in Mpumalanga, South Africa. Her colorful, geometric works are inspired by Ndebele jewelery, clothing, and wall paintings.

Beadwork

Crafts from across the continent

In Africa, beadwork takes many forms. Beads can be sewn onto backings of fabric or leather to create tunics, collars, hats, stools, and aprons, or strung on thin wire for support, as in Maasai collars and Dinka bodices. The most intricate beading techniques are used to create free-standing pieces, such as Mfengu necklaces.

△ **Kuba collar**
This collar, made by the Kuba people who live in the Democratic Republic of the Congo, utilizes glass beads and cowrie shells attached to a leather backing.
— Two-tone squares known as *lantshoong*

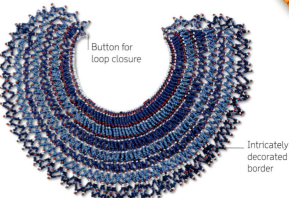

△ **Mfengu collar**
Ingqosha (collar) necklaces are worn by the Mfengu people, a Xhosa-speaking group who live in southeastern South Africa.
— Button for loop closure
— Intricately decorated border

- Animal horns said to give *oba* ability to speak with authority
- Neck design uses rare African jasper beads and the tiniest seed beads
- Crowns on either side of appliquéd face symbolize continuity of *oba*'s office

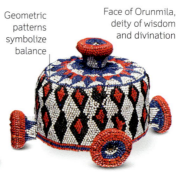

△ **Prestige cap**
Made by an artist from the Pende people of the Democratic Republic of the Congo, this *misango mapende* (royal crown) indicates high authority.
— Geometric patterns symbolize balance
— Face of Orunmila, deity of wisdom and divination

△ **Oba's crown**
This mid-19th century *oba*'s royal crown from Nigeria was created from a metal frame covered with printed cotton, onto which polished glass beads were embroidered.
— Top-knots often represent a town, city, or people

◁ **Royal Yoruba tunic**
Dating from around 1900 and intended to be worn by the *oba*, or king, this Yoruba v-neck tunic from Nigeria is covered with thousands of glass beads, expressing the wearer's high status.

BEADWORK | 279

▽ **Wedding necklace**
This type of collar, typical of the Maasai from southern Kenya and northern Tanzania, is associated with weddings and other special occasions.

Red beads symbolize bravery

Wire and metal spacers are used to create the collar's shape

MAASAI BEADED JEWELERY

Historically, the Maasai used local materials, such as shells, ivory, bone, wood, clay, copper, or brass, for their beadwork; today, glass beads are favored. Colors have symbolic meanings derived from the Maasai's deep connection with cattle, a key source of wealth and sustenance; for example, white represents purity by association with milk.

▷ **Dinka corset**
In the Dinka culture of southern Sudan, adolescents wore beaded corsets to indicate their stage of life. This example indicates a girl's eligibility for marriage.

Cowrie shells intended to promote fertility

Beaded cloth covering overlays wooden stool

Bead colors can identify different age groups

Strings at both sides would have been used to tie apron around wearer's waist

Leather (goatskin) backing

Base is a leopard, a symbol of power

△ **Beaded apron**
The seeds at the bottom of this cache-sexe, or loindress, identifies it as South Sotho in origin. Like similar Zulu pieces, it would be worn by an unmarried girl.

◁ **Royal stool**
This late 19th- or early 20th-century beaded stool would have been used by a king or courtier of the Bamileke people of western Cameroon. The glass beads represent wealth and the cowrie shells express fertility.

Small additional finger

△ **Ndebele apron**
This wedding apron, made by a Ndebele woman from South Africa, has seven "fingers," indicating that the owner was not the first wife; a first wife's apron would include only five "fingers."

Religions

Africa's faiths, old and new

Scores, if not hundreds, of Indigenous belief systems exist in Africa. Their tenets vary greatly, but they share common elements. Chief among these is a belief in a supreme deity. Its name varies from place to place. The Yoruba of West Africa call it Olodumare, for example; the Ruvu and Kamba people of East Africa refer to it as Mulungu. As in the ancient Greek, Roman, and Egyptian religions, the supreme deity often oversees lesser gods of the harvest, fertility, war, and so on.

Like most faiths, Africa's Indigenous belief systems are intensely spiritual, their aim being for believers to connect directly with the divine. Ancestor veneration is widely practiced, as are forms of belief in which rivers, trees, and other parts of the natural world are thought to be possessed by protective spirits whose favor is sought through offerings, prayers, and sacrifice. Often, contact with the divine or spirit world is made through intermediaries such as shamans, the *babalawos* ("medicine men") of West Africa, and the *Sangoma* healers of Southern Africa.

Fusion of beliefs

Today, fewer than 10 percent of Africans practice Indigenous faiths, but research shows that up to half of the populations of some states look to ancestors or spirits for protection from harm. Many Africans have faith in the protective power of charms and amulets, or juju. Indigenous beliefs are embedded in African cultures and hugely affect the way the continent's two largest religions, Islam and Christianity, are practiced.

△ **A celebration of creation**
Each October, the Yoruba of Ife, Nigeria, celebrate *Olojo* ("the day of the first dawn"). After a seven-day seclusion to commune with his ancestors for the welfare of the people, Ife's *ooni* (king) leads ritual processions through the city.

△ **Divine intermediaries**
Male and female priests, called *saltigues*, preside over the religious ceremonies of the Serer people of Senegal, such as at the *Xooy* ceremony, where they predict the future and commune with their creator-god, *Roog*. The *saltigues'* skills include casting cowrie shells and divining the meaning of the shapes they form.

△ **Woman of faith**
The dolls, beads, and carved stick carried by this priestess are totems in West Africa's Vodun religion. This faith's tenets of ancestor veneration and spiritualism (communicating with the spirits of the dead) reached the Americas as "Voodoo," via the slave trade.

> "We may have **different religions**...
> but we all belong to **one human race**."
>
> KOFI ANNAN, 2016

Of the two, Islam has been more accepting toward Indigenous beliefs. The *jinn*, a protective spirit revered by North Africa's Amazigh (Berber) people, became the "genie" of popular legend following the arrival of Arab Muslims from the 7th century. Islam has become the most popular faith in North and East Africa, with around 450 million followers. Devotees of both Islam and Christianity seek a personal relationship with their God and value the spiritual dimension, just as those who practice Indigenous beliefs do.

However, when Christianity spread in Africa during colonial times, its adherents openly disapproved of Africa's Indigenous belief systems. The hierarchy of the Catholic Church, in particular, disliked the more "democratic" approach of Indigenous beliefs, which allowed all followers to connect to the divine. But Indigenous beliefs persist, and an increasing number of so-called "breakaway" Christian churches have emerged to accommodate this. The Catholic Legio Maria Church and the Protestant Church of Christ in Africa both recognize ancestor veneration and polygamy among their congregations, for example. Pentecostalism, with its dynamic, energetic emphasis on the power of the Holy Spirit, is increasingly popular among Africa's 600 million Christians.

Africa's many religions and belief systems have developed in ways that are unique to the continent. Their differences are numerous, but it is their similarities, above all their shared spirituality, that is helping to ensure their continued success.

△ **Turning toward God**
Sudan has one of the world's largest Sufi communities. Sufism is a mystical branch of Islam. Its adherents achieve divine, spiritual ecstasy by spinning themselves into a trancelike state. These are the famous "whirling dervishes."

△ **A humble offering**
The *Irreechaa* is a ceremony performed by the Oromo people of Ethiopia and northern Kenya at the end of winter to thank the chief god, *Waaqa Tokkicha*, for the previous year's good fortune. Those who practice the *Waaqeffanna* faith believe lesser gods possess their bodies in order to communicate with them.

△ **A fusion of faiths**
South Africa's Nazareth Baptist Church fuses Zulu culture with Christianity. Founded around 1910 by the faith healer and preacher Isaiah Shembe, its roots in Indigenous beliefs are evident in its Pentecostal-like, ecstatic approach to worship.

Protecting environments
The challenge of climate change

Africa accounts for the smallest share of greenhouse gas emissions compared to regions such as the US, China, and Europe. Yet the continent has suffered some of the worst effects of climate change, and has begun searching for solutions.

Global warming from climate change is occurring across almost all the Earth's surface, causing extreme events, including flooding, heatwaves, and drought. Africa is responsible for less than 4 percent of global greenhouse gas emissions, yet is the most vulnerable region in the world to the changing climate, according to the UN's Environment Programme.

Perhaps the most significant impact of global warming on the continent is desertification, the process by which vegetation in arid and semi-arid lands, such as grasslands or shrublands, decreases, degrading the productivity of the land. The most affected areas include the Sahel region to the south of the Sahara and the Congo Basin in Central Africa.

Desertification occurs as a result of multiple interacting causes. In addition to anthropogenic (human-caused) climate change, factors include natural fluctuations in climate, deforestation, over-grazing and over-cultivation of crops, poor irrigation, and resource exploitation. Desertification leads to hotter and drier conditions, and more frequent and more severe droughts and famines. These conditions exacerbate existing food security issues by negatively impacting crop yields and livestock health. To help combat desertification, the African Union (see pp.304–305) adopted an initiative in 2007 known as the Great Green Wall. This mass planting of trees across the Sahel aims to prevent expansion of the Sahara and increase the amount of arable land.

Ecosystems and weather patterns

A serious issue in regions like the Congo Basin, where some of the largest rainforests in the world are found, is deforestation. Vast areas of this woodland have been cleared for logging, mining, agriculture, roads, hunting, and other purposes. This has resulted in the loss of habitat for many species and poses a global threat to the world's ecosystem, since rainforests are vital for trapping carbon that would otherwise be released into the atmosphere. The Democratic Republic of the Congo (DRC), home to the majority of the Congo Basin rainforest, has made commitments to

▽ **Great Green Wall**
The "greening" of a strip of land across Africa from the Atlantic Ocean to the Red Sea will help slow the progress of desertification and mitigate the effects of climate change.

◁ **Sustainable agriculture**
Women tend to crops in Senegal near the Great Green Wall. The initiative includes not only planting new trees, but also improving soils and setting up community gardens.

△ **Eroded soil**
This landscape in Kenya shows the effects of soil erosion. Activities such as building terraces, planting trees, and installing grass strips can help reduce the problem.

protect its rainforests by replanting trees and banning the export of raw timber. In other schemes, the DRC's government has granted local communities large tracts of land to manage sustainably, helping to halt the decline of the forest and alleviating poverty.

Climate change also increases the risk of floods, storms, and other natural disasters, which can cause famines, poverty, and the displacement of populations, putting pressure on neighboring lands. In Nigeria, which has experienced increasingly widespread flooding in recent years, the government has set a target to cut emissions by 45 percent by 2030 and initiated measures such as tree planting and land reclamation. Farmers in countries including Kenya, Uganda, Senegal, and Ethiopia have adopted solar-powered irrigation systems, which reduce power usage while increasing yields, while South Africa has invested in renewable energy production, especially solar and wind. Rwanda plans to connect households to solar mini-grids.

Battery minerals

As the world moves to electric vehicles, demand has grown for minerals used in their batteries, such as cobalt, lithium, and nickel. Africa is home to many of these minerals; the DRC, for example, produces more than 70 percent of the world's cobalt. The country has cooperated with neighboring Zambia on a "Green Minerals Strategy." The aims of the agreement are to reduce the environmental impacts of mining and to benefit local communities by developing the capacity not just to extract the minerals, but to assemble the batteries as well.

> "**Desertification** ... is the greatest environmental **challenge** of our time."
>
> LUC GNACADJA, BENINESE POLITICIAN, 2010

▷ **Panning for minerals**
Miners wash metal bowlfuls of sandy earth in the Lukushi River in the Democratic Republic of the Congo, looking for black nuggets of cassiterite (tin oxide ore).

Lagos

An iconic African megacity

Nigeria's unofficial capital, Lagos, is one of the world's largest urban areas. This thriving metropolis is an economic and cultural giant—and is so populous that it has been deemed one of Africa's three megacities.

The greatest cities of Africa are so large that it can be hard to know where they end and their hinterlands begin. However, Lagos in Nigeria (with a population of around 16 million), Kinshasa in the Democratic Republic of the Congo (16 million), and Cairo in Egypt (22 million) all qualify as megacities—urban areas with a population over 10 million. Megacities like these attract people and investment, but their rapid growth has brought inequalities and challenges in infrastructure, health, and education.

Lagos, the largest city in Nigeria, is a prime example of an African megacity. It began as Eko, a Yoruba fishing village on Lagos Island. Portuguese traders called it Lagos, from the Portuguese word for "lakes," and from the 17th century it became an increasingly important port for the trade in palm oil and enslaved people (see box, opposite). It stayed under Yoruba rule until the British occupied it by force in the mid 19th century and made it the capital of the colony of Nigeria.

Lagos expanded further under British rule, and, by the time Nigeria won its independence in 1960, it was a sizable coastal city surrounded by villages. Crude oil supercharged its development: in the 1970s, Lagos's role in oil exports from the Niger Delta saw its population reach two million as it expanded onto neighboring islands and the mainland. Eager to spread Nigeria's development more evenly, the government moved the capital to Abuja in 1991, but Lagos continued to thrive, and today stretches for more than 386 sq miles (1,000 sq km).

Challenges and successes

The development of Lagos was rapid but often haphazard. The British were focused on extracting resources, rather than building a sustainable city. The 1970s crude oil rush saw hastily erected warehouses crowd the shore and unplanned suburbs link the city with the villages around it. As a result, Lagos's infrastructure is uneven, and has struggled to keep up with its growing population. Today, congestion is common, and despite recent bridge and motorway construction, *keke* motorized tricycles and yellow *danfo* minibuses crowd the streets, as pedestrians and street vendors weave through the traffic.

Neighborhoods such as Ikoyi have sky-scraping luxury apartments and expensive boutiques, and if Lagos were an independent nation it would have one of Africa's biggest economies. Industries such as car manufacture, pharmaceuticals, software, electronics, and the oil sector are booming. Yet many residents

▽ **Crowded city**
Lagos's streets are often packed with bumper-to-bumper traffic. The yellow minibuses known as *danfo* are a city institution.

live in poor-quality housing with a lack of basic services such as piped water, health care, and education. In 2020, security forces opened fire on protesters against police brutality, while in 2023 currency shortages led to riots, and tensions continue between groups such as the Yoruba, Igbo, and Hausa.

For all its flaws, however, Lagos is a thriving cultural hub. Dishes from across Nigeria such as *eba* (a fried cassava snack) and *egusi* (melon-seed soup) are sold in restaurants and by street vendors and music is everywhere—Afrobeats stars Wizkid and Tiwa Savage were born in the city. Lagos Fashion Week is Africa's biggest fashion event, while Nollywood, Nigeria's film industry, is centered in Lagos. The city's vibrant locations have defined an industry that produces more than 2,000 films a year.

Cities of the future

Lagos's historic expansion may be just a taster for what is to come. At current rates, its population could hit 90 million by 2100. And Lagos is not alone. It and fellow megacities Cairo (the largest city in the Arab world) and Kinshasa (the world's largest French-speaking city) are set to be joined by other megacities.

Dar Es Salaam (Tanzania), Khartoum (Sudan), Nairobi (Kenya), and Luanda (Angola) are all due to pass 10 million inhabitants by 2050, as the urban population grows faster in Africa than on any other continent.

This growth will power economies and reshape global politics. Megacities will face familiar problems such as inequality and challenges with infrastructure and health care, as well as new ones, such as climate change. Investment and planning is critical if these cities of the future are to fulfill their potential.

GROWTH OF **A PORT CITY**

This print shows the port of Lagos in 1885. In the first half of the 19th century, Lagos was a Yoruba port that was integral to the trade in enslaved people and palm oil. In 1851, the British navy bombarded the city, ending the slave trade and installing a new Yoruba ruler, Akitoye, who had been ousted as *oba* by his nephew. In 1861, Britain invaded and annexed the city as a British colony. The British seized the remainder of Nigeria in 1886 with Lagos, now the colony's capital, gaining infrastructure such as railroads and street lighting.

▽ **Landmark bridge**
This cable-stayed bridge stretches for 0.84 miles (1.36 km) and connects the island neighborhoods of Lekki and Ikoyi.

Sports

Excelling at a range of sports

Africa has a long history of sports. Ancient Egyptians held swimming and athletics contests, while modern North African *fantasia* festivals of horsemanship have roots in ancient Numidia. Many sports were martial, such as the *dambe* boxing of Nigeria's Hausa and Angolan *engolo*, which developed into capoeira (a martial art that combines dance, acrobatics, and music).

Soccer has also been adopted. The Africa Cup of Nations is the continent's national tournament, pulling in millions of viewers. Successful men's teams include Cameroon, Egypt, Nigeria, Ghana, and Morocco—the first African side to reach the World Cup semifinals, in 2022. Egypt's Mohamed Salah, Cameroon's Samuel Eto'o, and George Weah (from 2018, Liberia's president) rank among the world's greatest players.

In athletics, East Africans dominate long-distance running, with Eliud Kipchoge of Kenya and Haile Gebrselassie and Kenenisa Bekele of Ethiopia setting multiple world records and winning several Olympic golds each. Other top athletes include triple and long jumper Hugues Fabrice Zango of Burkina Faso, and Kenyan middle-distance runner Faith Kipyegon.

Nigeria, the Democratic Republic of the Congo (DRC), Sudan, Senegal, and Cameroon are key basketball nations. As with soccer, many of the finest athletes have pursued their career overseas: in the United States' National Basketball Association (NBA), top players such as Hakeem Olajuwon of Nigeria, who played in the 1980s and '90s, and Dikembe Mutombo of the DRC, who played in the 1990s and 2000s, led

△ **Biniam Girmay (Eritrea)**
Eritrean road cyclist Biniam Girmay was African Cyclist of the Year in 2021, 2022, and 2023. At the 2022 *Giro d'Italia*, he triumphed in a Grand Tour stage and the 122-mile- (196-km-) long stage 10 after a sprint finish. In 2023, he won a Tour de Suisse stage.

△ **Tobi Amusan (Nigeria)**
Oluwatobiloba Ayomide "Tobi" Amusan is the World, Commonwealth, and African Champion in the 100 meter hurdles. She became the first athlete from Nigeria to win gold at the 2022 World Athletics Championships, setting a new world record of 12.12 seconds in the semifinal, followed by a 12.06 in the final.

△ **Africa Cup of Nations**
Africa's national soccer tournament, which takes place every two years, is popular on the continent and around the globe. Senegal (pictured) beat Egypt in the 2023 men's event, while South Africa defeated Morocco in the 2022 women's final.

> "I am running to **make history**, to show that no human is **limited**."
>
> ELIUD KIPCHOGE, KENYAN MARATHON RUNNER, 2019

the way for current stars such as Cameroonian Joel Embiid of the Philadelphia 76ers. The NBA is also a backer of the Basketball Africa League.

Cricket is popular in some nations that were British colonies, such as South Africa, Zimbabwe, and Namibia. South Africa has won several international tournaments, including the Champions Trophy in 1998. The country hosted the World Cup in 2003 and has its own T20 league. South Africa is also a global force in rugby union, and has triumphed in three World Cups. Namibia, Kenya, and Zimbabwe are increasingly competitive.

Wrestling and boxing are deeply rooted in African cultures, particularly in Senegal and Ghana, respectively. The wrestling style focuses on grappling. In West Africa in particular, competitions are held at festivals with drums and dances. Africans have also fought in Greco-Roman-style wrestling events including the Olympics. In boxing, some of the most successful African fighters on the global stage include Nigeria's Hogan Bassey and Dick Tiger, who were world champions in the 1950s and '60s. In the 1980s and '90s, Azumah Nelson of Ghana won multiple belts. Tennis is less popular, but Africa has produced some notable players, including Tunisian Ons Jabeur, the 2022 runner-up at Wimbledon and the US Open.

Many Africans outcompete the rest of the world at events first introduced by colonial powers. But in some countries, a lack of resources means top athletes move overseas to fulfill their sporting potential.

△ **Decorated runner**
In September 2018, Eliud Kipchoge of Kenya was awarded the gold medal at the 45th Berlin Marathon in Berlin, Germany.

△ **Phiwokuhle Mnguni (South Africa)**
Featherweight Mnguni won bronze at the 2022 Commonwealth Games, becoming the first female South African to win a major boxing medal. South Africa has a strong history of boxing—in 2003 Corrie Sanders became WBO World Champion.

△ **Rwanda vs South Sudan**
Kuany Ngor Kuany is pictured in possession for South Sudan's men's national basketball team during qualifiers for the 2023 World Cup. As a relatively new country and one enduring a cycle of war, South Sudan defied expectations by reaching the World Cup. It played alongside Egypt, Angola, Côte d'Ivoire, and Cabo Verde.

△ **Clive Madande (Zimbabwe)**
Madande is a rising star in Zimbabwean cricket. The wicketkeeper and batter, pictured here in Zimbabwe's capital, Harare, has an impressive record in test and one-day matches. He made his international debut for his country's cricket team in June 2022.

Feminisms

Fighting for women's rights

The struggle for equality for Africa's women has not been one of upward, linear progression. The considerable authority women lost during colonization had to be won again after it ended, resulting in feminisms that take different forms.

△ **Stamp of approval**
Born in 1918, South Africa's Albertina Sisulu—"Ma Sisulu"—led thousands of women in a march against apartheid laws in 1956.

In many African cultures, women customarily wielded power separately from men through familial structures and cultural and economic organizations. European colonizers imposed Victorian-era values of submissive femininity on the societies they controlled, disregarding the central role of women in producing, processing, and buying and selling food, and ignoring their important positions within their communities.

Finding a way to fight back

In response to this erosion of status, many women in Africa joined the anti-colonial struggle. The 1929 Aba Women's War (see p.219) and the 1947–1948 Egba Women's uprising in Nigeria (in which women opposed arbitrary taxes imposed on them by the colonial government) are examples of organized grassroots women's resistance. In Somalia, women used their own genre of poetry, *buraanbur*, to express their concerns and aspirations, while in Tanganyika (modern-day Tanzania) women gathered in dance clubs known as *ngoma* to form communal networks through which they could campaign for their political and social rights. This they sometimes did through performances in song and dance—although these were usually dismissed by colonial officials as little more than noisy entertainments.

Women also played an active role in armed uprisings, including Kenya's Mau Mau uprising of 1952–1960 (see pp.222–223), the Algerian War of Independence of 1954–1962 (see pp.234–235), and the Second Chimurenga in Zimbabwe of 1964–1979 (see pp.252–253). The names of political activists and feminists like Funmilayo Ransome-Kuti (Nigeria), Winnie Mandela (South Africa), Graça Machel (Mozambique), Hawo Tako (Somalia), and Aminatou Haidar (Western Sahara) are synonymous with nationalist movements in their countries.

In more recent times, literature has been an important—and often controversial—means of feminist expression. The protagonist of Egyptian novelist Nawal El Saadawi's *Woman at Point Zero* (1974)

△ **Charting progress**
Convened for the 10-year anniversary of 1975's International Women's Year, the UN-sponsored "Decade for Women" conference in Kenya drew attention to women's rights in Africa.

> "I generally **struggle with labels**, but I acknowledge the importance of **owning the word 'feminism.'**"
>
> MALEBO SEPHODI, SOUTH AFRICAN WRITER

△ **Lagos protests**
Protests against Nigeria's notoriously violent Special Anti-Robbery Squad (SARS) took place in 2020. One of SARS' most organized critics was the Feminist Coalition, founded that same year.

experiences genital mutilation and sexual abuse. Nigerian Flora Nwapa's *Efuru* (1966) depicts an Igbo woman's frustrations with married life. In 1965, Ghana's Ama Ata Aidoo became the first published African female dramatist, and she later went on to serve as her country's Minister for Education. The lives and careers of these women helped pave the way for post-millennial writers such as Zambia's Namwali Serpell, Zimbabwe's Tsitsi Dangarembga, Côte d'Ivoire's Véronique Tadjo, and Nigeria's Chimamanda Ngozi Adichie (see pp.302–303).

In the performing arts, the South African singer Miriam Makeba campaigned against apartheid, and for Black civil rights more generally, from the 1960s. She was followed by other outspoken South African singer-activists such as Brenda Fassie and Yvonne Chaka Chaka (see pp.296–297). The Beninese singer-songwriter Angélique Kidjo is a UNICEF ambassador and a campaigner for the rights of women and girls.

Africa's feminisms

Across the continent, women are working to improve women's lives. In 1982, for example, the Senegalese anti-FGM campaigner Awa Thiam founded the Commission for the Abolition of Sexual Mutilation, while Tanzania's Hope For Girls and Women, set up by Rhobi Samwelly, has been helping girls escape genital mutilation by providing safe houses and other services since 2017. African women who have been awarded Nobel Prizes include South Africa's Nadine Gordimer (Literature, 1991) and Yemen's Tawakkol Karman along with Liberia's Ellen Johnson Sirleaf (see pp.290–291) and Leymah Gbowee (Peace, 2011).

African women have adapted feminism to their own contexts. These feminisms take many forms, such as Womanism, which places special focus on the experiences of Black women, and Nego-Feminism, emphasizing negotiation as a way forward. Africa's feminisms remain irreducibly plural.

ECO FEMINISM IN AFRICA

Set up in 1977, the Green Belt Movement (GBM) mobilized women across rural Africa to plant 50 million trees to help prevent desertification. Established in Kenya, it was seen as a threat to male power in a patriarchal society. The movement put its members on the front lines of political engagement and protest for decades—none more so than the GBM's visionary founder Wangari Maathai (1940–2011, pictured here). With UN support, her organization expanded across the continent, involving tens of thousands of women in activism. In 2004, Maathai was awarded the Nobel Peace Prize.

Respected president Ellen Johnson Sirleaf is pictured here in 2011 after her reelection to the presidency. In office, she helped rebuild Liberia's infrastructure and economy and promoted peace and reconciliation.

Ellen Johnson Sirleaf

Liberian stateswoman and Nobel laureate

The first elected female head of state of an African country, Ellen Johnson Sirleaf served as the 24th president of the Republic of Liberia from 2006–2018, becoming an icon of good governance in her country after its long civil war.

Born in the Liberian capital, Monrovia, in 1938, Ellen Johnson Sirleaf was raised by her mother, a teacher, and her father, an attorney, and was educated at the prestigious College of West Africa. At age 17, she married a young agronomist, James Sirleaf, and the couple moved to the US in 1961. She earned an economics degree from the University of Colorado and a master's in public administration from Harvard University's John F. Kennedy School of Government.

In 1971, Johnson Sirleaf returned to Liberia and was appointed Assistant Minister of Finance a year later. Her public criticism of the government's financial mismanagement attracted national attention and in 1973 she left the Ministry to work for the World Bank in the US. In 1977, she returned to Liberia, becoming Deputy Finance Minister in 1977 and Finance Minister in 1979. The appointment proved short-lived: a coup led by Samuel Doe, a master sergeant, took place, and Johnson Sirleaf was forced to flee the country.

Return to politics

Johnson Sirleaf returned to Monrovia for the general election of 1985, hoping to run for vice president. Instead, she was repeatedly arrested for criticizing Doe's corrupt regime, which had now triggered a period of civil war. During a break in the hostilities in 1997, Sirleaf stood for the presidency, but it was not until the end of the second Liberian Civil War (1999–2003) that she reentered government. She won the 2005 general election, and in 2006 became the first female president of Liberia, ushering in a period of stability and a time for rebuilding the nation. She established the right to free education for children and passed laws to protect women from domestic violence. After serving a second term from 2011, she retired in 2017; the first peaceful transition of power in her country for 73 years took place in 2018.

△ **Nobel Peace Prize**
In 2011, Johnson Sirleaf was awarded the Nobel Prize for Peace, along with women's rights campaigners Leymah Gbowee of Liberia and Tawakkol Karman of Yemen.

◁ **Campaign for president**
Johnson Sirleaf was energetic in her campaigns for president. She is pictured here running for the first time in 1997, when she earned the epithet "Africa's Iron Lady."

1938 Born in Monrovia

1977 Appointed Deputy Minister of Finance and then Minister of Finance in 1979

1980 Flees Liberia after Samuel Doe seizes power, and works for banks in the US and Kenya

1985 Returns to Liberia and is arrested for criticism of the government; released in 1986 after international pressure

1992 Appointed Director of UN Development Programme's Regional Bureau for Africa

1997 First campaign for president; comes second to eventual winner, Charles Taylor

2005 Wins general election to become president

2011 Jointly awarded the Nobel Peace Prize for work enabling women to participate in the peace-building process

2018 Founds the Ellen Johnson Sirleaf Presidential Center for Women and Development

Cinema

Africa on the big screen

▷ **On the move**
Self-financed by director Djibril Diop Mambéty, *Touki Bouki* ("The Journey of the Hyena") is a Senegalese road movie.

If early films made by Europeans in and about Africa projected "exotic primitivism," films by Africans have opened up a completely different perspective. They show multiple depictions of Africa from the inside.

Many early "African" films reflected imperialist views. *De Voortrekkers* ("Pioneers," 1915) glorified white colonization in South Africa by the Boers (descendants of Dutch-speaking settlers), while the charismatic presence of Black American actor Paul Robeson in British-Hungarian director Zoltán Korda's *Sanders of the River* (1935) could not save it from promoting white "superiority." Other films, such as *Jim Comes to Jo'burg* (1949), perpetuated this message, as did educational documentaries made by colonial film units.

Independent filmmaking

After independence, African directors took over the lens, and film became a tool of revolution. In *Sambizanga* (1972), Sarah Maldoror dramatized Angola's anti-colonial struggle, while in Senegal, Ousmane Sembène's *Borom Sarret* ("The Wagoner," 1963), and *Black Girl* (1966) set the tone for a lifetime of radical filmmaking. In South Africa, anti-apartheid films like *Mapantsula* (1988) and *Sarafina!* (1993) led the way for post-apartheid films such as Ramadan Suleman's *Zulu Love Letter* (2004), in which two women struggle to come to terms with a legacy of political violence and trauma.

However, independent cinema developed in a piecemeal fashion due to a lack of investment. Funding or support from former colonial powers often came with strings attached: francophone nations could produce more films, but

▷ **Migrant story**
Ousmane Sembène's *Black Girl* follows a Senegalese woman who travels from Dakar to France, where she faces alienation and tragedy.

▷ **Futuristic horror**
Cameroonian director Jean-Pierre Bekolo describes his 2005 film *Les Saignantes* ("The Bloodettes") as a "stylized sci-fi-action-horror hybrid." The film is a futuristic vision of female power at play.

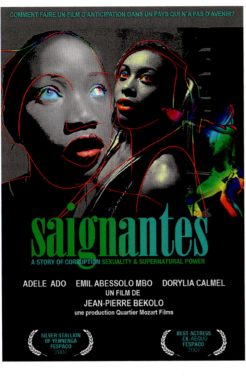

"I believe that **Africans**, in particular, must **reinvent cinema**."

DJIBRIL DIOP MAMBÉTY, SENEGALESE DIRECTOR

productions seen as critical of France were less likely to receive support. Directors such as Safi Faye in Senegal, Gaston Kaboré in Burkina Faso, and Souleymane Cissé in Mali made films distinguished by their meditative concentration on rural life and precolonial knowledge, and were dubbed "return to the source."

There were always many innovators. In Senegal, Djibril Diop Mambéty created a richly surreal world of startling juxtapositions that upended genre expectations. *Touki Bouki* (1973) is fast-paced and youthful, while *Hyenas* (1992) is a revenge tragedy set in the outskirts of Dakar. Guinean Mohamed Camara's *Dakan* ("Destiny," 1997), was the first African film to represent a same-sex love affair.

Contemporary cinema

African film has expanded into genres as diverse as futurism (*Pumzi*, or "Breath," 2009; *District 9*, 2009), LGBTQ+ love (*Rafiki*, 2017; *Inxeba/The Wound*, 2017), rom-com (*Tell Me Sweet Something*, 2015), Western (*Five Fingers for Marseilles*, 2017), thriller (*Nairobi Half Life*, 2012), political satire (*The Night of Truth*, 2004), and dramatized documentary (*Otelo Burning*, 2011).

Migration has meant filmmakers of African descent are active throughout the diaspora. European-based directors include French-Mauritanian Med Hondo, (*Soleil Ô*, or "Oh, Sun," 1970); Franco-Algerian Mounia Meddour (*Papicha*, or "Rebel Girl," 2019); and British/Ghanaian John Akomfrah, the UK's representative at the 60th Venice Biennale in 2024. Filmmakers born in one part of Africa but living and working in another include Mauritanian-Malian Abderrahmane Sissako, whose *Bamako* (2006) offers a severe critique of neoliberal economics and its resulting poverty; and Nigerian-South African Akin Omotoso, whose drama film *Man on Ground* (2011) responds to the phenomenon of township attacks on *makwerekwere*, or non-local "outsiders."

Though women have always been prominent as actors, recognition of their role as filmmakers has been slower to arrive. Today, female directors are making their mark across the continent. Wanuri Kahiu's *Rafiki* (or "Friend") was the first Kenyan film to be screened at the Cannes Film Festival, while women are central to Nigeria's "Nollywood," both as actors and directors, and sometimes—like Genevieve Nnaji (*Lionheart*, 2019)—both.

Hampered by lack of distribution, African cinema was for a long time confined to art house screenings and film festivals, notably the Panafrican Film and Television Festival of Ouagadougou (FESPACO). In the 1990s, new technology brought about a huge democratizing boom. Nollywood's sensational melodramas and comedies captivate local and diasporic audiences. Today, streaming services make African cinema more accessible than ever before.

▽ **Teen love story**
In *Rafiki*, Wanuri Kahiu offers a tale of lesbian love in a country—Kenya—where same-sex sexual relations are illegal. But this warm drama holds out hope that things may change.

Musical instruments
Music-making across Africa

Africa has a rich variety of Indigenous musical instruments, reflecting the many different musical styles of the continent. Percussion instruments, especially drums, are central to the ceremonies, dances, and songs of many African cultures, and melodic instruments, including various plucked and bowed strings and some wind instruments, are also widespread.

△ **Gourd rattle**
Shakers and rattles are found across Africa south of the Sahara. They are often made from hollow gourds containing seeds or loosely wrapped with a network of beads, shells, or nuts.

△ **African xylophone**
Various types of xylophone—tuned wooden percussion instruments—are found in Africa, including the *bala* (or *balafon*), seen here, from the Mande region of West Africa and the *marimba* from Southern Africa.

▷ **Jembe**
The *jembe*, a goblet drum played with bare hands, is said to derive its name from a saying by the Bambara people of West Africa, meaning "everybody gather in peace."

△ **Moroccan tar**
The *tar* is a variety of tambourine found across North Africa. This 19th-century example from Morocco consists of a decorated wooden frame with metal zills, or jingles, and a green animal skin.

△ **Zulu drum**
This simple drum in the Zulu style has animal-hide heads stretched over a hollow wooden shell. Drums such as these would accompany Zulu celebrations.

△ **Talking drum**
Squeezing the strings attached to the drumskins of this West African drum changes the pitch, allowing the player to mimic the cadences of human speech.

MUSICAL INSTRUMENTS | 295

▷ **Valiha**
The *valiha*, considered the national instrument of Madagascar, is a type of tube zither made from bamboo with attached, tensioned strings.

Carved wooden yoke

Bamboo tube

MUSICAL BOW

Particularly associated with peoples of Southern Africa, the musical bow consists of a single string, usually made of metal, stretched between the two ends of a flexible stick and then struck or plucked. To amplify the sound of the vibrating string, the player's mouth—or, sometimes, a gourd attached to the back of the bow—is used as a resonator.

◁ **Kora**
Found throughout the Mande diaspora in West Africa, the *kora* is a 21-string calabash (bottle gourd) harp plucked with the index fingers and thumbs.

Leather soundboard

Gourd resonator

△ **Mbira**
The tuned metal keys on a *mbira* are plucked with the thumbs and index fingers to produce sounds of different pitches.

△ **Begena**
The *begena* is a type of wooden lyre used as an accompanying instrument to the spiritual songs of the Amhara people of Ethiopia.

▽ **Bondjo**
The Congolese *bondjo* is a side-blown trumpet carved from elephant's tusk and wood, originally used in battle but nowadays employed in ceremonies.

Higher-pitched bell

Split gourd body

△ **Gankogui bell**
Originating from Ghana, Togo, and Benin, the iron double bell, called a *gankogui*, is struck with a wooden beater to produce two different pitches.

Carved mouthpiece

Decorated wooden extension

Popular music
The evolution of Indigenous African styles

With its many cultures and musical traditions, Africa has inevitably produced a diverse range of popular music over the course of the 20th and 21st centuries. Regions south of the Sahara in particular developed popular music that fused local styles with elements of Western genres such as jazz, pop, and rock.

Although a predominantly urban phenomenon, African popular music had its roots in the wealth of rural musical traditions, from Yoruba drumming to call and response forms—where a soloist sings a phrase, which is then repeated by backing singers—found across the continent. Colonialism in the 19th century brought exposure to Western folk and popular songs, which were gradually assimilated into the Indigenous styles. The process of assimilation accelerated in the 20th century with the advent of jazz and blues (themselves from African roots), which spread to an increasingly urban African audience.

One of the first countries to develop a characteristic popular genre was present-day Ghana, where "palm-wine music"—a fusion of jazz and local styles such as *sikyi*, an Akan genre of dance music—emerged in the pre–World War II period. By the 1950s, this had evolved into the Cuban-inspired highlife, featuring West African rhythms and melodies played on Western guitars and brass instruments, which quickly became popular throughout West Africa.

The 1960s saw the emergence of new hybrid genres, notably in the townships of apartheid-era South Africa. Singers such as Miriam Makeba popularized

△ **Miriam Makeba (1932–2008)**
In a more than 50-year career, South African singer Miriam Makeba became one of the first African musicians to achieve global acclaim, with Xhosa songs such as "Pata Pata" and "Qongqothwane" (the "Click song") inflected with elements of jazz.

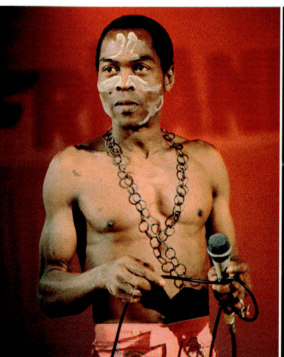

△ **Fela Kuti (1938–1997)**
Singer, multi-instrumentalist, bandleader, and political activist Fela Aníkúlápó Kuti is considered to be the originator of the highly influential hybrid Afrobeat genre in the 1960s. As the foremost Nigerian musician of his generation, he used his songs to campaign against Nigerian military rule and dictatorship.

△ **Stella Chiweshe (1946–2023)**
Zimbabwean musician Stella Chiweshe challenged the taboo against female players of the *mbira*, a Shona keyboard instrument. She supported nationalist and women's rights causes and brought Shona culture to a worldwide audience.

> "The **curious beauty** of African music is that it uplifts even as it **tells a sad tale**."
>
> NELSON MANDELA, *LONG WALK TO FREEDOM*

Xhosa songs with jazz inflections, while Zulu music formed the basis for *mbaqanga*, the pop-inspired music of urban Johannesburg. At the same time, a similar process was happening with the creation of *mbalax*, a Senegalese hybrid of local Wolof *sabar* drumming with influences from Latin genres.

Contemporary styles

The collective term "Afropop" refers to many regional varieties of African popular music that are truly Indigenous: African music absorbing Western genres, rather than Western music with an African flavor. As well as the integration of stylistic elements, the various genres of Afropop adopted the instruments of Western pop music, especially guitars, keyboards, and electronics. African instruments still featured strongly in most genres, but these were often amplified, and modern production techniques created a distinctively contemporary sound.

Perhaps paradoxically, these Western-influenced genres often came to symbolize the independence of postcolonial African countries. In Nigeria, for example, Fela Kuti blended Indigenous Yoruba music with highlife and African-American jazz and funk to create Afrobeat, which he used as a vehicle for sociopolitical comment. Less overtly political, but no less influential, was Youssou N'Dour, whose incorporation of multiple styles into Senegalese music stimulated a worldwide interest in African contemporary music.

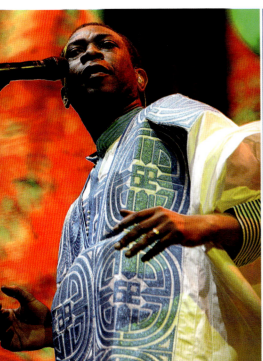

△ **Youssou N'Dour (1947–)**
Emerging from the *mbalax* dance music of 1970s Senegal, Youssou N'Dour gained an international following with his innovative fusion of Senegalese and other African genres with Islamic chants, jazz, and pop styles.

△ **Salif Keita (1949–)**
After some success as a member of the band Les Ambassadeurs, Salif Keita left his native Mali to pursue a solo career in Paris. Sometimes referred to as the "Golden Voice of Africa," Keita built a global reputation with his eclectic dance-music style, before returning to Mali's capital Bamako in the early 2000s.

△ **Yvonne Chaka Chaka (1965–)**
Born in the township of Soweto, Johannesburg, Yvonne Chaka Chaka became the leading light of South African *mbaqanga* music after her debut in the 1980s. An internationally famous singer, she has also been active in raising global awareness of issues including HIV/AIDS.

> "If you don't [handle] **the material**, the work might end up not **having a soul**."
>
> EL ANATSUI, 2011

Art and artist
El Anatsui stands in front of his 2004 sculpture *Sasa*, which is 27½ ft (8.4 m) tall. The artist chose the Ewe word *sasa*, meaning "patchwork," to refer to the carving up of Africa by European colonial powers.

Bottle-top sculptures

Metal mosaics made by groundbreaking Ghanaian artist

El Anatsui creates wall hangings that, on first glance, may be taken for woven tapestries. In fact, these works—which he makes by creating segments of flattened metal, including bottle caps, that are then stitched together—re-conceptualize the function and meaning of cloth, transforming it into an original form of sculpture. Anatsui's aesthetic draws on West African modes while being in dialogue with Western art. His wall hangings ironize Western art history through the transformation of discarded materials into objects of priceless beauty and grandeur. They also reference West African fabric styles, such as Ghanaian *kente* and Nigerian *aso-oke*, in which woven strips are sewn together in a process similar to his own.

New forms of expression

El Anatsui's practice chimes with that of other African and African-diaspora artists. By adorning 18th-century figures and interiors in wax-print fabric, British-Nigerian artist Yinka Shonibare similarly uses cloth to question the centrality of a Western perspective on history. With the help of a team of weavers based in Johannesburg, South African artist William Kentridge makes tapestries depicting sociopolitical conditions in his country. Romuald Hazoumè, a Yoruba artist from Benin, recycles jerry cans, and British painter Chris Ofili uses elephant dung, further exemplifying the infiltration of high art by a trash aesthetic.

Born in Anyako in southern Ghana, El Anatsui trained in sculpture in the central Ghanaian city of Kumasi in the 1960s. Formal art schools had proliferated in Africa during and after colonization. Exposure to a British-influenced school set Anatsui on a search for an Indigenous mode of expression. He began by experimenting with local materials, combining wooden trays used in markets with *adinkra* symbols, breaking and recombining pottery, and carving in wood. From 1975, he has lived in Nsukka, eastern Nigeria, where he works at the University of Nigeria as both artist and teacher.

In Nsukka, El Anatsui stumbled on the material for which he has become famous. The bottles of alcohol from which the discarded caps came had been a medium of colonial exchange. Struck by its historical resonances, he started by beating out the metal and stitching the segments together to form colorful patterns. He works with a team of assistants, laying out bottle caps in blocks of 200 to create a design, photographing them and playing with images on a computer, before painstakingly putting them together.

Displayed and purchased internationally, El Anatsui's hangings have draped the exterior of such buildings as the Alte Nationalgalerie in Berlin, the Royal Academy of Arts in London, and El-Badi Palace (Qasr al-Badīʻ) in Marrakech. In 2023, he created an installation for the Turbine (entrance) Hall at Tate Modern in London.

Combinations of metal caps and seals from bottles

Shimmering design
El Anatsui's 2021 artwork, *Wade in the Water*, recalls a song associated with the Underground Railroad. This secret network was established in the 19th century to help enslaved African Americans escape to freedom.

One of several sewn-aluminum sheets that are stitched together to create the piece

> "In my world, **every human is beautiful**."
>
> ZANELE MUHOLI, 2020

Art and activism

Identity-affirming photography by Zanele Muholi

Born in Umlazi, a township close to Durban, KwaZulu-Natal, in 1972, Zanele Muholi experienced firsthand the oppression of the South African apartheid regime, intensified by hostility directed at people whose sexuality was considered transgressive. Muholi is nonbinary, using the pronouns they/them, and their art focuses on issues of race, gender, and sexuality, observing and honoring the Black LGBTQ+ communities of South Africa.

Muholi's chosen medium is photography, including video and installation, but given their chosen subject matter, they prefer to describe themselves as a "visual activist" rather than a photographer or an artist. This reflects the motivation that runs through their work: to make both the positive and negative aspects of the lives of Black LGBTQ+ people visible. Muholi's first solo exhibition, *Visual Sexuality: Only Half the Picture*, in Johannesburg in 2004 presented images of survivors of hate crimes, their identity and even gender deliberately concealed. The effects of violence directed against South African Black LGBTQ+ people was a subject Muholi returned to in later exhibitions.

As well as highlighting oppressive attitudes toward race, gender, and sexuality, Muholi has devoted much of their work to celebrating especially Black lesbian and trans lives. This they did through portraits, such as those of lesbians in the *Faces and Phases* project which they began in 2006, and the *Brave Beauties* series of portraits of trans women shown in 2014.

Probably the most personal statement they have produced, however, is the series of 365 self-portraits titled *Somnyama Ngonyama* ("Hail the Dark Lioness" in isiZulu, the Zulu language), exhibited in New York in 2015 and in London in 2017, and subsequently published in book form. Photographed in various locations around the world, the arresting images portray Muholi as a series of alter egos, reflecting diverse African cultures, and often with a Zulu name.

In addition to their photographic work, Muholi was a cofounder of a Black lesbian organization, the Forum for the Empowerment of Women, in 2002, and more recently has concentrated on increasing educational opportunities in photography and art for underprivileged young people.

△ **Comb headdress**
In this photograph, entitled *Qiniso, The Sails, Durban* (2019), from the *Somnyama Ngonyama* series, Muholi wears a stylized headdress made of Afro combs, symbolizing pride in Black natural hair. *Qiniso* means "truth" in isiZulu.

▷ **Caught in coils**
Xiniwe at Cassilhaus, North Carolina (2016) captures one of Muholi's alter egos, Xiniwe, with an exaggerated hairstyle and wrapped in snake-like coils, highlighting exoticized representations of African cultures in the West.

Writers

Africa's literary history

African literature stretches back farther than that of any other continent. The first writing—Egyptian hieroglyphs—emerged around 3000 BCE. Religious texts were produced from around the 4th century CE in the Christian kingdom of Aksum (modern-day Ethiopia). In areas with an Islamic influence, including North Africa, the Sahel, and East Africa, texts mostly written in Arabic described religion and astronomy. The early Swahili epic poem *Utendi wa Tambuka* (The Story of Tambuka) dramatizes the conflicts between the Arabs, Ottomans, and Byzantines and was first written down in 1728.

Until the 18th century, African history and stories were passed on orally, in the form of proverbs, folklore (featuring animal tricksters such as spiders or tortoises), religious narratives, and love songs. In West Africa, storytellers called *griots* have told the history of a village or family in a mixture of poetry and music for hundreds of years. The tale of the Mandingo (Malinke) hero Sundiata (see pp.90–91) was told by *griots* for centuries and still shapes our understanding of the Mali Empire.

A wider circulation

When colonizers brought European literary traditions and written languages to Africa, Africans learned these languages and began to write in English and French. Firsthand accounts of enslavement such as the *Interesting Narrative of the Life of Olaudah Equiano* were written in English. A formerly enslaved Igbo man, Equiano (c. 1745–1797) bought his freedom and settled in London.

△ **Mariama Bâ (1929–1981)**
Born into a middle-class Muslim family in Senegal in the 1940s, Bâ took part in the country's feminist movement. She wrote the acclaimed *So Long a Letter* (1979) about a woman's painful experience of a polygamous marriage and the inequalities women face.

△ **Chinua Achebe (1930–2013)**
Nigerian novelist Achebe is known as the "father of African literature." He wrote in English, but used Igbo phrases in novels such as *Things Fall Apart* (1958), which explores the impact of colonial power on an Igbo village. His portrayal of a complex West African society challenged Western ideas of "primitive" Africa.

△ **Nawal El Saadawi (1931–2021)**
A graduate of Cairo University and a qualified doctor, El Saadawi was also a feminist who wrote novels, nonfiction, and short stories. Her focus was on social issues and the impact of religion on women, such as in the *The Hidden Face of Eve* (1977).

"If you **don't like** someone's story, **write your own**."

CHINUA ACHEBE, 1994

By the 20th century, Africans were writing in a range of Western genres. In the Gold Coast (now Ghana), J. E. Casely Hayford (1866–1930) wrote *Ethiopia Unbound* (1911), an influential philosophical novel about colonialism, while *The Girl Who Killed to Save: Nongqause the Liberator* by South African Herbert Isaac Ernest Dhlomo (1903–1956), published in 1935, is commonly regarded as the first English-language African play.

Independent voices

This trickle of new, often anti-colonial voices became a cascade in the decades that followed. Writers such as Chinua Achebe, Wole Soyinka, and Ngũgĩ wa Thiong'o used African as well as European languages to explore colonialism and identity. Since then, novelists including Tanzanian Abdulrazak Gurnah (1948–) and South Africa's J. M. Coetzee (1940–) have won Nobel prizes and achieved worldwide sales.

In the later 20th century, female writers became more prominent. Zimbabwean Yvonne Vera (1964–2005); Egypt's Nawal El Saadawi, who wrote in Arabic; and Senegal's Mariama Bâ have explored feminism and social issues. In the 21st century, a new generation, including Nigeria's Chimamanda Ngozi Adichie (1977–) and Franco-Senegalese novelist David Diop (1966–) are part of a diaspora of writers driving African literature forward. Authors such as American poet and photographer Teju Cole (1975–) and Jamaica's Marlon James (1970–) show that African writing is as wide-ranging and as vital as ever.

△ **Swahili wordsmith**
Tanzanian poet and author Shaaban bin Robert (1909–1962) wrote poetry, novels, and essays. He promoted the Tanzanian verse style and the Swahili language.

△ **Wole Soyinka (1934–)**
Soyinka's plays often target authority, and he has had to flee his native Nigeria during his career. His work explores Yoruba culture and Western themes and in 1986 he became the first person from Africa south of the Sahara to win the Nobel Prize for Literature.

△ **Ngũgĩ wa Thiong'o (1938–)**
Kenyan novelist, playwright, activist, and academic Ngũgĩ has been a force for change throughout his varied career. Although his first works were in English, he has written primarily in Gikuyu since the 1970s. He has pushed for the rebranding of "English literature" as simply "literature" across Africa.

△ **Chimamanda Ngozi Adichie (1977–)**
Globally successful writer Adichie was born in Nsukka, Nigeria, to Igbo parents. She studied politics and African history in Nigeria and the US. Her novel *Half of a Yellow Sun* (2006) is set during the brutal Nigeria–Biafra War (1967–1970) and has won several literary prizes.

The future of Africa

A new momentum

In most of Africa's 54 countries, 70 percent or more of the population is under the age of 30. In the 21st century, these overwhelmingly youth-dominated societies are looking to harness their economic and cultural potential.

△ **Symbol of solidarity**
The African Union emblem shows palm leaves (representing peace) and interlocking rings (showing solidarity) surrounding a continent without borders.

▽ **Nairobi skyline**
With a population of around 5 million, the Kenyan capital of Nairobi is one of Africa's fastest-growing cities.

In the 20th century, Africa freed itself from colonizing powers as nations across the continent forged their own paths. Now Africa is transforming again. Its population is projected to nearly double over the next few decades, reaching 2.4 billion by 2050, when one in four people around the world will live in Africa. By 2100, the figure is forecast to be one in three.

With a growing population, the demand for goods and services will increase, and Africa has the potential to become a major global player on its own terms. It is rich in resources such as oil, gas, and arable land, and holds around 30 percent of the world's mineral reserves, including gold, lithium, and cobalt (all used in batteries). Africa's biodiversity provides an opportunity to implement sustainable practices that protect the environment while supporting growth, and the potential of renewable energy such as wind, solar, hydro, and geothermal power is immense.

Turning this potential into long-term prosperity and stability will not be straightforward. Optimism is nothing new: in 1999, Thabo Mbeki, then president of South Africa, spoke of entering "the African century," but economic growth in the 2000s was followed by a dip in the 2010s due to lower commodity prices.

Countries including the Central African Republic, Burundi, and South Sudan regularly rank as the poorest in the world, and conflicts continue to affect several nations. Investment from powers such as China and Russia may have transformed infrastructure in some states, but also points toward the specter of a new imperialism.

Yet Africa's momentum is becoming unstoppable. The continent is experiencing a digital revolution, with advancements in technology and connectivity transforming various sectors. Mobile communication has played a significant role in leapfrogging traditional

infrastructure, empowering huge numbers of people through access to information, education, health care, and financial services.

Nigeria, South Africa, and Egypt had GDPs of more than $400 million in 2023, and Nigeria is expected to become one of the world's top ten economies in the next 50 years. These African superpowers are attracting more and more commercial opportunities, while other nations including Kenya, Côte d'Ivoire, and the Democratic Republic of the Congo (DRC) are among the fastest-growing economies in the world.

Collaboration and culture

To achieve their potential, African countries must address challenges such as poverty, inequality, and political instability, and ensure that the management of natural resources benefits their citizens and leads to stability and long-term growth.

Intergovernmental organizations such as the African Union (which replaced the Organization of African Unity in 2002) seek to encourage collaboration. The African Union has played a crucial role in promoting peace and its Agenda 2063 seeks to bring about a "prosperous Africa based on inclusive growth and sustainable development" via a road map for areas such as industrialization, infrastructure, and lowering trade barriers within the continent. The vision is positive, although—due in part to its consensus-building approach—progress has sometimes been slow.

Africa's future is more than just economic. There is strong interest in preserving Indigenous knowledge, promoting local languages, and reviving arts and crafts. Young and growing populations, as well as changing patterns of migration, will see Africa's cultures evolve and spread through the 21st century.

Popular music, notably West Africa's Afrobeats, has already become a global juggernaut, while African writers and filmmakers attract ever-larger international audiences. Cities such as Lagos, Kinshasa, Johannesburg, Cairo, Dakar, and Nairobi burst with creativity, and, as Africa builds a new future, the next big thing could come from anywhere on the continent.

△ **Edo Museum**
This digital visualization shows a planned exhibition space at Edo Museum of West African Art (EMWAA), which will focus on the history of the Kingdom of Benin. It is due to open in 2024 in Benin City, Nigeria.

▷ **Afrobeats**
Nigerian singer Wizkid performs at a tribute to musician Fela Kuti in 2017. In the 1960s, Kuti pioneered Afrobeat and influenced today's Afrobeats style, which also draws on hip-hop and other genres.

> "As Africans, we are **proud of our history**, as we are **optimistic** about **our future**."
>
> SOUTH AFRICAN PRESIDENT CYRIL RAMAPHOSA, 2023

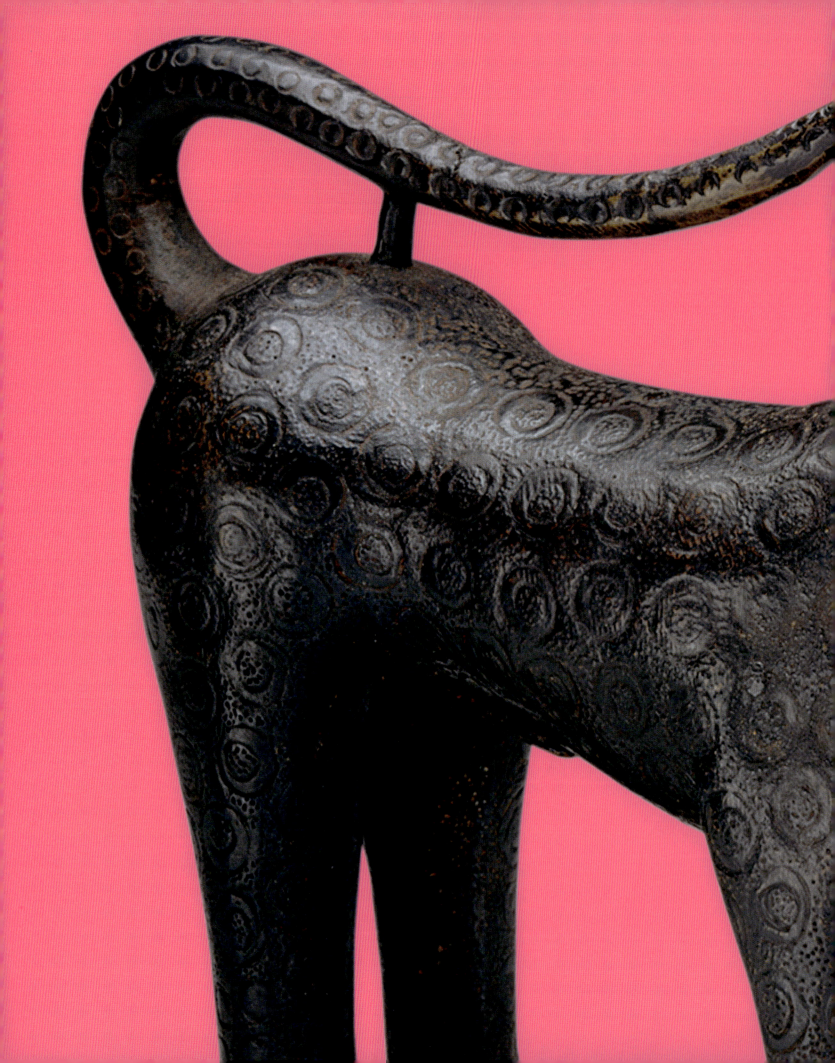

◁ **Benin water vessel**
This leopard-shaped bronze aquamanile, from Benin in modern-day Nigeria, was used for washing the hands. It was filled with water through an opening at the top of the head and emptied by pouring water out through the nostrils.

National histories

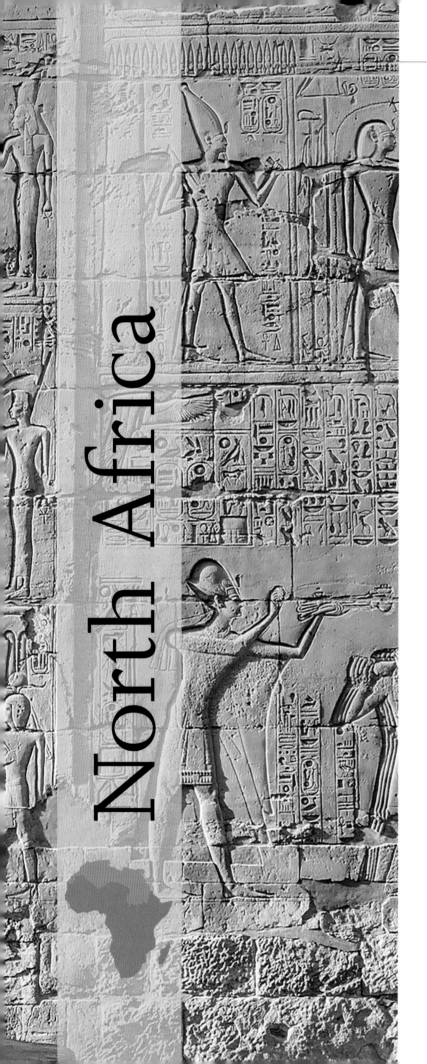

North Africa

Egypt

The site of one of the world's most ancient civilizations, born along the banks of the Nile River, Egypt has seen occupation by Persians, Greeks, Romans, Islamic empires, Ottoman Turks, the French, and the British, before emerging as a modern republic.

Official name: Arab Republic of Egypt
Date of formation: February 28, 1922
Official language: Arabic

Egypt is surrounded by deserts to the west and south, with the Mediterranean to the north and the Red Sea to the east. The nation's heartland is a 746-mile- (1,200-km-) long stretch of fertile land along the Nile River that is home to most of the nation's 107 million people (the third-largest population in Africa). Its ancient capital, Cairo, is Africa's largest, and Egypt's role as a leading Arab power and one of the Muslim world's largest economies gives it a unique sway. Its rich historical heritage, from the pyramids to ornate Islamic architecture, draws in millions of tourists every year.

Egypt of the pharaohs

As the Sahara region dried after 10,000 BCE, hunter-gatherers sought refuge along the fertile banks of the Nile, beginning farming around 5000 BCE. The kingdoms of the Badarian and Naqada cultures were united in around 3150 BCE by Narmer (or Menes). His successors ruled Egypt for more than 3,000 years, through 30 dynasties, supported by an ideology of royal power in which the pharaoh was seen as an embodiment of the god Horus. During the Old Kingdom era, (c. 2650–2130 BCE), Egypt enjoyed its first period of cultural and political power, and saw the building of the massive pyramids at Giza by the Fourth Dynasty pharaohs Khufu, Snefru, and Khefren between 2570 and 2530 BCE. Egypt's political unity dissolved after the Sixth Dynasty (2343–2181 BCE), but was restored by Mentuhotep II around 2055 BCE. He inaugurated the Middle Kingdom under which Egypt acquired an empire in the Eastern Mediterranean and sent trading expeditions to the Land of Punt (south of Egypt).

Another period of political disunity was followed by the even greater glories of the New Kingdom, during which pharaohs such as Hatshepsut, Thutmose III, and Ramses II (r. 1279–1213 BCE) reigned over a stable, prosperous land and engaged in military campaigns in Palestine and Syria, as well as building monuments such as the Temple at Luxor.

Foreign rule

As Egypt's power declined in the Late Period (after 1075 BCE), it was ruled by pharaohs from Libya and Nubia, occupied by

◁ Friezes at Karnak Temple, built around 1250 BCE

◁ In ancient Egypt, deities played a major part in life as well as death. This stela shows Ra-Horakhty-Atum, a god connected to the afterlife.

Assyrians and Persians, and was finally conquered by the Macedonian Alexander the Great in 332 BCE. Alexander's general Ptolemy founded a final dynasty of pharaohs, which lasted until 30 BCE when Cleopatra VII was defeated by the Romans. Egypt became a Roman province, its main role as a breadbasket for the empire interrupted only by sporadic revolts and a brief Persian occupation in 619–629 CE.

Islamic Egypt

Rome's rule over Egypt ended when Muslim Arab armies captured Alexandria in 641 CE. Egypt was ruled by the Umayyad caliphs (661–750) and then the Baghdad-based Abbasid caliphs. It regained autonomy under the Tulunids, a dynasty of Turkish origin, in 868, and the Ikhshidids, of Central Asian origin, who took over in 935. After this, the Fatimids, originally based in Tunisia, captured it, declaring their own caliphate in 969.

The great Kurdish general Saladin toppled the Fatimids and Egypt continued to prosper under the Ayyubid dynasty, which he founded in 1171. Under the Mamluks (1250–1517), Egypt continued to wield great political and military power. But the defeat by Sultan Selim I in 1517 began three centuries of Ottoman Turkish rule, administered by *beys* (governors) who became increasingly powerful. In 1805, after various power struggles, as well as a French invasion, the Ottoman Muhammad Ali Pasha took charge as sole ruler of Egypt.

British interference

Muhammad Ali and his *khedive* (viceroy) successors expanded Egypt's territory into Sudan, Syria, Arabia, and Greece, and undertook modernizing projects. His grandson Ismail II (r. 1864–1879) ran up debts in the process, including from investments in the Suez Canal, which was built under European management in 1869.

In 1882, after a revolt by army officer Ahmad Urabi against foreign influence, the British invaded. *Khedival* rule continued in principle, but Egypt was dominated by the British until the nationalist revolution of 1919, which led to the establishment of a formally independent kingdom under Fuad I in 1922. Yet, despite the efforts of the nationalist Wafd party, British influence continued. Tensions over this, and the British military presence in the Suez Canal Zone, boiled over in 1952, when Gamal Abdel Nasser's Free Officer Movement deposed Fuad's successor Farouk and declared a republic.

The Republic of Egypt

In 1957, Nasser defeated an Anglo-French invasion of Suez. He cofounded the Non-Aligned Movement and was a champion of Arab unity, leading to a brief merging of Egypt with Syria (1958–1961). Egypt went to war with Israel in 1956 and 1967.

After his death in 1970, Nasser was succeeded by Anwar Sadat, who was known for his economic liberalization and pro-US policies. In 1973, Egypt again went to war with Israel. A treaty signed with Israel in 1977 ended the conflict, but angered some Egyptians, and Sadat was assassinated by militants in 1981.

The new regime of Hosni Mubarak largely continued Sadat's policies, until it was overthrown during the Arab Spring protests of 2011. Egypt then experienced a brief rule by the Islamist Mohammed Morsi, before he was toppled in a 2013 military coup by Abdel Fatah el-Sisi. El-Sisi's presidency has been authoritarian, and in 2019 he changed the constitution to allow himself to run for a third term in 2024.

△ Cairo and the Nile, as seen from the city's 614-ft- (187-m-) tall Cairo Tower

Sudan

On an ancient trading and cultural crossroads between African kingdoms and the Muslim world, Sudan has seen recent violent conflicts.

Official name: Republic of Sudan
Date of formation: January 1, 1956
Official language: Arabic

Africa's largest country before 2011—when its southern part seceded—Sudan has a varied landscape, with the north largely barren desert and fertile land mainly confined to the south. Highlands in the south and east give way to southern plains watered by tributaries of the Nile. The population of 30 million is mainly Muslim—some 70 percent Arab, and the rest Nubian or eastern Sudanic groups such as the Nuba and Dinka. Sudan lost two-thirds of its oil fields in 2011, leaving its economy fragile.

Ancient states

The Kingdom of Kerma emerged along Sudan's Nile Valley around 2000 BCE, and was conquered by Egypt in about 1500 BCE. The region regained its independence c. 1070 BCE as the Kingdom of Kush, centered on the royal capital of Napata. Kush was strongly influenced by Egyptian culture, including the building of monumental temples to deities such as the lion god Apedemak. Under King Piye (r. 744–714 BCE), the Kushites invaded Egypt, ruling it for more than 80 years.

In the 6th century BCE, the Kushite kings moved farther south to Meroë. At this time, a new alphabet appeared and Egyptian influence receded. Meanwhile, the north was annexed by Egypt, and then by the Romans, until its reconquest by the Meroitic king Yesebokheamani in 298 BCE.

The Kushite kingdom collapsed in the 4th century CE, weakened by rebellions and invasion by Ethiopia's Aksumite kingdom. Sudan became divided between the kingdoms of Nobatia in the north, Makuria in the central region, and Alodia in the south, all of which became Christian by the 6th century.

Kingdoms and sultanates

Around 630, Nobatia occupied Makuria and, although it fought off invasion by Arab Muslim armies from Egypt, by the 12th century it—and Alodia—were in decline. In 1365, its former capital at Old Dongola was

△ Temple dedicated to the lion god Apedemak at Meroë, built in the 3rd century BCE

destroyed by groups including the Abdallab, who established an independent state in the north.

In 1504, a group known as the Funj moved up from the southern stretches of the White Nile. They defeated the Abdallab and established a sultanate at Sennar, on the banks of the Blue Nile. The Funj quickly adopted Islam and used Arabic as a language of administration. During its 17th-century peak, the kingdom stretched over much of what is now eastern Sudan, as well as Ethiopia and Eritrea. To the west, the Keira dynasty emerged among the Fur people in the early 17th century, and the region we now know as Darfur converted to Islam around this period.

Imperial rule

In 1821, the Funj, weakened by decades of factional infighting, were defeated by Muhammad Ali, the k*hedive* (hereditary monarch) of Egypt. Darfur survived for a few more decades before being absorbed into Egypt in the 1870s. When Egypt came under British control in 1882, Anglo-Egyptian forces spread through Sudan. Resentment of this colonial occupation helped fuel the rise of Mahdism, a highly conservative Islamic movement led by Muhammad Ahmad bin Abd Allah (who proclaimed himself the "Mahdi," or messianic redeemer of mankind). He raised a revolt in 1881, and established an independent state that lasted until 1898, when it was violently overthrown by Britain.

From 1899, Britain and Egypt shared rulership of the region. In practice, it was run as two separate British colonies, north (modern-day Sudan) and south (South Sudan), with a focus on cotton production for export and little reference to Sudanese interests. Calls for independence became increasingly vocal after World War II. Other tensions were growing: the south had long felt marginalized, and civil war broke out in 1955. In 1956, Egypt's President Nasser conceded independence, which Britain accepted.

A new nation

A military coup in 1958 was followed by protests in 1964, when the Sudanese people took to the streets and forced regime change. But in 1969 another coup brought Colonel Gaafar Nimeiry to power. Nimeiry signed a peace agreement with southern rebels in 1972, and consolidated his power, alternating conciliation and repression, and establishing Sharia law as the basis of Sudan's legal system in 1983.

Following protests against his regime, Nimeiry was overthrown in a 1985 military coup. New president Omar al-Bashir ran Sudan as a single-party state increasingly linked to Islamic fundamentalist groups such as al-Qaeda. The civil war in the south restarted again, spreading to new regions such as Darfur, where government-backed militias conducted widespread atrocities.

Beginning in 2005, peace agreements calmed the fighting and in 2011 South Sudan became independent, despite clashes between Sudan and rebel groups in the oil-rich region of Abyei, on the border with South Sudan.

Protests in 2018 culminated in a revolution that ended al-Bashir's regime. However, the new civilian Transitional Government was overthrown by a military coup in 2021, and in 2023 the army and paramilitaries unleashed large-scale violence in Khartoum and Darfur, displacing thousands of people.

South Sudan

Africa's newest state enjoys vast oil reserves but is still going through the difficult process of emerging from five decades of civil war.

Official name: Republic of South Sudan
Date of formation: July 9, 2011
Official language: English, with around 70 recognized national languages

South Sudan, which gained independence from Sudan in 2011, is tropical, with savanna and rainforests. Its population is around 15 percent Dinka and 5 percent Nuer, with dozens of smaller groups. Most people practice Christianity and local religions, with a Muslim minority.

Pastoralist peoples have been living in the region since about 3000 BCE. Around the 10th century CE, they were joined by the Dinka, who moved south from what is now Sudan with their cattle to avoid enslavers, and settled in the Sudd marshes.

In the 15th century, the Shilluk emerged along the White Nile, and by the 17th century they dominated its west bank, with a population density similar to that of the Egyptian Nile. The Shilluk clashed with rivals, including the Funj, over river trade.

The Dinka and Shilluk are both Nilotic groups, but to the south, the Azande have Central African roots. They entered the region in the 16th century and established a mosaic of kingdoms, with territories that stretched into the Democratic Republic of the Congo and the Central African Republic.

Under the rule of Muhammad Ali, Egypt claimed all of Sudan from the 1820s. Its grip on the south was initially weak, but incursions from enslavers, merchants, and Christian missionaries grew. In the 1880s, the Mahdist state occupied parts of South Sudan, before being crushed by the British in 1898.

Conflict and independence

From 1899, Britain and Egypt ruled both north and South Sudan, although they were effectively British colonies, with the south economically marginalized. As independence moved closer in the 1950s, it became clear that Sudan's two halves would be united, and in 1955, a first civil war erupted as the Anyanya rebels sought a separate destiny for a region that felt ignored by the largely Muslim north. War continued through independence in 1956, and a peace deal brokered in 1971 broke down in 1983. A new rebel group, the SPLA, led by John Garang, fought until a Comprehensive Peace Agreement in 2005 paved the way for a 2011 referendum in which 98 percent of South Sudanese people voted for independence.

However, border disputes with Sudan persisted over the oil-rich Abyei region. A civil war broke out in South Sudan in 2013 and, despite a 2018 peace deal, ongoing violence has hampered the government's efforts to begin reconstruction of the country.

Libya

Once a land of traders and corsairs, Libya has been ruled by Phoenicia, the Ottoman Empire, and Italy. Today, this oil-rich nation, nestled between the Sahara and the Mediterranean, is searching for stability after years of conflict.

Official name: State of Libya
Date of formation: December 24, 1951
Official language: Arabic

The fourth largest country in Africa, Libya was formed from the three historical regions of Cyrenaica (around the city of Benghazi) to the east, Tripolitania (centered on Tripoli) to the west, and Fezzan in the southwest.

Its fertile coastal strip houses most of the population, fringed by the Akhdar mountains and a vast desert hinterland plateau merging into the Sahara to the south. Libya's population is around 85 percent Arab and 10 percent Amazigh (Berber), and overwhelmingly Muslim. The country has the world's ninth largest oil reserves.

Early origins
The first known cultures in the territory of present-day Libya were the Tehenu, who fought several wars with Egypt from the late 4th millennium BCE, and the Garamantian, established by around 1000 BCE, with its capital at Garma in Fezzan to the southwest. While the Garamantes dominated the desert interior, the coast was settled by Phoenicians in the west around Oea (Tripoli) and Sabratha from about 700 BCE, and in the east by Greeks who founded colonies at Cyrene and Euhesperides (now Benghazi) in the east. While Cyrenaica (the Greek region) was absorbed into Egypt in 525 BCE, the west remained Phoenician until the fall of Carthage, and then Numidian until the Romans took it. In 74 BCE, Cyrenaica also fell into Roman hands. Leptis Magna in Tripolitania became a thriving city, the birthplace of the first African Roman Emperor, Septimius Severus (r. 193–211), who also finally conquered the Garamantian state around 202 CE.

Islamic rule
Like much of North Africa, Tripolitania fell to the Vandals in the 430s. They established a century-long Germanic state that ended with its reconquest by Eastern Roman Emperor Justinian in 534. This Byzantine renewal was short-lived. In 647, Arab Muslim armies captured Cyrenaica and Tripolitania. Libya enjoyed a measure of peace under the Umayyad and Abbasid caliphs and their Aghlabid governors and, from 909, under the Fatimids who replaced them, growing rich on the trade in gold and enslaved people from Sudanic Africa.

The Zirids, an Amazigh dynasty, broke away from the Fatimids in 972, and recognized the Abbasids as the rightful caliphs. The Fatimids retaliated by unleashing the Banu Hilal, a warlike Bedouin group, on the area. The resulting devastation undermined the Zirids, who were eventually forced from power by Normans from Sicily in 1148.

Ottoman conquest
In 1159, Libya was taken over by the Hafsids, a Sunni Muslim dynasty based in Tunis. It slowly recovered to become a center of art and scholarship, while trade grew with Europe and Hafsid caravans crossed the Sahara.

△ Decorative tiles in the 19th-century Gurgi Mosque, built in the Ottoman era

Tripoli was conquered by the Ottomans in 1551 although, as in much of Ottoman North Africa, real power was held by corsair leaders, who occupied the position first of *bey* (provincial governor), and then of *pasha* of Tripoli. Power then devolved to the *deys*, the leaders of the janissaries (elite troops), who ruled from 1611. Osman Saqizli Dey (r. 1649–1672) also conquered Cyrenaica. However, a Turkish officer, Ahmad Karamanli, killed the last of the *deys* in 1711, establishing a semiautonomous dynasty.

The Karamanlis survived until the Barbary Wars between the United States and Tripolitania ended with the suppression of the piracy on which they depended. The Ottomans retook Tripolitania and Cyrenaica in 1835, ruling the region for the next 77 years. The period saw the emergence of the Sanusiyya, an austere Islamic order founded in 1837. Its monasteries acted as a

△ Libya's president Muammar Qaddafi arrives at Tripoli airport in 1977

bastion against foreign influence but also as a limit on the power of the Ottomans.

Italian colonial rule
By the 20th century, European powers were putting the Ottoman Empire under increasing pressure. In 1911, the Italians, who wanted their own colonial empire in Africa to match the British and French, invaded. The Ottomans soon surrendered, and the Italians united the three provinces of the Ottomans under the Greek name "Libya." Local resistance, marshaled by the Sanusiyya, continued, only ending after the death of Omar al-Mukhtar, their leader, in 1931. Around half the Bedouin population were killed through disease or starvation in camps during the conflict.

The Italian Fascist regime of Benito Mussolini invested heavily in Libya, encouraging more than 100,000 Italians to settle, but the fighting during World War II devastated the country. After its conquest by the Allies in 1943, Libya's future, whether as a united country or broken down into its component regions of Fezzan, Tripolitania, and Cyrenaica, remained unclear.

Independent Libya
After prolonged discussion, the United Nations voted to make Libya a united monarchy under King Idris I, head of the Sanusiyya, and the country became independent in 1951.

The discovery of oil in 1959 brought wealth, but the king's pro-Western stance and failure to condemn Israel's 1967 invasion of Egypt precipitated a coup launched by junior officers in 1969. Their leader, Muammar Qaddafi, deposed Idris, nationalized the oil industry, and adopted a radical Pan-Arabist policy of union with Egypt and Tunisia, as well as vigorously supporting the Palestinian cause. His projects for Arab union soon soured, and in 1977 Qaddafi declared the Socialist Libyan Arab Jamahiriya, a state based on his own interpretation of socialism. This led to huge investments in welfare, but dissent was violently crushed by a vast security apparatus.

Qaddafi was a vocal champion of Pan-Africanism (see pp.232–233), and offered financial support to many African nations. But relations with Egypt deteriorated into war in 1977, and conflict with Chad over the Aozou Strip in the 1980s also undermined his claim to be a great unifier.

Accused of involvement in the 1996 Lockerbie bombing, Libya suffered sanctions and, in 2011, pent-up opposition sparked an uprising against Qaddafi. Helped by European countries who carried out air strikes on Libyan army positions, the rebels took Tripoli in August 2011 and killed Qaddafi two months later.

Post-Qaddafi Libya
Qaddafi's fall did not bring peace. The Transitional National Council, the main rebel faction, failed to unify the country, which fractured into rival governments based in Benghazi and Tripoli, complicated by the resurgence of former Qaddafi supporters and the growth of radical Islamist militias. In 2019, the eastern-based Libyan National Army marched on Tripoli, the seat of the internationally recognized government, but was pushed back by loyalist forces. A cease-fire was signed in 2020, and an interim unity government formed in 2021, but instability continues.

▷ This ancient Egyptian glazed tile shows a captured Tehenu chief, 2nd millennium BCE

Tunisia

Compact Tunisia has a grand history as a maritime empire, Roman province, Muslim emirate, French colony, and modern republic.

Official name: Republic of Tunisia
Date of formation: March 20, 1956
Official language: Arabic

The most northerly country in Africa and, at 63,000 sq miles (163,000 sq km), the smallest in North Africa, Tunisia is bounded by Algeria to its west and Libya to the southeast. Its highest mountains, the High Tell (an extension of the Saharan Atlas range), lie in the south, with the highest peak, Mount Chambi, soaring to 5,066 ft (1,544 m).

With a Mediterranean climate, the north is fertile, while the south endures hot, dry summers and the dusty sirocco wind from the Sahara. Tunisia's population is mostly of mixed Arab and Amazigh (Berber) heritage and is Sunni Muslim, while its economy relies heavily on petroleum, phosphates, and tourism.

Ancient civilizations

Tunisia was originally settled by Imazighen of the Capsian culture, who left rock art depicting hunting scenes. The first urban settlements—Utica around 1100 BCE and Carthage (see pp.64–65) some 300 years later—were founded by Phoenician traders. The Carthaginians soon built a maritime empire in the western Mediterranean, but commercial rivalry with the growing Roman Republic led to defeat in three Punic Wars between 264 and 146 BCE, after which the city was destroyed.

The area became the Roman province of Africa, centered on a rebuilt Carthage, which produced valuable grain to feed the large and populous Roman Empire.

As the empire waned, Africa was invaded by the Germanic Vandals. They took Carthage in 439 CE, establishing a kingdom that lasted until its reconquest by the Byzantine (Eastern Roman) armies of Emperor Justinian in 534.

Early Muslim states

Byzantine power waned in the 7th century, and in 698 Tunisia fell to the Arab armies advancing across North Africa. The Umayyads called the territory Ifriqiya, an Arabization of the Roman name Africa, and built cities at Kairouan and Tunis, abandoning Carthage.

After the Abbasids replaced the Umayyads in 750, the unity of the Muslim empire fractured, and Ifriqiya broke away in 800 under the Aghlabid dynasty. Great mosque builders, under whom Kairouan became the religious and cultural center of the Maghreb region, the Aghlabids expanded into Sicily, but in 909 they were overthrown by the Fatimids, an Islamic renewal movement. When the Fatimids in turn conquered Egypt in 969, their hold on Ifriqiya slackened and their Amazigh Zirid governors established an independent dynasty, lasting 972–1148. In the chaos that followed the Zirids' fall, Tunisia was divided between Normans from Sicily and Muslim Almohads from Morocco, until Abu Zakariya, a former Almohad governor, established the Hafsid dynasty in 1229.

Ottoman Tunisia

The Hafsids brought stability but by the 16th century were caught between Hapsburg Spain and the Ottoman Empire. The Ottomans finally annexed Tunisia in 1574, imposing a *pasha* to govern it as an Ottoman province. Real power, however, devolved to the *deys*, leaders elected by Turkish janissary soldiers, and the *beys*, who performed a similar role for local troops.

Dynasties of Muradid and Husaynid *beys* exercised power from 1640 to 1881, in later years seeking to establish modern industries and reform the Tunisian army.

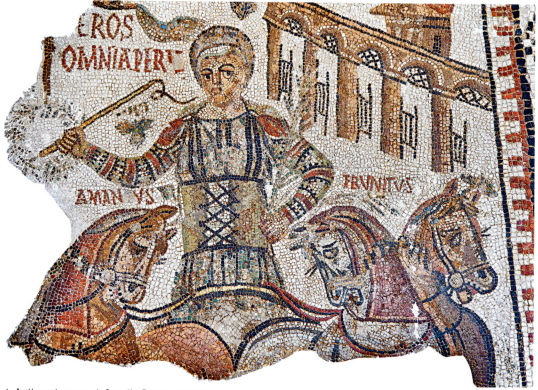

△ A 4th-century mosaic from the Roman ruins at Dougga, showing a charioteer identified as Eros

△ The Ksar Oued Sultane granary in southern Tunisia, typical of fortified stores built by Imazighen in the Maghreb

French colonialism

The expense of Tunisia's reform efforts bankrupted the Husaynids and, in 1881, France used the debt as a pretext to occupy Tunisia and make it a French protectorate. Although the *beys* remained in office, French officials wielded all power, and nearly 150,000 French colonists settled.

Nationalist parties quickly emerged, calling for Tunisian independence, especially after the foundation of the Destour (Constitution) Party in 1920, and Habib Bourguiba's Neo-Destour Party in 1934. World War II, during which Tunisia was governed by the pro-German Vichy regime, weakened French control further.

Independent Tunisia

After four years of unrest and negotiations, Tunisia gained independence in 1956. Bourguiba became first prime minister, and then president when the monarchy was abolished a year later. He occupied the position until 1987, and despite initial reforms, especially in education, his government became increasingly autocratic.

His successor, former general Zine al-Abidine ben Ali, promised reform, but while his Democratic Constitutional Rally (RCD) party maintained the appearance of democracy, he solidified autocratic rule. In 2010, anti-corruption protests spiraled into the Tunisian Revolution and the next month ben Ali fled.

In 2011, a moderate Islamist party, Ennahda, took power. Since then, progress has been decidedly mixed. Kais Saied, who was elected president in 2019, dismissed parliament in 2021 and has overseen police crackdowns and imprisoned his political rivals.

Algeria

Balanced between the Sahara and the Mediterranean, Algeria is Africa's largest country with its identity forged by multiple cultural influences. Algeria's Amazigh and Arab population has fought for independence for over 2,000 years.

Official name: The People's Democratic Republic of Algeria
Date of formation: July 5, 1962
Official languages: Arabic, Tamazight

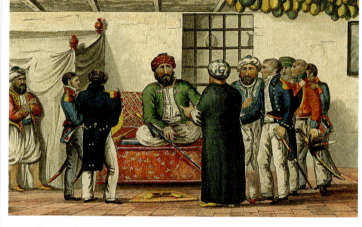

△ Dey Omar Agha negotiating with the British after the Anglo-Dutch bombardment of Algiers in 1816, intended to stop the enslaving of Europeans

Algeria, Africa's largest country at 920,000 sq miles (2.3 million sq km), is divided into two geographical zones. North of the Atlas mountains, a region with a mild Mediterranean climate and fertile soil is densely populated, with cities such as the capital, Algiers. To the south, a vast desert zone is dry, arid, and sparsely peopled.

Algeria's population is mainly Sunni Muslim, with around three-quarters of its people identifying as Arab, and a fifth Amazigh (Berber). A presidential republic, its economy is highly dependent on exports of natural gas and oil.

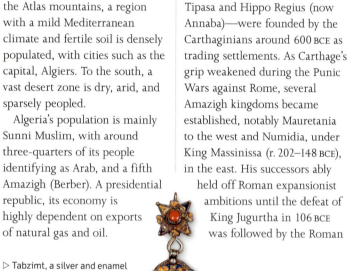

▷ Tabzimt, a silver and enamel ornament worn by Kabylie Amazigh women

Carthage and Rome

Algeria was settled by hominins for at least 2 million years. The first towns in Algeria—Tipasa and Hippo Regius (now Annaba)—were founded by the Carthaginians around 600 BCE as trading settlements. As Carthage's grip weakened during the Punic Wars against Rome, several Amazigh kingdoms became established, notably Mauretania to the west and Numidia, under King Massinissa (r. 202–148 BCE), in the east. His successors ably held off Roman expansionist ambitions until the defeat of King Jugurtha in 106 BCE was followed by the Roman annexation of part of Numidia and the progressive absorption of the rest. Mauretania's rulers had become clients of Rome, and after the murder of King Ptolemy in 40 CE the region was organized into two Roman provinces.

Apart from the serious revolts in 238 and 253 CE, the region remained quiescent under Roman rule, with Christianity becoming firmly established. The religion's most notable leader was St. Augustine, bishop of Hippo, whose book *City of God* suggested that the Vandals, Germanic peoples who conquered the region in the 420s, were a punishment from God. The Vandal Kingdom controlled Algeria until the reconquest of North Africa by Belisarius, general of the Eastern Roman emperor Justinian, in 534.

The coming of Islam

This reimposition of Roman rule was short-lived, however: in 670, Muslim armies under Uqba ibn Nafi began the conquest of the region, which by 711 was under Umayyad control. Later, the Rustamids, an Amazigh dynasty, established an independent state in 776, to be succeeded by the Zirids, who ruled Algeria from 972, expanding into Tunisia and Morocco. Their struggle with the Hamdanids, a rival Amazigh dynasty, allowed the Almoravids and then Almohads, both Moroccan-based Islamic renewal movements, to rule Algeria until the Zayyanids restored local control in 1235.

Ottoman Algeria

The weakening of the Zayyanids' emirate allowed the Spanish Hapsburg monarchs to occupy parts of northern Algeria, including Oran (1509), and for Muslim corsairs to take the rest. One of them, Kair ad-Din ("Barbarossa"), was appointed *pasha* (governor) of Algiers by the Ottoman sultan Suleiman I in 1518. He and his successors drove out the Spanish invaders and continued to raid ships run by Christian nations. The *pashas* and the *deys* (their successors from 1670) remained part of the Ottoman Empire for centuries, but were able to operate with a large degree of autonomy.

French rule

The Ottoman Empire came under increasing political, economic, and territorial encroachment by European powers in the 19th century, and in 1830 French troops invaded. Despite fierce resistance by Abd al-Kadir that lasted until 1847, France soon occupied most of Algeria. European settlers (or "pieds noirs") began to arrive in great numbers, and the country became a part of metropolitan France in 1881. French rule was harsh and violent: Indigenous Algerians were subject to settler colonial rule, including the dispossession of their lands and unequal treatment under the law.

An independence movement was fueled by the experience of Algerians who fought for France in the two World Wars but were never considered equals, by those such as nationalist leader Ferhat Abbas who had a French education but grew increasingly revolutionary, and by Muslim reformers. In 1945, thousands of Algerians were killed in a series of attacks by French troops and militia. Unsatisfied by the establishment of an Algerian Assembly in 1947, the nationalist *Front de Libération Nationale* (FLN) began a campaign of violence.

Independent Algeria

The War of Independence with France (1954–1962) was prolonged and brutal. Half a million French troops were sent to suppress the revolt, using tactics that pushed even moderate nationalists into the FLN camp. Around 8,000 villages across Algeria were destroyed as France attempted to "pacify" the country, and nearly 2 million Algerian people were detained in internment camps.

Faced with determined resistance and rising international pressure, the French government under Charles de Gaulle agreed to negotiations. In 1962, after a referendum that overwhelmingly backed independence, Algeria freed itself from colonial rule.

The new government of Ahmed ben Bella faced daunting challenges in reconstructing a country where over 500,000 had died and the infrastructure was devastated. He was overthrown in 1965 in a military coup by Houari Boumédiène. Both Boumédiène and his successor Chadi Benjedid (from 1978 to 1992) emphasized political authoritarianism and centralized economic policy over political freedom, helping to stoke new discontents that in 1991 provoked a civil war between Islamists and the government. Its suppression was as bloody as the war against France, and chilled any hope of political liberalization for decades.

In 2019, mass protests forced out Abdelaziz Bouteflika (the president since 1999), though his ultimate replacement, Abdelmadjid Tebboune, was also from the FLN party.

△ Algerians celebrating independence from French colonial rule on the streets of Oran, 1962

△ Elaborate decorative tile work on the mausoleum of Moulay Idris II, a ruler of the Idrisid emirate

Morocco

Great empires have flourished in Morocco, home to mighty mountains, a Mediterranean shore, and North Africa's only monarchy.

Official name: Kingdom of Morocco
Date of formation: April 7, 1956
Official languages: Arabic, Tamazight

Morocco is divided in two by the Rif and Atlas mountains, the latter rising to 13,665 ft (4,165 m) at Mount Toubkal. To the east are arid lowland and the fringes of the Sahara, and to the west the Moroccan plateau and a coastal Atlantic plain. Rainfall is plentiful near the mountains, and the coastal areas have a near Mediterranean climate. Around 60 percent of the population is Arab, and around a third Amazigh (Berber). Two coastal enclaves in northern Morocco, Ceuta and Melilla, are held by Spain, while Morocco itself occupies the disputed territory of Western Sahara.

The country is North Africa's only monarchy and more than 99 percent of its people are Sunni Muslim. It has the fifth largest economy in Africa.

Ancient Morocco

The oldest specimens of *Homo sapiens*, dating from 300,000 years ago, were found at Jebel Irhoud in western Morocco. From the 8th century BCE, Phoenicians began establishing coastal settlements such as Lixus and Mogador, trading with Amazigh peoples in the interior.

The independent Amazigh kingdom of Mauretania emerged around the 2nd century BCE. It dominated the area until it was reduced to a Roman vassal state under Juba II (r. 25 BCE–23 CE), and then annexed as the Roman province of Mauretania Tingitana in 44 CE.

Roman rule, based around cities such as Volubilis and Tingis (Tangier), was swept away by the Vandals, a Germanic people, in

429, before the Byzantine (Eastern Roman) Empire took back the region in the 6th century.

Islamic kingdoms

In 683, Muslim Umayyad armies conquered Morocco. Initially governed from Kairouan in Tunisia, in 740 Morocco shook off Umayyad control, as an Amazigh revolt led to the establishment of a number of emirates. The most powerful of these was the Idrisid, which was founded by Idris ibn Abdallah, who occupied the former Roman site of Volubilis in 788.

By the mid-9th century, Idrisid power had declined and Morocco broke apart. It was reunified from 1059 by the Almoravids, an Islamic reformist movement with its origins in nomadic Amazigh groups from the south, who founded a new capital at Marrakech. As Almoravid power waned, they were replaced by the similarly reformist Almohads, who ruled Morocco until defeat in Spain led to their collapse in 1269.

For the next two centuries, Morocco was held by the Amazigh Marinid dynasty, which by 1347 under Abu el-Hassan Ali ruled as far east as Tripoli in Libya. The Wattasids, who supplanted the Marinids in 1465, failed to hold off foreign intervention. It took a new dynasty—the Saadians, who seized Marrakech in 1524—to secure the kingdom by decisively defeating the invading Portuguese in 1578.

Succession wars in the early 17th century and growing opposition from Amazigh in the Atlas led to the eclipse of the Saadians, and the establishment in 1666 of the Alaouite dynasty. After a period of fragmentation, the Alouites eventually imposed their authority across Morocco under Muhammad III (1757–1790).

French and Spanish rule

The two Alaouite sultans Muhammad IV (r. 1859–1873) and Hassan I (r. 1873–1894) tried to reform the army and government. The French had bombarded Tangier in 1844 and war erupted with Spain in 1859–1860. The conflicts saddled Morocco with debt, which France and Spain used as a pretext to take control of Moroccan ports in 1906. In 1912, a French protectorate was declared in the south and a Spanish one in the north. The sultan remained the nominal head of state, but Morocco was subject to colonial rule.

In 1912, an uprising in the south spread to Marrakech, while the revolt of Abd el-Krim established the Republic of the Rif in 1921—it remained independent until 1926. In the 1940s, agitation for independence grew, headed by the nationalist Istiqlal party. France was already fighting to maintain control of Algeria, and in the face of mounting Moroccan pressure, it conceded independence in March 1956; Spain followed a month later.

Independent Morocco

In the beginning, Morocco had no parliament, and when elections were held in 1963, a pro-royalist party won. Parliament was dissolved in 1964 and not recalled until 1979, after which two abortive coups against King Hassan II led the monarchy's supporters to strengthen their grip on the political process.

A declining economy, a repressive government, and the costs of the war that Morocco was waging to retain control of Western Sahara (the region Spain had withdrawn in 1975) caused strains. Riots broke out in 1981 in Casablanca and the 1990s saw partial liberalization, as Hassan released thousands of long-serving political prisoners.

The accession of a young king, Muhammad VI, in 1999 brought some reforms in women's rights and the status of the Amazigh language Tamazight. The king navigated crises with Spain in 2002 over a small Spanish-occupied island, Islamist suicide bombings in Casablanca in 2003, and Arab Spring protests in 2011, which led to a new constitution and greater power for parliament.

The moderate Islamist PJD took power in 2011, but lost to the pro-royalist National Rally of Independents in 2021. Morocco, unlike many of its neighbors, had balanced reform and tradition without major upsets.

Western Sahara (disputed)

Western Sahara has seen a long war between Morocco and the Polisario Front, which declared it the Sahrawi Arab Democratic Republic.

Official name: Sahrawi Arab Democratic Republic (disputed)
Date of formation: February 27, 1976 (disputed)
Official languages: Arabic, Spanish

Spain evacuated Western Sahara in 1975, after Morocco sent a "Green March" of some 300,000 Moroccans into the territory. In 1976, the Polisario Front began a guerrilla war against Morocco and Mauritania (which also claimed a part of it, until a 1979 peace accord). A 1988 UN proposal stipulated a referendum on Western Sahara's status, but this has never been implemented. Despite periodic peace talks, little progress has been made: Morocco has built a "sand wall" to section off Polisario-controlled areas, and many Sahrawis remain in refugee camps. Western Sahara is currently recognized by 45 countries.

△ A train of camels crossing sand dunes in the Western Sahara desert

West Africa

◁ *Kente* cloth from Ghana, handmade from cotton and silk by Asante weavers and originally reserved for royalty

Mauritania

The predominantly desert state of Mauritania has been shaped by competing Arab, Amazigh, and Black African influences that have caused long-lasting political fault lines.

Official name: Islamic Republic of Mauritania
Date of formation: November 28, 1960
Official language: Arabic

Ninety percent of the northwest African country of Mauritania lies in the Sahara. Its population, concentrated in the milder south, is a mix of Amazigh (Berber)-Arab and the Haratin—Black Mauritanians who assumed an Amazigh identity—and a third made up of other Black ethnic groups, including the Tukulor and Fulani people. Most speak Arabic and are Sunni Muslim.

Although possessing significant reserves of iron ore and oil, the country relies mainly on fishing and agriculture. Mauritania has struggled since independence with human rights issues, only criminalizing slavery in 2007.

Early Mauritania

Rock art dating from around 3000 BCE and onward tells of prehistoric people living in the region, but not much is known of them. Amazigh groups migrated into Mauritania from the 3rd century CE, as the Sahara region dried. Arabs followed from the late 7th century, bringing with them Islam, but their expansion was blocked by Wagadou (ancient Ghana) as well as the Amazigh Sanhadja confederations of the Sahara. Islam eventually gained a hold among the Amazigh, generating an austere revivalist movement, the Almoravids, whose origins in the 1050s lay in *ribats*, fortified religious establishments in Mauritania and Western Sahara.

The Almoravids carved an empire in Morocco and Spain, but their fall to the Almohads in 1147 paved the way for Yemeni Arabs to enter Mauritania. Their conquest, fiercely opposed by local Amazigh peoples, was only completed after the Mauritanian Thirty-Year War (1644–1674).

By this time Europeans had penetrated the region, beginning with the Portuguese in 1442, and then Dutch and French traders in search of gum arabic used in textile manufacture. Gradually the French became dominant, expanding from their bases along the Senegal River, annexing the Waalo Kingdom and, in 1856, attacking the emirates of Trarza and Brakna north of the river, forcing a protectorate on them.

French colonialism

From 1900, the French governor Xavier Coppolani systematically undermined the emirates, encouraging *marabouts* (religious leaders) such as Shaykh Sidiya Baba to seek French protection.

The emirates fought back, and only by 1912 had the French defeated the key region of Adrar.

Skirmishes rumbled on until 1934, but didn't break French control. Little investment was made in developing Mauritania, which was joined to French West Africa in 1920 and treated as *Le Grand Vide* ("the great void"). Colonial administrators relied on the emirs of Trarza, Brakna and Adrar to ensure peace, but resentment gradually fueled a nationalist movement in the whole region, beginning with the Mauritanian Entente formed in 1946 by Senegal's emerging independence campaigners Léopold Senghor (see p.322) and Lamine Guèye.

Independent Mauritania

From 1956, France conceded limited autonomy to Mauritania, with the country's sole lawyer, Moktar Ould Daddah, as de facto prime minister. He steered the country to independence in 1960, imposing a one-party state in 1964, led by his *Parti du Peuple Mauritanien*. His authoritarian rule remained confirmed in unopposed elections in 1966, 1971, and 1976.

In 1975, Mauritania invaded Western Sahara, occupying the southern portion (Morocco took the north), beginning a war with the Sahrawi Polisario Front. The conflict destabilized Mauritania's economy and, in 1978, Daddah was deposed in a military coup. The new government of Colonel Haidallah made peace with the Sahrawi, and abolished slavery in 1981—but it was only criminalized in 2007, and is still widespread, with those born into slavery remaining enslaved. Haidallah was in turn deposed in a coup in 1984 by Maaouya Ould Taya.

Intercommunal violence between Black Mauritanians and Amazigh groups in 1989 led to the legalization of opposition parties in 1991, though Ould Taya continued to rule, persecuting political opponents, until he was toppled by a 2005 coup. A further coup in 2008 was followed by the restoration of civilian rule; in 2019 Mauritania experienced its first democratic transfer of power when opposition leader Mohamed Ould Ghazouani won presidential elections.

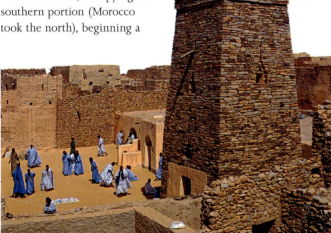
△ The square minaret of the 14th-century Chinguetti mosque in Adrar, Mauritania

The Gambia

One of Africa's smallest countries, the Gambia has succeeded in retaining its own diverse identity in a region dominated by larger powers.

Official name: Republic of the Gambia
Date of formation: February 18, 1965
Official language: English

Continental Africa's smallest country—in places only 30 miles (50 km) wide—the Gambia takes its name from the river that forms its core, and is surrounded by Senegal (except for its western coast). It is demographically and ecologically diverse, with mixed savanna-forest, pure savanna, and mangrove swamps. Among more than a dozen ethnic groups, about a third of Gambians are Mandingo, and around one fifth Fulani. More than 95 percent are Sunni Muslim. The Gambia's economy historically relied on the export of groundnuts.

Becoming the Gambia

The Gambia formed part of the mighty Mali and Songhai empires between the 13th and 16th centuries. Portuguese traders entered the region in 1445, followed by the British, who vied with the Dutch and then French, establishing a military post at Bathurst (now Banjul) in 1816. Because of the French presence in Senegal, the British couldn't expand beyond the land they controlled on both sides of the Gambia River, which they declared a protectorate in 1894.

An independence movement, beginning with Edward Small's National Congress of British West Africa in 1920, increased after World War II. By 1960, several political parties had emerged, leading to independence in 1965. Dawda Jawara, the first prime minister, was elected president in 1970 when the Gambia became a Republic, remaining in that post until 1994. A confederation with Senegal from 1981 to 1989 failed, and in 1994 Jawara was deposed in a coup by Yahya Jammeh, who banned opposition parties.

Multiparty democracy was restored in 1996, but Jammeh continued to win presidential elections in 2001, 2006, and 2016. His refusal to accept defeat by opposition candidate Adama Barrow in 2016 led to a military intervention by the ECOWAS grouping of West Africa states and his resignation in 2017.

△ Dawda Kairaba Jawara in 1969, just before becoming president

Senegal

Ethnically diverse Senegal lay at the edge of many historic West African empires. Its strong economy and relatively stable democracy, as well as a thriving culture and fashion scene, has made it a successful modern state, although lately plagued by unrest.

Official name: Republic of Senegal
Date of formation: April 4, 1960
Official language: French

At mainland Africa's westernmost point, Senegal sits where coastal and tropical rainforest ecosystems converge with semi-arid savanna. Its capital, Dakar, is an important trading center, exporting the fish, phosphate, and groundnuts that support the Senegalese industry. Historically politically dominant, the Wolof make up two-fifths of Senegal's people, with large Fulani, Tukulor, and Serer minorities; 97 percent of the population is Muslim.

The country has a rich cultural heritage, passed on by its famed *griot* storytellers, and explored by internationally renowned stars such as filmmaker Ousmane Sembène, author Mariama Bâ, and musician Youssou N'dour.

Evolving empires

Neolithic shell middens have been found in the estuaries of the Senegal and Casamance rivers, but it is the hundred or so stone circles built along the rivers, some time between the late 1st millennium BCE and the 1st millennium CE, that indicate the beginnings of more complex societies in Senegal.

The region lay at the western edge of several mighty medieval West African empires, including Wagadou (Empire of Ancient Ghana) from the 8th century, the Mali Empire in the 13th century, and its vassal state, the Jolof Kingdom, founded by Ndiadiane Ndiaye around 1350, whose territory lay largely in modern Senegal. The Jolof rulers, the *burs*, were at the height of their power when the Portuguese explorer Dinis Dias arrived at the Senegal River in 1444, beginning a trading relationship that soon undermined the Jolof Kingdom's power, as its constituent states, such as the Sine Kingdom, now gained an Atlantic outlet for their trade. By around 1600, the larger Jolof Empire had collapsed, with only its core remaining.

European encroachment

In 1627, the Dutch West India Company acquired Gorée Island off Dakar, building two forts there and escalating the existing European involvement in the transatlantic slave trade, which further undermined all local kingdoms in the region. In 1677, France seized Gorée, displacing the Dutch as the predominant European power in Senegal.

French colonial rule

The French confined themselves to the coast and posts along the Senegal River, though towns grew up at Saint-Louis, Dakar, Gorée, and Rufisque. From 1848, Africans living in these Four Communes had, in theory, the rights of French citizenship (while those living in other parts of the colony did not), although the process was lengthy and not fully implemented until 1918.

In 1854, the Tukulor religious leader al-Hajj Umar launched a jihad against French rule in West Africa, but didn't conduct any attacks in Senegal, which remained under French control. The French increased the cultivation of peanuts, a valuable export commodity that was already grown locally, and from 1879 built a railroad between Saint-Louis and Dakar, but otherwise did little to support further development. In 1895, Senegal became part of the new French West Africa Federation, with first Saint-Louis, then (from 1902) Dakar as its capital.

Many Senegalese soldiers were among the 200,000 West Africans who fought for France in World War I, with many also serving in World War II. The pro-Nazi Vichy regime (which controlled Senegal from 1940 to 1942) abolished all political rights of Black citizens of the Four Communes. But Black Senegalese politicians, despite temporarily losing their rights, continued to work for greater autonomy, and for voting rights for all Senegalese citizens, which were won in 1946.

△ Léopold Senghor, a Pan-Africanist politician and first president of Senegal

Independence

An alliance between the French-educated Senegalese, including the politician Léopold Senghor, and Muslim religious orders such as the Muridiyyah, began calls for independence. Senghor, himself a poet and philosopher, also championed the influential movement known as *Négritude*, which promoted Black African culture and identity.

Senegal gained independence in 1960, first as part of a federation with Mali that soon dissolved. Senghor was elected Senegal's first president, and consolidated his power after a 1962 alleged coup attempt. Political parties were banned, except for his Senegalese Progressive Union, and only re-legalized in 1976. Senghor remained in power through five terms, providing stability, if not political freedom, until stepping down in favor of Abdou Diouf in 1980.

Senegal since Senghor

Diouf permitted multiparty democracy, and in 1982 joined the Gambia in a Senegambian Confederation that lasted until 1989, making little real progress in integrating the two countries.

France's 1994 devaluation of the Central African Franc badly affected the Senegalese economy and, in 2000, Diouf was defeated by Abdoulaye Wade. In 2004, Wade negotiated a truce in the long-running conflict with separatists in the southern Casamance region, but the conflict is still rumbling on. In 2012, Macky Sall's presidential victory marked a third consecutive peaceful transition of power, and a 2016 referendum introduced a two-term limit. Sall won a second term in 2019 but since then, the country has faced increased civil and political unrest.

△ Fishermen harvest salt from the algae-tinted pink waters of Lake Reitba, northeast of the capital, Dakar

Guinea-Bissau

Once ruled by the Kaabu and linked to the Mali Empire via the gold and salt trade, Guinea-Bissau fought hard to free itself from centuries of Portuguese colonial rule.

Official name: Republic of Guinea-Bissau
Date of formation: September 10, 1974
Official language: Portuguese

One of West Africa's smaller countries, Guinea-Bissau includes the Bijagós archipelago with 15 main islands, a low-lying Atlantic coastline, and an inland plateau. Soil erosion and salination have damaged its agricultural land.

Guinea-Bissau has around 20 ethnic groups, of whom the Fula (at about 29 percent) and the Balanta (22 percent) are most numerous. Nearly half of the population speak Kriyol, a creole based on Portuguese. About 45 percent are Muslim, 20 percent are Christian, and 30 percent practice Indigenous religions.

Kaabu domination

Rice and sorghum farmers from farther inland reached Guinea-Bissau's Atlantic coast by the 13th century. They formed the state of Kaabu, subordinate to the Mali Empire farther north. Ruled by *mansabas*, Kaabu was extremely hierarchical with an elite warrior class. It profited from the trade in gold and salt and—after the arrival of the Portuguese in the area known as the Guinea Coast from the 1440s—also from the expanding slave trade.

Over the next four centuries, tens of thousands of people, mainly seminomadic Fulani, were taken to be enslaved on plantations in Cabo Verde and in the Americas, until the overthrow of the Kaabu kingdom by the Muslim Imamate of Futa Jalon at the Battle of Kansala in 1867.

Portuguese rule

After Kaabu's fall, Portugal began to expand from its coastal forts and occupy the interior. Guinean resistance was fierce, both on the mainland and on the islands, including a rebellion against hut tax in 1913, which was suppressed with appalling ferocity. The colony's economic development was neglected, except for peanut cultivation, and very few health clinics or schools were provided; by 1950, 99 percent of the population were still illiterate.

Independence and beyond

In 1956, the Pan-African theorist Amílcar Cabral founded the African Party for Independence of Guinea and Cabo Verde (PAIGC), envisaging that the two colonies would achieve independence together. After a strike by dock workers was violently crushed in 1959, the PAIGC launched an armed campaign in January 1963, and, although outnumbered, succeeded in gaining control of almost all the country outside the major towns by 1970. Cabral was assassinated in 1973, just a year before Guinea-Bissau achieved independence, when the new Lisbon government, installed following Portugal's Carnation Revolution, agreed to withdraw from its colonies.

Amílcar's half-brother Luís de Almeida Cabral became Guinea-Bissau's first president, but he was overthrown in a coup in 1980 by his prime minister João Vieira, which led to the severing of ties with Cabo Verde. Vieira won the first multiparty elections in 1994, but then lost power in 1999 after a year-long civil war with army mutineers. The first non-PAIGC government took over, led by Kumba Ialá, but despite initial optimism, Ialá's rule became increasingly autocratic and he was removed in a coup in 2003. Vieira, who returned from exile to resume the presidency, was assassinated in 2009, triggering widespread violence and a decade of instability and coups. In 2020, Umaro Sissoco Embaló took office as the first elected non-PAIGC president.

◁ Wooden statue of an *orebok*, a deity of the Bijagós islands, off the coast of Guinea-Bissau

Guinea

Modern Guinea has a proud history of fierce and long-lasting resistance to colonialism, and still possesses great mineral wealth.

Official name: Republic of Guinea
Date of formation: October 2, 1958
Official language: French

Guinea contains the sources of three major African rivers, the Gambia, Niger, and Senegal. It also houses much of the world's bauxite stock and large diamond and iron reserves. Its Atlantic coastal plain rises to inland plateaus with dense rainforest and the Fouta Djallon highlands, which reach 5,045 ft (1,538 m) at Mount Tamgué. The main ethnic groups are the Pular-speaking Fula, the Mandingo, and the coastal Sosso people. Eighty percent of Guineans are Muslim.

Early Guinea
Sosso and Mandingo peoples entered Guinea around 900 CE, and the area was incorporated into the Mali Empire in the mid-13th century. The Fulani, who arrived in the highlands around 1500, established a theocratic state in 1735, which survived until 1898, acting as a bastion of resistance to European advances. These came first in the form of the Portuguese in the mid-15th century, who began the centuries-long trading in enslaved people along the Guinea coast.

Guinea and France
The French started to penetrate the area in the early 19th century. In 1881, the *almamy* (ruler) of Futa Jallon accepted a French protectorate, but the independent Mandingo State of Samory Touré continued to resist the French until his capture in 1898.

From when French Guinea was established as a colony in 1891, the area saw little development. In the 1958 referendum on membership of the French Community, Guinea was the only remaining colony to vote against, precipitating independence with Sékou Touré as its first president. Cut off completely from French aid, Touré turned to the USSR and China for assistance, implementing policies such as the nationalization of land and removal of chiefdoms. As his rule became more autocratic, he also courted United States aid.

Modern struggles
Touré died in 1984 and was replaced by Colonel Lansana Conté, who re-legalized private ownership of businesses. A 1996 coup attempt and overspill from Sierra Leone's civil war in 2000 destabilized Guinea, but Conté stayed in power until his death in 2008. The outbreak of Ebola virus in 2014 damaged Guinea's economy, but an expansion of the bauxite industry under Alpha Condé offered a hope of growth until a military coup in 2021 stalled the country's progress.

Cabo Verde

Ecologically fragile, but politically relatively stable, the island state of Cabo Verde remains vulnerable to climatic variations.

Official name: Republic of Cabo Verde
Date of formation: July 5, 1975
Official language: Portuguese

The ten volcanic islands of the Cabo Verde archipelago, affected by soil erosion as well as water shortages, were uninhabited until the Portuguese settled in 1462. Most Cabo Verdeans are of mixed European/African descent, speak Cabo Verdean creole (known as Kriolu), and are Roman Catholic.

Island history
The Portuguese trafficked huge numbers of enslaved people through Cabo Verde on to Brazil. After the abolition of the trade, Cabo Verde became a steamboat refueling stop in the 1850s, which provided local jobs. In the early 20th century, islanders suffered from natural disasters and famine; as Portugal gave no assistance, discontent grew. The PAIGC movement (see p.324), achieved independence in 1975 under Aristides Pereira, who ruled until Antonio Mascarenhas Monteiro of the Movement for Democracy (MpD) replaced him in 1991, following Cabo Verde's first multiparty elections. Power has since alternated between the MpD and the PAICV (PAIGC's successor) and tourism boosts strong economic growth, now recovering after COVID-19.

△ An extinct volcano and lava field on the Cabo Verdean island of Fogo

Sierra Leone

Sierra Leone's wealth in diamonds has been a mixed blessing, bringing prosperity and fueling armed conflict in equal measure.

Official name: Republic of Sierra Leone
Date of formation: April 27, 1961
Official language: English

Sierra Leone has a varied climate, with savanna in the north and tropical rainforest in the south. Around 20 ethnic groups live here, of which the largest are the Temne and Mende, each about a third of the population. Among the minorities are the Krio, the descendants of formerly enslaved Black settlers. Muslims make up 80 percent of the population and Christians about a fifth. English is the official language, but around 97 percent of the population speak Krio, a creole related to English. The major economic sectors are agriculture and mining, especially of diamonds.

Early chiefdoms

Sierra Leone has been inhabited for at least 2,500 years. The Limba who migrated from the north were first, followed by the Bulom, Loko, Temne, Mende, and Fula, who established small states protected from outside interference by dense forest.

In 1462, the Portuguese explorer Pedro da Sintra arrived, and was soon followed by others who began trafficking enslaved people.

Foundation of Freetown

The British set up a base at Bunce Island in 1670, but as sentiment in Britain turned against slavery, abolitionists launched the Sierra Leone Resettlement Scheme. Its aim was to resettle the thousands of Black people who had ended up in Britain, from formerly enslaved workers to soldiers who had fought for the British. The first landed in 1787, founding Freetown five years later. Arriving later were Maroons (formerly enslaved rebels from Jamaica) and Africans freed from slave ships after the trade was abolished.

The British established a Crown Colony in 1808. They expanded inland, through treaties that were unfavorable to local chieftains, and a Protectorate was declared in 1896. Local resistance to a hut tax imposed on villages led to a serious uprising by the Temne chief Bai Bureh in 1898.

△ Chief Bai Bureh, leader of the Hut Tax revolt of 1898

Independence

Political activists began opposing colonial rule, but there were divisions between the Freetown Krio and leaders elsewhere. In 1951, many joined to form the Sierra Leone People's Party (SLPP), including Milton Margai, who became prime minister when independence was achieved in 1961. In 1968, Siaka Stevens of the All People's Congress (APC) took over, from 1971 as president, ruling a one-party state until 1985.

In 1991, the civil war in Liberia spilled over into Sierra Leone, and Revolutionary United Front (RUF) rebels seized many rural areas. The Abidjan Agreement, signed in 1996 between RUF leader Foday Sankoh and President Ahmad Tejan Kabbah, broke down. Sierra Leone spiraled into chaos, with Kabbah deposed by the military, and then restored by ECOWAS troops in 1998; the civil war came to an end in 2002. Since then, multiparty elections have seen power alternating between the SLPP and the APC, with Julius Maada Bio (SLPP) winning a second term in 2023.

△ Print from around 1790, showing ships anchored in the bay and river where Freetown was founded

Liberia

Declared independent by Black Americo-Liberians in 1847, Liberia later became the first country in Africa to elect a female president.

Official name: Republic of Liberia
Date of formation: July 26, 1847
Official language: English

Encompassing coastal mangrove plains in the south, mountains in the east, and tropical rainforest and deciduous forest inland, Liberia's biodiversity is threatened by illegal logging and hunting.

Liberia is a presidential democracy with an economy depending on rubber and timber export; extraction of diamonds, gold, and iron ore; and revenue acquired from Liberian-flagged ships (around 10 percent of global shipping tonnage). There are 16 main ethnic groups, of whom the Kpelle is the largest.

Early history

Liberia had been inhabited since at least the 12th century CE, when Kru, Bassa, and Kissi ethnic groups moved there, followed by further waves of migration after the collapse of the great Mali and Songhai empires in the 14th and 16th centuries. Although Europeans trafficked enslaved people from Liberia from the 16th century, it never saw the establishment of major European fortified bases.

Land of the free

Abolitionists in the United States saw Liberia as an area in which free Black Americans could live, and in 1820, 90 settlers set out on a ship organized by the American Colonization Society. A local ruler, Zola Duma, agreed to sell a piece of land and when the settlers arrived there in 1822, they built Monrovia as their capital.

Known as Americo-Liberians, the settlers grew in numbers, monopolizing power for over a century. In 1847, they declared independence as the Republic of Liberia, creating a nation state modeled on the United States. Politics was dominated by the True Whig Party from 1877, but Liberia faced constant pressure from the expansion of the French and British colonial presence, and lost much of its hinterland to them between 1885 and 1919.

Liberia suffered an economic crisis as demand for its products fell, but the establishment of a massive rubber plantation by the Firestone Tire and Rubber Company in 1926 reversed this, enabling the country to pay off all its foreign debt by 1951.

Modern Liberia

Liberia enjoyed stability during the six presidential terms of William Tubman from 1944 to 1971, but the oil shocks of 1973 and 1979 hit it hard. Tubman's successor, William Tolbert, was deposed in a coup by Samuel Doe (of the Indigenous Krahn group) in 1980, and in 1989 a civil war erupted between government forces and rebels led by Charles Taylor. Doe was killed in 1990 and Taylor's rebels overran most of the country except Monrovia.

The extreme brutality of the fighting scarred Liberia but after a 1995 peace deal, Taylor won elections. His rule was unpopular and when peacekeepers from ECOWAS (a union of West African states) pulled out in 1999, a new violent rebellion erupted, ultimately leading to Taylor's resignation, and his trial at The Hague in 2012 for human rights abuses.

In 2005, Ellen Johnson Sirleaf was elected head of state, and in 2011 was awarded a Nobel Peace Prize for promoting women's rights and post-war reconciliation. A disputed 2011 election, failure to eradicate corruption, and the impact of the Ebola epidemic in 2014 dogged Johnson Sirleaf's second term. Her party, the Unity Party (UP), lost the 2017 election to former professional soccer player George Weah in the first peaceful transfer of power since 1943.

△ Mask made of wood by the Bassa peoples in Liberia, 19th century

◁ Diviners' figures used by Baoulé seers to consult spirits

Côte d'Ivoire

 After decades of growth and political stability after independence, Côte d'Ivoire suffered two civil wars in the early 21st century, leaving the West African state with the hard task of reconstructing its political consensus and economic prosperity.

Official name: Republic of Côte d'Ivoire
Date of formation: August 7, 1960
Official language: French

Côte d'Ivoire's lagoon-studded Atlantic coastline merges inland with a zone of tropical rainforest, cleared forest plantations, and a high northern savanna. It harbors diverse wildlife, including pygmy hippopotamuses, elephants, West African manatees, chimpanzees, and more than ten separate species of antelope.

More than 60 ethnic groups live here: many, including the Baoulé, are Akan peoples, while 20 percent of the population is non-Ivorian, drawn in by West Africa's highest economic growth rate. The country is the world's biggest exporter of cocoa beans, mainly through the port of Abidjan, its largest city. Around 40 percent of the population are Muslim (mainly Sunni) and the same proportion Christian, with about 10 percent practicing Indigenous religions.

Early kingdoms

Since its dense rainforest belt acted as a barrier, Côte d'Ivoire was only partially absorbed into the Wagadou (ancient Ghana) and Mali empires, which in turn dominated the region between the 9th and the 16th centuries. Around 1600, political instability in the region led Kru peoples to migrate from Liberia, Senoufo from Mali and then, in the 18th century, Akan from Ghana.

In 1710, the Dioula, a Mande-speaking group from the former Mali Empire, established the Kong (or Wattara) Kingdom in northeastern Côte d'Ivoire, which disintegrated shortly after its founder Seku Wattara died in 1735. Its remnant, a decentralized city-state based on Kong, which traded in gold and kola nuts and acted as a focal point for the spread of Islam in the region, survived until 1898, when it was destroyed by the armies of the Mandingo religious leader Samory Touré (see p.217).

Other kingdoms appeared further south, notably the Bono state of Gyaman in the 17th century, and the Baoulé kingdom of Sakasso established by Akan refugees from the Asante Empire in the mid-18th century.

French colonization

A lack of sheltered harbors meant the slave trade was less developed than in other parts of West Africa (although a growing trade in ivory gave the region its later name). In the 1840s, the French began signing treaties with coastal chiefs, such as the king of Grand Bassam, but their presence was largely confined to commercial trading companies.

France withdrew its small number of garrisons in 1871, but in the aftermath of the Berlin Conference in 1884–1885—in which European colonial powers discussed how to divide large tracts of the African continent between themselves—it resumed its military presence to forestall other European powers.

Expeditions such as that of Captain Louis-Gustave Binger in 1887–1889 led to treaties with inland chiefs, and in 1893 France declared a protectorate. The Wassoulou Empire of Samory Touré continued to vigorously challenge the French presence until his defeat in 1898, and then the imposition of a much-resented hut tax sparked a series of revolts from 1908.

From 1904 to 1958, as part of the Federation of West Africa, Côte d'Ivoire's inland areas were allowed to retain their own customs, but forced drafting into work on French-owned mines and plantations, and on public works such as the railroad line to Upper Volta (now Burkina Faso), bred resentment. By 1939, however, 90 percent of cocoa production was in the hands of Ivorian smallholders.

The Houphouët-Boigny era

Racist legislation by the pro-Nazi Vichy regime in France from 1940 intensified opposition and in 1944, Félix Houphouët-Boigny formed the African Farmers Union to lobby for Ivorian rights. He secured a seat in the French National Assembly, and became Côte d'Ivoire's first president on independence in 1960.

△ Raffia-palm fiber cloth made by female weavers of the Dida, a Kru people in southern Côte d'Ivoire

A more conservative figure than many African nationalist leaders, he retained good relations with France, and nurtured a coffee industry that made Côte d'Ivoire a leading producer of coffee as well as of cocoa beans. But he was highly intolerant of dissent; his Parti Démocratique de la Côte d'Ivoire (PDCI) was the only political party permitted. In the 1980s, he spent huge sums in transforming his Baoulé home village Yamoussoukro into a new capital, although the former capital Abidjan has remained the country's economic hub.

Anti-corruption protests in 1990 forced the restoration of a multiparty democracy, and the death of Houphouët-Boigny in 1993 offered hopes for a new era.

Conflict and reconstruction

Houphouët-Boigny's successor, the PDCI's Henri Bédié, won the 1995 election—boycotted by two main parties—with a great majority, but longstanding ethnic and religious tensions emerged, and in 1999 he was overthrown in a military coup by Brigadier-General Robert Gueï. Military rule was short-lived, as a civilian president, Laurent Gbagbo, took office in 2000. Two years later, a failed coup ignited a civil war between rebels in the north and the government. Successive peace talks collapsed, until in 2007 a transitional government was installed with Guillaume Soro, a rebel leader, as acting prime minister. Presidential elections in 2010 were marred by violence and irregularities; the former prime minister Alassane Ouattara was declared winner, but the Constitutional Council overturned the result and handed back the presidency to Gbagbo.

This reignited the civil war, with Ouattara's forces seizing most of the country, leaving Gbagbo beleaguered in Abidjan. The intervention of a French-UN force led to Gbagbo's arrest and trial at The Hague (where he was acquitted in 2019). Ouattara, now president, enacted land reforms and changes to allow Côte d'Ivoire's many migrant workers to obtain citizenship, winning further terms in 2015 and 2020. Reconciling the civil war factions has proved a challenging part of this period of reconstruction.

Mali

The cradle of three powerful medieval empires, Mali became an important seat of Islamic learning, but controlling its vast desert hinterland and dealing with rising religious extremism have proved difficult challenges for its post-independence leaders.

Official name: Republic of Mali
Date of formation: September 22, 1960
Official language: French

Landlocked Mali is largely flat desert in the north and savanna in the south, with most of its fertile land lying along the banks of the Niger River. The largest ethnic group are the Bambara, with the Fulani, Mandingo, Dogon, and seminomadic Tuareg making up most of the rest. Gold mining, cotton production, pastoralism, and fishing are the main economic activities. Tourists, drawn by the ancient towns of Djenné and Timbuktu and the unique Dogon culture, provided much revenue until the 2012 Islamist coup made many areas inaccessible.

French is the official language, but Bambara is Mali's lingua franca, spoken by 80 percent of the population. Around 90 percent of Malians are Sunni Muslim, 5 percent Christian (mainly Roman Catholic), and the rest practice Indigenous religions, including that of the Dogon who venerate ancestral spirits.

Music is a large part of Mali's culture, ranging from ancient praise songs to Afropop, with musicians such as Salif Keita, Ali Farka Touré, and Oumou Sangaré spreading it around the world. Artists suffered from the ban on music after the 2012 Islamist takeover in northern Mali, but the music scene has recovered, at least in the capital, Bamako.

Trading empires

The first towns grew up along the middle Niger River, at Dia around 900 BCE and then at Djenné-Djenno from 250 BCE. Mali fell under the control of the Soninke kingdom of Wagadou (ancient Ghana) from the 7th century, but Wagadou's power waned and, in 1235, Sundiata Keita defeated the rival Sosso kingdom and established the Mali Empire. His armies secured the gold-producing area of Bambuk, and pushed as far north as Lac Débo and south to the Gambia.

Mali, under the rule of Keita's successors, the *mansas*, became rich, dominating the regional trade in gold and salt through their control of Timbuktu and Gao. One of them, Mansa Musa, made a pilgrimage to Mecca in 1324 that became legendary for the huge sums of gold he spent en route. His reputation attracted Muslim scholars and craftsmen, who built the great Djinguereber Mosque in Timbuktu. The already thriving trading hub developed into an emerging and soon key Islamic center of learning.

Mali's hegemony faltered under weaker *mansas*. In 1400, Gao broke away to become the capital of the new Songhai Empire. Under Sunni Ali (r. 1464–1492) and Askia the Great (r. 1493–1528) this became West Africa's most powerful state, although dynastic divisions weakened it after Askia's death and, in 1591, a Moroccan army captured Gao and Timbuktu, thus shattering Songhai's power.

The Moroccan conquest was followed by a period of anarchy. New Malian kingdoms gradually emerged, such as the Bambara state of Ségou in the early 18th century, controlled by Mamary Coulibaly. Under his rule, Ségou's military power grew, briefly even capturing Timbuktu.

New Muslim empires

The 19th century saw the rise of jihadist movements in Mali. By 1818, the Fulani Muslim teacher Sekou Amadou had

◁ Toumani Diabaté (left), one of Mali's finest griots, with one of his many 21-string *koras*

△ Market in front of Djenné's Great Mosque, a gigantic mud-brick structure replastered by its community once a year

defeated Ségou and founded the Masina Empire. Another Muslim cleric, the Tukulor al-Hajj Umar, conquered Masina in 1862. His death in a revolt by Masina two years later, divisions among his sons, and the intrusion of the French, who had established a post in western Mali in 1855, stemmed the Tukulor advance.

From the 1860s, the Mande leader Samory Touré (see p.217) preached a message of unity to oppose the European intruders. The Wassoulou Empire he created stretched from Guinea as far as modern Mali, Côte d'Ivoire, and Burkina Faso, but his growing power triggered the French to attack in 1882. Touré and his forces resisted vigorously, but the French took Timbuktu in 1894, and captured Touré in 1898.

Part of French West Africa from 1892, Mali saw little economic development beyond cotton cultivation (based on systematic forced labor), while cooperation with Muslim leaders, such as the Tijaniyyah brotherhood, blunted opposition to French rule.

Modern Mali

After years of debating the exact form of its relationship to France, Mali gained independence in 1960 with Modibo Keïta as its first president, initially as a federation with Senegal. Keïta strengthened ties with the USSR, implementing radical socialist economic policies, but opposition to these sparked a military coup in 1968 which brought Moussa Traoré to power. Civilian rule was restored in 1979, although Traoré remained president and his UDPM the only legal political party. He rebuilt relations with France and the United States, but demands for greater political freedom led to his fall and the election of Alpha Konaré as president in 1992.

A weakening economy, and the activities of Tuareg rebels in the north, contributed to the former general Amadou Toumani Touré being elected president in 2002. But the northern rebellion proved intractable and, in 2012, he was overthrown in a military coup. Tuareg rebels, allied with Islamist militias, declared an independent state of Azawad in the north and advanced as far as Timbuktu and Gao; it took military intervention by ECOWAS (see p.327) and France to push them back.

Presidential elections following a peace accord in June 2013 brought a new government under Ibrahim Boubacar Keïta, but Islamist violence persisted and the declining security situation led the army to arrest Keïta in 2020 and install a military junta.

Niger

Astride one of Africa's most ancient trade routes, Niger resisted colonization until 1922. The country won its independence in 1960, but has since struggled with a series of military coups and the rising influence of Islamism.

Official name: Republic of Niger
Date of formation: August 3, 1960
Official language: French

Landlocked Niger takes its name from Africa's third longest river, which runs through its southwest region, watering the fertile area of an otherwise largely arid country. Temperatures often reach 113°F (45°C) in the desert, where vegetation, such as date palms, is mainly confined to oases. The south harbors acacia, baobabs, and wildlife such as antelope, elephants, and warthogs.

Most of the population live in towns such as Agadez and the capital Niamey. Just over half are Hausa, with 20 percent Songhai, 10 percent Tuareg, and around 8 percent Fulani. The majority of Nigeriens are Muslim.

With an underdeveloped economy, Niger depends on subsistence agriculture, while uranium mining provides additional revenue.

Early and medieval Niger

Cattle-herding pastoralists lived in northern Niger as early as 7000 BCE, at a time when the Sahara was wetter. On a trade route from the Mediterranean to the Sahel, the ironworking Bura culture had appeared in the south by 300 CE, and the introduction of the camel in the early centuries CE enabled the development of the nomadic Tuareg society. At this time involved in prosperous trading thanks to the caravans passing through their area, the Tuareg would continue to influence Niger's later history.

By around 800 CE, Islam had entered Niger, spreading slowly among Tuareg peoples who lived dispersed until the foundation of the Tuareg kingdom of Takedda, to the west of the Aïr Massif, in the 14th century. Although conquered by the powerful Songhai Empire in 1500 (when the southeast of Niger fell to the sultanate of Kanem-Bornu, see pp.108–109), the kingdom regained its independence as the Sultanate of Agadez after Songhai's fall in 1591.

Niger between empires

Although Agadez was nominally under the control of the Ottoman Empire, in practice it—and other Tuareg confederations—acted independently. But warfare and a series of droughts, including the severe one of 1735–1736, led to a decline in the northern Tuareg's political power.

Usman dan Fodio's jihadist movement of 1804 (see p.194) pushed refugees into southern Niger, but otherwise outside influences remained muted until foreign explorers came searching for the source of the Niger River.

French colonization

France's initial forays into Niger were tentative. Only in 1899 did a concerted French campaign for conquest begin. The Tuareg resisted bitterly, aided by the harsh climate and landscape, and launched a major uprising against the imposition of French rule in 1915–1916, but by 1922 their power was broken. France imposed colonial administration, with Niger becoming part of French West Africa, governed from Dakar in Senegal. Niger received very little investment. Economic development came mainly in the form of the growth of cash crop cultivation among the Hausa of the south. Very few Nigeriens were able to gain an

△ Hausa horsemen in a parade celebrating Niger's independence

advanced education, however, and opposition did not coalesce until 1958, when trade union leader Djibo Bakary lobbied (unsuccessfully) for a vote against membership of the French Community, a newly formed organization intended to regulate the relationship between France and its remaining colonies.

Independent Niger

Bakary's cousin Hamani Diori of the Nigerien Progressive Party (PPN), who had argued for a vote to join the French Community, became president when Niger finally achieved independence in 1960. Diori outlawed other parties and ruled autocratically, and Niger became increasingly dogged by corruption. A series of Sahel-wide famines in the 1970s crystallized dissent, in part fueled by Diori's exclusion of Hausa and Fulani from positions of power. He was unseated in a 1974 coup led by Seyni Kountché, who headed a military regime until his death in 1987.

Modern-day challenges

Kountché's successor Ali Saibou gave way to calls for multiparty elections in 1993, in which the CDS candidate Mahamane Ousmane was elected president. But in 1995, in addition to an ongoing Tuareg rebellion, a tense standoff between Ousmane and his prime minister in the new coalition government, Hama Amadou of the opposition MNSD party, paralyzed politics; General Ibrahim Baré Maïnassara stepped in to overthrow Ousmane in 1996.

Instability continued as Baré Maïnassara was assassinated in 1999, but a civilian president, Mamadou Tandja, was elected the same year. Tandja won a second term in 2004, but faced a serious Tuareg uprising that began in 2007. At the end of his term in 2009, however, Tandja refused to step down and was arrested by the military, leading to another brief period of army rule before civilian government was restored by the 2011 general elections.

The new president, Mahamadou Issoufou, faced serious problems in the south, where the Nigerian Islamist group Boko Haram began to launch attacks. Islamist insurgency, poverty, and later also the effects of the COVID-19 pandemic dogged his attempt to break Niger's cycle of political instability. In 2021, Mohamed Bazoum of the PNDS party became the first president in Niger's history to enjoy a peaceful, democratic transfer of power, but he was ousted by a military coup in 2023.

△ Ruins of an ancient fort at Djado in Niger's Ténéré desert, in an area where traces of the earliest settlements date from around 7000 BCE

Burkina Faso

At the edge of the Sahara, the proudly named Burkina Faso ("land of the incorruptible") is vulnerable to desertification and Islamist groups.

Official name: Burkina Faso
Date of formation: August 5, 1960
Official language: French

Divided between a northern desert zone and a rockier southern part, Burkina Faso is relatively flat: Ténakourou, its highest mountain, is just 2,450 ft (747 m). Its three main rivers are the Black, White, and Red Volta, once featuring in the country's former colonial name, Upper Volta. Climatic variation is considerable, with rains often failing, creating severe food insecurity. Apart from agriculture, the economy depends on cotton production and mineral extraction of gold, manganese, and phosphates.

Around 63 percent of its population is Muslim and 23 percent is Christian. The Mossi peoples make up about half of the population, while other groups include the Gurma and Bwa.

Early kingdoms

Mossi peoples settled in the region by around 1200 CE. They established several kingdoms, including Tenkodogo, Yatenga, and Ouagadougou, the most powerful. Its *mogho naba* ("great lords") attacked the Songhai Empire in 1483 but were defeated, and suffered several Songhai invasions over the following century.

Later, the Gwiriko Empire, established around 1710 by Famagah Ouattara (brother of Sékou Ouattara, ruler of the Kong Empire in Côte d'Ivoire) became the region's dominant state.

French colonization

By the 1870s, during the reign of Ali Dyan, Gwiriko had lost most of its territory, leaving it unable to resist French advances that led to the declaration of a protectorate over the Yatenga Empire in 1895, and the rest of Burkina Faso in 1897. In 1915–1917, many thousands of rebels fought the French in the Volta-Bani war but, in 1932, France partitioned the colony between Côte d'Ivoire and French Sudan, hampering the development of further effective nationalist movements.

Independent Burkina Faso

As post-war France reorganized its colonies (see pp.234–235), Upper Volta became a single colony in 1947 and self-governing in 1958. It declared independence in 1960, with Maurice Yaméogo as president. He banned all parties save his own Voltaic Democratic Union, but he was overthrown in a 1966 coup by Sangoulé Lamizana, who remained as president until 1980.

◁ Carvings and friezes at the royal capital of the Kassena, in Tiébélé

△ Basi fish spirit mask of the Bwa people of central Burkina Faso

After widespread industrial unrest, Lamizana was deposed, but his replacement, Saye Zerbo, failed to restore calm, ultimately resulting in the seizure of power by Thomas Sankara's National Revolutionary Council in 1983.

Sankara renamed the country Burkina Faso and launched campaigns of infrastructure improvement, anti-corruption, mass vaccination, and women's rights. His popularity waned as the military's power grew and he was toppled in a 1987 coup by Blaise Compaoré. Programs were reversed, the economy stagnated, and opposition was ruthlessly suppressed, until protests against Compaoré's plans to extend his rule escalated and prompted his resignation in 2014.

The new military government of Isaac Zida struggled to restore order, and was itself overthrown in 2015, before international pressure led to free elections, won by Roch Kaboré. The new president faced a growing threat from Islamist militants, whose attacks left a million Burkinabé internally displaced. Although reelected in 2021, the following January he was overthrown in a military coup, the first of two that year that reflected the fragile state of the country's institutions.

Togo

Despite being home to a large number of ethnic groups, Togo has been dominated politically by the same family for more than 50 years.

Official name: Togolese Republic
Date of formation: April 27, 1960
Official language: French

A sliver of a country, just 93 miles (150 km) at its widest, Togo sits between far larger neighbors, Ghana to the west and Benin to the east. The tidal flats and beaches of its Atlantic coast encompass the capital, Lomé, also its main port for exporting the phosphates, coffee, cocoa, cotton, and groundnuts on which Togo's economy depends.

Togo has 40 different ethnic groups, of whom the Ewe in the south are the largest, at around a third of the population. Half of the inhabitants are Christian, a third practice Indigenous religions, and the rest are Muslim.

European disruption

Togo's main ethnic groups, the Ewe, Mina, and Gun, arrived in the region between the 11th and 16th centuries, but state formation was hampered by the ravages of centuries of slave trade following the arrival of the Portuguese in the late 15th century.

In 1884, several coastal chiefs signed treaties with the German explorer Gustav Nachtigal, which led to a German protectorate in 1885. The Germans established Lomé in 1897; their plantations were largely in private hands and development minimal. In 1914, Togo became a World War I battle scene, as France and Britain invaded from their neighboring colonies, using locally recruited soldiers. As a result of Germany's defeat in the war, without local input, Togo was divided between Britain and France under League of Nations mandates in 1922.

Independent Togo

In 1960, the part of Togo then called French Togoland claimed independence, with Sylvanus Olympio as its first president. Relations were difficult with Ghana, which had merged with British Togoland in 1956 before its independence and wanted to absorb the rest of Togo, and the economy suffered from Olympio's austerity policies. He was killed in a 1963 coup led by Gnassingbé Eyadéma, who later assumed the presidency and, in 1969, banned all political parties except the Togolese People's Rally (RPT).

Elections were not held again until 1979; Eyadéma won with great majority. A failed coup in 1986 and riots in Lomé in 1991 were the only significant threats to his regime until failed attacks by Ghanaian-based dissidents in 1993 and 1994. He died in 2005, and was replaced by his son Fauré, whose election as president and reelection in 2007 and 2015 were marred by fraud allegations. In power since 1967, the Gnassingbé Eyadémas are Africa's longest-lasting political dynasty.

△ Mud-brick tower house (*takienta*) in Togo's Koutammakou region

Ghana

With a history strongly influenced by the Akan people, modern Ghana—the first country in West Africa to achieve independence—enjoys a strong, diversified economy and a track record of peaceful democratic transitions of power.

Official name: Republic of Ghana
Date of formation: March 6, 1957
Official language: English

▷ A wooden *Akua Ba*, a figurine traditionally carried by Akan women hoping to conceive a child

Home to a varied landscape, ranging from coastal mangrove forest to inland tropical rainforest and northern savanna, Ghana also has a large riverine system. The dominant rivers are the Black Volta, White Volta, and Oti, interrupted by the vast artificial Lake Volta and the Akosombo dam, built in the 1960s. Logging has much reduced Ghana's forest cover. With a large service sector, a stable manufacturing base that includes ship construction, and rich oil, diamond, and gold deposits, Ghana has the third highest GDP in West Africa.

The largest ethnic group in Ghana—West Africa's second most populous nation—are the Akan (including the Asante and Fante), making up about 48 percent of the population, followed by the Mole-Dagbani and Ewe. About 60 percent are Christian and a fifth Muslim.

Early states

Although Ghana takes its name from the ancient empire that lay to the north, in modern Mali and Mauritania, its first known states, such as Dagomba and Mamprusi, emerged as Akan peoples arrived from the north around the 13th century. A century or two later, the Ga and Ewe, coming from modern Nigeria, founded states in the southeast; and then, in the early 17th century, the Mande set up the kingdom of Gonja in the center. As the terminus of trans-Saharan trade routes, the northern Ghanaian states came into contact with Mande and Hausa traders, but it was the arrival of the Portuguese along the coast in 1471 that had far more profound effects.

European intrusions

At first in search of gold, in 1482 the Portuguese built a fortress at Elmina Castle on what became known as the Gold Coast, and from it conducted a growing trade in enslaved people. By the mid-18th century, there were 40 Dutch, British, Danish, and Portuguese slaving forts.

This destructive activity also brought wealth to some local peoples, who had got involved. New kingdoms arose: the short-lived Akwamu Kingdom (1600–1730) and the Asante Kingdom in the central forest, founded by *Asantehene* (King) Osei Tutu, who had conquered much of the central and northern Akan states before he died in 1717.

△ Worshippers leaving the 15th-century mud-brick mosque at Larabanga, northwest Ghana

The outlawing of the slave trade in the British Empire in 1807 temporarily reduced European interference in the region, but the Asante expansion to the south, including their conquest of the southern Fan in 1806, led to a series of wars between the Asante and the British, starting in 1823. After the third, in 1874, the British declared the Gold Coast a protectorate. In 1896, they forced the *asantehene* to sign a treaty after British artillery bombarded the royal capital, Kumasi.

Until 1952, Britain ruled Ghana as a crown colony consisting of three territories: the Gold Coast, the Northern Territories, and Asante. The Gold Coast had a degree of self-government, with a legislative council set up in 1850. Cocoa bean cultivation spurred economic development; by the 1950s, the Gold Coast provided half the world's supply.

Independence

Pressure for independence grew in the 1940s and discontent intensified. When British troops shot at peacefully protesting Ghanaian World War II veterans in 1948, it led to riots. Among the campaigners was Kwame Nkrumah, who founded the Convention People's Party (CPP) in 1949. In the 1951 legislative elections, the CPP won almost all the seats. Despite local political unrest, they won again in 1956, and on March 6, 1957, Ghana achieved independence, the first country in West Africa to do so (see pp.240–241). In 1960, Prime Minister Nkrumah declared Ghana a republic. Now president, he sought rapid industrialization and the modernization of its educational system and, always a convinced Pan-Africanist, supported the liberation struggles of other African nations. But his rule became more autocratic and his reforms accrued crushing debts. In 1966, he was overthrown in a coup by Joseph Ankrah.

The debts and dependence on volatile cocoa prices undermined Ankrah's government and those that followed. In 1979, junior officers led by Jerry Rawlings seized power. After a brief return of democracy in 1981, Rawlings mounted a second coup, seeking to reform Ghana's politics and restructure its economy. He did so with a radical anti-inflationary drive, devaluing the currency and privatizing most state-owned companies. His free-market policies drove economic growth, but left many in poverty.

21st-century Ghana

Rawlings stood down in 2001, when John Kufuor won the election in the first peaceful democratic transfer of power since 1957. Kufuor, who pushed through health and education reforms, stepped down in 2009, peacefully succeeded by John Atta Mills and then John Mahama. In 2017, Nana Akufo-Addo was elected president, and Ghana confirmed its status as one of Africa's most stable democracies.

Benin

Cradle of the powerful Kingdom of Dahomey, Benin suffered severely from the effects of the Atlantic slave trade, but since independence it has maintained its identity and, despite enormous challenges, remained broadly democratic.

Official name: Republic of Benin
Date of formation: August 1, 1960
Official language: French

Situated in the Dahomey Gap, a transitional zone between the Central African rainforests and those of West Africa, Benin is relatively dry. The country's very narrow coastline—with Cotonou the main port—dominates its economic life, while subsistence agriculture (supplemented by cultivation of oil palms) is predominant in the fertile inland plateaus.

The Fon are two-fifths of the population, with the Aja and Mina around 15 percent, largely on the coast; the Yoruba, mainly in the southeast, an eighth; and the Bariba about a tenth. About half the population is Christian, around 30 percent Muslim, and 15 percent practice one of many local religions.

Benin derives its modern name from the Bight of Benin along which its coastline lies, not from the medieval kingdom of Benin (within modern Nigeria, see pp.128–129).

Kingdom of Dahomey

Before the 17th century, Benin was the site of a number of small kingdoms: Allada and Whydah in the south, and the Bariba kingdom of Nikki in the north, while parts of the east were occupied by the Oyo Empire (which lay largely in Nigeria, see pp.112–113). The Portuguese arrived along the Atlantic coast in 1471, and by the mid-16th century they (later joined by Dutch, English, and French merchants) were trading in enslaved Africans, mainly through the Kingdom of Ouidah. The Fon state of Dahomey (or Abomey), founded around 1600, gradually came to dominate all of these West African kingdoms.

Dahomey's expansion began under Wegebadja (c. 1645–1685), and under Agaja (r. 1708–1740), it conquered Allada (which became the new capital) and Ouidah. Although Dahomey became a tributary of Oyo in 1730, Agaja instituted an administrative apparatus with an annual tax-gathering ceremony (the "Annual Customs") in the capital.

Dahomey became a significant participant in the Atlantic slave trade, supplying around a fifth of all enslaved people. It reached

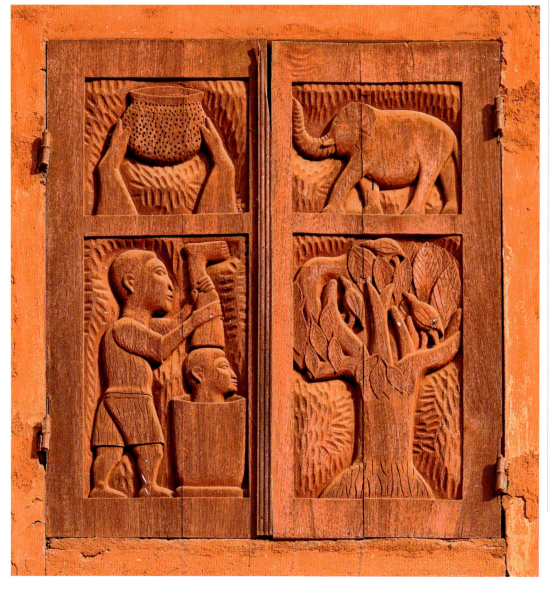

◁ Carved wooden shutters from the royal palace of Ghezo's son and successor, King Glele (r. 1858–1889)

△ Bas-relief of a lion from the palace of the Dahomean king Glele

the height of its power under King Ghezo (r. 1818–1858), whose standing army—including the *Mino* (meaning "our mothers"), a female regiment of frontline soldiers—provided a military advantage. He defeated Oyo in 1823, releasing Dahomey from its tributary status, but his attempts to expand east were checked by the state of Abeokuta (in modern Nigeria) in 1851 and 1864.

Treaties and colonization

Growing European interference, as well as commercial rivalry between local kingdoms, put pressure on Dahomey's rulers. In 1842, the French reoccupied a fort they had built at Ouidah in 1671 but later abandoned and, in 1851, France and Dahomey signed a treaty allowing French commercial activities in the area. Meanwhile, the trade in enslaved people had continued, with Brazil still a major player. In 1852, a British naval blockade to prevent further slave trade forced another treaty on Ghezo, making him turn to the production of palm oil as an alternative source of revenue.

During the reign of King Glele (r. 1858–1889), France established a protectorate over the Porto-Novo region in 1882. Glele's son, King Behanzin, who came to the throne in 1889, resisted an earlier agreement to hand over the port of Cotonou to France and fought hard to prevent further French takeovers. Under his rule, Dahomean raids on the French protectorates along the coast led to the Franco-Dahomean Wars in 1890 and 1892–1894, followed by the French occupation of Dahomey. Although the French at first ruled through a puppet king, in 1900 they deposed him, too, to rule Dahomey directly (from 1904 as part of French West Africa). The French authorities developed Cotonou's port and constructed sections of railroad; otherwise, the colonized area remained underdeveloped.

Independence and beyond

Dahomey became an overseas territory in 1946 and, taking part in the general transition toward independence in French West Africa through activism and pressure, in 1958 it became the self-governing Republic of Dahomey. It went on to gain full independence in 1960, with Hubert Maga as its first president.

Dahomey's unity was at risk from the emergence of regional parties in Porto-Novo, Abomey, and northern Dahomey, and economic difficulties destabilized the country. Six coups between 1963 and 1972 brought short-lived military regimes, with brief periods of civilian governments. In 1972, Major Mathieu Kérékou seized power and instituted radical communist reforms, nationalizing key industries and imposing state planning. In 1975, he renamed the country the People's Republic of Benin.

Kérékou's People's Revolutionary Party of Benin monopolized power until 1990, when he conceded a new constitution. Multiparty elections took place the following year. Dropping "People's" from Benin's official name, the victor, Nicéphore Soglo, reversed his predecessor's policy, reining in spending, but the resulting economic hardship led to his defeat in the 1996 elections and the return of Kérékou. Labor protests, as well as allegations of corruption and vote-rigging, dogged Kérékou's second and third terms. In 2006, the independent candidate Thomas Boni Yayi, focusing on economic development, anti-corruption, and improved access to education for women, was victorious.

Coup attempts—including by a former ally, Patrice Talon—and allegations that he planned, unconstitutionally, for a third term sullied Yayi's reputation. Fiercely fought elections in 2016 brought Talon to the presidency, a victory he repeated in 2021 with an 86 percent vote.

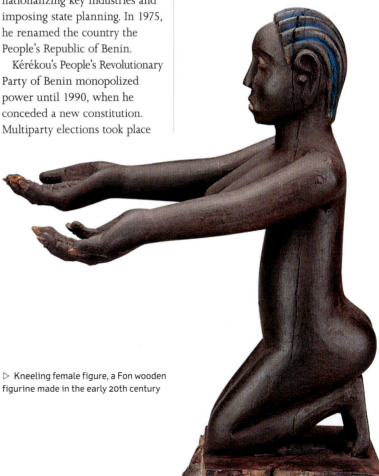

▷ Kneeling female figure, a Fon wooden figurine made in the early 20th century

Nigeria

Africa's most populous country and largest economy gave birth to powerful kingdoms, and since independence has navigated civil war, regional divisions, religious tensions, and periods of military rule to emerge as a vibrant democracy.

Official name: Federal Republic of Nigeria
Date of formation: October 1, 1963
Official language: English

The 36 states of the Federal Republic of Nigeria encompass over 250 ethnic groups; largest are the Yoruba of the southwest and the Igbo in the southeast (each about 20 percent) and the Hausa and Fulani (around 30 percent in total) in the north. The population is more or less equally divided between Muslims, who are predominant in the north, and Christians, a majority in the south, with Indigenous religions also being practiced. Now Africa's largest economy, Nigeria has rich oil fields and a growing financial sector, and is a major producer of oil, pharmaceuticals, and fertilizers.

Rise of kingdoms

Nigeria's first complex culture, the Nok, which flourished between 1500 BCE and 1 BCE on the Jos Plateau, produced striking terra-cotta figures (see pp.60–61). Around 900 CE, the Igbo-Ukwu culture of south-central Nigeria created exquisite bronzes, trading as far afield as Egypt. The northeast formed part of the Kingdom of Kanem-Bornu (see pp.108–109) from the 12th century; descendants of the sultans of Bornu are still hereditary rulers of the state of that name. The Hausa formed kingdoms such as Daura, Katsina, Kano, and Kebbi by the 14th century, heavily influenced by Islam, which spread southward through the trans-Saharan trade routes.

In the 11th century, the city-state of Ife (see pp.110–111) developed among the Yoruba to the south and west. Based around a divination center at Ife, it produced fine terra-cottas. From the 15th century, the Kingdom of Oyo (see pp.112–113) in the northern savanna controlled trade in salt, copper, and textiles, by the 17th century deploying a force of skilled cavalry through which it dominated Yorubaland.

The most powerful of the early Nigerian kingdoms was Benin in the southeast (see pp.128–129). Ruled by a line of *obas* from the late 12th century, it reached its largest extent under *Oba* Ewuare the Great (r. 1440–1473), who transformed his kingdom from a city-state to a great empire, its capital defended by a massive series of earthworks

Foreign trade

The Benin Empire produced a large number of striking bronzes, which adorned the palace of the *obas*, portraying important events in history. Some depict outsiders, the Portuguese, who began to trade with Benin and other states from the mid-15th century. By the 17th and 18th centuries, the

◁ A mask for the Owu masquerade, an Igbo New Year festival

△ The National Mosque in Nigeria's capital, Abuja, built in 1984

British and French, too, became involved in trafficking enslaved people here, with city-states in the delta such as Akwa Akpa (Calabar), founded in 1786, and the inland Igbo and Yoruba kingdoms supplying the trade with captives. By the early 19th century, these kingdoms were in decline, supplanted by others such as the Sokoto Caliphate, established in 1804 by Usman dan Fodio, a religious teacher who sought to purge Islam of accretions from local Hausa practices. By his death in 1817, Sokoto was the most powerful state south of the Sahara.

The British in Nigeria

The ban of the slave trade in the British Empire in 1807 led to a new kind of British involvement in Nigeria. The collapse of Oyo and a series of Yoruba wars (only ending in 1886) weakened local power and, in 1861, the British conquered Lagos. After a period of company rule by the Royal Niger Company, in 1900 Britain annexed the region as the Southern Nigeria and Northern Nigeria Protectorates. Resistance was strongest in the north, where the Sokoto Caliphate held out until its defeat in 1903. The two protectorates were united as a single colony in 1914, but Britain invested more in developing Southern Nigeria, leading to economic inequalities between the two areas that persist today.

Independence

As independence demands grew, Herbert Macaulay established the Nigerian National Democratic Party in 1923. In 1944, he and Nnamdi Azikiwe formed the National Council of Nigeria and the Cameroons, beginning a campaign that was partly stalled by the north's fears of southern domination. Among other key activists was Funmilayo Ransome-Kuti, who also campaigned for women's rights.

Nigeria achieved independence in 1960, was joined by the north of the former Cameroons in 1961, and became a republic with Azikiwe as president in 1963. But divisions between various regions of the country resulted in a series of military coups and countercoups. In 1967, civil war broke out as Odumegwu Ojukwu declared the independence of the Eastern region as the Republic of Biafra. An initial Biafran advance on Lagos was checked and, in 1970, Nigerian government forces completed Biafra's reconquest.

Contemporary Nigeria

General Yakubu Gowon, the federal president, ably reconciled the two sides, and a boom from newly discovered oil helped the

△ Biafran soldiers sit atop a destroyed Nigerian government military vehicle during the civil war, 1968

country's reconstruction. But in 1975, he was overthrown and eventually replaced by Lt-General Olusegun Obasanjo, who later oversaw a return to civilian rule. This ended in 1983, when Major General Muhammad Buhari seized power, to be overthrown by General Ibrahim Babangida two years later. Despite promises of reform, presidential elections were delayed until 1993, and initially annulled by Babangida.

Amid the rising chaos, Defense Minister Sani Abacha took power, dissolved parliament, and banned political parties. His sudden death in 1998 was followed by elections, which Obasanjo won. Now a civilian president, of the People's Democratic Party (PDP), he faced spiraling ethnic conflict and religious tensions, and a growing protest movement in the Niger Delta against the activities of oil companies. With Obasanjo barred from serving a third term, the 2007 elections were won by the PDP's Umaru Yar'Adua, whose illness led to his replacement by Goodluck Jonathan in 2010. Jonathan faced major challenges, such as a rising wave of attacks by Boko Haram. This Islamist movement, targeting churches, police barracks, and schools, was behind the 2014 mass kidnapping of schoolgirls in Chibok.

Jonathan lost the 2015 election to Muhammadu Buhari, now the leader of the All Progressives Congress (APC), in the first peaceful transfer of power from a defeated incumbent. Buhari had to contend with declining oil revenues and a serious recession, continued Boko Haram attacks, and the impact of COVID-19. Having served two terms, he could not stand in the 2023 elections, which the APC's Bola Tinubu won after a tightly fought contest.

Central Africa

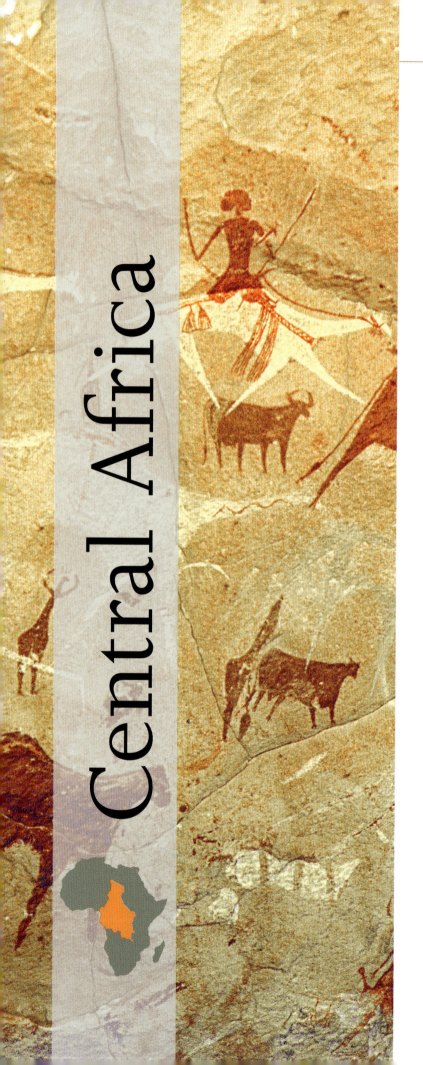

◁ Cave paintings in Chad's Ennedi Massif, one of many prehistoric sites in Central Africa

Cameroon

Cameroon's former division between different colonial powers has led to entrenched problems and separatist struggles, not resolved by its authoritarian leaders—all this endangering the progress of a country whose economic record has long been good.

Official name: Republic of Cameroon
Date of formation: January 1, 1960
Official languages: French, English

Famous for its huge geographical diversity, Cameroon's landscape encompasses an Atlantic coastline lined with vast mangrove forests around river estuaries, mountain ranges that include the volcanic Mount Cameroon, waterfalls, rainforest, savanna, and desert.

More than 200 ethnic groups live here, of whom the Bamileke (24 percent) and the Beti (21 percent) are the most numerous. About half of the population is Christian, with a fifth Muslim, and the same proportion practicing Indigenous faiths.

The majority of Cameroonians are engaged in subsistence agriculture, with cocoa, coffee, cotton, and bananas among the most important cash crops, and oil also providing export income. After a dip in 1987–1994, it has seen continued economic growth.

Early Cameroon

Northern Cameroon was first settled by humans around 30,000 years ago, while evidence of settlement in the south begins about 7,000 years ago, probably by ancestors of the Baka people.

▷ Ceremonial mask from the Bamileke people of southwestern Cameroon, made of cotton, glass beads, leather, and wood

By around 1000 BCE, Bantu-speakers had moved east from their probable homeland in the Nigerian-Cameroonian border highlands, displacing the Baka.

The first complex culture in Cameroon was the Sao, in the northeast around the basin of Lake Chad. They flourished in the late 1st millennium BCE and left intricately crafted terra-cotta statues. Between the 11th and 13th centuries CE, the influential Kanem-Bornu Empire (see pp.108–109) controlled part of northern Cameroon, bringing Islam into the area for the first time. Further Islamic influence came with Fulani pastoralists, who entered northern Cameroon in the 18th century. Their leader Modibo Adama, with the blessing of Usman dan Fodio (see p.194), fought a jihad against non-Muslim peoples. He founded the Adamawa Emirate, which later joined dan Fodio's Sokoto Caliphate.

Meanwhile, the south developed differently, and was a realm of *fons* or small chieftainships when the Portuguese arrived on the coast in 1472. The region became a major source of enslaved people in the transatlantic slave trade, many provided by inland kingdoms such as Bamum. The trade began to decline in the early 19th century, when Europeans turned to the establishment of rubber and palm oil plantations.

Colonial rule

Germany preempted growing British interest in Cameroon when the explorer Gustav Nachtigal signed protectorate treaties with local Duala leaders in 1884. The Germans set up an administration at Yaoundé and gradually pushed their control inland, fighting conflicts such as the Adamawa Wars (1899–1907) against the states of the north.

△ The 262-ft- (80-m-) high Ekom-Nkam waterfalls, one of Cameroon's most spectacular natural features

They established plantations and built railroads to bring tropical products to the coast, imposing harsh forced labor conditions that led to periodic rebellions. Germany's control ended after World War I, when its African territories, which had all seen battles, were reassigned by League of Nations mandates, in the case of Cameroon to France (the east) and Britain (the west).

Early independence

"French" Cameroon gained independence in 1960 after a long, often brutally repressed, campaign by the Cameroon People's Union (UPC), led by Ruben Um Nyobe, although its first president, Ahmadou Ahidjo, came from the Cameroon Union (UC). The northern part of "British" Cameroon voted in a plebiscite the following year to join Nigeria, while the south joined the now independent Cameroon in a federal structure. Ahidjo's rule became increasingly authoritarian, as he banned all opposition parties, leading to the Bamileke War, a rebellion by former UPC leaders, which was only put down in 1971.

Economically, Ahidjo was liberal, encouraging private investment, while the discovery of oil reserves in the 1970s provided an economic boost.

Cameroon under Biya

Ahidjo resigned in 1982 and was replaced by Paul Biya, his prime minister since 1975. Biya's initial attempt to continue to rule informally led, in 1984, to an uprising by the elite Republican Guard, which he put down. He retained the one-party state, leading to new tensions, as the Anglophone regions complained they were being marginalized. In 1990, Biya legalized opposition parties, but his CPDM party's near-loss of multiparty elections in 1992 brought a halt to reform. Cameroon soon faced a further challenge when Nigeria invaded the disputed oil-rich Bakassi Peninsula in 1993, where fighting continued for two years. Finally, in 2002, the International Court of Justice confirmed Cameroon's ownership of the area, which Nigeria eventually handed over in 2006.

In 2008, Biya announced he would remove presidential term limits, allowing him to stay in office; it led to violent protests and strikes. He was reelected in 2011, in his new term facing rising violence from border incursions by Boko Haram, Nigeria's militant Islamist group.

Tensions also rose with the Anglophone regions, which erupted in a series of protests in 2015, leading to harsh measures to repress the unrest. By 2017, armed separatists had declared the independent state of Ambazonia, as the struggle escalated into a civil war. Biya, though reelected in 2018, faced a fragile constitutional order in danger of unraveling.

Chad

Chad's precolonial kingdoms prospered from the trans-Saharan trade, but since independence its governments have struggled to contain insurgencies fueled by north-south ethnic and religious divisions and interference from its neighbors.

Official name: Republic of Chad
Date of formation: August 11, 1960
Official languages: Arabic, French

Africa's fifth largest country, Chad is a flat basin lined by mountains to the south and northeast. The north is largely desert, while most people live in the southern half, where cotton-growing and cattle-rearing provide subsistence.

Chad's many ethnic groups speak more than 100 languages. The Sara people are predominant in the south; a diverse population that includes Bagirmi, Kanuri, Fulani, Hausa, and Arabs inhabits the central region; and Toubou nomads live in the north. About 55 percent of Chadians are Muslim and 45 percent Christian.

Prehistoric Chad

Chad is one of the cradles of humanity: a 6- to 7-million-year-old skull of *Sahelanthropus tchadensis*, an early hominin, was discovered in northern Chad. By the 7th millennium BCE, this area was settled by hunter-gatherers who left thousands of cave paintings depicting game such as antelope, at a time when the Sahara was much wetter than today.

Early kingdoms

The first organized state was that of the Sao, from the 6th century BCE. The Sao built walled cities and produced sophisticated bronze statuary. By 900 CE, the Kanem state had arisen northeast of Lake Chad, growing rich from its control of trans-Saharan trade routes. Ruled from the late 11th century by *mais* (kings) of the Sayfawa dynasty who converted to Islam, Kanem reached its height under *Mai* Dunama Dabbalemi (ruled c. 1220–1259).

A series of weak *mais* and repeated attacks by Bulala people from the east forced the Kanem court to move on to Bornu, west of Lake Chad, around 1400. From there, able rulers such as Idris Alawma (r. 1571–1603) restored the empire's fortunes. But in 1808, Fulani warriors from Nigeria attacked Kanem-Bornu, capturing the capital. The empire never recovered, and the Sayfawa dynasty died out in 1846.

Southeast of Kanem-Bornu, the Bagirmi Kingdom was founded around 1520, converting to Islam under Sultan Abdullah about 1600. It prospered from the slave trade, but suffered depredations from Kanem-Bornu to the west and the Ouaddai Kingdom to the east. Founded about 1630, Ouaddai had broken away from the Sultanate of Darfur (see p.311) in the 1790s, taking control of a large share of the trans-Saharan trade under Muhammad Sabun (r. 1804–1815).

The French colonial period

All three kingdoms fell between 1883 and 1893, to the Sudanese warlord Rabih az-Zubayr, and then to the French, who sent in a series of military expeditions from 1898, which culminated in az-Zubayr's defeat and death at the Battle of Kousséri in 1900. Ouaddai resurged, holding out against the French until 1912, and other uprisings took place until 1917, by which time France controlled all of Chad.

Chad was initially governed from Brazzaville as part of French Equatorial Africa, and was not constituted as a standalone colony until 1920, when a governor moved in at Fort Lamy (N'Djamena). Investment in the colony was almost nonexistent save for cotton cultivation in the south, and control of the northern regions was intermittent.

Independence

In the 1950s, greater self-rule and increased political activity led to Chad's independence in 1960, under François Tombalbaye, a southern trade unionist. But longstanding tensions between the Muslim north and Christian

△ Prehistoric rock art from Manda Guili in Chad's Ennedi Massif

△ The sultan of Bagirmi returning home to his capital, Massenya, depicted in a 19th-century print

south ignited in 1961 when he joined most political parties into one and dissolved the National Assembly. Resentment prompted two opposition movements, the FNT in the east and FROLINAT in the north, to launch a civil war from 1966. Unable to control the insurgencies—as FROLINAT received aid from Muammar Qaddafi's regime in Libya—Tombalbaye called in French assistance before pivoting to sign a friendship treaty with Libya.

Tombalbaye was killed during a 1975 military coup that installed Félix Malloum, who was in turn replaced by a Libyan-backed regime under Goukouni Oueddei in 1979. A French-supported rebel group, the FAN, led by Hissène Habré, deposed Oueddei three years later. The Libyans occupied the disputed Aouzou strip on the border and much of northern Chad by 1983, before Habré drove them out with French and US support. Violent purges of opposition figures sapped support for his government and, in 1989, the former military adviser Idriss Déby launched a rebellion, taking N'Djamena the following year after Habré fled.

The Déby regimes

Déby faced two coup attempts, and a series of new rebel groups, but in 1996 he won multiparty elections marred by allegations of fraud. A peace deal with FARF and MDD rebels broke down in 1998, however, and a new group, the MDJT, appeared in the far northwestern region of Tibesti. Further instability was injected into Chad by refugees fleeing the crisis in Darfur in neighboring Sudan (see p.311).

Déby's brutal suppression of the opposition led to coup attempts in 2004 and 2006 and to new rebel offensives, one reaching the outskirts of N'Djamena, Chad's capital, in 2008. Déby went on to win heavily managed elections, but faced growing threats from Islamist militant groups, such as Boko Haram, and a resurgence in violence in the north, where CCMSR rebels began attacks in 2018. A new constitution, passed in the same year, would have permitted Déby to remain in power until 2033. He duly won presidential elections in April 2021, but just a day later it was announced that he had died in fighting with the northern rebels.

The military nominated Déby's son Mahamat Idriss Déby Itno as interim president. He launched a dialogue initiative with the rebels to try to bring peace to a country scarred by decades of civil war. But presidential elections were postponed and many issues—such as food insecurity and the ever-increasing number of Darfur refugees—remain unresolved.

Central African Republic

One of Africa's poorest countries despite its mineral wealth, and historically encroached on by enslavers, the Central African Republic has experienced coups, political instability, and civil wars that have, so far, prevented steady progress.

Official name: Central African Republic
Date of formation: August 13, 1960
Official languages: French, Sango

◁ Emperor Jean-Bédel Bokassa at his coronation in December 1977, seated on an eagle-shaped bronze throne

Formed of a large undulating plateau between the basins of Lake Chad and Congo River, the Central African Republic (CAR) is cut through by many rivers, including the Ubangi in the south, where the capital Bangui lies and most of the population resides. Largely treeless savanna in the north and tropical rainforest in the south harbor varied wildlife, from leopards and gorillas to forest elephants, hippos, and rare bongo antelope.

The country is home to around 80 ethnic groups, of which the most numerous are the Baya at 33 percent and the Banda at 27 percent. Christians make up about four-fifths of the population, with around an eighth practicing Indigenous religions. Agriculture is the largest economic sector, though the CAR possesses huge mineral resources, notably diamond, gold, and uranium.

Settlers and raiders

The earliest inhabitants were hunter-gatherers forced south by the desertification of the Sahara around 8000 BCE. By the mid-1st millennium BCE, they had begun farming and raised imposing megaliths in the Bouar region.

Few outsiders ventured far into the region until Muslim enslavers began raiding the interior in the 17th century. They partnered with the Bobangi people who used the Ubangi River to traffic enslaved people to the Atlantic coast. States dependent on the trans-Saharan slave trade formed in the 19th century; one such was Dar al-Kuti, which, however, became destabilized by the influx of arms as well as depopulation in the east, and collapsed in 1912.

The colonial era

Following the Berlin Conference in 1884–1885, France made a claim to the CAR, establishing a post at Bangui, the future capital, in 1889. Rabih az-Zubayr—a Sudanese warlord active in the slave trade, who had fled Sudan to establish an empire east of the Ubangi—confronted them. His death in battle against the French in 1900 left France in control of what was organized in 1903 as the colony of Ubangi-Shari.

Apart from levying taxes and forced labor, France left the CAR in the hands of private companies, leading to appalling abuses, while local rulers continued to carry out slaving raids. Western Ubangi-Shari was ceded to Germany in 1911, but reannexed by France after World War I, when some limited investment was made in infrastructure such as roads.

Independence and beyond

Resistance to colonial rule came in the large-scale Kongo-Wara rebellion in 1928, which went on for three years before ending in defeat, and through nationalist movements such as the former priest Barthélemy Boganda's Social Evolution Movement of Black Africa (MESAN). Boganda died in 1959, a year before independence, when politician David Dacko became the CAR's first president. Dacko outlawed all political parties except MESAN, and sought close relations with communist China, but an economic crisis in 1965 led to his deposition by the army-chief Jean-Bédel Bokassa.

The new president suspended the constitution and parliament, suppressing all opposition, in a regime that became increasingly autocratic and characterized by human rights abuse. In 1972,

△ A mural in the capital Bangui, encouraging national unity

Bokassa declared himself as president for life, and in 1976 emperor, followed by a costly coronation a year later; the CAR changed its name to the Central African Empire. But unrest grew. In 1979, following massacres of protesting students and other civilians, France sent in troops to oust Bokassa and reinstall Dacko, and the name reverted to CAR.

Dacko had many enemies and, in 1981, was toppled in a coup led by André Kolingba. The new president again suspended the constitution and only introduced free elections in 1993, which he lost to Ange-Félix Patassé, the country's first democratically elected president. With the CAR nearly bankrupt, rising public discontent, and facing three military coups, Patassé struggled to enact any reforms, despite the 1997 Bangui Accords signed with the opposition to devise solutions to the nation's problems.

Patassé was ousted in a coup in 2003 by François Bozizé, whose suspension of the constitution sparked the CAR Bush War as political opponents turned to arms. Peace agreements between 2007 and 2012 integrated various rebel movements into the army and political process, but faltered after Bozizé's reelection in 2011, widely seen as fraudulent.

In 2012, a new rebel front, the Séléka, emerged. After seizing Bangui in 2013, they established a transitional government. But the violence inflicted on the mainly Christian population in the south, by the largely Muslim Séléka rebels, soon led to the formation of Anti-balaka militias, and a near complete breakdown of order. Peacekeeping forces of the African Union and the UN stabilized the situation and, in 2016, Faustin-Archange Touadéra was voted president in bitterly contested elections. One faction of Séléka declared independence in the north, and other militias fought for control of the rest, while Russian Wagner group mercenaries were recruited for presidential protection in 2018. Touadéra was reelected in 2020, but he faced huge challenges in reasserting government control, let alone in beginning the long process of rebuilding the CAR's fragile society and economy.

▷ The prehistoric megaliths at Bouar, depicted on a 1967 postage stamp

Equatorial Guinea

Africa's only Spanish-speaking state has seen autocratic rule since independence, but its oil reserves could bring economic development.

Official name: Republic of Equatorial Guinea
Date of formation: October 12, 1968
Official languages: Spanish, French, Portuguese

A tropical country, Equatorial Guinea is split between a few small volcanic islands in the Gulf of Guinea—including Bioko with the capital, Malabo, and Annobón—and the mainland Río Muni region. The Fang make up 86 percent of the population, and Christianity is the main religion. Previously dependent on cocoa, coffee, and timber exports, from 1996 the nation has seen huge oil revenues, little of which have benefited its people.

Becoming a nation

Bantu-speaking peoples arrived in the region in the 12th–13th centuries. In 1474, the Portuguese claimed Bioko (calling it Fernando Pó) and Annobón. The Spanish, acquiring the mainland and islands in 1778, used them mostly as a conduit for their slave-trading to the Americas. Administered by the British from 1827 as a base for their anti-slave trade patrols, Bioko—now with a diverse population of local Bantu-speakers, formerly enslaved people from overseas, and Krio from Sierra Leone—was returned to Spain in 1843. Focusing on the mainland, the Spanish established cocoa plantations and encouraged migration from Spain, but made little effort to further develop the area economically.

With nationalism growing, in 1963 Equatorial Guinea achieved limited autonomy, and became independent in 1968, electing Francisco Macías Nguema as its president. Rapidly turning autocratic, in 1971 Macías instituted a one-party state and made himself president for life in 1972. Press was censored and foreign travel forbidden, schools closed, and the economy declined catastrophically, while thousands of his opponents were executed.

Macías was ousted in 1979 by his nephew Teodoro Obiang Nguema Mbasogo. The economy stabilized, but Obiang's regime has been repressive. He has faced allegations of severe human rights abuses and, despite multiparty elections being held since 1993, no opposition candidates have managed to successfully challenge his near-total majority results. After a 2004 failed coup attempt involving British mercenaries, a new constitution in 2011 further cemented his power, and he was reelected in 2016 and 2022.

São Tomé e Príncipe

The second-smallest state in Africa, though short of natural resources, is one of the continent's most stable democracies.

Official name: Democratic Republic of São Tomé e Príncipe
Date of formation: July 12, 1975
Official language: Portuguese

Consisting of two Atlantic islands, São Tomé (where the capital is located) and Príncipe, the country is home to three main ethnic groups: Mestiços (descendants of Portuguese colonists and enslaved Africans); Angolares (whose enslaved African ancestors were trafficked and shipwrecked here); and Forros (descendants of formerly enslaved people). Around 80 percent of the population are Roman Catholic. The economy depends mainly on agriculture, including cocoa, and fishing.

Island history

In 1470, Portuguese ships landed on the islands, which by the 16th century had become the world's largest sugar producer, their plantations worked by enslaved Africans taken here from the mainland. In the 19th century, coffee and cocoa became the key crops, and forced labor replaced slavery after its abolition in 1875.

Calls for independence got stronger after the 1953 Batepá massacre, in which hundreds of Forro protesters were killed by the Portuguese administration.

In 1975, the islands finally became independent, under Manuel Pinto da Costa. Their first multiparty elections took place in 1990, propelling Miguel Trovoada to power, since when São Tomé has experienced a series of democratic transitions.

△ The needle-shaped volcanic monolith of Pico Cão Grande, São Tomé

Gabon

With its wealth of natural resources such as oil and minerals, Gabon has strong economic potential, but it was ruled by the same family for decades and is struggling with a legacy of corruption.

Official name: Gabonese Republic
Date of formation: August 16, 1960
Official language: French

Close to the equator, Gabon has a warm and moist climate. Sparsely populated, it has over 40 ethnic groups, with the Fang (in the north), Nzebi, and Mbete the most numerous. Around 80 percent of Gabonese are Christian (mainly Roman Catholic), and about 10 percent Muslim.

Gabon's economy depends on mining; the country is one of the world's largest producers of manganese, with significant uranium, gold, and diamond extraction. The discovery of oil in the 1960s provided a boost to its budget, but corruption meant proceeds were often misdirected.

European intrusions

Bantu-speakers, notably the Fang, reached Gabon around 1000 CE. When the Portuguese arrived in 1472, local peoples were under the influence of the powerful Loango Kingdom. At first, the Europeans traded largely for wood and ivory, with the slave trade dominating from the 1760s.

Between 1839 and 1841, the French negotiated treaties with local chieftains and, in 1849, they founded a settlement for formerly enslaved people at Libreville, pushing French control as far as the upper Ogooué River by the 1880s. France left the economic development of the colony, part of French Equatorial Africa from 1910, to French companies that ruthlessly exploited local labor.

Independent Gabon

Political parties began to form, the first anti-colonial one in 1922. Like many other French colonies (see pp.234–235), Gabon achieved independence in 1960, with Léon M'ba as president; he faced a brief military uprising in 1964, put down with French help. After M'ba died in 1967, Omar Bongo became president. His Gabonese Democratic Party (PDG), the sole legal party, monopolized power until 1990 when, in response to austerity caused by globally declining gas prices, a national conference agreed on reforms.

Bongo narrowly won the next elections, and in 1993 was forced to include opposition figures in the government. Even so, the PDG reasserted its dominance and he remained president until his death in 2009. His son, Ali Ben Bongo Ondimba, sought to diversify Gabon's economy, but opposition grew and after two contested electoral victories in 2016 and 2023, Bongo was deposed in a military coup.

▷ A wooden mask worn by the Ngil, who were a Fang secret brotherhood responsible for dispensing justice

Democratic Republic of the Congo

A 19th-century ceremonial wooden royal stool of the Luba people

The DRC's great size and mineral wealth have proved mixed blessings, creating huge problems in maintaining the unity of a highly diverse country and contributing to violent civil wars aggravated by those seeking a share in its riches.

Official name: Democratic Republic of the Congo
Date of formation: June 30, 1960
Official language: French

The Democratic Republic of the Congo (DRC) is Africa's fourth-largest country by population and second by area. The east is dominated by high mountains and a lake system that includes Lakes Albert and Tanganyika. High grassland plateaus in the center merge with the world's second-largest rainforest, while the country has only a narrow 23-mile- (37-km-) long coastline. Dominating it all is the Congo River, historically the main means of inland transportation.

The DRC is rich in minerals, such as cobalt, cadmium, copper, gold, diamonds, and uranium, the profits from which have fueled the country's multiple post-independence civil wars.

Over 240 languages are spoken, with the Luba (at 18 percent) and Kongo (at 16 percent) being the largest ethnic groups. Nearly 95 percent of the DRC is Christian.

Early kingdoms

A series of kingdoms emerged in the DRC by the 16th century, notably the Kingdom of Lunda, the Kingdom of Luba, and the mighty Kingdom of Kongo. Founded in 1390, the latter, in the west of the DRC, southern Congo, and northern Angola, became the region's dominant power. Its rulers, the Manikongo, retained their independence against European encroachment from the mid-15th century, becoming vassals of Portugal only in 1862. The arrival of the Portuguese navigator Diogo Cão in 1483 on the coast of Kongo was followed by the inception of the Atlantic slave trade, which profited some rulers, but destabilized the region's people and political systems.

Belgian brutalities

After the Berlin Conference in 1884–1885, a large part of Kongo was, uniquely, handed over to a private individual, King Leopold II of Belgium. His Congo Free State was a colonial regime of almost unparalleled brutality. The extraction of ivory and rubber came at the cost of the deaths of hundreds of thousands of Congolese through violence or neglect and finally, in 1908, the Belgian government stepped in and annexed the territory

△ Patrice Lumumba with supporters after his removal as prime minister, 1960

Congo

Congo's oil and forestry wealth has saved it from the worst effects of a quarter century of autocratic rule and periodic civil unrest.

Official name: Republic of the Congo (also known as Congo-Brazzaville)
Date of formation: August 15, 1960
Official language: French

Sparsely inhabited except for its cities, most of Congo is covered in tropical rainforest, and cut through by the deep Congo River and its many tributaries. Forestry and petroleum extraction are the main economic sectors. The Kongo are the largest ethnic group (at around 50 percent), with Aka and Baka peoples at 2 percent. Some 88 percent of Congolese are Christian.

European encroachment

By the 15th century, organized kingdoms arose: Kongo in the southwest, Tio in the north, and Loango on the Atlantic coast. The Portuguese arrival in 1483 and the slave trade weakened them. French rule, which began with the signing of a treaty with Tio's ruler in 1880 and the declaration of a colony in 1891, involved forced labor on a railroad project that cost around 15,000 lives.

Modern struggles

After becoming an autonomous colony as part of the French Community in 1958, Congo achieved full independence in 1960. In 1964, Alphonse Massamba-Débat declared his MNR the sole legal party, launching socialist policies with Soviet aid. Denis Sassou-Nguesso moved to an even more radical Marxist-Leninist line from 1979. He was ousted in 1992, returning in 1997 with Angolan support. A two-year civil war broke out, but he was reelected in 2002 and 2016, despite disputed results.

directly. The Belgians did make some investment in mining and education; meanwhile western-educated Africans (then known as *évolués*) appeared and began to lobby for independence.

Lumumba and Mobutu

In 1958, the young Pan-Africanist Patrice Lumumba established the *Mouvement National Congolais* (MNC). When serious rioting forced the Belgians to grant independence in 1960, with Lumumba as prime minister, a crisis erupted, as the province of Katanga, under Moïse Tshombe, seceded. Lumumba turned to the Soviet bloc for aid, and the expanding civil war became a Cold War confrontation. As other provinces broke away, the US supported Joseph Mobutu's plan to overthrow Lumumba, who was assassinated in murky circumstances, and likely with foreign involvement, in 1961.

Mobutu declared himself president in 1965 and ruled the country, which he renamed Zaire in 1971, for the next 32 years. He imposed a one-party state and a campaign of *Authenticité*, which replaced Francophone names with Congolese ones. When the Cold War came to an end in 1990, Mobutu lost his Western sponsors and was forced to concede a multiparty system, which he evaded ever actually implementing. The spillover from the Rwandan crisis, after which large numbers of Hutu militia fled into Zaire, caused the Rwandan government to ally with opposition leader Laurent-Désiré Kabila, whose rebel forces took the capital Kinshasa—from which Mobutu had fled—in 1997.

The DRC after Mobutu

Kabila restored the country's former name, now as the DRC, and banned political parties. By 1998, new rebellions had already erupted, soon drawing an intervention from the DRC's neighboring countries. Kabila was assassinated in 2001, and succeeded by his son Joseph.

A peace deal in 2002 seemed to end a civil war in which three million had already died, but fighting continued in the east. Joseph Kabila clung on to power until 2017, after which presidential elections were won by Félix Tshishekedi. His victory was the first peaceful transfer of power in the DRC since 1960, a positive sign for a president facing a country devastated by decades of war.

△ President Denis Sassou-Nguesso at an Independence Day parade in 2014

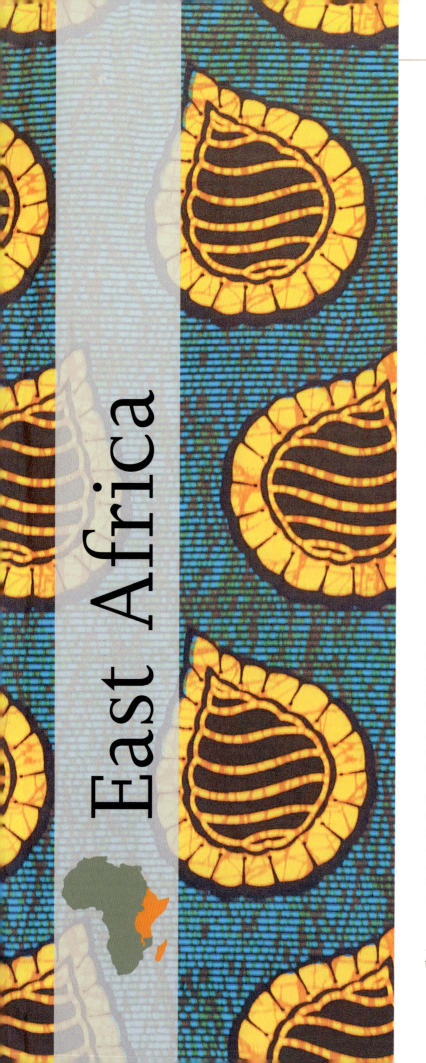
◁ Printed cotton kitenge fabric from Zanzibar, Tanzania

Madagascar

Madagascar's isolation allowed it to develop strong kingdoms and preserve its unique flora and fauna, but modern-day economic and political instability have hindered the island nation from further developing its economy and infrastructure.

Official name: Republic of Madagascar
Date of formation: June 26, 1960
Official languages: Malagasy, French

In the Indian Ocean, 250 miles (400 km) off Africa's east coast, Madagascar has experienced influences from the African mainland, the Arabian Peninsula, and southern Asia. Its isolated geographical position has meant it is home to an unparalleled range of wildlife unique to the island, including 40 species of lemurs.

More than 90 percent of the population is Malagasy, with the largest subgroups being the Merina on the central plateau, and the Betsimisaraka in the east. About half of Madagascans are Christian, while around 40 percent practice Indigenous religions. Madagascar's economy is heavily dependent on agriculture, fishing, and mining; the island has one of the world's largest reserves of titanium, and half the world's sapphires are sourced from here.

Settlements and kingdoms

The first known permanent human settlement on Madagascar occurred around 500 CE, when Austronesians, migrating from southeast Asia, made their home on the southeastern coast. Omani Arabs established small trading posts in the 7th century, introducing Islam and leaving the earliest written accounts of the island. Further Austronesian migrants came in the 8th century, followed by Bantu-speaking peoples crossing from mainland Africa. All these groups together became the Malagasy people.

By 1500, a mosaic of states had emerged, notably the Betsileo and Merina kingdoms in the central region and, in the 1630s, the southern theocratic state of Antemoro, which was one of the few to adopt Islam at this time. Meanwhile, the Portuguese had arrived in the early 16th century, French slave traders were active on the east coast by 1700, and pirates of various nationalities used the island as a base in the late 18th and early 19th centuries. Due to this ongoing increase in foreign activities, the Madagascan states coalesced into larger kingdoms.

Sakalava and Merina

In 1660, King Andriandahifotsy of Maroserana formed the Sakalava Empire, which came to dominate northern Madagascar for a century, after which it fractured into two parts. Both

Sakalava and the Betsimisaraka confederacy, which conquered much of the east coast under Ratsimilaho in the early 18th century, were then absorbed by Merina. Originally based around the central plateau, under King Radama I (r. 1810–1828), Merina forged an alliance with Britain by agreeing to help end the slave trade locally, and conquered most of the island. Radama's widow, Ranavalona I, succeeded him in 1828, expelling Christian missionaries and cutting off contacts with European traders.

End of the monarchy

Rainilaiarivony, who secured his power as prime minister by marrying three successive queens, reversed this isolationist policy, in 1869 adopting Protestantism, inviting missionaries to set up schools, and formulating a written law code. Modernization was hampered by the Franco-Merina war (1883–1885), which broke out over a disputed earlier treaty and ended with the French getting a foothold in the north. Despite diplomatic efforts by Queen

△ Queen Ranavalona III, photographed with her niece while in exile

Ranavalona III and the prime minister, in 1895 France took the rest of the island, established a protectorate, and exiled the prime minister. The queen was initially allowed to stay but in 1896, she, too, was exiled, living abroad until her death in 1917.

The French abolished slavery but used forced labor on their plantations. Large-scale revolts in 1895 and 1904–1905 did not lead to improved conditions for the workers. While railroads, roads, and schools were built, the focus on producing rice, manioc, and rubber—and later coffee, vanilla, cloves, and tobacco—for export precluded industrial progress.

The first republic

Nationalist sentiment rose again in the 1940s, and a revolt against French rule broke out in 1947. Brutally suppressed, it ended in 1949 with more than 11,000 dead. Madagascar finally achieved independence in 1960, with Philibert Tsiranana of the Social Democratic Party as president. He espoused a form of socialism aimed at improving the situation for the peasantry, until he was deposed in 1972. After a period of instability, Didier Ratsiraka became president in 1975. He nationalized industries and banks, seeking closer diplomatic ties to the Soviet bloc and allowing only a few left-wing parties. Crippling debt and a declining economy forced him to adopt free market policies in the early 1980s, but he remained in power until the first multiparty elections in 1992–1993 saw his defeat by Albert Zafy.

Modern Madagascar

After a rising tide of protests ended with Zafy's impeachment in 1996, Ratsiraka was reelected. He increased presidential powers and stabilized the economy, but the 2001 elections led to a crisis when his defeated opponent Marc Ravalomanana claimed he had won, and declared himself president. Clashes broke out, and Ratsiraka fled after the United States and France recognized Ravalomanana. He was reelected in 2006 but violent protests in 2009 in the capital, Antananarivo, led the army to seize power and hand the presidency to the city's mayor, Andry Rajoelina.

As chaos mounted, Rajoelina, Ravalomanana, Zafy, and Ratsiraka signed a pact to form a transitional unity government, which soon collapsed. Constitutional order was restored in 2014 with the election of Hery Rajaonarimampianina, who remained in power until 2018, when Rajoelina returned as president. Since then, the country has had to deal with a famine caused by the drought of 2021–2022.

△ A 20th-century frieze near the Royal Palace in Madagascar's capital Antananarivo, depicting scenes from the country's history

Tanzania

Inhabited since the era of the first hominins, Tanzania has been shaped by complex influences that didn't prevent a comparatively peaceful path to independence, but have yet to yield the self-reliant prosperity the nation's first president hoped for.

Official name: United Republic of Tanzania
Date of formation: April 26, 1964
Official languages: Swahili, English

Mainland Tanzania lies mostly on high ground, with plateaus punctuated by mountains such as Kilimanjaro, Africa's highest at 19,340 ft (5,895 m), though it also encompasses parts of the large lakes Victoria, Malawi (Nyasa), and Tanganyika, reaching depths of 4,823 ft (1,470 m). The climate varies from hot and humid on the coast to temperate in the highlands, and hot and arid on the inland plateaus. It has a rich variety of wildlife, including zebras, giraffes, lions, leopards, and hippopotamuses across its 21 national parks, but poaching poses a serious threat.

Offshore lies the autonomous archipelago province of Zanzibar, with large islands such as Unguja and Pemba, and many smaller ones, some of which are busy sea bird breeding grounds.

Some 120 languages, most belonging to the Bantu family, are spoken by as many ethnic groups, although Swahili is the lingua franca. Around 63 percent of Tanzanians are Christian and a third are Muslim. Agriculture is the largest economic sector, while coffee and cotton export, and gold mining, provide large income, but the country still has high levels of poverty.

Changing communities

The *Australopithecus afarensis* fossils excavated in Tanzania's Olduvai Gorge represent some of the earliest of humankind's ancestors. San hunter-gatherer communities who settled here were displaced 2,000 years ago by Bantu-speakers and then by Nilotic peoples migrating from the Sudan.

The first towns appeared on the coast, where Persian and Arab merchants came to trade in gold and ivory with Bantu-speaking African traders. Settlements with mixed populations, such as Kilwa (see pp.146–147), were established around 1000 CE and Swahili developed as a language of exchange, and of poetry.

The Portuguese captured Zanzibar in 1505, but never got far into the mainland interior. In the 18th century, they were driven out of most areas by an alliance of Swahili rulers and the Sultan of Muscat. Arab merchants who traded in enslaved people reached the region of Lake Tanganyika in the 1830s, where Ujiji soon became an important trading center. In 1840, Sultan Sayyid Said moved his court from Muscat to Stone Town on Zanzibar's main island, cementing Arab rule there.

▷ An ornately carved wooden doorway in Stone Town, Zanzibar, a sign of the area's historic links with the Arab and Islamic world

European colonization

By then, Europeans had begun to explore the interior, the British reaching Lake Tanganyika in 1857–1858. In 1884, the German Carl Peters made several treaties with coastal chiefs. The 1886 Anglo-German Agreement made these areas a German sphere of influence and then, after a revolt by local Arab and Swahili people in 1888, they became a formal German protectorate in 1891. Resistance to German expansion into the interior was fierce. The Hehe, under Chief Mkwawa, defeated an expedition in 1891 and resisted for seven years, and the more widespread Maji Maji revolt, which began in 1905 as a movement against forced labor, cost the lives of 300,000 Africans before it was put down in 1907.

After World War I, during which fighting between colonial powers took place in the region (see pp.228–229), German East Africa was handed to Britain as a League of Nations Mandate, administered from 1920 as the Tanganyika Territory. When the British loosened restrictions on local organizations, it led to

△ A postage stamp commemorating Julius Nyerere, who led Tanzania for nearly a quarter of a century

the foundation of the Tanganyika African Association in 1929, which became the seedbed of the later nationalist movement.

Independent Tanzania

Founded by the activist and politician Julius Nyerere in 1954, the Tanganyika African National Union (TANU) pushed strongly for independence, which came in 1961 with Nyerere as first prime minister. Converting Tanganyika into a republic in 1962, Nyerere instituted a one-party state. It expanded in 1964 by the addition of Zanzibar, a former British protectorate (1890–1963), where a revolution by Black nationalists led by John Okello shortly after independence in 1963 had overthrown the ruling sultan.

Nyerere sought closer relations with Eastern Bloc countries, notably China, and in his Arusha Declaration of 1967 set forward a policy of *ujamaa*, an ideology of self-reliance and socialism. The main practical manifestation of this was a collectivization of agriculture, which proved highly unpopular among villagers and led to sharp falls in production. Deteriorating relations with Idi Amin's Uganda, which in 1978 occupied part of northwest Tanzania, led Nyerere to send his army into Uganda and oust Amin from power in 1979.

In 1985, Nyerere stepped down from the presidency. Succeeding him, Ali Hassan Mwinyi soon denationalized key industries, accepted foreign aid from non-communist countries, and permitted the first multiparty elections in 1995, in which the CCM's Benjamin Mkapa was elected president. Tanzania faced new strains, with an influx of refugees from Rwanda and the DRC (see pp.266–267) and, in 1998, the US embassy in Dar es Salaam was bombed by Islamist terrorists, killing 11 people.

Mkapa's reelection in 2000 came amid allegations of fraud and violent demonstrations, and the CCM's Jakaya Kikwete won presidential elections in 2005 and 2010. Corruption dogged his terms in office, leading to the dismissal of six ministers in 2012.

John Magufuli succeeded Kikwete as president in 2015, despite a strong challenge from Ukawa, a new opposition alliance. He announced infrastructure policies and a crackdown on corruption, but also became increasingly authoritarian, soon imposing restrictions on the media and legal measures against same-sex sexual acts. Magufuli was returned in 2020 with a huge majority, in elections whose fairness was widely doubted.

After Magufuli's death related to COVID-19 in 2021, Samia Suluhu Hassan became Tanzania's first female president. Focusing on improving education and the economy, she has also revoked Magufuli's ban on political opposition rallies and worked for stronger international relations.

▷ A Makonde tree of life carving, in a style that became popular in the 1950s

Malawi

Inhabited since prehistoric times, for much of its post-independence era Malawi was controlled by the autocratic Dr. Hastings Banda.

Official name: Republic of Malawi
Date of formation: July 6, 1964
Official language: English

The Great Rift Valley cuts right through Malawi, creating a varied and dramatic landscape. The mountainous areas around the rift, rising to 7,875 ft (2,400 m), have a mild climate, while the lowlands are hot, especially in the far south. Wildlife such as elephants, hippos, and rhinos abound, with fish and waterfowl plentiful in the deep, clear Lake Malawi. This large rift lake takes up a fifth of the nation's area, creating a long, watery border with Tanzania and Mozambique.

Among ten major ethnic groups, the Chewa make up around a third, the Lomwe 19 percent, and the Yao 14 percent of the population. English is the official language, but over 60 percent of Malawians speak Chichewa. More than three-quarters are Christian, and close to 15 percent Muslim. Around 80 percent of the workforce in Malawi is occupied with subsistence farming, with agricultural exports such as tobacco, sugarcane, and cotton the main earners.

Early kingdoms

The remains of hominins dating back to two million years ago have been found in Malawi. Much later, Bantu-speaking peoples arrived from the north in several waves between the 1st and 15th centuries CE and, by 1480, they had established the Maravi Confederacy, whose leader, the *Karonga*, ruled most of central and southern Malawi. The Maravi traded ivory and enslaved people via the Swahili states along the east coast of Africa (see pp.146–147), and from the 16th century with the Portuguese.

The migration of the Ngoni, fleeing from the Zulu expansion in southern Africa, and of the Yao from Mozambique, precipitated the state's decline in the early 19th century. Both the Ngoni, who established a militarized system similar to the Zulu, and the Yao engaged in slave trading, while the Jumbe, who were Swahili-speaking slave traders, brought Islam into Malawi from 1840 onward. Christianity came through missionaries such as the Scot David Livingstone who explored the area in the 1860s.

Colony and independence

Increasing British activity in the region eventually culminated in the establishment of the British Central Africa Protectorate in 1891 (to be renamed Nyasaland in 1907). The colonial regime built roads and railroads and encouraged European settlers to grow cash crops, but little effort was put into supporting African agriculture and many Malawians became migrant laborers in neighboring countries.

In 1953, Britain merged the Nyasaland colony with Southern and Northern Rhodesia to create the Federation of Rhodesia and Nyasaland. This artificial union caused severe resentment and fostered growth in support for nationalist movements, in particular the Nyasaland African Congress (NAC), founded in 1944.

△ Chongoni Forest Reserve on the Malawi plateau, where many of the rugged hills feature ancient Chewa rock art

△ Dr. Hastings Banda giving a speech in 1960

The Federation was dissolved in 1963 and Dr. Hastings Banda, leader of the Malawi Congress Party (successor to the NAC), became prime minister when Malawi achieved independence in 1964. He soon faced a serious crisis when three ministers were dismissed for plotting against him, but in 1966 he became president as Malawi chose to be a republic; in 1971, he declared himself president for life.

Modern Malawi

Imposing a one-party state under the MCP, Banda clamped down ruthlessly on all opposition and enforced highly conservative legislation (including censorship of films and the press), and he was one of the few African leaders not to cut ties with the apartheid regime in South Africa. A declining economy as well as mounting dissent within Malawi led him to concede multiparty elections in 1994. The opposition UDF won a majority and Bakili Muluzi became president.

Muluzi was reelected in 1999, but faced serious unrest when sectarian violence broke out as Christians protested against the growing influence of southern Muslims (of whom Muluzi was one). His last years in office were marred by a famine in 2002, while his UDF successor Bingu wa Mutharika's election victory in 2004 was tainted by allegations of vote rigging.

Mutharika tried to purge his party of corrupt officials, but the impact of the HIV/AIDS epidemic slowed down reforms. Protests against his increasingly autocratic rule became violent in 2011, but his death the following year and replacement by vice-president Joyce Banda calmed tensions.

Banda devalued the currency to reduce inflation, doubled the growth rate, and launched a clampdown on corruption, but critics blamed her for not acting firmly enough against the 2013 "cash-gate" scandal, in which government funds were embezzled. When she tried to annul the 2014 elections, the High Court stepped in and Peter Mutharika (the brother of the former president) was elected president. The court annulled the next elections, which Mutharika had won, and his opponent Lazarus Chakwera was sworn in as president in 2020, vowing to continue fighting corruption.

Comoros

Divisions between its three islands have troubled the Comoros, hindering attempts to improve the economy of an already poor country.

Official name: Union of the Comoros
Date of formation: July 6, 1975
Official languages: Comorian, Arabic, French

A string of three volcanic islands northwest of Mozambique, the Comoros have been subject to African, Arab, Malagasy, and French influences. Their fertile valleys suffer from soil erosion aggravated by deforestation from logging. Around 97 percent of the population is Comorian (a mixture of Bantu, Malagasy, and Arab descent). The most common language is Comorian, a variant of Swahili, and Islam is the main religion. The economy is largely based on subsistence agriculture and fishing. Mayotte, the archipelago's fourth island, is still administered by France.

History

The Comoros islands were settled by Malayo-Polynesians around 500 CE, and from Madagascar and East Africa in the 9th to 13th centuries. On a major sea route, the islands were involved in the Indian Ocean slave trade, while European influence was muted until the cession of Mayotte to France in 1843, followed by a French protectorate in 1886.

In 1974, three islands voted for independence. The new president Ahmed Abdallah also claimed Mayotte, but France refused to accept this, and withdrew all aid. Abdallah was overthrown by Said Mohamed Jaffar in 1975, but later restored in a 1978 coup led by French mercenary Bob Denard. Abdallah's rule continued until he was assassinated in 1989.

More coups, and secessionist movements on the Anjouan and Mohéli islands, rocked the Comoros, until a coup in 1999 brought Colonel Azali Assoumani to power. He negotiated an agreement on rotation of political rule between the three islands and, in 2016, it became his turn to govern again. His holding of a referendum to allow a second consecutive term and his victory in the subsequent 2019 elections caused a crisis, but he stayed on. In 2023, the Comoros was appointed to chair the African Union for the first time.

▷ Pre-independence stamp issued by the Comoros in 1962

△ A spectacular granite boulder-fringed beach on La Digue, the Seychelles' third most populated island

Seychelles

An archipelago nation in the Indian Ocean, the Seychelles has been exposed to the competing interests of colonizing European nations, and to political conflicts following independence. It is now taking action against the local effects of climate change.

Official name: Republic of Seychelles
Date of formation: June 29, 1976
Official languages: French, English, Seychellois Creole

The 115 islands of the Seychelles lie some 930 miles (1,500 km) east of the African mainland. The archipelago's population, at only around 100,000, is the lowest of any African nation, and is 97.5 percent Seychellois Creole. Three quarters of the population are Catholic.

While the main islands are hilly, forested granite formations, those scattered further out are flat coral islands barely reaching above sea level. The surrounding waters contain large seagrass meadows, forming important ecosystems. Unique species, such as the Aldabra giant tortoise, live on and around the islands, which also host giant seabird colonies.

Wildlife and pristine beaches attract a growing number of visitors and the nation's economy is heavily dependent on high-end, increasingly "green" tourism, thus being sensitive to challenges such as COVID-19. The second-largest industry is fishing.

Plantation era
Although Arab and Malay voyagers across the Indian Ocean might have explored the islands, the first known recorded landing on the Seychelles was in 1609 by the British East India Company. France claimed possession in 1756, and the two nations contested the islands until the Treaty of Paris formally awarded them to Britain in 1814. By then, the population was made up of descendants of the Africans and Indians forcefully brought to the plantations here, as well as of white planters. The abolition of slavery in 1833 caused a shift from plantation-based cotton crops to other cash crops.

Independent Seychelles
Early political movements were dominated by privileged planters, interested mainly in their own gains. It took until the 1960s for a socialist party to form, which campaigned for independence. In 1976, the Seychelles became an independent republic but its first president, James Mancham, was ousted the next year. The prime minister, France-Albert René, succeeded Mancham as president, instituting a one-party socialist state under the Seychelles People's United Party (later the SPPF) in 1979. Surviving a number of coup attempts in the 1980s, over time René abandoned socialist policies and privatized most state agencies, to attract offshore financial companies.

A new constitution in 1993 legalized opposition political parties, but René won successive elections until 2004, when he resigned in favor of his vice-president, James Michel. The SPPF continued to dominate politics, with Michel winning reelection, albeit very narrowly, in 2015, until he stepped down in 2016. In 2020, the opposition won the Seychelles presidency for the first time, with the victory by Wavel Ramkalawan of the Seychellois Democratic Alliance (LDS). The nation is now making efforts to tackle climate change; its tourism and fishing, and the islands themselves, are under threat.

Mauritius

An island republic in the Indian Ocean, Mauritius has experienced high growth that has been one of Africa's economic success stories.

Official name: Republic of Mauritius
Date of formation: March 12, 1968
Official language: English

Mauritius and its smaller islands occupy most of the Mascarenes, a volcanic island chain located around 560 miles (900 km) east of Madagascar. Two-thirds of Mauritians are of South Asian origin, and about a quarter are of Creole (African and French) ancestry; the lingua franca of the islands is Mauritian Creole. About half of the population is Hindu and a third Christian.

Early history
Arab sailors, and others on the medieval Indian Ocean trade routes, knew of the island by the 10th century, and the Portuguese recorded landing there in 1505. A Dutch colony, founded in 1638, was abandoned in 1710 after cyclones rendered the settlement unviable. The French occupied Mauritius in 1721, calling it Île de France, and transported enslaved Africans to work on its sugar cane plantations. In 1810, the British took the island, ending slavery in 1835 but instead bringing in large numbers of South Asian workers to provide a new labor force. Competition from beet sugar, and the Suez Canal opening in 1869, dented Mauritius's prosperity, amplifying calls for independence.

Independent Mauritius
Severe riots erupted during the last three years of British rule, and in 1968 Mauritius gained its independence, with Seewoosagur Ramgoolam as prime minister. In 1965, though, Britain had transferred the Chagos islands, which Mauritius claimed, to the British Indian Ocean Territory, thus beginning a still unresolved dispute over their ownership.

▷ Monument in memory of enslaved people who lived and died on Mauritius

Mauritius initially struggled with falling sugar prices, prompting its leadership to diversify the economy and, in 1992, declare a republic. Although the country has faced the impact of Indian Ocean piracy, its governments, led since 2019 by President Prithvirajsing Roopun, have succeeded in attracting financial services and tourism, and Mauritius now has one of the highest GDP per capita in Africa.

Réunion

An overseas department of France, Réunion still relies heavily on sugar cultivation, while functioning as a French military base.

Official name: Réunion
Date of formation: March 19, 1946 (as Overseas Department of France)
Official language: French

Retained by France, Réunion is situated some 110 miles (180 km) southwest of Mauritius. The island is dominated by a series of extinct volcano cones and linking plateaus. Its active volcano, Piton de la Fournaise, regularly erupts, its vast lava flows adding new contours to the already dramatic landscape. High rainfall lends Réunion a relatively cool climate, though it is subject to frequent tropical cyclones. Réunionese, of mixed European, South Asian, African, Creole, and Chinese descent, make up 85 percent of the population, about 83 percent of whom are Christian and about 7 percent Hindu. French is the official language, but most people speak Réunion Creole. Sugarcane cultivation is the key industry.

European occupation
Portuguese explorers visited the uninhabited island in the early 1500s but France claimed it in 1642, then founding a small settlement in 1665 and naming it Réunion in 1793. The French established coffee and sugarcane plantations, worked by enslaved Africans. During the Napoleonic Wars, the island was briefly occupied by Britain in 1810–1814.

In the 1840s, vanilla-growing supplemented sugar and, when slavery was abolished in 1848, it was mainly indentured workers from Southeast Asia and India who labored on the plantations. But competition from beet sugar and the 1869 Suez Canal opening, which shifted trade routes, led to a prolonged economic depression.

Modern Réunion
In March 1946, Réunion was made an overseas department (département d'outre-mer) of France and, because of its strategic location, in 1973, it became the headquarters for French military forces in the Indian Ocean. The high rate of unemployment on the island has led to periodic demonstrations and, in 1991, rioting. Since 2014, a campaign to raise awareness of the many children who were forcefully resettled in France between 1966 and 1982 has led to some of them being able to return to Réunion for the first time.

Rwanda

Rwanda's long history has been marred by divisions between its Hutu and Tutsi peoples, culminating in the 1994 genocide.

Official name: Republic of Rwanda
Date of formation: July 1, 1962
Official languages: Kinyarwanda, French, English, Swahili

Forested hills and mountains, including the volcanic Virunga range where mountain gorillas live, dominate much of Rwanda. The principal ethnic groups are the Hutu, around 80 percent of the total; the Tutsi, around 10 percent; and a small minority of Twa. Forty percent of Rwandans are Roman Catholic, and a third Protestant. The country is heavily dependent on agriculture, most importantly coffee for export.

Tutsi kingdoms

Rwanda was settled by Twa hunter-gatherers before 3000 BCE, followed in the 15th century by Bantu-speaking Hutu farmers and Tutsi pastoralists. By the 16th century, the Tutsi had established kingdoms. Most important of these was Rwanda, founded by King Gihanga, which reached its maximum extent under King Kigeli IV Rwabugiri (r. 1853–1895).

In 1894, Germany asserted a claim from the 1884–1885 Berlin Conference. King Yuhi V Musinga (r. 1896–1931) came to the throne during the unrest that followed Rwabugiri's early death, and collaborated with the Germans to secure support for his rule. Germany administered Rwanda mainly through diplomatic agents at the royal courts, favoring an ethnic hierarchy in which a Tutsi ruling class dominated the Hutu.

After World War I, Belgium was given a League of Nations mandate over Rwanda as one part of Ruanda-Urundi. Coffee was introduced as a cash crop, and the Tutsi elite were free to use Hutu workers for forced labor.

Opposition to Belgian rule took on an ethnic cast, with separate parties emerging in the 1950s: Parmehutu for the Hutu, founded by Grégoire Kayibanda, and the UNAR for the Tutsi. Violence broke out and after an attempted assassination of a Hutu dignitary in 1959, around 100,000 Tutsi were murdered before Belgian troops intervened. Many others went into exile in Uganda where they formed rebel groups.

Independence and beyond

Following a general nationalist, anti-colonial push in the region, and a referendum that rejected the Tutsi monarchy, Rwanda became an independent republic in 1962. Tutsi guerrillas tried but failed to overthrow Kayibanda's Hutu-dominated government, and more Tutsi refugees fled to neighboring countries.

In 1973, Kayibanda's defense minister Juvénal Habyarimana overthrew him, forced remaining Tutsi out of official positions, and made Rwanda a one-party state under his MRND. In 1990, he faced an invasion from Uganda by Tutsi of the Rwandan Patriotic Front (RPF), led by Paul Kagame. The 1993 Arusha Accords halted the fighting, but Habyarimana's death in April 1994—when his plane crashed in circumstances that are still disputed—led to a violent backlash. The Rwandan army and Hutu militia groups began a mass slaughter, killing around 800,000 Tutsi in three months, before a further RPF advance halted the carnage.

By the time Kagame's Tutsi troops entered Kigali in July 1994, two million Hutu refugees had fled, including to Zaire (now called the DRC), where they became involved in a complex civil war (see pp.266–267). In 1996, Rwanda's new government invaded Zaire in pursuit of the Hutu militia, its troops remaining there until 2002.

Kagame, president since 2000, held multiparty elections in 2003 and attracted international aid to rebuild Rwanda's shattered society and economy. His rule grew more authoritarian, and the 2010 elections were marred by persecution of opposition politicians, while in 2017 he pushed through a constitutional amendment allowing him to remain president until 2034.

△ Stained-glass window in Kigali's Genocide Memorial, commemorating victims

Burundi

Burundi's ethnic divisions have flared up into violence several times in recent history, hindering political and economic progress.

Official name: Republic of Burundi
Date of formation: July 1, 1962
Official languages: Kirundi, French, English

Hilly and mountainous, Burundi has a temperate climate. Its border with the Democratic Republic of the Congo to the west is largely taken up by Lake Tanganyika, while that with Rwanda to the north follows several rivers. Burundi is primarily rural and dependent on agriculture, making the soil erosion of its deforested slopes a severe problem.

Most of the population are Hutu (around 85 percent), about 14 percent Tutsi, and less than 1 percent Twa. Around 90 percent of Burundians are Christian (mainly Roman Catholic), with small numbers practicing Islam or Indigenous religions.

Early history
Originally populated by Twa hunter-gatherers, Burundi was settled by Hutu farmers and Tutsi agriculturalists from 1000 CE. By the 17th century, a Tutsi kingdom had emerged, founded by Ntare Rushatsi. Its rulers, the *mwamis*, established a system in which the Hutu were subordinated (although it was still possible for a rich Hutu to acquire the social status of a Tutsi).

Burundi's isolation and its mountainous terrain had made it hard for outsiders to penetrate. But after the Berlin Conference in 1884–1885, Germany made its claim, and in 1903 Burundi became a colony when King Mwezi Gisabo signed a treaty which in effect meant ceding his lands to Germany. After World War I, Burundi was granted to Belgium in 1924 as part of the League of Nations mandate of Ruanda-Urundi.

Escalating tensions
Calls for independence grew in the 1950s, with the foundation of political parties such as Unity for National Progress (UPRONA) in 1958. The assassination in 1961 of Prince Rwagasore, the popular leader of UPRONA, which represented both Hutu and Tutsi, meant ethnic tensions were heightened when Burundi gained its independence in 1962.

In 1965, Prime Minister Pierre Ngendandumwe, a Hutu, was killed by a Tutsi gunman. When King Mwambutsa IV sought to appoint a Tutsi, Léopold Biha, as successor, a chaotic situation ensued—the king went into exile, the monarchy was abolished, and Michel Micombero, a Tutsi, became president in 1966.

In 1972, violence broke out, in which 200,000 Hutu were killed and tens of thousands fled into exile. In 1976, Micombero was overthrown by Jean-Baptiste Bagaza who, though Tutsi, sought to reconstitute the multiethnic UPRONA. Bagaza's Second Republic ended in 1987 when Pierre Buyoya, at the head of a military junta, overthrew him. Buyoya, another Tutsi, initially did little to ease the plight of impoverished rural Hutu and in 1988, another spasm of killing erupted and 20,000 Hutu died.

Buyoya reached out to Hutu political leaders, formed a cabinet that had a Hutu majority, and set up a commission to find ways to resolve the ethnic divide. A new constitution in 1992 decreed that all parties must be multiethnic, and in 1993 the country held its first free elections, in which Melchior Ndadaye, a Hutu, won the presidency from Buyoya.

Civil war and aftermath
Ndadaye was assassinated in a coup attempt four months later and, in the ensuing violence, 150,000 Tutsi were killed. His replacement, the Hutu Cyprien Ntaryamira, died in the same plane incident that killed Rwandan president Juvénal Habyarimana in April 1994, leading to a new flare-up in fighting. The Tutsi-Hutu power-sharing government that then took office was overthrown in a military coup in 1996, which reinstalled Buyoya as president. After international sanctions, in 2000 Buyoya signed the Burundi Arusha Accords with Hutu rebels. This led to a power-sharing constitution, the dispatch of a UN peacekeeping force, and the election of Pierre Nkurunziza, a Hutu, as president in 2005.

With the civil war finally over, Burundi began to rebuild, joining the East African Community in 2006, and investing in vital infrastructure. However, the 2010 elections were marred by violence and fears that Nkurunziza's CNDD-FDD party was building a one-party state.

In 2015, as Nkurunziza sought an unconstitutional third term, a coup attempt against him failed and, despite protests on the streets, he won a large majority. Violence flared up again with attacks on military bases and revenge killings by security forces. In 2020, with Nkurunziza having stepped down, the CNDD-FDD's candidate, the Hutu civil war veteran Évariste Ndayishimiye, won the election against opposition leader Agathon Rwasa.

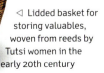

◁ Lidded basket for storing valuables, woven from reeds by Tutsi women in the early 20th century

Uganda

Uganda's heritage of powerful kingdoms and the fertility of its soil could not overcome ethnic divisions and the corrosive effect of the Amin dictatorship, and its recent stability and economic growth have come at the cost of political freedoms.

Official name: Republic of Uganda
Date of formation: October 9, 1962
Official languages: English, Swahili

△ Bwindi Impenetrable National Park, home to wild mountain gorillas

Landlocked in the Great Lakes region, Uganda includes much of Lake Victoria, Africa's largest freshwater lake. The climate is hot, with high rainfall, and the country is home to abundant wildlife, including the mountain gorillas that live on the forested slopes of Bwindi Impenetrable National Park and by the snow-capped Rwenzori Mountains.

Uganda's highly fertile soil supports the agriculture on which it depends, notably coffee-growing, its principal export earner. Expanding tourism and services sectors have also contributed to strong economic growth.

The country's south is largely inhabited by Bantu-speakers, of whom the Ganda (about a sixth of the population) are most numerous. The north is the heartland of Nilotic language groups, such as Acholi and Lango. Swahili, a national language since 2022, is a lingua franca in much of the north, and Luganda is spoken by many. About four-fifths of the population are Christian and an eighth Muslim.

Rise of Buganda

Bantu-speaking agriculturalist peoples arrived around 1000 BCE, and by the 15th century, states had begun to emerge. In the south, Bunyoro-Kitara—whose *omukama* leaders combined religious and secular power—dominated, but it weakened in the 18th century, when Buganda, on the northern shores of Lake Victoria, deployed flotillas of canoes to subdue the lakeside communities. In the 19th century, however, Egyptian and Sudanese slave traders became increasingly active in Buganda. Its ruler, *Kabaka* Mutesa I (r. 1856–1884), sought support from the British, an act that also led to the arrival of Christian missionaries.

British protectorate

Kabaka Mutesa's successor Mwanga II, who saw Christianity as a threat to Bugandan culture, was deposed in 1888 amid a civil war between rival religious groups. This led to foreign intervention, first by Germany. Mwanga then got British help, on the condition that he retracted the treaty with the Germans, and instead accepted Buganda becoming a British protectorate in 1894. Named Uganda by the British, the protectorate expanded rapidly, signing treaties with the Toro and Ankole kingdoms, and launching a military expedition against Kabarenga, ruler of Bunyoro. Meanwhile, Mwanga revolted against British rule in 1897, but failed and was exiled in 1899. Chiefs backed by rival Christian groups also caused unrest. This led to the 1900 Buganda Agreement, which recognized the *kabaka* as ruler, gave his royal council, the *lukiiko*, official status, and secured land tenure for the Buganda chiefs.

Britain's rule in Uganda was in consequence less direct than elsewhere in Africa. Cash crops, in particular cotton, were grown on plantations largely owned by Africans. Schools were opened, such as King's College Budo, which produced a generation of graduates, who in 1919 established the Young Baganda Association to lobby for reform.

Push for independence

Local discontent mounted as the British kept control of the prices at which small producers could sell their cash crops, and in 1949 serious rioting broke out. Attempts to establish a pro-independence party

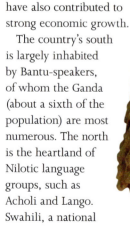

▷ The Mpanga terra-cotta head found at a Buganda shrine at Luzira dates from around 1000 CE and is made of hollow baked clay, with details separately applied

foundered when the Uganda National Congress collapsed in 1954, but fear that Uganda would be incorporated into a Central African Federation, dominated by white Kenyan settlers, crystallized Ugandan opposition to British rule. People also resented the colonial government's attempts to bypass the royal court of the *kabaka* and regional chiefs in favor of Western-educated men (who the British assumed would be more amenable). When a ministerial system in which only five out of eleven ministers were Africans was introduced, Bugandans largely ignored it.

Kabaka Mutesa II—at the time referred to by the British press as "King Freddie"—had received his university education in Britain and served in the Grenadier Guards, but he was an ardent champion of Bugandan autonomy. When in 1953 he feared this would be snuffed out, he pressed for complete independence for Buganda, supported by the *lukiiko*. The alarmed British authorities exiled Mutesa, which resulted in a backlash and his restoration in 1955.

Political parties had begun to emerge by the late 1950s, and Mutesa formed an alliance of convenience between his own royalist *Kabaka Yekka* ("king only") party and the Uganda People's Congress, established by Milton Obote in 1960. This alliance won the Legislative Assembly elections in April 1962—against the conservative, Catholic-oriented Democratic party, which sought a more unitary Uganda. Mutesa and Milton Obote became the key interlocutors with whom the British negotiated Uganda's self-government, and then full independence in October 1962, and Obote became Uganda's first prime minister.

Obote and Mutesa's cooperation was short-lived; disagreements between them led to Obote suspending the 1962 constitution in 1966. The fragile coalition between the Democratic Party and *Kabaka Yekka* broke up, Mutesa fled to Britain, dying there in 1969, and Obote faced several assassination attempts.

The Amin regime

In January 1971, the army chief Idi Amin overthrew Obote. His coup was initially welcomed, but he installed a brutal military dictatorship, relying on a small core of supporters from his own Kakwa people. He turned to Muammar Qaddafi's Libya and the Soviet Union (USSR) for aid, and instituted an "Africanization" policy, in 1972 expelling the 80,000-strong Asian community, whose ancestors were recruited as railroad workers in the 1890s, and who had since come to occupy a key role in Uganda's economy.

The government and economy came close to collapse, as Amin's State Research Bureau unleashed a reign of terror, including mass execution of opponents. In 1978, Tanzania's president Julius Nyerere reacted to a Ugandan cross-border incursion against anti-Amin exiles by launching an invasion. Tanzanian troops took Uganda's capital Kampala in April 1979, and Amin fled. After a brief transition, elections in 1980 returned Milton Obote to power, but an insurgency led by Yoweri Museveni's National Resistance Army soon broke out among elements of the opposition unreconciled to Obote's victory. This led to Obote's overthrow in 1985 after Museveni had secured most of the country.

▷ *Kabaka* Mutesa II, ruler of the Kingdom of Buganda from 1939 to 1966

The Museveni presidency

As Museveni became president in 1986, he faced huge problems of interethnic rivalry, the decay of government, and a variety of armed rebel groups, including the Lord's Resistance Army. This diffuse movement, led by Joseph Kony from 1987, abducted more than 30,000 Ugandan children, indoctrinating and recruiting them to serve in its forces, and caused waves of displaced people.

Museveni also intervened in the war in the Democratic Republic of the Congo (DRC) in the 1990s, supporting rebel groups there, and only finally withdrawing Ugandan troops from the DRC in 2003. Reelected as president in 1996, Museveni stabilized Uganda's economy but this came at the cost of political pluralism, with political parties other than his NRM banned until 2005, when a referendum result led to multiparty elections being held.

In the elections of 2006, 2011, and 2016, Museveni defeated Kizza Besigye of the Forum for Democratic Change, the second and third victories beset by allegations of fraud. Having amended the constitution to allow him to stand again in 2021, Museveni beat the entertainer Bobi Wine, and thus continued his long reign as president.

Kenya

Once home to some of our earliest hominin ancestors, and later Bantu-speaking cultures and wealthy Swahili port cities, Kenya has struggled with political instability and a string of disputed elections since the death of its first president in 1978.

Official name: Republic of Kenya
Date of formation: December 12, 1963
Official languages: Swahili, English

Kenya has a diverse geography, including snow-capped Mount Kenya—Africa's second-highest peak at 17,000 ft (5,199 m); temperate highlands; forests and savanna; the lakes of the Rift Valley, once formed by Africa's largest volcanic fault; the arid north; and mangroves, beaches, and islands. Its population is equally varied, with more than 70 ethnic groups, among them the Kikuyu, Luhya, Kalenjin, and Luo, who make up just over half the total. Around 85 percent of Kenyans are Christian, and 10 percent Muslim.

Kenya's economy relies on the export of tea, coffee, and cut flowers, and on the tourists who come to see lions, zebras, and wildebeest in national reserves such as the Masai Mara.

Human origins

A 6-million-year-old specimen of *Orrorin tugenensis* discovered in the Tugen Hills in central Kenya is the second-oldest hominin ever found, while the oldest stone tools ever discovered, dating to around 3.2 million years ago, were unearthed at Lomekwi near Lake Turkana. In the 3rd millennium BCE, a pastoral people speaking a Southern Cushitic language moved south into Kenya, where they built great burial mounds and stone circles. In around 700 BCE, Southern Nilotic peoples came here, and Bantu-speakers with knowledge of iron smelting. Their Urewe culture produced iron pots and pottery with fine geometric patterns and dents.

Swahili city-states

From around 800 CE, traveling Arab merchants trading ivory and enslaved people from the interior for spices and other luxury goods visited trading communities along the coast. These grew to towns

△ Zebras and wildebeest on the vast Masai Mara grasslands, observed by visitors on safari

such as Lamu, Malindi, and Mombasa, and Kilwa (in what is now Tanzania), in which the Swahili culture was born of the interaction between Arab and African peoples and customs (see pp.146–147). When the Arab traveler Ibn Battuta visited in 1331, he described towns with many Muslim inhabitants and mosques. With inland as well as overseas connections, these towns were part of an extensive Indian Ocean trade network.

The Portuguese navigator Vasco da Gama reached Mombasa in April 1498 on his way to India, leading to a Portuguese naval and military presence in the region and ultimately the construction in 1593 of Fort Jesus in the town. The Sultans of Oman challenged Portuguese rule, capturing Fort Jesus in 1698 and transferring their own capital from southern Arabia to Zanzibar in 1840. The Omanis encouraged economic development by establishing clove and coconut plantations, but this led to an increasing trade in enslaved people—70,000 were trafficked through Zanzibar each year by the 1860s.

The colonial period

Once Britain had abolished its own slave trade, its attempts to clamp down on the slave trade of other nations, and the increasing prosperity of the Swahili coast, led it in 1895 to claim part of the region's interior. Large numbers of white settlers arrived in this East Africa Protectorate. Its Highlands region was reserved for them—the only Africans allowed were laborers working on the burgeoning white-owned coffee plantations; Asians who had come over from the Indian subcontinent were also excluded.

From 1903, Britain drove out the Kikuyu, Kamba, and Maasai peoples, reallocating the lands they had farmed or used as pasture for many centuries to Europeans. This left a legacy of bitterness that seeded Kenyan nationalism. The East African Association (EAA) was formed in 1921, and promptly banned by the British, while the Kenyan African Union (KAU), founded in 1944, grew to provide a political voice for African Kenyans. At a local level, movements such as Mumboism, a prophetic cult that predicted that the British would be driven out, also gained support.

Kenyatta's Kenya

In 1947, Jomo Kenyatta became president of the KAU, attracting leaders of the Luo people to join what had until this point been a largely Kikuyu movement. Pressure for independence grew steadily, and in 1952 this ignited the violent Mau Mau uprising (see pp.240–241), which drew mainly Kikuyu support. The uprising ended in 1956 after British military action and an extremely harsh campaign of repression, during which many Kikuyu were held and tortured in detention camps and nearly 13,000 of their people died.

The independence campaign continued, and in 1963 Britain finally gave way. Jomo Kenyatta, only recently released from prison and forced exile, became the nation's first prime minister, and KANU (a merger of KAU and two other parties) the ruling party. In a bid to promote interethnic harmony, Kenyatta appointed the Luo leader Oginga Odinga as his vice president, but quarrels between the two over economic policy led the alliance to collapse. Odinga's new party, the socialist KPU, was banned in 1969 and he was jailed. After his release, Odinga's criticism of Kenyatta's transfer of land to prominent Kikuyu officials of KANU led to a one-party state in 1974.

Modern Kenya

Kenyatta remained president until his death in 1978, when he was succeeded by Daniel Arap Moi, a member of the minority Kalenjin people. Fears the loss of Kenya's independence leader would cause instability proved unfounded, but Moi gradually gathered more power to himself, banning all parties but KANU in 1982 and jailing opponents.

In 1991, multiparty elections were reinstated, in which Moi was reelected. The opposition coalesced around the Forum for the Restoration of Democracy (FORD), which lobbied against

△ Jomo Kenyatta, Kenya's first president, portrayed in 1973

what it saw as Moi's increasing corruption. Moi stepped down in 2002, when FORD's leader Mwai Kibaki defeated Jomo Kenyatta's son, Uhuru Kenyatta, to become Kenya's first non-KANU president. Accusations of corruption dogged the new presidency. The 2007 election, in which Kibaki narrowly defeated Raila Odinga, Oginga Odinga's son, was marred by violence in which over 1,000 people died.

Uhuru Kenyatta narrowly defeated Raila Odinga in the 2013 election, which passed off peacefully, but the new administration faced problems of increasing Islamic militant activity by the Somali-based al-Shabaab group, which in 2013–2015 engaged in several bloody attacks. Kenyatta won a resounding electoral victory in the 2017 presidential elections, after Odinga withdrew.

Years of political instability seemed at an end when Odinga and Kenyatta announced a rapprochement in 2018, but the 2022 elections again ended in a disputed result when Odinga, who ran against Kenyatta's former deputy, William Ruto, refused to accept the result until the Supreme Court confirmed it.

Somalia

Once a renowned part of ancient trade networks, Somalia has long been fought over by foreign rulers as well as local clans. Its transition to statehood was troubled, and it later descended into a civil war exacerbated by clan-based loyalties and fragmentation.

Official name: Federal Republic of Somalia
Date of formation: July 1, 1960
Official languages: Somali, Arabic

Somalia's narrow coastal plain gives way to mountain ranges and broad plateaus, a divided terrain that has encouraged a tendency to fierce regional and clan loyalties. The climate is arid in the north and dry in the center and south, where fertile land is concentrated and agriculture has always been primarily pastoral, often leading to overgrazing.

Disputed western borders with Ethiopia, Djibouti, and Kenya, a devastating legacy of colonial administrations, mean the Somali people today are split between many countries. Almost all Somalis are Sunni Muslim, and most speak Somali, with Arabic writing and reading taught. Civil war has left Somalia's economy and infrastructure in ruins, with foreign aid and remittances from expatriates the main source of national income.

Historic kingdoms

At the nexus of ancient maritime trade routes linking Africa to the Arabian Peninsula, Somalia was probably the Land of Punt, which traded spices, gold, and ivory to pharaonic Egypt. Between the 3rd and 7th centuries CE, its northwest regions were part of the Kingdom of Aksum (see pp.62–63), in modern-day Ethiopia.

Islam reached this corner of Africa in the late 7th century, and several Islamic sultanates arose, including Adal, Ifat, Mogadishu (founded around 900 CE) and, from the 13th century, the Ajuran Empire. These dominated the Indian Ocean trade and vied with the Christian rulers of Ethiopia for control of the border regions. In 1531, Sultan Ahmed Gran of Adal invaded and conquered most of Ethiopia, only being turned back with the help of a force of Portuguese musketeers. The Ajuran and Adal states collapsed by the 17th century but successors, such as the Isaaq Sultanate, based at the port of Berbera, exercised some control over an increasingly fragmented region.

European colonization

Britain's 1839 annexation of the strategically placed port of Aden, near the entrance to the Red Sea, intensified European interest in Somalia. Taking advantage of a vacuum left after a brief Egyptian occupation of Berbera, the British signed protectorate treaties with northern Somali clans in 1884–1886. By 1889, Italy had also acquired protectorates, in northeastern Somalia, and leased a portion of the southern Somali coast from the sultan of Zanzibar.

Indigenous resistance to both Italy and Britain grew in the 1890s. The local religious leader Mohammed Abdullah Hassan led an uprising against the British, lasting until the 1920s. In the south, separate clans revolted against the Italians, whose use of forced labor and control of ports threatened regional trade; the Banadir Resistance, led by the Biimal clan for 22 years, was one of the longest-running.

Independence

After World War II, Italian Somalia and British Somaliland both came under British administration, until they were separated again in 1949. In 1960, both territories voted for independence as one united country. Somalia's first president, Aden Abdullah Osman, faced huge challenges in overcoming

◁ Egyptian soldiers taking part in a trading expedition to Punt, believed to have been located in Somalia, on a relief dating from the 15th century BCE

△ The Adal sultan Ahmed Gran defeating Ethiopian forces (top), before being shot by Portuguese musketeers (bottom), as depicted in a modern Ethiopian painting

long-established clan loyalties. The southern-based Somali Youth League came to dominate the government but when it won all but one seat in 1969, the military stepped in, installing a Supreme Revolutionary Council led by General Mohamed Siad Barre.

Siad Barre adopted an ideology of "scientific socialism" and soon courted assistance from China and the USSR. His rule was authoritarian, with clan elders being subordinated to regional committee, although a mass literacy campaign in 1973 gained some success. In 1977, Siad Barre launched an invasion of Ogaden (which he claimed as Western Somalia), reaching as far as the city of Harar before Ethiopian troops, with Soviet and Cuban support, drove Somali forces back.

Civil war

Two Somali opposition groups, the SSDF and SNM, began attacks from Ethiopia in 1982 and Siad Barre's hold on power started to weaken. In 1991, the United Somali Congress, a rebel group, ousted him, clan-based militias seized control of vast swathes of territory, and the SNM declared the former British protectorate independent as the Republic of Somaliland. The rest of Somalia descended into civil war between the SNA alliance of Muhammad Farah Aydid and the SSA forces of Ali Mahdi Muhammad. A UN intervention force from 1992 to 1994 achieved little but securing parts of Mogadishu, and in 1998 Puntland, the SSDF-controlled region of the northeast, declared itself autonomous.

Successive attempts at peace talks all foundered, and the Transitional Federal Government (TFG), formed in 2002, had to rule in exile from Kenya until establishing a tenuous foothold in Baidoa, a state capital, in 2006. The same year, the Islamic Courts Union (ICU) seized Mogadishu and southern Somalia, including Baidoa, sparking an Ethiopian intervention to prevent radical Islamists gaining power. The ICU disintegrated but the country remained fractured. Growing attacks by al-Shabaab, an Islamist terrorist group, posed challenges, and the government was dogged by corruption allegations.

Indirect elections—controlled by clan elders—in 2017 brought the former prime minister Mohamed Abdullahi Mohamed to the presidency. In 2022, he was replaced in a similar election by Hassan Sheikh Mohamud. But Mohamud's political power barely reached outside Mogadishu, and definitely not into Somaliland, which, despite failing to gain international recognition, has continued to assert its own independence from Somalia.

△ One of many wall paintings in the capital, Asmara, this mural represents life in the agricultural center of Barentu

Eritrea

With a history closely linked to Ethiopia since ancient times, Eritrea has struggled to assert its independence and borders.

Official name: State of Eritrea
Date of formation: May 24, 1993
Official language: None; Tigrinya is the most widely spoken

Eritrea's 600-mile (1,000-km) Red Sea coastline opened it to influences carried along by trade, including Islam and Christianity, each of which roughly half the country's population practices today. The fertile coastal plain and the barren Danakil plain in the south represent the extremes of a diverse geography, which includes central highlands rising to just over 10,000 ft (3,000 m).

Around 55 percent of the population is Tigrinya, and some 30 percent is Tigre. Minorities, such as the Afar, Saho, Bilen, and Kunama peoples, make up most of the remainder. Agriculture is the main economic sector, with some mining of salt and gold.

Early and medieval states

By 3500 BCE, early settlements had appeared along the Eritrean coast, which may have been part of the Land of Punt referred to in ancient Egyptian texts. Inland, on a plateau rich with prehistoric cave art, is an area that from the 8th century BCE to the 6th century CE successively formed part of the Ethiopian kingdoms of D'mt—where settlements such as Qohaito expanded into busy trade route centers—and Aksum (see pp.62–63). The hold of the Ethiopian Solomonids from the 12th century was more tenuous, however, as Tigrayan lords asserted some measure of independence. Eritrea became the Medri Bahri, the "land between the seas," later partially conquered by the Ottoman Turks in the 16th century, while in the south it was dominated by the Aussa Sultanate from 1577.

Italian and Ethiopian rule

In 1869, the opening of the Suez Canal led the Italian shipping company Rubattino to purchase land along the Red Sea near the port city of Assab, an area that Italy annexed in 1882. Italy landed troops in 1885, steadily expanding its control from the coast farther into the highlands. The 1889 Treaty of Wichale between Ethiopia and Italy recognized the land conquered so far as Italian territory, but Ethiopia's emperor Menelik II thwarted the Italians' ambitions to expand any further by defeating them in battle at Adwa in 1896.

Instead, Italy then focused on Massawa and Assab, building roads and railroads, and sending over tens of thousands of Italian settlers, who appropriated the best agricultural land. After Italy's defeat in World War II, Ethiopia lobbied for Eritrea to be returned to its control and, in 1952, the two were joined in a federal state.

Gradually, Ethiopia squeezed Eritrea's identity, banning all political parties and, in 1962, abolishing its federal status. Tigrinya lost its standing as an official language to the Amharic of Ethiopia; this fueled a separatist revolt by the Eritrean Liberation Front (ELF) that began in 1960.

Wars and independence

By 1977, an enlarged separatist group, the EPLF, was on the verge of capturing all of Eritrea from Ethiopia, but the new Ethiopian Derg regime (see p.371) retook most of the land. Yet the EPLF regrouped, and in 1991 seized power when the Derg collapsed. A referendum in 1993 led to independence, and Isaias Afwerki became Eritrea's first president.

Relations with Ethiopia got worse over the disputed territory of Badme, resulting in a war in 1998–2000. An international commission awarded the area to Eritrea but Ethiopia refused to hand it over. In 2008, another border war erupted, now with Djibouti, and Eritrea also became embroiled in the Somali Civil War (see p.367). These conflicts stifled economic progress and accelerated a slide into autocracy.

Afwerki's People's Front for Democracy and Justice (PFDJ) became the only legal party and human rights violations such as press censorship and torture of opponents became routine. After a summit in 2018, relations with both Ethiopia and Djibouti were restored, and Eritrea got involved on Ethiopia's side in the 2020–2022 Tigray War, although there has been little sign internally of any meaningful political reform.

△ The ruined temple of Mariam Wakino in the pre-Aksumite city of Qohaito

Djibouti

In a key position where the Red Sea meets the Gulf of Aden, the small nation of Djibouti has always attracted foreign interest.

Official name: Republic of Djibouti
Date of formation: June 27, 1977
Official languages: Arabic, French

On the west side of the strategic Bab el Mandeb Strait that links the Red Sea to the Gulf of Aden, Djibouti has thrived on trade since ancient days. In modern times, its location has attracted foreign military bases, including those of France, the US, China, and Saudi Arabia. Djibouti City, its capital, is a busy modern port.

Despite its small size, Djibouti is geographically varied, from mountains in the north to low desert plains and the eerie Abbe salt lake in the south. It lies on a geological fault line; its active Ardoukoba volcano last erupted in 1978. The dominant ethnic groups are the Somali (70 percent) and Afar (30 percent); most Djiboutians are Muslim.

Early history

Prehistoric stone tools and other remains tell of the first, largely pastoral, people living in the area. It was probably part of the Land of Punt with which Pharaonic Egypt traded, and was later ruled by the Ethiopian kingdom of Aksum until the 7th century CE.

As Islam reached East Africa, Djibouti was under the sway of the Adal Sultanate from the 10th century and the Ifat Sultanate after 1285, before returning to Ethiopian rule in the 1330s. In 1862, France purchased land at Obock, a key position near the entrance to the Red Sea, then steadily expanding its protectorate until 1897, when its borders were recognized by an agreement with the Ethiopian emperor Menelik II. Djibouti became the capital of French Somaliland, its trade facilitated by a railroad to Addis Ababa completed in 1917.

Modern Djibouti

In 1957, Djibouti was granted limited self-government but a referendum held in 1967 resulted in Djibouti remaining under French rule. Calls for self-rule resumed in the early 1970s and, in 1977, a new referendum strongly supported independence. Djibouti's first president, Hassan Aptidon, established a one-party state under his People's Rally for Progress (RPP), eventually sparking a civil war with Afar FRUD rebels that dragged on from 1991 to 1994.

Aptidon served five terms as president before stepping down in 1999, in favor of his nephew Ismail Omar Guelleh. Tension between the Afars and the dominant Somalis has continued, despite FRUD joining the ruling coalition. In 2008, Djibouti fought a brief border war with Eritrea, but Guelleh has continued to win sometimes disputed elections, beginning his fifth term in 2021.

Ethiopia

One of Africa's oldest countries, the only one to defy European colonization, and the center of an ancient empire and venerable Indigenous culture, Ethiopia was an obvious choice as the headquarters of the Organization of African Unity and the African Union.

Official name: Federal Democratic Republic of Ethiopia
Date of formation: 4th century CE
Official languages: Afar, Amharic, Oromo, Somali, Tigrinya

The second most populous country in the Horn of Africa, Ethiopia is a mountainous state, its Western Highlands rising to 14,872 ft (4,533 m) at Mount Ras Dejen. The Rift Valley runs through the country, its southern section elevated and with many lakes that provide fertile soil, as do the banks of the Blue Nile, though soil erosion and failure of seasonal rains render Ethiopia highly prone to drought.

Near 100 languages are spoken, with the largest groups being the Oromo (around 35 percent) and Amhara (about 27 percent). About 63 percent of Ethiopians are Christians (with two-thirds Ethiopian Orthodox), and around a third Muslim. Coffee is the top export, but despite some recent strong economic growth, Ethiopia remains a poor country.

Ancient Ethiopia

The 3.2 million-year-old skeleton of a female *Australopithecus afarensis* nicknamed "Lucy," excavated in the Afar Depression, shows how long people have lived in this region (see pp.22–23). The first Ethiopian kingdom, D'mt, appeared around 1000 BCE in the northern Tigrayan highlands.

D'mt's control of trade routes in ivory, gold, and enslaved people was increasingly challenged by the rival state of Aksum, which in the 1st–5th centuries BCE rose to become the main trading power in the region (see pp.62–63). Converting to Christianity under King Ezana (r. c. 330–350 CE), Aksum expanded west, but a Persian invasion in 572 broke its grip on trade routes, and by the 9th century it had collapsed.

Medieval Ethiopia

Around 1100, the Zagwe dynasty emerged, its capital named for King Gebre Lalibela (r. c. 1181–1221). Eleven enormous rock-cut churches were built; legend says all by King Lalibela, but some are more likely by later Zagwe rulers (see pp.118–119). The Zagwe were overthrown in 1270 by Yekuno Amlak, who claimed descent from the biblical monarch Solomon. Under Amda Seyon I (r. 1314–1344), the Solomonids became dominant in the Horn of Africa, and established a strong military

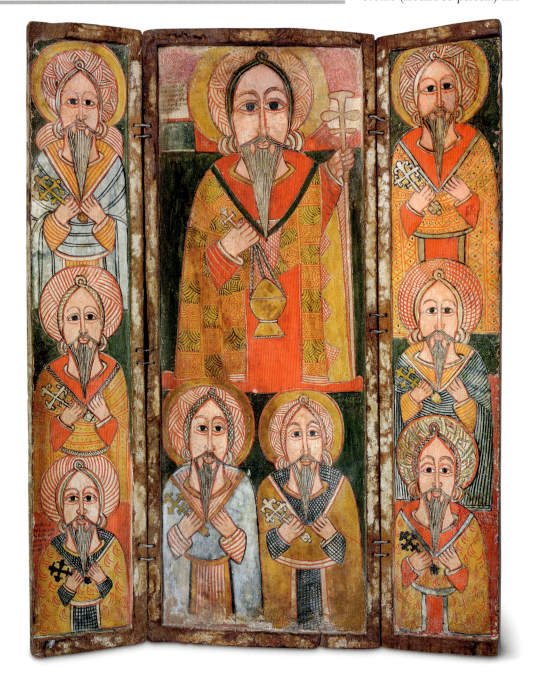

◁ A 17th-century triptych of the 14th-century religious reformer Ewostatewos and eight disciples

to defend against the southern Muslim sultanates. Ahmad Gran, the sultan of Adal, invaded in 1528, and Emperor Galawdewos (r. 1540–1559) used Portuguese assistance to defeat and kill him. By 1600, however, the Solomonids lost control of much of the south to the pastoral Oromo people.

Portuguese influences led to Emperor Susenyos (r. 1607–1632) converting to Catholicism. This, however, resulted in his deposition in favor of his son Fasilides (see pp.120–121), who built a capital at Gondar. The power of the throne was reestablished, sparking a cultural renaissance in literature, painting, and architecture. But by 1769, its central authority had collapsed, and during the Zamana Masafent ("Age of the Princes"), regional lords held more power than the emperor.

The modern empire

In 1855, Kassa Hailu declared himself Emperor Tewodros II, restoring order by reuniting the disparate Ethiopian statelets. But his attempted reforms alienated the Ethiopian Church, whose lands he seized, and his arrest of a British envoy led to a British attack in 1868 and his defeat and suicide. A period of turmoil followed as the new Emperor Yohannes IV vied with the rival king of Shewa, Sahle Mariam, and also fought against Italian intrusion on the Eritrean coast.

After Yohannes's death in 1889, Sahle Mariam became emperor as Menelik II. He signed a treaty with Italy, recognizing Italian rule in Eritrea, but repudiated the treaty when Italy claimed that this gave it a protectorate over the whole country. When the Italians invaded, Menelik defeated them at Adwa in March 1896, in a signal victory for an African army over a European colonial force.

A victorious Menelik modernized the capital Addis Ababa and built railroads, schools, and roads. Haile Selassie, who became emperor in 1930, continued the modernization process but, in 1935, the Italian fascist leader Benito Mussolini invaded from Eritrea, forcing him into exile. The emperor returned in 1941 with British aid and, in 1952, the United Nations awarded Eritrea back to Ethiopia.

The reformist zeal of the early part of Emperor Selassie's reign, however, was now tempered, although an elected parliament was introduced in 1955. An attempted army coup in 1960, which led to a reimposition of autocracy, an insurrection that began in Eritrea in 1960, and the forced imposition of the Amharic language across all regions of the country dissolved most ties of loyalty to the monarchy.

Ethiopia under the Derg

In June 1974, Ethiopian army officers under Mengistu Haile Mariam mutinied and set up a coordinating committee, known as the Derg, seizing control of the government. Haile Selassie was deposed and later murdered. The Derg declared a socialist regime, nationalizing large properties and turning to the USSR for military aid to fight an Eritrean rebellion by the EPLF (see p.369) and a Somali invasion of the Ogaden in 1977–1978.

The Derg ruthlessly suppressed any opposition, but a series of severe droughts from 1980 and a devastating famine in 1983–1985 fatally undermined its power-base. The EPLF allied with the TPLF, a Tigrayan rebel group, to form the EPRDF, and advanced steadily. In May 1991, they took power in Addis Ababa, and overthrew the Derg.

△ Emperor Menelik II, shown with members of his family in 1900

Contemporary Ethiopia

The new government under Meles Zenawi conceded Eritrean independence in 1993 (which in fact meant that Ethiopia lost its Red Sea coastline), and passed a federal constitution based on regionalism and ethnic autonomy. The EPRDF won the first free elections in 1995, but a war with Eritrea over the disputed territory of Badme and the splintering of the party took its toll. In 2005, violent protests broke out, and Zenawi was forced to send troops into Somalia in 2006 to bolster the frail transitional government there. Elections in 2015 gave every seat in parliament to the EPRDF and its allies, now led by Hailemariam Desalegn, but increasing dissatisfaction with lack of political reforms led the EPRDF to replace him with Abiy Ahmed, the country's first Oromo leader.

Ahmed released thousands of political prisoners, privatized more businesses, and signed a peace deal with Eritrea over Badme. He was rewarded with Ethiopia's first Nobel Peace Prize in 2019. But Tigray's TPLF felt sidelined, and tensions exploded into conflict in 2021, threatening new turmoil for a country which had finally begun to feel some hope of new stability and growth.

Southern Africa

◁ Neolithic rock painting made by the San people of South Africa

Angola

The world's second-largest Portuguese-speaking country, Angola collapsed into a 27-year civil war after independence, but thanks to its mineral resources its economy has recovered strongly and the country is slowly rebuilding itself.

Official name: Republic of Angola
Date of formation: November 11, 1975
Official language: Portuguese

Angola's landscapes encompass part of the semi-desert known as the "Skeleton Coast," rainforest in the interior, and a high central plateau. In the far north lies the disputed exclave of Cabinda, cut off from the rest of Angola by land that is part of the Democratic Republic of the Congo. Angola's three largest ethnic groups are the Ovimbundu (who make up 37 percent of the population), the Mbundu (23 percent), and the Bakongo (13 percent).

The majority of Angolan people speak Portuguese, but there are more than 40 national languages, including Umbundu, Kikongo, and Kimbundu. Over 90 percent of Angolans are Christian. Angola has rich deposits of oil, diamonds, gold, and copper and has become one of Africa's fastest-growing economies.

Great kingdoms

The Bantu ironworking cultures that appeared from the 6th century CE evolved into larger kingdoms, most notably Kongo, founded by Lukeni lua Nimi around 1390 in the south (see pp.182–183), and the Ndongo Kingdom located in the central highlands. Portuguese explorers had reached Kongo in 1483, and the local people began to trade and exchange ideas with them.

In 1491, the *manikongo* (king) Nzinga a Nkuwu converted to Christianity, changing his name to João I. His son, taking the name Afonso, built churches and schools, modernizing his kingdom and continuing to adapt Portuguese practices as it suited him. Portugal's ever-expanding involvement in the slave trade and its increasing local impact was, however, something he objected to and tried to regulate. Afonso and his successors fended off Portugal's advances and absorbed rival kingdoms, despite the foundation of a Portuguese colony at Luanda in 1575.

Queen Njinga Mbande of Ndongo and then of Matamba (see pp.180–181) allied with the Dutch to force the Portuguese out of Luanda and to regain her control of Ndongo, which she had temporarily lost to a king installed by the Portuguese. Her resistance by wars and diplomacy lasted until her death in 1663, although deals she struck with the Portuguese in later life facilitated their slave trading.

Portuguese colonization

A huge loss of population in the region due to the slave trade, and the lack of a united front, eventually led to the Portuguese taking over much of the coast. While the slave trade was banned in 1836, after which the economy turned to cotton, sugar, and coffee cultivation, slavery in the colony was legal until 1878. After that, many formerly enslaved people remained on plantations as indentured laborers.

The Portuguese intruded further into the highlands from 1902; their systematic invasion of the interior continued until the 1920s. Angolans strongly resented the land confiscations and forced cultivation, as well as a lack of access to education and health services, and a revolt broke out in northern Angola in 1961.

Independence and conflict

The ensuing nationalist guerrilla campaign was hampered by splits between the Marxist MPLA led by Agostinho Neto (with strong Mbundu support), the FNLA (mainly Bakongo) led by Holden Roberto, and the predominantly Ovimbundu UNITA under Jonas Savimbi. Then, Portugal's 1974 Carnation Revolution resulted in Angola's independence (see pp.248–249). The MPLA seized the capital Luanda in 1975, announcing Neto as president, while the FNLA and UNITA established rival administrations. Angola, led from 1979 by the MPLA's José Eduardo dos Santos, faced 27 years of civil war, stoked by Cold War interference.

UNITA, backed until 1988 by South Africa, forced a cease-fire and participated in multiparty elections in 1992, but accusations of fraud by the MPLA led the civil war to reignite again. The Lusaka Protocol in 1994 established a new power-sharing government, but this collapsed and peace only came when Savimbi died in 2002.

After the civil war

Dos Santos and João Lourenço (his successor from 2017) faced severe problems in reconstructing a country whose civil war had cost a million lives and displaced millions more, and where a long separatist armed conflict in the province of Cabinda flared up anew in 2016. Dissent continues at the monopolization of power by MPLA, as the party again won disputed elections in 2022.

△ President Agostinho Neto and Fidel Castro during a state visit to Cuba in 1976

Ascension Island

Small, rugged Ascension Island has served as a naval base since the 19th century and is still linked to Britain as an Overseas Territory.

Official name: Ascension Island
Date of formation: September 12, 1922 (as part of a UK Overseas Territory)
Official language: English

A mostly barren, volcanic peak, 1,600 miles (1,000 km) west of continental Africa, Ascension Island was first mentioned by Portuguese navigators who sailed past in 1501 and 1503. It remained uninhabited until 1815, when the British (who had claimed it since 1659) set up a garrison and it became an important stopping-off point for ships in the South Atlantic. Previously governed by the Admiralty, it was made a dependency of St. Helena in 1922, administered by executives of the Cable & Wireless Company until 1964. It houses Wideawake (a US airbase), as well as British signal monitoring stations, and was used as a staging post for British forces during the 1982 Falklands War. No permanent residents live there, while there are important turtle and seabird populations.

St. Helena

This remote, rocky Atlantic island, 1,180 miles (1,900 km) west of the African continent, today relies on British aid and tourism.

Official name: St. Helena
Date of formation: April 22, 1834 (as British Crown Colony)
Official language: English

In 1502, Portuguese ships were the first to visit the uninhabited St. Helena; the British made landfall in 1588. In 1659, the English East India Company took control, and the population consisted mainly of the garrison and its enslaved laborers, who often rebelled. It became a busy stopping-off point for ships and, in 1815–1821, a place of exile for the French emperor Napoleon Bonaparte. The island was made a Crown Colony in 1834 but, after the opening of the Suez Canal, ships stopped calling and St. Helena's economy declined. Limited autonomy was introduced in 2021.

Namibia

Despite a prolonged colonial period, including a brutal genocide, Namibia has emerged as a stable democracy, buoyed by mineral resources.

Official name: Republic of Namibia
Date of formation: March 21, 1990
Official language: English

One of the world's most sparsely inhabited countries, Namibia has two vast deserts—the Namib, a coastal desert, the northern part of which is nicknamed the "Skeleton Coast" due to the many wrecks stranded along its dunes, and the Kalahari, which reaches across the borders into Botswana and South Africa. With low soil fertility, little water, and high summer temperatures, not much land is suitable for arable agriculture and most people live in the slightly less arid north.

The main ethnic groups are the Ovambo (nearly half of the population), the Kavango (9 percent) and the Herero (7 percent). Around 88 percent of Namibians are Christian. Poverty levels are high, and half the population derive their livelihood from subsistence agriculture. Namibia's economy is heavily dependent on mining, including diamonds and uranium oxide, and there have been recent discoveries of natural gas. Tourism has grown recently, now accounting for about a fifth of all employment.

Settlers and intruders

Namibia's earliest people left rock paintings depicting hunting scenes, made in the Brandberg mountains in about 2000 BCE. San hunter-gatherers and Damara and Nama pastoralists—ancestors of ethnic groups that are present in Namibia today—settled the area. By the 17th century CE, various Bantu-speaking groups had arrived, too, including the Ovambo and Kavango, who settled in the north where the climate was better for farming, and the animal-keeping Herero and Himba peoples, mainly in the northeast and central regions.

Although Portuguese explorers landed in Namibia in 1486, there was little contact with Europeans until the 18th century, when Afrikaner traders from the Dutch Cape Colony began to enter the region. In the 1830s, the Oorlam-Nama people formed, a mixed group of Khoisan and Nama who had assimilated the Afrikaans language and the use of horses and guns. They established a kingdom in the central grasslands ruled by *Kaptein* Jonker Afrikaner. Another mixed Afrikaner-African community, the Basters, also arrived, founding the "Free Republic of Rehoboth" in 1872.

△ Skeletal tree-trunks and strikingly colored sand dunes in Namibia's Namib-Naukluft, the largest national park in Africa

Colonization and uprisings

The British established a base at Walvis Bay in 1797, annexed to the Cape Colony in 1878. A possible further British expansion attracted the attention of the Germans. In 1884, Adolf Lüderitz purchased a stretch of land around Angra Pequena from a Nama chief, and the following year persuaded Chancellor Otto von Bismarck to establish the colony of German South West Africa. The narrow Caprivi strip was added by a 1890 treaty.

In 1896, Chief Kahimemua Nguvauva led a Herero uprising against the Germans, who shipped in elite troops to end it. But sporadic fighting continued and, in response, the Germans established a Red Line. This was a system initially intended to control the spread of animal diseases but, from this point on, it came to separate the area of strong colonial control in the south from that of more indirect rule in the north.

German settlers came to the south in increasing numbers, and in 1904, Herero fighters began attacking German farms that encroached on their land. The war that resulted, from 1904 to 1907, was extremely brutal. The Herero, led by Samuel Maharero and joined by the Nama, were pushed into waterless regions where many died of starvation or by drinking from wells that the Germans poisoned. Three quarters of all Herero and half of the Nama died in the genocide.

South African rule

In 1920, South Africa was given a League of Nations Mandate to administer Namibia. The South Africans exploited Namibia's diamond reserves and, after 1945, developed a cattle and fish export business, creating prosperity that benefited white settlers, but left the Black population in poverty; apartheid laws were introduced in 1948. In 1966, the United Nations forfeited the mandate, and nationalist resistance to South African rule grew, with trade union activism resulting in a major strike in 1971–1972. The main force for independence was the South West African People's Organization (SWAPO), which since 1960 had fought an armed struggle from bases in Zambia and Angola.

Despite international efforts to resolve the Namibian conflict, fighting continued for nearly 30 years. But the cost to South Africa grew, and when an intervention in southern Angola to attack SWAPO bases there was defeated in 1988, the South African government began negotiations for a transition to independence.

Independent Namibia

SWAPO, led by Sam Nujoma, decisively won UN-facilitated parliamentary elections in 1989, and Nujoma became Namibia's first president after independence in March 1990, although South Africa retained control of an enclave around Walvis Bay until 1994. SWAPO consolidated its hold on power in the early independence years, with Nujoma winning a third term in 1999, though some dissent was caused by his decision to send Namibian troops to intervene in the Democratic Republic of the Congo in 1998.

The HIV/AIDS epidemic, with a fifth of Namibians infected by the year 2000, and difficulties in land reform caused problems. But SWAPO retained power after Nujoma stepped down in 2004, winning successive elections, with Hage Geingob securing a second term in 2019.

Lesotho

While completely encircled by South Africa, Lesotho has retained its own identity and is one of Africa's few remaining sovereign monarchies.

Official name: Kingdom of Lesotho
Date of formation: October 4, 1966
Official languages: Sesotho, English

Most of Lesotho is mountainous, rising to 11,424 ft (3,482 m) at Thabana Ntlenyana, and it has a relatively mild climate. A central plateau forms the basis of the country's important cattle-raising industry. The Basotho make up 99 percent of the population, which is mainly Christian.

History

Lesotho was founded by the Basotho chief Moshoeshoe I in 1824, after his people fled the *Mfecane* ("the crushing"), the violence accompanying the Zulu expansion (see pp.206–207). Britain annexed the kingdom in 1868. Despite attempts to transfer it to South African control in 1910, Lesotho remained a British colony (Basutoland), ruled through the Basotho paramount chiefs, successors to Moshoeshoe.

Lesotho became independent as a monarchy in 1966, with the pro-royalist Basotho National Party (BNP) in government. When the opposition Basutoland Congress Party (BCP) won a majority of parliamentary seats in the 1970 election, the BNP prime minister Leabua Jonathan suspended the constitution; he remained in power until 1987, when a military council deposed him. In 1992, limited democracy returned with elections that chose the BCP's Ntsu Mokhehle as prime minister. There was further political turbulence as the king attempted to take control in 1995, the BCP split, and the new Lesotho Congress for Democracy (LCD) led by Pakalitha Mosisili took power in 1998. A wave of violent protests erupted, in which South African forces intervened.

The LCD fractured and, in 2012, Motsoahae Thabane's All Basotho Convention (ABC) won most seats. Thabane lost to Mosisili in 2015 but came back as prime minister in 2017, until resigning in 2020. His successor, Moeketsi Majoro, also resigned and the businessman Sam Matekane was elected prime minister in 2022.

△ Moshoeshoe I, king of Lesotho from 1824 until he died in 1870, aged 93

Botswana

Botswana's diamond wealth and strong sense of its Tswana identity has enabled it to build a strong, stable democracy.

Official name: Republic of Botswana
Date of formation: September 30, 1966
Official language: English

Occupying a central point in Southern Africa, landlocked Botswana has borders with five countries; that with Zambia, at only 500 ft (150 m) long, is the world's shortest international frontier. The Kalahari Desert covers around 70 percent of Botswana, with the major sources of water being in the Okavango Delta and surrounding marshes. Most vegetation is dry savanna grassland, but Botswana has abundant wildlife, including 30 species of bats and 460 of birds. Its many fish species include the notoriously aggressive tiger fish.

More than three quarters of Botswanans belong to the Tswana people, with around 18 percent Kalanga (mainly living in the northeast), and 2 percent San. The modern nation derives its name from "Batswana," meaning "The people of Tswana." Tswana is also the root of Setswana, the main spoken language of Botswana (English is the official government language). Around 60 percent of the population is Christian, and a third practice Indigenous religions.

With little land suitable for arable cultivation, agriculture in Botswana is primarily pastoral. High economic growth since the 1960s means it has one of the highest GDP per capita in Africa, its economy strongly supported by mining (it is the world's second-largest producer of diamonds) and safari tourism. HIV/AIDS has affected Botswana gravely, and by 2014, as much as 20 percent of the population had been infected, but progress is being made.

Early settlement

The earliest traces of settlement in Botswana date from around 17,000 BCE, when ancestors of today's Khoikhoi and San people lived in the Tsodilo Hills.

By around 200 CE, Bantu-speaking ironworkers had entered the area, and farming settlements emerged around Molepolole and in the Okavango Delta by about 500 CE. Around the 7th century CE, the Toutswe state arose, its wealth deriving from cattle herding and trading along the Limpopo River. It dominated Botswana until its conquest in the 13th century by the Mapungubwe kingdom, of the Kalanga people, to the east.

The Tswana kingdoms

In the 14th century, new states began to appear among the Tswana people, including the Kwena and Hurutshe dynasties. They established stone-walled villages around 1700 and, by 1795, had founded the Ngwaketse chiefdom, which controlled much of the Kalahari and valuable copper-producing areas around Kanye in the south. Another Tswana people, the Tawana, also established a state around Lake Ngami in the late 18th century. The Tswana states suffered attacks by Kololo peoples from the southeast and by the Ndebele of western Zimbabwe (see p.380). By the 1840s, however, they had regained control of the ivory trade to Cape Colony under great rulers such as Sechele of the Kwena (r. 1829–1892) and Khama III of the Ngwato (r. 1875–1923).

European pressure on the Tswana grew after the Berlin Conference in 1884–1885, as German attempts to join its colony in South West Africa to the Transvaal and Tanganyika clashed with British efforts to expand their colonies through Botswana into Zimbabwe.

British protectorate

In 1885, Britain declared a protectorate over the Ngwato, extending this to the Tawana in 1890. Tswana chiefs resisted attempts to make them hand over what was now the Bechuanaland

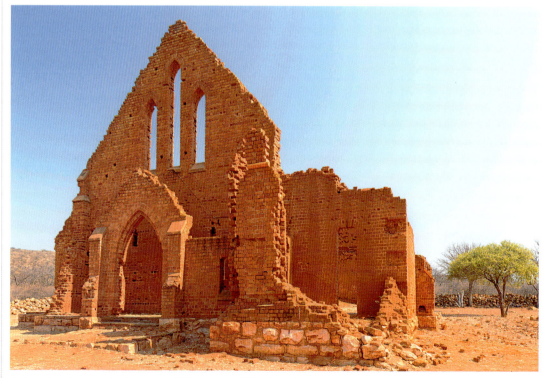

△ The ruins of a red mud-brick church at Old Palapye, built in 1892–1894

Protectorate to the direct administration of Cecil Rhodes's British South Africa Company; three of them, led by Khama III, traveled to London in 1895 to put their case to Queen Victoria. But Rhodes's company wielded significant power, building a railroad through Bechuanaland to Rhodesia. The British government neglected the protectorate, with little investment save short-term plans to develop mining and agriculture in the 1930s.

In 1952, Seretse Khama, the exiled chief of the Ngwato, began to organize calls for independence, leading to the foundation of the Bechuanaland Democratic Party (BDP) in 1962. The British acceded, building a new capital at Gaborone in 1965 (Bechuanaland had long been administered from Mafeking in South Africa) and in 1966, the country gained independence as the Republic of Botswana, with Khama as its first president.

Independent Botswana

Initially almost completely depending on British financial aid, Botswana's prospects were transformed by the discovery of diamonds at Orapa, in the northeast, in 1967. The income this generated fed investment in infrastructure, allowing Khama and the BDP to win consistent majorities until his death in 1980. Although he was politically dominant, Khama did not impose a one-party state, and the Botswana National Party (BNP), an alliance of conservative chiefs and socialist politicians, posed the main opposition.

Internationally, Khama aligned Botswana with the "Frontline States" (Zambia, Tanzania, Mozambique, and Angola), which brought pressure on Zimbabwe and South Africa to grant Black majority rule. In 1980, he helped reform these into a formal body, known as the Southern African Development Co-Ordination Conference (SADCC), which in 1992 evolved into the Southern African Development Community.

Khama's long-term deputy, Quett Masire, succeeded him in July 1980. Grievances over high unemployment and the gap in wealth between urban and rural areas, aggravated by a slowing economy, as well as deteriorating relations with South Africa (which raided Gaborone in 1985 and 1986), tarnished Botswana's previous successes. The growing impact of the HIV/AIDS epidemic also weighed heavily on the country.

Masire stepped down in 1998 to be replaced by Festus Mogae, again from the BDP, who was reelected in 1999 and 2004 before stepping down in 2008. His successor Ian Khama, son of Seretse Khama, won a full term as president in 2009, but soon faced a damaging split in the BDP when a breakaway faction formed the Botswana Movement for Democracy (BMD) in 2010. As a result, an opposition alliance, the Umbrella for Democratic Change (UDC), won almost a third of the seats in parliament in 2014. But Ian Khama remained in power until his resignation in 2018, just before his term was ended.

His successor Mokgweetsi Masisi removed all of Khama's allies, leading Khama to form his own Botswana Patriotic Front, which joined the UDC. Even so, the BDP won two-thirds of seats in the 2019 elections. Although it had never previously experienced a change of ruling party, the country's peaceful independence transition and maintenance of multiparty democracy has been a model for others.

Eswatini

Africa's second-smallest mainland country and its only surviving absolute monarchy has retained its identity in the face of much larger neighbors.

Official name: Kingdom of Eswatini
Date of formation: September 6, 1968
Official languages: Swazi, English

Despite its tiny size, Eswatini is geographically varied, with the densely populated Highveld zone, the Lowveld of thorny bush, and the Lubombo escarpment. The Swazi make up 84 percent of the population and the Zulu 10 percent; both are part of the large Northern Nguni group of peoples. Around 90 percent of Swazi are Christian.

History

The ancestors of the modern Swazi migrated from Mozambique in the 1740s, establishing the Ngwane kingdom around 1770, under Ngwane III. In the 1820s, during the *Mfecane* ("crushing"), the ruling Dlamini clan was forced northward by Zulu pressure. Their king, Sobhuza I (r.1815–1850), survived by establishing a Zulu-style military state, which evolved into the Swazi kingdom. In 1894, Britain and the Boer South African Republic signed a convention, assuming legal control over Eswatini, which from 1903 became the Swaziland Protectorate.

Political pressure for self-rule increased with the forming of parties in the 1960s, including King Sobhuza II's Imbokodvo National Movement (INM), and in 1968, Eswatini became an independent monarchy again. Sobhuza resisted parliamentary government, but the country made economic progress before his death in 1982. The accession of Mswati III was the start of a period of increasing autocracy. In 2002, widespread protests demanded reform, but a new constitution in 2006 only slightly diluted royal power and did not formally legalize opposition parties. In 2018, the king announced the official new name of the country as Eswatini.

△ Lidded wooden vessel made by artisans of the Northern Nguni people

△ A monument in Cape Town honoring South Africa's four Nobel Peace Prize winners

South Africa

Emerging from apartheid in 1993, South Africa has become a vibrant multiracial democracy, though still facing social and economic issues.

Official name: Republic of South Africa
Date of formation: May 31, 1910
Official languages: Afrikaans, English, Ndebele, Sepedi, Sesotho, Setswana, Swati, Tshivenda, Xhosa, Xitsonga, Zulu

The bulk of Africa's southernmost country is a high plateau, which encompasses plains known as the veld, the shrubland of the Great Karoo, and the true desert of the Kalahari, with abundant wildlife such as leopards and giraffes proving a tourist draw. To the south and east, the plateau ends abruptly in the Great Escarpment, which includes the steep, rugged Drakensberg, part of which forms a natural border with Lesotho.

Black South Africans (including Zulu, Xhosa, and Southern Ndebele) make up 79 percent of the population; white South Africans 9 percent; people of mixed European and African descent 9 percent; and people of Indian or Asian descent 2.5 percent. The economy, which is Africa's third largest, is highly developed, with mining its most significant sector, especially of platinum, chromium, and gold.

Early settlement

Human ancestors lived in South Africa at least 3 million years ago—that is the date of a skull of a young *Australopithecus africanus* found at Taung (see pp.22–23). *Homo sapiens* had arrived in the area by 150,000 BCE. San hunters and gatherers roamed the land, on which Khoikhoi people then were herding their animals by 2000 BCE. Bantu-speaking peoples reached the region by 300 CE, and it was these ironworking farmers who gradually developed larger urban centers, such as the gold-mining Mapungubwe by the 11th century (see pp.136–137).

Invasions and resistance

The cultures and lives of local peoples were, however, to be radically disrupted and altered by the arrival of the Dutch East India Company. The Dutch established a first settlement at Cape Town in 1652 (see pp.168–169). The Khoisan, initially trading with the newcomers, soon had to deal with ever-increasing intrusions on the land they used as pasture, and friction grew. This led to wars, which resulted in many Khoisan becoming displaced. Later, Dutch settlers known as the *trekboers* continued moving inland and, by the late 18th century, they had collided with Bantu-speaking agricultural peoples who lived there.

The Zulu Kingdom

In 1806, Britain seized Cape Colony from the Dutch. This caused Dutch settlers (the Boers) to move out and, in 1835, they crossed the Orange River (in the *voortrek*), encroaching on the realms of African states. These states were, however, coalescing; by 1825, Shaka Zulu had welded the disparate Zulu groups into a powerful military kingdom, which often clashed with their neighboring peoples, including the Ndebele. During this time, known as the *Mfecane* ("the crushing"), many peoples fled north or east (see pp.206–207). The Zulu also put the *voortrekkers* in Natal under so much pressure that the Dutch evacuated, which, however, meant that the British annexed Natal in 1843.

A vigorous response by Xhosa leaders—such as the Sotho king Moshoeshoe—to prevent further British encroachment led to a temporary British retraction to Cape Town, but this enabled the Boers to establish independent states in Transvaal (1852) and the Orange Free State (1854). Britain, further incentivized by the discovery of diamonds in the North Cape interior in 1866, and gold in 1886, pushed forward in 1879–1880. The Zulu, no longer as strong as under Shaka, fought but in the end could not stop the British, who deposed the Zulu king Cetshwayo. In 1899–1902, Britain fought a war with the self-declared Boer Republics. The war had a deep impact on the Black population, many thousands of whom were detained and perished in British prison camps, which were separate from those holding Boer prisoners of war.

The apartheid regime
In May 1910, Britain's former Southern African colonies and the Boer republics joined as the Union of South Africa. Resisting this development, Black political leaders formed the South African Native National Congress in 1912, which in 1923 became the ANC (see pp.254–255).

The marginalization of South Africa's Black population, set in law, culminated in 1948 with the electoral victory of the National Party, which instituted a series of extreme segregationist policies known as apartheid. The Group Areas Act (1950) separated urban areas by race, and other measures forbade interracial marriages and controlled the movements of Black Africans. From 1976, the government set up "Bantustans" (homelands) in which Black South Africans had residency in politically powerless quasi-states.

The international community sought to isolate South Africa with sanctions—first imposed by a UN resolution in 1966—and arms embargoes. But the apartheid regime responded with more repression, as well as with raids on neighboring states such as Zambia and Angola, both of which were supporting the anti-apartheid ANC. A massacre of Black Africans, mainly teenage students, in Soweto in 1976 heightened international and internal pressure, and the South African Army's defeat in Angola in 1988 also suggested apartheid's days were finally numbered.

Post-apartheid nation
The National Party leader F. W. de Klerk began negotiations with the imprisoned ANC leader Nelson Mandela (see pp.270–271), who was released in February 1990 and became president after South Africa's first-ever elections under universal suffrage in 1994. In 1993, Mandela and de Klerk were both awarded the Nobel Peace Prize, joining previous South African Nobel laureates: the ANC activist and politician Albert Lutuli (awarded the peace prize in 1960), and Archbishop Desmond Tutu (in 1984).

The new ANC government swept away the apartheid laws, while Mandela's conciliatory rhetoric and the establishment of the Truth and Reconciliation Committee in 1995 aided the healing process.

Mandela stepped down in 1999, to be replaced by Thabo Mbeki as post-apartheid South Africa entered an era in which disappointed hopes, high crime rates, rising unemployment, and allegations of corruption weighed down on the ANC's zest for reform, and where HIV/AIDS was not effectively tackled. In 2008, Mbeki was forced to resign. Jacob Zuma, his former deputy, led the country until 2018 when, dogged by financial scandals, he was replaced by Cyril Ramaphosa, a former trade union leader. Concern over poor economic performance and the slow pace of land reform meant the ANC's victory in the 2019 elections was its narrowest yet, though the party retained its grip on power.

Tristan da Cunha

The six small volcanic islands of Tristan da Cunha are one of the most remote inhabited places in the world.

Official name: Tristan da Cunha
Date of formation: January 12, 1938 (as dependency of St. Helena)
Official language: English

With a population of just less than 300, almost all living in the only settlement, Edinburgh of the Seven Seas, Tristan da Cunha lies 1,300 miles (2,100 km) south of St. Helena, off Southern Africa's west coast. With no airstrip, Tristan da Cunha is accessible only by boat. The islands, now with a marine protection zone, are home to rare elephant seals.

Colonial history
First sighted by the Portuguese explorer Tristão da Cunha in 1506, the islands were visited by the Dutch in 1643. The British placed a garrison there in 1816, but after a year all left except one soldier and his family. Over time a handful of others migrated there, including people of mixed Asian, African, and European ancestry from St. Helena and African women from Cape Colony. The original founder, William Glass, ruled the island colony until 1853, its inhabitants surviving by seal-fishing and raising crops. A bad winter in 1885 and a plague of rats almost caused the colony's evacuation, as did a potato blight in 1906.

In 1938, the islands became a dependency of St. Helena (see p.373), and were used as a Royal Navy radio station during World War II. The eruption of Queen Mary's Peak in 1961 caused people to sail to Southampton, UK, but most returned in 1963. A cyclone in 2001 badly damaged the settlement, highlighting the community's vulnerability.

△ Southern Ndebele women in front of a house decorated in the Ndebele style

Zimbabwe

Once the heart of a great African civilization, Zimbabwe has had a troubled path to statehood, with a prolonged independence war followed by severe economic mismanagement from the late 1980s to 2017, leaving it struggling to reconstruct.

Official name: Republic of Zimbabwe
Date of formation: April 18, 1980
Official languages: Chewa, Chibarwe, English, Kalanga, Khoisan, Nambya, Ndau, Ndebele, Shangani, Shona, Sign Language, Sotho, Tonga, Tswana, Venda, Xhosa

A landlocked nation, Zimbabwe is dominated by the elevated ridge of the Highveld, which covers a quarter of the country. As cultivated areas are expanding, wildlife has suffered, but giraffes, elephants, eland, and the chacma, the largest form of baboon, still thrive. More than two-thirds of Zimbabweans are Shona-speakers, and about a sixth Ndebele; there are 14 other official languages. Around 85 percent are Christian, mostly of Protestant denominations.

Zimbabwe's economy shrank dramatically from the 1990s, as land reforms and hyperinflation hit. Agriculture, the largest sector, includes sugar and beef exports. There is some platinum and gold mining, and large diamond finds.

Rising kingdoms

Bantu-speakers arrived between the 5th and 10th centuries CE, displacing San hunter-gatherers.

Around 900 CE, the Mapungubwe people of southern Zimbabwe, grown rich from the ivory trade, created a state that soon became a substantial kingdom. Its royal enclosure, ringed by a great stone wall, was the first *zimbabwe* (Shona for "stone house"). This style of building was taken up by the Kingdom of Great Zimbabwe (see pp.136–139), which by around 1300 had supplanted Mapungubwe. By 1450, though, Great Zimbabwe was in decline due to shifting trade routes for gold, ivory, and copper,

◁ A contemporary soapstone statue in Shona style from the Chapungu Sculpture Park, Harare

and was overtaken by the Mutapa Empire established in the north by Nyatsimba Mutota, a former Great Zimbabwe prince. Mutapa expanded to the coast, vying with the Torwa Kingdom of the south.

Attempts by the Portuguese, who reached the area in 1511, to seize the trade routes undermined Mutapa and, in the 1680s, Rozvi emerged as a powerful kingdom. The new rulers, the Mambos, dominated the area until the 19th century, when migrations linked to the Zulu expansion (see pp.206–207) destabilized Rozvi.

Rhodesia

Most impactful of the peoples moving north were the Ndebele in 1838–1839; their new kingdom absorbed Rozvi in 1866. After lengthy negotiations, in 1888 the Ndebele king Lobengula granted the Rudd Concession to Cecil Rhodes, giving him exclusive rights—for a monthly fee, and weapons—to exploit minerals. Rhodes used this to establish the British South Africa Company (SAC) in 1889. However, in 1893, in response to Ndebele raids on other peoples in the area, Rhodes attacked Lobengula's capital Bulawayo, forcing him to flee.

By 1894, Ndebele resistance had collapsed, and the SAC had taken control of what it called Southern Rhodesia. Ndebele and Shona rebelled in 1896–1898 but the SAC governed until 1923, creating a settler colony—with 34,000 Europeans migrating there by 1922. All productive land was held by white Europeans and Black Africans were forced to move into marginal areas and be tied to onerous labor contracts.

In 1953, Southern Rhodesia was joined with Northern Rhodesia (Zambia) and Nyasaland (Malawi) to form a single federation. The move was widely resented and fostered nationalist sentiment under leaders such as Joshua Nkomo, who founded the Zimbabwe African People's Union (ZAPU) in 1961, and Robert Mugabe, who joined the Zimbabwe African National Union (ZANU) in 1963.

The UDI era

The federation was dissolved in 1963 but, in 1965, fearing Britain might grant independence to the Black majority, Rhodesia's prime minister Ian Smith announced a Unilateral Declaration of Independence (UDI). Britain declined to recognize this, and in 1966 obtained a UN Resolution imposing mandatory sanctions, while Smith passed measures to solidify white power and in 1970 declared Rhodesia a republic.

ZAPU and ZANU began an armed struggle (see pp.252–253) whose ferocity increased after the two movements formed the Patriotic Front (PF) in 1976, operating from bases in Mozambique. By 1979, Smith conceded an "internal settlement" under which the moderate Black nationalist Bishop Abel Muzorewa led government.

Becoming Zimbabwe

ZANU and ZAPU wanted more, and negotiations at Lancaster House in London brought a new settlement. Southern Rhodesia returned briefly to British colonial control but, in 1980, emerged as an independent Zimbabwe. Mugabe, as prime minister, and Nkomo, home affairs minister, only shared power uneasily. In 1982, Mugabe accused the ZAPU leader of planning a coup and dismissed him, starting a civil war in Matabeleland in which thousands were killed. It only ended in 1987 with the merger of ZANU and ZAPU as ZANU-PF.

△ The ruins of the Hill Complex, the oldest section of Great Zimbabwe, and possibly its religious center

Zimbabwe became a one-party state with Mugabe as president and Nkomo as vice-president. The challenge of developing national education and health systems proved hard, as soaring unemployment, the high cost of intervening in the wars in the DRC (see pp.266–267), and the significant agricultural impact of the confiscation of white-owned farms hit the economy.

Dissent against ZANU-PF rule rose, and in the 2000 elections, the Movement for Democratic Change (MDC) won almost half the seats. But Mugabe continued his increasingly autocratic rule, and by 2008, the economy was collapsing, with inflation reaching 10 million percent. Presidential elections indicated the MDC's Morgan Tsvangirai was in the lead, but with less than 50 percent, thus necessitating a run-off, a result widely believed to have been manipulated by ZANU-PF. Tsvangirai boycotted the second vote, precipitating a crisis that only subsided when Mugabe and Tsvangirai signed a power-sharing agreement. Mugabe, however, sidelined Tsvangirai, retaining control of the security apparatus, and the elections of 2013 returned him with a large majority. By now in his early 90s, he faced growing opposition from those in his own party who opposed his plan to hand the succession to his wife Grace.

As the economy deteriorated once more, demonstrations broke out and when Mugabe fired the vice-president, and potential successor, Emmerson Mnangagwa in 2017, the army stepped in and Mugabe was forced to resign.

Zimbabwe after Mugabe

Mnangagwa, sworn in on November 24, 2017, reached out to white farmers and applied to rejoin the Commonwealth, but in the elections that followed, his vote share of just over 50 percent was widely believed to be manipulated. Serious protests that followed an increase in fuel prices in 2019 showed that the government was again struggling to establish its credibility, not just with the international economic and political community but with its own people, too.

Zambia

Landlocked Zambia's destiny has long been dependent on copper, which attracted European colonization and provided funds for its post-independence governments to attempt to boost the economy of an ethnically and politically diverse country.

Official name: Republic of Zambia
Date of formation: October 24, 1964
Official language: English

At the heart of Southern Africa, Zambia's high plateaus are riven by the great river valleys of the Zambezi and Congo drainage basins. Its moderate tropical climate allows abundant wildlife to flourish, including over 700 species of birds, but poaching and habitat loss has meant larger mammals, such as elephants, lions, and African buffaloes, are scarce outside national parks.

More than 70 ethnic groups live in Zambia, of which the Bemba (21 percent), Tonga (14 percent), Chewa (7 percent), and Lozi (6 percent) are the most numerous. Over 95 percent of Zambians are Christian (four-fifths of those Roman Catholic). The population is heavily concentrated around the capital Lusaka in the south and the Copperbelt in the north, which lies at the heart of the economy's most important sector. Recently, the government has sought diversification into other areas such as tourism and hydroelectric power.

Copper kingdoms

Homo sapiens skeletons dating back to 100,000 years ago have been found at Kalambo Falls, and Zambia was settled by ancestors of the Khoisan and Batwa peoples before Bantu-speakers moved south into the area in the 6th century CE. They were the first to mine copper, and by 1000 CE were trading with the port cities on the east coast of Africa. Their territory lay on the borders of several great empires. The Luba Kingdom, which arose in the southern Democratic Republic of the Congo around 1585, dominated trade routes across the breadth of Africa. East of Luba, the Lunda Kingdom ruled an extensive domain, including parts of northwest Zambia, until Chokwe invaders brought it down in the late 19th century. Parts of Zambia also lay in the territory of the Kingdom of Mutapa (in modern-day Zimbabwe) from the 14th to the 17th centuries.

By that time, other, smaller kingdoms had appeared in Zambia, among them the Chewa of the east, the Bemba of the northeast, and the Lozi of the Upper Zambezi. By the 1760s, Portugal was trading cotton with these kingdoms in exchange for ivory and copper and did not seek to colonize or control them politically. But political instability in the 1840s, as Kololo herdsmen invaded the Lozi Kingdom, and in the 1860s, when Ngoni from the south conquered Chewa, combined with the devastating impact of the slave trade, had weakened local power in the region, which by now had begun to attract British interest.

Foreign exploitation

In 1889, Britain granted a charter to Cecil Rhodes's British South Africa Company (BSAC), giving it the right to make treaties with African rulers, and with other European powers. Although the Ngoni fought hard against BSAC troops in 1898, disease, famine, and a belief that the British might be useful allies against other Europeans allowed Rhodes's company to gain control of significant territories and their mineral resources. The company exploited copper deposits and transported local laborers to gold and coal mines farther south.

◁ Lidded food container of the Lozi people, with bowls for sorghum meal at the bottom and stew above

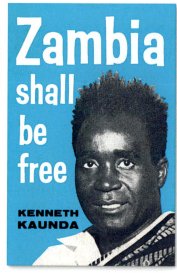

△ Kenneth Kaunda on the front cover of his 1962 political autobiography, which called for Zambian independence

This and company-levied taxes led to resistance, such as by the local Watchtower Movement from 1908, which preached social reforms for mineworkers. In 1924, the BSAC handed over what was then known as Northern Rhodesia to the British government as a protectorate.

New copper deposits were discovered in 1928 but they brought little prosperity to Africans as profits went to the colonizers and, in the late 1940s, local trade unions began to form among the mineworkers.

In 1953, Northern Rhodesia was joined with Southern Rhodesia and Nyasaland in the Central African Federation. There was an economic boom caused by a rise in copper prices, but when this ended—leading to soaring unemployment—the focus on independence increased again. Nationalist leaders, led by Kenneth Kaunda and his UNIP party, demanded the federation's breakup and an independent Zambia. A campaign of civil disobedience in 1962 convinced the British to accede, and in 1964 Zambia gained independence with Kaunda as president.

Zambia under Kaunda

Buoyed by copper prices rising once more, President Kaunda was able to invest in infrastructure and education, establishing the University of Zambia in 1965. The country suffered, however, due to UN sanctions imposed on Rhodesia after its white minority government (see p.381) declared independence the same year, which caused Zambian trade to the south to dry up. As copper prices fell, a recession hit and the government became authoritarian, imposing a one-party constitution in 1973. By this time, Zambia had become a base for anti-apartheid and anti-colonial parties from its neighboring nations, including the ANC (see pp.254–255).

Poverty in the growing cities bred discontent and in 1986 and 1990 there were large-scale food riots. In 1990, Kaunda conceded the return of a multiparty system and the following year was resoundingly defeated in elections by Frederick Chiluba, ending his 37-year presidency.

Modern Zambia

Chiluba and his Movement for Multiparty Democracy (MMD) attempted economic reforms, privatizing key industries, but his constitutional maneuvers in preventing Kaunda from standing in the 1996 elections, followed by a coup attempt in 1997, tarnished people's hopes for a freer political atmosphere. Chiluba was banned from running a third term in 2001. The political reforms of his MMD successor, Levy Mwanawasa, were hampered by ill health. In 2008, Mwanawasa died, to be replaced by his party colleague Rupiah Banda, who won elections that his main opponent, Michael Sata of the Patriotic Front (PF), claimed were rigged. Sata did, however, win in 2011, promising economic growth and social freedoms, neither of which transpired before he, in turn, died prematurely in 2014.

Edgar Lungu of the PF won the special election that followed and the presidential election in 2016. His launch of large infrastructure projects was hit by the onset of the COVID-19 pandemic in 2020, and his reputation by increasing harassment of opposition media. Despite some election-period violence, Lungu conceded to his UPND opponent Hakainde Hichilema after losing in 2021. Zambia's economy might remain dependent on copper, but its politics have diversified.

△ The Mosi-oa-Tunya (Victoria Falls) in the Zambezi River on the border with Zimbabwe, one of Zambia's most spectacular natural features

Mozambique

Undermined by the slave trade, Portuguese colonialism, and a long civil war, Mozambique has only recently begun to recover, allowing it to make use of its strategic position astride Indian Ocean trade routes and its own natural resources.

Official name: Republic of Mozambique
Date of formation: June 25, 1975
Official language: Portuguese

Mozambique's extensive coastline facing the Indian Ocean has long laid it open to outside influences, and provided riches from trade as well as from exploitation of maritime resources. Low in the south, Mozambique's terrain climbs toward the north and center, rising to 7,992 ft (2,436 m) at Mount Binga in the Chimoio highlands. The Zambezi River dominates the country, draining more than 87,000 sq miles (225,000 sq km) in the center and providing rich and fertile soils. The climate is tropical with a strong monsoon in the north.

Ethnically diverse, the country has more than 40 Bantu languages. About half of the population speak Makua or Lomwe, while Tsonga is used by around a seventh; though official, Portuguese is not universally spoken. Some 55 percent of Mozambicans are Christian, a quarter practice Indigenous faiths, and a sixth are Muslim. The main economic activity is agriculture, with cashew nuts and cotton grown for export, while electricity production (mainly transmitted to South Africa) and aluminum smelting also contribute.

Early settlements

Iron-using, Bantu-speaking agriculturalists arrived in the region in the 3rd century CE, slowly pushing out the San peoples who had preceded them and establishing small chiefdoms, or *nyika*. By the 13th century, a small *zimbabwe* fortification was built at Manekweni in southern Mozambique, which was linked to the Kingdom of Great Zimbabwe (see pp.136–139) and prospered on cattle-raising and control of the gold trade. Swahili trading posts (see pp.146–147) had by the 14th century spread southward from the Tanzanian coastline as far as Angoche, creating long-distance land and sea networks for the trade in gold, ivory, and enslaved people.

Struggle for dominance

The Portuguese first arrived in Mozambique in 1498, en route to India. By 1505, they had set up their first trading post, at Sofala, gradually extending their control over the coast and, by the 1550s, trading with the peoples of the interior. Portugal's trafficking of enslaved Africans from this region, mainly to Brazil, went on for centuries. The Arab capture of Fort Jesus (Mombasa) in 1698, however, eclipsed the Portuguese, with Mazrui and Omani Arabs once again dominating the Indian Ocean trade, conducted through centers such as Kilwa and the Island of Mozambique.

Already destabilized by the slave trade, the region suffered further disruption in the early 19th century, caused by militarized groups operating in the south, on the edges of the Zulu State. One of these, the Ngoni, led by their ruler Soshangane, went across the Limpopo River and founded the Gaza State, which came to dominate southern Mozambique until the 1890s.

Portuguese colony

By the 1880s, the Portuguese were confined to coastal enclaves such as Lourenço Marques (later Maputo). But as Gaza began to decline, neighboring African states allied with the Portuguese, whose army destroyed Gaza in 1897 and took control of southern Mozambique. Over the next two decades, Portugal took the center, too, and defeated the coastal sheikhdoms of Angoche.

The Portuguese wanted to connect Mozambique to their colony in Angola, but Britain resisted this and, in 1891, Portugal accepted Mozambique's current borders. The colony became neglected, ruled by private chartered companies, which imposed forced labor, poverty wages, and high taxation on the African population. Limited attempts at development of infrastructure began in the 1950s, but with Portuguese companies retaining monopolies and a flux of European settlers, the Mozambicans became increasingly discontented.

Nationalist movements first developed in exile, with the foundation of the Mozambique Liberation Front (FRELIMO) under Eduardo Mondlane in Tanzania in 1962. Trained by the USSR, FRELIMO guerrillas began attacks in 1964. Led by Samora Machel (see pp.250–251) from 1969, the struggle intensified, and by 1974, FRELIMO controlled large parts of the north.

Independent Mozambique

Portugal's Carnation Revolution in 1974 accelerated Portuguese decolonization (see pp.248–249) and Mozambique became independent in June 1975. As president of a one-party state, Machel ended forced labor and nationalized key industries, partially collectivizing agriculture, which, however, led to marked opposition and the policy's abandonment in 1985. FRELIMO's support for armed nationalists in Rhodesia and South Africa led those governments to fund RENAMO, an anti-FRELIMO militant movement, whose attacks devastated Mozambique's

▷ Mozambican 1937 stamp showing a *dhow*, an Indian Ocean trading vessel

economy. In 1984, South Africa and Mozambique signed the Nkomati Accord, agreeing to end support for their respective opposition groups—the ANC (see pp.268–269) operated from Mozambique—but RENAMO fought on until a 1992 peace agreement (finalized in 1994).

Joaquim Chissano, who had become president after Machel's death in a plane crash in 1986, sanctioned multiparty elections which took place in 1994, giving RENAMO a strong representation in parliament. Mozambique joined the Commonwealth in 1995, the first former colony of a country other than Britain to do so. But the demining of huge swathes of Mozambique, the demobilization of thousands of guerrillas, and the return of 1.7 million refugees sapped the nation's resources. By 2004, when FRELIMO's Armando Guebuza was voted president, economic growth had resumed, but tensions with RENAMO and its leader Afonso Dhlakama simmered, and in 2013 small-scale fighting broke out.

A new peace accord was signed by Dhlakama and Guebuza in 2014, but collapsed again in 2015. Although fighting died down, the next peace agreement was only signed in 2019 and instability, drops in the price of commodities on whose export Mozambique depended (which led to a partial default in 2017), a devastating cyclone in 2019, and the impact of COVID-19 all weighed heavily on the economy. Nonetheless, RENAMO performed badly in the 2019 elections, so FRELIMO's grip on power that had lasted for over 40 years could continue.

▷ An *ujamaa* sculpture symbolizing the strength of community, by the Makonde people of northern Mozambique

Glossary

A

Abbasid Caliphate (750–1258 CE) A Muslim empire that stretched across modern-day Iran, Iraq, Saudi Arabia, and North Africa as far as Tunisia.

Afrikaner (or Boer, from the Dutch for "husbandman," or "farmer") Describes South Africans descended from predominantly Dutch settlers who arrived in 1652.

African Union An organization founded in 2002 to replace the Organization of African Unity (OAU). It promotes solidarity between African states and international cooperation to further economic development on the continent.

Aghlabid dynasty (800–909 CE) An Arab dynasty that ruled modern-day Tunisia, eastern Algeria, and parts of Southern Italy and Sicily in the 9th and early 10th centuries.

Akan An ethnolinguistic grouping of peoples who settled in what is now Ghana, Côte d'Ivoire, and parts of Togo in the 11th–18th centuries.

Aksum (c. 150–1000 CE) A kingdom in East Africa and the Arabian Peninsula.

Almohad Caliphate (1121–1269 CE) An Amazigh (Berber) Muslim empire that stretched across much of North Africa (the Maghreb) and the Iberian Peninsula (al-Andalus).

Almoravid Caliphate (1050s–1147 CE) An Amazigh Muslim empire that encompassed North Africa (the Maghreb) and the Iberian Peninsula (al-Andalus).

Amazigh (pl. Imazighen) A diverse grouping of distinct ethnic groups in North Africa, descendants of pre-Arab inhabitants of the region. Also known as Berber, from the Greek for "[non-Greek speaking] foreigner."

annexation The proclamation of sovereignty by one state over territory outside its domain; often preceded by conquest and military occupation.

anthropoids The group of primates that includes living and fossil monkeys, apes, and humans.

apartheid In South Africa and southwest Africa, the system of institutionalized racial segregation that existed from 1948 to 1994.

Arab Describes Arabic-speaking people who came from the Arabian Peninsula and inhabited much of the Middle East and North Africa.

Asante Empire (1701–1901 CE) A West African state that occupied the area that is now southern Ghana.

Assyria An ancient empire in southwestern Asia that was at its height from about 750 to 612 BCE.

autonomy The right or condition of self-government.

Ayyubid Sultanate (1171–1260 CE) A Muslim empire—founded by Salah al-Din Yusuf ibn Ayyub (commonly known as Saladin) in Egypt—that encompassed much of the Middle East and North Africa.

B

Bamum A Central African kingdom established in the 14th century in what is now northwest Cameroon.

Bantu-speaking people Speakers of any of the approximately 500 Bantu languages spoken in Central and Southern Africa.

Biafra A state that declared its independence from Nigeria in May 1967 and existed until January 1970.

Boer See Afrikaner.

Buganda (c. 14th century–1967, reestablished in 1993) A kingdom in Uganda, Central Africa, that was at its most powerful in the 18th and 19th centuries.

Bunyoro (c. 12th century–1967, reestablished in 1993) A kingdom in western Uganda that was at its height from the 16th to the 19th centuries.

C

caliph A Muslim civil and religious ruler, regarded as a successor of the Prophet Muhammad.

caliphate An Islamic state, especially one ruled by a single religious and political leader.

Chimurenga A Shona word meaning "uprising" (the Ndebele equivalent is *Umvukela*, meaning "revolutionary struggle"). It refers to the Shona and Ndebele insurrections against the British South Africa Company during the late 1890s—known as the Second Matabele War, or the First *Chimurenga/Umvukela*. In the 1960s and '70s, the Second *Chimurenga/Umvukela*, also known as the Zimbabwe War of Independence, was fought between African nationalist guerrillas and the predominantly white Rhodesian government.

city-state In the ancient world, a city and surrounding land with its own government.

client king A term used in ancient Rome for a ruler in a harmonious but unequal alliance with Rome.

Coptic Christianity One of the oldest churches of Christianity, based in Egypt and said to have been founded by Mark, an apostle and evangelist, in the middle of the 1st century CE.

crown colony A British colony that was administered by a governor appointed by the British monarch on the advice of the UK Government.

Cushite A word used in the Hebrew Bible to refer to Africa and Africans. Cush is identified with the Kingdom of Kush (c. 1070 BCE–c. 550 CE), also known as ancient Sudan.

D

Dahomey Kingdom (c. 1625–1904 CE) A West African power that flourished in the 18th and 19th centuries in southern Benin.

diaspora A population that shares a cultural and regional origin, but currently resides elsewhere. Diasporas come about through immigration and forced movements of people.

Dogon An ancient ethnic group in Mali and Burkina Faso, known for their mask dances and dry stone buildings.

dynasty A line of rulers or leaders from the same family or group, or a period of time when a country or region is ruled by them.

E

emirate A Muslim state ruled by a military commander called an emir.

Ethiopian Empire (1270–1974 CE) A state in the region that is now Ethiopia and Eritrea, founded by the Solomonic dynasty.

F

Fatimid Caliphate (909–1171 CE) A Muslim empire that spanned North Africa to western Saudi Arabia.

forced labor Work that is performed involuntarily—not, as with slavery, because the worker is "owned" (seen as a piece of property), but because of threats such as of violence or death.

French Community An association of states set up in 1958 between France and its remaining African colonies; by the end of 1960, its African members had declared their independence and left, although the association was only officially abolished in 1995.

Fulani Empire (or Sokoto Caliphate) (c. 1800–c. 1900 CE) A West African Muslim theocracy in Cameroon, Burkina Faso, Niger, and Nigeria.

G

Gao A town on the Niger River in Mali that gave rise to a kingdom that, by the end of the 13th century, had become part of the Mali Empire.

Ge'ez An ancient language of Ethiopia that influenced modern Ethiopian languages such as Amharic and that survives as the liturgical language of the Ethiopian Church.

Great Zimbabwe The stone-built capital city of a great medieval kingdom in modern-day Zimbabwe.

H

Hajj The pilgrimage that Muslims are required to make to Mecca—Islam's holiest city—in Saudi Arabia.

Hausa Kingdoms (c. 1000–1815 CE) A loose alliance of trading states in what is now northern Nigeria.

hominid A group consisting of all living and extinct great apes (modern humans, chimpanzees, gorillas, and orangutans, and all their immediate ancestors).

hominin A group consisting of *Homo sapiens* (modern humans) and extinct ancestors such as *Homo erectus* and *Homo neanderthalensis*.

hut tax Taxation introduced by British colonizers in Africa on a per hut or household basis, payable in money, labor, grain, or stock.

I

Ilé-Ifè (or Ife) A city in southwestern Nigeria, founded by the 4th century BCE and considered to be the oldest city-state of the Yoruba people.

Indentured servitude A contracted period of labor without salary to pay off an indenture or loan.

J

Jolof (or Wolof) Empire (c. 1200–c. 1600 CE) A West African trading state that dominated inland modern-day Senegal.

K

kandake A title for queens and queen mothers of the Empire of Kush (also known as Nubia) in what is now northern Sudan and southern Egypt.
kabaka The title of the king of Buganda in what is now Uganda.
Kanem-Bornu (c. 800–1893 CE) A trading empire that controlled the area around Lake Chad in West Central Africa.
Khoikhoi Indigenous peoples of Southern Africa, traditionally nomadic herders and hunter-gatherers.
Kongo Kingdom (c. 1390–1862 CE) A western Central African state located in present-day northern Angola, Congo, and the western Democratic Republic of the Congo.

L

Lozi Kingdom (c. 1700s–1890 CE) A state inhabiting the area that is today western Zambia in Central Africa.
Luba Kingdom (1585–1889 CE) A power that arose in what is now the southern Democratic Republic of the Congo.
Lunda Kingdom (c. 1665–c. 1887 CE) A confederation of states in what is now the Democratic Republic of the Congo, northeastern Angola, and northwestern Zambia.

M

madrasa The Arabic word for a place of learning, either religious or secular.
Maghreb The western part of the Arab world, comprising western and central North Africa, including Mauritania (disputed), Western Sahara, Morocco, Algeria, Tunisia, and Libya.
Mali Empire (1230–1660 CE) A state in West Africa renowned for the wealth of its rulers, especially Mansa Musa.
Mamluk dynasty (1250–1517 CE) A dynasty that ruled Egypt and Syria, established by formerly enslaved soldiers turned generals.
Mandingo Also known as Mandinka or Malinke, an ethnic group primarily found in southern Mali, the Gambia, and eastern Guinea.
megacity A very large city, typically with a population of over 10 million.

Meroë A city of ancient Kush in present-day Sudan; also the name of the area surrounding the city.
Mfecane The Zulu name (meaning "destruction" or "crushing") for an upheaval among Indigenous peoples in Southern Africa in the first half of the 19th century during the formation of the Zulu Kingdom. Also known by the Sesotho names *Difaqane* or *Lifaqane* (meaning "forced migration").

N

Napata An ancient city of Nubia and Kush, situated in present-day Sudan.
Négritude An anti-colonial movement founded in the 1930s by French-speaking African and Caribbean writers living in France.
Neocolonialism A term first used after World War II to describe the use of economic, political, cultural, or other pressures exerted by one state on another, particularly former colonies.
Nri Kingdom (900 CE–present) A state in what is now Nigeria.

O

oba A ruler among various peoples in the Benin region of West Africa.
Organization of African Unity (OAU) A body founded in 1963 to promote self-government, respect for territorial boundaries, and social progress throughout the African continent.
Ottoman Empire (c. 1299–1922 CE) One of the mightiest and longest-lasting dynasties in world history, which controlled much of southeast Europe, North Africa, and western Asia.
Oyo Empire (c. 1300–1896 CE) The largest Yoruba state in West Africa, located in present-day eastern Benin and western Nigeria.

P

palette In ancient Egypt, a decorated stone on which cosmetics were mixed.
Pan-Africanism A worldwide movement that aims to unite and strengthen the relationship between people of African descent.
Phoenicia (c. 2500–64 BCE) A maritime state that extended along the coastal regions of modern-day Lebanon and parts of Syria and Israel.
protectorate A state or region that is nominally independent, but whose external affairs are controlled by a protector country.

Punic Wars (or Carthaginian Wars) (264–146 BCE) A series of three wars between the Roman Republic and the Carthaginian (Punic) Empire in modern-day Tunisia, as a result of which Rome took control of the western Mediterranean, destroyed Carthage, and enslaved its people.

S

Sahel The semiarid region of West and northern Central Africa extending from Senegal eastward to Sudan.
San Indigenous hunter-gatherer peoples of Southern Africa, and the oldest surviving cultures of the region.
Semitic Relating to or denoting a family of languages that includes Hebrew, Arabic, Amharic, and Aramaic, as well as certain ancient languages such as Phoenician.
Shia Islam One of two main branches of Islam (the other being the Sunni), which regards Muhammad's cousin and son-in-law Ali ibn Abi Talib and his descendants as the Prophet's rightful successors.
Songhai Empire (1464–1591 CE) A trading state of West Africa, which replaced the Mali Empire as the most important power in the region.
Solomonic dynasty The ruling dynasty of the Ethiopian Empire from the 13th to the 20th centuries.
sphere of influence The claim by one state to have control over a foreign area or territory.
stela (pl. stelae) In the ancient world, an inscribed stone or wooden slab set up for a monumental purpose.
Sufism An Islamic belief and practice in which adherents seek the truth of divine love and knowledge through direct personal experience of God.
sultanate A state or country that is ruled by a sultan, or Muslim sovereign.
Sunni Islam The largest of the two major branches of Islam (the other being the Shia), which recognizes the first four caliphs as the Prophet Muhammad's legitimate successors.
Swahili Bantu-speaking people of Zanzibar and the adjacent coast of Africa; also the language spoken.

T

Tellem The name (meaning "those who were before us") used by the Dogon for the people who inhabited their region in Mali before them.

theocracy A system of government by religious leaders.
Tifinagh The script used to write Amazigh languages.
tributary state In premodern times, the subordinate relationship of one state to another, involving the sending of regular tokens of submission, or tributes, such as gold, goods such as cattle or crops, or enslaved people.
Tukulor Empire (c. 1850–1893 CE) A Muslim theocracy in West Africa founded by cleric Al-Hajj Umar Tal.

U

Umayyad Caliphate (661–750 CE) The second Muslim caliphate established after the death of the Prophet Muhammad, which, at its peak, controlled the Middle East, parts of India, much of North Africa, and Spain.

V

vassal state A country that has limited independence and only has the rights and privileges that a more powerful country has given to it.
Vodun A West African religion practiced by peoples in Benin, Togo, Ghana, and Nigeria; elements of it are found in the Haitian religion of Vodou, brought there by enslaved Africans.

W

Wagadou Empire (or ancient Ghana) (600–1000 CE) A trading empire in parts of what is now Mauritania and Mali.

X

Xhosa An group of related peoples in Southern Africa who speak Xhosa, a Bantu language.

Y

Yoruba A West African ethnic group who inhabit parts of Nigeria, Benin, and Togo, a region known as Yorubaland.

Z

Zagwe Kingdom (c. 900–c 1200 CE) A dominant state in the northern parts of Ethiopia and Eritrea that was ruled by the Zagwe dynasty, whose best-known emperor, Lalibela, is said to have built the magnificent rock-hewn churches named after him.
Zulu Kingdom (1816–1887 CE) A monarchy in Southern Africa founded by Shaka kaSenzangakhona (known as Shaka Zulu).

Index

Page numbers in **bold** refer to main entries.

A

A-group 50
Aba Women's Protest 219, 288
Abacha, Sani 263
Abbas, Ferhat 234
Abbasid dynasty 98
Abbasiya 98
Abd al Mu'min 103
Abd-al-Kadir 228
Abdallah ibn Yasin 100
Abdelkader, Emir 217
Abdullah II of Ifriqiya 98
Abdurrahman dan Abi Bakar, Caliph 195
abolition movement 149, 163, 215
Abu Abdullah al-Shii 98
Abu Bakr ibn Umar 100
Abu Ibrahim Ahmed 98
Abu Ishaq al-Sahili 93
Abu Simbel 45
Abu Yazid 99
Abydos **42**
Abyssinia 72
Achebe, Chinua 302, 303
Acheulean tools 28
Actium, Battle of 43
Adal Sultanate 119
Adherbal 66, 67
Adichie, Chimamanda Ngozi 289, 303
Adinkra symbols 59, 151
Adlam script 59
administration, colonial **222–3**, 259
Adwa, Battle of 218, 219
Afonso I of Kongo 182, 183
Africa Cup of Nations 275, 286
Africa Nova 67
Africa Proconsularis 70, 74
African National Congress (ANC) 228, 254–5, 268, 269, 271, 274
African Union 261, 274, 277, 282, 304, 305
Africanus, Leo 105
Afrikaners 209, 217
Afro-Asiatic languages 80
Afro-Turk community 215
Afropop 297
Agadez, Sultanate of 105, 106, 109
Agaja of Dahomey 178
Agenda 2063 305
Aghlabid dynasty **98**
agriculture
    and Bantu migrations 36, 37
    development of 31, **34–5**
    sustainable 282
Ahmad al-Mansur, Sultan of Morocco 89
Ahmadu Tal 196, 197
Ahmose I, Pharaoh 42
Ahmose-Nefertari 42
Aidoo, Ama Ata 289

Ajami script 59, 96
Akan people 59, 151, 190, 192, 296
Akhenaten, Pharaoh 134
Akomfrah, John 293
Aksum, Kingdom of 10, 40, 41, 55, **62–3**, 72, 74, 78, 118, 205, 302
Akyem people 192
al-Adil I, Sultan 124
al-Aghlab, Ibrahim ibn 98
al-Bakri, Abu al-Aziz 85
al-Fazari, Ibrahim 84
al-Ghazi, Ahmad ibn Ibrahim 119
al-Idrisi, Mohammed 83
al-Jamali, Badr 99
Al-Kahina, Queen of the Imazighen 73
al-Kamil, Sultan 125
al-Kanemi, Muhammad 109
al-Katib, Jawhar 99
al-Mansur, Caliph 99
al-Masudi 85
al-Muizz, Caliph 99
al-Mukhtar, Omar 236
al-Mustansir, Caliph 99
al-Salih, Sultan 125
al-Umari 119
al-Ya'qubi 85, 108
Alexandria 71, 74, 75, 205
Algeria 216–17, 223, **316–17**
    Fatimid 99
    independence 227, 234–5, 317
Algerian War of Independence 234, 235, 288, 317
Ali Gaji 109
'Ali ibn Yusuf 103
Allada people 178
Allied Democratic Forces (ADF) 266
Almohad dynasty **100–101**, 103
Almoravid dynasty 78, 85, 89, 90, **100–101**, 135
Alodia Kingdom 74–5
Alvaro I of Kongo 182
Alvor Agreement 249
Amanikhatashan, Queen of Kush 55
Amanirenas, Queen of Kush 55
Amanishakheto, Queen of Kush 54, 55
Amazigh kingdoms 41, **66–7**
Amazigh languages 59, 67, 70, 80
Amazigh people 100, 101, 126, 150
Amba Geshen 119
Amda Seyon I of Ethiopia 119
Amenhotep III, Pharaoh 42
Americas
    Atlantic slave trade **162–3**, 166
    colonial empires 160
Amhara people 118
Amin, Idi 263, 363
Amusan, Oluwatobiloba Ayomide "Tobi" 286
ancestor worship 156, 280
Andriamandisoarivo of Boina 170
Andriamanetiarivo of Menabe 170
Andriamisara of the Sakalava 170

Andrianampoinimerina of the Merina 170, 173
Andriandahifotsy of the Sakalava 170
Anfao, Battle of 106
Anglo-Asante Wars 191, 216, 217, 221
Anglo-Belgian India Rubber Company 213
Anglo-Boer War 217, 379
Anglo-Zanzibar War 187
Anglo-Zulu War 209
Angola **372–3**
    civil war 246, 247, 373
    colonial rule 223
    independence 247, 248, 249, 373
    and Kingdom of Kongo 182, 183
    Njinga Mbande 180–81
animal legends 156–7
ankara 151
Anna Pepple House 221
anti-apartheid movement **256–7**, 268–9, 379
anti-slavery movements 215
Antony, Mark 43, 67
Aoudaghost 84, 85, 100
apartheid 207, **254–5**, 379
    dismantling of **268–9**, 271
    resistance to **256–7**
Apuleius 65
Arab Spring 274
Arab travelers 84, **85**
Arabia, trade with 82–3, 146
Arabic script 59
Arafat, Yasser 239
Ardipithecus ramidus 23
Arochukwu 115
art and artifacts
    Aksum 62
    in anti-apartheid struggle **256–7**
    beadwork **278–9**
    Benin bronzes 128, 129, 130, **132–3**, 276
    bottle-top sculptures **298–9**
    colonial theft of 276
    contemporary Africa 274, 277
    Egyptian **48–9**
    Great Zimbabwe soapstone birds 137
    Igbo 114, 115, 116
    Kerma civilization 50
    Kongolese *mangaaka* **184–5**
    Luba 142, **144–5**
    Nok culture **60–61**
    Nri bronzes 115, **116–17**
    prehistoric 14, 15, 30
    textiles **150–51**
    visual cultures of West Africa **198–9**
    Yoruba 110
    Zanele Muholi **300–301**
    see also rock art
Asante Empire 10, 78, 79, 112, 135, 150, 151, 156, 160, **190–91**, 216, 218, 228
    Osei Tutu **192–3**
Ascension Island **373**
Ashurbanipal of Assyria 57
Askia Muhammad I of Songhai 105, **106–7**

Askia Musa of Songhai 106
Aspelta of Kush 54
Assyrians 40, 43, 57, 64
athletics 274, 286
Atlantic Charter 226, **231**
Atlantic slave trade 149, **162–3**, 214–15
Atlas Mountains 16, 17, 21
Augustine, St **71**
Augustus, Emperor 55
Australopithecus afarensis 14, 22, 23, 354, 378
Australopithecus anamensis 23
Australopithecus boisei 23
Autshumao (Khoi chieftain) 169
Awadghust 89
Aybeg, Sultan of Egypt 125
Ayyubid dynasty **124–5**, 135
az-Zubayr, Rabih 109
Azikiwe, Nnamdi 240, 241, 260, 261

B

Bâ, Mariama 302, 303
babalawos (medicine men) 280
Badari culture 42
Baga of Mauretania 66
Baganda Kingdom/people 151, 241
Bamako 276
Bambara Empire 197
Bambatha kaMancinza of the Zulu 228
Bambuk goldfields 88, 91, 104
Bambuti people 267
Bamum, Kingdom of 202
Bamum, map of **202–3**
bana balute (memory men) 144
Banana, Canaan 253
Banda, Hastings 260–61
Bankole-Bright, Herbert 229
Bantu languages 80, 81, 147
Bantu migrations 15, 35, **36–7**, 136, 152, 206
Bantu-speakers
 mythology 156
 sea trading 82, 146
Bantustans 255
Banu Hilal 99
Banu Marin 101
Banu Sulaym 99
Barghash bin Said, Sultan 188, 189
Barotseland 143
Barre, Siad 265
Barth, Heinrich 201
basketball 286–7
battery minerals 283, 304
beadwork **278–9**
Bedouin 10, **126–7**
Belgian Congo 183, 213, 219, 259, 266, 350–51
Belgium
 colonial empire 142, 160, 161, 183, 210–11, 219, 223
 and Congo Free State **212–13**, 350–51
 continued influence in Africa 263
 exploration of Africa 200
 and Rwanda and Burundi 177
Ben Bella, Ahmed 263
Benguela 162
Benin 178, **338–9**
 independence 235, 339
Benin City 128, 129, 130

Benin, Kingdom of 112, 115, **128–9**, 216, 217
 Benin Bronzes **132–3**, 276
 Oba Ewuare **130–31**
Berber *see* Amazigh; Imazighen
Bere festival 113
Berlin Conference 160, 161, 163, 210, 211, 212, 216, 221, 248
Bete Giyorgis (Lalibela) 122–3
Betsimisaraka people 170
Biafra War 227, 264
Bibi Titi Mohammed 226, 227
Biko, Stephen Bantu **268**
biodiversity 304
Bismarck, Otto von 210
Biya, Paul 261, 343
Black Consciousness Movement (BCM) 233, 268
Black nationalism 226, 243
Black Power 233
Blyden, Edward Wilmot 232
Boer War *see* Anglo-Boer War
Boers 207, 254, 292, 378, 379
Boina, Kingdom of 170
Boko Haram 275, 345
Bondu goldfields 91
Bonny Island 221
Book of the Dead 43, 48
borders, arbitrary drawing of 211, 258, 259
Borgawa people 228
Bornu Empire 109, 135
Botha, P. W. 268
Botswana 263, 265, 274, **376–7**
bottle-top sculptures **298–9**
Bourguíba, Habíb 234
Boussouma 140
boxing 287
brain development 25, 30
Brandenburg African Company 167
Brazil 162, 214
Britain
 abolition of slavery 149, 163
 and Afrikaners/Boers 217
 and Asante Empire 190, 191, 216, 218
 and Bunyoro and Buganda 174–5
 and Cape Colony 166, 169
 decolonization 226, 227, 228, 229, 230, 231, **240–41**, 262
 early intervention in Africa 166
 and Egypt 125, 237, 239, 246, 309
 exploration of Africa 200, 201
 and Gambia 166
 and Gold Coast/Ghana 166, 242–3
 and Igbo states 115
 imperialism 11, 129, 160, 161, 210, 211, 231
 independence from **240–41**
 and Kenya 222, 223, 365
 and Kingdom of Benin 129, 216, 217
 and Libya 236
 and Lozi Kingdom 143
 missionaries 205
 and Nigeria 211, 219, 221, 223, 284, 285, 341
 and Rhodesia 166, 218, 252–3
 share of colonial Africa 223
 and Sierra Leone 166, 326
 slave trade 166, 167
 and Sokoto Caliphate 195
 and South Africa 166, 271, 378–9
 trade 129

World War II 230, 231, 241
 and Zanzibar 187, 189
 and Zulu Kingdom 207, 208, 209, 217, 218
British Somaliland 230
British South Africa Company 166, 218, 222, 228, 252, 382
British West Africa 230
Broom, Robert 22
Buffalo Horns 206
Buganda Agreement 175
Buganda Kingdom 135, **174–5**, 362
Bulala pastoralists 109
Bunyoro Kingdom 134, **174–5**, 241
Bure goldfields 89, 104
Burkina Faso **334**
 independence 235, 259, 334
 Tuareg people 127
Burton, Richard 201
Burundi 201, 304, **361**
 independence **177**, 361
 Kingdom of 176, 177, 361
Byzantine Empire 62, 63, 67, 72, 73, 149

C

C-group 50
Cabo Verde 200, **325**
 independence 249, 325
Cabral, Amílcar 248, 249, 325
Caesar, Julius 67
Caetano, Marcelo 249
Cairo 99, 124, 125, 274, 284, 285, 305
calendars, Igbo 114
calypso 215
Camara, Mohamed 293
camels
 caravans 88–9
 dromedary 21
 nomadic peoples 126–7
Cameroon 261, 263, **342–3**
 independence 235, 343
Canaanites 50
Canary Islands 277
Candomblé 111, 215
Cannae, Battle of 69
Canning, George 187
Cão, Diego 182
Cape Colony 160, 161, 166, 169, 207, 209, 378
Cape of Good Hope 160, 162, 168, 200
Cape Town 160, 166, **168–9**
Cape Verde 160
Capua, Siege of 69
Caracalla, Emperor 71
Caribbean, African diaspora 214–15
Carthage/Carthaginians 10, 40, 41, 58, **64–5**, 66, 70, 71, 75
 Hannibal **68–9**
 Muslims sack 73
cartography **202–3**
Casely Hayford, J. E. 303
Casement, Roger 213
Cato, Marcus Porcius 65
cattle
 conflicts over 169
 pastoralists 126, **152–5**
 as wealth/power 136, 170
cave paintings *see* rock art

Central African Republic 304, **346–7**
  independence 235, 346–7
ceramics *see* arts and artifacts
Césaire, Aimé 229, 233
Cetshwayo of the Zulu Kingdom 207, **208–9**, 217, 379
Chad **344–5**
  independence 235, 344–5
Chad, Lake 20
Chadic languages 80
Chaka Chaka, Yvonne 289, 297
Chaminuka 157
children
  child mortality 274
  enslaved 162
Chilembwe, John 226, 228, 229
Chimurenga, first and second 228, 252–3, 288
China
  interests in Africa 247, 261, 262, 264, 274, 304
  trade with 82, 83
Chiweshe, Stella 296
Chokwe people 143
Christian Highland Kingdom 119
Christianity
  in Aksum 62
  arrival in Africa 10, 40
  and colonialism 160, 258
  in contemporary Africa 281
  Coptic 125
  in Ethiopia 118–21, 370
  and European intervention 166, 167
  Igbo people 115
  and independence movements 228
  and indigenous beliefs 280–81
  in Kongo 182, 183
  missionaries and conversions **204–5**
  in North Africa 71, **74–5**
  and state power 78
Church of Christ 281
Church Missionary Society 205
churches, rock-cut 118, 122–3
Churchill, Winston 231
Chwa II Kabalega of Bunyoro 174–5
cinema 274, 277, **292–3**, 305
Cissé, Souleymane 293
citizenship, Roman 71
civil wars **264–5**, 274
  colonial origins of 258, 264
civilizations, first 10, 14, 31
Cleopatra VII of Egypt 43, 67
click languages 81
climate 16–17
  Sahara **20–21**, 42
climate change 275, **282–3**
  historical 14, 28–9, 36, 126, 137
Cochoqua people 169
Coetzee, J. M. 303
coffins, Egyptian 49
Coillard, François 205
Cold War
  Africa and 11, 231, **246–7**, 262
  and decolonization 226
Cole, Teju 303
collaboration, African 305
colonialism
  Belgian colonial corruption **212–13**
  British in West Africa 129
  colonial wars **216–17**

European 11, **160–61**, 163, 167
  exploration and 201
  governance **222–3**
  legacy of colonization **258–9**, 262
  and religion 205
  resistance to 181, 184, 216–17, **218–19**, 223, 226
  and royal power 135
  Scramble for Africa **210–11**
Columbus, Christopher 162
Commission for the Abolition of Sexual Mutilation 289
communism 263
Comoros **357**
  independence 235, 357
companies, administrative 222
concentration camps 222
Congo **351**
  independence 235
Congo Basin 201, 282–3
Congo Crisis 247
Congo Free State 142, 143, 161, 183, 201, 210, **212–13**
Congo War
  First 266
  Second **266–7**
Convention People's Party (CPP) 243
Coptic Christianity 40, 74–5
corruption 262, 263, 264, 265, 266, 291
Côte d'Ivoire 167, 261, 305, **328–9**
  civil war 275, 329
  independence 234, 235, 329
cotton 166, 259
coups, military **262–3**
COVID-19 274
cowrie shells 113
creation myths 156, 157
Creole languages 81, 215
cricket 287
crops 34, 35, 166, 259
  and climate change 282
Crowther, Samuel Ajayi 205
Crusades 99, 101, 124, 125
Cugoano, Ottobah 232
culture
  birth of 14, **30–31**
  and European exploration 201
  impact of African diaspora on 215
  impact of colonialism on 258
  preservation of indigenous 305
  reclaiming cultures **276–7**
Cushites 82
Cushitic languages 80
cycling 286
Cyrenaica 40, 41, 70, 71, 205, 236

D

da Gama, Vasco 160, 200
Dabous Giraffes 33
Dahomey, Kingdom of 11, 78, 112, 160, 162, **178–9**, 228, 338–9
Dakar 305
dance 33, 127, 157, 199, 276, 288, 294, 296, 297
Dangarembga, Tsitsi 289
Dankaran Tuman of Mali 91
Dar Es Salaam 285
Dart, Raymond 22
DaSilva, Roger 244–5
Davis, Angela 233

De Klerk, F. W. 268, 269, 271, 379
dead, burial of the 31
Déby, Idriss 345
Déby Itno, Mahamat Idriss 345
decolonization 215, **226–7**
  legacy of colonization **258–9**, 262
  military coups following **262–3**
  new political generation **260–61**
  see also independence movements; Pan-Africanism
deforestation 20, 282–3
Delany, Martin Robison 232
Democratic Republic of the Congo 201, 210–11, 213, 226, 229, 261, 263, 274, 282–3, 305, **350–51**
  Second Congo War **266–7**
Demotic script 58
Denkyira 190, 192
Denmark, abolition of slavery 163
Denshawai Incident 237
Derg regime 247, 371
desertification 282, 289
deserts 16, 17, 18–21
Destour 229
Dhar Tichitt 84
Dhlomo, Herbert Isaac Ernest 303
Diaba Lompo of Fada N'gorma 140
Diagne, Blaise 229
diamonds 166
Dias, Bartolomeu 160, 162
diaspora, African **214–15**, 232–3, 293
Dingiswayo of the Zulu 206
Dinka people 153, 258
Diop, David 303
direct rule 223
disease
  in contemporary Africa 274, 275
  indigenous people and European 162, 167
  on slave ships 163
Djenné 88, 104, 105, 106
  Great Mosque of 90
Djibouti **369**
  independence 235, 369
Djinguereber Mosque 94–5
Djoser Pyramid 42
D'mt Kingdom 40, 41
DNA 25
Doe, Samuel 291, 327
Dogon Kingdom/people 86–7, 104, 157
Dogon language 80
Donatism 75
Dorze people 151
Douglass, Frederick 215
drought 20, 282
drums, talking 81, 294
Du Bois, W. E. B. 215, 227, 232, 233
Duhaga II of Bunyoro 175
Dunama Dabbalemi of Kanem-Bornu 109
Dunama of Kanem-Bornu 108–9
Dunama Lefiami of Kanem-Bornu 109
Dutch East India Company (VOC) 166, 168, 378
Dyabe Sissé of Wagadou 84

E

Early Dynastic Period 42, 43
early humans **22–3**
East African Sultanates **146–7**
Ebola virus 275

eco feminism **289**
economies 304, 305
ecosystems 282
Ede-Ile 113
Edo people 128
education
   colonialism and 258–9, 260
   missionaries and 205
Efik people 115
Egba people 228
Egba Women's uprising 288
Egypt **308–9**
   Arab Spring 274
   Ayyubids, Mamluks and Ottomans **124–5**
   British protectorate 125
   Coptic Christianity 74
   economy 305
   Fatimid dynasty 99
   Gamal Abdel Nasser **238–9**, 262
   independence 227, 236, **237**, 309
   Islamic conquest 72, 309
   return of valuable objects to 276
Egypt, ancient 10, 40, **42–9**, 308–9
   agriculture 35
   and Kerma and Kush 50–51, 54
   mythology 156
   Nubian pharaohs 54, 56–7
   Roman rule 70, 71
   royal power 134
   slavery 149
   writing 58
Egyptian Revolution 237, 262
Ehengbuda of Benin 129
El Anatsui **298–9**
El Saadawi, Nawal 288–9, 302, 303
el-Sadat, Anwar 239
elephants, Hannibal's 69
Elissa (Dido), Queen of Carthage 64
Eltekeh, Battle of 57
empires, medieval era **78–9**
English language 81
engravings 32
enslaved people
   in Cape Colony 169
   see also slave trade
environmental issues **282–3**
Epic of Sundiata 91, 96
Equatorial Guinea **348**
Equiano, Olaudah **115**, 215, 232, 302
Eritrea 211, 218, 230, 264, **368–9**
Esarhaddon of Assyria 57
Eswatini 135, **377**
Ethiopia 261, **370–71**
   Christianity 74, 75, 370
   civil war 264
   Cold War 247
   Gondar **120–21**
   Islam 72
   medieval **118–19**, 370–71
   resistance to colonialism 211, 218, 219
   World War II 230, 231
Ethiopian Empire 78
ethnicity 33, 40
Europe
   Atlantic slave trade **162–3**, 166
   colonization of Africa 160–61, **210–11**
   continued influence in Africa 261

early intervention in Africa **166–7**
exploration of Africa 160, **200–201**
legacy of colonization **258–9**
Scramble for Africa **210–11**
Europeanization 201
evolution, human **22–3**
Ewe people 259
Eweka II of Benin 129
Ewuare of Benin 128, 129, **130–31**, 133
exploration, European 160, **200–201**
exports 259
Eyasu II of Ethiopia 120
Ezana I of Aksum 62, 63, 74, 370
Ezana Stone 41

F

Fada N'gourma 140
Fagg, Bernard 60
faïence 50
famine 175, 282, 283
farming *see* agriculture
Farouk I of Egypt 239, 262
Fasil Ghebbi (Royal Enclosure) (Gondar) 121
Fasilides of Ethiopia 119, 121
Fassie, Brenda 289
Fatimid Caliphate 78, **98–9**, 100, 124, 135
Faye, Safi 293
female genital mutilation (FGM) 289
feminisms **288–9**, 303
Fertile Crescent 34
Fès 98
Feyiase, Battle of 190, 192
Fezzan 236
film *see* cinema
fire 14, 25, 30
First Hijra 72
floods 282, 283
folklore **156–7**
Fon people 178
football 274, 286
Force Publique 212, **213**
forced labor 173, 253
foreign investment 274, 304
Forum for the Empowerment of Women 300
fossils **22–3**, 25, 28
Fouta Djallon 196
France
   and Algeria 216–17, 223, 316–17
   colonial empire 11, 171, 173, 210, 211, 223
   continued influence 261, 263
   and Dahomey 178, 339
   decolonization 226, 227, 228, 229, 231, **234–5**, 262
   early intervention in Africa 166–7
   and Egypt 125, 237, 239, 246
   exploration of Africa 200
   and Libya 236
   Mandinka Resistance Wars 217
   and Mossi States 141
   and Tukulor Empire 196, 197
   World War II 231
free-trade areas 160
FRELIMO (*Frente de Libertação de Moçambique*) 248–9, 251, 384, 385
French Revolution 226
French Union/French Community 234–5

Frente Nacional de Libertação de Angola (FNLA) 248, 249
Frere, Henry Bartle 209
Fuad I of Egypt 237
Fulani Caliphate 109, 111, 113, 195, 196, 197
Fulani Kingdom 104, 106, 165
Futa Toro 196
future of Africa **304–5**

G

Gabon **349**
   independence 235, 349
Gambia, the 160, 166, 200, **321**
Gao 88, 91, 93, 104, 105, 106
Garvey, Amy Jacques 232
Garvey, Marcus 215, 226, 227, 232–3
Gaynt Qirqos, Battle of 118
Gbowee, Leymah 289
GDP 305
Gedara of Aksum 62
Gedi 82
Ge'ez script 59
gemsbok 18–19
gender and sexuality 33
General Act 211
genocide, Rwandan 177
German East Africa 177
Germany
   colonial empire 211, 218–19, 223, 228
   early intervention in Africa 167
   exploration of Africa 200
   and Rwanda and Burundi 177
Ghana 216, 217, 229, 246, 265, **336–7**
   independence 226, 240, 241, 260, 337
   Kwame Nkrumah **242–3**, 260, 337
   military coups 262–3, 337
Ghana Empire *see* Wagadou (Ghana) Empire
Ghana Youth Party 277
Ghezo of Dahomey 178
Gihanga I of Rwanda 176
Girmay, Biniam 286
Gladstone, William Ewart 208
Gobir, Kingdom of 194, 195
gold
   mining 50, 137, 159, 166, 223
   trade 10, 78, 83, 84, 85, 88–9, 90, 91, 93, 104, 105, 113, 118, 126, 128, 136, 137, 146, 147, 149, 162, 182, 200
Gold Coast, the 166, 240, 243, 260
Golden Stool 190
Gondar 119, **120–21**
Gonnema (Khoi chieftain) 169
Gordimer, Nadine 289
government, colonial **222–3**
Great Enclosure (Great Zimbabwe) 136, 137, **138–9**
Great Green Wall 282
Great Lakes
   Bunyoro and Buganda Kingdoms **174–5**
   Maasai **126–7**
   Rwanda and Burundi **176–7**, 201
Great Pyramids of Giza 42
Great Rift Valley 14, 16, 17, 174
Great Trek 169
Great Zimbabwe 78, 79, **136–9**, 380
Greece, ancient 40, 41, 43, 65, 200
Greek Orthodox Church 75

Green Belt Movement (GBM) 289
greenhouse gas emissions 282
griots 91, 164–5, 302
guerrilla warfare 248
Guinea 160, 200, 246, **325**
   independence 234, 235
Guinea-Bissau **324**
   independence 248, 249, 324
Gurnah, Abdulrazak 303

H
Haïdar, Aminatou 288
Haïdara, Abdel Kader 96
Haile Selassie, Yohannes 22, 23
Haitian Revolution 226, 232
Hajj Ali of Kanem-Bornu 109
hamada 21
Hamoud ibn Mohammed of Zanzibar 187
Hannibal 65, **68–9**
Hasdrubal 69
Hastie, James 171
Hatshepsut, Pharaoh 42, 43, 48
Hausa Kingdoms 104, 105, 106, 115, 165, 194, 195
Hausa-Fulani people 211, 258
Hausaland 109
Hazoumè, Romuald 298
Helm, Charles 205
Henry the Navigator 160
Herero people 218–19
Herodotus 200
Hertzog Bills (South Africa) 254
Hierakonpolis 42
hieroglyphs 43, 49, **58**, 302
Himyarite Kingdom 63
Hittites 45
HIV/AIDS 271
Holocene Epoch 36
homelands, Black 255
Homer 200
hominids 14, **22–3**, 25
Homo erectus 14, 15, 25, 28, 30
Homo ergaster 25
Homo habilis 14, 25
Homo heidelbergensis 25, 28
Homo sapiens 14, 15, **24–5**, 28–9, 30, 382
Hondo, Med 293
Hope For Girls and Women 289
Hor-Aha 42
Horus 134
Houphouët-Boigny, Félix 234, 329
House of Wonders (Zanzibar) 188, 189
Huguenots 254
Humai ibn Salamna of Kanem-Bornu 108
human spirits 157
humans, first 14, **22–5**, 364, 370, 378, 382
hunter-gatherers 14, 25, 34–5, 37, **152–3**
Hutu people 176–7, 265, 266–7
Hyksos 50

I
Ibadan 113
Ibadism 187
Ibibio people 115
Ibn al-Nadim 108

Ibn Battuta 20, 89
Ibrahim II of Ifriqiya 98
ice ages 14
ideographic scripts 59
Idris Katakarmabe of Kanem-Bornu 109
Idris, Muhammad/Idris I of Libya 236
Idrisid dynasty 98
Ifat Sultanate 119
Ife Empire 78
Igbo people 114, 116, 130, 211, 258, 264, 265, 277
Igbo states **114–15**, 134
Igbo-Ukwu 114
Ikshidid dynasty 99
Ilé-Ifè 60, 110, 128
Ilesha 110
Ilunga Tshibinda of Lunda 142
Imazighen 70, 73
independence movements 11, 219, **226–7**
   colonial response to 229
   early **228–9**
   impact of World War II **230–31**
   independence from Britain **240–41**
   independence from France **234–5**
   independence from Portugal **248–9**
India
   Siddi people 215
   trade with 82, 146, 147
Indian Ocean
   East African trade 82, 146
   slave trade 149
indirect rule 223
Industrial Revolution 210
industrialization 305
inequality 305
infrastructure
   colonial legacy 259
   contemporary Africa 274
   foreign investment in 304
   future 305
Inkatha Freedom Party (South Africa) 269
internment 222
iron-making
   Bantu migrations 36, 37
   Nok culture 60
irrigation 283
Isandlwana, Battle of 161, 209, 217
Ishaq ibn Ali, Emir 100
Islam
   and Aksum 63
   Almoravid and Almohad dynasties **100–101**
   arrival in Africa 10, 40, **72–3**
   East African Sultanates 119, **146–7**
   and East African trade 83
   Fatimid Caliphate **98–9**
   Ibadism in Zanzibar 187
   and indigenous beliefs 280–81
   and royal power 135
   scholarship 96–7, 124
   Shia 83, 98, 99, 124, 147
   Sokoto Caliphate **194–5**
   Songhai Empire 105
   spread via trade routes 88, 105
   and state power 78
   Sunni 83, 124, 147, 194, 217
   Tukulor Empire **196–7**
   veil-wearing 106

Ismail Pasha 237
Israel 28
   and Egypt 239
Italy
   colonial empire 211
   and Ethiopia 218, 219, 371
   exploration of Africa 200
   and Libya 236, 313
   World War II 230
iyoba (queen mother) 135

J
Jaja of Opobo **220–21**
James, Marlon 303
Jamshid bin Abdullah Al Said of Zanzibar 187
Java Man 28
jazz 215
Jerusalem
   Crusades 124, 125
   siege of (701 BCE) 57
Jesuits 160
jewelery *see* arts and artifacts
jihad 194–5
João I of Kongo 182
Johannesburg 305
Johnson Sirleaf, Ellen 289, **290–91**, 327
Jolof Empire 78, 79
Juba I of Numidia 66, 67
Juba II of Numidia 66, 67
Jubogha, Jubo *see* Jaja of Opobo
Judah 57
Jugurtha of Numidia 66–7
Jugurthine War 67
Justinian I, Emperor 63

K
Kabila, Joseph 266, 267
Kabila, Laurent-Désiré 266, 267
Kaboré, Gaston 293
Kabyle people 277
Kadesh, Battle of 44, 45
Kagame, Paul 260, 261
Kaguvi, Sekuru 218
Kahiu, Wanuri 293
Kairouan 88, 98
   Great Mosque of 72–3, 98
Kalahari Desert 17
Kalala Ilunga of Luba 142
Kaleb of Aksum (St. Elesbaan) 63
Kanem-Bornu Kingdom 88, **108–9**, 149
Karman, Tawakkol 289
Karnak 43, 44, 45, 56, 57
Kashta of Kush 54
Kato Kintu of Buganda 175
Kaunda, Kenneth 382–3
Kawa 57
Keïta, Modibo 263
Keita, Salif 297
Keïta, Seydou 244
Kemoko Kanté of Sosso 90
Kentridge, William 298
Kenya 211, 222, 223, 263, 305, **364–5**
   independence 241, 261, 365
Kenya Land and Freedom Army 223

Kenyanthropus platyops 23
Kenyatta, Jomo 241, 261, 365
Kerma civilization 10, 40, 41, **50–51**, 54, 310
Khālid ibn Barghash of Zanzibar 187, 189
Khami 137
Kharga oasis (Sudan) 58
Khartoum 285
Khoi-Dutch Wars 169
Khoikhoi people/language 81, **152**
Khoisan people 25, 168–9, 276
Khrushchev, Nikita 247
Kidjo, Angélique 289
Kigeli IV of Rwanda 177
Kikuyu people 223, 261
Kilwa Kisiwani 147
Kilwa Sultanate 147
Kimbangu, Simon/Kimbanguism 219, 228–9
Kinshasa 274, 284, 285, 305
Kirina, Battle of 91
Kitara Empire 174
Kitombo, Battle of 183
Kizimkazi Sultanate 147
Kongo, Kingdom of 11, 78, 79, 162, **182–3**, 205
    mangaaka power figures **184–5**
Kongo-Portuguese Wars 182
Kongolo Mwamba of Luba 142
Kony, Joseph 265
Korda, Zoltán 292
Koumbi Saleh 84–5
Koutoubia Mosque (Marrakech) **102–3**
Krotoa 169
Kuany, Kuany Ngor 287
Kuba people 150, 212
Kumasi 216
Kush, Kingdoms of 10, 41, **50–51**, **54–5**, 57, 310
Kuti, Fela 296, 297
Kwaman Alliance 190, 192
Kwaman, Kingdom of 192
Kwararafa 109
KwaZulu-Natal 206, 207, 255

L

Lagos 274, **284–5**, 305
Lalibela 63, 118
    rock-cut churches 122–3
Lalibela, Gebre Meskel, King of Zagwe dynasty 78, 118, 134
Lancaster House talks 253
land reform 253
land rights 277
language **80–81**
    development of 15, 30, 31
    suppression of indigenous 276
Las Navas de Tolosa, Battle of 101
laws, European 259
Leakey, Louise 23
Leakey, Mary 22–3
Leakey, Meave 23
Lebanon 64
Legio Maria Church 281
Leninism 243, 251
Leopold II of Belgium 142, 160, 161, 201, 210, 212–13, 266
Leptis Magna 71
Lesotho 150, **375**
LGBTQ+ communities 293, 300

Liberia 211, **327**
    civil war 265, 327
    Ellen Johnson Sirleaf **290–91**, 327
Libya 43, 45, 65, 211, **312–13**
    civil war 274, 313
    independence 226, 227, **236**, 313
    Islamic conquest 72, 312
    Roman 70, 71
Libyco-Berber script 59
life expectancy 274
literacy 258
literature 274, **302–3**, 305
    feminist 288–9
Little Ice Age 137
livestock
    domestication 15
    management of 34, 35
    pastoralists 126, **152–3**
    see also cattle
Livingstone, David 201, 205, 212
London Missionary Society 205
Lord's Resistance Army (LRA) 265, 266
lost wax process 133
Lozi Kingdom/people **143**, 205
Luanda 162, 181, 248, 285
Luba Kingdom 79, 134, **142**, 144–5
Lucy 22, 23, 370
lukasa 144–5
Lukena lua Nimi of Kongo 182
Lumumba, Patrice 263, 351
Lunda Kingdom **142–3**
Luo script 59
Luxor 43, 47

M

Maasai 10, **126–7**, 276, 279
Maathai, Wangari 289
Macedonians 40, 43
Machel, Graça 288
Machel, Samora 243, 249, **250–51**, 384–5
Madagascar 160, **170–71**, **352–3**
    independence 226, 235, 353
    Ranavalona I **172–3**, 353
Madande, Clive 287
Maghan of Mali 91
Maghreb 66, 72, 73, 75, 228
Maharero, Samuel 218
Maji-Maji uprising 219, 228
Majid, Sultan of Zanzibar 187
Makapansgat pebble 14
Makeba, Miriam 289, 296–7
Makuria Kingdom 74–5, 310
Malagasy 81
malaria 210, 274
Malawi 226, **356–7**
    independence 253, 260–61, 356–7
Malawi, Lake 174
Malcolm X 233
Maldoror, Sarah 292
Mali 263, **330–31**
    civil war 274, 331
    independence 226, 235, 331
    Tuareg people 127, 331
Mali Empire 10, 78, 79, 85, 89, **90–91**, 96, 104, 140, 302, 330
    Mansa Musa **92–3**, 330

Mambéty, Djibril Diop 293
Mamluks 124, **125**
Mande language 80
Mande/Mandingo 90–91, 104, 165, 302
Mandela, Nelson 254, 255, 257, 268, 269, **270–71**, 274, 379
Mandela, Winnie 269, 288
Mandinka Empire 217
Mandinka Resistance Wars 217
Mansa Musa of Mali 78, 79, 89, 91, **92–3**, 94, 135, 330
Mansouri, Lazhar 244
mapping techniques 202
Mapungubwe 136–7
Maputo 249
marginalization, colonialism and 201, 258, 259
Marrakech 100, 101
    Koutoubia Mosque **102–3**
marriage, prohibition of mixed 254
Marxism 243, 251
Mashonaland 252
Masina 197
Masinissa of Numidia 66
masks 141, 198–9, 276
Masmuda Amazigh 100
Massina Empire 140
Massylii and Masaesyli 66
Mastanabal 66
Matabeleland 252
Matamba 181
Mau Mau rebellion 222, 223, 241, 288
Mauretania 41, **66–7**, 70, 167
Mauritania **320–21**
Mauritius 274, **359**
mbalax 297
Mbanda Kasi, Battle of 182
Mbandi of the Mbundu 181
Mbanza Kongo, Battle of 182
mbaqanga 297
Mbeki, Thabo 304, 379
Mbudye (Bambudye) Society 144
Mbundu people 181
Mbuti people 151
Mbuyazi 209
Mecca, pilgrimage to 93, 106
Meddour, Mounia 293
Medu Art Ensemble 256
megacities 284–5
Memphis 42, 57
Menabe, Kingdom of 170
Menelik I of Ethiopia 118
Menelik II of Ethiopia 218, 371
Menes, King 43
Mentewab, Empress of Ethiopia 121
Merina people 170, 173
Meroë 10, 40, 41, 51, **54–5**, 63, 78
Meroitic kingdom 74
Meroitic script 58
metalwork *see* art and artifacts
Mfecane 207
Middle Kingdom 40, 42, 50
Middle Passage 162–3
migrations
    African diaspora **214–15**
    Bantu 15, 35, **36–7**
    early human 15, 25, **28–9**
    from Sahara 21
military coups 11, **262–3**

minbars 103
mining 213, 223, 259, 282, 283
minority rule, white 253
mission civilatrice 229
missionaries 11, 160, 170, 173, 200, 201, 210, 212
    and conversions 167, **204–5**, 258
    resistance to 221
Mitochondrial Eve 25
Mnguni, Phiwokuhle 287
Mnyele, Thami 256
Mobutu Sese Seko 263, 266, 267, 274, 351
Mondlane, Eduardo 249, 251
Mongol Empire 125
monsoons 20, 21
Montuhotep II, Pharaoh 42
Morel, E. D. 213
Morocco 135, 263, **318–19**
    Aghlabid and Fatimid 98–9, 319
    independence 234, 319
    Islamic conquest 73, 319
Moshoeshoe I of Lesotho 150
Mossi States/Empire 93, 104, **140–41**
mountains 16
Movimento Popular de Libertação de Angola (MPLA) 247, 248, 249, 371
Mozambique 149, 160, 201, 223, 253, **384–5**
    independence 247, 248–9, 384
    Samora Machel **250–51**, 384–5
Mozarabs 204
Mpande of the Zulu Kingdom 209
Mswati III of Eswatini 135
mudbrick architecture 50
Mugabe, Robert 243, 252, 253, 380–81
Muhammad Ali Pasha 124, 125
Muhammad Bello, Sultan of Sokoto 196
Muhammad ibn Tumart 100
Muhammad, the Prophet 72
Muhammadu Attahiru II, Caliph 195
Muhammed Bello, Caliph 195
Muholi, Zanele **300–301**
Mundari people 154–5
Musa Ibn Nusair, General 73
Museveni, Yoweri 265, 363
music 33
    contemporary 274, 277, 289
    indigenous African styles **296–7**, 305
    instruments **294–5**
Mutapa Kingdom 137
Mutara III of Rwanda 177
Mutesa I of Buganda 175
Muzorewa, Bishop Abel 253
Mwambutsa IV of Burundi 177
Mwezi Gisabo of Burundi 177
Mwitanzige, Lake 174
mythology **156–7**

N

Naguib, Mohamed 239, 262
Nairobi 285, 304, 305
Najasi of Aksum 72
Namib Desert 16, 17, 18–19
Namibia 211, 218, 223, 265, **374–5**
Namibian War of Independence 247
Napata 10, 51, **54–5**, 57, 78
Naqada culture 42
Narmer, King 40, 42

Nasser, Gamal Abdel 237, **238–9**, 246, 247, 262
Natal 209
National Association for the Advancement of Colored People 232
National Party (South Africa) 254, 269
nationalism 177, 226, 229, 237, 240–41, 253, 259, 277
    Arab 239
    see also independence movements
Natives Land Act (South Africa, 1913) 254
Natives (Urban Areas) Act (South Africa, 1923) 254
natural resources 160, 166, 212–13, 216, 304
    colonial exploitation of 166, 201, 210, 222, 223, 258, 259, 284
    management of 305
    ongoing thirst for Africa's 262, 263
Nazareth Baptist Church 281
Ndebele people 205, 218, 228, 252, 277
Ndondakusuka, Battle of 209
Ndongo 181
N'Dour, Youssou 297
Neanderthals 14, 15, 29, 30
Necho I, Pharaoh 57
Nefertari, Queen 45
Nefertiti, Queen 134
Nego-Feminism 289
Négritude 229, 233
Nehanda, Mbuya 218
neocolonialism 259, 261, 274, 304
Neolithic era
    A-group 50
    agriculture 34
    rock art **32–3**
    tools **26–7**
Netherlands
    colonial empire 11, 160, 161, 168–9, 181, 183, 223
    trade 166
Neto, Agostinho 248, 371
Netshitenzhe, Joel 262
New Kingdom 40, 42–5, 50, 51
Ngazargamu 109
Ngwale, Kinjikitile 219
Niger **332–3**
    independence 235, 333
Niger Delta 284
Niger-Congo languages 80
Nigeria 219, 223, 228, 229, 263, 305, **340–41**
    civil war 264–5, 341
    colonial legacy 258
    colonial rule 211, 341
    Igbo people **114–15**
    independence 129, 226, 227, 240, 241, 260, 341
    Jaja of Opobo **220–21**
    Lagos **284–5**
    Yoruba people 111
Nigerian National Democratic Party 229
Nijmi 108, 109
Nile Delta 16, 21, 42
Nile River/Valley 10, 16, 200
Nilo-Saharan languages 80–81
Nilotic languages 80, 81
nisi makondo 184
Njinga Mbande, Queen of the Mbundu 134, **180–81**
Njoya, Ibrahim of Bamum 202
Njuu language 81
Nkomo, Joshua 253, 380, 381
Nkrumah, Kwame 227, 229, 233, 241, **242–3**, 246, 260, 262–3, 337

Nnaji, Genevieve 293
Nobatia Kingdom 74–5, 303, 310
Nobel Prizes 268, 269, 289, 291
Nok culture 10, 40
    terra-cotta figures **60–61**
Nollywood 274, 285, 293
nomadic peoples 63
    Bedouin, Tuareg, and Maasai **126–7**
Non-Aligned Movement (NAM) 246
Northern Rhodesia 223, 380, 382
    see also Zambia
Nri Kingdom/culture 115, **116–17**, 134
Ntare I of Burundi 177
Ntare IV of Burundi 177
Ntim Gyakari of Denkyira 190, 192
Nubia/Nubians 40, 41, 43, 45
    Christianity 74, 205
    Kerma and Kush **50–51**
    Lion Temple (Naga) 52–3
    Napata and Meroë **54–5**
    Ottomans and 125
Nuer people **153**
numeracy 258
Numidia 40, 41, **66–7**
Nupe people 112
Nuri 57
Nwapa, Flora 289
Nyasaland 226, 228, 229, 380
Nyerere, Julius 233, 241, 246, 261, 355
Nzinga of Kongo 182

O

Obalufon II of Ilé-Ifè 110
Oduduwa of the Yoruba 110, 112
Ofili, Chris 298
Ogaden War 247
Ohen of Benin 130
oil 262, 284, 304
Okello, John Gideon 187
Okomfo Anokye 78, 190, 191, 192
Old Kingdom 40, 42, 88
Olduvai Gorge 23, 28
Oman, Sultanate of 147, 186
Omotoso, Akin 293
Onitsha 115
Opobo **220–21**
Opoku Ware I of Asante 191, 192
oral history 165, 302
Orange Free State 217
Oranmiyan, Prince 112, 128
Organization of African Unity (OAU) 227, 233, **261**
Oromo people 153, 277, 281
Osadebe, Dennis 274
Osei Kwadwo of Asante 135
Osei Kwame Panyin of Asante 191
Osei Tutu of Asante 78, 190, **192–3**
Ottoman Empire 109, 124, **125**, 175
    and Libya and Egypt 236–7, 309, 312
Otumfuo Nana Prempeh I of Asante 190
Ouadane 85
Ouagadougou dynasty 140
Ouagadougou of Tenkodogo 140
Ouattara, Alassane 261
Oubri 140
Ouédraogo 140, 141
Ovonramwen of Benin 129

Oyo Empire 78, 79, 110, **112–13**, 134, 178
Oyo-Ile 112
Ozolua of Benin 128, 130

P

painting *see* art and artifacts; rock art
paleoclimate 20
Palestinian Liberation Organization (PLO) 239
palm oil 221
palm-wine music 296
Pan African Women's Organization 277
Pan Arabism 239
Pan-African Congress 227, 232, 233, 241, 255, 261
Pan-Africanism 215, 226, **229**, **232–3**, 243, 256, 261
Panafrican Film and Television Festival of
    Ouagadougou 277, 293
Pangaea 14
Paranthropus robustus 23
Park, Mungo 161, 200
*Partido Africano para a Independência da Guinée
    Cabo Verde* (PAIGC) 249
pastoralists 126, **152–3**
Pedro V of Kongo 183
Peking Man 28
Pemba 83
Pentecostalism 281
Persia/Persians 43
    trade with 146, 147
petroforms 32
petroglyphs 32, 33
pharaohs **42–3**, 134
    Nubian 54, 56–7
Pharos of Alexandria 71
Philip the Evangelist 74
Phoenicians 40, 41, 58, 64, 137, 236
photography 300–301
pictograms 59
pictographs 32
pigments 33
plantations 162, 166, 214
Polisario Front 275
politics
    contemporary political map 275
    political renewal 277
    post-colonial **260–61**
Pompey 67
popular music **296–7**
population
    African 275, 304
    age profile 304
    megacities 284, 285
Portugal
    and Angola 181, 248, 373
    arrival in Africa 89, 166
    colonial empire 11, 223
    and East African Sultanates 147
    exploration and colonization 160, 161, 166, 200
    independence from **248–9**
    Kingdom of Kongo 182–3
    and Mozambique 248–9, 251, 384
    slave trade 162, 181
    trade 91, 128, 129, 130, 137
poverty 264, 283, 304, 305
Pr-Ramesses 45
predynastic Egypt 42, 50
prehistory **14–15**

Prempeh I of Asante 216
Prempeh II of Asante 135
priest-kings 115, 134
protectorates 125, 160
Protestant missionaries 205
Proto Saharan 58
proxy wars 246–7
Ptolemaic dynasty 43
Punic script 58
Punic Wars 65, 66, **68–9**, 70
pyramids
    Egyptian 42
    Nubian 41, 54–5, 57

Q

Qaddafi, Muammar 236, 313
quinine 210
QwaQwa 255

R

racism 201, 231, 233
    see also apartheid
Radama I of Madagascar 170–71, 173
Radama II of Madagascar 173
Rafohy, Queen of the Merina 170
railroads 259
rainforests 10, 16–17, 282
Ramaromanompo of Betsimisaraka 170
Ramses II, Pharaoh 43, **44–5**, 47
Ramses III, Pharaoh 43, 47
Ramses XI, Pharaoh 43
Ramesseum 45, **46–7**
Ranavalona I, Queen of Madagascar 171, **172–3**, 353
Ransome-Kuti, Funmilayo 226, 227, 288
Rashidun Caliphate 63, 67, 72
Rassemblement Démocratique Africaine (RDA) 234–5
Rawa of Zondoma 140
Rawlings, Jerry John 263, 337
Red Sea, trade 125
reeducation camps 250
reggae 215
religion **280–81**
    Carthaginian 64
    and colonialism 160
    creation myths 156
    Egyptian 42
    fusion of beliefs 280–81
    hybrid 215
    indigenous belief systems 280–81
    Mossi States 141
    mythology and folklore **156–7**
    Neolithic 33
    Nubian 53
    and royal power 135
    Songhai 105
    see also Candomblé; Christianity; Islam; Vodun
RENAMO (*Resistência Nacional Moçambicana*) 251,
    384, 385
renewable energy 283, 304
Republic of the Congo 263, 266
Réunion **359**
Rhapta 82
Rhodes, Cecil 160, 166, 252, 382
Rhodesia 166, 218, 223, 380
    independence 227, 241, 251, **252–3**

Rhodesia Front 253
Rialé 140, 141
Riebeeck, Jan van 160, 161, 166, 168–9
rivers 16
Robert, Shaaban bin 303
Roberto, Holden 248
Robeson, Paul 292
rock art 15, 20, 24, 27, 29, 31, **32–3**
Roha (Adefa) 118
Roman-Jewish Wars 55
Rome
    Africans in Empire 214
    and Aksum 62
    and Carthage 64, 65, 68–9
    and Egypt 43
    exploration of Africa 200
    and Nubia 55
    and Numidia and Mauretania 66–7
    Roman Empire 40, 41
    Roman North Africa 70–71
    slavery 149
Roosevelt, Franklin D. 231
Royal African Company (RAC) 167
royal power **134–5**
Royal West African Frontier Force (RWAFF) 230–31
rubber 160, 212–13
Russia, interests in Africa 247, 262, 264, 304
Rwanda 201, 261, **360**
    civil war and genocide 177, 265, 266, 274, 360
    independence 177, 259, 360
    Kingdom of **176–7**, 360

S

Saadi dynasty 105
Saguntum, sack of 69
Sahara Desert 17, **20–21**, 42, 282
    Bedouin and Tuareg **126–7**
    trans-Saharan trade routes **88–9**, 104, 200
Saharan languages 80
Sahel 20, 282
Sahelanthropus tchadensis 23
Sakalava people 170
Saladin (Salah al-Din Yusuf ibn Ayyub) 99, 101, 124,
    125, 134, 135
Salazar, Antonio 249
Sall, Macky 261
Sallust 66, 200
salt trade 62, 105, 126, 174
saltigues (priests) 280
Samwelly, Rhobi 289
San people 80, 81, 136, **152**, 156, 168, 276
    rock art 27, 29, 33, 37
Sandawe language 81
Sangoma healers 280
Sanhaja 100
Sanniquellie Declaration 233
Santeria 215
Sao civilization 40, 41
São Tomé e Príncipe 162, 249, **348**
Saqqara 42
Sassanian Empire 63
Saudi Arabia 29
Savimbi, Jonas 246, 248
Sayfawa dynasty 108–9
Sayyid Said of Zanzibar 186–7, 188
Sayyida Salme **186**

Schism of 451 75
Scipio Africanus 69
scorched earth policy 175
Scramble for Africa 160, 163, **210–11**, 216
Second Intermediate Period 50
Seidman, Judy A. 256
Selene II, Queen of Numidia and Mauretania 67
Seleucid Empire 69
self-determination 231, 241, 274
self-government 226
self-reliance 259
Sembène, Ousmane 292
Semitic languages 80
Senegal 160, 167, 200, 229, 261, 263, **322–3**
   independence 226, 235, 261, 323
Senghor, Léopold 233, 261, 323
Sennacherib of Assyria 57
Senzangakhona kaJama of the Zulu 206
Septimius Severus, Emperor 71, 214
Serer people 280
Serpell, Namwali 289
Seti I, Pharaoh 43, 45
settlements
   agriculture and 34–5
   desert 20
settler rule 223
sexuality 300
Seychelles 241, **358**
Shabaka, Pharaoh 57
Shaka Zulu 78, 79, **206–7**, 378
shamans 280
Shanakhdakheto, Queen of Kush 55
Shanga Sultanate 83, 147
Sharpeville Massacre 255
Sheba, Queen of 62, 63, 118
Shell, boycott of 268
Shiraz 147
Shirkuh 124
Shona civilization/people 78, **136–7**, 138, 157, 218, 228, 252
Shona language 80
Shonibare, Yinka 298
Sicily 64, 65, 98, 99
Siddi people 215
Sierra Leone 166, 229, **326**
   missionaries 205
Sijilmasa 88, 100
Sissako, Abderrahmane 293
Sisulu, Walter 254
Six-Day War 239
slave ships 11, 162–3
slave trade
   and African diaspora **214–15**
   Asante Empire 191
   Benin Kingdom 128
   and colonization 218
   Dahomey 178
   Eastern **148–9**
   end of 222
   Igbo people 115
   Lunda Kingdom 142–3
   Stone Town (Zanzibar) 188–9
   trans-Saharan 89, 105, 149, 200
   transatlantic 89, 160, **162–3**, 166
   Yoruba 111, 113
   Zanzibar 186–7
Smith, Ian 253, 380

society
   birth of 14, 30
   Egyptian 42
   Igbo 114–15
   impact of Europeans on 167
   Khoisan 168
   Meroitic 55
   Mossi 141
   Songhai 104
soil erosion 283
Sokoto Caliphate 111, 140, **194–5**, 196
Solanke, Ladipo 229
solar power 283, 304
Solomon, King 118, 135, 137
Solomonid dynasty 78, 79, 118–19, 135
Somali Democratic Republic 247
Somalia 211, 231, **366–7**
   civil war 265, 367
   independence 226, 366–7
Somaliland 275
Songhai Empire 10, 78, 79, 89, 91, 93, 96, **104–5**, 140, 165
   Askia Muhammad I **106–7**
Songhai languages 81, 96
Soninke Kingdom 84, 85, 104
Sosso Kingdom 90, 104
South Africa 169, 263, 305, **378–9**
   anti-apartheid movement **256–7**, 268, 379
   apartheid **254–5**, 259, 379
   early Dutch involvement 166, 378
   end of apartheid **268–9**, 379
   independence 226, 254
   Nelson Mandela **270–71**
   Zulu people 206, 207, 378–9
South Africa Defense Force (SADF) 256
South African Native National Congress 229
South Sudan 304, **311**
   civil war 265, 311
   independence 153, 258, 264, 275, 277, 311
Southern Rhodesia 252–3, 380, 382
   independence 241
   see also Zimbabwe
Soviet Union, Cold War 231, 246–7, 262, 264
Soweto 254, 268
Soyinka, Wole 303
Spain
   al-Andalus 100
   exploration and imperialism 160
   Punic Wars 65, 69
Speke, John Hanning 200, 201
Sphinx 42
spice trade 126
Spinola, General Antonio 249
sport 274, 275, **286–7**
St. Helena **373**
Stanley, Henry Morton **201**, 212
stelae, Aksum 62
stencils 32
Stone Age tools **26–7**
Stone Town (Zanzibar) 149, **188–9**
storytellers 302
Sudan 263, **310–11**
   civil war 264, 311
   colonial legacy 258
Sudanic languages 80
Suez Canal 237, 239, 246
Sufism 100, 196, 236, 281

sugar plantations 162, 166
Suleman, Ramadan 292
Sultanates, East Africa **146–7**
Sumanguru of Sosso 90, 91
Sundiata Keita of Mali 78, 89, 90, **91**, 93, 302
Sunni Ali Ber of Songhai 79, 104–5, 106
Sunni Dao of Songhai 106
sustainability 282, 283, 304, 305
Swahili Kingdoms 136, 365
Swahili language/people 80, 83, 147
Syria 45, 64, 125, 239

T

Tabarka, Battle of 73
Tadjo, Véronique 289
Taghaza salt mines 104
Taharqa, Pharaoh 56–7
Taieb, Maurice 23
Tako, Hawo 288
Takrur 84, 85
Tambo, Oliver 254
Tamisso, Kingdom of 223
Tanganyika 219, 228, 241
Tanganyika, Lake 174
Tangier 73
Tanzania 211, 246, **354–5**
   independence 226, 227, 241, 261, 355
   Maasai people 127
   and Zanzibar 187
Tarikh al-Sudan **104**
Taylor, Charles 265
tectonic plates 14
Tenkodogo 140
tennis 287
Tewahedo Church 75
textiles **150–51**, 276
Thapsus, Battle of 67
Thebes 45, 46–7, 50, 57
Thiam, Awa 289
Thiong'o, Ngũgĩ wa 276, 303
Thutmose III, Pharaoh 42
Thuwaini, Sultan of Oman 187
Tidiani Tal 197
Tifinagh/Neo-Tifinagh script 59
Tigray people 277
Timbuktu 88, 91, 104, 105, 197
   Djinguereber Mosque **94–5**
   Manuscripts **96–7**, 276
   sack of 89
   as seat of learning 93, 104, 105
Timgad 71
Tippu Tip 149
tobacco plantations 162
Togo 211, 223, **335**
   independence 235, 335
tools
   agricultural 34
   stone 23, 25, **26–7**, 28, 29, 30–31
topography 10, **16–17**
Touré, Ahmed Sékou 217, 233, 234, 246
Touré, Samory 217, 228, 325, 331
townships 253
trade
   Aksum 62
   Benin Kingdom 128, 129, 130
   Bunyoro and Buganda 174

Carthaginian 64, 66
development of East African **82–3**
East African Sultanates **146–7**
future 305
Lunda Kingdom 142–3
Madagascar 170
Mali Empire 91
medieval African empires 10–11, 78
Mossi States 140
Numidia and Mauretania 66
palm oil 221
Roman North Africa 70
sanctions against South Africa 268–9
Shona Empire 136, 137
Songhai Empire 104–5, 106
Swahili 136
textiles 151, **259**
trans-Saharan trade routes 84, 85, **88–9**, 104, 126, 127
triangular 166
Wagadou (Ghana) Empire 84
Yoruba 110–11
see also slave trade
trade unions 229, 255
trading posts 222, 223
transhumance 20
Transkei 255
Transvaal 217
Traoré, Moussa 263
treaty system **223**
tribute 51, 85, 112, 113, 128, 182, 192, 195, 207
Tripoli 72, 88
Tripolitania 236
Tristan da Cunha **379**
Truth and Reconciliation Commission 271
Truth, Sojourner 214, 215
Tshisekedi, Félix 267
Tuareg 10, 80, 91, 96, **126–7**, 197, 277
Tukulor Empire 165, **196–7**, 331
Tunisia 229, **314–15**
　Arab Spring 274
　Fatimid 99, 314
　independence 234, 315
　Islamic conquest 72, 314
Tunka Menin of Wagadou 85
Turgut Reis, Pasha 109
Turkana Boy 25
Tutankhamen, Pharaoh 42, 43
Tutsi people 176–7, 259, 265, 266, 360
Twa people 176–7, 267
Tyre 64

U

Ubaydullah al-Mahdi 98
Ubeidiya archaeological complex (Israel) 28
Uganda 263, 266, **362–3**
　civil war 264, 265, 363
　kingdoms 174, 175, 362
Ulundi, Battle of 209
Umar, Caliph 72
Umar, Sheikh of Borno 109
Umar Tal, Al-Hajj 196–7
Umayyad Caliphate 67, 72–3, 99
Umkhonto we Sizwe (Spear of the Nation) 271
União dos Populações de Angola (UPA) 248
União Nacional para a Independência Total de Angola (UNITA) 248, 249, 371

United African National Council (UANC) 253
United Arab Republic 239
United Gold Coast Convention 243
United Nations 267, 268
　Universal Declaration of Human Right 226, 227
United States
　abolition of slavery 163, 215
　and African self-determination 231
　Cold War 246–7
　continued influence in Africa 261, 262, 263, 264
　interests in Africa 247, 262
　people of African decent 214
Universal Negro Improvement Association 232
Uqba Ibn Nafi, General 72–3
Urabi Revolt 237
Usman dan Fodio, Caliph 109, 194–5

V

Valley of the Kings 43
Vandals 67
vegetation 15, 16–17
　and climate change 36
Vera, Yvonne 303
Verwoerd, Hendrik 255
Victoria, Lake 174, 175
Victoria, Queen of the United Kingdom 208, 209
Virgil 64
Vodun religion (Vodou/Voodoo) 178, 215, 280
Volubilis 67
Voyages of exploration **160–61**

W

Wafd Party 229, 237, 239
Wagadou (Ghana) Empire 10, 78, **84–5**, 88, 89, 90, 135, 149
Walata 106
Wassoulou Empire 217, 228
water
　preservation of 137
　supply 29
weapons
　and colonization 210
　trade in European 167
weaving see art and artifacts
West Africa, Atlantic slave trade **162–3**
West African Student's Union (WASU) 229
Western Sahara 275, **319**
Whydah people 178
wildlife 16, 17
　in rock art 32, 33
Williams, Henry Sylvester 226
Wobgo of Ouagadougou 141
Wolof language 297
Womanism 289
women
　Dahomey Mino soldiers 179
　enslaved 162
　feminisms **288–9**
　and Zimbabwean independence **253**
Wonderwerk (South Africa) 58
World Cup (South Africa, 2010) 274
World War I
　African troops 228
　Germany loses colonies 177
　weakening of colonial power 161, 226, 228–9

World War II
　African troops 230–31
　and decolonization 11, 226, **230–31**, 234
wrestling 287
writing systems **58–9**, 78

X

Xhosa language 81
Xhosa people 169, 297

Y

Yaa Asantewaa **217**
Yahya ibn Umar 100
Yao Nawedji of Lunda 142
Yatenga 140
Year of Africa 226
Yekuno Amlak 118, 119
Yemen, Civil War 239
Yennenga, Princess 140, **141**
Yitbarek, King of the Zagwe dynasty 118
Yombe people 184
Yoruba people 10, 78, 115, 128, 130, 150, 151, 156, 157, 165, 211, 215, 241, 258, 280, 284, 285, 296, 297
　Oyo Empire **112–13**
　rise of **110–11**
Younger Dryas 36
youth movements 277
youth-dominated societies 304
Yuhi V of Rwanda 177
Yunfa of Gobir 194–5

Z

Zaghawa people 108
Zagwe dynasty 63, 78, 79, 118
Zaire 263, 265, 266, 274
　see also Democratic Republic of Congo
Zama, Battle of 65, 69
Zambezi River 143, 205
Zambia 143, 201, 253, **382–3**
　independence 253, 382
ZANU-PF 253
Zanzibar Revolution 187
Zanzibar, Sultanate of 11, 147, 149, **186–7**
　Stone Town **188–9**
Zewde, Sahle-Work 261
Zimbabwe 137, 211, 227, 228, **380–81**
　creation of 241, 247, **252–3**, 274, 380–81
Zimbabwe African National Union (ZANU) 253, 380, 381
Zimbabwe African People's Union (ZAPU) 253, 380
Zimbabwe culture 136–7
Zirid dynasty 99
Ziyadat Allah I of Ifriqiya 98
Ziyadat Allah III of Ifriqiya 98
Zondoma 140
Zoungrana 140
Zulu Kingdom 10, 78, 79, 135, 157, 161, 167, 169, 205, 217, 218, 228, 252, 276, 297, 378–9
　Cetshwayo 207, **208–9**
　Shaka Zulu **206–7**
Zulu language 80, 81

Acknowledgments

DK would like to thank the following for their help with this book:
Professor Gérard Chouin at William & Mary University, Virginia, US, and Professor Mark Gillings at Bournemouth University, UK, for assistance with the Oyo-Ile walls map (p.112); James Anthony Gardner, Tony Humphries, Keith Shiri, and Dr. Hengameh Ziai for additional consultancy; Sophie Adam, Diana Loxley, and Bonnie Macleod for editorial assistance; Jessica Tapolcai for design assistance; Sarah Smithies for picture research advice; Steve Crozier, Butterfly Creative Services Ltd. for image retouching; Manpreet Kaur for picture logging; Mrinmoy Mazumdar, Raman Panwar, and Vishal Bhatia (Creative Technical Support team); Diana Vowles for proofreading; and Helen Peters for indexing.

The publisher would like to thank the following for their kind permission to reproduce their photographs:

(Key: a-above; b-below/bottom; c-center; f-far; l-left; r-right; t-top)

1 Photo Scala, Florence: The Metropolitan Museum of Art / Art Resource. **2-3 Alamy Stock Photo:** funkyfood London - Paul Williams. **4 Photo Scala, Florence:** Princeton University Art Museum, / Art Resource NY (c). **5 The Metropolitan Museum of Art:** Rogers Fund (tc); The Michael C. Rockefeller Memorial Collection, Gift of Nelson A. Rockefeller, 1964 (tr). **Science Photo Library:** Pascal Goetgheluck (tl). **6 Bridgeman Images:** North Carolina Museum of Art (tl). **Photo Scala, Florence:** The Metropolitan Museum of Art / Art Resource (tc, tr). **7 Photo Scala, Florence:** Princeton University Art Museum, / Art Resource NY (r). **8-9 Bridgeman Images:** The Keir McGuinness Collection of African Textiles / Lyon & Turnbull (b). **10-11 The Metropolitan Museum of Art:** Gift of Mr. and Mrs. Klaus G. Perls. **12 Science Photo Library:** Pascal Goetgheluck. **14 Alamy Stock Photo:** Natural History Museum, London. **15 Alamy Stock Photo:** Greatstock / SATourism (tr); Naveed Hussain (cra); Jack Maguire (crb). **16-17 naturepl.com:** Hougaard Malan (t). **17 Alamy Stock Photo:** Marian Galovic (cra); Wilmar Topshots (b). **18-19 naturepl.com:** Sergey Gorshkov. **20 Alamy Stock Photo:** NASA Image Collection (cb); robertharding / Michael Runkel (crb). **Getty Images:** The Image Bank / Oliver Strewe (clb). **21 Alamy Stock Photo:** Michele Falzone (clb); Ami Vitale (cb); (crb). **22-23 Getty Images / iStock:** znm (t). **22 Alamy Stock Photo:** Andrea Izzotti (clb). **23 Alamy Stock Photo:** blickwinkel / McPHOTO / OTF (crb). **Yohannes Halle-Selassie, Cleveland Museum of Natural History:** (bc). **24 Alamy Stock Photo:** DPK-Photo. **25 Alamy Stock Photo:** agefotostock / M&G Therin-Weise (br); Sabena Jane Blackbird (crb). **Science Photo Library:** S. Entressangle / E. Daynes (cra). **Shutterstock.com:** DevonJenkin Photography (bl). **26 Alamy Stock Photo:** UPI / MPI EVA Leipzig / Mohammed Kamal (ca/x3). **Courtesy of Smithsonian. ©2023 Smithsonian:** Chip Clark (clb). **Science Photo Library:** Pascal Goetgheluck (r, clb/Scraper, crb). **27 Alamy Stock Photo:** Nick Greaves; Agfa Awards Winner (tr). **Science Photo Library:** Pascal Goetgheluck (tl, tc, cl, cb, cb/Axe, cr). **28 Ian Cartwright, Palaeodeserts Project:** (ca). **29 Africa Image Library:** Ariadne Van Zandbergen (tl). **Getty Images:** Roger de la Harpe / Education Images / Universal Images (br). **30 Courtesy of Smithsonian. ©2023 Smithsonian:** Chip Clark (cl). **Courtesy of Professor Christopher Henshilwood:** (ca). **Pierre Jean Texier:** (br). **31 Alamy Stock Photo:** Album (tr). **Courtesy of Professor Christopher Henshilwood:** (b). **32 Alamy Stock Photo:** DPK-Photo (crb); imageBROKER.com GmbH & Co. KG / Michael Runkel (clb); Mike P Shepherd (b). **33 Alamy Stock Photo:** Design Pics Inc / Alberto Arzoz / Axiom (crb); GFC Collection (clb); Frans Lemmens (cb). **National Museum of Namibia:** (tr). **34 Alamy Stock Photo:** Album (bl); The Print Collector / CM Dixon / Heritage Images (t). **35 Alamy Stock Photo:** imageBROKER.com GmbH & Co. KG / Egmont Strigl (br). **36 Gallerie Estensi, Biblioteca Estense Universitaria, Modena:** 3394=Alfa.V.10.18 (ms. Araldi, A) (bl). Rexford Nkansah: (ca). **37 Getty Images / iStock:** brytta. **38-39 The Metropolitan Museum of Art:** Rogers Fund. **40 Alamy Stock Photo:** World History Archive. **41 Getty Images / iStock:** geogif (tl); mbrand85 (tc); Goddard_Photography (tr). **42 Alamy Stock Photo:** Art Collection 2 (cla/x2). **Getty Images / iStock:** CircleEyes (bl). **43 BiblePlaces.com / Todd Bolen:** (tr). **Bridgeman Images:** NPL - DeA Picture Library (cra). **The Metropolitan Museum of Art:** Rogers Fund, 1929 (bl). **44 Museo Egizio, Torino:** (l, br). **45 akg-images:** NEW PICTURE LIBRARY SRL / De Agostini Picture Lib. / S. Vannini (tr). **Getty Images / iStock:** FevreDream (crb). **46 Alamy Stock Photo:** Universal Images Group North America LLC / DeAgostini / G. Dagli Orti (tc). **47 Alamy Stock Photo:** MET / BOT (tc). **48 Alamy Stock Photo:** © Fine Art Images / Heritage Images (clb, br). **Bridgeman Images:** National Trust Photographic Library / Derrick E. Witty (cla); Photograph © 2023 Museum of Fine Arts, Boston. All rights reserved. / Harvard University Boston Museum of Fine Arts Expedition (c). **The Metropolitan Museum of Art:** Gift of Edward S. Harkness, 1917 (tr); Rogers Fund, 1951 (cr); Rogers Fund, 1927 (cb/x2). **49 Alamy Stock Photo:** Cultural Archive (c); Funkyfood London - Paul Williams (tl/Jar, tc, tr). **The Metropolitan Museum of Art:** Rogers Fund, 1919 (clb); Rogers Fund, 1918 (tl); Funds from various donors, 1886 (r); Rogers Fund and Edward S. Harkness Gift, 1922 (bc). **50 Alamy Stock Photo:** robertharding / Andrew McConnell (c). **Getty Images:** Sepia Times / Universal Images Group (bl). **51 The Metropolitan Museum of Art:** Rogers Fund, 1930 (t); Gift of Norbert Schimmel Trust, 1989 (br). **52-53 Alamy Stock Photo:** Hemis / Frumm John. **54-55 Getty Images / iStock:** Martchan (t). **54 Alamy Stock Photo:** Album (bl). **55 Alamy Stock Photo:** Album (br). **56 akg-images:** Herv Champollion. **57 Alamy Stock Photo:** Vladislav Gajic (tr). **Getty Images:** Werner Forman / Universal Images Group (clb). **58 Alamy Stock Photo:** Goran Bogicevic (clb); Peter Horree (cb); Eddie Gerald (crb). **59 Alamy Stock Photo:** Roberto Esposti (cb); The Picture Art Collection (crb). **The Metropolitan Museum of Art:** Rogers Fund, 1998 (clb). **Pitt Rivers Museum, Oxford:** (tr). **60 Alamy Stock Photo:** CPA Media Pte Ltd / Pictures From History (clb). **61 Alamy Stock Photo:** World History Archive. **62 Alamy Stock Photo:** Andrew Holt (cl). **© The Trustees of the British Museum. All rights reserved:** Eon, Ezanas, Aksumite Kingdom (br/x3). **63 Alamy Stock Photo:** Paul Strawson (t). **Wikipedia:** (br). **64 Alamy Stock Photo:** GRANGER - Historical Picture Archive (cra); Peter Horree (bl). **64-65 Alamy Stock Photo:** Jesse Kraft (b). **66 Alamy Stock Photo:** Penta Springs Limited / Artokoloro (cr); YA / BOT (crb). **Bridgeman Images:** © NPL - DeA Picture Library (cra); Tarker (b). **67 Alamy Stock Photo:** Fine Art Images / Heritage Images. **68 akg-images. 69 Alamy Stock Photo:** CBW (clb). **© The Trustees of the British Museum. All rights reserved:** (cra/x2). **70 Alamy Stock Photo:** Oliver Gerhard (br). **Getty Images:** Moment / Bashar Shglila (t). **71 akg-images:** New Picture Library Srl / De Agostini / Biblioteca Ambrosiana (bl). **Alamy Stock Photo:** GRANGER - Historical Picture Archive (tr). **72 Alamy Stock Photo:** Volgi archive (clb). **72-73 Getty Images:** Deagostini / DEA / G. Dagli Orti (c). **73 Alamy Stock Photo:** Cultural Archive (cra). **74 Alamy Stock Photo:** agefotostock / J.D. Dallet (cla). **Biblioteca Apostolica Vaticana:** (bl). **Getty Images:** Sepia Times / Universal Images Group (cr). **75 The Metropolitan Museum of Art:** Rogers Fund, 1998 (r). **76-77 The Metropolitan Museum of Art:** The Michael C. Rockefeller Memorial Collection, Gift of Nelson A. Rockefeller,. **78 akg-images:** Andr Held (bl). **79 Alamy Stock Photo:** Neil Bowman (crb); Christopher Scott (tr); Matyas Rehak (cra). **80 Alamy Stock Photo:** Sunny Celeste (crb); Ben McRae (cb). **Getty Images:** Icas94 / De Agostini Picture Library (cb). **81 Alamy Stock Photo:** Bildagentur-online / McPhoto-Nilsen (clb); Greenshoots Communications / GS International (cb). **Getty Images:** Deaan Vivier / Beeld / Gallo Images (crb). **Pitt Rivers Museum, Oxford:** (tr). **82 akg-images:** Werner Forman Archive (cla). **Alamy Stock Photo:** Ariadne Van Zandbergen (bl). **83 akg-images:** Pictures From History (t). **84 Photo Scala, Florence:** RMN-Grand Palais (bl). **85 Alamy Stock Photo:** Roberto Cornacchia. **86-87 Alamy Stock Photo:** Stephanie Rabemiafara / Danita Delimont. **88 © The Trustees of the British Museum. All rights reserved.:** (cra). **88-89 Bridgeman Images:** (b). **89 Alamy Stock Photo:** Cultural Archive (tr). **90 Alamy Stock Photo:** Alissa Everett (t); SBS Eclectic Images (bl). **91 Getty Images:** Werner Forman / Universal Images Group (tr). **The Metropolitan Museum of Art**: Purchase, Buckeye Trust and Mr. and Mrs. Milton F. Rosenthal Gifts, Joseph Pulitzer Bequest and Harris Brisbane Dick and Rogers Funds, 1981 (br). **92 Alamy Stock Photo:** IanDagnall Computing. **93 Alamy Stock Photo:** Horst Friedrichs (tr); Ian Nellist (crb). **95 Getty Images:** AFP / Michele Cattani (tr). **UN/DPI Photo:** Tiecoura N'daou (br). **96-97 Getty Images:** Xavier ROSSI / Gamma-Rapho. **98 Bridgeman Images:** G. Dagli Orti / © NPL - DeA Picture Library (crb). **The Metropolitan Museum of Art:** Theodore M. Davis Collection, Bequest of Theodore M. Davis, 1915 (cl). **99 Bridgeman Images:** Freer Sackler Gallery / Freer Gallery of Art, Smithsonian Institution. **100 akg-images:** Album / Oronoz (cra). **Alamy Stock Photo:** Luis Dafos (bc); The Picture Art Collection (cla). **101 Alamy Stock Photo:** Album. **103 akg-images:** Erich Lessing (r). **Alamy Stock Photo:** VPC Travel Photo (cr). **104 Bibliotheque de l'Institut de France:** Ms 2414 f.151 A verso (crb). Courtesy of the New Orleans Museum of Art: Acc.No.97.138 (bl). **105 Bridgeman Images:** Pictures from History (tl). **The Metropolitan Museum of Art:** Gift of John and Evelyn Kossak, The Kronos Collections, in honor of Martin Lerner, 1983 (r). **106 Alamy Stock Photo:** Horst Friedrichs (cla). **Reuters:** Florin Iorganda (crb). **107 Bridgeman Images:** Heini Schneebeli. **108 Alamy Stock Photo:** Chronicle (t). **Getty Images:** Universal Images Group / Werner Forman (bl). **109 akg-images:** Andr Held (br). **Alamy Stock Photo:** Album (tr). **110 Alamy Stock Photo:** Omoniyi Ayedun Olubunmi (cl). **Bridgeman Images:** Dirk Bakker (br). **111 akg-images:** Andrea Jemolo (r). **Alamy Stock Photo:** CMA / BOT (tl). **112 © The Trustees of the British Museum. All rights reserved:** (bl).

113 Alamy Stock Photo: Penta Springs Limited / Artokoloro (br). The Charles Deering McCormick Library of Special Collections and University Archives: Justine Cordwell Papers, Northwestern University Archives (tl). **114 The National Archives:** (bl). **Photo Scala, Florence:** Christie's Images, London (cra). **115 Alamy Stock Photo:** Historic Images (br); World History Archive (tc). **Wikipedia:** Peoples of All Nations by Northcote W. Thomas, The Amalgamated Press Ltd, London, 1922 (cra). **116 akg-images:** Andr Held (c); Andrea Jemolo (b). **Bridgeman Images:** Dirk Bakker (cl, tr, cr). **© The Trustees of the British Museum. All rights reserved:** (cr/Pendant). **117 akg-images:** Andr Held (t); Werner Forman Archive / British Museum, London (br). Bridgeman Images: Dirk Bakker (cr, bl); Andrea Jemolo (cl). **118 Alamy Stock Photo:** History and Art Collection (cl). **The Metropolitan Museum of Art:** Mariana and Ray Herrmann Gift, 2015 (bc). **119 Alamy Stock Photo:** The Picture Art Collection (br); Tim Wege (t). **120 Alamy Stock Photo:** Thomas Cockrem. **121 Alamy Stock Photo:** John Elk III (bl). **122-123 Getty Images:** Moment / Jon Bratt. **124 Getty Images:** Pictures from History / Universal Images Group (cla, br). **125 Alamy Stock Photo:** Album (br). **126 Alamy Stock Photo:** Dorling Kindersley ltd (cra). **Bridgeman Images:** Photo Josse (bc). **127 Alamy Stock Photo:** Old Books Images (t). **Getty Images:** Eric Lafforgue / Art in All of Us / Corbis (br). **128 Alamy Stock Photo:** Florilegius (cla). **Getty Images:** Universal Images Group / Werner Forman (bc). **129 akg-images:** Pictures From History. **130 Alamy Stock Photo:** MET / BOT (crb). **The Metropolitan Museum of Art:** Gift of Mr. and Mrs. Klaus G. Perls, 1991 (clb). **131 The Metropolitan Museum of Art:** The Michael C. Rockefeller Memorial Collection, Bequest of Nelson A. Rockefeller, 1979. **132 The Metropolitan Museum of Art:** The Michael C. Rockefeller Memorial Collection, Gift of Nelson A. Rockefeller, 1965. **133 The Metropolitan Museum of Art:** The Michael C. Rockefeller Memorial Collection, Gift of Nelson A. Rockefeller, 1972 (crb). **134 Alamy Stock Photo:** imageBROKER.com GmbH & Co. KG / Stefan Auth (crb). **Bridgeman Images:** Zev Radovan (cb). **Getty Images:** DDP / Oliver Lang (clb). **135 Alamy Stock Photo:** Chronicle (cb). **Getty Images:** Popperfoto (crb). **The Metropolitan Museum of Art:** Mr. and Mrs. Klaus G. Perls, 1991 (clb). **136 Alamy Stock Photo:** Christopher Scott. **137 Alamy Stock Photo:** Fine Art Images / Heritage Images (bl). **© The Trustees of the British Museum. All rights reserved:** (tr). **138 Alamy Stock Photo:** Gallo Images / Denny Allen (tc). **140 Alamy Stock Photo:** INTERFOTO / History (bl); robertharding / Ian Griffiths (br). **141 Bridgeman Images:** Heini Schneebeli (t). LOT-ART: (br). **142 Getty Images:** Werner Forman / Universal Images Group (bl). **Photo Scala, Florence:** Image copyright The Metropolitan Museum of Art / Art Resource (c). **143 The Metropolitan Museum of Art:** Rogers Fund, 1988 (crb); The Michael C. Rockefeller Memorial Collection, Gift of Nelson A. Rockefeller, 1969 (c). **144-145 Brooklyn Museum:** Gift of Marcia and John Friede (b). **145 Mary (Polly) Nooter Roberts:** (tl). **146 Alamy Stock Photo:** John Warburton-Lee Photography / Nigel Pavitt (t). **© The Trustees of the British Museum. All rights reserved:** (br). **147 Alamy Stock Photo:** The Picture Art Collection (br). **Getty Images:** Universal Images Group / Pictures from History (tc). **148 Getty Images:** Dea Picture Library / De Agostini. **149 Alamy Stock Photo:** CPA Media Pte Ltd / Pictures From History (ca); World History Archive (br). **150 Alamy Stock Photo:** Aninka Bongers-Sutherland (crb); Tribaleye Images / Tribal Textiles / Jamie Marshall (cb). The Metropolitan Museum of Art: Purchase, Mrs. Howard J. Barnet Gift, 2012 (clb). **151 Alamy Stock Photo:** Thomas Cockrem (clb); Nick Greaves; Agfa Awards Winner (cb). **Getty Images:** Sepia Times / Universal Images Group (crb). **152 Alamy Stock Photo:** Eric Lafforgue (bl). **Dorling Kindersley:** Dave King / Pitt Rivers Museum, University of Oxford (ca). **152-153 Alamy Stock Photo:** Art World (b). **153 Dorling Kindersley:** Dave King / Pitt Rivers Museum, University of Oxford (t). **154-155 Alamy Stock Photo:** Tariq Zaidi / ZUMA Wire. **156-157 Courtesy of the New Orleans Museum of Art:** Francoise Billion Richardson Fund, 90-306 (c). **156 Alamy Stock Photo:** Interfoto / Fine Arts (bc). **Photo Scala, Florence:** The Metropolitan Museum of Art / Art Resource (l). **157 Alamy Stock Photo:** Jon Arnold Images Ltd / Gavin Hellier (cra). **158-159 Bridgeman Images:** North Carolina Museum of Art. **160 The Metropolitan Museum of Art:** Gift of Mr. and Mrs. Klaus G. Perls, 1991 (bl). **161 akg-images:** Heritage Images / Fine Art Images (crb). **Alamy Stock Photo:** Pictorial Press Ltd (tr). **Getty Images:** DEA / G. DAGLI ORTI / De Agostini (cra). **163 Alamy Stock Photo:** GRANGER - Historical Picture Archive (t). Library of Congress, Washington, D.C.: LC-USZ62-34160 (b). **164-165 Alamy Stock Photo:** VTR. **166 The Metropolitan Museum of Art:** Louis V. Bell and Rogers Funds (bl). **167 Alamy Stock Photo:** Pictorial Press Ltd (tr). Rijksmuseum Amsterdam: (b/x3). **168 Alamy Stock Photo:** ART Collection (bl); Chronicle (t). **169 Alamy Stock Photo:** Album (br); Florilegius (tc). **170 Alamy Stock Photo:** World History Archive (ca). University of Southern California: (bl). **171 The Metropolitan Museum of Art:** Purchase, The Fred and Rita Richman Foundation Gift and Rogers Fund, 2000. **172 Alamy Stock Photo:** history_docu_photo. **173 Alamy Stock Photo:** Old Images (clb); World History Archive (cra). **174 Alamy Stock Photo:** North Wind Picture Archives (cr); Ariadne Van Zandbergen (bl). **175 Mary Evans Picture Library:** (t). **176 Alamy Stock Photo:** Oscar Espinosa (t); Boaz Rottem (bl). **177 Bridgeman Images:** Heini Schneebeli (bl). **Getty Images:** Popperfoto / Paul Popper (tr). **178 Alamy Stock Photo:** Historic Images (cla). **Fowler Museum at UCLA:** (b). **179 Bridgeman Images:** Look and Learn. **180 National Portrait Gallery, London. 181 Getty Images:** Archive Photos / Fotosearch (cb); Hulton Archive / Heritage Images (cra). **182 Alamy Stock Photo:** Science History Images (cla). **The Metropolitan Museum of Art:** Gift of Ernst Anspach, 1999 (c). **183 Alamy Stock Photo:** Penta Springs Limited / Artokoloro (c). **Dreamstime.com:** Fabian Plock (tr). **184-185 The Metropolitan Museum of Art:** Purchase, Lila Acheson Wallace, Drs. Daniel and Marian Malcolm, Laura G. and James J. Ross, Jeffrey B. Soref, The Robert T. Wall Family, Dr. and Mrs. Sidney G. Clyman, and Steven Kossak Gifts, 2008. **185 The Metropolitan Museum of Art:** Purchase, Lila Acheson Wallace, Drs. Daniel and Marian Malcolm, Laura G. and James J. Ross, Jeffrey B. Soref, The Robert T. Wall Family, Dr. and Mrs. Sidney G. Clyman, and Steven Kossak Gifts, 2008 (tr). **186 Alamy Stock Photo:** CPA Media Pte Ltd / Pictures From History (cla); UtCon Collection (br). **© The Trustees of the British Museum. All rights reserved:** (bl). **187 Alamy Stock Photo:** WBC ART (r). **189 Alamy Stock Photo:** CPA Media Pte Ltd / Pictures From History (tl). **190-191 Bridgeman Images:** British Library Board. All Rights Reserved (t). **190 Alamy Stock Photo:** INTERFOTO / Fine Arts (br). **191 Dorling Kindersley:** Wallace Collection, London / Geoff Dann (cr). **192 Alamy Stock Photo:** Album (cla); Holden History (cb). **193 The Metropolitan Museum of Art:** The Michael C. Rockefeller Memorial Collection, Purchase, Nelson A. Rockefeller Gift, 1967. **194 Alamy Stock Photo:** Chronicle (crb); Jorge Fernandez (l). **195 Bridgeman Images:** Archives Charmet / Bernatz, Johann Martin (1802-1878) (after) / German (tr). **196-197 Photo Scala, Florence:** Muse de l'Arme, Paris. Dist. RMN-Grand Palais (b). **196 Getty Images**: De Agostini (cla). **197 Alamy Stock Photo:** Historic Images (t). **198 Alamy Stock Photo:** Penta Springs Limited (bl); Stock Imagery (tr). **Photo Scala, Florence:** The Metropolitan Museum of Art / Art Resource (cra, c, cl, br). **199 akg-images:** François Gunet (tr). **Bridgeman Images:** Brooklyn Museum / Gift of Marcia and John Friede (br). **The Metropolitan Museum of Art:** Purchase, Mrs. Howard J. Barnet Gift, 2015 (bc); The Michael C. Rockefeller Memorial Collection, Purchase, Nelson A. Rockefeller Gift, 1967 (l); The Michael C. Rockefeller Memorial Collection, Bequest of Nelson A. Rockefeller, 1979 (tc); The Michael C. Rockefeller Memorial Collection, Gift of Nelson A. Rockefeller, 1972 (c). **Photo Scala, Florence:** The Metropolitan Museum of Art / Art Resource (cr). **200 Alamy Stock Photo:** The History Collection (cra). **Getty Images:** Photo12 / Universal Images Group (bl). **201 Alamy Stock Photo:** World History Archive (bc). **Getty Images:** DeAgostini (t). **202-203 Library of Congress, Washington, D.C.:** Njoya, Sultan Of Bamoun, 1876?-1933, Cartographer. Bamum. [Cameroon: producer not identified, Between to 1919, 1912]. **204 Alamy Stock Photo:** Universal Images Group North America LLC / PHAS / UIG. **205 Alamy Stock Photo:** Colaimages (cra); Scherl / Sddeutsche Zeitung Photo (br). **206 Getty Images:** Gamma-Rapho / Jean-Noel De Soye (bl). **207 Alamy Stock Photo**: Historica Graphica Collection / Heritage Images (tr, b). **208 Alamy Stock Photo:** GL Archive. **209 Alamy Stock Photo:** CBW (crb); Pictorial Press (tr). **© The Trustees of the British Museum. All rights reserved:** (ca). **210 Alamy Stock Photo:** Chronicle (cla). **210-211 Alamy Stock Photo:** Granger - Historical Picture Archive (b). **211 Alamy Stock Photo:** Svintage Archive (tc). **212 Alamy Stock Photo:** Svintage Archive (bl). **Brooklyn Museum:** Arts of Africa / Purchased with funds given by Mr. and Mrs. Alastair B. Martin, Mrs. Donald M. Oenslager, Mr. and Mrs. Robert E. Blum, and the Mrs. Florence A. Blum Fund (cra). **213 Alamy Stock Photo:** Photo12 / Archives Snark (tr). **The New York Public Library:** (bc). **214 Alamy Stock Photo:** IanDagnall Computing (bl); Science History Images (t). **215 Alamy Stock Photo:** Chronicle. **216 Alamy Stock Photo:** Zuri Swimmer (cla). **Getty Images:** Universal Images Group (br). **217 Alamy Stock Photo:** Alto Vintage Images (tr); Ariadne Van Zandbergen (tc). **218 Alamy Stock Photo:** Historic Images (cra); Vinard Collection (bl). 219 © The Trustees of the British Museum. All rights reserved. **220 Alamy Stock Photo:** Classic Collection 3. **221 © The Trustees of the British Museum. All rights reserved:** (crb). **Dreamstime.com:** Dolphfyn (ca). **222 Alamy Stock Photo:** The Print Collector / Heritage Images (crb). **Getty Images:** Bert Hardy / Picture Post / Hulton Archive / Stringer (t). **223 Alamy Stock Photo:** Art Collection 2 (bl); Prisma Archivo (tr). **224-225 Photo Scala, Florence:** The Metropolitan Museum of Art / Art Resource. **226 Getty Images / iStock:** E+ / PictureLake (bl). **227 Alamy Stock Photo:** Everett Collection Historical (cra); World History Archive (tr). **Getty Images:** Hulton Archive / Keystone / Stringer (crb). **228 Alamy Stock Photo:** Alto Vintage Images (br); Peregrine (cra). **229 Alamy Stock Photo:** Agefotostock / Historical Views (t). **Getty Images:** James O Jenkins / Bolton & Quinn / AFP (br). **230 Alamy Stock Photo:** NBP / piemags. **231 Alamy Stock Photo:** Associated Press (bl); D and S Photography Archives (tr). **Getty Images:** Universal Images Group Editorial / Photo 12 (tc). **232 Alamy Stock Photo:** History and Art Collection (crb); Pictorial Press Ltd (clb). **Getty Images:** Bettmann (cb). **233 Getty Images:** AFP / STF (clb); Lipnitzki / Roger Viollet (cb); Bettmann (crb). **Photo Scala, Florence:** RMN-Grand Palais / Dist. / Diouf, Ibrahima (20th cent.) (tr). **234 Alamy Stock Photo:** Dragan Ilic (cla); Photo12 / Ann Ronan Picture Library (bl). **235 TopFoto:** Heritage-Images. **236 Alamy Stock Photo:** Charles O. Cecil (cr). **237 Alamy Stock Photo:** The Print Collector / Heritage Images (tr). **Getty Images:** Bettmann (b). **238 Getty Images:** AFP / STR / Stringer. **239 Alamy Stock Photo:** Photo12 / Ann Ronan Picture Library (ca). **Getty Images:** Rolls Press / Popperfoto (crb). **240 akg-images:** African Pictures (PTY) Ltd (bl). **Getty**

Images: Bettmann (t). **241 Getty Images:** Bettmann (br). **Shutterstock.com:** Mirt Alexander (tr). **242 Getty Images:** Bettmann. **243 Alamy Stock Photo:** Historic Collection (crb); Sura Nualpradid (c). **244-245 Josef and Anni Albers Foundation:** Courtesy of Xaritufoto and Le Korsa.. **246 Alamy Stock Photo:** Grant Rooney (br). **Getty Images:** AFP / Trevor Samson (ca). **247 Getty Images:** Hulton Archive. **248 Getty Images:** Archive Photos / Ben Martin (cla); Archive Photos / David Hume Kennerly (bl). **249 Getty Images:** Corbis Historical / Michael Nicholson (b). **250 Getty Images:** CILO / Gamma-Rapho. **251 Alamy Stock Photo:** Keystone Press (clb). **Getty Images:** AFP / Alexander Joe / Staff (cra). **252 Alamy Stock Photo:** Peter Jordan (t). **Getty Images:** AFP / Alexander Joe / Staff (crb). **253 Alamy Stock Photo:** Brian Harris (br). **254 Getty Images:** Sygma / Alain Nogues (cla); Sygma Premium / William Campbell (bl). **255 Alamy Stock Photo:** Mike Abrahams (b). **Photo Scala, Florence:** Photo Smithsonian American Art Museum / Art Resource (tr). **256-257 Photo Scala, Florence:** The Art Institute of Chicago / Art Resource, NY. **258 Alamy Stock Photo:** Pictorial Press Ltd (br). **Getty Images:** Keystone-France / Gamma-Keystone (cl). **259 Alamy Stock Photo:** Borislav Marinic (br). **Getty Images:** Michel Huet / Gamma-Rapho (tr). **260 Alamy Stock Photo:** GFC Collection (t). **261 Alamy Stock Photo:** Associated Press / Uncredited (bc); Marion Kaplan (c). **262 Getty Images:** - / AFP. **263 Alamy Stock Photo:** Contraband Collection (tl). **Getty Images:** Pierre Guillaud / AFP (br). **264 Alamy Stock Photo:** Mike Goldwater (cb); Trinity Mirror / Mirrorpix (clb). **Getty Images:** Marco Di Lauro / Stringer (crb). **265 Alamy Stock Photo:** Associated Press / Samir Bol (crb). **Getty Images:** Corbis / VCG / David Turnley (cb); Sygma / Patrick Robert - Corbis (clb). **266 Getty Images:** Patrick Durand / Sygma (ca). **266-267 Getty Images:** Paris Match Archive / Gysembergh Benoit (c). **267 Getty Images:** AFP / Pascal Guyot / Staff (br). **268 Getty Images:** AFP / STF / Staff (bc). **Reuters:** Juda Ngwenya (cla). **269 Alamy Stock Photo:** Associated Press / Denis Farrell (t). **Getty Images:** AFP / Keith Schamotta / Staff (br). **270 Getty Images:** Thomas Imo / Photothek. **271 Getty Images:** Eli Weinberg / Apic / Hulton Archive (tr); The Chronicle Collection / Allan Tannenbaum (crb). **272 Photo Scala, Florence:** The Metropolitan Museum of Art / Art Resource. **274 Courtesy of SMAC Gallery/Southern Guild:** (bl). **275 Alamy Stock Photo:** AfriPics.com (tr). **Getty Images:** AFP / Issouf Sanogo (cr); AFP / Pius Utomi Ekpei (crb). **276-277 Jennifer Okpoko:** (tc). **276 Getty Images:** Gallo Images Editorial (bl); Hulton Archive / Heritage Images (cr). **Jennifer Okpoko:** (tl). **277 Getty Images:** AFP / Gulshan Khan (b). **Jennifer Okpoko:** (tr). **278 Alamy Stock Photo:** LMA / AW (crb); Universal Images Group North America LLC / DeAgostini / A. Dagli Orti (cra). **Photo Scala, Florence:** Princeton University Art Museum, / Art Resource NY (tc, bl); Princeton University Art Museum / Art Resource NY (crb/Cap). **278-279 Dreamstime.com:** Fabrizio Cianella (t). **279 Alamy Stock Photo:** CPA Media Pte Ltd. / Pictures From History (cr); John Warburton-Lee Photography / Nigel Pavitt (tr); Penta Springs Limited / Artokoloro (crb). **Brooklyn Museum:** Gift of Thomas Alexander (cb). **Photo Scala, Florence:** The Metropolitan Museum of Art / Art Resource (bl). **280 Alamy Stock Photo:** Nature Picture Library / Christophe Courteau (crb); Omoniyi Ayedun Olubunmi (clb). **© UNESCO:** DCP, 2011 (cb). **281 Alamy Stock Photo:** Africa Media Online / Rogan Ward (crb); Eric Lafforgue (clb). **Reuters:** Tiksa Negeri (cb). **282 Science Photo Library:** Thierry Berrod, Mona Lisa Production (bl). **283 Alamy Stock Photo:** Martin Harvey (t). **Getty Images:** Junior Kannah / AFP (br). **284 Getty Images:** Anadolu Agency (bl). **285 Alamy Stock Photo:** Antiqua Print Gallery (tc). **Shutterstock.com:** Dr Craig (b). **286 Getty Images:** AFP / Glyn Kirk (cb); Velo / Tim de Waele (clb); AFP (crb). **287 Alamy Stock Photo:** Associated Press / Markus Schreiber (cra). **Getty Images:** Anadolu Agency (cb); Robert Cianflone (clb); Gallo Images (crb). **288 Alamy Stock Photo:** Peregrine (cla). **Collection IAV-Atria:** Copyright unknown (br). **289 Getty Images:** Micheline Pelletier / Corbis (bc). **Reuters:** Temilade Adelaja (t). **290 Getty Images:** Micheline Pelletier / Corbis. **291 Alamy Stock Photo:** NTB / Cornelius Poppe / Scanpix Norway / POOL (cra). **Getty Images:** AFP / Issouf Sanogo / Staff (clb). 292 Alamy Stock Photo: Photo 12 / Cinegrit (t). **Posteritati:** (br). **293 Alamy Stock Photo:** Lifestyle pictures (br); Photo 12 / A7A collection (tc). **294 Alamy Stock Photo:** Chrisstockphoto (cla); Yuri Kevhiev (tr); Zoonar / Aliaksei Hintau (br). **Dreamstime.com:** Dario Lo Presti (cb). **The Metropolitan Museum of Art:** The Crosby Brown Collection of Musical Instruments (bl). 295 Alamy Stock Photo: Chrisstockphoto (bl); Fortune Fish (c); Eric Lafforgue (cra). **Getty Images:** Universal History Archive / Universal Images Group (cr). **Photo Scala, Florence:** The Metropolitan Museum of Art / Art Resource (br). **296 Getty Images:** PoPsie Randolph / Michael Ochs Archives / Donaldson Collection (clb); David Corio / Redferns (cb); Frans Schellekens / Redferns (crb). **297 Alamy Stock Photo:** Mariano Garcia (cb). Getty Images: Suhaimi Abdullah (clb); Michael Loccisano / Staff (crb). **298-299 © El Anatsui. Courtesy of El Anatsui Studio:** Photo courtesy Brandywine Workshop and Archives.. **298 Alamy Stock Photo:** Independent / Tom Pilston (tc). **300 Yancey Richardson Gallery:** Courtesy of the Artist and Yancey Richardson, New York. **301 Yancey Richardson Gallery:** Courtesy of the Artist and Yancey Richardson, New York. **302 africamediaonline.com:** (clb). **Getty Images:** David Degner (crb). **Shutterstock.com:** The LIFE Picture Collection / Carlo Bavagnoli (cb). **303 Getty Images:** Awakening / Simone Padovani (cb); Gamma-Rapho / Frederic Reglain (clb); LightRocket / SOPA Images (crb). **304 Getty Images:** Photodisc / Buena Vista Images (b). **305 Alamy Stock Photo:** Associated Press / Sunday Alamba (crb). **Edo Museum of West African Art:** (t). **306-307 The Metropolitan Museum of Art:** Gift of Mr. and Mrs. Klaus G. Perls. **308 Dreamstime.com:** Iigo Arza Azcorra (l). **309 Alamy Stock Photo:** agefotostock / Anton Aleksenko (br). **Getty Images:** Atilano Garcia / SOPA Images / LightRocket (tl). **310 Alamy Stock Photo:** MJ Photography (b). **312 Alamy Stock Photo:** Frans Lemmens (tr). **Getty Images:** Bettmann (bl). **313 Alamy Stock Photo:** agefotostock / Tolo Balaguer (r). **314 Alamy Stock Photo:** funkyfood London - Paul Williams (br). **315 Alamy Stock Photo:** Prisma by Dukas Presseagentur GmbH / Raga Jose Fuste. **316 Alamy Stock Photo:** Everett Collection Inc / Ron Harvey (tr); Universal Images Group North America LLC / DeAgostini / A. Dagli Orti (bl). **317 Alamy Stock Photo:** Associated Press. **318 Dreamstime.com:** Alexey Pevnev (t). **319 Dreamstime.com:** Maria Grazia Bertano (br). **320 Getty Images / iStock:** E+ / alantobey (l). **321 Alamy Stock Photo:** Images&Stories (bl). **Getty Images:** Hulton Archive / Keystone / Stringer (cr). **322 Getty Images:** Felix Man / Stringer / Picture Post / Hulton Archive (bc). **323 Alamy Stock Photo:** Michel Renaudeau / Onlyworld.net. **324 akg-images:** NEW PICTURE LIBRARY SRL / De Agostini Picture Lib. / G. Dagli Orti (br). **325 Alamy Stock Photo:** Renato Bordoni (br). **326 Alamy Stock Photo:** The History Collection (tr). **Bridgeman Images:** British Library Board. All Rights Reserved (bl). **327 Photo Scala, Florence:** RMN-Grand Palais. **328 Photo Scala, Florence:** Image copyright The Metropolitan Museum of Art / Art Resource (l). **329 Photo Scala, Florence:** Image copyright The Metropolitan Museum of Art / Art Resource. **330 Alamy Stock Photo:** Horst Friedrichs (bl). **331 Alamy Stock Photo:** AGF Srl / Hermes Images. **332 akg-images:** Paul Almasy (tr). **333 Alamy Stock Photo:** robertharding / Michael Runkel. **334 Alamy Stock Photo:** Guiziou Franck / Hemis.fr (bl); Peter Horree (tr). **335 Alamy Stock Photo:** Michele Burgess (r). **336 Alamy Stock Photo:** The Consoli Collection (l). **337 Alamy Stock Photo:** Greenshoots Communications / GS International. **338 Alamy Stock Photo:** Michele Burgess (bl). **339 Alamy Stock Photo:** Alida Latham / DanitaDelimont (tl); Penta Springs Limited / Artokoloro (br). **340 Alamy Stock Photo:** Johnny Greig (bl); PRAWNS (tr). **341 Alamy Stock Photo:** Trinity Mirror / Mirrorpix. **342 Alamy Stock Photo:** CMA / BOT (br). **Getty Images:** Christian Sappa / Gamma-Rapho (l). **343 Alamy Stock Photo:** jbdodane. **344 Alamy Stock Photo:** Hemis.fr / Charton Franck (bl). **345 Alamy Stock Photo:** Antiqua Print Gallery (t). **346 Alamy Stock Photo:** Keystone Pictures USA / ZUMA Press, Inc. (bl). **347 Alamy Stock Photo:** Historic Collection (br). **Reuters:** Joe Penney (t). **348 Alamy Stock Photo:** imageBROKER / Michael Runkel (br). **349 Alamy Stock Photo:** Nikreates (r). **350 The Metropolitan Museum of Art:** Purchase, Buckeye Trust and Charles B. Benenson Gifts, Rogers Fund and funds from various donors, 1979 (l). **351 Alamy Stock Photo:** Everett Collection Historical (tl); Xinhua / Liu Kai (br). **352 Alamy Stock Photo:** GarryKillian (l). **353 Alamy Stock Photo:** Fanika Zupan (b). **Getty Images:** Universal History Archive (tc). **354 Alamy Stock Photo:** John Warburton-Lee Photography / Nigel Pavitt (br). **355 Alamy Stock Photo:** Sabena Jane Blackbird (r); Neftali (tl). **356 Alamy Stock Photo:** Julian Lott (b). **357 Alamy Stock Photo:** Panther Media GmbH / Zatletic (br). **Getty Images:** Central Press / Hulton Archive (tl). **358 Alamy Stock Photo:** Jakub Gojda (t). **359 Alamy Stock Photo:** Travelib Culture (cra). **360 Alamy Stock Photo:** Minkimo (tr). **361 Photo Scala, Florence:** The Metropolitan Museum of Art / Art Resource (br). **362 Alamy Stock Photo:** Art Wolfe / DanitaDelimont (tr). **© The Trustees of the British Museum. All rights reserved:** E J Wayland (bc). **363 Getty Images:** Universal History Archive (br). **364-365 Getty Images / iStock:** E+ / brittak (b). **365 Alamy Stock Photo:** Marion Kaplan (tr). **366 Dreamstime.com:** Dietmar Rauscher (bl). **367 Alamy Stock Photo:** Science History Images / Photo Researchers (l). **368 Alamy Stock Photo:** Jack Malipan Travel Photography (t). **369 Alamy Stock Photo:** HomoCosmicos (bl). **370 The Metropolitan Museum of Art:** Louis V. Bell Fund, 2006 (bl). **371 Alamy Stock Photo:** colaimages (tr). **372 Alamy Stock Photo:** Sueddeutsche Zeitung Photo / Czychowski / Timeline Images (l). **373 Alamy Stock Photo:** Associated Press / Anonymous (bl). **374 Alamy Stock Photo:** mauritius images GmbH / Rene Mattes (b). **375 Alamy Stock Photo:** ART Collection (cr). **376 Alamy Stock Photo:** THP Creative (b). **377 The Metropolitan Museum of Art:** Richard, Ann, John, and James Solomon Families Foundation, Adam Lindemann and Amalia Dayan, and Herbert and Lenore Schorr Gifts, Rogers Fund (br). **378 Alamy Stock Photo:** Erik Koole (tl). **379 Alamy Stock Photo:** Horizons WWP / Jochem Wijnands (bl). **380 Alamy Stock Photo:** Robert Fried (bl). **381 Alamy Stock Photo:** Marcus DeYoung. **382 Alamy Stock Photo:** World History Archive (tr). **Photo Scala, Florence:** Image copyright The Metropolitan Museum of Art / Art Resource (bl). **383 Getty Images / iStock:** E+ / guenterguni. **384 Alamy Stock Photo:** Peregrine (bc). **385 Alamy Stock Photo:** Peter Horree (r)

All other images © Dorling Kindersley

BRINGING HISTORY TO LIFE

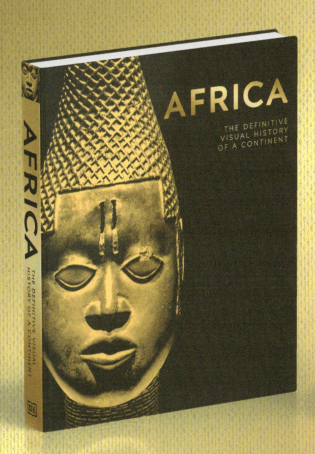
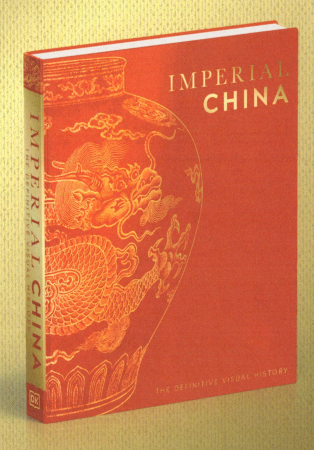
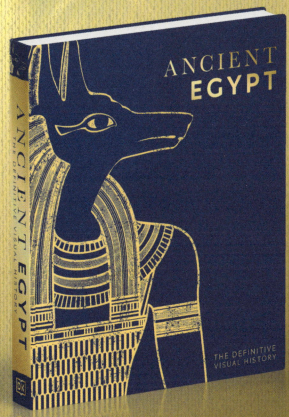
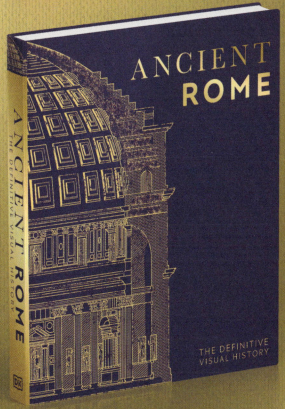

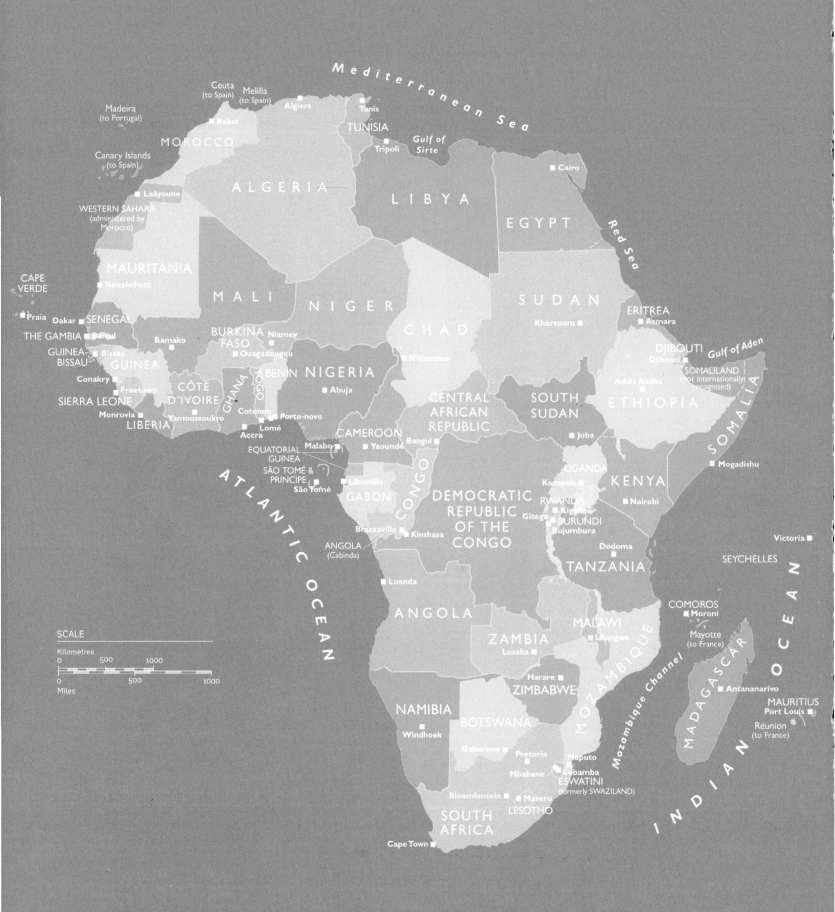